Dynamics of Production in the Ancient Near East

1300–500 BC

Dynamics of Production in the Ancient Near East

1300–500 BC

Edited by

Juan Carlos Moreno García

OXBOW | books
Oxford & Philadelphia

Published in the United Kingdom in 2016 by
OXBOW BOOKS
10 Hythe Bridge Street, Oxford OX1 2EW

and in the United States by
OXBOW BOOKS
1950 Lawrence Road, Havertown, PA 19083, USA

Paperback Edition: ISBN 978-1-78570-283-9
Digital Edition: ISBN 978-1-78570-284-6 (epub)

A CIP record for this book is available from the Library of Congress and British Library

Printed in the United Kingdom by Hobbs the Printers Ltd

For a complete list of Oxbow titles, please contact:

UNITED KINGDOM
Oxbow Books
Telephone (01865) 241249, Fax (01865) 794449
Email: oxbow@oxbowbooks.com
www.oxbowbooks.com

UNITED STATES OF AMERICA
Oxbow Books
Telephone (800) 791-9354, Fax (610) 853-9146
Email: queries@casemateacademic.com
www.casemateacademic.com/oxbow

Oxbow Books is part of the Casemate Group

Cover: Kudurru (stele) of King Melishipak I (1186–1172 BC): Jacques de Morgan, currently on display at the Louvre Museum, Paris. Drachma from Bruttium (210 BC); Ancient camel from Persepolis; Gold mask of Shoshenk II; Babylonian kudurru from the late Kassite period, found near Baghdad: Creative Commons.

Certains hommes sont des collines
Qui s'élèvent entre les hommes
Et voient au loin tout l'avenir
Mieux que s'il était présent
Plus net que s'il était passé

To Pascal Vernus, with gratitude and admiration

Contents

List of contributors ix

Introduction xi

Juan Carlos Moreno García

1. Economies in transition: trade, "money", labour and nomads at the turn of the 1st millennium BC 1
   Juan Carlos Moreno García

2. Oil and wine for silver? The economic agency of the Egyptian peasant communities in the Great Oasis during the Persian Period 41
   Damien Agut-Labordère

3. Urban craftsmen and other specialists, their land holdings, and the Neo-Assyrian state 53
   Heather D. Baker

4. Beyond capitalism – conceptualising ancient trade through friction, world historical context and bazaars 75
   Peter Fibiger Bang

5. Phoenician trade: the first 300 years 91
   Carol Bell

6. The contribution of pottery production in reconstructing aspects of local rural economy at the northern frontier of the Neo-Assyrian Empire 107
   Anacleto D'Agostino

7. Silver circulation and the development of the private economy in the Assyrian Empire (9th–7th centuries BCE): considerations on private investments, prices and prosperity levels of the imperial *élite* 125
   Salvatore Gaspa

8. Long-distance trade in Neo-Babylonian Mesopotamia: the effects of institutional changes 167
   Laetitia Graslin-Thomé

9. The empire of trade and the empires of force: Tyre in the Neo-Assyrian and Neo-Babylonian periods 187
Caroline van der Brugge & Kristin Kleber

10. Temples and agricultural labour in Egypt, from the Late New Kingdom to the Saite Period....................223
Juan Carlos Moreno García

11. North-east Africa and trade at the crossroads of the Nile Valley, the Mediterranean and the Red Sea 257
Robert G. Morkot

12. Temples, trade and money in Egypt in the 1st millennium BC 275
Renate Müller-Wollermann

13. From "institutional" to "private": traders, routes and commerce from the Late Bronze Age to the Iron Age 289
Susan Sherratt

14. Intercultural contacts between Egypt and the Arabian Peninsula at the turn of the 2nd to the 1st millennium BCE 303
Gunnar Sperveslage

15. Interactions between temple, king and local elites: the *hanšû* land schemes in Babylonia (8th–6th centuries BC)....................331
John P. Nielsen & Caroline Waerzeggers

16. Organisation and financing of trade and caravans in the Near East 345
Jean-Baptiste Yon

17. Aegean economies from Bronze Age to Iron Age: some lines of development, 13th–7th centuries BC....................357
Julien Zurbach

List of contributors

Damien AGUT-LABORDÈRE: damien.agut@gmail.com

Heather D. BAKER: heather.baker@utoronto.ca

Peter Fibiger BANG: pbang@hum.ku.dk

Carol BELL: carol.bell@ucl.ac.uk

Anacleto D'AGOSTINO: anacleto.dagostino@gmail.com

Salvatore GASPA: gaspasal@libero.it

Laetitia GRASLIN-THOMÉ: laetitia.graslin@univ-lorraine.fr

Kristin KLEBER: k.kleber@vu.nl

Juan Carlos MORENO GARCÍA: jcmorenogarcia@hotmail.com

Robert G. MORKOT: r.g.morkot@exeter.ac.uk

Renate MÜLLER-WOLLERMANN: renate.mueller-wollermann@uni-tuebingen.de

John P. NIELSEN: jpnielsen@bradley.edu

Susan SHERRATT: s.sherratt@sheffield.ac.uk

Gunnar SPERVESLAGE: gunnar_sperveslage@yahoo.de

Caroline VAN DER BRUGGE: cbvanderbrugge@casema.nl

Caroline WAERZEGGERS: c.waerzeggers@hum.leidenuniv.nl

Jean-Baptiste YON: jean-baptiste.yon@mom.fr

Julien ZURBACH: julien.zurbach@gmail.com

Introduction

Juan Carlos Moreno García

This volume presents the results of the European Science Foundation (ESF) Exploratory Workshop entitled *"Dynamics of production and economic interaction in the Near East in the first half of the 1st millennium BCE"*, which was held at the University Charles-de-Gaulle Lille 3, 28–30 June 2011. The application for the organisation of the Workshop was approved by the ESF Standing Committee for the Humanities, and the Workshop was totally financed by the ESF according to the ESF Exploratory Workshops scheme. According to the ESF Exploratory Workshops rules, Prof. Dr Juan Carlos Moreno García (CNRS) acted as the Convenor of the Workshop and Dr Barry Dixon, member of the Standing Committee for the Humanities of the ESF, participated in the Workshop offering a presentation of the ESF at the opening and chairing the final discussion where suggestions were put forward for developing a research network.

The workshop was devoted to the study of the transition of Near Eastern economies from the Late Bronze to the Early Iron Age, roughly between 1100 and 600 BCE. This was a period in which some monarchies collapsed but others (as well as some of their most important institutions) had to cope with a new economic environment. An era where expanded trade networks, private "entrepreneurs", innovative juridical practices and new forms of currency transformed the way in which former palatial structures operated. The nature, scope and social impact of the economic adaptations underwent by these monarchies were thus analysed in an interdisciplinary perspective, aiming to integrate recent Egyptological research into a broader Near Eastern and Mediterranean perspective. By getting together specialists from different fields, the workshop intended to promote interdisciplinary discussion and to establish the guidelines for future collaborative research. The workshop was structured into four main thematic areas: *"Declining institutions versus raising private sector? Economies in transition in the 1st millennium"*, *"The archaeology of trade"*, *"The dynamics of change from the perspective of temples"* and *"Trade, markets and investment in a new economic environment"*. The papers presented and the discussions that followed provided an excellent opportunity for the analysis of recent research, to explore new venues for comparative studies and to address the pertinence (and the limits) of methodologies "imported" from other disciplines to the domain of ancient Near Eastern studies. As Convenor of the workshop, I am deeply grateful to the ESF for their financial support and expertise in order to achieve these goals.

The main tasks of the ESF Standing Committee for the Humanities (SCH) are:

- to encourage interdisciplinary work through the independent evaluation of collaborative research proposals emanating from the scholarly community;
- to identify priority research areas and to play an integrative and co-ordinating role by creating links between research communities which in the Humanities are often small and fragmented;
- to contribute to the development of the ESF science policy agenda and to provide expert advice on science policy actions at the European level in the field of its responsibilities.

In this perspective, I hope that the stimulating conference held in 2011, and the proceedings published in this volume, are useful expressions of the role played by the ESF as the only European Agency where the Humanities have a place next to the other sciences and where European projects are reviewed, developed and subsequently operated.

Chapter 1

Economies in transition: trade, “money”, labour and nomads at the turn of the 1st millennium BC

Juan Carlos Moreno García

Two sets of texts may illustrate the fact that deep changes intervened after the crisis of the Late Bronze Age palatial system. In the first case a passage in the report of Wenamun (around the very end of the 2nd millennium BC) records the demands that the king of Byblos made of Egyptian rulers in exchange for the delivery of wood. Alongside precious items such as five gold and silver vessels and several garments of fine linen, more prosaic goods were also sent to the Libanese city, including 500 linen mats, 500 ox-hides, 500 ropes, 20 sacks of lentils and 30 baskets of fish (Lichtheim 1976, 227). The text also evokes the conditions prevalent in the preceding era, when Egyptians paid for timber in hard cash (1000 *deben* of silver – or 91 kg – on a single occasion). In fact, the harsh negotiations between Wenamun and the Byblite king are hardly reminiscent of the glamorous correspondence of the Amarna era, when gold circulated profusely between royal courts and cemented a dense network of diplomatic, matrimonial and trade contacts at the highest level between international powers (Liverani 1990). However the possibility cannot be excluded that such a contrast between two eras is somewhat artificial and that, in fact, we are simply dealing with two very different spheres of interaction between partners, wherein bargaining was in any case essential, even when kings were involved. On the one hand a world of diplomatic contacts fuelled by the delivery of gifts and the exchange of precious items (including royals and highly sought after specialists, such as craftsmen and doctors), and in which gold played a crucial role. On the other hand a more materialistic world of purely commercial exchanges based on silver.

Both spheres were evoked together, for instance, in the second set of texts to be mentioned, two letters of the Amarna correspondence sent by the king of Alasiya (Cyprus) to the pharaoh. The first letter is typical of the courteous epistolary exchanges between peers. In exchange for a delivery of 100 talents of copper to Egypt, the king of Alasiya expected the delivery of precious goods (perfumes, ebony furniture, horses, a chariot with gold ornaments, luxury garments, etc.) which, in fact, were also readily available in his kingdom as other letters make clear. His requirements thus appear to have been inspired not by need but by diplomacy, as this kind of exchange was reserved for peers, that is to say to acknowledged "great kings" (or candidates aspiring to such a status) equal in power, rank and wealth. In the second letter the tone is nevertheless quite different, albeit still courteous. The dispatch of 500 talents of copper was to be followed by a payment in silver:

> "You are my brother. May he send me silver in very great quantities. My brother, give me the very best silver, and then I will send you, my brother, whatever you, my brother, request". (EA 34 and 35: Moran 1992, 105–109; see also Kassianidou 2009)

When considering both sets of texts together it appears somewhat reductive to interpret Wenamun's claims as proof of an Egyptian decline in the international trading sphere in the late 2nd millennium. In fact, the king of Byblos reminds Wenamun in another passage that former pharaonic missions also arrived into his city to "do business", even if accompanied by ships loaded with precious gifts. In this vein, Queen Hatshepsut also recalled in her Punt inscriptions that her forebears brought precious goods from this exotic land "in exchange of numerous payments" (Sethe 1961, 344). But what appeared perhaps as a shocking novelty in Wenamun's times is that modest commodities (hides, ropes, lentils, fish) were now exchanged even at the highest level, a practice that was nevertheless also recorded in the Amarna letters (Fletcher 2012).

This is probably the crucial question underlying the economic changes that occurred between the Late Bronze and Early Iron periods in the Near East. Traditional narratives routinely equate the simultaneous end of several Near Eastern states with invasions, poverty, climate change and economic crisis, usually under the apparently self-explanatory term "collapse" (a recent example: Cline 2014). The Late Bronze Age is no exception, and these narratives have focused their attention on the 12th century BC and argued that "usual suspects" such as climate change and, especially, sudden foreign invasions (Libyans, Arameans, Sea Peoples, etc.) disrupted trade circuits and urban life and precipitated the end of many vibrant palatial societies, from small Levantine city-states to "great powers" like the Hittite kingdom. In other cases, the emphasis is placed on internal factors as causes of the collapse, the most noteworthy being internal divisions and the struggle between different factions of the ruling elite and, from a more socio-economic point of view, excessive taxation and the subsequent impoverishment of large sectors of the peasantry. Yet these interpretations are not free from some weaknesses.

First of all, if invaders attacked coastal areas, disorganised exchange networks and provoked "collapse", this means that trade had an astonishingly disruptive power in a world that was supposedly based chiefly on agriculture and peasant labour, and which was largely self-sufficient, with limited small-scale exchanges (both in range and volume) and where trade was usually reduced to prestige exchanges between palaces involving a very limited demand (issued from the palatial elite) as well as highly selected commodities. How the reduction, even the end of such limited and specialised circuits, could finally precipitate the end of the whole socioeconomic structure of the Near East thus remains a mystery.

Secondly, the very notion of a sudden collapse is highly reductive. Recent archaeological research shows that the alleged "collapse" or decline was longer than previously estimated and its local effects quite uneven; while some areas were not affected by it at all (they even thrived), others simply experienced a change in their political organisation (like the emergence of Neo-Hittite kingdoms), while others experienced similar crises but, significantly, quite later (as in the case of the Elamite, Kassite and Assyrian kingdoms; Bachhuber & Roberts 2009; Venturi 2010; Babbi *et al.* 2015).

Thirdly, the role of "invaders" as destructive forces is somewhat misleading and it is not impossible that their emergence was more the consequence than the cause of the problems encountered by the palatial systems. Parallels from other periods (such as the Viking Age: Skre 2007; 2013; Graham-Campbell *et al.* 2011) reveal that changes in the demands of states and in the organisation of circuits of exchanges had intense effects on populations specialised in transport and mediation activities, especially in coastal areas. These populations could then be forced partly to turn to predatory practices (piracy, smuggling), partly to develop new alternative circuits of exchanges, partly to settle in new areas (Sherratt 2003; for Aramaeans: Bunnens 2009). Fourthly, it seems strange that societies with, apparently, quite different political structures, ranging from the allegedly centralised Egyptian monarchy to the almost "federal" Hittite kingdom, not to speak of the "feudal" Kassite state, in some cases relatively distant from the core areas touched by invasions, all suffered similar consequences. What is more, these societies suddenly proved strangely unable to integrate the new actors (pastoral populations, maritime communities, etc.) within their structures when they had previously been doing so for centuries.

Two alternative historical models provide a more sophisticated narrative. In the first model, internal socioeconomic factors are privileged. Liverani, for instance, considers that the increasing exploitation of the labour force, especially dependent people working for the palace sector, led to a gradual demographic and fiscal crisis of the state, aggravated by the flight of impoverished peasants into marginal areas and the abandonment of settlements. The consequence was that the growth of territories and populations that escaped the control of palaces progressively weakened these institutions, to the point that internal rebellions and the incursions of external raiders finally precipitated the end of these monarchies (Liverani 1987). While the persuasive arguments of Liverani are based on abundant documentation from Ugarit, they do not seem to extend to other regions and states. As for the second model, the emphasis is put on trade and in changes in the organisation of demand during the Late Bronze Age. According to this perspective, Sherratt (2003) suggests that the intensification of exchange then stimulated the expansion of a new demand based on goods both humbler and different from those requested by the palatial elites. This, in turn, stimulated technological innovation (such as iron metallurgy, more accessible than copper and tin) and new trade circuits that complemented but also circumvented those controlled by the states.

The increasing importance of these new activities and exchange networks, operating on the fringes of the palatial circuits, finally precipitated the crisis of the palatial economies. But what followed was not "collapse" or "crisis" but a reorganisation of economic activities on a different basis.

Also in this vein, Liverani postulates that the changes that occurred at the end of the Late Bronze Age saw the emergence of new state structures (national and ethnic states), as well as of more decentralised forms of exchange that further highlighted the rigidity and difficulties of adaptation of the old palatial systems (Liverani 2002). In any case, the crisis was only relative. Cypriot and later Phoenician traders, the expansion of the incense route in Arabia, the emergence of a lucrative commerce based on silphium around Cyrenaica as well as the continuity of trade routes through the oases of the Western Desert in Egypt, not to speak of the quest for metals from the western Mediterranean, nevertheless proves the importance of exchange following the crisis of Late Bronze imperial powers. Such importance is probably related to a fact evoked by Susan Sherratt, the appetite for metal goods observable in many areas of the Mediterranean at the end of the 2nd millennium. An appetite that contributed, possibly quite significantly, to the transformative intercultural effects of an economic, cultural and technological as well as ideological nature within European and Mediterranean societies during the period from the late 13th century until well into the early centuries of the 1st millennium (Sherratt 2012).

Henceforth trade appears as a crucial element in the economic changes observed during the Late Bronze Age and early Iron Age, especially in the case of exchanges occurring outside the palatial sphere. In other words, while official sources frequently refer to commercial operations revolving around palaces, they probably only refer to the tip of the iceberg (Monroe 2009 and 2010; Sauvage 2012). Furthermore it is quite probable that the bulk of exchange was based on modest commodities, rarely documented at all, while their traces in the archaeological record are scarce because of their perishable and transformable nature (metals, textiles, hides, plants, etc.), contrary to the expensive luxury items found in elite tombs or represented in the official iconography (Heymans & van Wijngaarden 2011; Sherratt 2003). In general, it also seems that the centrality ascribed to the palatial economy is somewhat illusory and unbalanced, a mirage due to the fact that monarchies and their personnel not only produced the immense majority of the documents preserved but, in many cases, the goods they produced and sought are easily detected in the archaeological record and enjoy a high prestige as works of art (exotic pottery and ornaments, objects in gold and silver, statues, etc.). Palatial economies thus appear to be somewhat oversized while private operations risk going unnoticed because of the absence of textual sources and the difficulty of detecting the goods involved (Wilkinson 2014). As for the lure of precious metals and the astonishing capacity of small polities to accumulate huge quantities of them (as the plunder brought back from Palestine into Egypt by Sheshonq I in the late 10th century BC shows), these phenomena are hardly understandable if "money" (mainly silver) did not circulate broadly in internal and external exchanges, had not permeated the whole society (not only its more privileged sectors) and could not be accumulated thanks to customs duty, taxes, etc. (Holladay 2006; 2009). In the absence of powerful monarchies regulating international exchange, temples appear instead as guarantors of the quality of precious metals used in commercial operations (Dercksen 1999; Jurman 2015). Only later would states gradually assume this function for their own fiscal and economic interests.

From a political point of view, the gradual end of the Late Bronze monarchies, first in the Eastern Mediterranean basin, later in Mesopotamia and western Iran, was not followed by anarchy but by what could be called a "Levantine political system", made up not of large states and "empires" but by a cluster of petty polities and city-states. Some of the former "big powers" survived, but on a much reduced scale, sometimes even divided (Egypt, Assyria, Babylonia, Elam); occasionally they launched military campaigns seeking to regain control over lucrative nodes of trade (for example the Elamite incursions into Mesopotamia or the campaign of Shesonq in Palestine), but these attempts proved to be ephemeral, failed to expand and consolidate new borders and, quite the reverse, were succeeded by increasing political fragmentation and decline in their homelands. By contrast, petty small polities specialising in trade and in the production of coveted goods (metals, incense) thrived. In all, this was a world where decentralisation prevailed, characterised by a renewal of mobile life-styles (Libyans, Arameans, Chaldeans), political instability, flourishing trade and new forms of demand. In fact, the reduced weight of traditional states was concomitant with the development of both new commercial routes escaping their control and new economic practices seeking to secure and facilitate exchange, such as the generalisation of common sets of juridical expressions and the use of coined metals.

Finally, what happened to former palatial institutions? Late Bronze Age "imperial" elites, depending on revenue from foreign tribute, military and court positions and, perhaps, income derived from taxes on trade and the circulation of commodities, were most exposed to the changes that took place during the final Late Bronze Age and were strongly affected by the increasing autonomy of economic actors. Under these conditions, local elites rose to a more prominent position and, judging from the best documented cases (Egypt, Assyria, Babylonia) it seems that they followed a two-fold strategy. On the one hand they "ruralised" themselves as land became their main source of income. On the other hand, they became closely associated with temples, the only institutions which could still provide income (in the form of landed assets and prebends), institutional security in the long term and which, moreover, preserved substantial political power in the local sphere. Neo-babylonian and later Mesopotamian evidence reveals, for instance, that "entrepreneurs" mediated in trading operations involving the commercialisation of the production of temples and invested in date plantations, real estate, the acquisition of temple prebends, etc. (Stolper 1985; Bongenaar 2000; Abraham 2004; Jursa 2010). The commercialisation and externalisation of operations imply that temples (and perhaps what remained of the "public" sector: domains of the elite and the royal family, etc.) also contributed to the flows of exchange, as the case of Wenamun shows. Finally, temples appear as guarantees of economic transactions (Babylonian *kudurrus* were placed in sanctuaries), beneficiaries of donations (as revealed by the Egyptian donation stelae) and surveyors of the quality of precious metals in circulation. However, little is known about the forms of wealth accumulation, investment, etc., outside the elite sector during the very late 2nd and early 1st millennium BC in the ancient Near East, not to speak of the organisation of production in the countryside and the characteristics of peasant and urban demand.

Bearing in mind the importance and extent of the economic changes that occurred during the transition between the Late Bronze and Early Iron Ages, in the following pages I intend to highlight some of the most conspicuous in a long-term perspective.

Trade and geopolitics in the late 2nd–early 1st millennium BC

The expansion of trade activities and new networks of exchange, which were not controlled or dominated by the main institutions and "big powers" of the Late Bronze Age, had a deep influence on the changes that occurred in the Eastern Mediterranean and the Near East from the beginning of the Iron Age. They also help explain how the surviving monarchies tried to adapt themselves to a new economic and political scenario, a process that culminated in the emergence of the first "world empires" of the 1st millennium BC, from Neo-Assyrians to Achaemenids (Sherratt 1998; 2000; 2003; 1998; Sherratt & Sherratt 2001). Egypt was not alien to these transformations and, in fact, it is quite possible that the increasing participation of the Nile Delta in trade activities with the Levant finally precipitated the advent of the so-called Third Intermediate Period, an era marked by the division of the country into many distinctive polities and by the development of the Delta (Sherratt 2003, 49). In a context in which trade and exchange played an increasing role in the distribution of goods, animals and people in the Near East and in the diffusion of artistic styles (Mumford 2007, 259; Feldman 2014), often outside the palatial sphere, Lower Egypt emerges as an important point of arrival and a centre of distribution of the traffic with the Levant (Holladay 2006, 327).

Susan Sherratt has shown how crucial changes affected the organisation of commercial networks during the Late Bronze Age, when modest merchants used the trade networks established by the institutions to their own profit, trading with their own goods. This led to a flourishing small-scale trade, to the development of new trade routes, to the emergence of specialised communities heavily involved in trade (Greek, Phoenician and South-Arabian city-states: Sherratt 2001; Liverani 1997a; 1997b, 111), to the multiplication of exchange regardless of states, thus precipitating the crisis of Late Bronze Age monarchies, as more and more traffic escaped their control, monopoles and tax-systems (as in the route used by smugglers that connected Nubia and Cyrenaica through the oases of the Egyptian Western Desert: Kuhlmann 2002, 163–165; 2013). Under these circumstances, Lower Egypt appears as a region with an ideally privileged position in the new commercial circuits that were emerging in the Eastern Mediterranean and the Near East. On the one hand, Cypriot archaeology reveals the existence of new trade routes linking the Iberian Peninsula, the Aegean, Cyrus, Phoenicia and Palestine (Demand 2004); on the other, the development of the incense route from the end of the 2nd millennium was concomitant with the ephemeral Egyptian effort to control this emerging land route from Arabia (as revealed by the discovery of an inscription of Ramesses III in the oasis of Tayma: Somaglino & Tallet 2011), with the end of the Egyptian presence in Palestine (a network of centres emerged in the Neguev seeking to control caravan trade, sometimes from South Arabia: Faust 2006; Thareani-Sussely 2007), with the last Egyptian expedition sent to Punt (the area of the southern Red Sea) in order to obtain a direct supply of incense and other products from this land and, finally, with the domestication of dromedary (Jasmin 2005). The incense route was fully operative towards the beginning of the 1st millennium (Liverani 1992; Kitchen 2001).

Upper Egypt apparently failed to become an active prtagonist in this new scenario, as the Theban region remained relatively isolated from the Mediterranean, without any apparent control over Nubian territory and resources and it was involved in occasional political turmoil. By contrast, Lower Egypt entered into a new era of urban development, agricultural expansion (judging from the donation stelae) and active trade with the Levant and beyond; the tale of Wenamun, for instance, mentions 20 ships in Byblos that traded with pharaoh Smendes, while another 50 ships in Sidon did business with a certain Werket-el (probably an Asiatic partner or agent of Smendes) and had sailed to his domain (Lichtheim 1973, 226; Liverani 1990, 247–254). A century later, when future pharaoh Sheshonq I established a cultic endowment for his father, his contribution included 15 *deben* of silver provided by his agents, two "*foreigners from Khor*" (=Syria and Palestina: Blackman 1941). "Esamon, the man from Gaza" appears as borrower of a certain amount of silver, together with a herder, in the Theban papyrus Michaelides 2, from around 700 BC (Donker van Heel 2004, 162–166). Further evidence confirms the increasing importance of trade in Egypt, even in Upper Egypt, as well as of activities related with it, such as loans, credit, a broader use of silver as money and contracts (Malinine 1953; Lüdeckens 1960; Martin 1995; Jasnow 2001, 39–43, and 2003, 804–810; Bleiberg 2002, 257, 270; Manning 2003, 843–852; Muhs 2005, 3–5), even the compilation of the first "juridical manuals" (Donker van Heel 1990; Lippert 2004). So terms such as *ḫbr* "to trade/do business" appear in some papyri of the Theban area around the end of the 11th and the beginning of the 10th centuries BC (Müller 2009, 262), while an expression like *jrt šwj* "to trade" is mentioned in a context of transactions such as leases, quotas, etc. in a stela of the 10th–9th centuries BC (Meeks 1995).

Another characteristic of Lower Egypt that is reminiscent of the Levant is the fragmentation of its territory into numerous political powers. This probably explains the abundance in this region of land donation stelae from the very end of the 2nd millennium and the first centuries of the 1st millennium, as if local elites sought institutional stability and security through their association with local sanctuaries. While such donations were extremely rare in Upper Egypt and may correspond to a strategy of "ruralisation" of the local elites there, conditions were radically different in Lower Egypt. Here donations were quite abundant (more than a hundred donation stelae are known from this period) and their frequency coincides with a flourishing local urbanism, the emergence of several capital cities, the consolidation of several independent kingdoms and the growth of local temples, from 950 BC. It is probably quite significant that no trace of donation stelae is known in Lower Egypt prior to this date. To sum up, the increasing integration of Lower Egypt in the trade networks of the Eastern Mediterranean may be partly explained by its flourishing agriculture, the cultivation of new spaces and a growing urban life whose prosperity led to the foundation of richly endowed sanctuaries. As linen, natron, papyrus, horses, ox-hides, fish, etc., were then traded with the Near East, it is quite probable that agriculture, cattle raising and the exploitation of the natural resources of the Delta provided goods for exportation (including cereals, as in the late 2nd millennium), paid with silver (Mumford 2007; Morkot 2007; Briant & Descat 1998, 80–81; Pope 2014, 155–156).

From a geopolitical point of view, however, an expanding trade also fostered rivalries and competition between powers in order to capture and control flows of wealth and networks of exchange (as for the notion of capture of trade circuits: Banaji 2007). In this vein, Kushites and Assyrians (later on, Neo-Babylonians) conquered, respectively, strategic crossroads such as Egypt and Syria in their attempts to control the Levant, the region where some of the most important maritime and caravan routes of the Iron Age converged. In fact, the Kushite conquest of Egypt may probably be explained by the emergence, after the collapse of the Ramesside empire in Asia, of several trade routes that directly linked important producing areas such as South Arabia, Eritrea and Ethiopia to the Mediterranean coast (Philistia, Phoenicia), thus by-passing the Nile Valley. Furthermore, from 800 BC these areas were politically organised as states for the first time and contacts between them, across the southern Red Sea seem to have been intense: on the one hand, South Arabia appears to have been divided into several kingdoms while, on the other hand, the Ethiopian kingdom of *D'MT* was ruled by kings who held titles typical of South Arabian monarchs, like *MKRB* and *MLK*, and peoples from South Arabia are attested in the Ethiopian plateau from 850 BC (Curtis 2004; Fattovich 2004; Philips 2004; Pope 2014). So it seems that an Ethiopian state (or several states) blocked in some way the traditional direct access of Nilotic powers to the Southern Red Sea by land (in this case, the Kushite state), thus forcing them to seek new, alternative ways of controlling this lucrative traffic. Thus, the Kushite conquest or, perhaps better, hegemony over a divided Egypt was only the first step in a strategy that led the Nubian armies towards Palestine and Syria, where they were brought face to face with the powerful Assyrian armies, sometimes with success. Later on the Saite kings would continue the same policy, this time against the Neo-Babylonian Empire. In any case, Kushite kings celebrated the arrival of beams from the cities of the North as well as of Asiatic copper employed in their monuments; they also mention the arrival of ships loaded with Syrian goods, while the expression "man of the North" became synonymous with slave (Morkot 2001, 248–251; Pope 2014, 113, 119 and 131). Recent discoveries prove that they mastered iron technology in the production of high-quality weapons (Smith 2008).

From an Assyrian perspective, it is possible to get a better perspective of the interests at stake. The use of dromedaries as a new means of transportation made it possible for the palatial powers along the Euphrates valley and in the area between the Euphrates and the Levant to accumulate huge quantities of exotic goods and precious metals within a few decades. According to the Assyrian booty lists, these included myrrh, frankincense and other spices from Arabia, as well as African goods (ivory, elephant tusks, elephant hide, gold, and ebony) and Indian goods (e.g. rosewood) arriving through the same trade routes. So the early Assyrian strategy sought to control the long-distance trade hub of the Middle Euphrates, where the traditional routes along the river converged with the newly established overland routes. So, in the first third of the 9th century BC, Ashurnasirpal II (883–859 BC) built a new city here and named it after himself, Kār-Ashurnasirpal, while his 9th century successors also conquered or built cities in this area and (re)named them with the element *kār* "port of trade, emporium" (Vér 2014, 791–792). Later on, within a few years (743–734 BC), the Assyrian army subjugated the vast territory between the band of the Euphrates and Egypt and established nine *kārus* in the Levant, from the mouth of the Orontes to Gaza, with the goal of supplying the Empire. Sargon II (721–705 BC) pushed the Assyrian border to the south of Gaza and seized an important commercial centre in the border zone:

> "The Egyptians and the Arabians – I made them overwhelmed by the glory of Aššur, my lord. At the mention of my name their hearts trembled, they let down their hands. I opened the sealed [harbo]ur of Egypt. The Assyrians and the Egyptians I mingled [to-]gether and I made them trade [with each other]." (Vér 2014, 793)

Sargon II also led campaigns towards the Zagros and the valleys of the Great Khorasan Road – which connected Mesopotamia and Iran, and which later became a very important route of the Silk Road – and created there six new *kārus*. Finally Sennacherib (704–681 BC) and his son, Esarhaddon (680–669 BC) established *kārus* in the Zagros, Phoenicia, Philistia and in the Delta of the Nile as well (Vér 2014, 794). So Assyria succeeded in controlling the most important trade routes in the Near East as well as strategic goods, thus making it possible to outrival enemies and competitors, such as when Assyria forbade the export of cedar beams to Egypt (Vér 2014, 798–799), a prohibition somewhat circumvented by Sidonian and Tyrian timbermen and private merchants (Semaan 2015, 98). At the same time, however, the consolidation of the Assyrian Empire also increased the opportunities for commercial expansion (Fletcher 2012).

In the end, palatial policies seeking control of the main trade routes crossing the Near East, the Red Sea and north-eastern Africa promoted more global ambitions and inspired a new kind of geopolitical vision, especially when compared with their Late Bronze Age precedents. The result was the emergence of the first "world-empires" spreading over two, sometimes three continents: the Assyrian Empire and the Achaemenid Empire. Their economic impact, however, encompassed a much broader area (Aruz *et al.* 2014).

Wages, hired labour and temples as centres of pre-monetisation

Certain economic features that were well documented in some near eastern societies during the 1st millennium BC can be traced back, in fact, to the last centuries of the 2nd millennium if not earlier. One of the most important, because of its economic and social consequences, is the increasingly decentralised management of land owned by temples and the crown and, consequently, the increasing presence of workers not directly dependent on these institutions. So private "entrepreneurs" as well as labour forms based on contracts, hired workers and wages become more frequent in the documentary record.

In the case of New Kingdom Egypt, for instance, temples and especially the Domain of god Amun and the memorial temples of the kings, became immense production centres that possessed considerable resources in land, herds, personnel as well as other resources, from mines to fisheries and textile workshops (Grandet 1994; Haring 1997). This marked a new era, as temples now replaced older forms of institutional agricultural and labour management based on networks of royal agricultural centres (such as the Old Kingdom *ḥwt*) and labour camps (most notably Middle Kingdom *ḫnrt*) as well as on relatively modest provincial temples. If figures evoked in documents such as the papyrus Harris I, the Wilbour Papyrus and other administrative documents are correct, New Kingdom temples became enormous economic machines, crucial poles in the agricultural and economic organisation of the countryside, able to produce huge amounts of agricultural and textile produce and promoting their own mining, trading, gathering and cattle-rearing operations. But their economic role went much further as they also specialised in the management of crown land. Under these conditions, the cultivation of the fields under their care (whether their own or those belonging to the crown) was made possible by the simultaneous use of several complementary work systems, including the utilisation of their own dependent workforce (compelled to deliver standard quotas of grain), of corvée and, increasingly, agricultural "entrepreneurs" and "free" tenants who leased land and delivered part of the harvest, even gold, to the owning institution (Moreno García 2008; 2010; 2014b). Under this decentralised system, temples and the crown saved resources (especially the sustenance of a permanent workforce only needed seasonally), could cultivate dispersed fields without the need to create an administrative infrastructure and obtained huge amounts of grain and silver as income. And here lay two capital questions. On the one hand, the considerable amounts of silver delivered by the temples as taxes to the crown reveal that they commercialised part of their production (about a ton of silver in just one case: Grandet 1994, 238). On the other hand, entrepreneurs had at their disposal a workforce that could be used when and where it was required, thus implying the possibility of hiring workers and the existence of wages. However the weight of hired work and wages in relation to other forms of work, especially serfdom and dependent workers, is difficult to evaluate (Moreno García 2008; 2010; 2014b).

Two sets of sources from the second half of the 3rd millennium BC nevertheless give some possible clues. In the first case, owners of mastabas declare that they had paid the artisans and workers who built their funerary monuments. One example is Akhetmehu at Giza: "with regard to this my tomb of eternity, it was made for bread and beer; every workman who worked on it thanks all the gods for me. I gave them clothing, oil, copper and grain in great quantity" (Strudwick 2005: 252). These and many other similar statements suggest that some economic activities outside the institutional sphere were based on agreements between workers and individuals on a "contractual" basis, with wages paid for work and services, as in the inscription of Intef son of Myt, dating from the late 3rd millennium BC: "I have hired (by contract) a *ka-priest*" and "I have hired (by contract) a lector-priest". Later on, during the New Kingdom, dozens of agreements between individuals and artisans stipulate the delivery of high-quality funerary equipment (such as coffins) in exchange for payments, and these transactions took place outside the economic circuits dominated by the palatial sphere (Cooney 2007). As for the use of "contractual" agreements and hired work in the agricultural sphere prior to the 1st millennium BC, a second set of sources might cast some light. Several private inscriptions from the late 3rd millennium BC evoke the acquisition of fields, ships, herds of cattle, goats and assess, even people, while some wealthy individuals even boasted about not having enslaved people (usually women) in periods of distress. In other cases, indebtedness and problems related to inheritance and divisions of property led to the dissolution of private patrimonies, to the extent that preserving and bequeathing the familial assets intact (lit. "the house of the father") to the next generation became a major concern and a source of pride in private inscriptions. Hence both sets of documents reveal that wages and hired work were not unknown in Egypt from the late 3rd millennium BC, including wages partially paid in metals. Furthermore, debts, hard times, problems due to inheritances, people deprived of their fields, etc., put at the disposal of both institutions and wealthy individuals a workforce compelled to sell their labour and to integrate themselves into patronage networks in order to survive. The correspondence of Heqanakht, for instance, reveals that the household of this well-off landowner included several subordinates employed in the cultivation of his fields (Allen 2002).

Two final points regarding Egypt should be considered. The first one is the existence of a "commercial" private agriculture, mainly recorded when taxes were paid, centred on the cultivation of date-palms, flowers, orchards and vineyards and important enough to justify the use of new irrigation tools such as the *shaduf*. The introduction of this irrigation device around the middle of the 2nd millennium BC made possible the perennial irrigation of small plots and expanded the possibilities for horticulture, especially in peri-urban areas. The papyrus Louvre E 3226 (dated from 1450 BC), for instance, records the exchange of grain and dates (one sack of grain for one sack of dates). While the grain was controlled by institutional granaries, the dates were produced and delivered by individuals (Megally 1977, 254–257; Moreno García 2014b, 49). Other New Kingdom papyri record the delivery of flowers, dates and other horticultural produce made by individuals to ships sent by institutions (Janssen 1961). As for the second point, New Kingdom documents reveal the increasing use of precious metals in everyday transactions, including the acquisition of slaves, fields and cattle. Especially significant is the case of fishermen, who were paid in silver and who also paid their taxes in silver, thus suggesting the commercialisation of their catches. As for the tomb and temple robberies of the late New Kingdom, when huge amounts of silver and gold were stolen, the Ramesside documents reveal that robbers used the booty for the acquisition of fields, slaves, etc. In all cases traders appear as crucial elements in the transformation of agricultural produce into precious metals and their activities seem crucial not only in the service of temples and the crown but also individuals (Moreno García 2014a; 2014b). The extent of such operations is difficult to evaluate but, judging from the evidence in the Papyrus Harris I and other contemporary texts, it seems to have been quite important. In fact, it also appears that Egyptian grain was exported, partly at least in the context of agreements between states. Liverani, for instance, suggests a possible link between the exports of Egyptian grain to the land of Hatti and the depreciation of the value of silver in Egypt around the reign of Merenptah (from a ratio silver/copper of 1:100 to only 1:60 *deben*), suggesting that huge quantities of this metal had arrived into Egypt as payments for the grain delivered (Liverani 1990, 235–236; Moreno García 2014b, 67–72). To sum up, an increasing role of traders and silver in institutional and everyday transactions, the commercialisation of agricultural produce (both produced by institutions and individuals, especially horticultural goods), the availability of hired work and decentralised management appear to be related phenomena in New Kingdom Egypt. A tendency that would continue during the 1st millennium BC with the first land leases.

Similar conditions also prevailed in contemporary Mesopotamia. Here, the use of silver in private economic activities as well as activities carried out by private "entrepreneurs" goes back to the 3rd millennium BC (Ouyang 2013; Garfinkle 2012; Steinkeller 2004; Paoletti 2008; Peyronel 2010; Rosa 2011; Bulgarelli; Widell 2008; Wilcke 2014; Cripps 2014), while hired labour is well attested in Ur III times. Then antichretic loaning arrangements procured extra labour, when the interest on a barley loan was repaid in human labour, usually in the form of harvest work. In fact, both the provincial economies and the royal sector were forced to hire workers for wages, usually paid in barley although the occasional use of silver is documented as well (Steinkeller 2015). As for temples, they played a dominant (but not exclusive) role in the economic life of the country from the late 4th millennium, as the cuneiform archives reveal (Steinkeller 2004; Schrakamp 2013; Selz 2014). A position that still prevailed in southern Mesopotamia during the second half of the 2nd millennium in spite of the increasing importance of business and private entrepreneurs (Van de Mieroop 1992). In fact, private entrepreneurs appear in these documents partly working for themselves and partly carrying out missions for temples and palaces.

Later on, while many documents from Kassite Babylonia still remain unpublished, temples appear nevertheless as beneficiaries of royal land grants. This was a period of an apparently increasing ruralisation of society, when the trend towards smaller settlements accelerated. Nevertheless it also witnessed the expansion of the indirect management of land, as *kudurru* documents prove. These texts concern "state land" allocated by the king to high officials, such as viziers, high priests etc. and, to a lesser extent, to temples. An example is Itti-Ezida-lummir, a dignitary whose private archive mainly deals with real estate sales concerning houses and house plots but which also includes a *kudurru*, unfortunately quite damaged. He appears to have been a well-off Babylonian, in possession of some houses in Babylon, as well as of a land donation of a larger estate in this province or in others close to Babylon itself. These royal grants enabled the king to relinquish direct control over his land by parcelling it out to favoured members of the elite. This had the double advantage of rewarding loyal service while absolving the state of the need to manage the exploitation of the land itself (Baker 2011, 304–306; Paulus 2013; 2014). Similarly, during the Neo-Babylonian and Achaemenid periods, institutions like temples and the royal palace itself often preferred not to manage their agricultural holdings directly but rather delegated agrarian management to others by various means, including the participation of entrepreneurs (Stolper 1985; Bongenaar 2000; Abraham 2004; Wunsch 2012). Alongside *kudurru*, several private archives have also been identified in Kassite Babylonia, often containing sale and loan contracts but, for some reason, it seems as though some restriction affected large property sales, to the point that only small estates like private fields around towns, gardens or houses and building plots could be freely sold (Paulus 2013; 2014). There is also evidence of thousands of people forming a mass of slaves in Kassite times, being allowed to live in family groups but ascribed to compulsory work for the state and often trying to run away (Tenney 2011). It appears then that the consolidation of a wealthy landed elite was concomitant not only with royal grants of land, but with land sales of small plots and the existence of serfs and slaves.

A similar pattern emerges in northern Mesopotamia and Syria, where many documents from the first half of the 2nd millennium concern fields sold by private individuals to other private individuals. According to Zaccagnini, the overall pattern of private land ownership from the late 3rd to the mid-1st millennium in these regions (Nuzi, Ebla, Ugarit, Alalakh, Emar, Ekalte, Assyria in the Late Bronze Age) is characterised by the disproportion between a relatively small number of large patrimonies owned by individual large landowners and a vast number of small plots of family land. The agricultural activities carried out for the absentee landlords were performed by a subordinate workforce formed by local peasants who were the former owners of the land, which they had to sell in order to settle economic difficulties and were thus reduced to the condition of debtors or workers for powerful men. As the deeds of transfer reveal, the great majority of privately owned fields were too small to represent the exclusive source of maintenance for an average family. Many peasants were compelled to seek additional income. The basic trend is thus one of a progressive impoverishment of the rural strata and a generalised disintegration of rural family properties that were conveyed to single individuals building up vast land patrimonies (Zaccagnini 1999). This explains why so many texts refer to the loss of property or the right to cultivate communal land to the profit of buyers whose interests sometimes extended over considerable areas encompassing several villages (Renger 1995, 304–307; Beckman 1997; 2008). Under these conditions, hired work flourished, to the point that a special formula for hiring contracts was developed in private documents (Farber 1978, 30–35; Klengel 1987, 163–165; Dosch 1987, 231–232).

The Old Babylonian period palaces also benefited from similar conditions as they could now avoid maintaining a permanent labour force; instead they granted economically viable activities such as herding, farming, selling agricultural products, collecting obligations owed to the palace and recruiting seasonal labourers, to individuals ("middle-men", "entrepreneurs") who bore the risks, who could make some profit and who could mobilise the workforce necessary to cultivate the land. This is the *Palastgeschäfte* system (Goddeeris 2002, 338–346, 352–353; Földi 2014, with previous bibliography). Thus the "Laws of Eshnunna" (18th century BC) and the "Code of Hammurabi" (around 1700 BC), provide some of the earliest sources of information about the wages of (putatively "free") hired labourers (Scheidel 2010, 438–440). Moreover documents relating to the hiring of workers in the Old Babylonian period reveal that silver was always valued above barley in the payment of wages; workers hired for one year received proportionately less than those hired for a month, while those paid on a daily basis received the equivalent of the highest monthly wage (Farber 1978, 30–35). In any case the gradual impoverishment of certain sectors of the peasantry was a tendency that continued in northern Mesopotamia during the second half of the 2nd millennium, when strain from states on the working population and on its capacity to reproduce itself, an increasingly impoverished rural population, the flight of peasants and of urban underclasses joining with nomads to plunder the countryside, contributed to a slow breakdown of the palace-centred economy, especially in Syria-Palestine, during the late second millennium (Liverani 1987). Later on, during the middle of the 1st millennium BC, hired work represented a substantial part of the workforce employed by institutions, and their wages (partly in silver, partly in foodstuff) far exceeded the salaries of the institutional personnel (Jursa *et al.* 2010, 660–681; Rader 2015; Jursa 2015).

Egypt and Mesopotamia thus reveal that the second half of 2nd millennium was a period in which indirect forms of land management were concomitant with an increasing recourse to traders and agricultural entrepreneurs, in a context of a growing commercialisation and "monetisation" of agricultural produce. While the role of such intermediaries is well attested in ancient Mesopotamia from the 3rd millennium, in the case of pharaonic Egypt it is during the New Kingdom when inscriptions attest for the first time the importance of traders at the service of temples and institutions, and when many expressions reveal the role played by trade and business in the institutional sphere. Not only do traders (*šwtjw*) appear for the first time in administrative documents, but their role was considered important enough to appear in the literary genre of the satires of trades as an occupation attractive enough for scribes-to-be. Furthermore, many Semitic terms related to trade and business then entered the Egyptian vocabulary. In fact, the role of traders was crucial in the commercialisation of agricultural produce and its transformation into precious metals that could be subsequently taxed by the state. In any case, the scarcity of Egyptian sources when compared with Mesopotamia hardly conceals the fact that many parallels existed between both regions and that the role of temples as economic agencies in the second half of the 2nd millennium was related to the increasing role of trade, "money" and decentralised forms of agricultural management in the institutional sphere (Moreno García 2014b, 67–72).

Precious metals and proto-monetary forms of exchange

The famous papyrological dossier on the tomb robberies in the late Ramesside period reveals that huge quantities of precious metals were being robbed from temples and royal tombs in the Theban area, and that robbers operated in collusion with priests, policemen, officials and necropolis workers. In the same documents traders appear as crucial mediators in order to "launder" the gold and silver stolen as they enabled robbers to buy fields, slaves and cattle with their part of the booty. In other cases they helped melt down metals (Vernus 1993, 64–73). However royal burials and temples were far from being the only target of robbers during these troubled times. Other texts also reveal that modest tombs, such as those owned by the artisans at Der el-Medina, were affected in the same way and that the metallic objects stored in them were avidly sought after (Cooney 2014). Sherratt has stressed that tomb looting in search of metals became a generalised phenomenon in the late 2nd and early 1st millennium BC, when the decentralised circulation of bronze (sometimes in the form of objects, sometimes in scrap or recyclable form) in ever-increasing quantities, combined with the circulation of itinerant metalworkers, meant that bronze and bronze goods had become available directly to almost anyone who wanted them. This subverted the tight control which eastern Mediterranean ruling elites had once attempted to exert over the bulk circulation and centralised redistribution of copper and tin, and contributed to their "collapse" at the end of the East Mediterranean Bronze Age. Furthermore, this bronze inflation must have affected the value of bronze in the eastern half of the Mediterranean and promoted the increasing production of traditionally highly precious materials like iron. Finally, she also argues that it encouraged the search for silver, the traditional standard of exchange in the East, leading Cypriot and Phoenician activities further and further west, culminating in the Phoenician arrival at Huelva (Spain) by the end of the 10th century (Sherratt 2000; 2012; cf. also Yule in press). Other scholars such as Rehren have emphasised the existence, alongside a mainstream bronze economy closely administered by institutions like temples and the state, of a small-volume uncontrolled scrap metal economy serving the archaeologically often less visible peasant and migrant populations (Rehren & Pusch 2012). The discovery at Bate's Island around Marsa Matruh, about 300 km west of Alexandria, of furnaces and traces of a modest metallurgical production (needles, pins, etc.), in the context of informal small-scale trading activities dominated by Libyan populations, provides an example of such activities (White 2002, 47–53, 168–174). Decentralised circuits of exchange, together with the increasing use of metals (including silver) in everyday activities, reveal the growing importance of trade and the transformation of commodities into silver and gold, thus leading to what could be called a proto-monetary system led by merchants.

The case of Egypt during the New Kingdom is particularly noteworthy. An exceptional document from this period, the papyrus Harris I, records the massive donations made by pharaoh Ramesses III (1184–1153 BC) to several temples during his reign. Several passages enumerate the huge amounts of goods paid as annual taxes by the servants of the royal mortuary temple and later donated by the king to the temples. Along with linen, cattle, agricultural produce, gold from Nubia and the Eastern Desert, etc., the text also mentions enormous quantities of silver, a metal not produced in Egypt and which, consequently, could only arrive to the Nile Valley through trade and tribute. Only the Theban temples, for example, received three assignments of silver for an amount of, respectively, 10,964.9 *deben*, 3606.1 *deben* and 4204.7 *deben*, that is to say 997.8 kg, 328 kg and 382 kg (Grandet 1994: 238 and 325). How those servants obtained such considerable quantities of silver is unfortunately not stated, but it is quite reasonable to think that the commercialisation of part of the harvests of the temples, as well as taxes levied from temple fisheries and herds, trading activities, etc., made it possible for these institutions to accumulate substantial amounts of silver and pay the taxes in silver on a regular, annual basis.

Other sources reveal that the crown levied taxes in gold and silver, among other goods, from temples and towns in New Kingdom times (Jursa & Moreno García 2015, 149–151). In any case, exchange and the transformation of agricultural produce into metals imply the existence of markets and commercial operations in which traders played a crucial role. Their role as intermediaries in the economic activities led by temples is described in several inscriptions from this period, when they appear at the service of the crown and the temples, to the point that overseers of merchants became part of the temple personnel. In other cases, however, they led their own commercial activities (including missions for wealthy Egyptians) and were taxed by the crown (Castle 1992; Moreno García 2013, 94–96; 2014, 67–72). Traders were thus indispensable not only for transporting, buying and selling goods at different places but also in the transformation of agricultural produce into precious metals and vice-versa, as in the case of traders, apparently at the service of a temple, who exchanged gold for foodstuff (Peet 1934; Megally 1974; 1975). Official missions also involved the use of silver, as in the case of a scribe working for an institution and in charge of the delivery of 46 ingots of silver as well as quotas of other goods (fish, wool, etc.) in the context of trading operations involving the participation of several ship captains (Wente 1990, 120–122). As for fishermen, several sources reveal that they routinely paid their taxes in silver. Ramesside ostracon Gardiner 86, for instance, mentions workers involved in herding and gathering activities in the Delta, who delivered animals, salt, natron and plants to the Domain of Amun while fishermen instead paid a fixed amount of silver.

Later on, when Kushite pharaoh Taharqa endowed a sanctuary in the Memphite region, part of the revenue granted to the temple consisted again of silver delivered by fishermen as taxes. Likewise when Herodotus evoked centuries later the Egyptian tribute paid to the Persian treasury, he specified that it consisted of 700 talents of silver as well as silver delivered by the fishermen of lake Moeris (Moreno García 2013, 94–96). Finally, a single Ramesside official in charge of the production of natron in the area of Fayum delivered to the royal treasury an astonishing amount of 91 kg of gold as his annual tax, thus suggesting that this gold came from customs revenue or from exports, especially when considering that natron was then crucial in the production of glass, a flourishing industry in the Near East during the Late Bronze Age (Moreno García 2013, 96).

Small-scale trade also involved the use of silver and gold (Castle 1992, 256–263). A scribe, for instance, wrote to a colleague to forbid him to behave in such a reprehensible way again as he had done in the past, when he set aside part of the rations under his care in order to convert them into silver (Wente 1990, 114). Three tenants who cultivated some royal land assigned to a temple, are said to have paid gold into the Pharaoh's treasury (Wente 1990, 130–131). A papyrus recording the collection of diverse goods along the Nile evokes the delivery of silver to a woman at the *meryt* "quay, marketplace" (Condon 1984, 63–65), and a market scene from the tomb of Niankhkhnum and Khnumhotep (around 2400 BC) records the exchange of a piece of cloth in exchange for 6 *shaty*, a unit of value currently used with gold and silver (Moussa & Altenmüller 1977, 85, fig. 10, pl. 24). And, as stated before, traders played a crucial role in the tomb robberies of the late New Kingdom, as they recycled the stolen metals into other goods, thus suggesting that the circulation of precious metals was quite common within Egyptian society and that the sudden appearance of gold and silver in the hands of commoners did not arouse particular suspicion. In some cases stolen gold was melted in the houses of priests (Demarée 2010, 57). How did precious metals circulate at the local, small-scale level?

The discovery of a small treasure at El-Amarna may provide some clues. In a small open space beside a public well in the North Suburb a pottery jar was buried, containing 23 bars of gold and a quantity of silver fragments and roughly made rings, as well as a silver figurine of a Hittite god. The total weight of the gold was 3375 g (about 37 *deben*), while the total weight of the silver came to 1085 grams (about 12 *deben*). As Kemp has stated, this discovery illustrates easily convertible wealth poised on the point of re-entering the economy at a private level (Kemp 1992, 244–246). Some texts confirm this impression. Ostracon BM 5631 from Deir el-Medina, dated from the 19th dynasty (1295–1186 BC), contains a statement made by an individual, in which he mentions the discovery of a sealed jar bearing two seal impressions and inscribed with a list of its contents: 10 *deben*-weights of silver, 2 *mine*-weights of gold, 7 heart amulets, 7 chains (?) of gold, and 20 gold signet rings (Wente 1990, 146). Quite significantly, other metallic objects also found by the same individual are said to belong to Pharaoh, but apparently it was not the case of the jar; it may then be assumed that, quite probably, it belonged to an individual. As in the case of the Amarna treasure, an amalgam of different objects and pieces of precious metals were stocked together. So precious metals circulated in the private sphere in different forms, and Castle has emphasised that some contemporary units of value (*sha(y)t*, *deben*) referring to metals (copper, silver, gold) derived from verbs meaning "to cut" (Castle 1992, 267–268).

This evidence, both archaeological and textual/linguistic, points to a crucial aspect of the circulation of precious metals in everyday operations, that discs, rings, wires, pieces of metal, etc., were stocked, cut, exchanged and held in houses. The recent discovery at the Ramesside garrison city of Beith Shean, in Israel, of three small silver hoards found in the 20th dynasty levels is of particular interest, since they contained "chocolate bar" silver ingots and used silver objects that had a monetary function, and could have been used to pay the wages of Egyptian officials or mercenaries. Silver came from southeast Turkey and Greece (Thompson 2009, 597–607; Kelder 2015). Such small hoards are well known in Early Iron Age contexts in the Levant and have inspired some discussion of pre-monetary practices in the Near East and the role played by bullion *hacksilber* that had to be cut and weighed out in every transaction (Balmuth 2001; Kletter 2003; 2004; Thompson 2003; Gitin & Golani 2004; Peyronel 2010, 931; cf. also Jursa 2010, 479–480).

But what transpires from discoveries like those at Amarna and Beith Shean is that such practices were also common in the Late Bronze Age (Gestoso Singer 2010) and their precedents can be traced back even earlier, to the late 3rd and early 2nd millennium, as revealed by about a dozen hoards of silver from beneath the floors of private houses in several Mesopotamian cities (Powell 1996, 236; Goddeeris 2002, 391; Peyronel 2010; Kroll 2011, 15) as well as by an Old Assyrian hoard found at Kanesh/Kültepe, in Anatolia (Pálfi 2014, 222–223), an Old Babylonian one at Larsa and an Old

Syrian one at Ebla (Peyronel 2010). Also since the middle of the 2nd millennium, but especially from the 1st millennium BC on, silver and precious metals also circulated in the form of sealed bags of a given weight, both in Egypt and the Near East, such as the bag with 11 *deben* of silver mentioned by Wenamun (examples: Vargyas 2004; Holladay 2009, 215; Jursa 2010, 490; Földi 2014, 101–102, 110).

In the case of ancient Mesopotamia, silver replaced copper as a weight currency from the late Early Dynastic III, and fixed exchange ratios for silver to copper and silver to barley regulated the flow between these categories of staple goods *versus* currency. Also from the late Early Dynastic III varying degrees of purity were acknowledged for silver, while taxes and tributes were paid in silver, usually in the shape of spirals and rings. Finally the tendency to establish value rates on silver became further fixed and standardised when administrative unification and standardisation accompanied the rise of the Akkadian empire and its expansion into the famous "silver mountains" and the land of copper (Helwing 2014). In fact, the use of silver, the commercialisation of agricultural produce through markets and the crucial mediating role played by merchants between institutions and producers is well attested from the 3rd millennium (Neumann 1999; van Driel 2002, 1–30; Steinkeller 2002; 2004; Paoletti 2008; Bulgarelli 2011; Ouyang 2013; Cripps 2014). The sophistication of the commercial operations and the uses of silver involved in them is apparent in the extraordinary archive of the Old Assyrian merchants at Kanesh/Kültepe, in Anatolia, who transported textiles and tin to Anatolia in exchange for silver and gold carried back to their homeland (with profits of 100% on tin and 200% on textiles). Silver unambiguously functioned as money and not only as a standard of value and means of payment, but also as an indirect means of exchange, while markets, fluctuating prices, creditors and credits, assurances, long-term trade ventures, etc., are also well documented in the texts from Kanesh (Dercksen 1996; Veenhof 1997, 1999; 2010). The importance of silver in private and institutional economic operations continued during the 2nd millennium, as in the Old Babylonian period (Farber 1978; Van de Mieroop 1992; 2002; Pomponio 2003; Saporetti 2009; Földi 2014), in the Middle Assyrian kingdom (Rosa 2011), in Kassite Babylonia (Del Monte 2009), and are particularly well documented in the 1st millennium, during the Neo-Babylonian period (Jursa 2010, 469–753).

A final aspect to be dealt with is the integration of economies over large areas and its "monetary" implications. In the case of pharaonic Egypt, copper appears to have been the dominant metal in the rare private transactions recording the use of metals prior to the middle of the 2nd millennium BC. High officials used copper (among other goods, such as textiles) to pay artisans for their work, as seen *supra*, while Heqanakhte, in the early 2nd millennium, requested their subordinates to "send 24 *deben* of copper for the lease of land" (letter II) and to "collect the copper of those two female servants" of his household (letter P') (Allen 2002, 17, 21, 119). Silver was then only used in the production of precious objects, jewellery, etc. (some 3rd millennium examples are mentioned in Posener-Krieger 1976, 162; Strudwick 2005, 125). But with the advent of the New Kingdom silver became synonymous with "money" and "payment" and was widely used as a means of fixing and expressing the prices of commodities and services (Castle 1992, 261–262). Quite significantly, a unit of value used from the middle of the 3rd millennium and restricted to gold and silver (never to copper), the *shaty*, was equivalent to one-twelfth of a *deben* in the New Kingdom (Janssen 1975, 102–105); its duodecimal basis appears as an oddity given the decimal system of measures then prevailing in Egypt, probably because of near-eastern influence. However, balance weights appear in the vast region between the Aegean and western India around 2600 BC, while weight units are surprisingly uniform over large areas from the 3rd millennium, and the Egyptian "small" standard gold *deben* (13.6 g.) and the "large" copper *deben* (27.3 g.), in use from at least the early 2nd millennium if not earlier (Marcus 2007, 149, with references), had the same weight as the unit used contemporaneously in the sexagesimal Eastern Mediterranean system (13.7 g) and in the Indus area (13.71 g), the same regions where lapis lazuli and silver had been imported since the 3rd millennium (Rahmstorf 2006, especially 13–18; 2010, 100–102; 2012, 315–316; see also Wilkinson 2014, 146–151, 200). The alleged abundance of gold in Egypt (from the Eastern Desert and Nubia) meant that the ratio between gold and silver was usually 1:2, and that of silver and copper 1:100 (Černy 1954, 905–908).

If gold was relatively cheap in Egypt and silver comparatively expensive, this circumstance could have opened many possibilities for trade with neighbouring regions. For example, the usual purchase rate of copper at the trade colony of Kanesh, in Anatolia, during the Old Assyrian period, was 120:1 in silver, while the sales rate was 60:1, thus the copper trade assured a 100% profit, apart from expenditure (Dercksen 1996, 158). In fact, during the early 2nd millennium, the circulation of silver suddenly expanded among Egyptian high society (Pierrat-Bonnefois 2014, 174) and considerable quantities of silver, copper and bronze were imported from the Levant, such as the 22.79 kg. of silver, 133.28 kg. of bronze and 435.73 kg. of copper brought by two ships from Lebanon in a single expedition (Marcus 2007, 141, 148 n. 34, 152). Silver arrived into Egypt, Byblos and Mari in the early 2nd millennium BC (Wiener 2013). However, what Egyptians exported in exchange remains largely unknown, but it is possible that gold figured as an important commodity, especially when considering that an active trade with gold then took place in the Egyptian fortresses in northern Nubia. In fact, in contemporary Assyria, silver was usually the high-range money, but gold appeared sporadically in a money function and in joint-ventures from the early 2nd millennium BC as an extra-high-range money, and the ratio silver/gold was then about 1:8 (Powell 1996:229).

As for Babylonia, the dramatic increase in the value of silver relative to gold (from a ratio of 9:1 to 3:1) over about three generations, just until Hammurabi's 35th year (middle of the 18th century BC), was due to the fact that gold became much more abundant at that time. Later on, during the Kassite, Middle Assyrian, and Middle Babylonian periods, the texts reveal the utilisation of gold in increasing quantities, to the point that by the Kassite period, commodities were for the first time valued, although not necessarily paid for, in gold (Farber 1978, 3–7; Powell 1996, 229, 230–231). The ratio silver/gold was then 4:1 for first-class (lit. "bright") gold. In my opinion, it is quite noteworthy that the lowest ratio silver/gold in the Mesopotamian area is attested at Ebla and Mari, where it oscillated between 6:1 and 2:1 (Powell 1990, 80–81). Both cities were important commercial nodes between the Mediterranean Sea and Mesopotamia, and contacts between Ebla and Egypt are well attested in the Early and Middle Bronze Age; furthermore the ratio 2:1 is the usual one in Egypt. In fact, the early 2nd millennium BC witnessed an increasing production of prestigious items while gold work became characterised by the application of advanced technologies like filigree, granulation and soldering, first developed in Syria around 2300 BC and which significantly expanded at the beginning of the 2nd millennium BC, especially in Byblos around 2000 BC, in Mari around 2200–1900 BC and in the royal tombs at Ebla around 1825–1700 BC (Prévalet 2014). It could be possible that Nubian and Egyptian gold entered into Mesopotamia through these centres. Later on and according to the Great Abydos inscription of Ramesses II, traders operating in Egypt "trade with their consignments, their revenue thereof being gold, silver and copper" (Castle 1992, 250–251).

The years preceding the New Kingdom also witnessed the increasing importance of gold in Egyptian transactions, including as a unit of value (Lacau 1933, 14, 24–25, 31; Redford 1997, 12 no. 63; Beylage 2002, 403–411). While the value of silver relative to gold appears to have been quite stable during the New Kingdom (2:1 and in one case 5:3), as well as that of silver and copper (around 1:100), the latter experienced some changes during the 20th dynasty, when it dropped to 1:60 during the later years of Ramesses II or the reign of Merenptah, a ratio still in use by the year 7 of Ramesses IX (around 1119 BC: Janssen 1975, 106–107). Liverani has suggested that this shift in the silver/copper rate from 1:100 to 1:60 took place in a period when Egypt shipped grain to the Hittite empire (Hittites also imported grain from northern Syria then) and that this could be the result of massive Hittite payments in silver for grain (Liverani 1990, 235–236): Queen Puduhepa claimed in a letter to Ramesses II that there was no grain in her lands and, around the same time, Hittite prince Heshmi/Hishmi-Sharrumma was sent to Egypt to arrange the prompt shipment of a consignment of wheat and barley to the Hittite land. Later on, pharaoh Merneptah declared that he had sent shipments of grain to Hatti; finally, Hittite king Tudhaliya IV wrote to the king of Ugarit demanding a ship and crew for the transport of 450 tonnes of grain to Hatti and stressing the need to act without delay (Bryce 2002, 94–95). The extraordinary hoard found at Tell Basta confirms the increasing presence of silver in Egypt then (Lilyquist 2012).

Quite significantly, the end of the Egyptian empire in Nubia and the Levant (and the income obtained therefrom), and the disruption of the *institutional* circuits of exchange dominated by the palatial powers of the Late Bronze Age, hardly affected the ratio silver/gold in Egypt, as silver continued to flow in the Nile Valley. Thus the high priest Menkheperre, who lived in the time of Psusennes I (1039–991 BC), bought many land tenures from over two dozen Theban tenants and paid generously for them: instead of the "official" rate of one *deben* of silver for 60 *deben* of copper he accepted an exchange rate of 1:100 (lines 9, 13, 27); furthermore he delivered to them five sacks of emmer for 10 *deben* of copper instead of the three sacks customary in those days (lines 13 and 28; Ritner 2009, 130–135). Silver then returned to the rate current before the reign of Merenptah and which was dominant for most of the New Kingdom, suggesting that the supply of this metal continued uninterrupted, a circumstance confirmed by the massive silver coffin of Psusennes I himself. As stated *supra*, Sherratt has stressed the appetite for metals observable in the Eastern Mediterranean basin *after* the collapse of the old palatial system, when new forms of demand and small-scale trade fuelled exchange (Sherratt 2000 and 2012).

In all, the price of cereals suffered a gradual increase from the reign of Ramesses III and peaked during the reigns of Ramesses VII to Ramesses IX; it then decreased but remained above (about double) that prevailing in Ramesses III times and prior. However, the evolution of the price of cereals was not matched by those of wages and other commodities (like vegetables, garments, basketry, cattle), oil being a possible exception (Janssen 1975, 112–132, 550–558). This marks a notable difference in respect to another well documented period in near eastern history, the Neo-Babylonian period. Here, Jursa has shown a general trend of increasing prices from about 550 to 500 BC, dramatic in the case of barley and less pronounced, but still quite strong, for other commodities (dates, sesame, sheep, slaves). They follow roughly the same long-term trend and reflect a single economic system, with prices determined primarily by the interplay of supply and demand. The origins of this development are manifold, one being monetary (inflation) due to the huge influx of silver into the Babylonian economy up to the Persian conquest, another being higher productivity per capita owing to agricultural changes (Jursa 2010, 469–753; data summarised in Jursa 2014a; 2014b).

Three conclusions may be inferred concerning Egypt. First, the increase in prices in the late Ramesside period affected cereals, not other commodities, so it is inappropriate to refer to the late New Kingdom as a period of generalised staple shortages, inflation and economic crisis. Secondly, the increment in the price of cereals seems to have been linked to the arrival of silver into Egypt and the subsequent devaluation of this metal, *but only in respect to copper not to gold.* It appears then that some kind of market system was operative in Egypt, at least for exportable items such as cereals and, perhaps, oil. This could explain some cases of massive grain robbery by Egyptian officials, like the 6000 sacks recorded in the Turin Indictment Papyrus, about 1150 BC (Porten 1996, 52–54), as these could yield enormous profits to the thieves (the price of one sack of grain was usually 2 *deben* of copper; so, 6000 sacks were equal to 12,000 *deben* of copper or 200 *deben* of silver, about 18.2 kg of this metal). Finally, the overall stability of prices suggests that the abundance of silver did not result in a generalised inflationary process, thus pointing either to a limited circulation of silver and, consequently, to the reduced importance of "monetisation" and the market economy in Egypt or, on the contrary, to a period of abundance because of *real* low (and *nominally* stable) prices (with the exception of cereals).

Given the apparent ease with which huge quantities of precious metals were recycled within the Egyptian economy, the overall appetite for metals at the end of the 2nd millennium (Sherratt 2012; Cooney 2014), and the private demand for luxury objects (Cooney 2007; 2012; 2014), including huge quantities of high quality funerary figurines paid for with "refined silver" (Edwards 1971), the second option seems more plausible and finds some support in the fleets of Egyptian and Levantine traders evoked in the tale of Wenamun, which suggests that trade continued to flourish in the last years of the 2nd millennium BC (Moreno García 2014a, 22–34). In any case, it must be stressed that much prize data from this period comes from Deir el-Medina, a relatively isolated community of specialised artisans working for and supplied by the crown, with many goods delivered to them in the form of rations/quotas ("wages") and not through markets, thus making it difficult to make generalisations from this locality. But the role played by silver and prices in the gradual integration of territories and activities over vast areas of the Near East opens many venues for future research (Warburton 2010; 2013; on prices and price formation in the ancient Near East cf. also the methodological warnings formulated by Zaccagnini 1997).

Mobile populations and new trade routes

It seems obvious that institutional archives mainly concern the economic activities carried out by these institutions (palaces, temples, management of the possessions of the elite, etc.), usually within an official and diplomatic framework. Furthermore, to their rather biased and selective content it must be added that the usual depiction of the Late Bronze Age as an era of sophisticated urban life, refined culture and intense international contacts is also based on the archaeological evidence provided by prestigious monuments (palaces, temples, residences of the elite). So there is a high risk of focussing excessive attention on the demands of the ruling elites, and considering these to be the main force behind the economic changes that occurred at this time. However, occasional references in official sources reveal the existence of small-scale exchange and economic activities whose aggregated value could have had an enormous impact on the long-term, even if this is difficult to detect in the epigraphical record (Moreno García 2014a, 22–26). Archaeology thus becomes essential in order to provide clues about barely visible in-deep movements, silent trade and gradual changes in the demand and then to help balance interpretations exclusively based on written sources. Several authors have rightly stressed the role played by such small demand activity in long-term economic transformations, partly by bypassing the circuits dominated by the palatial institutions, partly by producing and distributing goods to broader social sectors without the intervention of monarchies (Sherratt 2001; 2003; Bachhuber & Roberts 2009; Heymans & van Wijngaarden 2011; Babbi *et al.* 2015). Then as before (such as at the beginning of the 2nd millennium

BC) mobile populations and non-institutional actors played an important role in the development of new trade routes, in the exploitation of minerals and goods and in the diffusion of new techniques and ideas (Kepinski 2007; Fuller & Boivin 2009; Boivin & Fuller 2009; Fuller *et al.* 2011). A "silent trade" rarely evoked in the written record but whose enduring impact contributed to the transformation of the economic organisation of the ancient Near East (Moreno García 2013, 94–99; compare with Morrison & Junker 2002).

Mining is but one example. Many examples from the 2nd millennium reveal that mobile populations, even peasants, exploited metallic ores and commercialised copper and gold without the intervention of the palaces and their agents. The recent analysis of some gold objects from several Middle Kingdom and Second Intermediate Period tombs in Abydos and Qurneh reveal that the precious metal employed in their manufacture was of alluvial origin, not mined (Tissot *et al.* 2015; Troalen *et al.* 2014). In fact, archaeological research at Hosh el-Guruf, in the region of the Fourth Cataract of the Nile, has revealed the presence of many grinding stones usually associated with gold mining, an activity apparently carried out on a seasonal basis by local populations during the first centuries of the 2nd millennium BC. The gold extracted was then exported to Kerma (Meyer 2010) but it is possible that this was just one of its destinations, as Nubian gold was traded in the Egyptian fortresses (perhaps more precisely trade outposts) in the area of the Second Cataract, where many weights used for weighing gold have been discovered; furthermore small caravans of Nubians travelled there in order to trade. Another destination is suggested by the local ceramics from the Fourth Cataract retrieved, together with others from Kerma, at the Red Sea harbour of Mersa/Wadi Gawasis; inversely, Red Sea shells have been discovered in the area of the Fourth Cataract, thus proving that direct contacts existed between these two regions (Manzo 2012;2014).

Also during the same period, Egyptians extracted copper and other minerals from Sinai, partly by expeditions from Egypt, partly by local populations whose role was crucial in mining, transporting and providing security and logistics for the miners from the late 3rd millennium BC (Bietak 2010, 147–150; Jirásková 2011; Goldwasser 2013). As for the galena mining operations attested at Gebel Zeit, near the Red Sea coast, during the first half of the 2nd millennium BC, they involved the participation of "Asiatics", judging from a Syrian cylinder-seal found at this site (Régen & Soukiassian 2008, 329–330) and from the famous Asiatic caravan loaded with galena depicted in the tomb of Khnumhotep II at Beni Hassan. Finally, Pan-Grave Nubians travelled across the Egyptian Nile Valley and the oases of the Western Desert during this period, apparently as peddlers, and their small cemeteries were spread all over Egypt (Näser 2010; 2013).

A similar pattern is discernible in the late 2nd millennium BC in northwest Saudi-Arabia, as revealed at Qurayyah and Tayma, on the pilgrim and trade route connecting Yemen with the Levant, where an autonomous local production of copper and pottery emerges from the archaeological record. A locally produced multi-chrome ware (the Qurayyah Painted Ware, QPW) has been widely identified across north-west Arabia, the oasis of Tayma, Jordan (including the Wadi Arabah), the Southern Levant and, significantly, also in the Egyptian mining and smelting site at Timna and a number of sites in the Negev. Furthermore, copper smelt, alloyed and refined in Qurayyah and Tayma was of local (perhaps also Mediterranean) origin (Liu *et al.* 2015, 501).

As for the small scale resumption of copper production along the Arabah Valley (Timna, Feynan), this is probably linked to the economic and political changes that occurred during the transition between the Late Bronze Age and the Iron Age, especially because of the disruption of commercial connections between Cyprus and the Levant at the end of the 13th century BC and the vacuum in political power in the region after the decline of Egyptian influence. The evidence from Faynan indicates that the resumption of copper production at the very end of the Late Bronze and Early Iron Age was opportunistically initiated by local semi-nomadic tribal societies (Ben Yosef *et al.* 2010; Levy *et al.* 2012). What is more, the introduction of domestic camels as pack animals to the southern Levant occurred not earlier than the last third of the 10th century BC and coincided with a major reorganisation of the copper industry of the region (Grigson 2012; Sapir-Hen & Ben-Yosef 2013). Finally a decentralised system of copper production also appears in Late Bronze Age Cyprus, and seems to have been mainly based on small private family enterprises (Pickles & Peltenburg 1998).

In general, mobile populations and private producers were active in the circulation of goods, techniques and ideas in the Late Bronze and Early Iron Age, often in competition with the palatial systems, thus being characterised as invaders, prowlers and pirates in the written record. This is the case of the Sea Peoples (Hitchcock & Maeir 2014), but also, for instance, the Libyans. During the Ramesside era, Libyans suddenly appear depicted as invaders and as a source of armed conflict in pharaonic inscriptions and scenes. However, far from being the starving wandering herders evoked in Egyptian texts, they appear instead to have been well integrated in international networks of exchange, both with the Levant and inner Africa, while they also occupied settlements in the Western Delta. So conflicts can probably be best explained by competition for the control of lucrative trade routes as well as for the resources of Lower and Middle Egypt. Particularly when pharaohs promoted an intense agricultural development in these areas (as revealed by wine and oil labels as well as by documents such as the Wilbour Papyrus) and founded a huge capital in the Eastern Delta, Pi-Ramesses, with an estimated population of about 250,000–300,000 dwellers. The supply requirements of such a city must have weighed heavily on the resources of the Delta, thus exacerbating conflicts with other potential users (Moreno García 2014). Finally, Libyans also appear more and more involved in the life of the oasis of the Western Desert since the end of the 2nd millennium, when the exploitation of precious commodities like silphium, as well as the control of caravan routes from Nubia (bypassing the Nile Valley) and later the Middle Niger made the oasis of Siwa a crucial crossroads from the first half of the 1st millennium BC at least if not earlier (Richardson 1999; Kuhlmann 2002; 2013; Liverani 2014).

In Arabia the activities of mobile populations, a growing small-scale trade, and the introduction of new pack animals also enabled exchange circuits formerly in the hands of pharaohs to be bypassed. The origins of this process obey a complex set of circumstances, partly related to the new opportunities opened when the authority of formerly powerful states over areas under their control began to fade away. That was apparently the case of the development of a land route connecting incense producing southwest Arabia to the Mediterranean coast, thus avoiding the maritime route through the Red Sea controlled by the Egyptian kings. Archaeological research reveals how these circumstances also worked together in southeast Arabia, when the use of *qanats* from the very end of the 2nd millennium BC was a local response to increasing aridity. Domesticated camels were also introduced there as an adaptive strategy and, for the first time, all major environmental zones in that area were occupied, including coastal, desert and inland settlements, all of them displaying a uniform material culture. In each of these settlements, the columned hall became the centre of political and religious power, with banqueting playing an important social role and where incense, probably imported from southwest Arabia, was commonly used. The combination of elite banqueting equipment and objects that may have been used in a religious context within these columned buildings, provides evidence of increasing social and economic differentiation. However there is no evidence that these oasis polities ever exercised authority over large territories, but their occasional specialisation (camel breeding, cereal cultivation) points to economic integration and exchange as no individual settlement, or environmental zone, contained all the necessary resources to maintain social order and economic viability. The viability of settlement in the entire region was ultimately dependent, therefore, on the ability to maintain intraregional trade contacts with other settlements. The uniformity of banqueting practices in columned buildings at Rumeilah, Bida Bint Saud, and Muweilah suggests that such activity provided a powerful context in which to ensure communication and trade and to forge economic and political ties, apparently within a framework of parity between settlements (Magee 2007). Also at Tayma, a rectangular building surrounded by at least one row of columns has produced a great quantity of small cups, probably used during rituals or ceremonial meals, as well as prestige items in ivory, wood, faience and bone (Hausleiter 2010, 230–231). Small desert settlements like Muweilah show their integration in inter- and intraregional trade routes thanks to the abundant imported ceramics discovered and traded down the Persian Gulf and then inland, such as pseudo-Barbar ceramics from Bahrain, torpedo-shaped jars from Mesopotamia, and several smaller vessels that may have been imported from Iran. The recovery of imported and local metals (iron, bronze) implies that the control of some trade goods formed a key component in the existence of hierarchies at the settlement, while a brief inscription in Monumental South Arabian attests to contacts with the south Arabian kingdoms that were emerging during this period (Magee 2007).

Under these "decentralised" conditions based on autonomous local populations, south Arabian goods reached the Mediterranean through a network of routes and settlements thanks to the use of the camel from the middle of the 12th century BC (Jasmin 2005). The recently found inscription of Ramesses III in the oasis of Tayma probably represents an ephemeral attempt to control this emerging route, especially as he also sent the last recorded expedition to the land of Punt in the 2nd millennium BC. Also at the same time, towards the end of the 2nd millennium/early 1st millennium BC, the first south Arabian inscriptions appear in the regions of Jawf, Hadramawt and Wadi Bayhan thus pointing to an increasing political organisation in that area and the emergence of monarchies (Arbach 2010, 17). The oases of northwest Arabia were important nodal points in the overland caravan routes between south and north Arabia, acting also as markets for the exchange of goods. The emergence and development of the Arabian incense trade route from around 1000 BC made this region a crucial junction between the southern Arabian Peninsula and cultures and states in Mesopotamia, the Eastern Mediterranean and the Arabah. Besides aromatics, copper is recognised as one of the main goods flowing along this route (Liu *et al.* 2015, 492). In addition, other export items, such as precious metals and stones, were traded, especially during the initial phase of trade.

Consequently, the level of cultural and economic exchange between the Arabian peninsula and its neighbours reached a previously unparalleled degree of intensity, embedded in the general economic growth of the early Iron Age (Hausleiter 2012, 818). At Tayma, certain parts of the *c.* 10 km long city wall were constructed out of mudbrick during the 2nd millennium BC. A number of Egyptian and Egyptianising objects have been recovered together with prestige goods of a Syro-Levantine type from an apparently isolated structure at Tayma, while the recently discovered cartouche of Pharaoh Ramesses III in the vicinity of Tayma may indicate a stronger political connection between Egypt and northwest Arabia than previously assumed. Slightly earlier finds had already strongly indicated links between northwestern Arabia and Syria and the Levant during the Middle and Late Bronze Age, thus underlining the northwestern orientation of cultural contacts (Liu *et al.* 2015, 493).

Although evidence is scarce, it appears plausible that some time after the reign of the Assyrian king Tiglath-pileser I (1114–1076 BC), commercial contacts between Arabia and Mesopotamia began, as indicated by Assyrian cuneiform sources. Assyrian interest in aromatics in Arabia features in the cuneiform sources from the 9th century BC onwards. Camels, the only suitable means for crossing desert areas (probably apart from donkeys), were mentioned amongst the booty collected by the Assyrian king Tukulti-Ninurta II (890–884 BC) from tribes along the Euphrates; Arabs were mentioned for the first time by Shalmaneser III (858–824 BC) as members of a coalition of Syrian cities against the Assyrian army in 853 BC (Hausleiter 2012, 820), while recent archaeological evidence shows that cultural influences between Mesopotamia and the kingdoms of South Arabia can be firmly rooted prior to 750 BC (Mazzoni 2010; Avanzini 2012); finally, Aramaean tribes of southern Syria were essential for establishing contacts between the inhabitants of northern Arabia and the populations of Syro-Mesopotamia (Hausleiter 2012, 818).

In fact, new mobile populations such as Aramaean and Chaldeans emerge in the Near-Eastern sources as crucial political and economic actors and, as in the case of the Libyans, quite often in conflict with states and benefiting from their decline (Bunnens 2009). An overall long-term trend for the period between the 12th and the late 8th century BC in lower Mesopotamia is marked by a general decline in population levels, by a diminution of urbanism, with a corresponding increase in economic and social ruralisation and by extensive abandonments of settlements. In general, compared to the Chaldean groups, the family units of the Arameans prove to have had a far great mobility, not only infiltrating themselves between one enclave and another, but even giving rise to interregional movements, between the Middle Euphrates and Lower Mesopotamia and with contacts with northern Arabia. The Euphrates was one of the most important trade routes in ancient Syria and was under the control of the Aramaeans, who may have quickly resumed trade and exchange trade connections between northern Arabia, Syria, and Mesopotamia. This trade activity is clearly attested in the rich booty from the Aramaean groups in the middle Euphrates collected by Tiglath-Pileser I in the 11th century B.C. and by Assurnasirpal II at the dawn of the 9th century BC: precious metals, ivory, sheep, and dyed textiles. The slave-trade also seems to have played a certain role in this activity. This revival of trade is attested as early as the 11th century at several sites by the presence of imported pottery. The settled communities could have intensified their own level of production to participate in this active commerce, as evidenced, for example, by the flourishing textile industry attested in Tell Afis and in the sheep and dyed textiles that are constantly mentioned as part of the booty collected from Aramaean groups (Sader 2014, 22). Territorial claims and the control of the trade routes that linked the Arabian Peninsula (King's Highway) and the Mediterranean to north Syria appear to be behind the lasting Israelo-Aramaean conflicts (Sader 2014, 35), while the aggressive Assyrian expansion towards the Middle Euphrates and the Zagros was followed by the creation of *kārus* or trade emporia (Vér 2014). The immense wealth accumulated through trade taxes, etc., by some of the small polities that flourished along these trade routes can be discerned when considering the amount of tribute collected by Assyrian kings (Holladay 2006; 2009). Later on, the Neo-Babylonian king Nabonidus conquered the oasis of Teima, a strategic commercial crossroads where some texts refer to caravans going back and forth between Arabia, including Teima, and Babylonia (Beaulieu 2013, 48).

As for Chaldeans, while nominally retaining a social and political structure based on kinship ties, they appear to have taken on a basically sedentary way of life in their southern Euphrates enclaves, with occupations in agriculture, stock raising, and intra-regional trade. Their structures for communal living comprised not only rural villages and small townships, but also walled cities. But the strategic position of the main Chaldean enclaves along the westernmost and southern axes of the alluvium also had crucial implications for commerce. The lists of precious goods already offered in the 9th century, and then again under Tiglath-pileser III, by the

Chaldean chiefs as tribute to the Assyrians, which included elephant hides and tusks, ebony and sissoo wood, prove that the Chaldean tribes had gained full control of the trade routes cutting through the Babylonian region, and were thus on the receiving end of a vast commercial network which reached Mesopotamia from the Levant, Northern Arabia, and Egypt by land. Furthermore a "southern Mesopotamian axis" of trade, based on seamanship and the recently introduced large-scale exploitation of the camel as a pack-animal, was progressively constituted, so as to antagonise the northern Mesopotamian routes dominated by the Assyrian empire -and which would eventually replace the latter. Bearing in mind the presence of Arabian allies in the military efforts by the Chaldeans, a strong thrust for political and military cooperation offered by the Elamite state on the basis of economic advantage, and evidence of direct contacts with the Levant, it is possible to understand the political substructure behind this new commercial axis. Merodach-baladan is explicitly said by Tiglath-pileser to have brought his own enormous tribute (of gold, pearls, beams of ebony, medicinal plants, multi-coloured garments, cattle and sheep; Fales 2011, 91–97; Frame 103).

Conclusion

The end of the Late Bronze Age had a deep impact on the palatial systems, but the crisis of the East Mediterranean and Near Eastern monarchies was not followed by the end of exchange. As had occurred during the Middle Bronze Age, flourishing trade and exchange occurred in the absence of big powers and, in many cases, visible contemporary phenomena only gained in importance during the following periods, culminating in the 1st millennium BC. The first of these was the gradual incorporation of new areas to the traditional core of contacts in the Near East; during the Late Bronze Age, commercial interests expanded towards the central and western Mediterranean and, consequently, pivotal areas also moved westward. While the Levant still retained much of its role as point of contact between north-eastern Africa, Arabia and the Near East, later on the Aegean took on this function. The second phenomenon is that the control over such expanding networks took the form of increasingly greater monarchies, a process culminating in the emergence of the first "world-empires", going well beyond the traditional frontiers of their core areas: Assyria, Babylonia, even Egypt with its expansion into Cyrenaica. The Achaemenid Empire achieved this process with its expansion into Central Asia and Greece. Increasing contacts and the need to obtain resources when and where they were needed in greater areas probably revealed the limits of former tributary structures; this led to the third phenomenon, the emergence of "money" as a means to promote both exchange with other regions and to collect and mobilise wealth, ready to be used when needed. This, of course, would be impossible if entrepreneurs and trade could not have their goods *prêt-à-porter* for monarchies, from supplies to mercenaries. So decentralisation and private trade may be considered the fourth characteristic of this period of transition between the Late Bronze Age and the Iron Age, thus continuing and deepening economic and administrative trends going back to the 3rd millennium.

Bibliography

Abraham, K. (2004) *Bussiness and Politics under the Persian Empire: The Financial Dealings of Marduk-nāṣir-apli of the House of Egibi (521–487 BCE)*, Potomac.

Allen, J. P. (2002) *The Heqanakht Papyri*, New York.

Arbach, M. (2010) Aux origines de l'établissement des royaumes sudarabiques. Saba et les cités-États du Jawf aux VIIIe–VIe s. av. J.-C., *Chroniques yéménites* 16: 15–27.

Aruz, J., S. Graff & Y. Rakic (ed.) (2014) *Assyria to Iberia at the Dawn of the Classical Age*, New York.

Avanzini, A. (2012) The Sabean presence in Jawf in the eighth–seventh centuries BC. Notes on the oldest phase of ancient South Arabian culture and its relationship with Mesopotamia. In G. B. Lanfranchi, D. Morandi Bonacossi, C. Pappi & S. Ponchia (eds), *Leggo! Studies Presented to Frederick Mario Fales on the Occasion of His 5th Aniversary*, 37–52, Wiesbaden.

Babbi, A., F. Bubenheimer-Erhart, B. Marín-Aguilera & S. Mühl (eds) (2015) *The Mediterranean Mirror. Cultural Contacts in the Mediterranean Sea between 1200 and 750 B.C.*, Mainz.

Bachhuber, Ch. & R. G. Roberts (eds) (2009), *Forces of Transformation. The End of the Bronze Age in the Mediterranean*, Oxford.

Baker, H. D. (2011) Babylonian land survey in socio-political context. In G. J. Selz (ed.), *The Empirical Dimension of Ancient Near Eastern Studies*, 293–324 (Wiener Offene Orientalistik 6), Vienna,.

Balmuth, M. S. (ed.) (2001) *Hacksilber to Coinage: New Insights into the Monetary History of the Near East and Greece* (Numismatic Studies 24), New York.

Banaji, J. (2007) Islam, the Mediterranean and the Rise of Capitalism, *Historical Materialism* 15: 47–74.

Beaulieu, P.-A. (2013) Arameans, Chaldeans, and Arabs in cuneiform sources from the Late Babylonian Period. In A. Berlejung & M. P. Streck (eds), *Arameans, Chaldeans, and Arabs in Babylonia and Palestine in the First Millennium B.C.*, 31–55, Wiesbaden.

Beckman, G. (1997) Real property sales at Emar. In G. D. Young, M. W. Chavalas, & R. E. Averbeck (eds), *Crossing Boundaries and Linking Horizons. Studies in Honor of Michael C. Astour on His 80th Birthday*, 95–120, Bethesda.

Beckman, G. (2008), A small town in Late Bronze Age Syria, *Zeitschrift für Assyriologie* 98: 211–220.

Ben-Yosef, E., T. E. Levy, T. F. G. Higham, M. Najjar & L. Tauxe (2010) The beginning of iron Age copper production in the southern Levant: new evidence from Khirbat al-Jariya, Faynan, *Antiquity* 84: 724–746.

Beylage, P. (2002) *Aufbau der königlichen Stelentexte von Beginn der 18. Dynastie bis zur Amarnazeit* (Ägypten und Altes Testament 54), Wiesbaden.

Bietak, M. (2010) From where came the Hyksos and where did they go? In M. Marée (ed.), *The Second Intermediate Period (Thirteenth-Seventeenth Dynasties). Current Research, Future Prospects* (OLA, 192), 139–181, Louvain-Paris-Walpole.

Bleiberg, E. (2002) Loans, credit and interest in ancient Egypt. In M. Hudson & M. van de Mieroop (eds), *Debt and Economic Renewal in the Ancient Near East*, Bethesda, 257–276.

Boivin, N. & D. Q. Fuller 2009) Shell middens, ships and seeds: exploring coastal subsistence, maritime trade and the dispersal of domesticates in an around the ancient Arabian Peninsula, *Journal of World Prehistory* 22/2: 113–180.

Bongenaar, A. C. V. M. (ed.) (2000) *Interdependency of Institutions and Private Entrepreneurs*, Leiden.

Briant, P. & R. Descat (1998) Un registre douanier de la satrapie d'Égypte à l'époque achéménide (TAD C3,7). In N. Grimal & B. Menu (eds), *Le commerce en Égypte ancienne*, 59–104, Cairo.

Brinkman, J. A. (2006) Babylonian royal land grants, memorials of financial interest, and invocation of the divine, *Journal of the Economic and Social History of the Orient* 49: 1–47.

Bryce, T. (2002) *Life and Society in the Hittite World*, Oxford.
Bulgarelli, O. (2011) Financial and economic activity in Mesopotamia. In G. Barjamovic, J. L. Dahl, J. G. Westenholz, U. S. Koch & W. Sommerfeld (eds), *Akkade is King. A Collection of Papers by Friends and Colleagues Presented to Aage Westenholz on the Occasion of His 70th Birthday*, 37–53 (PIHANS 118), Leiden.
Bunnens, G. (2009) Assyrian empire building and aramization of culture as seen from Tell Ahmar/ Til Barsib, *Syria* 86: 67–82.
Castle, E. W. (1992) Shipping and trade in Ramesside Egypt, *Journal of the Economic and Social History of the Orient* 35: 239–277.
Černy, J. (1954) Prices and wages in Egypt in the Ramesside period, *Cahiers d'histoire mondiale* 1: 903–921.
Charpin, D. (2002) Chroniques bibliographiques. 2. La commemoration d'actes juridiques: à propos des kudurrus babyloniens, *Revue d'assyriologie* 96: 169–191.
Cline, E. (2014) *1177 BC: The Year Civilization Collapsed*, Princeton.
Condon, V. (1984) Two account papyri of the late Eighteenth Dynasty (Brooklyn 35.1453 A and B), *Revue d'Égyptologie* 35: 57–82.
Cooney, K. M. (2007) *The Cost of Death. The Social and Economic Value of Ancient Egyptian Funerary Art in the Ramesside Period*, Leiden.
Cooney, K. M. (2012) Objectifying the body: the increased value of the ancient Egyptian mummy during the socioeconomic crisis of Dynasty Twenty-One. In J. Papadopoulos & G. Urton (eds), *The Construction of Value in the Ancient World*, 139–159, Los Angeles.
Cooney, K. M. (2014) Private sector tomb robbery and funerary arts reuse according to West Theban documentation. In J. Toivari-Viitala (ed.), 16–28 (Deir el-Medina Studies), Helsinki.
Cripps, E. L. (2014) Money and prices in the Ur III economy of Umma, *Wiener Zeitschrift für die Kunde des Morgenlandes* 104: 205–232.
Curtis, M. C. (2004) Ancient interaction across the southern Red Sea : new suggestions for investigating cultural exchange and complex societies during the first millennium BC. In P. Lunde & A. Porter (eds), *Trade and Travel in the Red Sea Region. Proceedings of the Red Sea Project I*, 57–70, Oxford.
Del Monte, G. (2009) La formazione dei prezzi delle derrate in età cassita, *Rivista di Storia Economica* 25: 103–142.
Demand, N. (2004) Iron Age Cyprus : Recent finds and interpretative strategies. In R. Rollinger & C. Ulf (eds), *Commerce and Monetary Systems in the Ancient World: Means of Transmission and Cultural Interaction*, 257–269, Stuttgart.
Demarée, R. J. (2010) Ramesside administrative papyri in the Civiche Raccolte Archeologische e Numismatiche di Milano, *Jaarbericht "Ex Oriente Lux"* 42: 55–77.
Dercksen, J. G. (1996) *The Old Assyrian Copper Trade in Anatolia* (PIHANS 75), Leiden.
Dercksen, J. G. (ed.) (1999) *Trade and Finance in Ancient Mesopotamia*, Leiden.
Donker van Heel, K. (1990) *The Legal Manual of Hermopolis (P. Mattha). Text and Translation*, Leyde.
Dosch, G. (1987) Non-slave labor in Nuzi. In M. A. Powell (ed.), *Labor in the Ancient Near East* (American Oriental Series 68), 223–235, New Haven.
Edwards, I. E. S. (1971) Bill of sale for a set of ushabtis, *Journal of Egyptian Archaeology* 57: 120–124.
Fales, F. M. (2011) Moving around Babylon: On the Aramean and Chaldean Presence in Southern Mesopotamia. In E. Cancik-Kirschbaum, M. Van Ess & J. Marzahn (eds), *Babylon. Wissenskultur in Orient und Okzident*, 91–111, Berlin-Boston.
Farber, H. (1978) A price and wage study for northern Babylonia during the Old Babylonian period, *Journal of the Economic and Social History of the Orient* 21: 1–51.
Fattovich, R. (2004) The 'pre-Aksumite' state in northern Ethiopia and Eritrea reconsidered. In P. Lunde & A. Porter (ed.), *Trade and Travel in the Red Sea Region. Proceedings of the Red Sea Project I*, Oxford, 71–77.

Faust, A. (2006) The Negev 'fortresses' in context : reexamining the 'fortress' phenomenon in light of general settlement processes of the eleventh-tenth centuries B.C.E. *Journal of the American Oriental Society* 126: 135–160.
Feldman, M. H. (2014) *Communities of Style. Portable Luxury Arts, Identity, and Collectiva Memory in the Iron Age Levant*, Chicago.
Fletcher, R. N. (2012) Opening the Mediterranean: Assyria, the Levant and the transformation of Early Iron Age trade, *Antiquity* 86: 211–220.
Földi, Z. (2014) On Old Babylonian Palastgeschäft in Larsa. The meaning of *sūtum* and the 'circulation' of silver in state/private business. In Z. Csabai & T. Grüll (ed.), *Studies in Economic and Social History of the Ancient Near East in Memory of Péter Vargyas* (Ancient Near Eastern and Mediterranean Studies, 2), 79–117, Budapest.
Frame, G. (2013) The political history and historical geography of the Aramean, Chaldean, and Arab tribes in Babylonia in the Neo-Assyrian Period. In A. Berlejung & M. P. Streck (eds), *Arameans, Chaldeans, and Arabs in Babylonia and Palestine in the First Millennium B.C.*, 87–121, Wiesbaden.
Fuller, D. Q. & N. Boivin (2009) Crops, cattle and commensals across the Indian Ocean: current and potential archaeobiological evidence, *Études Océan Indien* 42–43: 13–46.
Fuller, D. Q., N. Boivin, T. Hoogervorst & R. Allaby (2011) Across the Indian Ocean: the prehistoric movement of plants and animals, *Antiquity* 85: 544–558.
Garfinkle, S. J. (2012) *Entrepreneurs and Enterprise in Early Mesopotamia. A Study of Three Archives from the Third Dynasty of Ur*, Bethesda.
Gestoso Singer, G. (2010) Forms of payment in the Amarna Age and in the Uluburun and Cape Gelidonya shipwrecks, *Ugarit Forschungen* 42: 261–278.
Gitin, S. & A. Golani (2004) A silver-based monetary economy in the seventh century BCE: a response to Raz Kletter, *Levant* 36: 203–205.
Goddeeris, A. (2002) *Economy and Society in Northern Babylonia in the Early Old Babylonian Period (ca. 2000–1800 BC* (OLA 109), Leuven-Paris.
Goldwasser, O. (2013) Out of the mists of the alphabet – redrawing the "brother of the ruler of Retenu", *Ägypten und Levante* 22: 353–374.
Graham-Campbell, J., S. M. Sindbæk & G. Williams (2011) *Silver Economies, Monetisation and Society in Scandinavia AD 800–1100*, Aarhus.
Grandet, P. (1994) *Le Papyrus Harris I (BM 9999)*, vol. I, Cairo.
Grigson, C. (2012) Camels, copper and donkeys in the Early Iron Age of the Southern Levant: Timna revisited, *Levant* 44: 82–100.
Haring, B. J. (1997) *Divine Households. Administrative and Economic Aspects of the New Kingdom Royal Memorial Temples in Western Thebes* (Egyptologische Uitgaven 12), Leiden.
Hausleiter, A. (2010) L'oasis de Taymâ'. In A. I. Al-Ghabban, B. André-Salvini, F. Demange, C. Juvin & M. Cotty (eds), *Routes d'Arabie. Archéologie et histoire du royaume d'Arabie Saoudite*, 219–239, Paris.
Hausleiter, A. (2012) North Arabian kingdoms. In D. T. Potts (ed.), *A Companion to the Archaeology of the Ancient Near East*, 816–832, Chichester.
Helwing, B. (2014) Silver in the early state societies of Greater Mesopotamia. In H. Meyer, R. Risch & E. Pernicka (eds), *Metalle der Macht – Frühes Gold und Silber*, 411–421, Halle (Saale).
Heymans, E. & G. J. van Wijngaarden (2011) Low-value manufactured exotics in the Eastern Mediterranean in the Late Bronze and Early Iron Ages. In A. Vianello (ed.), *Exotica in the Prehistoric Mediterranean*, 124–136, Oxford.
Hitchcock, L. A. & A. M. Maeir (2014) Yo-ho, yo-ho, a *seren*'s life for me! *World Archaeology* 46: 624–640.
Holladay, J. S. (2006) Hezekiah's tribute, long distance trade, and the wealth of nations ca. 1000–600 B.C. In S. Gitin, J. E. Wright & J. P. Dessel (eds), *Confronting the Past. Archaeological and Historical Essays on Ancient Israel in Honor of William G. Dever*, 309–331, Winona Lake.
Holladay, J. S. (2009) How much is that in ...? Monetization, money, royal states, and empires In J. D. Schloen (ed.), *Exploring the Longue Durée. Essays in Honor of Lawrence E. Stager*, 207–222, Winona Lake.

Janssen, J. J. (1961) *Two Ancient Egyptian Ship's Logs: Papyrus Leiden I 350 Verso and Papyrus Turin 2008+2016*, Leiden.

Janssen, J. J. (1975) *Commodity Prices from the Ramessid Period. An Economic Study of the Village of Necropolis Workmen at Thebes*, Leiden.

Jasmin, M. (2005) Les conditions d'émergence de la route de l'encens à la fin du IIe millénaire avant notre ère, *Syria* 82: 49–62.

Jasnow, R. (2001) Pre-demotic Pharaonic sources. In R. Westbrook & R. Jasnow (eds), *Security for Debt in Ancient Near Eastern Law*, 35–45, Leiden-Boston.

Jasnow, R. (2003) Third Intermediate Period. In R. Westbrook (ed.), *A History of Ancient Near Eastern Law. Volume I* (Handbuch der Orientalistik, I.72), 777–818, Leiden-Boston.

Jirásková, L. (2011) Relations between Egypt and Syria-Palestine in the latter part of the Old Kingdom. In K. Duistermaat & I. Regulski (eds), *Intercultural Contacts in the Ancient Mediterranean*, 539–568, Leuven-Paris-Walpole.

Jurman, C. (2015) Silver of the treasury of Herishef – considering the origin and economic significance of silver in Egypt during the Third Intermediate Period. In A. Babbi, F. Bubenheimer-Erhart, B. Marín-Aguilera & S. Mühl (eds), *The Mediterranean Mirror. Cultural Contacts in the Mediterranean Sea between 1200 and 750 B.C.*, 51–68, Mainz.

Jursa, M. (2014a) Factor markets in Babylonia from the late seventh to the third century BCE, *Journal of the Economic and Social History of the Orient* 57: 173–202.

Jursa, M. (2014b) Economic development in Babylonia from the late 7th to the late 4th century BC: economic growth and economic crises in imperial contexts. In H. D. Baker & M. Jursa (eds), *Documentary Sources in Ancient Near Eastern and Greco-Roman Economic History*, 113–138, Oxford.

Jursa, M. (2015) Labor in Babylonia in the First Millennium BC. In P. Steinkeller & M. Hudson (eds), *Labor in the Ancient Labor*, 345–396, Dresden.

Jursa, M. & J. C. Moreno García (2015) The ancient Near East and Egypt. In A. Monson & W. Scheidel (eds), *Fiscal Regimes and the Political Economy of Premodern States*, 115–165, Cambridge.

Jursa, M. J. Hackl, B. Janković, K. Kleber, E. E. Payne, C. Waerzeggers & M. Weszeli (2010) *Aspects of the Economic History of Babylonia in the First Millennium BC: Economic Geography, Economic Mentalities, Agriculture, the Use of Money and the Problem of Economic Growth*, Münster.

Kassianidou, V. (2009) "May he send me silver in very great quantities" EA 35. In D. Michaelides, V. Kassianidou & R. S. Merrillees (es.), *Egypt and Cyprus in Antiquity*, 48–57, Oxford.

Kelder, J. M. (in press) Mycenae, rich in silver. In K. Kleber & R. Pirngruber (eds), *Silver, Money and Credit. A Tribute to Robartus J. van der Spek on the Occasion of His 65th Birthday, Festschrift R. J. van der Spek*, 309–319, Leiden.

Kepinski, Chr. (2007) Mémoires d'Euphrate et d'Arabie, les tombes à tumulus, marqueurs territoriaux de communautés en voie de sédentarisation, in Chr. Kepinski, O. Lecomte & A. Tenu (eds), *Studia euphratica. Le Moyen Euphrate iraquien révélé par les fouilles préventives de Haditha*, 87–128 (Travaux de la Maison René-Ginouvès 3), Paris.

Kitchen, K. A. (2001) Economics in ancient Arabia. From Alexander to the Augustans. In Z. H. Archibald, J. K. Davies, V. Gabrielsen & G. J. Oliver (eds), *Hellenistic Economies*, 157–173, London.

Klengel, H. (1987) Non-slave labour in the Old Babylonian period: the basic outlines. In M. A. Powell (ed.), *Labor in the Ancient Near East* (American Oriental Series 68), 159–166, New Haven.

Kletter, R. (2003) Iron Age hoards of precious metals in Palestine – an underground economy, *Levant* 35: 139–152.

Kletter, R. (2004) Coinage before coins? A response, *Levant* 36: 207–210.

Kroll, J. H. (2011) Money of the Greeks and their near Eastern neighbors before the advent of coinage, and after. In M. P. García-Bellido, L. Callegarin & A. Jiménez Díaz (eds), *Barter, Money and Coinage in the Ancient Mediterranean (10th–1st centuries BC)* (Anejos de AespA 58), 15–23, Madrid.

Kuhlmann, K. P. (2002) The "Oasis Bypath" or the issue of desert trade in Pharaonic times. In R. Kuper (ed.), *Tides of the Desert. Contributions to the Archaeology and Environmental History of Africa in Honour of Rudolph Kuper* (Africa Præhistorica 14), 125–170, Köln.

Kuhlmann, K. P. (2013) The realm of "two deserts": Siwah Oasis between east and west. In F. Förster & H. Riemer (eds), *Desert Road Archaeology in Ancient Egypt and Beyond* (Africa Præhistorica 27), 133–166, Köln.

Lacau, P. (1933) *Une stèle juridique de Karnak*. Cairo.

Levy, Th. E., E. Ben-Yosef & M. Najjar (2012) New perspectives on Iron Age production and society in the Faynan region, Jordan. In V. Kassianidou & G. Papasavvas (eds), *Eastern Mediterranean Metallurgy and Metalwork in the Second Millennium BC*, 197–214, Oxford.

Lichtheim, M. (1973) *Ancient Egyptian Literature, vol. II: The New Kingdom*, Berkeley.

Lilyquist, Chr. (2012) Treasures from Tell Basta: Goddesses, officials, and artists in an international age, *Metropolitan Museum Journal* 47: 9–72.

Liu, S., T. Rehren, E. Pernicka & A. Hausleiter (2015) Copper processing in the oases of northwest Arabia: technology, alloys and provenance, *Journal of Archaeological Science* 53: 492–503.

Liverani, M. (1987) The collapse of the Near Eastern regional system at the end of the Bronze Age: the case of Syria. In M. Rowlands, M. Larsen & K. Kristiansen (eds), *Centre and Periphery in the Ancient World*, 66–73, Cambridge.

Liverani, M. (1990) *Prestige and Interest. International Relations in the Near East ca. 1600–1100 B.C.*, Padoue.

Liverani, M. (1992) Early caravan trade between South-Arabia and Mesopotamia, *Yemen* 1: 111–115.

Liverani, M. (1996) Dal "piccolo regno" alla "città-stato". In E. Acquaro (ed.) *Alle soglie della classicità, il Mediterraneo tra tradizione e innovazione. Studi in onore di Sabatino Moscati, vol. I: Storie e culture*, 249–259, Pisa.

Liverani, M. (1997a) Beyond deserts, beyond oceans. In A. Avanzini (ed.), *Profumi d'Arabia: atti del convegno*, 557–564, Rome.

Liverani, M. (1997b) Ramesside Egypt in a changing world. An institutional approach. In G. Colonna (ed.), *L'impero Ramesside. Convegno internazionale in onore di Sergio Donadoni*, 101–115, Rome.

Liverani, M. (2002) Stati etnici e città-stato: una tipologia storica per la prima età del Ferro. In M. Molinos & A. Zifferero (ed.), *Primi popoli d'Europa. Proposte e riflessioni sulle origini della civiltà nell'Europa mediterranea*, 33–47, Florence.

Liverani, M. (2003) The influence of political institutions on trade in the ancient Near East (Late Bronze to Early Iron Age). In C. Zaccagnini (ed.), *Mercanti e politica nel mondo antico*, 119–137, Rome.

Liverani, M. (2014) The Sahara during antiquity: structure and history. In C. C. Lamberg-Karlovsky, B. Genito & B. Cerasetti (eds), *"My life is like the summer rose". Maurizio Tois e l'archeologia come modo di vivere. Papers in Honour of Maurizio Tosi for His 70th Birthday*, 443–447, Oxford.

Lüddeckens, E. (1960) *Ägyptische Eheverträge*, Wiesbaden.

Magee, P. (2007) Beyond the Desert and the Sown: Settlement Intensification in Late Prehistoric Southeastern Arabia, *Bulletin of the American Schools of Oriental Research* 347: 83–105.

Malinine, M. (1953) *Choix de textes juridiques en hiératique "anormal" et en démotique (XXVe-XXVIIe dynasties)*, Paris.

Manning, J. G. (2003) Demotic law. In R. Westbrook (ed.), *A History of Ancient Near Eastern Law. Volume I* (Handbuch der Orientalistik, I.72), 819–862, Leiden-Boston.

Manzo, A. (2012) From the sea to the deserts and back: New research in Eastern Sudan, *British Museum Studies in Ancient Egypt and Sudan* 18: 75–106.

Manzo, A. (2014) Beyond the Fourth Cataract. Perspectives for research in Eastern Sudan. In J. R. Anderson & D. A. Welsby (eds), *The Fourth Cataract and Beyond* (British Museum Publications on Egypt and Sudan, 1), 1149–1157, London.

Marcus, E. (2007) Amenemhat II and the sea: maritime aspects of the Mit Rahina (Memphis) inscription, *Ägypten und Levante* 17: 137–190.

Martin, C. J. (1995) Marriages, wills and leases of land : some notes on the formulae of demotic contracts. In M. J. Geller & H. Maehler (eds), *Legal Documents of the Hellenistic World*, 58–78, London.
Mazzoni, S. (2010) Arabia in the first millennium BC: the Near Eastern background. In A. Avanzini (ed.), *Eastern Arabia in the First Millennium BC* (Arabia Antiqua 6), 17–27, Rome.
Meeks, D. (1995) Une borne commémorative hiératique, *Chronique d'Égypte* 70: 72–83.
Megally, M. (1974) À propos du papyrus CGC 58070 (Papyrus Boulaq XI), *Bulletin de l'Institut Français d'Archéologie Orientale* 74: 161–169
Megally, M. (1975) Le papyrus CGC 58081. Suite du papyrus CGC 58070 (Papyrus Boulaq XI), *Bulletin de l'Institut Français d'Archéologie Orientale* 75: 165–181.
Megally, M. (1977) *Recherches sur l'économie, l'administration et la comptabilité égyptiennes à la XVIIIe dynastie d'après le papyrus E 3226 du Louvre* (Bibliothèque d'étude 71), Cairo.
Meyer, C. (2010) The Kingdom of Kush in the 4th Cataract: archaeological salvage of the Oriental Institute Nubian Expedition 2007 season. Part II: grinding stones and gold mining at Hosh el-Guruf, Sudan, *Gdańsk Archaeological Museum and Heritage Protection Fund African Reports* 7: 39–52.
Monroe, Ch. M. (2009) *Scales of Fate. Trade, Tradition, and Transformation in the Eastern Mediterranean ca. 1350-1175 BCE*, Münster.
Monroe, Ch. M. (2010) Sunk costs at Late Bronze Age Uluburun, *Bulletin of the American Society of Oriental Research* 357: 19–33.
Moreno García, J. C. (2008) La dépendance rurale en Égypte ancienne, *Journal of the Economic and Social History of the Orient* 51: 99–150.
Moreno García, J. C. (2010) Les *jḥwtjw* et leur rôle socio-économique au IIIe et IIe millénaires avant J.-C. In J. C. Moreno García (ed.), *Élites et pouvoir en Égypte ancienne* (Cahiers de Recherche de l'Institut de Papyrologie et d'Egyptologie de Lille 28), 321–351, Villeneuve d'Ascq.
Moreno García, J. C. (2013) The limits of Pharaonic administration: patronage, informal authorities, mobile populations and 'invisible' social sectors. In M. Bárta & Hella Küllmer (eds), *Diachronic Trends in Ancient Egyptian History: Studies Dedicated to the Memory of Eva Pardey*, 88–101, Prague.
Moreno García, J. C. (2014a) Penser l'économie pharaonique, *Annales. Histoire, Sciences sociales* 69: 7–38.
Moreno García, J. C. (2014b) L'organisation sociale de l'agriculture pharaonique: quelques cas d'étude, *Annales. Histoire, Sciences sociales* 69: 39–74.
Moreno García, J. C. (2014c) Invaders or just herders? Libyans in Egypt in the thrid and second millennia BCE, *World Archaeology* 46: 610–623.
Morkot, R. (2001) Egypt and Nubia. In S. E. Alcock, T. N. D'Altroy, K. D. Morrison & C. M. Sinopoli (eds) *Empires. Perspectives from Archaeology and History*, 227–251, Cambridge-New York.
Morkot, R. (2007) War and the Economy : the international 'arms trade' in the Late Bronze Age and after. In T. Schneider & K. M. Szpakowska (eds) *Egyptian Stories. A British Egyptological Tribute to Alan B. Lloyd on the Occasion of His Retirement*, 169–195, Münster.
Morrison, K. D. & L. L. Junker (edd) (2002), *Forager-Traders in South and South-East Asia. Long-Term Histories*, Cambridge.
Moussa, A. M. & H. Altenmüller (1977) *Das Grab des Nianchchnum und Chnumhotep*, Mainz am Rhein.
Muhs, B. P. (2005) *Tax Receipts, Taxpayers, and Taxes in Early Ptolemaic Thebes*, Chicago.
Müller, M. (2009) The "El-Hibeh"-archive : introduction and preliminary information. In G. P. F. Broekman, R. J. Demarée & O. E. Kaper (eds), *The Libyan Period in Egypt. Historical and Cultural Studies into the 21st-24th Dynasties*, 251–264, Leiden-Louvain.
Mumford, G. (2007) Egypto-Levantine Relations during the Iron Age to early Persian Period (Dynasties Late 20 to 26). In T. Schneider & K. M. Szpakowska (eds) *Egyptian Stories. A British Egyptological Tribute to Alan B. Lloyd on the Occasion of His Retirement*, 225–288, Münster.
Näser, Cl. (2012) Nomads at the Nile: Towards and archaeology of interaction. In H. Barnard & K. Duistermaat (eds), *The History of the Peoples of the Eastern Desert* (Cotsen Institute of Archaeology Monograph 73), 81–92, Los Angeles.

Näser, Cl. (2013) Structures and realities of Egyptian-Nubian interactions from the late Old Kingdom to the early New Kingdom. In S. J. Seidlmayer, D. Raue & Ph. Speiser (eds), *The First Cataract of the Nile: One Region – Diverse Perspectives*, 135–148, Berlin.

Neumann, H. (1999) Ur-Dumuzida and Ur-DUN. Reflections on the relationship between state-initiated foreign trade and private economic activity in Mesopotamia towards the end of the third millennium BC. In J. G. Dercksen (ed.), *Trade and Finance in Ancient Mesopotamia*, 43–53, Leiden.

Ouyang, X. (2013) *Monetary Role of Silver and Its Administration in Mesopotamia during the Ur III Period (c. 2112–2004 BCE): A Case Study of the Umma Province* (Biblioteca del Próximo Oriente Antiguo 11), Madrid.

Pálfi, Z. (2014) Some questions of prices, metals and money in "Old Assyriology". In Z. Csabai & T. Grüll (eds), *Studies in Economic and Social History of the Ancient Near East in Memory of Péter Vargyas* (Ancient Near Eastern and Mediterranean Studies 2), 217–225, Budapest.

Paoletti, P. (2008) Elusive silver? Evidence for the circulation of silver in the Ur III state. *KASKAL* 5: 127–158.

Paulus, S. (2013) The limits of Middle Babylonian archives. In M. Faraguna (ed.), *Archives and Archival Documents in Ancient Societies* (Legal Documents in Ancient Societies IV), 87–103, Trieste.

Paulus, S. (2014) *Die babylonischen Kudurru-inschriften von der kassitischen bis zur frühneubabylonischen Zeit – Untersucht unter besonderer Berücksichtigung gesellschafts- und rechtshistorischer Fragestellungen* (Alter Orient und Altes Testament 51), Münster.

Peet, T. E. (1934) The unit of value *šty* in Papyrus Boulaq 11. *In Mélanges Maspero* I/1, 185–199, Cairo

Peyronel, L. (2010) Ancient Near Eastern economies: the silver question between methodology and archaeological data. In P. Matthiae, F. Pinnock, L. Nigro & N. Marchetti (eds), *Proceedings of the 6th International Congress of the Archaeology of the Ancient Near East*, vol. I, 925–948, Wiesbaden.

Philips, J. (2004) Pre-Aksumite Aksum and its neighbours. In P. Lunde & A. Porter (eds), *Trade and Travel in the Red Sea Region. Proceedings of the Red Sea Project I*, 79–85, Oxford.

Pickles, S. & E. Peltenburg (1998) Metallurgy, society and the bronze/iron transition in the East Mediterranean and the Near East. *Report of the Department of Antiquities, Cyprus*, 67–100.

Pierrat-Bonnefois, G. (2014) Les échanges entre l'Égypte et le Proche-Orient. In F. Morfoisse & G. Andreu-Lanoë (eds), *Sésostris III pharaon de légende*, 174, Ghent.

Pomponio, F. (2003) Aspetti monetari e finanziari del periodo neo-sumerico. In L. Milano & N. Parise (eds), *Il regolamento degli scambi nell'antichità (III–I millennio a.C.)*, 59–108, Roma-Bari.

Pope, J. W. (2014) Beyond the broken reed: Kushite intervention and the limits of *l'histoire événementielle*. In I. Kalimi & S. Richardson (eds) *Sennacherib at the Gates of Jerusalem. Story, History and Historiography*, 105–160, Leiden-Boston.

Porten, B. (1996) *The Elephantine Papyri in English. Three Millennia of Cross-Cultural Continuity and Change*, Leiden-New York-Köln.

Posener-Krieger, P. (1976) *Les archives du temple funéraire de Néferirkarê-Kakaï (Les Papyrus d'Abousir): Traduction et commentaire* (BdÉ 65). Cairo.

Powell, M. A. (1990) Identification and interpretation of long term price fluctuations in Babylonia: more on the history of money in Mesopotamia, *Altorientalische Forschungen* 17: 76–99.

Powell, M. A. (1996) Money in Mesopotamia, *Journal of the Economic and Social History of the Orient* 39: 224–242.

Prévalet, R. (2014) Bronze Age syrian gold jewellery – technological innovation. In H. Meyyer, R. Risch & E. Pernicka (eds), *Metalle der Macht – Frühes Gold und Silber* (6. Mitteldeutscher Archäologentag), 423–433, Halle.

Radner, K. (2015) Hired labor in the Neo-Assyrian empire. In P. Steinkeller & M. Hudson (eds), *Labor in the Ancient Labor*, 329–343, Dresden.

Rahmstorf, L. (2006) In search of the earliest balance weights, scales and weighing systems from the East Mediterranean, the Near East and Middle East. In M. E. Alberti, E. Ascalone & L. Peyronel (eds), *Weights in Context. Bronze Age Weighing Systems of Eastern Mediterranean. Chronology, Typology, Material and Archaeological Contexts* (Studi e Materiali 13), 9–45, Rome.

Rahmstorf, L. (2010) The concept of weighing during the Bronze Age in the Aegean, the Near East and Europe. In I. Morley & C. Renfrew (eds), *The Archaeology of Measurement. Comprehending Heaven, Earth and Time in Ancient Societies*, 88–105, Cambridge.

Rahmstorf, L. (2012) Control mechanisms in Mesopotamia, the Indus Valley, the Aegean and Central Europe, c. 2600–200 BC, and the question of social power in early complex societies. In T. L. Kienlin & A. Zimmermann (edd), *Beyond Elites : Alternatives to Hierarchical Systems in Modelling Social Formations* (Universitätsforschungen zur prähistorischen Archäologie 215) vol. II, 316, Bonn.

Redford, D. B. (1997) Textual sources for the Hyksos Period. In E. D. Oren (ed.), *The Hyksos: New Historical and Archaeological Perspectives*, 1–44, Philadelphia.

Régen, I. & G. Soukiassian (2008), *Gebel el-Zeit II. Le matériel inscrit, Moyen Empire-Nouvel Empire* (Fouilles de l'Institut Français d'Archéologie Orientale 57), Cairo.

Rehren, T. & E. B. Pusch (2012) Alloying and resource management in New Kingdom Egypt: the bronze industry at Qantir – Pi-Ramesse and its relationship to Egyptian copper sources. In V. Kassianidou, & G. Papasavvas (eds), *Eastern Mediterranean Metallurgy and Metalwork in the Second Millennium BC*, 215–221, Oxford.

Renger, J. (1995) Institutional, communal, and individual ownership or possession of arable land in ancient Mesopotamia from the end of the fourth to the end of the first millennium B.C., *Chicago-Kent Law Review* 71: 269–319.

Richardson, S. (1999) Libya domestica: Libyan trade and society on the eve of the invasions of Egypt, *Journal of the American Research Center in Egypt* 36: 149–164.

Ritner, R. K. (2009) *The Libyan Anarchy. Inscriptions from Egypt's Third Intermediate Period*, Atlanta.

Rosa, D. F. (2011) Argento, *annaku* e il problema della moneta e del denaro nel periodo Medio Assiro (XIV–XI sec. a. C.), *Rivista di Storia Economica* 27: 113–131.

Sader, H. (2014) History. In H. Niehr (ed.) *The Aramaeans in Ancient Syria* (Handbuch der Orientalistik 1.106), 11–36, Leiden-Boston.

Sapir-Hen, L. & E. Ben-Yosef (2013) The introduction of domestic camels to the southern Levant: evidence from the Aravah Valley, *Tel Aviv* 40: 277–285.

Saporetti, Cl. (2009) L'argento come mezzo di scambio nell'economia paleo-babilonese. *Rivista di Storia Economica* 25: 91–103.

Sauvage, C. (2012) *Routes maritimes et systèmes d'échanges internationaux au Bronze Récent en Méditerranée orientale*, Lyon.

Scheidel, W. (2010) Real wages in early economies: Evidence for living standards from 1800 BCE to 1300 CE, *Journal of the Economic and Social History of the Orient* 53: 425–462.

Schrakamp, I. (2013) Die 'Sumerische Templestadt' heute. Die sozioökonomische Rolle eines Temples in frühdynastischer Zeit. In K. Kaniut, A. Löhnert, J. M. Miller, M. Roaf & W. Sallaberger (eds), *Tempel im Alten Orient. 7. Internationales Colloquium der Deutschen Orient-Gesellschaft*, 445–466, Wiesbaden.

Selz, G. (2014) Aspekte einer Sozialgeschichte der spät-frühdynastischen Zeit. Das Beispiel Lagash, oder: "The inhabited ghosts of our intellectual ancestors". In Z. Csabai & T. Grüll (eds), *Studies in Economic and Social History of the Ancient Near East in Memory of Péter Vargyas* (Ancient Near Eastern and Mediterranean Studies 2), 239–281, Budapest.

Semaan, L. (2015) New insights into the Iron Age timber trade in Lebanon. In R. K. Pedersen (ed.), *On Sea and Ocean: New Research in Phoenician Seafaring*, 95–119, Marburg.

Sherratt, A. & S. Sherratt (2001) Technological change in the East Mediterranean Bronze Age: capital, resources and marketing. In A. J. Shortland (ed.), *The Social Context of Technological Change. Egypt and the Near East, 1650-1550 BC*, 15–38, Oxford.

Sherratt, S. (1998) 'Sea Peoples' and the economic structure of the late Second Millennium in the Eastern Mediterranean", in S. Gitin, A. Mazar & E. Stern (eds), *Mediterranean Peoples in Transition: Thirteenth to Early Tenth Centuries BCE*, 292–313, Jerusalem.

Sherratt, S. (2000) Circulation of metals and the end of the Bronze Age in the Eastern Mediterranean. In C. F. E. Pare (ed.), *Metals Make The World Go Round: The Supply and Circulation of Metals in Bronze Age Europe*, 82–98, Oxford.

Sherratt, S. (2001) Potemkin palaces and route-based economies. In J. Killen & S. Voutsaki (eds), *Economy and Politics in the Mycenaean Palace States* (Cambridge Philological Society, Supplementary Vol. 27), 214–238, Cambridge.

Sherratt, S. (2003) The Mediterranean economy : 'Globalization' at the end of the second millennium B.C.E. In W. G. Dever & S. Gitin (eds), *Symbiosis, Symbolism and the Power of the Past. Canaan, Ancient Israel, and Their Neighbors from the Late Bronze Age through Roman Palaestina*, 37–62, Winona Lake.

Sherratt, S. (2012) The intercultural transformative capacities of irregularly acquired goods. In Joseph Maran and Philipp W. Stockhammer (ed.), *Materiality and Social Practice. Transformative Capacities of Intercultural Encounters*, 152–172, Oxford.

Skre, D. (2007) Dealing with silver: economic agency in south-western Scandinavia AD 600–1000. In D. Skre (ed.), *Means of Exchange: Dealing with Silver in the Viking Age* (Kaupang Excavation Project Publication Series 2), 343–355, Oslo.

Skre, D. (2013) Money and trade in Viking-Age Scandinavia. In M. Bogucki & M. Rębkowski (eds), *Economies, Monetisation and Society in the West Slavic Lands 800–1200 AD*, 75–87, Szczecin.

Smith, S. T. (2008) Tombs and the transition from the New Kingdom to the Napatan Period in Upper Nubia. In W. Godlewski & A. Łajtar (ed.), *Between the Cataracts. Proceedings of the 11th Conference for Nubian Studies. Part One: Main Papers*, 95–115, Varsow.

Somaglino, Cl. & P. Tallet (2011) Une mystérieuse route sud-orientale sous le règne de Ramsès III, *Bulletin de l'Institut Français d'Archéologie Orientale* 111: 361–369.

Steinkeller, P. (2002) Money-lending practices in Ur III Babylonia: The issue of economic motivation. In M. Hudson & M. van de Mieroop (ed.), *Debt and Economic Renewal in the Ancient Near East*, 109–137, Bethesda.

Steinkeller, P. (2004) Toward a definition of private economic activity in third millennium Babylonia. In R. Rollinger, Ch. Ulf (ed.), *Commerce and Monetary Systems in the Ancient World: Means of Transmission and Cultural Interaction* (MELAMMU Symposia 5), 91–111, Wiesbaden.

Steinkeller, P. (2015) Introduction. Labor in the early states: an early Mesopotamian perspective. In P. Steinkeller & M. Hudson (eds.), *Labor in the Ancient World*, 1–35, Dresden.

Stolper, M. W. (1985) *Entrepreneurs and Empire. The Murašû Archive, the Murašû Firm, and Persian Rule in Babylonia* (PIHANS 54), Leiden.

Tenney, J. S. (2011) Household structure and population dynamics in the Middle Babylonian provincial "slave" population. In L. Culbertson (ed.), *Slaves and Households in the Near East*, 135–146 (Oriental Institute Seminars 7), Chicago.

Thareani-Sussely, Y. (2007) Ancient caravanserai : an archaeological view from 'Aroer, *Levant* 39: 123–141.

Thompson, C.M. (2003) Sealed silver in Iron Age Cisjordan and the "invention" of coinage, *Oxford Journal of Archaeology* 22: 67–96.

Thompson, C.M. (2009) Three 20th Dynasty silver hoards from the Egyptian garrison. In N. Panitz-Cohen & A. Mazar (eds), *Excavations at Tel Beth-Shean 1989-1996* (Beth-Shean Valley Archaeological Project Publications 3), Vol. III, 597–607, Jerusalem.

Tissot, I. Troalen, L. G., Manso, M., Ponting, M., Radtke, M., Reinholz, U., Barreiros, M. A., Shaw, I., Carvalho, M. L. & Guerra, M. F. (2015) A multi-analytical approach to gold in Ancient Egypt: Studies on provenance and corrosion, *Spectrochimica Acta Part B* 108: 75–82.

Troalen, L. G., J. Tate & M. F. Guerra (2014) Goldwork in Ancient Egypt: workshop practices at Qurneh in the 2nd Intermediate Period, *Journal of Archaeological Science* 50: 219–226.

Van de Mieroop, M. (1992) *Society and Enterprise in Old Babylonian Ur*, Berlin.

Van de Mieroop, M. (2002) Credit as a facilitator of exchange in Old Babylonian Mesopotamia. In M. Hudson & M. van de Mieroop (eds), *Debt and Economic Renewal in the Ancient Near East*, 163–173, Bethesda.

van Driel, G. (2002) *Elusive Silver. In Search of a Role for a Market in an Agrarian Environment. Aspects of Mesopotamia's Society*, Leiden.

Vargyas, P. (2004) La monétisation de l'économie rurale en Babylonie et en Égypte pendant le 1er millénaire av. J.-C. In B. Menu (ed.), *La dépendance rurale dans l'Antiquité égyptienne et proche-orientale*, 109–120, Cairo.

Veenhof, K. R. (1997) "Modern" features in Old Assyrian trade, *Journal of the Economic and Social History of the Orient* 40: 336–366.

Veenhof, K. R. (1999) Silver and credit in Old Assyrian trade. In J. G. Dercksen (ed.) *Trade and Finance in Ancient Mesopotamia*, 55–83, Leiden.

Veenhof, K. R. (2010) Ancient Assur: The city, its traders and its commercial network, *Journal of the Economic and Social History of the Orient* 53: 39–82.

Venturi, F. (ed.) (2010) *Societies in Transition: Evolutionary Processes in the Northern Levant between Late Bronze Age II and Early Iron Age*, Bologne.

Vér, A. (2014) Neo-Assyrian *kārus* in the Zagros. In Z. Csabai & T. Grüll (eds), *Studies in Economic and Social History of the Ancient Near East in Memory of Péter Vargyas* (Ancient Near Eastern and Mediterranean Studies 2), 789–810, Budapest.

Vernus, P. (1993) *Affaires et scandales sous les Ramsès. La crise des valeurs dans l'Égypte du Nouvel Empire*, Paris.

Warburton, D. (2010) The Egyptian economy: sources, models and history. In A. Hudecz & M. Petrik (ed.), *Commerce and Economy in Ancient Egypt*, 165–175, Oxford.

Warburton, D. (2013) Integration by price in the Bronze Age. In D. Frenez & M. Tosi (eds), *South Asian Archaeology 2007. Volume I: Prehistoric Periods*, 287–296, Oxford.

Wente, E.F. (1990) *Letters from Ancient Egypt*, Atlanta.

White, D. (2002) *Marsa Matruh II: The Objects*, Philadelphia.

Widell, M. (2008) The Ur III metal loans from Ur. In S. J. Garfinkle & J. C. Johnson (eds), *The Growth of an Early State in Mesopotamia: Studies in Ur III Administration* (Biblioteca del Próximo Oriente Antiguo 5), 207–223, Madrid.

Wiener, M. H. (2013) Contacts: Crete, Egypt, and the Near East circa 2000 B.C. In J. Aruz, S. B. Graff & Y. Rakic (eds), *Cultures in Contact from Mesopotamia to the Mediterranean in the Second Millennium B.C.*, 34–43, New York.

Wilcke, C. (2007) Markt und Arbeit im Alten Orient am Ende des 3. Jahrtausends v. Chr. In W. Reinhard & J. Stagl (eds) *Menschen und Märkte. Studien zur historischen Wirtschaftsanthropologie*, 71–132, Vienna-Köln-Weimar.

Wilkinson, T. C. (2014) *Tying the Threads of Eurasia. Trans-Regional Routes and Material Flows in Transcaucasia, Eastern Anatolia and Western Central Asia, c. 3000–1500 BC*, Leiden.

Wunsch, C. (2012) Neo-Babylonian entrepreneurs. In D. S. Landes, J. Mokyr & W. J. Baumol (eds), *The Invention of Enterprise: Entrepreneurship from Ancient Mesopotamia to Modern Times*, 40–61, Princeton.

Yule, P. A. (2015) The ʿIbrī/Selme Hoard from al-Ẓāhirah Province – 30 years after. In *The Archaeological Heritage of Oman*, 133–140, Muscat.

Zaccagnini, C. (1997) Prices and price formation in the ancient Near East. A methodological approach. In J. Andreau, P. Briant & R. Descat (eds), *Économie antique: Prix et formation des prix dans les économies antiques* (Entretiens d'archéologie et d'histoire Saint-Bertrand-de-Comminges 3), 361–384, Saint-Bertrand-de-Comminges.

Zaccagnini, C. (1999) Economic aspects of land ownership and land use in northern Mesopotamia and Syria from the late 3rd millennium to the Neo-Assyrian period. In M. Hudson & B. A. Levine (eds), *Urbanization and Land Ownership in the Ancient Near East*, 331–341, Cambridge (MA).

Chapter 2

Oil and wine for silver? The economic agency of the Egyptian peasant communities in the Great Oasis during the Persian Period

Damien Agut-Labordère

In the Western desert, 200 km from the Nile Valley, the Kharga Oasis stretches along a narrow depression of 160 km long. Located at its southern end, around Tell Douch, the sandy site of Ayn Manawir has been since 1994 the subject of excavations conducted on behalf of the Institut français d'archéologie orientale by a team led by the late Michel Wuttmann. The settlement dates back to the 5th and 4th centuries BC. A small mud-brick temple and a settlement structure were grouped at the foot of a sandstone mound dug with deep *galeries de captage*[1] that enabled the extraction of water from a perched water table. However, the excavation of the temple (MT sector) and different sectors of habitats and a survey carried out on the adjacent site of Ayn Ziayâda yielded hundreds of ostraca inscribed in demotic (O.Man). Entrusted to Michel Chauveau (EPHE-IV) assisted by the author 461 documents are now transliterated and translated. All these texts will be available online on www.achemenet.com directed by Pierre Briant (Collège de France).

During the 1990s, the principle interest of scholars concerning the Ayn Manawir excavations was focused on the technique used for extracting hidden water (Briant 2001). In a second phase, a very important article published by Michel Chauveau in 2000 pointed out that the earliest textual attestation of the Athenian staters in Egypt appears in some O.Man to date from the end of the 5th century, demonstrating that the local oasian community was integrated into a monetised economic channel (Chauveau 2000, completed by Agut-Labordère 2014). The aim of this paper is to explore this paradoxical situation whereby the northern Greek coins are mentioned for the first time in texts written on the periphery of a periphery of the deep South of Egypt.[2]

In the absence of any evidence of the presence of Greek mercenaries in the Kharga Oasis during the Persian Period, historians are deprived of the classical explanation of the staters' diffusion (Faucher *et al.* 2012, 160–161). This leads us to give priority to internal economic factors. A possible explanation for the early mentions of staters in the O.Man could lie in local economic dynamics. In order to test this hypothesis we need to consider the export capacity of the small settlement of Ayn Manawir.

Identifying the marketable productions: vessels, plant remains and texts

Lisa Giddy is one of the first authors to have stressed the role of exports in the economy of the settlements of the Western Oasis. She particularly emphasised the importance of basketry among the oasis productions by analysing the tributary scenes from the Theban tombs of the 18th dynasty (Giddy 1980, 121–124; 1987, 75, 88, 97, 156–157). The import of "baskets from the Oasis" (*t̠bs.t n Wḥ3.t*) is confirmed by lists of supplies written on two Theban ostraca dated to the end of the 19th dynasty (n°25677 v°20–21 et 25678 v°2: Černy 1935). Based on the analysis of the ceramic assemblage of the New Kingdom found in Ayn Asil (Dakhlah Oasis) and on the sealing and inscriptions of these containers, Sylvie Marchand and Pierre Tallet have recently succeeded in following the wine exports of the Dakhleh Oasis from the place of production to their place of consumption in the valley (Marchand & Tallet 1999).

Traces of oasis exports during the Persian Period: the ceramic evidences

Concerning the 1st millenium BC and, more precisely, the Saite and Persian Periods, Oasis exports are well attested by the dissemination of at least two locally produced ceramic types in many parts of the valley.[3] Even if, for the moment, no ceramic production site has been identified at Ayn Manâwir, the manufacture of containers with local clay seems to have been quite dynamic, especially with regard to the *siga*.

- *siga* are heavy and thick vessels identifiable by their elongated shape surrounded by a neck set in the vase widens. Contemporary examples tend to show that *siga* were intended to transport liquids: water (Heinen 1997, 161–167) but also milk and cheese (Defernez 2012, 396 note 38). No reliable residue was identified in the *siga* dated to the Persian period. However, two elements show that they were also intended for the carriage of liquids; in some cases the neck had a large diameter filter, and could be closed hermetically by a clap made with clay and a piece of textile. The oldest attested *siga* dated from the 27th Dynasty. The type 1 in the 'Ayn Manâwir typology (also called "grande *siga*") is now identified at Elephantine, Edfu, Dendera, Karnak (Masson 2007), Abydos and Tebtynis (Defernez 2012, 495).
- Oasian made lenticular flasks were also attested in much smaller quantities and are spread in the Delta from the 26th dynasty and in the Theban area (Hope *et al.* 2006). Their relatively neat decoration tells us that they contained a valuable product, most likely a cosmetic.

The oasis containers were loaded onto donkey caravans to be sent to the cities of the valley.

Identifying the productions: plant remains and texts

In 2013, Claire Newton and the author published a study concerning the vegetal economy in 'Ayn Manawir for the Persian Period. By cross-referencing the textual and archaeobotanical data, this work allows us to identify wine and castor oil as productions which are likely to have been exported to the Nile valley (Agut-Labordère & Newton 2013, 14–17).

In the absence of a study concerning the market value of wine in Saite and Persian Egypt, it is impossible to estimate the role of this production in the Egyptian inner and outer exchanges. However, consistent evidence demonstrates the importance of Egyptian viticulture before the Macedonian conquest (Defernez 2012, 391–394). In the Ayn Manawir documentation, an ostracon dated to 380 BC concerning the establishment of an annuity rent (O.Man 5469) gives to us a very complete equivalence list to the value of the 16 (artaba) of "beautiful barley"[4] (*i͗t nfr*) which constituted the rent. Such a quantity of cereal is equivalent to "2 (hin) of honey = 4 (hin) of pure wine (*wʿb i͗rp*) = 8 (hin) of castor and 2⸢4⸣ (artaba) of wheat." The fact that wine comes second in the list clearly illustrates its value inside the Oasian community.

The botanical remains analysed by Claire Newton show the importance of the culture of the vineyard: the charred remains of vines are attested in 70% of the samples. These are seeds, whole but also fragmented, fully formed or immature and peduncles. These features are not compatible with consumption only in the form of fruits, fresh or dried, since the seeds are usually ingested with the fruit. Charred residues are probably used by-products of the pressing of fruit as a domestic fuel. Their ubiquity in the archaeological sediment would tend to show a large amount of juice was produced; sufficient for the sub-products to have been stored and used regularly as fuel. In addition, the presence of vine wood in charcoal confirms that it was a local culture.

The castor plant (*ricinus communis*) is indigenous to the southeastern Mediterranean Basin, Eastern Africa, and India.[5] Today it is widespread throughout tropical regions. In areas with a suitable climate, castor establishes itself easily and can often be found on wasteland. It likes exposure to heat and prefers to be planted in full sun and watered as and when it grows. Castor is a plant of rapid growth: planted in May, in 5 months it can reach 3 m high. When the plant is young (during the first month), castor requires a good deal of water but when it grows old, it has less need to be refreshed because its deep roots allow it to withstand drought thanks to a narrowing of the leaves or their extinction. The sandy soils irrigated by the oasis channels are therefore suitable for such cultivation. In addition the hardiness of the castor plant allows it to fit into the culture system without competing against the food crop. This means that developing castor plantations didn't necessarily interfere with the cereal and vegetable production and helped to cultivate previously underused areas, as confirmed by a passage of Herodotus. Travelling in Egypt during the rule of Artaxerxes I, Herodotus provides details on the cultivation of castor he observed in the Delta, noting that it was sown only on the banks [II.94]:

> [1] *The Egyptians who live around the marshes use an oil drawn from the castor-berry, which they call kiki. They sow this plant, which grows wild in Hellas, on the banks of the rivers and lakes;* [2] *sown in Egypt, it produces abundant fruit, though malodorous; when they gather this, some bruise and press it, others boil after roasting it, and collect the liquid that comes from it. This is thick and useful as oil for lamps, and gives off a strong smell.* (trans. A. D. Godley. Cambridge, Harvard University Press 1920).

This text is of great interest because it also tells us how the castor oil was extracted from seeds.[6] It also specifies that, because of its high flammability, castor oil was used to produce light for small lamp-wicks.[7]

The price of castor oil, fixed under the state control of oil production known as the *P.Rev.Laws* during the rule of Ptolemy II, shows that it was an expensive commodity (30–48 drachmas per 12-chous metretes: Muhs 2005, 73). Even in earlier times, under the reign of Amasis, the priests of Amun of Teudjoi who tried to influence Kherkhonsou son of Hor, a musician depending directly on the king, provided him with an annuity made up of "300 bags of grain, 200 hin of castor oil, 50 hin of honey and 30 geese" (P.Ryl. 9.16.18).[8] As a high value product, castor oil could be exported by the inhabitants of Ayn Manawir. Textual and archaeobotanical data perfectly coincide to indicate that castor oil was produced in important quantities by the Oasian peasants (Agut-Labordère & Newton 2013, 14–16). Furthermore, the high value of castor inside the community is proven by O.Man.5488, an acknowledgement of debt established in spring 392 BC. The debt concerns 19 artaba of "beautiful barley" (*ỉt nfr*) and 2 (artaba) of castor seed (*pr.t tgm*). The fact that castor seeds are loaned and associated with the "beautiful barley", the local currency commodity (Agut-Labordère 2014), illustrates the importance of castor in the local economy. Furthermore, the transaction is also guaranteed by a penalty in silver.

An Aramaic letter dated to the late 6th to early 5th century illustrates the fact that castor oil was a consumer product in the valley during the Persian Period. Makkibanit who stayed in Memphis wrote to Tashi, his wife, who lived in Elephantine to ask her, among other things, to send him "handfuls of castor oil" (Kuhrt 2007, 759–760 no. 29). This document also shows that castor oil was not produced in the northern part of Egypt at this time. Thus, with Elephantine (and probably other areas of Upper but also Middle Egypt), Kharga was a producing region of castor oil.

Nevertheless, we can assume that the castor oil from the oasis suffered a major disadvantage compared to that produced elsewhere in the valley: its price would include the cost generated by its being conveyed to the banks of the Nile. To remedy this it is possible that the Oasians used their castor oil to make more sophisticated products that bore the extra costs generated by the transport through the desert. On this point a Ptolemaic period ostracon (O.Daba 1) published by Michel Chauveau and whose origins are in Dabasheya, north of the town of Kharga, causes us to suppose that Oasian castor oil was not only used to power lights (Chauveau 2009, 3–4). The author of this letter calls repeatedly refers to "commercial quality oil" (*wʿ nḥḥ šwṱ*, l. 3) to produce a colouring product for the skin similar to henna (*qpr*). In this letter, it may also be about a matter of mortar (⌜*ḥ.t*⌝-*n*ʿ, l.10). Castor oil obtained by cold pressing (with a mortar) is characterised by a very high viscosity (this is the densest vegetable oil). Thanks to this original texture, castor oil is an excellent wetting and dispersing agent for pigments and, more generally, for all kinds of skin care (Schoske *et al.* 1992, 245).

If the examination of the diffusion patterns of the Oasian trade containers illustrates the dynamics of some local productions, the analysis of the vegetal economy in Ayn Manawir during the Persian period allows us to identify the potentially marketable production. Seen from the site of Ayn Manawir, the south of Kharga appears to be part of a rent-Oasis producing one or several commodities of great value, comparable to dates in the contemporary Western Sahara oasis of Tunisia, Algeria and Morocco.[9]

Analysing a production system through an inadequate documentation

Having analysed the Oasis exports to the Nile valley as far as possible, we can turn to the system of wine and castor oil production. Here we encounter one of the main difficulties caused by the nature of the written documentation. The problem is that the vast majority of the texts discovered in Ayn Manawir concerning the plant economy originate not from private persons but from a local institution: the temple of Osiris-iou (Agut-Labordère & Newton 2013, 7 graph. 5). This is therefore a relatively inadequate documentation for analysing a phenomenon concerning commercial agriculture because, as we will see, wine and mainly castor appear in the temple documents first as products which can be levied for the benefit of this institution.

Indeed, in Ayn Manawir during the Persian period, castor is peculiarly attested in a specific kind of receipt in which a certain amount of castor is given to the temples of Osiris-iou.

O. Man. 4047 (Year 4 of an unspecified king):

Recto
1. Hor son of Horkheb greets
2. Unamenheb son of Harsiese:
3. "You gave to me 1/2 of castor
4. (for) supplying the lamp
5. of Osiris-iou (6) in the year 4.

Verso
1. (I) have received it from your hand.
2. My heart is satisfied."
3. Written by Nesinher.
4. Dictation of Hor son of Horkheb.

The formulation is rather elliptic. Whether we are dealing with castor oil or castor seeds, it is impossible to know: it may be half an artaba (=15 l.) of beans or half a hin

(= 40 cl.) of oil. What is remarkable in this document is how the levy is "theologically" legitimated: "for the supply of the god's lamp of Osiris-iou" (*r t3 ḫrỉ(.t) ẖbs n Wsỉr-ỉw*). We found a similar formula on the Saite lamp donation stelae: *ẖr ẖbs m-b3ḥ* + the name of a god, translated "endowment for a god's lamp" by Anthony Leahy (Leahy 1981: 38-39). These stelae concern the revenue of a land given to a temple to supply the oil for the maintenance of lamps used in the liturgy (Meeks 1972, 109 [206]; 1979, 650 n. 24; El-Sayed 1975, 61). The mention of a *p3 šmw n n3 3ḥ.w nty ẖr p3 ẖbs* "the harvest of the fields which feed the lamp" is also attested in the P.Saq.Sekhemkhet (l.5) an incomplete and isolated saito-persian papyrus found in Saqqara (Cruz-Uribe 1990). During the Saite and the Persian Period a portion of the divine domain of some Egyptian temples was thus intended to produce fuel for lighting. On this point, Leahy made an incisive remark concerning the use of the stelae he studied:

> "The majority of these stelae were set up, not by the benefactor to record his generosity, but by temples, either as a boundary marker or in the temple enclosure, to provide a permanent record of an institution's right to the revenue of a piece of property ...". (Leahy 1981, 41)

Another ostracon, a receipt formulated as a letter, helps us to precise the elliptic formulary attested in the receipts concerning the fuelling of the god's lamp in castor oil.

O. Man. 3984 (Year 4 of an unspecified king):

Recto
1. [Horkheb] son of Horkheb greets
2. [Unamenheb] son of Harsiese. May Phre
3. prolong his life! You gave to me [...] of castor for
4. the supplying the lamp of Osiris-iou
5. (made) from castor taken from the harvest
6. of the year 4. (I) have received that. My heart
7. is satisfied. Written by
8. Nesinher son of Hor.
9. [ ]

Verso
1. Horkheb son of Horkheb.

Thereby some cultivators of Ayn Manawir were submitted to an annual levy on crops in castor. Technically this levy operated by the temples on the crops harvested on their agricultural domains must be related to the well-known *šmw*-tax given in cereals by the tenants of the temples (Donker van Heel 1995, 43–45).

The conditions under which this castor tax was levied are highlighted by O.Man. 4316, a document establishing the conditions of the partnership between two persons,

Hor son of Horkheb and Onnophris son of Petemanheb, who had been hired by the temple of Osiris-iou to collect the castor for the lamp of the god.

O. Man. 4316 (430 BC, 8 April–7 May)

Recto
1. Year 35 month of Tybi of Pharao[l.p.h.] Artaxerxes[l.p.h.],
2. the agreements concluded between Hor son of Horkheb and Onnophris son of
3. Peteamenheb to whom was given the quarter of the castor of Osiris-iou.
4. We agreed on collecting this quarter
5. on the cultivators of the village. Any of us who
6. will defect to his companion and will not
7. collect with him, he will have to give 3 deben of silver melt in the Treasure of Ptah
8. to his companion and we will
9. deliver in spite of that castor.

Verso
1. To the priests of Osiris-iou.
2. [ ]
3. Written by Nesinher son of Hor.
4. In the year 25 month of Tybi day 1.

Through the levy system, we can observe how the castor was produced by the Oasian peasants; the oasis farmers gave over a portion of their fields for the cultivation of this plant, and when they leased land of the Osiris-iou temple they had to give a quarter of their production to this institution.

Nevertheless, the allusiveness of the formulation raises the question of what was actually collected by the Horkheb and Onnophris. In other words, was this tax paid in beans or in oil? In her comprehensive study consecrated to the religious association, Françoise de Cenival concluded that the word *tgm/dgm* must always be translated as "castor oil" and not "castor seeds".[10] Above we have seen that Petubastis son of Inaros the scribe of the O.Man.5488 specified that castor part of the annuity income was in the form of seeds (*pr.t tgm*) and not in oil which could mean that the word *tgm* alone could designate "castor oil". Nevertheless, we have to be very cautious on this point. Another receipt concerning castor (O.Man. 4042, year 5 of an unspecified king) explicitly mentions the transfer of "10 of ⸢60 hin⸣ of castor" by Unamenheb son Harsiese to Hor son of Diameniry. 60 hin could correspond to one artaba (Depauw 1997, 166) of seeds ... but it may also be relative to 600 hin of castor oil corresponding to 2400 l. a little more than the capacity of a 10 Burgundian barrels of 228 l.[11]

In any case, as the temple draws a quarter of the production of castor it implies that a large majority of the oil produced from the seeds remained in the hands of these tenants who could use it for domestic lighting and most likely entered in the commercial circuit that can be estimated from the dissemination of the local containers. The absence of any commercially written documentation prohibits a definitive conclusion concerning the issue of the commercialisation of castor oil and wine produced in the Great Oasis during the Persian Period.

Conclusion

We have now to go back to our first question: Oil for silver? Maybe. The peasant families who lived in Ayn Manawir produced goods that were quite likely exported outside the Great Oasis and could be traded against the Greek coins circulated in the Nile Valley at this time. Thus the assumption of an internal economic development leading to an early arrival of the silver coin deserves to be posited. Can it be proven? Not in the present state of our documentation. The indications we have are not sufficient to assert that staters attested in the texts came from the export of wine, cosmetic and lighting oil. Nevertheless, for the moment, this hypothesis remains the least improbable one.

However, trying to answer the question of the origin of staters allows us to pinpoint some of the dynamics of the local agriculture, highlighting the fact that it wasn't fully oriented toward subsistence. This question refers to the issue of the agency of the Egyptian peasant communities that produced commodities for self-consumption but also for trade.[12] The castor tax rate shows that ¾ of the castor (oil or beans) production remained in the hands of the tenants of the sacred land. The temple of Osiris-iou could take a fairly limited amount of the valuable crops grown on its land. It can thus be assumed that the decision to devote part of their efforts to this cash production had been taken beforehand by the peasant families themselves. The local religious institutions intervened a second time to tax this kind of lucrative production.

The advantage of this hypothesis is twofold:

- First, the possibility of producing high value commodities such as wine or lighting oil in the Great Oasis could explain the efforts to dig the *galeries de captage* accomplished by local peasant groups.[13] It is therefore noteworthy that apart from the payment of a "village tax" to the Governor of Dush[14] none of the 460 demotic ostraka found in Ayn Manawir mention a Royal agent. There is no evidence that the Persian king attempted to mould the territory in the South of the Great Oasis.
- On the contrary, analysing the development of this area during the Persian Period using the assumption of the agency of the local peasant communities helps to explain the fact that the *mw* (lit. "water"), the basic elements of the water irrigation system, frequently bear the name of private individuals who were probably at the head of the first families which dug the *galeries de captage*.

We must therefore consider the hypothesis that the economic development of the South of the Great Oasis was due to a free peasantry renting sometimes sacred lands. The capacity for self-exploitation among these families (Ouzoulias 2014) could explain the fact that the price of the Oasian wine and oil remained competitive in the Valley in spite of the transport cost handicap. In this scenario, the cultivation of new lands and the development of an agricultural community in Ayn Manawir could be the result of internal factors relating to the demography of the Great Oasis and not the result of a Royal will to create a Saharan pioneer front. A significant increase in the local population could be the cause of a creative pressure which obliged the inhabitants of the south of the Great Oasis to cultivate new lands. It is important to note here that this type of demographic stimulus was necessarily peculiarly powerful in an Oasis where the carrying capacity of the land is very low.[15]

This hypothesis breaks with the classic analysis of the development of the Ancient Egyptian economy that it was the Pharaonic State and the temples which were at the origin of the agricultural initiatives.[16] It may well be that the diachronic analysis of the economic history of the Oasian peasant communities will help us to have a less naïve and more balanced approach. A brief history of the production and taxation of castor production shows that the temples and the Royal state did not pioneer its cultivation but followed local initiatives which remain undocumented due to the lack of appropriate documents. As the written sources are largely of an institutional origin, philologists are unable to perceive the agricultural changes when they affect the temples or the Crown. Therefore the textual sources can only strengthen the illusion that these institutions were the sole initiators of economic changes creating a strong bias in the analysis of agricultural history. We have to be aware of the type of scenario that the nature of the written documents leads us to favour (Eyre 1998; 1999; 2004; Moreno-García 2011, 3–4). Cross-referencing different kinds of documents (text and archaeological data) and making use of the theoretical models advanced by rural sociology and history are ways to avoid falling into a simplistic narrative that deprive the peasants of Ancient Egypt of their creativity and capacity to take the initiative.

Concerning castor oil production, Anthony Leahy made a very important comment in his article concerning the donations for the gods' lamps: "the complete absence of 'lamps' from the extant donation stelae of the Dynasties 22–25 and even those from the reign of Psametik I suggests an increase in some aspect of their use in the course of the Saite Period."[17] The ostraka of Ayn Manawir shows that part of the lighting oil production was captured by some temples at least as far back as the First Persian domination. Two centuries later, the castor tax levied by the religious institutions came under Royal control. The great fiscal reform of Ptolemy II held that the tax farmers paid to the cultivators was only three quarters of their harvest in castor: for the Egyptian peasants, the rate of the tax remained unchanged. It is probable that much later the Royal state found another way of attaining income from the production of castor oil. A tax on the castor oil press is therefore attested by P.Thmouis (Mendesian nome) dated to the second half of the second century AD.[18] In the history of castor taxes, the King comes in last place – after the temples – to capture one part of the wealth created by the cultivation of this plant thanks to the effort of the Egyptian peasantry.

Notes

1. This term is borrowed from Boucharlat 2001.
2. The architectural and archeological remains signal the importance of the city of Hibis located in the north of the Kharha Oasis.
3. Marchand 2007. On Desert roads, see now Förster & Riemer 2013.
4. Agut-Labordère 2014, 86.
5. Battisti 2005, 100. *Ricinus communis* seems to be of Abyssinian origin. Today this plant grows spontaneously in the whole Sahara.
6. For more references drawn from Classical sources, see Manniche 1989, 142–143. Note that Dioscorides (I.38) mentions castor-oil extractions with baskets.
7. Manniche 1989, 142 for other Classical references. Salt was often mixed with oil in order to dry the oil to avoid the flame cracklings (Bussière 1973).
8. Vittmann 1998, 531. As an indicator, in a Ptolemaic marriage contract, the husband was obliged to provide to his wife with 2 hin of castor oil per month (P.Ryl. 10 = P.Ehe 10 quoted by Muhs 2005, 75 n 533).
9. Battisti 2005, 20. The Oasian economies based on auto consumption, in which the entire production is consumed by the inhabitants themselves, are fairly rare.
10. De Cenival 1972, 19–20. The term used to designate castor in O.Man. is *tgm* and not *k3k3* well attested in the place names (Leahy 1988: 185 [d]; Vittmann 1998: 583) from which the Greek word κίκι derives (Muhs 2007, 53).
11. Maybe this huge quantity of castor is proportionate to the political importance of the recipient: someone called Hor son of Diameniry is also mentioned in another receipt as "the governor of Dush" (*p3 sḥn (n) Gš*, O.Man 6857, l.3, year 3 of an unspecified king) concerning no less than 62 (artaba) of barley given, this time, by Hor. It is therefore impossible to know firmly whether the levy allocated in the name of the Osiris-iou temple was in seeds or in oil.
12. Concerning the Roman Economy, Kron 2008 also underlines the importance of "Roman smallholders [which] remained a vital force in Roman agriculture and society" (p. 108).
13. This hypothesis fits perfectly with the one formulated in Boucharlat concerning the polygenic origins of the "galeries de captage" (2001, 178–179). The hypothesis of the importation in Egypt of a Persian technique for extracting hidden water has no documentary foundation. If we add that there is no proof of the existence of qanawat in Iran before the Islamic Period, it can be seen to be baseless.
14. See note 10.
15. It is also possible that the dual constraints of the poverty of the lands and of the transport cost induced many Oasian peasants to adopt new production strategies, see the case of cotton production during the Roman Period highlighted in Tallet *et al.* 2012.
16. On this point see the fundamental analysis of Moreno García 2014a; 2014b.
17. Leahy 1981, 43 n. 2. An even older short decree establishing a series of donations to fuel the Amon-Re lamp is attested in the "Chronicle of Prince Osorkon" (Caminos 1985, 61–65).
18. Blouin 2007. Note that O.Leipzig 2200 (a late Ptolemaic ostracon from Thebaid) contains mention of the milling of *tkm* (translated by "Ölsaat" by Kaplony-Heckel 2010, 142–143).

Bibliography

Agut-Labordère, D. (2014) L'orge et l'argent. Les usages monétaires à Ayn Manâwir à l'époque perse, *Annales Histoire Sciences Sociales* 69: 75–90.

Agut-Labordère, D. & C. Newton (2013) L'économie végétale à 'Ayn Manâwir à l'époque perse: archéobotanique et sources démotiques. *ARTA* 2013.005 (Available online: http://www.achemenet.com/document/ARTA_2013.005-Agut-Newton.pdf

Battesti, V. (2005) *Jardins au désert, Évolution des pratiques et savoirs oasiens, Jérid tunisien*, Paris. http://hal.archives-ouvertes.fr/halshs-00004609

Blouin, K. (2007) Environnement et fisc dans le nome mendésien à l'époque romaine. Réalités et enjeux de la diversification, *Bulletin of the American Society of Papyrologists* 44: 136–166.

Boucharlat, R. (2001) Les galeries de captage dans la péninsule d'Oman au premier millénaire av. J.-C.: questions sur leur relation avec les galeries du plateau iranien. In P. Briant (ed.), *Qanat et canalisations souterraines en Iran, en Égypte et en Grèce*, 157–183, Paris.

Bussière, J. (1973) Sur une mèche de lampe, *Antiquités africaines* 7: 255–257.

Caminos, R. A. (1958) *The Chronicle of Prince Osorkon*, Roma.

Černy, J. (1935) *Ostraca hiératiques* CGC 25502-25832, Cairo.

Chauveau, M. (2000) La première mention du statère en Egypte, *Transeuphratène* 20: 137–143.

Chauveau, M. (2009) Résumé des conférences. Démotique. Progamme de l'année 2007–2008, *Annuaire de l'École pratique des hautes études, section des sciences historiques et philologiques*: 3–4. http://ashp.revues.org/609?file=1

De Cenival, Fr. (1972) *Les associations religieuses en Égypte d'après les documents démotiques*, Cairo.

Cruz-Uribe, E. (1990) A note on Early Demotic grain formula, *Enchoria* 17: 55–68.

Defernez, C. (2012) Sur les traces des conteneurs égyptiens d'époque perse dans le Delta. In C. Zivie-Coche & I. Guermeur (eds), *"Parcourir l'éternité". Hommage à Jean Yoyotte*, 387–408, Paris.

Depauw, M. (1997) *A Companion to Demotic Studies*, Brussels.

Donker van Heel, K. (1995) *Abnormal Hieratic and Early Demotic texts collected by the Theban choachytes in the reign of Amasis. Papyri from the Louvre Eisenlohr lot*, Dissertation, Leiden.

Eyre, C. (1998) The market women of Pharaonic Egypt. In N. Grimal & B. Menu (eds), *Le commerce en Égypte ancienne*, 173–191, Cairo.

Eyre, C. (1999) The village economy in Pharaonic Egypt. In A. Bowman & E. Rogan (eds), *Agriculture in Egypt: From Pharaonic to Modern Times*, 33–60, Oxford.

Eyre, C. (2004) How relevant was personal status to the functioning of the rural economy in Pharaonic Egypt? In B. Menu (ed.), *La dépendance rurale dans l'Antiquité égyptienne et proche-orientale*, 157–186, Cairo.

Faucher, Th., W. Fischer-Bossert & S. Dhennin (2012) Les monnaies en or aux types hiéroglyphiques *nwb nfr*, *Bulletin de l'Institut Français d'Archéologie Orientale* 112: 147–169.

Förster, F. & H. Riemer (2013) *Desert Road Archaeology in Ancient Egypt and Beyond*, Köln.

Giddy, L. (1980) Some Exports from the Oases of the Libyan Desert. In *Le Livre du Centenaire*, 119–125, Cairo.

Giddy, L. (1987) *Egyptian Oases: Bahariya, Dakhla, Farafra and Kharga during Pharaonic Times*, Warminster.

Heinen, N. H. (1997) *Poteries et potiers d'Al Qasr, oasis de Dakhla*, Cairo.

Hope, C. A., M. A. J. Eccleston, O. E. Kaper, D. Darnell & S. Marchand (2001) Kegs and flasks from the Dakhleh Oasis, *Cahiers de la ceramique égyptienne* 6: 189–231.

Kaplony-Heckel, U. (2010) Theben-Ost III, *Zeitschrift für Ägyptische Sprache und Altertumskunde* 137: 127–144, pls xi–xx.

Kron, G. J. (2008) The much maligned peasant. Comparative Perspectives on the productivity of the small farmer in Classical Antiquity. In L. de Ligt & S. Northwood (eds), *People, Land, and Politics. Demographic Developments and the Transformation of Roman Italy 300 BC–AD 14*, 71–119, Leiden-Boston.

Kuhrt, A. (2007) *The Persian Empire: A Corpus of Sources of the Achaemenid Period*, London.

Leahy, A. (1981) Saite lamp donations, *Göttinger Miszellen* 49: 38–39.

Leahy, A. (1988) The earliest dated monument of Amasis and the end of the reign of Apries, *Journal of Egyptian Archaeology* 74: 183–199.

Manniche, L. (1989) *An Ancient Egyptian Herbal*, London.

Marchand, S. (2007) Les conteneurs de transport et de stockage de l'oasis de Kharga. De la Basse Époque (XXVIIe–XXXe dynasties) à l'époque ptolémaïque. In S. Marchand & A. Marangou (eds), *Amphores d'Égypte de la Basse Époque à l'époque arabe* (Cahiers de la Céramique égyptienne 8), 489–502, Cairo.

Marchand S. & P. Tallet (1999) Ayn Asil et l'oasis de Dakhla au Nouvel Empire, *Bulletin de l'Institut Français d'Archéologie Orientale* 99: 307–352.
Masson, A. (2007) Le quartier des prêtres du temple de Karnak: rapport préliminaire de la fouille de la Maison VII, 2001–2003, *Karnak* 12: 593–655.
Meeks, D. (1979) Les donations aux temples dans l'Égypte du Ier Millénaire avant J.C. In E. Lipiński (ed.), *State and Temple Economy in the Ancient Near East II*, 661–681, Leuven.
Moreno-García, J. C. (2011) Village. In E. Frood & W. Wendrich (eds), *UCLA Encyclopedia of Egyptology*, Los Angeles. http://digital2.library.ucla.edu/viewItem.do?ark=21198/zz0026vtgm
Moreno-García, J. C. (2014a) Penser l'économie pharaonique, *Annales. Histoire Sciences Sociales* 69: 7–38.
Moreno-García, J. C. (2014b) The cursed discipline? The peculiarities of Egyptology at the turn of the 21st century. In W. Carruthers (ed.), *Histories of Egyptology: Interdisciplinary Measures*, 50–63 London.
Muhs, B. P. (2005) *Tax Receipts, Taxpayers and Taxes in Early Ptolemaic Thebes*, Chicago.
Ouzoulias, P. (2014) *Nos natura non sustinet*. À propos de l'intensification agricole dans quatre terroirs du nord des Gaules, *Gallia* 71/2: 307–328.
Schoske, S., B. Kreißl & R. Germer (1992) *"Anch" Blumen für das Leben. Pflanzen im alten Ägypten*, München.
Tallet, G., C. Gradel & F. Letellier-Willemin (2012) «Une laine bien plus douce que celle des moutons» à El-Deir (oasis de Kharga): le coton au cœur de l'économie oasienne à l'époque romaine. In S. Guedon (ed.), *Entre Afrique et Égypte*, 119–141, Bordeaux.

Chapter 3

Urban craftsmen and other specialists, their land holdings, and the Neo-Assyrian state

Heather D. Baker

In recent years, increasing attention has been devoted to the study of the Neo-Assyrian countryside with a view to elucidating the state's influence on the nature of rural settlement and modes of agricultural exploitation. The need to supply the increasing urban populations was a major factor behind the drive to intensify cultivation within and beyond the hinterlands of the major urban centres. Recent archaeological research has highlighted the role of massive state investment in extensive canal systems that helped to reduce the risks associated with agriculture in an area of unpredictable rainfall and facilitated intensification (Wilkinson *et al.* 2005; Ur 2005; Kühne 2012). However, the Neo-Assyrian heartland itself – the so-called "Assur-Nineveh-Arbela triangle" (Radner 2011) – had not been subject to intensive survey until the recent renewal of archaeological investigation in this region. Current work by, among others, the "Land of Nineveh Regional Project" (dir. D. Morandi Bonacossi) and the "Erbil Plain Archaeological Survey" (EPAS, see Ur *et al.* 2013), is sure to shed welcome new light on these issues; see also Altaweel 2008 on the Assur region. Evidence for changing social organisation has been detected in the dispersed pattern of rural settlement of the Jazira, which differs markedly from the tell-based landscapes of the Early Bronze Age, and the role of state intervention has been emphasised: "... a good case can be made for the distinctive pattern of settlement being a direct or indirect result of the umbrella of imperial authority" (Wilkinson *et al.* 2005, 49). This pattern has not yet been verified for the heartland region, where the necessary reconnaissance work has only very recently begun in earnest, but preliminary results from EPAS are pointing towards "a planned and imposed agricultural colonization" and a landscape "composed of uniformly small villages or farmsteads" (Ur *et al.* 2013, 14, 22–23). Further, text-based studies of Neo-Assyrian land include Postgate (1974a: a critical discussion of the Harran Census tablets), Fales (1990: on the rural landscape) and Radner (2000: on the king's attitude towards the land and its resources).

Behind these physical traces of imperial authority lay a human landscape of changing social and economic relations engendered by the (re)forming of local communities as a result of (re)settlement or relocation (whether enforced or voluntary) in combination with changing conditions of land ownership or tenure. With this background in mind, the present paper explores the situation of the middle and lower-ranking city dwellers from the perspective of their access to agricultural land. These are the people who, among the Neo-Assyrian populace in general, are the most difficult to study: "our discipline has extraordinary knowledge of the highest ranks of the elites, but near-complete ignorance of the rest of society" (Ur *et al.* 2013, 1). Indeed, althout the "lower stratum families" are numerically well represented in the extant written sources, the information we have about them is qualitatively different from that relating to the élite, as Galil (2007, 4) has noted.

At the upper end of the social spectrum, the actors involved and their relationships with the land are relatively well attested and researched: alongside the king and members of his family, the so-called "magnates" (the seven highest office-holders of the land, see Mattila 2000) and other generally high-ranking officials feature prominently in the documentation in various capacities, especially as owners of estates or as beneficiaries of royal grants. Whether their lands were held *ex officio* or in a private capacity (or indeed, both), such estates would have provided for the support of the individual and their household or department and would in all likelihood also have formed the basis for their personal wealth. At the lower end of the social scale, numerous (semi-)dependent individuals and families are attested in association with the rural estates to which they were tied. Many of these are likely to have been deportees, as has been suggested in the case of the tablets of the so-called Harran Census (Fales & Postgate 1995, xxx–xxxiv). In any case, it seems that these people were typically attached to estates owned by high officials. When such an estate was sold the people who lived and worked on it were transferred too, as we know from the documents recording the purchase of land and people (e.g., State Archives of Assyria [=SAA] 6 314–315). Similar conditions apply to the land grants (e.g., SAA 12 26) and the associated schedules detailing the estates and their workers (e.g., SAA 12 27). These people attached to rural estates make up a substantial proportion of the "lower stratum families" recently studied by Galil, together with slaves, pledged people and deportees in general (Galil 2007, with reviews by Radner 2008 and Baker 2009). It is not at all clear, however, to what extent these people tied to large estates are representative of the rural population in general. Postgate (1974a, 231) has cautioned against taking the information presented in the Harran Census tablets as giving a true picture of conditions in the Assyrian countryside, since the estates documented in them need not be typical for all property in the area.

In between these two extremes formed by the members of the élite on the one hand and the (semi-)dependent class on the other, the urban middle- and lower-ranking personnel, including the craftsmen and other specialists, feature less prominently in the sources in connection with land outside of the city. The private archives from

Assur are the best source of information on these people (see Pedersén 1986, whose numbering scheme for the archives is followed here, and also Faist 2007). These archives contain tablets relating to the various activities of the key protagonists who include craftsmen and specialists such as goldsmiths (archive N33) and *ḫundurāius* (N9–10) as well as traders (Radner forthcoming) and representatives of foreign communities, especially Egyptians (N31). For an overview of the population of Assur in the 7th century see Fales (1997), and for a detailed study of the organisation of the communities of goldsmiths and other specialists see Radner (1999b). Such people and their access to agricultural land, examined in the wider context of the food supply for the cities of the Assyrian heartland, will be the focus of the present paper. I shall first discuss the sources of information concerning their access to land, and then I shall examine some evidence that has not yet been brought to bear on this issue.

The evidence from the royal inscriptions is relatively sparse. According to a text preserved in several exemplars from Assur, king Esarhaddon (ruled 680–669 BC) re-established the *kidinnūtu*-status (i.e., freedom from tax and labour obligations) of (the inhabitants of) the city of Assur, including freedom from agricultural taxes (*šibšu* and *nusāḫē*, straw tax and corn tax respectively) (Leichty 2011, 124, no. 57 iii 3–15). As Postgate (1974b, 239) noted, this was presumably in response to the letter now edited as SAA 16 96, from the mayor and elders of Assur to the king, complaining that officials were engaged in exacting corn and straw taxes. This episode suggests that a substantial number of Assur's city-dwellers had a personal stake in the countryside and relied on its produce, either directly (for their own sustenance) or as a source of income, whether by selling the surplus or using it as a medium of exchange to acquire other goods and services. Esarhaddon's father, Sennacherib (r. 704–681 BC), claimed to have subdivided meadowland upstream of the city of Nineveh, creating plots of two *pānu* each for the inhabitants in order for them to plant gardens (Grayson and Novotny 2012, 39, no. 1:88). Such a plot amounted to approximately 2.16 ha (Powell 1987–1990, 487). Both of these royal inscriptions thus attest to the possession by the ordinary city inhabitants of land in the urban hinterland, though in neither case is it possible to determine how widespread this phenomenon was, nor the extent to which these people depended on it for their families' sustenance.

Further evidence for the ownership of rural land by urban inhabitants who were not among the higher officials comes from the everyday legal documents. Before considering this evidence in greater detail, it seems advisable to briefly evaluate the extant corpus of documents relating to the sale of productive land (whether arable, or gardens/orchards, or a combination). Essentially this corpus can be divided into two phases. Practically all of the land sale documents from the end of the 9th century and from the 8th century down to the earlier part of the reign of Tiglath-pileser III (r. 744–727 BC) come from the city of Kalhu, because that is where the earlier archival material originates. The later material, from *c.* 734 BC on, comes overwhelmingly from Nineveh, and is among the tablets edited in volumes SAA 6 and 14. The tablets recording land sale or rental contracts from Nineveh published in the volumes SAA

6 and SAA 14 mostly involve personnel associated with the royal court who typically owned estates in different parts of the empire, often quite distant from the imperial centre, such as the royal charioteer Rēmanni-Adad (Fales 1987; 2002 [no. 4]). Of the documents from this later phase that involve productive land (whether through sale, lease, inheritance or debt security), around 85% belong to the Ninevite corpus, while only around 11% come from Assur. This is despite the relative size of the two corpora of legal documents, with 829 from Nineveh and at least 521 known to me from Assur. These figures put into sharp relief the difficulty of studying the ownership of land by the kinds of people represented in the private archival documents from Assur. Either land sales are poorly represented among the Assur texts because of archival/record-keeping factors, or because they actually were much less common and their scarcity relects the actual situation. In fact, there is some indirect evidence for the ownership of productive land on the part of the inhabitants of Assur that suggests it was more common than is suggested by the land sale documents alone.

In a recent publication, Galil (2008, 79, n. 7) listed 17 sales of productive land from Assur (apparently counting StAT 2 60 and 61 as representing original and duplicate of one text on account of their similar contents, although both are sealed). Four documents are to be removed from his list because they concern unbuilt land that was located within the city (VAT 8270 = StAT 3 104; VAT 9361 = StAT 3 77; VAT 9764 = StAT 3 5; VAT 21000). Two further texts are to be added: StAT 3 32 and SAAB 9 136. In any case, the number is not great. However, among the legal contracts we find other kinds of documents that are relevant for the present theme. These include contracts mentioning harvesters: such contracts do not deal directly with land, but they are nevertheless of interest because they presuppose rural land ownership on the part of those for whom the harvester(s) were to work. The transactions represent ways of procuring the necessary workers for harvest time, when labour was generally in short supply. They can be divided broadly into two categories: in the first place, labour contracts which record the hiring of a worker explicitly for carrying out harvesting work, and in the second place, debt notes which require the debtor to supply his creditor with harvesters at harvest time.

Of the former category, only one such text has so far been published, in the context of a study of hired labour in Assyria (Radner 2007, 205–206, no. 4). It belongs to the archive of the trader Dūrī-Aššūr that was excavated recently at Assur (Cancik & Radner 1999 [no. 9]; the archive will be edited in full by Radner (forthcoming)). The tablets of Dūrī-Aššūr's archive are primarily concerned with his overland trading ventures, but this labour contract indicates that he had agricultural land at his disposal, presumably in the vicinity of Assur. The hired man is said to come from the household of the goldsmith Aššūr-šarru-uṣur, so he was certainly a local.

The second document category – debt notes stipulating the supply of harvesters by the debtor – is considerably better represented. These texts, and the data drawn from them, have been collected by Radner (1997, 14–17), who notes elsewhere that the obligation upon a debtor to supply harvesters often replaced the charging of

interest on the sum owed (Radner 2007, 194). Some of these documents betray a clearly institutional background, for example ND 5469 (Nabû temple, Kalhu) and CTN 2 105 (the palace at Kalhu), since legal contracts were not confined to the private sphere but were also used in an administrative context to record obligations between different bureaux. These have no bearing on the present theme and may be excluded from consideration. We are then left with a handful of individuals about whom we mostly lack further background information. One exception is Urdu-Aššūr who is well attested as one of the central figures in tablets from the archive N31 from Assur (Baker 2011a [no. 5]). Many of the central figures and witnesses who feature in the tablets of this archive were of apparently Egyptian extraction, so Urdu-Aššūr may have been too. He held the military rank of "commander-of-fifty" (*rab ḫanšê*) and was involved in a range of activities including the procurement of horses via the *iškāru* system. Urdu-Aššūr was the creditor in the tablet StAT 2 228 which records a debt of 3 2/3 shekels of silver; the debtor was obliged to carry out harvesting for Urdu-Aššūr or else repay double the amount of silver owed.

This piecemeal evidence drawn from the (mainly 7th century) legal documents (see Table 3.1 for a summary) sheds some light on land ownership by the city-dwellers who were not members of the élite, but it is too fragmentary to permit more wide-ranging conclusions to be drawn. It attests to the fact (or presumed fact) of land holding, but reveals little about the actual conditions of ownership or tenure. To supplement this shadowy picture I shall now discuss written evidence that, I suggest, attests to the allocation of agricultural land by the state to collectives of craftsmen and specialists in the Assyrian heartland. This evidence, that has been largely overlooked in previous studies of the Assyrian countryside, takes the form of compound toponyms which include terms for specific crafts or professions, such as:

ālu-ša-X (profession)	"town/village of X"
kapru-ša-X (profession)	"village/hamlet/farmstead of X"

The specialist occupations which occur in toponyms of this kind are: bakers; bow makers; brewers; donkey-drivers; fullers; gardeners; goldsmiths; hatters; hoisters; horse-trainers; merchants; plumbers; potters; shepherds; smiths, and temple-enterers (details are presented in Table 3.2).

The evidence collected here reflects a phenomenon in need of further explanation: what was the reality behind these toponyms? It has sometimes been assumed that such a toponym represents a city-district where specialists in a particular profession lived and worked. For example, in her recent study of Neo-Babylonian laundry workers, Caroline Waerzeggers writes: "It is likely that washermen grouped in certain quarters or districts, as was the case in the Neo-Assyrian period ..." (Waerzeggers 2006, 96). This was not an unreasonable assumption to make, since social clustering by occupation in urban residential neighbourhoods is very well attested for many different periods and places (Smith 2010). On the other hand, it would rather contradict the model put

Table 3.1: Land ownership in the private archival tablets from Assur

Details	*Archive*	*Text & date*
Sale of garden in Kar-Nabû (= Kišešlu) which the vendor, Sīn-aḫū'a-uṣur, a "third man" (on the chariot) of a prefect, had acquired as a gift from the prefect	N2	StAT 3 15 (715)
Court record concerning a dispute over land (details quite broken). The witnesses include officials and temple personnel from Nineveh, Kalhu, Assur and Raṣappa.	N3	StAT 3 27 (715)
Sale of a field, details lost.	N5	StAT 3 32 (708)
12 homers of land are leased to Nabû-rēmanni	N9	SAAB 5 57 (date lost, 7th century)
Mannu-kī-Adad owes 10 š silver to Aššur-mudammiq and must bring in his harvest or pay 50 š silver.	N10	StAT 2 17 & 18 (639*)
Sale of field by Bušî to Nagaḫî for 8 shekels of silver.	N18	StAT 2 60 (621*)
Fragmentary sale of field by Bušî.	N18	StAT 2 61 (621*)
Purchase of cultivated land by Mar-[...] from [...], son of Šulmu-[...], for 6 1/2 shekels of silver.	N18	SAAB 9 99 (660)
Babilaiu owes [x barley] to Šarru-iqbi, to be repaid at the threshing floor.	N20	StAT 2 72 (668)
Šulmu-aḫḫē son of Lā-tubašanni-ilu, from the town Sukarana, owes [x] barley to Šarru-iqbi, to be repaid [at the threshing floor]; in the meantime the debtor's wife is given as security.	N20	StAT 2 73 (658)
Purchase of a field by Bābu-šumu-iddina from Dan(?)-Aššūr and Erība-Aššūr.	N24	SAAB 9 136 (642*)
1 homer 2 *sūtu* of barley owed by Qibīt-Issār son of Adad-uballiṭ to Ubru-šarri, to be repaid at the threshing floor or it will increase by 1 homer 5 *sūtu*.	N25	StAT 2 111 (649)
A small, slightly fragmentary administrative document (edition: "harvest report") listing amounts (of grain) and their allocation to different people, as well as 100 bales of straw (l. 6) and 30 harvesters (r. 1).	N26	StAT 2 133 (not dated)
27 sheaves of straw owed by Bēl-rēmanni, son of Nabû-tariṣ, to Quwāiu, to be repaid at the threshing floor or it will increase (= bear interest, amount not specified).	N27	StAT 2 38 & 39 (647*)
6 homers [n *sūtu*] of barley are owed by Ana-šēp-šarri-iddina, son of Šulmu-aḫḫē, from Ekallati, to Aššūr-šallim-aḫḫē at 5 *sūtu* per homer interest. The debtor is to supply 1 harvester; he also gives a house as security.	N27	StAT 3 40 (618*)
Šēp-Aššūr, son of Abu-erība, owes barley (details lost) at 5 *sūtu* per homer interest. The debtor is to supply 1 harvester.	N27	StAT 3 43 (630*)
Ka''unānu owes 3 homers 3+n? *sūtu* of barley to Aššūr-šallim-aḫḫē at 5 *sūtu* per homer interest. The debtor is to supply 1 harvester.	N27	StAT 3 48 (622*)

(Continued)

Table 3.1: Land ownership in the private archival tablets from Assur (Continued)

Details	*Archive*	*Text & date*
Šamaš-ibni, son of Šamaš-rēmanni, owes 12 homers 2 *sūtu* barley to Aššur-šallim-aḫḫē at 5 *sūtu* per homer interest. The debtor is to supply 1 harvester.	N27	StAT 3 52 (622*)
A 20-homer (c. 36 ha) field is given as security by its owner for a debt of 1 mina of silver that he owes to the creditor; the document is styled as a 6-year lease contract.	N28	StAT 3 70 (676)
An estate of [11(+?n)] homers 5 *sūtu* near the town Benuḫše is sold by Nabû-tariṣ from Assur to Sagībī for 1 mina 7? shekels of silver.	N28	StAT 3 74 (date lost, perhaps c. 672–657)
Purchase of a 20-homer field by Nergal-šarru-uṣur, [...] of the household of the king of Babylon (Šamaš-šum-ukīn), from Nabû-tariṣ. Details mostly lost.	N28	StAT 2 134 (667)
A letter of Aššūr-šumu-iddina containing two missives, the first to Šummu-Aššūr, the second to Šummu-ussēzib who is told "Collect the harvest ..." (r. 11).	N30	StAT 2 163 (not dated)
Dilušeri(?) owes 3 2/3 shekels of silver and is obliged to carry out harvesting for Urdu-Aššūr or he must repay double the amount of silver owed.	N31	StAT 2 228 (not dated)
Nabû-šumu-iškun, a dispatch rider(?) of the chief treasurer, owes 4 shekels of silver to Šumma-Aššūr; the debtor is to supply [x] harvester(s).	N33	StAT 1 2 (654)
Šamaš-ibni-aḫḫē buys three fields in different places.	–	KAN 4 1 (date lost)
Bābu-šumu-šukna, a priest of Gula and son of Ḫu-māmāti, sells a garden which is (part of) his inheritance share to the priest Ninurta-nādin-aḫḫē for 80 minas of copper.	–	KAN 4 19 (date lost, probably late 8th century)
Nabû-bēlu-šallim, chief eunuch of the great commander-in-chief Iaḫalu (Aia-ḫalu), buys land in Potters' Town (see Table 2).	–	KAV 75 (820)
Baṭṭūṭu exchanges a field from his paternal estate with another property.	–	MAss 69 (PNA 278 s.v. Baṭṭūṭu 1.) (637*).
Purchase of 10-homer field, details mostly lost.	–	StAT 2 256 (date lost)
Mannu-kī-Arbail owes 3 shekels of silver, property of Aššur and Ištar of Arbail, to Qibīt-Aššūr and gives his share of a field in Nineveh as security for 7 years.	–	TCL 9 66 (646*?)
Urdu-Dādi son of Ša-lā-Aššūr-mannu owes 15 harvesters to Šamaš-šēzib; if he does not carry out the harvesting, he will be liable for 2 homers of grain, the expenditure of the threshing floor, and he will pay double the amount of silver.	–	TCL 9 60 (640*)
Sangi-ili buys land from some men (priests?) from Assur	–	VAT 10430 (PNA 1089 s.v. Sangi-ili) (date lost, attributed to reign of Sennacherib)

Note: Dates after 649 BC follow the sequence of post-canonical eponyms published by S. Parpola in Radner (ed.) (1998 (PNA 1/I), xviii–xx) forward by Elizabeth Stone for Old Babylonian urban neighbourhoods, which is one of social mixing (Stone 1987, 123–131). For Babylonia in the first millennium BC the picture seems to be more complicated (Baker 2011b, 543–544). In the case of Assyria the issue has not been considered in detail, but if this assumption that we are dealing with specialised city quarters were correct, then it might shed some interesting light on the spatial organisation of the Neo-Assyrian city. However, I believe it to be incorrect, for reasons that I shall now explain.

In the first place, all of the supplementary evidence that we can extract from the tablets concerning these settlements indicates that they were not part of the urban fabric but were located in the countryside. Whenever the tablets mention topographical features adjoining these settlements, they make it clear that we are dealing with a rural context and not an urban one. They frequently mention fields, or features such as roads leading to a major city (e.g. Potters' Town, SAA 6 10//11). In other cases the context itself, such as a grant of land, makes it clear that we are dealing with a settlement in the countryside. In the light of these circumstances, there remain two possibilities. The first is that we are dealing with rural settlements primarily occupied – at least originally – by specialists in the particular craft or profession denoted by the toponym. In fact, Postgate (1979, 198, Chart 2) classified the following under "rural industries":

- palm/reed artefacts
- leather-working
- textiles
- pottery
- salt, soap, gypsum etc.

Out of these industries classified by Postgate as "rural", two ("pottery" and "metallurgy") are among the professions that are attested as a component of a toponym (see Table 3.2, Potters' Town and Smiths' Town). However, I think that a general assumption that such a toponym reflects a rural settlement where workers in that particular craft actually lived is unwarranted. The range of professions incorporated into these toponyms include some which seem highly unlikely to have been concentrated in a rural setting outside of the major urban centres. I am thinking here of professions such as goldsmith, smith, brewer, and merchant, to name but a few. These specialists are more likely to have carried out their activities in proximity to those whom they supplied or served. In the case of the "Temple-enterers' Town", as the name implies, these were consecrated temple personnel who were permitted to enter the shrine of the deity they served, so this was certainly an urban-based occupation.

If these craftsmen were not actually settled in the villages whose names reflect their occupations, then the other possibility is that these settlements represent land-holdings originally assigned for sustenance to collectives of specialists who actually lived and worked in the city. In fact, when we take into account whatever topographical clues we can find in the tablets as to their location, then these clues

Table 3.2: Toponyms formed on a professional designation in Neo-Assyrian sources

Toponym	*Writing*	*Details*	*Sources*	*Date*
Bakers' Town (Āl-āpiāni)	URU–*a-pi-a-ni*	40 ha of land there are assigned to Barbiru the Gurrean in a "Schedule of Estate Assignments"	SAA 11 228 ii 7′	not dated (probably reign of Sargon II)
	[UR]U–⸢LÚ. NINDA.MEŠ-*ni*⸣/ [URU–LÚ]. ⸢NINDA.MEŠ⸣-*ni*	Land there was originally exempted and given by Adn III to 3 men to provide offerings for the gods Aššur and Bābu; it had become abandoned and Sargon now gave land in the Town of the Temple-Enterers (q.v.) near Nineveh to the descendants of the 3 men, taking in return the land in Bakers' Town	SAA 12 19: 23′, r. 10 (cf. van Driel 1970, 172 re the earlier reading *šaknūtu*, 'settled' people)	(Adn III–) Sg II
Bakers' Village (Kapar-āpiāni)	URU.ŠE–NINDA. MEŠ-*ni*	In a list of towns and villages, in a section of settlements under the authority of Ezbu	ND 2618 r. 5	not dated (Tiglath-pileser III or Sargon II)
Bow-makers' Town (Āl-sasinnī)	URU–⸢ZADIM?⸣. MEŠ	This administrative document mentions estates in various towns in the vicinity of Dur-Šarrukin, including 38 homers in Bow-makers' Town	ND 2476 i 5′	not dated (Sargon II or later)
Brewers' Town (Āl-sirāšê)	URU–⸢LUNGA⸣. MEŠ	This administrative document mentions estates in various towns in the vicinity of Dur-Šarrukin, including 24 homers 1 *qa* in Brewers' Town	ND 2476 i 4′	not dated (Sargon II or later)
	URU–DUMGAL. MEŠ	Asqūdu son of Qurdi-ilāni from Brewers' Town owes grain	CTN 3 11: 8	1-IX-624*
Donkey Driver Town (Āl-rādi-imāri)	URU–UŠ–ANŠE	Witnesses to the purchase of a well include Aššūr-šarru-uṣur, a bow-maker from Donkey Driver Town	SAA 14 271 r. 12′	date lost (probably 7th century)
	URU–UŠ–ANŠE-*a-a*	The third sealer named on this land sale tablet is Ululaiu, a bow-maker(!) (edition: "tanner", but cf. the Index) from Donkey Driver Town	SAA 14 140: 2	653
Farmers' Town (Āl-ikkāri)	URU–ENGAR. MEŠ	Cultivated land, a threshing floor and house in Farmers' Town are purchased by Nergal-aḫu-uṣur from Ubri-šarri for 200 (minas of) copper	SAA 14 210: 8′	date lost (8th or early 7th century)

(Continued)

Table 3.2: Toponyms formed on a professional designation in Neo-Assyrian sources (Continued)

Toponym	*Writing*	*Details*	*Sources*	*Date*
Farmers' Village (Kapar-ikkāri)	URU.ŠE–LÚ.ENGAR	In a list of land leased, several estates are summed up as totalling 60 ha in Farmers' Village; the land is among a total of 210 ha in the land of Halahhu that is rented by Aḫīja-qāmu	SAA 11 224 r. 1	date lost
Fullers' Town (Āl-ašlākī)	URU—LÚ*.TÚG.UD.MEŠ	The sealer of the tablet is Nabû-rēḫtu-uṣur, son of Amurṭēše, a Hasean under the authority of Urdu-Issār, from Fullers' Town	SAA 14 161: 4	1-VI-623*
Gardeners' Town (Āl-nukaribbī)	URU–NU.GIŠ.SAR.[MEŠ]	1 grove in Gardeners' Town, in the farmland of the town Sa[...], is listed in a list of groves	SAA 11 231: 7′	not dated
Goldsmiths' Town (Āl-ṣarrāpī)	URU–SIMUG.KU[G.GI.MEŠ] / UR[U]–SIMUG.KUG.GI.M[EŠ]	Administrative document listing amounts of grain, including 23 homers (from) Goldsmiths' Town in the eponymy of Nabû-[...], then 20 homers (from) Goldsmiths' Town in the eponymy of Šamaš-šarru-ibni (612*)	CTDS 1 i 13′, ii 5′	612* or later
	URU–SIMUG.KUG.G[I] / URU–SIMUG.KUG.GI.MEŠ	An estate of 14 ha of cultivated land, a house, a threshing floor and an orchard in Goldsmiths' Town are purchased by Šumu-lēšir for 20 minas of copper from 4 sons of Itu'āiu. One witness, Sūsīa, is a goldsmith of the Vizier's household, as is his son, the next witness Ilumma-le'i (cf. another witness who is a weaver of the same household); another, Riba-aḫḫē, is from Goldsmiths' Town (r. 9′)	SAA 6 19:6, r. 9′	26-IX-734
	URU–SIMUG.KUG.GI	Atâ, a witness to this record of a court decision, is city lord (*bēl āli*) of Goldsmiths' Town	SAA 14 183 r. 2	date lost
Hatter's Town (Ālu-ša-kubšātēšu)	URU?–LÚ.*šá*–TÚG.U.SAG.MEŠ-*šú*	A fragment belonging to SAA 12 27, a schedule to a land grant in favour of Nabû-šarru-uṣur, mentions [...] Hatter's Town [...]	SAA 12 28:35	657

(Continued)

Table 3.2: Toponyms formed on a professional designation in Neo-Assyrian sources (Continued)

Toponym	*Writing*	*Details*	*Sources*	*Date*
Hoisters' Town (Ālu-ša-ḫābīšu)	URU–*ša–ḫa-bi-šu*	Adad-nerari III grants land to the god Aššur to provide offerings. He takes land in Kadišhu in the province of Kurbail and names it town [...]; it adjoins the road from Hoisters' Town to Kurbail	SAA 12 1:11	788
Horse-Trainer Town (Āl-sūsāni)	URU.2–LÚ.GIŠ. GIGIR	According to an Assurbanipal type schedule to a land grant, a [x]-ha field in Horse-Trainer Town is in the care of Tuqūnu-ēreš, the farmer, and his people, and Aḫu-iddina, farmer, and [his people]. The land is in the vicinity of Arbail (cf. l. 7)	SAA 12 50: 1	Assurbanipal
	URU–*su-sa-nu*	Mannu-kī-Aššūr, of Horse-Trainer Town, is one of the people named in a list of fugitives in the province of Šimu	SAA 11 163 i 5	not dated
	URU–LÚ*.GIŠ. GIGIR.MEŠ-*a-a*	Ṣalmu-šarri-iqbi, [...] from Horse-Trainer Town, owner of the field being sold, is named as sealer of the tablet	SAA 14 258:2	date lost (probably 7th century)
	šá LÚ*.GIGIR-*a-a*	List of quantities (of grain), including 8 homers of the *horse trainer villagers*	StAT 2 133	not dated
Limestone-man's Town (Āl-ša-pūlīšu)	URU–[*š*]*a*?–*pu-li-šu*	Admininistrative document in which Limestone-man's Town is one of 33 towns listed as having delivered UDU.MEŠ *ka-ru-ia*	Billa 82:7′	late 9th century
Merchants' Town (Ālu-ša-tamkārē)	URU–*šá*–LÚ.DAM.QA[R(.MEŠ?)]	In a letter to the king concerning repair work on temples, [Aššūr-bani] says: "Let them write to Kiṣir-Aššūr that he should make available the straw in Merchant Town and Šitabni, so that we can use it for the work"	SAA 1 114 r. 8	Sargon II
Plumber's Town (Āl-ša-rāṭātēšu)	URU–*ša–ra-ṭa-ṭi-šú*	Adad-nerari grants land to Aššur in order to provide for offerings. He takes land in Kadišhu in the province of Kurbail and names it town [...]; it adjoins Plumber's Town of the governor of Kurbail	SAA 12 1:11	788

(Continued)

Table 3.2: Toponyms formed on a professional designation in Neo-Assyrian sources (Continued)

Toponym	*Writing*	*Details*	*Sources*	*Date*
Potters' Town (Āl-paḫḫārāni)	URU–*pa-ḫa-ra-a-ni*	Land in Potters' Town is purchased by Nabû-bēlu-šallim, chief eunuch of Aia-ḫalu, great commander-in-chief	KAV 75: 6′	820
	URU–LÚ.BAḪÁR.MEŠ / URU.LÚ.[BAḪÁR.MEŠ]	An estate in Potters' Town is among those purchased by Inūrta-ilā'ī; some of the other estates adjoin the road to Kalhu	SAA 6 10: 11, 17 (& duplicate SAA 6 11:5′)	16-XI-717
Shepherds' Town (Āl-rā'iāni)	URU–LÚ.SIPA.MEŠ *ša* DUMU–LUGAL	[x] ha of field in Shepherds' Town of the Crown Prince is in the care of Gurdî, farmer, and his people, according to an Assurbanipal type schedule to a land grant	SAA 12 50 r. 18′	Assurbanipal
Smiths' Town (Āl-nappāḫi, Ālu-ša-nappāḫi)	URU—SIMUG.ME	Inūrta-šarru-uṣur is to cultivate and harvest 1 ha of exempt land in Smiths' Town for Ilā-erība, village manager of the chief treasurer's household	SAA 14 434: 7	28-VI-612*
	URU–*ša*–LÚ*.SIMUG.MEŠ	Letter which mentions the feeding of plants in Smiths' Town and in Bit-gabiu near Nineveh	StAT 2 12	not dated
Temple-Enterers' Town (Āl-ērib-bēti)	URU–LÚ.TU!.MEŠ–É / URU–LÚ.TU.MEŠ–É	For details see above s.v. Bakers' Town	SAA 12 19: 30′, r. 10	(Adad-nerari III–) Sargon II

point towards a location in the immediate hinterland of the major cities, Nineveh, Kalhu and Dur-Šarrukin, which tends to support the scenario I am proposing. And if we accept that some of these groups had an urban base, then this remains at least a theoretical possibility for the others too. If this proposal is correct – that we are dealing with settlements in the hinterland of the major cities which were named after rural land-holdings assigned to collectives of specialists who lived and worked in the city – then it is unlikely that the landholders themselves would have worked the land. Their responsibilities within the city are likely to have precluded a very active role, and the actual working of the land must have been down to tenants or tied workers.

Before developing this argument further, a few of these particular toponyms require more explanation. Among those listed in Table 3.2, we find several which

include terms for professions that are of a particular type, with the formation *ša-x-šu*. The range of professions with names formed on this pattern, literally "the one of commodity X", has recently been studied by Radner (1999a) in her article on "Traders in the Neo-Assyrian Period". It had long been thought that the equivalent expression in Neo-Babylonian was to be interpreted as "peddlar of commodity X". However, Radner showed quite clearly that this cannot be the case in Neo-Assyrian. The evidence of the topoymns provides us with four further attestations of these profession-types, two of which represent new professions which can be added to the repertoire listed by Radner. These four new cases have interesting implications for the subject that I am addressing. Before I go into those implications, I should first explain in greater detail these attestations and what they represent (the two new *ša*-x-*šu* professions are indicated by an asterisk):

> *Āl-ša-ḫabīšu (URU–*ša-ḫa-bi-šu*)
> "hoister" (SAA series; cf. CAD Ḫ 19: *ḫabû*, Ass. *ḫapû* "to draw water or wine")
>
> Āl-ša-kubšātēšu (URU?–^{LÚ}*šá*–^{TÚG}U.SAG.MEŠ-*šú*)
> "the one of the cap" (SAA series: "hatter")
>
> Āl-ša-pūlīšu (URU–[š]*a*?–*pu-li-šu*)
> "the one of limestone"
>
> *Āl-ša-rāṭātēšu (URU–*ša-ra-ṭa-ṭi-šú*)
> "plumber" (SAA project). Cf. Fales 1990, 85, who translates "(the town of) the drainage channels". Note CAD R 219f. s.v *rāṭu* "channel, runnel" (for irrigation, drainage). A *rāṭu* could also be used for conducting liquids for libations or offerings; for these contexts CAD offers various translations: "conduit", "trough", "runnel". It is not clear which of these meanings belongs with the profession discussed here, but it seems that a cultic connection cannot be ruled out. If we are dealing with drainage or irrigation channels then the contexts do not indicate a domestic setting and thus "plumber" is not apposite.

In her study of these *ša*-x-*šu* professions Radner (1999a, 125) concluded "... the contextual evidence indicates that the professionals are in subordinate and dependent positions, mainly as part of the palace or the temple household". This picture agrees entirely with what I am suggesting, based on the evidence of the toponyms discussed so far. Within an urban context it seems quite possible that some categories of craftsmen might come to concentrate in certain parts of the city without any formal state intervention. However, the settlements I am discussing here are of an entirely different nature, and it is likely that they represent what was originally a formal land allocation scheme implemented by the central government. This observation in turn has important implications for our interpretation of the organisation of craftsmen and other professionals. If my suggestion is correct then it means that without question these crafts and professions were, at one time, recognised by the state as having a collective identity, and that on this basis they were integrated into the state administration. Moreover, the earliest attestation among the cases that I have listed indicates that this phenomenon goes back to at least the later 9th century BC, in the reign of Shalmaneser III ("Limestone-man's Town", attested in the Šibaniba tablet Billa 82).

If this interpretation is correct, then this evidence for a collective identity of craftsmen and specialists prefigures the rather better known evidence for associations of craftsmen from the 7th century. This later evidence, which comes primarily from Assur, has been discussed especially by Radner (1999b, 25–33) in relation to the goldsmiths. As she noted, a similar kind of collective organisation is attested for the bakers of Assur, and probably for the oil-pressers too. It holds true also for the people known as *ḫundurāius*, whose exact function is unclear (possibly carpet-weavers?); these latter workers have been discussed in detail by Fales and Jakob-Rost (1991, 21–26) in their publication of tablets from the archives N9 and N10. In the case of the *ḫundurāius*, we know that they collectively owned land within the city of Assur, because we have a record of a sale made by thirty of them acting jointly. As Fales and Jakob-Rost suggested, we seem to be dealing in their case with common residence, property and activity.

To place these settlements in context, it is rather well known that members of the Neo-Assyrian royal family and high officials could own substantial estates, and some of these are also attested in our sources in the form of toponyms. These included the crown prince, the princess, and the queen, as well as the commander-in-chief, the cupbearer, the treasurer, the vizier, the eunuchs, and the magnates (see Table 3.3 for details). In the case of Eunuchs' Town and Magnates' Town, the settlements appear to have been assigned on a collective basis, in the same way as those associated with the craftsmen and other professionals discussed above. Like key members of the royal family, several of the individual magnate's offices also had their own settlements. It is worth noting that a servant of the chief eunuch is attested as coming from Eunuchs' Town in 742 BC, while servants of the vizier and the chief cupbearer are attested in 710 BC in connection with land near to Magnates' Village (see Table 3.3). These associations suggest that we are not dealing here with mere "fossil" place names. In addition to these toponyms relating to officials, we also find settlements whose names indicate an association with the deities Ištar, Nabû and Šamaš; their land was presumably intended for the supply of offerings for these deities.

To summarise the findings outlined so far, it is possible to identify in the Neo-Assyrian texts settlements which I believe must represent allocations of land originally made by the state to craftsmen and other specialists on a collective basis, for their sustenance. This picture is supported by a certain amount of other evidence, for example in the tablet CTN 2 35 from Kalhu, dated around the early 8th century. In relation to this tablet, Postgate (1989, 145) writes of a "consortium of temple personnel as joint owners of land (4 singers and a lamentation priest)". Such a scenario might well have had its origins in a collective land allocation scheme of the kind proposed here. At least some of these settlements were located in the hinterland of the major

Table 3.3: Toponyms associated with a member of the royal family or a high-ranking office

Toponym	*Writing*	*Details*	*Sources*	*Date*
Crown Prince's Town (Ālu-ša-mār-šarri)	URU–šá–A–MAN	In a record of food offerings from officials, one section listing various foodstuffs is summed up as "Total, Šulmu-bēlī-lāmur, of the administrative district of (ša NAM) Crown Prince's Town"	SAA 7 161 ii 22	no year date
Crown Prince's Village (Kapar-mār-šarri)	⌜URU.ŠE⌝–A–MAN	Ezbu, majordomo of the Crown Prince, son of Balāṭu-ēreš, from Crown Prince's Village, is named as the sealer of a receipt document	ND 3412:2	date lost
Princess's Town (Ālu-ša-mār'at-šarri)	URU.2–DUMU.MÍ–LUGAL	A schedule of estates assigned to officials mentions an estate of the *sartennu* Adad-dān (comprising) 8 people, 20 ha land, and 150 sheep in Princess's Town	SAA 11 221:4	reign of Assurbanipal (before 652; see Mattila 2000, 78)
	URU–ša–DUMU.MÍ–MAN	Settlement of lawsuit brought against Arbail-ḫammat, daughter of Sanānu, and her son Nabû-erība, both from Princess's Town	VS 1 96:4	638*
Queen's Village (Kapar-sēgalli)	[UR]U.ŠE–MÍ.É.GAL	Queen's Village is mentioned in a very fragmentary purchase of land and people, probably as the home of one of the witnesses	SAA 14 401 r. 6′	date lost
Lady-of-the-House's Town (Ālu-ša-Bēlet-bīti)	[U]RU.*a-lum-ša*–GAŠAN–É	A fortified settlement of the land of Rašu which is mentioned in an inscription of Sennacherib	*Archiv für Orientforschung* 20, 83:25	Sennacherib (704–681)
Commander-in-Chief's Village (Kapar-turtāni)	URU.ŠE–LÚ*.*tar-ta-ni*	Slave sale document; the witnesses include Ahuānu, mayor of Commander-in-Chief's Village	CTN 2 4 r. 9	13-I-769
Vizier's Town (Āl-sukkalli)	URU–LÚ.SUKKAL	This small fragment of a letter mentions Vizier's Town in very broken context.	SAA 15 153:6′	(Sargon II?)

(Continued)

Table 3.3: Toponyms associated with a member of the royal family or a high-ranking office (Continued)

Toponym	*Writing*	*Details*	*Sources*	*Date*
Vizier's Village (Kapar-sukkalli)	URU.ŠE–LÚ*.SUKKAL	Nabû-sakip donates two slaves and an estate to the god Nabû of Kalhu. The donated estate of 7 ha is situated in the town Ṣabat-lukun and adjoins the road to Vizier's Village, among other landmarks.	SAA 12 96:8	25-VII-616*
Cupbearer's Village (Kapar-šāqî)	URU.ŠE–KAŠ.LUL	101 homers 4 *sūtu* of grain are listed in connection with Cupbearer's Village as part of barley described as *nakamtu ša rab-danibāte*	ND 2465:9	not dated
Treasurer's Town (Āl-masenni)	[UR]U–⌜LÚ⌝.IGI.DUB?	Very fragmentary sale of unbuilt plot and house, probably situated in Treasurer's Town as it is mentioned in the property description	SAA 14 230:2′	date lost
Magnates' Village (Kapar-rabûti)	URU.ŠE–GAL.MEŠ	An estate sold by Paršidu (name of buyer lost) adjoins the road of Magnates' Village; witnesses include a servant of the vizier and a servant of the chief cupbearer	SAA 6 30:7	15-XII-710
Eunuchs' Town (Ālu-ša-rēšāni)	URU–LÚ.SAG.MEŠ	Purchase of slaves by Mušallim-Issār. A witness, Aššūr-nādin-aḫḫē, is said to come from Eunuchs' Town; he is one of 9 people described as servants of the [chief] eunuch (the other 8 are from Til-Inurta)	SAA 6 1 r. 16	26-XI-742
	URU.2–LÚ*!.SAG!.MEŠ	In a fragmentary estate sale, two witnesses, Nabû-nāṣir and Iadī', are said to be from Eunuchs' Town.	SAA 6 277 r. 8′	VII–674

cities, Nineveh, Kalhu, and Dur-Šarrukin. They are dated at the earliest in the later 9th century, and settlements of this kind continue to be mentioned in our sources until around the time of the fall of the empire, in 612 BC. Of course, the date of a text mentioning a toponym only tells us that the place was still known by that name; it tells us nothing of the social reality at the time the tablet was written. Without independent confirmation we cannot tell whether such a town or village was still associated with the specialists to whom it was originally allocated. Similarly, Stolper (1985, 72) writes of the *ḫadrus* in the region of Nippur in late Achaemenid Babylonia: "... the texts provide no real evidence that *ḫadru* names actually characterise the members' professional or social statuses, that is, that the names have descriptive as well as identifying value", though he goes on to cite indirect evidence in support of a correlation between the *ḫadru* names and their social composition. Thus the names of the *ḫadrus* – which certainly had a territorial correlate – have played a central role in reconstructing the topographical and social landscape of the Nippur region in the later 5th century BC. They refer to groups of men with a shared background often comprising an ethnic grouping but including also professions, and so they provide a parallel, very broadly speaking, for the elements of the Assyrian toponymy that are the present focus, although the operation of the "land-for-service" system in late Achaemenid Nippur is considerably better documented and understood (see Stolper 1985, especially 70–103; Beaulieu 1988; van Driel 2002, 308–310; Jursa 2010, 247). In fact, Stolper (1985, 99) characterised the *ḫadrus* as "a functional successor to earlier Mesopotamian administrative regimes which managed state-controlled lands by granting benefices to state workers". Van Driel (2002, 309), discussing the pre-Achaemenid history of the *ḫadrus* in Babylonia, suggested a connection with the Neo-Assyrian *kiṣru* (a term denoting a military cohort) and noted the likelihood that the assignment of land was involved, given the incorporation of cohorts of foreign troops into the Assyrian *army*. This seems quite plausible. It is also worth noting the existence in Babylonia too of the kinds of toponyms discussed here, e.g. *Ālu-ša-aškāpē* ("Leather-workers' Town") and *Ālu-ša-rē'ê* ("Shepherds' Town"), both in the Nippur region (Zadok 1985, 9, 18).

It is beyond the scope of the present study to trace these connections in greater detail, but it is clearly in this general context that these Assyrian rural settlements should be seen. Their creation and chronological development remains obscure, thanks to the nature of the evidence which means that there is no way of determining how much time had elapsed between the founding and/or naming of the settlement, and its attestation in our written documentation. By that time the composition of the settlement might have changed dramatically, as might the circumstances of tenure/ownership. A direct connection between the eponymous craft/profession and the people known to be associated with that toponym is also difficult to establish, perhaps again on account of the time-lapse between the settlement's creation and the date of the textual source(s) in which it is mentioned. In some cases there is no evident connection at all: for example, we know of two different bow-makers from

Donkey Drivers Town. Nevertheless, some of the available evidence indicates that the phenomenon itself goes back at least as far as the later 9th century. This kind of land allocation scheme may be one factor contributing to the survival in Neo-Assyrian land sale documents of communal restraints on private ownership, as seen for example in the references to potential claims by officials or others associated with the seller, such as the *šaknu*, *ḫazannu* or *bēl ilki* (Postgate 1976, 19). This issue is also significant for taxation: as Postgate (1989, 144) wrote, "... there is ample evidence that the village remained the organisation through which land law and customs were administered ... *ilku* service and other forms of taxation were exacted through the villages".

The phenomenon of land allocated by the state to urban-based craftsmen and other specialist professionals on a collective basis, as suggested here, would fit in rather well with the archaeological evidence pointing to a managed rural landscape that is the "direct or indirect result of the umbrella of imperial authority" (see above). Whether the proposed system survived through to the 7th century or had broken down over time, to be superseded by alternative conditions of tenure, including perhaps a greater prevalence of private ownership, cannot be determined in the absence of further (and better quality) information. Many questions remain open, but it is hoped that the material presented and discussed here will contribute to the ongoing debate concerning the development of rural settlement in the Neo-Assyrian heartland.

Acknowledgements
The research presented here was conducted as part of the project "Royal Institutional Households in First Millennium BC Mesopotamia," led by the author at the University of Vienna and funded by the Austrian Science Fund (FWF) grant S 10802–G18 as part of the National Research Network "'Imperium' and 'Officium': Comparative Studies in Bureaucracy and Officialdom". The work was facilitated by the possibility of using the Helsinki electronic text corpus CNA (Corpus of Neo-Assyrian), kindly granted by Simo Parpola.

Bibliographical abbreviations

Billa: Finkelstein, J. J. (1953). Cuneiform texts from Tell Billa. *Journal of Cuneiform Studies* 7, 111–176.
CAD: Gelb, I. J. *et al.* (1956–2010). *The Assyrian Dictionary of the Oriental Institute of the University of Chicago*, Chicago.
CTN 2: Postgate 1973.
ND: Siglum of texts excavated in the British excavations at Nimrud (Kalhu); for details see Radner 1998–1999, B-32.
PNA: Radner 1998–1999; Baker 2000–2011.
SAA 6: Kwasman & Parpola 1991.
SAA 12: Kataja & Whiting 1995.
SAA 14: Mattila 2002.
SAA 16: Luukko & Van Buylaere 2002.
SAAB 9: Deller *et al.* (1995).
StAT 2: Donbaz & Parpola 2001.
StAT 3: Faist 2007.

Bibliography

Altaweel, M. (2008) *The Imperial Landscape of Ashur: Settlement and Land Use in the Assyrian Heartland*, Heidelberg.

Baker, H. D. (ed.) (2000–2011) *The Prosopography of the Neo-Assyrian Empire, 2/I: Ḫ-K* (2000); *2/II: L-N* (2001); *3/I: P-Ṣ* (2002); *3/II: Š-Z* (2011), Helsinki.

Baker, H. D. (2009) Review of G. Galil (2007), The lower stratum families in the Neo-Assyrian Period, *Journal of the American Oriental Society* 129: 343–344.

Baker, H. D. (2011a) Urdu-Aššūr. In H. D. Baker (ed.), *The Prosopography of the Neo-Assyrian Empire, 3/II: Š-Z*, 1399–1401, Helsinki.

Baker, H. D. (2011b) From street altar to palace: reading the built environment of urban Babylonia. In K. Radner & E. Robson (eds), *The Oxford Handbook of Cuneiform Culture*, 533–552. Oxford.

Beaulieu, P.-A. (1988) An early attestation of the word *ḫadru*. *NABU* 1988/54.

Cancik, E. A. & K. Radner (1999) Dūrī-Aššūr. In K. Radner (ed.), *The Prosopography of the Neo-Assyrian Empire, 1/II: B-G*, 390. Helsinki.

Deller, K. H., F. M. Fales & L. Jakob-Rost (1995) Neo-Assyrian texts from Assur. Private archives in the Vorderasiatisches Museum of Berlin, Part 2, *State Archives of Assyria Bulletin* 9: 1–137.

Faist, B. (2007) *Alltagstexte aus neuassyrischen Archiven und Bibliotheken der Stadt Assur* (Studien zu den Assur-Texten 3), Wiesbaden.

Fales, F. M. (1987) Prosopography of the Neo-Assyrian Empire, 1: The Archive of Remanni-Adad, *State Archives of Assyria Bulletin* 1: 92–114.

Fales, F. M. (1990) The rural landscape of the Neo-Assyrian empire: a survey, *State Archives of Assyria Bulletin* 4: 81–142.

Fales, F. M. (1997) People and professions in Neo-Assyrian Assur. In H. Waetzoldt & H. Hauptmann (eds), *Assyrien im Wandel der Zeiten* (Heidelberger Studien zum Alten Orient 6), 33–40, Heidelberg.

Fales, F. M. (2002) Rēmanni-Adad. In H. Baker (ed.), *The Prosopography of the Neo-Assyrian Empire, 3/I: P-Ṣ*, 1038–1041, Helsinki.

Fales, F. M. & L. Jakob-Rost (1991) Neo-Assyrian texts from Assur: private archives in the Vorderasiatische Museum of Berlin, Part 1, *State Archives of Assyria Bulletin* 5/1–2.

Fales, F. M. & J. N. Postgate (1995) *Imperial Administrative Records, Part I. Provincial and Military Administration* (State Archives of Assyria 11), Helsinki.

Galil, G. (2007) *The Lower Stratum Families in the Neo-Assyrian Period* (Culture and History of the Ancient Near East 27). Leiden.

Galil, G. (2008) A new look at a Neo-Assyrian sale of 'land and people'. In M. Cogan & D. Kahn (eds), *Treasures on Camels' Humps. Historical and Literary Studies from the Ancient Near East Presented to Israel Eph'al*, 75–85, Jerusalem.

Grayson, A. K. & J. Novotny (2012) *The Royal Inscriptions of Sennacherib, King of Assyria (704-681 BC), Part 1* (Royal Inscriptions of the Neo-Assyrian Period), Winona Lake.

Jursa, M. J. Hackl, B. Janković, K. Kleber, E. E. Payne, C. Waerzeggersand M. Weszeli (2010) *Aspects of the Economic History of Babylonia in the First Millennium BC. Economic Geography, Economic Mentalities, Agriculture, the Use of Money and the Problem of Economic Growth* (Alte Orient und Altes Testament 377), Münster.

Kataja, L. & R. Whiting (1995) *Grants, Decrees and Gifts of the Neo-Assyrian Period* (State Archives of Assyria 12), Helsinki.

Kühne, H. (2012) Water for Assyria. In R. Matthews & J. Curtis (eds), *Proceedings of the 7th International Congress on the Archaeology of the Ancient Near East, 12 April-16 April, the British Museum and UCL, London. Volume 1. Mega-cities & Mega-sites; The Archaeology of Consumption & Disposal; Landscape, Transport & Communication*, 559–569, Wiesbaden.

Kwasman, K. & S. Parpola (1991) *Legal Transactions of the Royal Court of Nineveh, Part I. Tiglath-Pileser III through Esarhaddon* (State Archives of Assyria 6), Helsinki.

Leichty, E. (2011) *The Royal Inscriptions of Esarhaddon, King of Assyria (680–669 BC)* (Royal Inscriptions of the Neo-Assyrian Period 4), Winona Lake.

Luukko, M. & G. Van Buylaere (2002) *The Political Correspondence of Esarhaddon* (State Archives of Assyria 16), Helsinki.

Mattila, R. (2000) *The King's Magnates. A Study of the Highest Officials of the Neo-Assyrian Empire* (State Archives of Assyria 11), Helsinki.

Mattila, R. (2002) *Legal Transactions of the Royal Court of Nineveh. Part II. Assurbanipal through Sin-Šarru-Iškun* (State Archives of Assyria 14), Helsinki.

Pedersen, O. (1986) *Archives and Libraries in the City of Assur. A Survey of the Material from the German Excavations* (Studia Semitica Upsaliensia 8), Uppsala.

Postgate, J. N. (1973) *The Governor's Palace archive* (Cuneiform Texts from Nimrud 2), London.

Postgate, J. N. (1974a) Some remarks on conditions in the Assyrian countryside, *Journal of the Economic and Social History of the Orient* 17: 225–243.

Postgate, J. N. (1974b) *Taxation and Conscription in the Assyrian Empire* (Studia Pohl Series Maior 3), Rome.

Postgate, J. N. (1976) *Fifty Neo-Assyrian Legal Documents*, Warminster.

Postgate, J. N. (1979) The economic structure of the Assyrian empire. In M. T. Larsen (ed.), *Power and Propaganda. A Symposium on Ancient Empires*, 193–221, Copenhagen.

Postgate, J. N. (1989) The ownership and exploitation of land in Assyria in the 1st millennium B.C. In M. Lebeau & P. Talon (eds), *Reflets des deux fleuves: volume de mélanges offerts à André Finet* (Akkadica Supplementum 6), 141–152, Leuven.

Powell, M. A. (1987–90) Masse und Gewichte. *Reallexikon der Assyriologie* 7: 457–517.

Radner, K. (1997) Erntearbeiter und Wein. Neuassyrische Urkunden und Briefe im Louvre. *State Archives of Assyria Bulletin* 11, 3–29.

Radner, K. (1999a) Traders in the Neo-Assyrian period. In J. G. Dercksen (ed.), *Trade and Finance in Ancient Mesopotamia (MOS Studies 1). Proceedings of the First MOS Symposium (Leiden 1997)* (PIHANS 84), 101–126, Leiden.

Radner, K. (1999b) *Ein neuassyrisches Privatarchiv der Tempelgoldschmiede von Assur* (Studien zu den Assur-Texten 1), Saarbrücken.

Radner, K. (2000) How did the Neo-Assyrian king perceive his land and its resources? In R. M. Jas (ed.), *Rainfall and Agriculture in Northern Mesopotamia (MOS Studies 3). Proceedings of the Third MOS Symposium (Leiden 1999)* (PIHANS 88), 233–246, Leiden.

Radner, K. (2007) Hired labour in the Neo-Assyrian empire, *State Archives of Assyria Bulletin* 16: 185–226.

Radner, K. (2008) Review of Galil 2007, *Zeitschrift für Assyriologie und Vorderasiatische Archäologie* 98: 295–297.

Radner, K. (forthcoming) Die beiden neuassyrischen Privatarchive. In P. Miglus, K. Radner & F. M. Stepniowski, *Untersuchungen im Stadtgebiet von Assur: Wohnquartiere in der Weststadt*, Teil 1 (WVDOG), Wiesbaden.

Smith, M. E. (2010) The archaeological study of neighborhoods and districts in ancient cities, *Journal of Anthropological Archaeology* 29: 137–154.

Stolper, M. W. (1985) *Entrepreneurs and Empire: The Murašû Archive, the Murašû Firm, and Persian Rule in Babylonia*, Istanbul.

Stone, E. C. (1987) *Nippur Neighborhoods* (Studies in Ancient Oriental Civilization 44), Chicago.

Ur, J. (2005) Sennacherib's northern Assyrian canals: new insights from satellite imagery and aerial photography, *Iraq* 67/1 (CRRAI 49/2): 317–345.

Ur, J., L. de Jong, J. Giraud, J.F. Osborne and J. MacGinnis. (2013) Ancient cities and landscapes in the Kurdistan region of Iraq: the Erbil Plain Archaeological Survey 2012 season, *Iraq* 75: 1–29.

van Driel, G. (1970) Land and people in Assyria: some remarks, *Bibliotheca Orientalis* 27: 168–175.

van Driel (2002) *Elusive Silver. In Search of a Role for a Market in an Agrarian Environment. Aspects of Mesopotamia's Society* (PIHANS 950), Istanbul.
Waerzeggers, C. (2006) Neo-Babylonian laundry, *Revue d'assyriologie et d'archéologie orientale* 100: 83–96.
Wilkinson, T. J., J. Ur, E. Barbanes Wilkinson & M. Altaweel (2005) Landscape and settlement in the Neo-Assyrian Empire, *Bulletin of the American Schools of Oriental Research* 340: 23–56.
Zadok, R. (1985) *Geographical Names According to New- and Late-Babylonian Texts* (Répertoire Géographique des Textes Cunéiformes 8), Wiesbaden.

Chapter 4

Beyond capitalism – conceptualising ancient trade through friction, world historical context and bazaars

Peter Fibiger Bang

"To my master ... Dorotheos greetings ... Know that by the grace of our savior and righteous prayers we set off and came to Chaireu after 17 days and suffered no harm, nor have we given any "backsheesh/gratuity" on the river, apart from only 300 myriads ..., and we gave another 1200 myriads at the mouth of the canal ... And the commander (stratelates) came to me, but did nothing bad, nor did he keep any soldiers at all. As I was delayed on the way, because of that I did not catch Alphios, nor Markarios. By the grace of God, I completed the disposal of the small sacks (sakkion) by/for the love of our martyrs. Business is still completely deadlocked in Alexandria. Thus you do not want to accept a letter of credit from anyone after I release these and come up to Oxyrhynchus. And ... Heraeiskos sent Theodoros, his assistant, to Kaisarea with his little sacks again and ... to Kaisarea with his sacks ..."

Here is a fascinating report from the daily life of a 5th century merchant.[1] The letter was sent from Alexandria in Egypt to his master upstream in the city of Oxyrhynchus. Leaving aside the missive's shaky Greek literacy, difficult to convey in translation, we are given a vivid sense of a concrete commercial universe and the practical conduct of ancient trade. The hazards of travel, the payment of baksheesh or gratuities to people along the route, delays, possible abuse by soldiers and magistrates, an unforeseeable standstill in business, the need to travel on in search of a market in an alternative location, the many topics touched upon by the writer form a list which will be familiar to most students of pre-industrial society. However, even if these aspects of pre-modern trading life are commonplace, they are, nevertheless, not to be mistaken for trivial. Commerce may seem to invite description in a well-oiled language of movement and communication, of transfer and integration, in sum, of connectivity, but it was and is a physical, tangible and social process; it was shaped, so the letter reminds us, by elements of friction.

"A wheel turns because of its encounter with the surface of the road, spinning in the air it goes nowhere", the anthropologist Anna Tsing has objected against the eager advocates of abstract globalisation theory. The forces of movement and exchange are only articulated through "the grip of encounter."[2] People used to a world where staggering capital sums can be transferred from one end of the globe to the other in a split second may tend to forget such tangible truth. Ancient historians, by contrast, are confronted by the opposite problem. Our worlds did not enjoy the luxury of dramatically shrinking time-distance horizons. From a modern perspective, extensive movement of men and things in a distant past without access to motorised transport seems almost unimaginable and yet movement there was. So a common response has been to downplay the obstacles to travel and transport and instead emphasise the positive capacity to get around (Horden & Purcell 2000, chap. 9; Adams 2007). But in doing so, we risk missing half the story, as it were. After noting the basic mobility of materials and people, that other half would go on to analysing how specific trades were shaped by concrete processes: how they were channeled by physical geographies, how their pulse would beat to the rhythm of the seasons and how goods would often be anchored in specific ecologies and social environments. Only by paying close attention to these dimensions of friction will we be able to capture and portray the character of a commercial universe in which economic integration developed against the backdrop of a mode of life where the forces of localism were so much stronger than they are today.[3] Life-cycles may be traced for commodities, just as for people.[4] That archaeologists have found building bricks, produced in the environs of Rome, in North Africa is not simply a reflection of the strength, in any abstract sense, of marketing networks in the Roman empire. Rather, the surprising transfer of such bulky items over such distances, only makes economic sense against the need of grain freighters for ballast on the return journey from the gluttonous city on the Tiber; the cost of transport had already been covered by the government sponsored deliveries of wheat from the outbound trip. By the same token, the trade in pottery from Bronze/Iron Age Cyprus, discussed by Susan Sherratt in this volume, is probably best explained as rising on the back of a commerce in the far more precious copper, mined on the island. Anchoring this export of ceramics in the Cypriot metal trade, however, should not be seen as an attempt to belittle or trivialise the phenomenon. Quite the reverse: it offers a richer, more densely textured understanding than a narrative about the rise of markets in general. André Tchernia, the pioneer of amphora studies, has recently introduced the notion of a *commerce imbriqué, entangled trades*. This is what we should be studying, commercial activity embedded in the manifold concrete processes of life.[5]

***

But the language of "thick description" needs to be wedded to economic analysis. Many historians, myself included, have been turning towards the so-called New Institutional Economics for that purpose (Bang 2009; Morris *et al.* 2007; Jursa 2010).

There is a body of economic theory attuned to giving history its due, by insisting that economic performance is decisively shaped by specific organisation and institutional constellation, by context or, to put it in another way, by the different historical trajectories taken by societies.[6] In the implementation of analysis, however, there may be a tendency to jump from the existence of an institution to the conclusion that it was economically efficient. But, as Sheilagh Ogilvie has forcefully objected, that would be a mistake. Institutions have not been created to benefit the economy at large, but only those people and groups that control them. Often institutions simply siphon off wealth or rents from one group in society to another. One might, for instance, argue that the many kinds of merchant associations – which can be found across pre-industrial Eurasia – served to form networks of social capital that facilitated the activities of traders and thus promoted commerce. However, Ogilvie observes, it was far more important that these organisations often hampered the expansion of economic activity by making it more difficult for outsiders to enter the market and by using their social power to redistribute economic resources in their own favour. More than economic activity and expansion, these associations promoted rent-seeking. Only as commerce was given free and the influence of merchant associations was pushed back during the early-modern period, did the economy experience growth and development (Ogilvie 2011).

Quite apart from the salutary reminder that in analysing institutions it is *de rigueur* to work out the balance between the redistribution of rents and economic efficiency, Ogilvie's argument reveals something even more important. Our discussions remain caught up in a distorting early-modern teleology. Either institutions are efficient and produce modern conditions or they are rent-seekers that prevent economic development. But that is not really the problem facing the student of ancient societies; the analytical choice handed out to us is unsatisfactory, the perspective unnecessarily confined. To put it bluntly, the historical context is wrong. *We* study the development in antiquity of the complex form of society which was to be transformed when, much later, modern economies began to develop. Even Plato, with his well-known aristocratic and agrarian disdain for everything commercial, recognised that a civilised life of the former, more traditional, type also required traders and a division of labour.[7] Within this division of labour, the majority of the population was based in agriculture, but a substantial minority developed other specialisations as aristocratic warriors and servants, priests and scribes, craftsmen and traders. Social hierarchies of honour and divine truth were more firmly and elaborately articulated than among more loosely organised tribal societies, and became fixed in writing, cities and command of the agricultural surplus.[8] How did trade fit into this form of society that the victorious bourgeoisie of the 18th and 19th centuries has taught us to think of as aristocratic and traditional? Our question, well identified in the title of a recent monograph, is that of *Commerce before Capitalism*.[9] It was precisely the kind of economic institutions that capitalism broke away from, as traditional and constricting which had enabled the development of early civilised societies. At the level of intercontinental trade, for instance, the rise of early-modern capitalism saw an intensification and the emergence of an ability to organise and command the long-distance trade routes as a whole. Before, the values circulating in this commercial artery of spices, precious metals and cloths – stretching across Eurasia, from the Bronze Ages onwards, to service the needs of the elites for numinous rarities and strategic goods – had certainly been anything but negligible. However, the system was, as Yon makes clear in his contribution below, only loosely joined together and carved up into regional segments.[10] No one really knew the network from beginning till end, let alone was able to create a commercial organisation that spanned across the length and breadth of it. This was "world trade" before capitalist hegemony.[11]

Perhaps, many of the economic institutions which sustained our sort of "traditional" society may look inefficient from a modern perspective and geared to rent-taking. But long ago Schumpeter observed how, under conditions of economic uncertainty, rent seeking might be economically beneficent and productive; it enabled investment to be made with some certainty that a profit could be earned. This may have been the situation in the ancient world.[12] The high friction universe of pre-industrial societies, as the opening letter served to illustrate, would have been one of considerable uncertainty. Yet, economic agents developed ways of tackling, managing and coping with uncertainty. Sometimes these methods appear to us moderns as brakes on further development; but they formed part of an institutional matrix which generated greater social power and tapped more energy than alternative modes of life available.

Historians continue to argue about whether these societies in their most flourishing moments were capable of generating growth and raising living standards. Most of the time, the evidence is too fragmentary to allow precise, let alone definitive answers.[13] In his discussion of pre-industrial growth, however, Persson has elegantly argued that to sustain cities complex agrarian societies would, a priori, have had to raise average per capita incomes above what was found in simpler economies. Urbanisation could barely be financed by merely siphoning off wealth from the countryside; production had to be increased (Persson 1988, chap. 3). On the other hand, the experience of the Black Death in medieval Europe makes one pause. As population figures and economic activity plummeted in the wake of the plague, living standards can be seen to have risen in spite of the fall-off in city-life and social complexity. Whatever gains might have been achieved in per capita incomes, they were too modest and feeble not to be undermined by the growing population of the high middle ages – more mouths to feed. In the long run, Malthusian pressures kept living standards from rising substantially in our kind of world.[14] But recognising this does not saddle the student of antiquity with a bleak history of stagnation. It might look so, if we concentrate only on per capita growth. But the emphasis on such intensive growth, diverts attention away from a far more significant and powerful story.

Often treated as the poor relation by economists interested in the miracle of industrialisation, extensive growth deserves to be put centre stage in discussions of the ancient world. Irrespective of whether some areas were capable of temporarily producing some modest growth in per capita incomes, complex agrarian societies everywhere used resources more intensively and could sustain (even depended on) higher levels of population. The denser the number of people on the land, the more intensive the method of cultivation – this was the classic insight of Boserup (Boserup 1965). The consequences were palpable. Everywhere, the establishment of this mode of life was accompanied by a fluctuating, yet inexorable tendency to expand horizontally as population rose. The history of complex agrarian societies may be charted as a slow glacial, expansive drift from small beginnings in fertile flood valleys. The late second millennium/early first millennium trade of copper and pottery, as Susan Sherratt is right to intimate, needs to be situated in a context of westward expansion from the Levant further out into the Mediterranean. Our story then is not one of a stalled modernity, but of the gradual outward march and then consolidation of complex or civilised agrarian societies – a trend that may be reflected in the movement from small city-states to universal empire detectable first in the history of the ancient Near East and then repeated by the Greeks and Romans.[15]

***

Karl Polanyi, in days gone by, attempted to explore the problem of "commerce before capitalism" through a set of three ideal-types: reciprocity, redistribution and market-exchange (Polanyi 1957). But drawn from the simple pre-state societies studied by economic anthropology, these distinctions were too crude and they saddled our disciplines with a number of unhelpful debates about non-market versus market societies that nevertheless still inform our discourse. Several papers in this volume, for instance, apply a distinction between institutional and free market trade. But neither the reciprocity of gift-giving nor political redistribution of economic resources on their own will do as analytical keys to the ancient world on their own; nor will the connected Polanyi-esque notion of market-less trading, one might add. Of all people, it was Finley who had to insist that Greco-Roman society, at least, was one of markets.[16] Students of the Ancient Near East have, emphatically, made the same point. To be sure, much economic activity in a pre-industrial economy remained outside markets. A significant proportion of the agricultural yield will have been allocated and consumed within the households of peasant producers. Likewise, monarchs, noble lords, temples and urban governments would customarily receive in kind a part of the proceeds, deriving from their domain lands as well as from other dues. Their needs, though, were far more diverse than the main products of the agricultural sector from which they drew most of their income. So access to markets was crucial to exchange the staples of the agricultural economy into the wider range of products necessary to sustain the splendid life-styles of elites and to enable consumption away from the point of production. Serving as transformers, markets were significant in mobilising the agricultural surplus.[17] In short, the ancient economy was too complex to be placed under a single label, be it market or redistribution; it must be analysed as a compound set of inter-woven institutions: peasants households, temple domains, aristocratic estates, taxing states, cities – and markets.

About the latter Braudel once proffered an inspired intuition when he remarked about markets that they were far from identical with capitalism. Capitalism hovered in a sphere above the market and was based on organisational muscle, the ability and power to control markets, "the anti-market"; its history was one of only gradual evolution.[18] Braudel himself was inclined to detect traces of capitalist development in the earliest of historical times; but, as argued here, these developments may more profitably be described rather in terms of the expansion of civilised society, while capitalism proper is better reserved for the transformation that followed in the footsteps of the rise of the commercial system, so well analysed in Braudel's mighty tomes, centred in northwestern Europe particularly from the 16th century onwards. At any rate, Braudel opened a window for exploring other dimensions of markets and identifying a more differentiated typology. Some ancient historians, for instance, have turned to the periodic markets and fairs of peasant society for guidance (De Ligt 1993). But ancient society was also an urban one. If general knowledge of periodic markets has vastly refined our understanding of concrete commercial processes in the ancient countryside, where might we look to achieve something similar for the permanent markets of the cities?

Perhaps, the most attractive model on offer is Clifford Geertz's of the bazaar (Geertz 1979). For many, of course, the bazaar will be inseparably linked to the Muslim cities of the Middle East. But historically the characteristic physical layout of the bazaar, as it appears to us today, is merely what emerged as the myriad shopkeepers and other commercial people of the Greco-Roman cities moved out from their positions among the colonnaded walk ways and spilled over into the broad monumental streets when urban authorities ceased periodically to clear the path sometime in late antiquity.[19] Structurally, Geertz's analysis of the bazaar, may be summarised in a number of key features: many small actors, opaque and uncertain information, volatility of prices and fragmentation of markets. All these usefully highlight some characteristic and well-known dimensions of pre-industrial trade. Business was generally organised on the basis of households and personal partnerships rather than much larger impersonal firms. Uncertainty and unpredictability of conditions in the market were common, a result of the friction which the papyrus opening letter cited above served to evoke. A further result would have been considerable variation between or fragmentation of markets. Illustration may be provided by another document from late antiquity, a set of papyri compiled by the Roman provincial authorities, listing prices for a number of goods current in the cities of the middle Egyptian province of Arcadia over a year. A striking feature is the considerable differences existing between the grain prices recorded across individual cities. The records also fail to register much interannual variation. This may be a reflection that the market in food grains was perhaps less significant, at least to the government which collected a grain tax in kind, than that of the main cash crop, wine. Here the variation in prices between cities is smaller and inter-annual fluctuation is recorded with greater precision. Even so, the prices show some differences in development over the year. Here we have an instructive snapshot of the uneven character of the formation and integration of markets to be expected in most cities of pre-industrial society and which no other model seems to capture better than Geertz's notion of the bazaar.[20]

It might be objected (as some have already done) that "the bazaar" underestimates the level of economic integration, the extent of trade between localities. But the bazaar is not a model of primitive or trifling trade.[21] The field work of Geertz took place in cities that were bigger than an ancient city of average size and the model does not preclude even considerable exchange of goods between localities. What it does, however, is to emphasise that the character of this integration would often have been lumpy and uneven; considerable fragmentation would have remained. Maps of archaeological finds, charting widespread distributions of some goods and objects, may be thought to contradict this expectation. The truth may be less straightforward. Such maps reveal patterns accumulating over several decades, even centuries. Many of the shifting inter-annual local variations are likely to even out in the picture of the very long run recovered by archaeological distributions. When our historical record becomes more fine grained, extensive trade flows can be seen to co-exist with considerable local fragmentation. Not before the introduction of the railway, for instance, did markets in bulky materials such as grain really become integrated across territories in Europe (Persson 1999). Prior to the 19th century, integration ran in narrower, particularly well-connected circuits. In a study of the grain market in the Roman Empire, Paul Erdkamp has demonstrated how this expectation of uneven integration is reflected in the meagre evidence available to the ancient historian.[22]

So far, in this essay, the discussion of the bazaar as a useful model of urban markets in antiquity, has concentrated on the irregularities, on the limits of its ability to integrate. This was where Geertz started, too, in the 1950s and early '60s when modernisation theory still dominated the agenda. *Peddlers and Princes* analysed the economy of Indonesian towns through two elegant ideal types. The commercial sector was in the hands of multitudes of bazaar merchants, peddlers with lots of enterprising spirit, but little organisational capacity. Conversely, agriculture and industry were dominated by aristocratic households, with plenty of capacity to organise, but dismissive of business and wedded to traditional values even as they tried to meet the challenge of modernisation. Development remained hampered by the misfit between rationalising entrepreneurship and organisation (Geertz 1963, 139–140). Two decades later, the faith in modernisation theory had faded and the analytical perspective changed, describing an intellectual journey that closely resembles the goal of this essay. In the study of the bazaar of the Moroccan city of Sefrou, Geertz produced a more sensitive model of its trading universe (Geertz 1979). From a modern perspective, to be sure, integration was limited. Nonetheless, considerable activity took place and more attention was now given, by Geertz, to the enabling features of bazaar organisation. To navigate the high friction universe of the bazaar, merchants had developed a set of strategies for coping with fragmentation and uncertainty. These may be grouped under three headings: clientelisation, community and protection.[23] All these speak directly to concerns that are, and perhaps increasingly so, central to the student of pre-modern commercial life.

Clientelisation focuses on the forging of interpersonal relationships and networks of mutual exchange of favours and patronage, a field of study to which rising numbers are turning under the banner of network analysis (Broekaert 2012; 2013; Seland 2013). Here one would also have to place various forms of commenda relationships, where a sedentary investor provides the working capital for a junior, often travelling partner.[24] Community asks us to explore the cultural, religious and communal life of merchants as central for the formation of norms and the articulation of social hierarchies. In a world where the state provided relatively few services and left much to the self-help capacity of individuals and groups, these activities would have been crucial to make commercial society work.[25] Organisation in associations, societies of co-worshippers and ethnic diasporas, therefore, become important to the working of the bazaar.[26] Finally, protection costs have been shown to be one of the most important variables by students of better recorded periods of pre-modern trade.[27] But it is clearly a dimension to which much more attention ought to be given in the analyses of the ancient world.[28] The attraction of the bazaar, however, is not merely to suggest these themes, but to combine them into a coherent whole, a portrait of markets in what from a modernisation perspective would still have to be described as a traditional society dominated by agriculture. As any reader of C. A. Bayly's classic *Rulers, Townsmen and Bazaars* will know, this may still be a very vibrant, dynamic and alluring setting. The model of the bazaar, in short, aims to embed our analysis of trade in a web of interpersonal, communal and political relations of power and thereby anchor it in a concrete societal context. What anthropologists refer to as local knowledge, therefore, becomes crucial. To navigate the universe of the bazaar successfully, it is never enough to know or describe trade in general, one must appreciate the specifics of actual commercial relations and processes, the properties of products and how they fit together. To understand commerce in the bazaar, one must study trade in the concrete; and it was precisely with the need for just such a model that this essay began.

Postscript

A macro-historical and comparative framework, such as has been outlined here, may meet with suspicion and scepticism in some quarters. Offering a broad sketch of historical development, generalisation of this type is claimed to be unduly reductive, shoehorning culturally specific societies into overly simple categories. This is a form of critique which is often voiced by anthropologists against (neo-colonial) development schemes that insist on scoring societies against a checklist of abstract norms, one size fits all. But the instinctive dislike of such universalising forms of knowledge fails its purpose. That they constitute an enormously powerful mode of thinking and analysis is not in itself a good reason simply to make them an object of complaint, call for their abandonment and wish them to go away. Quite the contrary, it ought precisely to be an incitement to produce better, more historically and culturally sensitive macro-models.[29] Universalising comparison is too forceful and effective a field of analysis to be vacated by the humanities. The historian, certainly, cannot easily do without a general and consciously articulated sense of societal evolution.

This essay has attempted to substitute a more nuanced version of past development for the tendency to rank ancient phenomena according to a binary teleology, from traditional to modern. Ancient history, that is the claim, should not be ranged primarily or solely in relation to early-modern Europe; this would be rushing ahead of time and it distorts our vision. Instead, the bazaar has been offered as a framework for exploring common ground between Greco-Roman and Levantine antiquity, not to mention other pre-industrial societies. Equally a simplifying generalisation, the bazaar has the great advantage of foregrounding some significant characteristics of pre-industrial trade which tend to be disregarded as irregularities by a more overtly modernising perspective. In its capacity to capture this "irregular" dimension as an integral part of ancient commercial life, the model is bound to say something both significant and right, irrespective of whether it under-estimates the extent of economic exchange and integration or not. Perhaps, the model will turn out to be better suited for the modest, average urban community than for the few most bustling and well-connected commercial hubs of the ancient world. But that is a job for comparative history to decide and explore.

A particular attraction of the bazaar, in this connection, is that it situates locally specific conditions within a generalised model of commercial life. If one danger of comparative analysis is the overly abstract claims occasionally found in the social sciences, practitioners within the humanities are normally more prone to the other pitfall of comparison: analysis as a catalogue of similarities and, especially, differences carefully listed and recorded in the minutest detail. Often this procedure is little more than a certain recipé to avoid generalisation, the uniqueness of each example seemingly confirmed.[30] Indeed frequently juxtaposition, with little or no analytical contact, of separate cases is considered quite enough. But if we distrust the ability to generalise from a small set of cases, why bother with the juxtaposition in the first place? Moreover, there is such a thing as over-privileging the uniqueness of each case and individual society; and the price to pay for it, we normally refer to as the prejudice of small differences. Nations claim to be singular to distinguish themselves from their neighbours, yet they all turn out to be singular in remarkably similar ways. There is no end to the number of cultural markers that may be claimed to distinguish the Levant from the Greco-Roman world; yet the more carefully we look, the more impressive the commonalities seem to become. The "invention" of coinage, for instance, it is clear from the contributions in this volume, was probably of less moment, in economic terms, than we might tend to assume. Given that there is thus far little tradition for treating our two worlds of antiquity together within a shared frame, let us not rush immediately into the false security of particularism.

Acknowledgements
I am grateful to Juan Carlos Moreno García and, as so often before, Peter Garnsey who both offered critique and helpful suggestions to various draft versions of this essay. Moreover, thanks are due to Niels Brimnes for introducing me to the work of Anna Tsing and Gojko Barjamovic for letting me see his forthcoming analysis of old Assyrian trade, and to Kristian Kristiansen for sending me his introduction to a forthcoming volume theorising "trade and civilization".

Notes

1. *P.Oxy*.56.3864. On this papyrus letter, see the discussion, commentary and translation (which I have felt free to modify and vary in the quotation above) by the editor, Sirivianou, and the analysis of Hidetaro 1999/2000, especially for the occurrence of apragia, business standstill. Further bibliography and text available from: http://papyri.info/ddbdp/p.oxy;56;3864?rows=3&start=11&fl=id%2Ctitle&fq=series_led_path%3Ap.oxy%3B56%3B*%3B*&sort=series+asc%2Cvolume+asc%2Citem+asc&p=12&t=23#to-app-choice31. Arietta Papaconstantinou has deftly suggested that the expression translated by the editor as "by the love of our martyrs", be translated "for the feast of our martyrs." This is a possibility, but does perhaps not chime so well with the whole business context of the letter. There, yet another pious exclamation is probably preferable, even if it seems stylistically clumsy. N. Gonis has pointed out that the letter could also date to the 4th century.
2. On the concept of friction, in the globalising world of today, see Tsing 2005, quotations from p. 5.
3. Scheidel 2014 & http://orbis.stanford.edu/ for a recent attempt to emphasise the significance of the physical geography in shaping patterns of movement and communication in the Greco-Roman world.
4. Life-cycles, or "biographies" as Kopytoff 1986 termed it.
5. Tchernia 2011, 155 and p. 159 for discussion of return cargoes from Rome. McCormick 2001, chap. 4 is also strong on such connections.
6. North 1990 and Greif 2006 for two strong and influential examples.
7. Plato, *The Republic* II, 369D–371E.
8. On the character of complex agrarian societies, e.g. Gellner 1988; Crone 1989; Haldon 1993.
9. Howell 2010. The opposite approach, to search for precursors of modern capitalism back from the earliest ages of history, is exemplified by the recent two volume *The Cambridge History of Capitalism* (2014). But the drawback of this approach is to reduce most of human history to a group of failed attempts at modernity before capitalism came into its own in the 17th–19th centuries. The guiding question of the first volume, as the editor states, then becomes "Why did capitalism and modern economic growth take so long to get started in the first place?" The answer, the editor Neal carries on, "essentially, is that it was hard - very hard (p. 2)". But if that is so, perhaps it would be more productive not in our analysis to impute to these societies a history which tended to get stuck in its tracks and was never really unfolded.
10. See further Barjamovic forthcoming and 2011 confirming this impression of a long distance trade organised in regional stages through an analysis of the 19th century BC trade in tin and textiles from Assur to Anatolia.
11. To play on the title of Abu-Lughod 1989.
12. Cf. Bang 2012, 210–214. Schumpeter 2010 [1943], 76–79. The relevance of Schumpeter for pre-modern economic history more broadly has been demonstrated forcefully by North *et al.* 2009.

13. Analysis of archaeologically recovered skeletal remains, though, will improve our understanding; but the material is very complex and far from unequivocal. Careful and systematic exploration of the Italian material suggests that the more intense form of social organisation following in the wake of successful imperialism, also brought considerable health stresses, with a notable drop in average height of the Romano-Italian population, see Gowland & Garnsey 2010.
14. Scheidel 2007 on the basic Malthusian character of the ancient economy, but also pointing out the significance of the ability to spread outwards; one of Rome's most important effects in economic history was to push the urban "frontier" westwards and northwards. Further, see still Braudel 1979, vol. 1, 69–78, and Scheidel 2002 for a (contested) attempt to analyse the Antonine Plague in the light of the Black Death and the rising living standards following hard on its heels.
15. Barjamovic 2013 for the city-state to empire pattern in Mesopotamian history. The gradual, slow outward expansion of complex agrarian societies may be read in the distinction made in Lieberman 2009 between an old zone in Eurasia, exposed to nomadic attack, and a new, protected zone developing from AD 800 onwards in Europe and Southeast Asia. In general, here, I find myself in a constructive, but critical dialogue with Kristian Kristiansen. We agree about the significance of expanding civilisation. But Kristiansen is less inclined to make a fundamental distinction between complex agrarian society and "early modernity" which to him is already present during the bronze ages. See Kristiansen (forthcoming).
16. Finley 1970: "... price variations according to supply and demand were a commonplace in Greek life in the fourth century B.C.", a comment made in constructive opposition to Polanyi (p. 14); and further 1985, 28–29 making a distinction between the private property and trade characteristic of the Greco-Roman world, and the bureaucratic "rationing" of Near Eastern societies. Few would accept this distinction today, because markets and private property are now seen as equally important for the economy of ancient Mesopotamia and Egypt, thus Bedford 2005. Further Van der Spek, Van Leeuwen & Van Zanden 2015, chap 1. The long-term pattern of market performance discussed by the group of editors in this chapter as well as their chapter 21 seems broadly compatible with the general framework proposed in this essay: some development of markets, perhaps with a slowly rising trend, before the new turn marked by European capitalism in the 18th and 19th centuries.
17. Bang 2008, chap. 2 and 2007, toying with the notion of port-folio capitalists.
18. Braudel 1979, vol. II, 192–207, in particular 196–97 "contre-marché" (in the English ed. pp. 223–239, in particular 229–30). The discussion of the concept of capitalism, of Polanyi and much else on these pages remains highly rewarding. The model distinguishing between capitalism, the market and an immobile "natural" economy outside the market, "material life", is further explicated in the avant-propos both to volume 1 and 2.
19. A good example would be the *suq* which had encroached on the old Roman Via Recta in Damascus. Kennedy 1985, complemented by Holleran 2012: 115 & 126, for a basic discussion of the redevelopment of the broad colonnaded streets of Roman times to the narrow, in part covered bazaars and the pressure on the Roman street from vendors already during the Republic and Principate. The numerous *tabernae* of ancient Roman cities already constituted a bazaar, so Maier 2012, 74–75.
20. I summarise and develop here on the analysis in Bang 2008, chap. 3 of *P. Oxy.* 3628–3633/36. The set of papyri was edited and accessibly presented by J. R. Rea; Lo Cascio 1998 for a basic discussion of the price reports submitted by Egyptian professional associations to the imperial authorities. The image of uneven integration conveyed by the late Roman Egyptian material seems well paralleled in Jursa 2015's analysis of Babylonian markets, a degree of integration combined with fragmentation and price volatility. But, of course, the model can then be further differentiated and developed on the rich Babylonian material. The easy access to rivers made transport between markets far more feasible than in land-locked regions.
21. The different positions in this debate are conveniently collected and juxtaposed in "A forum on trade", chap. 14 of Scheidel 2012. But discussions continue, e.g. Tchernia 2011, 109–110 in favour; Problome & Brughmans 2014 for a new kind of critique while Hawkins 2012 has gone

on to study urban craftsmen in the Roman empire in a way very congenial to the bazaar, emphasising the importance of risk and seasonality for keeping businesses small and forming social "subcontracting networks." Additional references are provided in the following footnotes.
22. Erdkamp 2005. Temin 2011, chap. 2 has attempted to show that the Roman Empire during the late Republic and Principate had come to form an integrated grain market. But the evidential support is very weak, a handful of prices drawn from several centuries of history. In fact, the evidence we do have from the Principate reveals fragmentation, cf. Scheidel 2014, 27–30 and Bransbourg 2012, just as the late antique papyri prices from the province of Arcadia would lead us to expect.
23. Bang 2008, chaps 3–5 for an extensive discussion of these dimensions of the bazaar and the character of Roman trade.
24. Barjamovic forthcoming, the structure described by him for Assyrian Bronze Age trade, with many "modest" households participating, some big merchants, commercial partnerships, the spreading of risk, and collective caravans would be interesting to explore in terms of clientelisation and commenda.
25. Terpstra 2013 for an attempt to explore this dimension of Roman trade further, emphasising the significance of information uncertainties and limited government enforcement of legal rules.
26. Brokaert 2011f develops this argument further for Roman history. Much work is being done on associations in antiquity in these years, Cf. Dondin-Payre & Tran 2012 and the Copenhagen Associations project which will undoubtedly add significantly to our understanding of the culture of associational life in the Greco-Roman world.
27. The studies of Lane remain crisp and fundamental, conveniently collected in Lane 1966, part 3. See Steensgaard 1974 for an inspired, if contested attempt to employ Lane's conceptualisation to understand early modern world trade; Bang 2007 for an attempt to apply the work of Lane to Roman imperial history; Corocci & Collavini 2014 for a discussion in relation to medieval European history.
28. Cottier 2008 and France 2001 for some recent work on customs tolls in the Roman empire.
29. I read Tsing 2005 as an attempt in this direction, all though less eager for grand meta-history than this signature. Pandey 2013, 8–9 similarly recognises and shares the critique of universalising macro-models of social evolution, but nevertheless proceeds to write a comparative history.
30. Bang 2014, 32–58 for a discussion of the contrasting habits of comparison within the humanities and the social sciences. See further Moreno García 2014 for a discussion of the recent work in ancient comparative history, perhaps with slightly different emphasis and view of the comparative enterprise.

Bibliography

Abu-Lughod, J. L. (1989), *Before European Hegemony: The World System A.D. 1250–1350*, New York.

Adams, C. (2007), *Land Transport in Roman Egypt*, Oxford.

Bang, P. F. (2014), *Irregulare Aliquod Corpus? Comparison, World History and the Historical Sociology of the Roman Empire. I: Theoretical and Methodological Introduction and Summary*, Copenhagen.

Bang, P. F. (2012) Predation. In W. Scheidel (ed.), *The Cambridge Companion to the Roman Economy*, 197–217, Cambridge.

Bang, P. F. (2009) The Ancient Economy and New Institutional Economics, *Journal of Roman Studies* 99: 194–206.

Bang, P. F. (2008), *The Roman Bazaar: A Comparative Study of Trade and Markets in a Tributary Empire*, Cambridge.

Bang, P. F. (2007) Trade and empire – in search of organizing concepts for the Roman economy, *Past & Present* 195: 3–54.

Barjamovic, G. (2013) Mesopotamian Empires. In P. F. Bang & W. Scheidel (eds), *The Oxford Handbook of the State in the Ancient Near East and Mediterranean*, 120–160, New York.

Barjamovic, G. (2011) *A Historical Geography of Anatolia in the Old Assyrian Colony Period*, Copenhagen.
Barjamovic, G. (forthcoming) Interlocking commercial networks and the infrastructure of trade in western Asia during the Bronze Age. In K. Kristiansen, T. Lindkvist & J. Myrdal (eds), *Trade and Civilization in the Pre-Modern World*, Cambridge.
Bayly, C. A. (1983), *Rulers, Townsmen and Bazaars: North Indian Society in the Age of British Expansion, 1770–1870*, Cambridge.
Bedford, P. R. (2005) The economy of the Near East in the first millenium BC. In I. Morris & J. Manning (eds), *The Ancient Economy. Evidence and Models*, 58–83, Stanford.
Boserup, E. (1965) *The Conditions of Agricultural Growth: The Economics of Agrarian Change under Population Pressure*, Chicago.
Bransbourg, G. (2012) *Rome and the Economic Integration of Empire*, ISAW Papers 3 (http://dlib.nyu.edu/awdl/isaw/isaw-papers/3/).
Braudel, F. (1979) *Civilisation matérielle, économie et capitalisme, XVe–XVIIIe siècle*, vols 1–3, Paris.
Broekaert, W. (2011) Partners in business. Roman merchants and the potential advantages of being a collegiatus, *Ancient Society* 41: 221–256.
Broekaert, W. (2012) Vertical integration in the Roman economy, *Ancient Society* 42, 109–125.
Broekaert, W. (2013) Financial experts in a spider net. A social network analysis of the archives of Caecilius Iucundus and the Sulpicii, *Klio* 95/2: 471–510.
Corocci, S. & S. M. Collavini (2014) The cost of states. Politics and exactions in the Christian west (sixth to fifteenths centuries). In J. Hudson & A. R. López (eds), *Diverging Paths? The Shapes of Power and Institutions in Medieval Christendom and Islam*, 125–158, Leiden.
Cottier, M. *et al.* (2008), *The Customs Law of Asia*, Oxford.
Crone, P. (1989), *Pre-Industrial Societies*, Oxford.
Dondin-Payre, M. & N. Tran (eds) (2012), *Collegia - Le phénomène associatif dans l'Occident romain*, Bordeaux.
Erdkamp, P. (2005) *The Grain Market in the Roman Empire. A Social, Political and Economic Study*, Cambridge.
Finley, M. I. (1970) Aristotle and economic analysis, *Past & Present* 47: 3–25.
Finley, M. I. (1985) *The Ancient Economy, 2nd ed.*, London.
France, J. (2001), *Quadragesima Galliarum: l'organisation douanière des provinces alpestres, gauloises et germaniques de l'Empire romain (1er siècle avant J.-C.-3er siècle après J.-C)*, Rome.
Geertz, C. (1963) *Peddlers and Princes. Social Development and Economic Change in Two Indonesian Towns*, Chicago.
Geertz, C. (1979) Suq: The bazaar economy in Sefrou. In C. Geertz, H. Geertz & L. Roan (eds), *Meaning and Order in Moroccan Society*, 123–225, Cambridge.
Gellner, E. (1988), *Plough, Sword and Book. The Structure of Human History*, Chicago.
Gowland, R. & P. Garnsey (2010) Skeletal evidence for health, nutritional status and malaria in Rome and the empire. In H. Eckhardt (ed.), *Roman Diasporas: Archaeological Approaches to Mobility and Diversity in the Roman Empire* (*Journal of Roman Archaeology* Supplement 78), 131–156, Portsmouth (RI).
Greif, A. (2006), *Institutions and the Path to the Modern Economy: Lessons from Medieval Trade*, Cambridge.
Haldon, J. (1993), *The State and the Tributary Mode of Production*, London.
Hawkins, C. (2012) Manufacturing. In W. Scheidel (ed.), *The Cambridge Companion to the Roman Economy*, 175–194, Cambridge.
Hidetaro, I. (1999/2000) The transfer of money in Roman Egypt. A study of epitheké, *Kodai* 10: 83–104.
Holleran, C. (2012) *Shopping in Ancient Rome: The Retail Trade in the Late Republic and the Principate*, Oxford.
Horden, P. & B. N. Purcell (2000) *The Corrupting Sea. A Study of Mediterranean History*, Oxford.
Howell, M. C. (2010) *Commerce before Capitalism in Europe, 1300-1600*, Cambridge.

Jursa, M. (2010) *Aspects of the Economic History of Babylonia in the First Millennium BC. Economic Geography, Economic Mentalities, Agriculture, the Use of Money and the Problem of Economic Growth*, Münster.
Jursa, M. (2015) Market performance and market integration in Babylonia in the 'long sixth century' BC. In R. J. Van der Spek, B. Van Leeuwen & J. L. Van Zanden (eds) (2015), *A History of Market Performance: From Ancient Babylonia to the Modern World*, 83–106, Abingdon.
Kopytoff, I. (1986) The cultural biography of things: commoditization as process. In A. Appadurai (ed.), *The Social Life of Things. Commodities in Cultural Perspective*, 64–94, Cambridge.
Kristiansen, K. (forthcoming), Theorizing Trade and Civilization. In K. Kristiansen, T. Lindkvist & J. Myrdal (eds), *Trade and Civilization in the Pre-Modern World*, Cambridge.
Lane, F. C. (1966) *Venice and History. The Collected Papers of Frederic C. Lane, Edited by a Committee of Colleagues and Former Students with a Foreword by Fernand Braudel*, Baltimore.
Lieberman, V. (2009) *Strange Parallels. Southeast Asia in Global Context, c. 800–1830. Vol. 2: Mainland Mirrors: Europe, Japan, China, South Asia, and the Islands*, Cambridge.
Ligt, L. de (1993) *Fairs and Markets in the Roman Empire: Economic and Social Aspects of Periodic Trade in a Pre-industrial Society*, Amsterdam.
Lo Cascio, E. (1998) Considerazioni su circolazione monetaria, prezzi e fiscalità nel IV secolo. *In Atti dell'Academia Romanistica Costantiniana. XII Convegno Internazionale sotto L'Alto Patronato del Presidente della Republicca in honore di Manlio Sargenti*, 121–136, Naples.
Maier, E. (2012) *The Ancient Middle Classes. Urban Life and Aesthetics in the Roman Empire, 100 BCE–250 CE*, Cambridge (MA).
McCormick, M. (2001) *Origins of the European Economy: Communications and Commerce, A.D. 300–900*, Cambridge.
Moreno García, J. C. (2014) Ancient states and Pharaonic Egypt: An agenda for future research, *Journal of Egyptian History* 7: 203–240.
Neal, L. & J. G. Williamson (2014) *The Cambridge History of Capitalism. Volume 1: The Rise of Capitalism. From Ancient Origins to 1848*, Cambridge.
North, D. C. (1990) *Institutions, Institutional Change, and Economic Performance*, Cambridge.
North, D. C., J. J. Wallis & B. R. Weingast (2009) *Violence and Social Orders. A Conceptual Framework for Interpreting Recorded Human History*, Cambridge.
Ogilvie, S. (2011) *Institutions and European Trade: Merchant Guilds, 1000–1800*, Cambridge.
Persson, K. G. (1988) *Pre-Industrial Growth*, Cambridge.
Persson, K. G. (1999) *Grain Markets in Europe, 1500–1900: Integration and Deregulation*, Cambridge.
Polanyi, K. (1957) *Trade and Market in the Early Empires: Economies in History and Theory*, Glencoe.
Problome, J. & T. Brughmans (2014) Roman bazaar or market economy?: An agent-based network model of tableware trade and distribution in the roman east. In *Social Simulation Conference*, Bellaterra, Cerdanyola del Vallès. Diposit digital de documents de la Universitat Autònoma de Barcelona (http://ddd.uab.cat/record/126344?ln=en).
Scheidel, W. (2007) Demography. In W. Scheidel, I. Morris & R. Saller (eds), *The Cambridge Economic History of the Greco-Roman World*, 38–86, Cambridge.
Scheidel, W. (ed.) (2012) *The Cambridge Companion to the Roman Economy*, Cambridge.
Scheidel, W. (2014) The shape of the Roman world: modeling imperial connectivity. *Journal of Roman Archaeology* 27: 7–32.
Scheidel, W., I. Morris & R. Saller (eds) (2007) *The Cambridge Economic History of the Greco-Roman World*, Cambridge.
Schumpeter, J. A. (2010 [1943]) *Capitalism, Socialism and Democracy. With a New Introduction by Joseph E. Stiglitz*, London & New York.
Seland, E. (2013) Networks and social cohesion in ancient Indian Ocean trade: geography, ethnicity, religion, *Journal of Global History* 8: 373–390.

Steensgaard, N. (1974) *The Asian Trade Revolution of the Seventeenth Century: the East India Companies and the Decline of the Caravan Trade*, Chicago.
Tchernia, A. (2011) *Les Romains et le commerce*, Naples.
Temin, P. (2013) *The Roman Market Economy*, Princeton.
Terpstra, T. T. (2013) *Trading Communities in the Roman World: A Micro-economic and Institutional Perspective*, Boston.
Tsing, A. L. (2005) *Friction. An Ethnography of Global Encounter*, Princeton.
Van der Spek, R. J., B. Van Leeuwen & J. L. Van Zanden (eds) (2015), *A History of Market Performance: From Ancient Babylonia to the Modern World*, Abingdon.

Chapter 5

Phoenician trade: the first 300 years

Carol Bell

This paper will consider the question: what do we really know about the initial trajectory of expansion of Phoenician trade in the earliest Iron Age? We know what the Phoenicians did but not how they did it (Kopcke 1992; Vella 1996) and the material evidence is, to say the least, patchy. But, to paraphrase Donald Rumsfeld (2002), knowing what we do not know is a crucial step in moving the debate forward, especially when this research question calls for coordination across such a wide geographical area and so many disciplines.

Consistent with the objectives of the workshop, I will also consider how one might analyse the material correlates of these complex interactions. As Vella pointed out some years ago, some historic approaches have been "expecting the impossible" from rather a small body of textual evidence (Vella 1996, 247). While not ignoring these sources, where they exist, my approach will consider how we might measure the degree of long-distance interaction and how this changes through time.

The Early Iron Age (EIA) expansion of Phoenician commercial activity – broadly speaking the period between 1200 and 900 BC – is obscure compared with later periods. Large scale syntheses of Phoenician history, such as Markoe (2000) and Aubet (1993), understandably, spend very little time on the economic aspects of this period. There are many problems, not least lack of data from the Phoenician heartland in modern-day Lebanon. This is due to several reasons:

1. The continuous inhabitation of Tyre, Sidon and Arwad to this day.
2. The political situation within the region over the past four decades

The absence of contemporaneous of textual sources adds to the challenge of working on trade in the EIA, as does lack of scientific analysis of e.g. pottery finds and absolute dating in the excavations that have been published for key sites in Lebanon. Adding further to the complexity of unravelling the development of Phoenician overseas interests, Phoenicia itself is a collection of city states with diverse interests and international aspirations and what may be true for Tyre's long distance trade connections may not apply to Sidon.

It is vital to commence any discussion of this nature with a clear definition of terms and scope and nowhere is this more crucial than when dealing with the terms "Phoenicia" and "Phoenician". How do we define the cultural area known as Phoenicia when its own inhabitants considered themselves first as belonging to a city-state rather than a larger social unit? As Lehmann (2008) has pointed out, the emergence of the Phoenicians as a cultural phenomenon dates to *c.* 1200 BC with the appearance of epigraphy in the Phoenician alphabetic script. Their material culture, on the other hand, is the result of continuous development from the Bronze Age repertoire (Lehmann 2008).

From the close of the LBA forward, the coastal area between Arwad in the north (in modern Syria) to Tel Dor in the south (in northern Israel) shares a common material culture that can be labelled Phoenician (see Figure 5.1 for location of the sites discussed). Although the geographical location of Arwad, an offshore island close to the mainland, very much fits the bill for a Phoenician establishment, its material culture is almost completely unknown and its identification as a Phoenician site hinges on historical and linguistic references (Lehmann 2008). Tel Dor, however, has been the subject of a substantial excavation and publication programme for many years and provides much material relevant to this subject (Gilboa *et al.* 2008, 114).

We may continue to lament the lack of well stratified new archaeological excavations from the Phoenician heartland in modern Lebanon across the LBA/Iron Age transition but arguably, we do not pay give the ones that do exist (Sarepta and Tyre) the attention they disserve (Nunez Calvo, 2008). What we do know is that, during this period, this part of the Levantine littoral did not suffer the destructive events that permanently removed Ugarit from Eastern Mediterranean trading circuits or the disruption experienced at ports on the southern Levantine coast, which were destroyed but recovered rapidly (Bell 2006, 137).

The stratigraphic sequence excavated by James Pritchard at Sarepta, which is located between Tyre and Sidon close to the mouth of the Litani river, is the only fully published continuous sequence across the LBA/Iron Age transition from a major excavation in Lebanon (see Bell 2006, 41–42, 99 for discussion and references). This sequence contains no destruction horizon corresponding the destruction of Ugarit and other sites in coastal Syria and Israel and the same is true for the sequence excavated by Bikai from a limited sounding at Tyre (Bikai 1978). This lack of destruction surely placed these Phoenician cities at an advantage when major ports to both north and south were out of action.

To begin at the beginning, therefore, what was the nature of the Late Bronze Age (LBA) trading system from which the Phoenician mercantile phenomenon evolved? The textual evidence excavated from the houses of merchants of Ugarit dating to the final decades of the LBA is the best starting point. These texts have been analysed by Christopher Monroe (2009a) as part of a wider study of Eastern Mediterranean

Fig. 5.1. Sites mentioned in the text.

textual material from this period. They cast a unique spotlight on the role of individual merchants, whom we know by name, in facilitating the flow of goods and commodities on which LBA society had come to rely. The evidence from Ugarit does not fit neatly into the conception of trade and international relations usually portrayed in large scale syntheses of the Eastern Mediterranean in for this period, for example Van De Mieroop 2007 (Monroe 2009b). Documenting the multifaceted relationships of individual merchants with the Royal Palace of Ugarit, these texts disserve integration into supra-regional syntheses of the political economy of this period. I will not reprise the substantivist/formalist debate here (see Bell 2006 and McGeough 2007 for recent discussions). Suffice it to say that the rather black and white positions these opposing paradigms portray of nature of trade seem to contradict the rather complex, and often personal, relationships that emerge from the texts from Ugarit. I prefer the position put forward recently in a major global and multi-period review of the archaeology of trading systems by Oka and Kusimba (2008) which sees traders being governed by social, political and ideological constraints as well as economic calculations.

Sometimes these merchants acted as agents for the state, by supplying pack animals for example in Rapanu's case, but also they put their own capital at risk. The scale of transactions they handled was impressive: one of Yabninu's documents records a consignment of 600 kg of tin – equivalent to 60% of the quantity found on the Uluburun wreck (Bell 2012). This should make us think twice about assuming that all metal-rich cargoes emanating from the Levant were necessarily royal.

Sherratt and Sherratt (2001) referred to the transformation of the economy from the palace to the hands of merchants as privatisation. The evidence from the texts of Ugarit suggests that this process was firmly underway before the end of the LBA and it is no longer feasible to envisage wholesale replacement of palace administered exchange with entrepreneurial trade at the beginning of the Iron Age. Although Phoenicia has so far not yielded a comparable body of texts to Ugarit, it is not unreasonable to assume that a similar relationship between the state and merchants may have existed at Phoenician ports, which were counterparties to, and destinations for, trade from Ugarit (Bell 2012). Furthermore, any regulatory influence the Egyptian imperial authorities had on the Phoenician ports is likely to have been relatively "light-touch" in the years between the battle of Kadesh and the end of the LBA as Egyptian control of coastal Lebanon appears to have been low (Sherratt 2003; Stieglitz 1990).

Arguably, therefore, what happened after the destructions that affected coastal cities both to the north and south of Phoenicia can be seen in terms of restructuring long distance relationships by concentrating on routes that continued to be both feasible and profitable. This included exporting both raw materials and manufactured goods that were locally sourced to acquire unavailable necessities such as copper and other metals and, in due course, exotic luxuries.

Shortly after 1200 BC, the merchants of Phoenicia would have had no need for direction from a higher authority to reshape the scope and geographical reach of their activities. Nor would such direction have been necessary to identify the products they could continue to trade. For example, Phoenicia would have had timber, olive oil, textiles and wine to exchange for copper from Cyprus. The archaeological evidence from Sarepta shows that manufacturing olive oil and purple dye continued, along with a major potting industry to manufacture the jars in which to ship its wine (Pritchard 1978). Sarepta's bronze industry also continued to function and, as well as being a supplier of copper, Cyprus was an ideal platform for western expansion for the Phoenicians.

It goes without saying that there is no hope of being able to address the evidence for this expansion to beyond the straits of Gibraltar without a finely resolved pottery sequence in the homeland (Gilboa *et al.* 2008, 192). Until recently, the main sources for dating Phoenician pottery were Patricia Bikai's volume on the pottery of Tyre (Bikai 1978) and her work on the Phoenician pottery of Cyprus (particularly Bikai 1983; 1987), together with William Anderson's publication on Sarepta (Anderson 1988).

EIA horizons from recent and ongoing excavations Beirut at Sidon have not been published yet and the evidence from the Tyre al-Bass cemetery are of relatively little use for dating purposes (Gilboa *et al.* 2008, 17). It is fortunate, therefore, that Tel Dor has furnished a superb ceramic sequence and dozens of absolute dates. Tel Dor has been excavated almost continuously since 1990 and was occupied between the Middle

Bronze Age II (MB II) and the Roman Period. Since 2003, excavations have been directed by Gilboa and Sharon, who have contributed many important articles to the question of Early Iron Age chronology (Gilboa & Sharon 2001; 2003; Gilboa 2005 and Gilboa *et al.* 2008). Tel Dor has yielded a detailed ceramic sequence (including imports) from reliable contexts in substantial EIA exposures. Moreover, extensive radiometric dating has been carried out, making Dor the ideal Levantine case study for this earliest Iron Age period (Gilboa *et al.* 2008, 117). For a site located in the heartland of the Biblical narrative, relating the ceramic sequence, for groups of wares, to absolute chronology, rather than tenuous historical connections, is a major breakthrough (Gilboa *et al.* 2008, 117). The fact that these ceramic groups travel far by ship and are the markers of early Phoenician trade activity makes the Dor data unique.

Historically, Dor was considered to be part of the territory of the "Sea Peoples", specifically that of the Šikila (Gilboa *et al.* 2008, 114), based mainly on the 11th century BC "*Story of Wenamun*" and the "*Onomasticon of Amenope*", which dates to the end of the 12th–beginning of the 11th century BC (Stern 1990), both being Egyptian sources. This conventional wisdom contrasts strongly with the archaeological evidence from the now extensive excavations of this horizon, which appears to be early Phoenician (Stern 1990). The excavators describe the material culture as having a marked continuity with previous Canaanite traits, with some Cypriot input (Gilboa *et al.* 2008, 117) and characterise the town as a "thriving urban center in this period of general decline" with commercial contacts in Cyprus, Egypt, Philistia and possibly Syria. Petrographic evidence from Cyprus identifies the Carmel Coast as the place of manufacture of Phoenician commercial containers in this period (Gilboa *et al.* 2008), confirming the involvement of this southern part of Phoenicia in trade.

The stratigraphic sequence of Dor parallels those of Sarepta and Tyre (Gilboa *et al.* 2008) in this period. From the point of view of determining the timing of trading contacts with Cyprus and Spain, Gilboa, Sharon and Boaretto published an important article that concentrates on small decorated Phoenician containers and commercial jars (the former being much better chronological indicators than the latter).

Figure 5.2 shows a synthesis of the chronology of the stratigraphic and pottery phases for key Phoenician sites in Lebanon. This figure also includes the Cypriot sequence in order to assist in pinpointing the earliest arrival of Iron Age Phoenician wares there. In the interest of brevity, I will only be able to mention some of the earliest relevant Phoenician finds in Cyprus (and I will not discuss the ceramic traffic going the other way from Cyprus to Phoenicia).

The LBA/EIA transition appears to be missing at Dor so far and the story must be taken up in Ir 1a (in the terminology of the excavators). A pre-Phoenician bichrome horizon has been identified at Dor that correlates in Cyprus to the LC IIIB and its transition to Cypro Geometric I (Gilboa *et al.* 2008, 130). The radiometric dates at Dor are slightly lower than the conventional date shown on Figure 5.2 of 1050 BC for the transition between the Ir 1a and Ir 1b (or LC IIIB and CG I by implication) but not

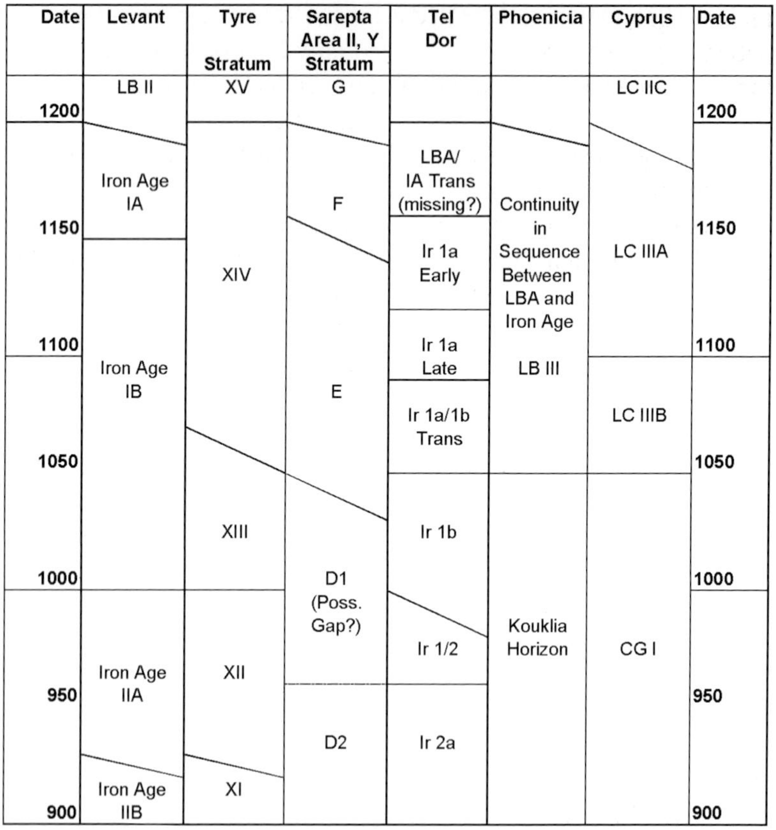
Date
Levant
Tyre
Stratum
Sarepta
Area II, Y
Stratum
Tel
Dor
Phoenicia
Cyprus
Date
LB II
XV
G
LC IIC
1200
1200
LBA/
IA Trans
(missing?)
Iron Age
IA
F
Continuity
in
Sequence
Between
LBA and
Iron Age
1150
1150
Ir 1a
Early
LC IIIA
XIV
1100
1100
Ir 1a
Late
Iron Age
IB
LB III
E
Ir 1a/1b
Trans
LC IIIB
1050
1050
XIII
Ir 1b
1000
1000
D1
(Poss.
Gap?)
Kouklia
Horizon
Ir 1/2
CG I
Iron Age
IIA
XII
950
950
D2
Ir 2a
Iron Age
IIB
XI
900
900

Fig. 5.2. Chronological chart. Source: Mazar (1993, 30) for the Levant; Nunez (2004, 286, fig. 138) for Tyre, Phoenicia, Cyprus and the Aegean post-1100 BC; Anderson (1988, 422–423) for Sarepta; Gilboa & Sharon (2003, 55, table 21) for Tel Dor and Tyre pre-1100 BC; Steel (2004, 13, table 1.1) for Cyprus pre-1100 BC.

radically so (somewhere in the third quarter of the eleventh century BC) (Gilboa *et al.* 2008, 184).

Gilboa *et al.* (2008, 131) have made the point that, for some reason, this earliest Iron Age phase is left out from discussions on Phoenician pottery in Cyprus, which normally start with the appearance of Phoenician Bichrome and the onset of the Kouklia Horizon. At Dor, this earliest horizon marks the appearance of a few small closed containers (mainly flasks, but also jars), that are decorated mainly with concentric circles and which are descendants of LBA antecedents (Gilboa *et al.* 2008, 124–125). A parallel is made with regard to this early phase to a flask found in Kouklia-*Xerolimini* Tomb 9 in the Palaepaphos region of Cyprus (Gilboa *et al.* 2008, 131; fig 5, 128). It is relatively safe to deduce, therefore, that the first stage of Iron Age of Phoenician maritime trade involves Cyprus before the end of LC III. By Ir 1b period, these small beginnings have developed into a "geographically limited but intensive Cypro-Phoenician interaction sphere" (Gilboa *et al.* 2008, 190).

Palaepaphos, on the west coast of Cyprus, is unique within the Cypriot archaeological record because of the continuity of this site from LC IIIB into the CG I period, being neither destroyed, abandoned nor transferred to another site (Maier 1999). It has also proved to be a crucial site with regard to the identification of early Phoenician imports. Prior to the discovery of the tombs at Palaepaphos-*Skales* in 1979 (excavated by Karageorghis and published in 1983), it was generally believed that Tyre and Sidon had not begun their westward expansion until the 9th century, at the earliest (Bikai 1994) with a traditional date for the founding of the colony of Kition of 830–810 BC (Miles 2010, xiii). The excavations Palaepaphos-*Skales* pushed the date at which meaningful quantities of Phoenician pottery appear in Cyprus earlier by two centuries. Palaepaphos' other name, Kouklia, gives its name to the earliest horizon of Phoenician overseas ceramic exports and is sometimes referred to as a pre-colonisation period (Gilboa *et al.* 2008, 118).

I have presented elsewhere (Bell 2009) the evidence Bikai put forward for parallels between storage jars at Palaepaphos-Skales and Tyre and Sarepta, in the earliest Iron Age and noted her striking comments about the similarity between these jars and their likely origin (Bikai 1983). All the evidence from Palaepaphos, unfortunately, currently comes from tombs and we must hope for some excavation of the settlement in due course.

I have also argued elsewhere that commercial contacts between Phoenicia and Cyprus, particularly with the west of the island, may have endured across the LBA/Iron Age disruption (Bell 2009). This accords with Bikai's view but, as Karageorghis (2008) has pointed out, we do not have firm evidence for this in Cyprus itself yet.

Back on the mainland, at Sarepta, Cypriot ceramic imports continue in Stratum F and include LCII and LC III wares as well as, in all probability Mycenaean IIIC style deep bowls manufactured on the island (Anderson 1988, 390). Although these strata mark a low ebb in the ceramic imports at Sarepta (Gilboa & Sharon 2003, 51), there is nevertheless evidence of continuity of contact with Cyprus.

Moving westwards, prior to the excavations at Kommos in southern Crete, the earliest evidence of Phoenician pottery in Crete came from Knossos, with the discovery of Phoenician jugs dating to approximately 800 BC (Bikai 2000). Early in the excavation of the Greek sanctuary area of Kommos, fragments of Phoenician pottery were recognised and Patricia Bikai was invited to write the short chapter thereon in the excavation report, which was published in 2000. The majority of the sherds had the characteristics of the Phoenician coast (soft fabric with many also having soft red ferrous inclusions). Bikai remarked that the number of Phoenician vessels that found their way to this area of Kommos was not high. She also noted that the fragmentary material recovered at Kommos would have hardly been noticed at a mainland site and it is a credit to the excavators that they were noticed at all (Bikai 2000, 310).

Unfortunately, as well as being fragmented, the assemblage at Kommos consists of storage jar sherds which, as already noted, are less useful for precise dating. For the period that concerns us here, some of the storage jar handle fragments found are of interest. Bikai (Bikai 2000, 308) cites similarities between one of these (cat. no 5: Bikai 2000, 310; pl. 4.63), with an inscription with a finger impression at the base of the handle, which has parallels in Tyre Stratum XIII (in the first half of the 11th century). It is impossible to deduce the form of this jar, but Bikai has cited parallels from Tyre (Stratum XV: 1200–1050 BC) or Palaepaphos-*Skales* Tomb 49 (1050–950 BC) that also have handles with incised marks (Bikai 2000, 308). The context at Kommos in which they were found is that in the first layer of reoccupation after the Minoan levels and the occupation gap at the site lowers the earliest possible date to about 925 BC (Bikai 2000, 310) – right at the end of the period under consideration in this paper.

Several rim sherds with incised bands below the rim were also found, that date to 920–880 BC approximately – the earliest phase of this temple. Parallels between these sherds and ones from Sarepta (unfortunately, from a disturbed context) led Bikai to suggest that the workshop that produced the Kommos jars was Sarepta and she mentions Anderson's hypothesis that Sarepta (with its substantial pottery industry) was the packaging branch of Sarepta Inc (Bikai 2000, 309). Be that as it may, the Kommos excavations pushed back the date at which the earliest Phoenician pottery appears on Crete by a century to around 900 BC. Prophetically, Bikai stated that it was only a matter of time before earlier Phoenician wares were found in the west (which then stood at 800 BC at Huelva) and it is to the evidence from Spain that we must now finally turn.

The Greek and Roman historical tradition puts the initiation of Phoenician expansion to the far west at the late 12th century BC (Neville 2007, 1) with the foundation of Gadir (modern Cadiz) and Lixus (in Morocco). Until rescue excavations were conducted in Huelva, in Southern Spain, however, there was no incontrovertible proof of Phoenician settlement anywhere near as early as this in the Atlantic and Western Mediterranean (Neville 2007; Gonzales de Canales *et al.* 2009).

The location of Huelva, close to the Riotinto polymetallic ore deposits, was no doubt of great interest to the Phoenicians, notably as an embarkation port for iron, silver, gold and copper. Like so many other Phoenician sites, it remains occupied to the present day, being such good harbour. The oldest Phoenician finds come from 7–13 Méndez Nuñez Street/12 Las Monjas Square which excavations were undertaken during 1998 in the old city of Huelva. Due to issues with the water table, pumping was necessary to get to levels earlier than the late 8th century BC. Some 8009 diagnostic sherds were catalogued (about 9% of those collected; Gonzalez de Canales *et al.* 2008) and, after limiting the count to rim and base fragments, Phoenician sherds represented 3233 sherds compared with 3000 local fabrics (Gonzalez de Canales *et al.* 2009). Gonzalez de Canales and colleagues then proceeded to analyse these Phoenician sherds armed with Bikai's work on Tyre and the Phoenician horizons of

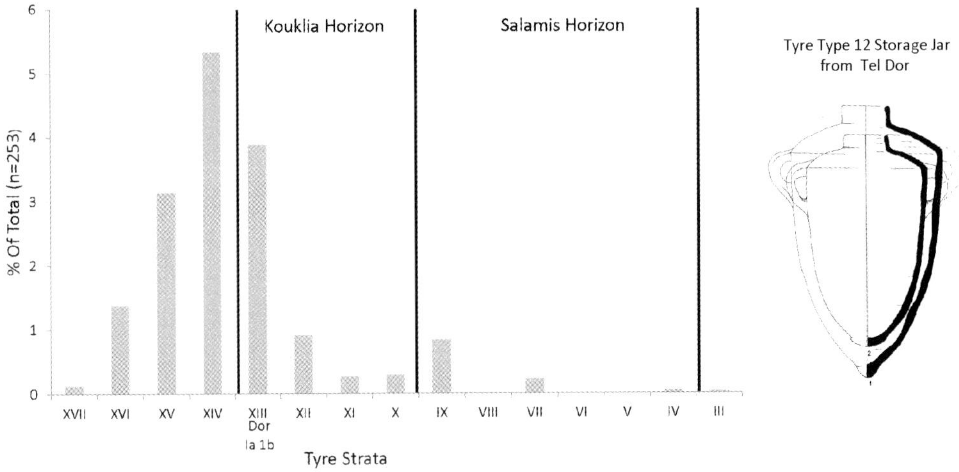

Fig. 5.3. Chronological distribution of Tyre Type 12 Storage Jars at Tyre. Source: *Bikai (1978, 44 table 10A); Gilboa & Sharon (2003, fig. 4: 1 and 2).*

Cyprus (Bikai 1978; 1987) together with Anderson's work on the Sarepta sequence (Anderson 1988).

Two points stand out about the Huelva finds from this earliest context. The first is that the excavators recognised many similarities between the ceramics of Huelva and those of Tyre (Gonzalez de Canales *et al.* 2008, 634) accepting the colour changes brought about through the action of the water table at Huelva. They assigned the majority of the Phoenician ceramics to the Salamis horizon (Strata IX–IV at Tyre), which comes after the end of the Kouklia Horizon and the period under consideration in this paper. However, they did attribute some of the Phoenician wares to the Kouklia Horizon (Tyre Strata XIII–X: 1050–900 BC, see Figure 5.2).

Such examples were few in number but included examples of the Tyre Type 12 Storage Jar, of which 11 examples were found at Huelva. This type of jar is virtually unknown in Tyre after Stratum IX and drops off very substantially in quantity after Stratum XIII (Gonzalez de Canales *et al.* 2006; Bikai 1978, table 10A). Figure 5.3 charts the appearance of this type of jar at Tyre to illustrate this point.

Moreover, the Huelva Type 12 Storage Jars are practically identical to those at Dor where they are prolific in Ir 1a, present in Ir 1b and are virtually absent thereafter (Gilboa & Sharon 2003, 48 table 17), which is consistent with the tail off in this vessel at Tyre after Stratum XIII.

Only three radiocarbon dates have been determined from this horizon at Huelva (on cattle bones) and these suggest a range of 1000–820 cal BC, with the weighted average of the three dates being 930–830 BC (Gonzales de Canales *et al.* 2009). Overall, the excavators date the beginning of the stratum excavated at Huelva to about 900

BC, without excluding the possibility that it could have begun in the closing decades of the 10th century BC.

The second point I should like to make is that, unlike the situation at Kommos, a substantial quantity of Phoenician material was recovered at Huelva, even if most of it dates to slightly later periods than concerns us here. This argues for a significant early contact between Huelva and Phoenicia.

Casting our minds back to Cyprus briefly, the concentration of earlier Phoenician finds in the Kouklia (Palaepaphos), and the possibility that some of the pottery at Kommos and even as far west as Huelva comes from the Kouklia Horizon, suggests that the Phoenicians used Western Cyprus as a staging post for westward voyages.

Having summarised the so far "known knowns" about Phoenician maritime trade expansion towards the west in this earliest period, I shall now turn to the "known unknowns" (Rumsfeld 2002). What do know that we do not know and how might we address these issues?

First, we do not have a good enough sequence from the central Levantine heartland across the LBA/Iron Age transition. We only have the meticulous but relatively limited excavations at Sarepta, which was not one of the leading cities at this time, albeit it did have a substantial industrial activity and its fair share of imported goods. Unfortunately, Stratum XIV at Tyre is far too long and undifferentiated to be used to resolve issues of continuity across the LBA/IA transition and Gilboa and Sharon (2003, 44) have also raised issues about the recording of this sequence. Meanwhile, the LBA/IA transitional horizon seems to be missing so far at Tel Dor (Gilboa & Sharon 2003, 44).

In Cyprus, of course, the evidence from funerary contexts from Kouklia/Palaepaphos is later, as is that so far published from the Tyre al-Bass cemetery. We must await the publication of the results of the most recent season which was undertaken in 2008–2009 at Tyre al-Bass.

Further excavations of settlement contexts both in Phoenicia and Cyprus – particularly the west of the island would be an important step forward in addressing this question. We must hope that Claude Doumet-Serhal's Sidon excavations find the earliest Iron Age, but it is possible, given the limited extent of these excavations, they may not. The best opportunity to clarify this sequence in the Phoenician homeland in the near term may come on the "island" of Tyre where Maria Eugenia Aubet and her colleagues have recently been asked by the Lebanese authorities to work close to Bikai's excavations (M.°E. Aubet, pers. comm. May 2012). Tel Dor may also yield something but perhaps a return to Sarepta for an extensive campaign would be appropriate, given that this site has not been overbuilt since the 1970s excavations finished? The excavation of a settlement context at Palaepaphos would also be invaluable (although that site, like Sidon, Arwad and much of Tyre, suffers from current occupation).

Logistically, the Phoenicians must have called at several ports en route to Huelva but so far, I am not aware of any ceramic evidence west of Kommos that dates to this earliest period. I have not mentioned Italy, but that must be another fruitful area for enquiry, particularly Sicily and Sardinia. A theme that emerged at a conference in 2010 in Cyprus on cooking pots, drinking cups, loomweights and ethnicity in Bronze Age Cyprus and neighbouring regions was that more and more Italian pottery is being recognised (e.g. Charaf 2012) suggesting a greater degree of interaction with the Central Mediterranean than hitherto thought during this period. There is no break in Sardinia's connections with the Eastern Mediterranean across the LBA/EIA transition and the Nuragic culture continues (Dyson & Rowland 2007, 102). There is no evidence of permanent Phoenician settlements on the island this early, but it is nevertheless possible that it served as a stopping off point *en route* to Iberia.

It is also possible that new research on North African coastline may yield some insights, for example Linda Hulin's Western Marmarica Coastal Survey in Libya, east of Tobruk (which was initiated in 2008).

Having discussed the data, and the lack thereof, it is appropriate to conclude briefly with some methodological challenges and opportunities. Recent developments in the far west and at Tel Dor provide grounds for optimism about the integration of ceramic sequences from the Levant to Atlantic Spain, alongside a few absolute dates. This is a necessary first step when tackling broader questions about trade, especially the motivation behind such an expansion and the degree to which the Phoenicians put down permanent roots over time beyond the homeland in this earliest, and text-free, phase.

One of the reasons for selecting this subject for inclusion in this volume is, like the LBA merchants of Ugarit, the part Phoenicians played is often overlooked in broader syntheses of the region in the first half of the 1st millennium BC in favour of discussions of what went on in more conventional empires from which texts, mercifully, do exist. While this conference's stated objectives refer by name to Assyria, Babylonia, Persia and Egypt, I am most grateful to the organisers for granting the Phoenicians their seat at the table. Not only were they the prime-movers in long distance maritime trade of manufactured goods and raw materials in the Early Iron Age but also they transmitted arguably two of the most useful technologies to come out of the Eastern Mediterranean and Levant: an alphabetic script and the knowledge of iron working (even if they did not invent the latter technology).

Sherratt and Sherratt (1993) suggested that breakthroughs in the production and working of iron in Cyprus in the 12th century BC spread along the old trade routes that were used to supply copper and tin. I would contend that the Phoenicians certainly played their part in keeping some of these routes alive in the aftermath of the destructions at the close of the LBA. Papasavvas (2003) has put forward the argument that Cyprus continued to be an active copper producer and exporter after the end of LC IIC (or the destruction of Ugarit). Certainly, the material culture of the island is rich in terms of bronze in LC IIIB–CG II period, as evidenced by the bronze tripods found in graves at Palaepaphos-*Skales* and Kourion-*Kaloriziki* (*ibid.*) at the western end of the island, with which Phoenicia had contact. Interestingly, also, evidence from the Palaepaphos-*Eliomylia* tomb suggests a pioneering role of this site in western Cyprus in adoption of iron for tools (Karageorghis 1990, 84).

Perhaps the nature of Phoenicia's political structure, based on the city rather than being a unitary state, lies behind the difficulty in conceptualising these early stages of if its expansion? Perhaps the fact that this expansion seems to have been, on the whole, friendly and not aimed at gaining territorial control or agricultural resources to satisfy demographic constraints (with the possible exception of the expansion south towards Tel Dor in Israel)? Instead, it appears that Phoenicians inserted themselves at key points in the supply chain, without seeking to control the whole chain by conquest or colonisation (Braudel 1984, 65).

The only visible means of payment for the acquisition of metals that definitely originated from the Phoenician homeland are the decorated containers and storage jars and, presumably, their contents. In terms of landfall, Phoenicians looked for compact settlement areas with natural borders that were easy to defend, such as an island or a spit of land jutting out to sea, with good harbours and access to resource rich hinterlands (Niemeyer 1990). The initial Phoenician strategy with regard to Cyprus seems to have been motivated by trade, particularly with the west of the island and the first Phoenician colony to be confirmed by archaeology on the island, Kition, is not established until the 9th century BC (Aubet 1993, 42).

Most recent scholarship would certainly place the exciting evidence from the early context at Huelva firmly in a pre-colonial setting (e.g. Gonzalez de Canales *et al.* 2009). Nor can this initial contact with the far west be tied to the later neo-Assyrian demand, with menaces, for iron and bullion that emerged at the time of Tiglatpileser III (Aubet 2008; 1993, 46). Perhaps the initial voyages to the west were driven only by the need to acquire metals for domestic consumption or onward trade with others?

The study of economic interactions is beset by a number of theoretical oppositions (usually ending in –ism). I have mentioned in passing substantivism and formalism and how the activities of the merchants of Ugarit, as recorded in texts, appear more complex than either of these two oppositions can accommodate. Trade on their own account was possible, but this was surely governed by social norms.

Another feature of the development of Phoenicia in this period is one of gradual rather than abrupt change and one of the challenges for archaeologists is to obtain data that are sufficiently fine-grained to detect this. An abrupt end is undoubtedly what happened to prosperous Ugarit, Alalakh and Emar on the important tin route from the Euphrates to the Mediterranean. Phoenicia did not suffer the same abrupt end, nor even the temporary disruption experienced elsewhere in the Levant at the close of the Bronze Age. Things were really never that dark in Phoenicia, even if the quantity of imports from Cyprus did drop for a time. The merchants, and perhaps the leaders, of the Phoenician city states knew what to do to keep trade flowing.

On the subject of the measurement of the volume of trade and interaction, archaeologists do not always succeed in differentiating between the importance of a handful of imported sherds and material quantities thereof (perhaps the collective noun for sherds should be shedloads)! Finding a way of measuring the intensity of trade, and how this changes through time, must be a priority. Given the nature of the material record, this will inevitably result in an even greater focus on ceramics than is healthy, so we must beware the pots = people equation and hope for help from the scientific disciplines and for architectural and other evidence of lifeways from settlement contexts.

The European academic establishment in general, and archaeology in particular, is facing a difficult time with regard to funding research projects at the moment, which I know only too well from my vantage point as Treasurer of the British School at Athens. In crisis years such as these, the drive is on to make all research in the humanities and social sciences count with a growing emphasis on funding multidisciplinary, cross regional and scientific research to the detriment of stand-alone excavation projects. This publication and the workshop that inspired it are prime examples of this trend. Ironically, such collaborative approaches can only help in uncovering the steps through which the Phoenicians rose to such prominence from the ashes of that other economic crisis at the end of the 2nd millennium BC.

Acknowledgements
I should like to thank Juan Carlos Moreno García, the Université Charles-de-Gaulle and the European Science Foundation for organising the workshop whose proceedings this publication documents and for inviting me to participate. This contribution is based largely on work carried out while taking up a Tytus Fellowship at the University of Cincinnati in 2010, for which I thank that university very much.

Bibliography

Anderson, W. (1988) *Sarepta I: The Late Bronze and Iron Age Strata of Area II, Y*, Beyrouth.
Aubet, M. (1993) *The Phoenicians and the West*, Cambridge.
Aubet, M. (2008) Political and economic implications of the new Phoenician chronologies. In C. Sargona (ed.), *Beyond the Homeland: Markers in Phoenician Chronology* (Ancient Near Eastern Studies Supplement 28), 247–259, Leuven.
Bell, C. (2006) *The Evolution of Long Distance Trading Relationships across the LBA/Iron Age Transition on the Northern Levantine Coast: Crisis, Continuity and Change* (BAR S1574), Oxford.
Bell, C. (2009) Continuity and change: the divergent destinies of LBA ports in Syria and Lebanon across the LBA/Iron Age Transition". In C. Bachhuber & G. Roberts (eds), *Forces of Transformation: The End of the Bronze Age in the Mediterranean*, 180–187, Oxford.
Bell, C. (2012) The merchants of Ugarit. Oligarchs of the LBA trade in metals? In V. Kassianidou & G. Papasavvas (eds), *Eastern Mediterranean Metallurgy and Metalwork in the Second Millennium BC*, 180–187, Oxford.
Bikai, P. (1978). *The Pottery of Tyre*, Warminster.
Bikai, P. (1983) The imports from the East. In V. Karageorghis (ed.), *Palaepaphos-Skales: an Iron Age cemetery in Cyprus*, 396–406, Konstanz.
Bikai, C. (1987) *The Phoenician Pottery of Cyprus*, Nicosia.
Bikai, C. (1994) The Phoenicians in Cyprus. In V. Karageorghis (ed.), *Cyprus in the 11th Century B.C.*, 177–188, Nicosia.

Bikai, C. (2000) Phoenician ceramics in the Greek sanctuary. In J. M. Shaw & M. Shaw, *Kommos IV*, 302–312, Princeton.

Braudel, F. (1984) *The Perspective of the World. Civilization & Capitalism 15–18th Century*, Vol. 3, London.

Charaf, H. (2012) Over the hills and far away: handmade burnished ware and Mycenaean cooking pots at Tell Arqa (Lebanon). In V. Karageorghis & O. Kouka (eds.), *On Cooking Pots, Drinking Cups, Loomweights and Ethnicity in Bronze Age Cyprus and Neighbouring Regions*, 203–218, Nicosia.

Dyson, S. & R. Rowland (2007) *Archaeology and History of Sardinia from the Stone Age to the Middle Ages. Shepherds, Sailors, and Conquerors*, Philadelphia.

Gilboa, A. (2005) Sea peoples and Phoenicians along the southern Phoenician coast – a reconciliation: an interpretation of Sikila (SKL) material culture, *Bulletin of the American School of Oriental Research* 337: 47–78.

Gilboa, A. & I. Sharon (2001) Early Iron Age radicometric dates from Tel Dor. Preliminary implications for Phoenicia, and beyond, *Radiocarbon* 43/3: 1343–1351.

Gilboa, A. & I. Sharon (2003) An archaeological contribution to the Early Iron Age chronological debate: alternative chronologies for Phoenicia and their effects on the Levant, Cyprus, and Greece, *Bulletin of the American School of Oriental Research* 323: 7–80.

Gilboa, A., I. Sharon & E. Boaretto (2008) Tel Dor and the chronology of Phoenician "pre-colonisation" stages. In C. Sargona (ed.), *Beyond the Homeland: Markers in Phoenician Chronology* (Ancient Near Eastern Studies Supplement 28), 113–204, Leuven.

González de Canales, F., L. Serrano & J. Llompart (2006) The pre-colonial Phoenician emporium of Huelva ca 900–770 BC, *BABesch* 81: 13–19.

González de Canales, F., I. Serrano & E. Boaretto (2008) The emporium of Huelva and Phoenician chronology: present and future possibilities. In C. Sargona (ed.), *Beyond the Homeland: Markers in Phoenician Chronology* (Ancient Near Eastern Studies Supplement 28), 631–655, Leuven.

González de Canales, F., I. Serrano & J. Llompart (2009) Two phases of Phoenician colonisation. Beyond the Huelva finds, *Ancient West and East* 8: 1–20.

Karageorghis, V. (ed.) (1983) *Palaepaphos-Skales: an Iron Age Cemetery in Cyprus*, Konstanz.

Karageorghis, V. (1990) *Tombs at Palaepaphos. 1. Teratsudhia 2. Eliomylia*, Nicosia.

Karageorghis, V. (2008) Les Phéniciens à Chypre. In C. Doumet-Serhal (ed.), *Networking Patterns of the Bronze and Iron Age Levant. The Lebanon and its Mediterranean Connections*, 189–214, Beirut.

Kopcke, G. (1992) What role for Phoenicians? In G. Kopcke & I. Tokumaru (eds), *Greece Between East and West: 10th–8th centuries BC*, 103–113, Mainz.

Lehmann, G. (2008) North Syria and Cilicia. In C. Sargona (ed.), *Beyond the Homeland: Markers in Phoenician Chronology* (Ancient Near Eastern Studies Supplement 28), 205–246, Leuven.

Maier, F.-G. (1999). Palaipaphos and the transition to the Early Iron Age: continuities, discontinuities and location shifts. In M. Iacovou & D. Michaelides (eds), *Cyprus: The Historicity of the Geometric Horizon*, 79–94, Nicosia.

Markoe, G. (2000) *Phoenicians*, London.

Mazar, A. (1993) *Archaeology of the Land of the Bible*, Cambridge.

McGeough, K. (2007) *Exchange Relationships at Ugarit* (Ancient Near Eastern Studies Supplement 26), Leuven.

Miles, R. (2010) *Carthage Must be Destroyed. The Rise and Fall of an Ancient Civilization*, London.

Monroe, C. (2009a) *Scales of Fate, Trade, Tradition and Transformation in the Eastern Mediterranean ca. 1350–1175 BCE* (Alter Orient und Altes Testament Band 357), Münster.

Monroe, C. (2009b) Seeing the world, *Bulletin of the American Schools of Oriental Research* 356: 81–87.

Neville, A. (2007) *Mountains of Silver and Rivers of Gold. The Phoenicians in Iberia* (University of British Columbia Studies in the Ancient World 1), Oxford.

Niemeyer. H.-G. (1990) The Phoenicians in the Mediterranean. Between expansion and colonisation: a non-Greek model of overseas settlement and colonisation, *Descœudres:* 469–489.

Nuñez Calvo, F. (2004) Preliminary Report on the Ceramics. In M. Aubet (ed.), *The Phoenician Cemetery of Tyre-Al Bass. Excavations 1997-1999* (BAAL Hors Serie), 281–373, Beirut.
Nuñez Calvo, F. (2008) Phoenicia. In C. Sagona (ed.), *Beyond the Homeland: Markers in Phoenician Chronology* (Ancient Near Eastern Studies Supplement 28), 19–95, Leuven.
Oka, R. & C. Kusimba (2008) The archaeology of trading systems, part 1: towards a new trade synthesis, *Journal of Archaeological Research* 16: 339–395.
Papasavvas, G. (2003) Cypriot casting technology I: the stands, *Report of the Department of Antiquities Cyprus*, 23–52.
Pritchard, J. (1978) *Recovering Sarepta. A Phoenician City*, Princeton.
Rumsfeld, D. (2002) White House Press Briefing 12 February, 2002.
Sherratt, A. & S. Sherratt (1993) The growth of the Mediterranean economy in the Early First Millennium, *World Archaeology* 24/3: 361–378.
Sherratt, A. & S. Sherratt (2001) Technological change in the East Mediterranean Bronze Age: capital, resources and marketing. In A. Shortland (ed.), *The Social Context of Technological Change: Egypt and the Near East, 1650-1550 B.C.*, 15–38, Oxford.
Sherratt, S. (2003) Visible writing: questions script and identity in Early Iron Age Greece and Cyprus, *Oxford Journal of Archaeology* 22/3: 225–242.
Steel, L. (2004) *Cyprus Before History. From the Earliest Settlers to the End of the Bronze Age*, London.
Stern, E. (1990) New evidence from Dor for the first appearance of the Phoenicians along the northern coast of Israel, *Bulletin of the American School of Oriental Research* 279: 27–34.
Stieglitz, R. (1990) The geopolitics of the Phoenician littoral in the Early Iron Age, *Bulletin of the American Schools of Oriental Research* 190: 9–12.
Van de Mieroop, M. (2007) *The Eastern Mediterranean in the Age of Ramesses II*, Oxford.
Vella, N. (1996) Elusive Phoenicians, *Antiquity* 70: 245–250

Chapter 6

The contribution of pottery production in reconstructing aspects of local rural economy at the northern frontier of the Neo-Assyrian Empire

Anacleto D'Agostino

Introduction

The analysis of changes to the archaeological remains of ancient societies can provide a valuable means of observing the impact of empires upon the social, political and ideological development of a region (Matthews 2003, 127–154). In particular, the material evidence, when read in conjunction with the written record, can reveal much about the economic profile of a region and the way in which that profile was determined and altered by the needs and demands of newcomers and the interaction between local and external components of that society.

The contribution of pottery studies to the topic of this volume, "Dynamics of production and economic interaction in the near East in the first half of the 1st millennium BC", has been noticeably marginal but can shed some light on aspects of the basic economic setting of the territories at the northern edge of the Assyrian controlled area. This state of neglect is due in part to the fact that excavation at the northern frontier of the Assyrian controlled area has so far failed to produce meaningful evidence of ceramic manufacturing processes and contexts. For instance, no pottery workshops have been identified and the organization of the pottery production remains basically obscure. In addition, systematic research on clay sources and mineral/chemical compositions of vessels has not been undertaken or, at best, is limited to restricted sample groups. Ascertaining the distribution patterns of the main categories of vessels, where the vertical and horizontal sequences can be sketched in outline only, is also difficult. As things stand, the study of pottery as potential indicator of the changing economic fabric of the region is drastically reduced but however productive in terms of alternative evidence next to, the traditional interpretative tools as texts, architectures and seals.

Generally the quantity of pottery sherds is remarkable when compared with other categories of finds and their presence, not only in stratified contexts but also on the surface of non-excavated sites, makes them one of the most reliable tools for characterizing the material production of these specific geographical areas. As well as providing material evidence of the daily activities performed in household contexts, pottery is also a primary product of certain manufacturing facilities that produced items for the locality and sometimes markets further afield. Thus, the value of studying sherds lies not just in what they tell us about everyday life and practices but also, by analyzing the regional ceramic profile, they can provide useful information about the wider features of the local economy, definitely of secondary aspects of it compared with other main activities. Although it is fair to say that in terms of economic income the production of pottery for daily purposes was not the main priority of a village or family – there existed other more basic and main concerns such as agriculture and animal husbandry – the manufacture of ceramics was, nevertheless, an integral part of the economic life of the settlement and as such would have been responsive to external constraints affecting the local economic system as a whole. As one of the key material indicators of this phenomenon, the study pottery should, in theory at least, provide us with additional information about the impact of Assyria's hegemony over its subject populations, broadening the documentary basis we have in hands.

How can aspects of the economy be revealed by the archaeological record? Changes in the archaeological profile of some settlements allow us to formulate hypotheses about changes in social systems and economic strategies. Indeed, socioeconomic factors combined with certain modes of craft production and transmission may act as critical conditions both for fixing technological traits and explaining change in material culture (Roux 2008, 83–84).

Since houses and households formed one of the primary focuses of local economic activity, the objects utilised within these contexts assume certain relevance when defining the modalities by which basic economic agencies operated. The organisation of ceramic production, domestic or otherwise, would have formed part of the production and distribution of goods that were possibly controlled or administrated by ruling elites and local leaders. In the case of Assyria, its territorial expansion during the 1st millennium BC resulted in the adaptation and transformation of different economic areas within an integrated and centrally administered system of control. These changes doubtlessly affected the economic environment for the manufacture of pottery. conditioning potters activity and local demand.

The purpose of the present article is to explore how the archaeological record can contribute to our knowledge of the economic organisation of the northern regions at the time of Neo-Assyrian Empire.[1] In doing so particular attention will be shown to the evidence for wheel- and hand-shaped techniques in pottery production as well as the presence of certain types of vessel distributed over the region.

Brief geographical description of the northern territories and historical background for the 1st millennium BC

The geographical setting of our investigation encompasses the area between northeastern Syria and southeastern Turkey, namely the upper catchment of the Khabur river, part of the Jezirah plains and the Upper Tigris valley, at the foot of the Tauros Mountains (Fig. 6.1). Situated within the wider region of the Upper Mesopotamia and South-eastern Anatolia, the plains of the Khabur and the valley of the Tigris River represent two different types of landscape. The Jezirah is a large undulating alluvial plain, extending across northeastern Syria, northern Iraq and southeastern Anatolia whereas the Tigris valley is a narrow valley cut by the river between the foothills of the eastern Tauros ranges. Although fertile soils and good agricultural productivity are the hallmarks of these regions, each area differs significantly from the other in terms of climatic regime, ecology and relative harvest success. These environmental differences pose obvious challenges to any like-for-like comparison, a task that is made even more difficult by the highly fragmentary condition of the archaeological evidence. Only a few key-sites provide us with stratified levels dating to the first part of the 1st millennium and of these most show limited diversity in terms of function with the result that one suspects that the sample provides a very incomplete understanding of the rural settlement pattern for both areas.

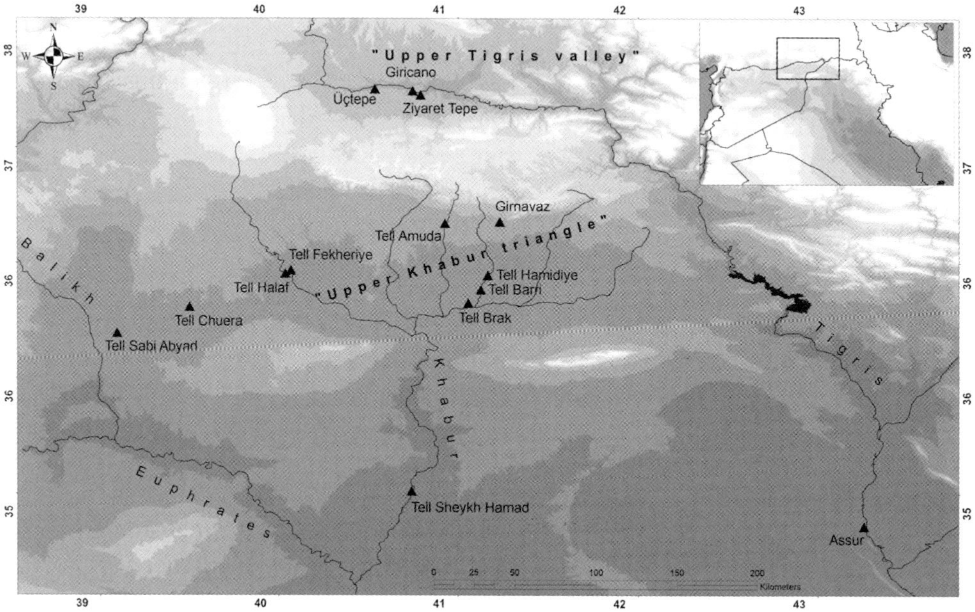

Fig. 6.1. The Upper Khabur and the Upper Tigris with location of some sites mentioned in the text (M. Raccidi).

The Khabur plains are separated from the Tigris valley by the Tur Abdin mountains. However, this natural east-west boundary does not appear to have acted as a serious obstacle to communication between the two areas. Several tracks and paths pass through the range following the courses of small rivers and streams that flow in opposite directions, towards north and south (Radner 2006, 277; Ponchia 2004). The interconnections among people living on both sides of the mountains were probably active over the course of many centuries, a fact that is strongly reflected by a shared cultural heritage and dimorphic social system typical of the great part of Upper Mesopotamia and southeastern Anatolia. Communities of sedentary farmers, semi-nomadic and nomadic shepherds were co-players in this cultural development and it was the changes in balance of these social components that arguably triggered the historical and political events at the turn of the millennium.

Both textual and archaeological evidence suggest that the plains of the northern Jazirah and the valley of the Tigris river, north of the Tur Abdin, had been the target of Assyrian expansionism for centuries and were initially incorporated into the Assyrian system of political and economic control at the time of the first Middle Assyrian expansion and again later during the so-called Neo-Assyrian "re-conquest" in the 1st millennium BC (Liverani 1988; Radner 2006, 72, 113–118) when the region became primary focus of the foreign policy of the Assyrian kings. For the period between these two events, the historical sources suggest that the region enjoyed a level of autonomy characterized by the existence of both local well-established dominions, which probably continued to be loyal to Assur whilst possessing independent status (Kühne 1995, 77), and the formation of new polities such as Bit Bakhiani and Bit Zamani (Sader 2000, 68–76; Lipínski 2000a, 109–110; Matney 2010). At the turn of 1st millennium these regions were affected by far-reaching population movements that resulted in an influx of new settlers, farmers, semi-nomads, and pastoralists (Assyrians, Arameans, Mushki, Kasku and Urumu from Anatolia). This change gave rise to a complementary network of cities, fortified towns, new villages, farmsteads, and temporary campsites indicative of agricultural colonisation and the exploitation of natural resources (grazing land, animals, wooden, raw materials, etc.). The friction between the two parts, Assyrians and tribes – depending firstly on the changing capacity in force projection and efficiency of the Assyrian army to control and protect the net of communication and flow of goods – was alternate in the course of the time, and characterised by various vicissitudes until the Assyrian obtained the control of the region and the conquest was completed with the establishment of provinces. The effects of these events on the settlement system and material assemblages are fairly visible in the archaeological record. Notable features include the rise of urban centres, the growth of small sites spreading over the territory, the use of writing (indicative of the introduction of bureaucracy) and the appearance of new external elements of material culture in the form of ceramics, seals and other artefacts.

Ceramics as measure of changes between politics and tradition

The ubiquity of pots sherds, essentially representing the bulk of what we find in the field, should make them the basis of any investigation. The value of pottery for the study of regional economic trajectories is not at issue here and in this case can be shown to produce a useful snapshot of the basic production activities at work at the edges of the Assyrian Empire. Pottery is no longer considered almost exclusively as a tool for dating whereby changes in pottery types are related to chronological periods, but also as a key to social and economic organisation (Gaimster & Freestone 1997, 12). Pottery types can also be an indicator of the specific distribution of populations or cultural uniformity between different groups as well as a measure of changes arising in accordance with external influences. In fact the production and distribution of material culture, even utilitarian goods such as ceramics, are often affected by political changes whereby centralised political systems act to control the production and distribution of goods that serve both political and economic ends (Sinopoli 1991, 159; Matthews 2003, 144–145). Modes of ceramic production, including the technological and manufacturing processes, the organisation and scale of manpower, and the relationship of pottery making to the physical environment are all subject to changes in political power and the shifting economic priorities of complex societies.

Additionally, pottery types and decorative styles can often be means of social and cultural expression, conveying messages of affiliation and identity through self and group representation as well as the rank and status of the consumer within the context of social and political strategies performed by the community. There are other factors to consider too. For instance, the nature of the subsistence economy and the range of foodstuffs it produced would have determined the types of pots made and their uses. In many cases this functional feature emerges more clearly than others. Ceramics, like all material products of anthropic activity, are used and produced in a social context and are determined by it. In the local productive chain, forms of vessels and manufacturing techniques are passed down from generation to generation in a system of meaning and are replicated in order to meet the demands of users in accordance with tradition. As for the products used in routine activities such as the cooking and consumption of food, these items conform to a conservative form of production characterised by functionality and a tendency to shirk innovation and eccentricity. Most of these vessels remain largely unaltered over several centuries and only occasionally register political and cultural change. Non-utilitarian wares, on the other hand, tend to be more reactive to the needs of market and are therefore more prone to sudden modifications (Rice 1987, 460, 464). This model of a regional pottery repertoire as a heterogeneous set of traditional and new types has yet to be investigated in any depth in the case of the northern territories at the time of Assyrian Empire.

Networking Assyrian related and indigenous sites in the subjected territories

An overview of the main archaeological arguments is necessary in order to provide a general framework for the territories and the period under consideration. Field research concerning the rural settlement pattern of the Upper Jezirah provides us with little evidence. In fact systematic surveys of the Late Bronze–Iron Age period remains have either concentrated on very limited areas or are often too extensive with a focus on selected and mainly mounded sites. Moreover, the limited understanding of the ceramic repertoire of the so-called "Dark Centuries" represents a serious hindrance for dating surveyed sites and makes it hard to understand the stages of settlement development across the plains. However, despite all the evident distortions in the survey data caused by these factors, the generally accepted reconstruction of Iron Age settlement envisages a pattern of rural and dispersed occupation consisting of small, low-lying settlements or extensive lower towns (Wilkinson 2002; Wilkinson & Barbanes 2000). Between the end of the Late Bronze Age and the Middle Iron Age the distribution of sites appears to have remained substantially unaltered showing continuity of occupation and a significant increase in the number of small settlements dating to the Late Assyrian period. Smaller sites, like the villages, hamlets and farmsteads mentioned in textual records (Fales 1990), were scattered on the plains alongside watercourses and depended on a few large-sized urban centres.

Relatively better known are the large mound settlements of the Upper Khabur. However, while Late Bronze Age and Middle Iron Age levels have been found at various sites (Tell Fekheriyeh, Tell Hamidiye, Tell Amuda, Tell Brak, Tell Mohammed Diyab, Tell Aqab), the excavations were not extensive enough to reveal consistent stratified deposits or coherent contexts for the transitional period in question. Thus far, remains dating between the mid-11th and the mid-9th century BC are scant and as a consequence we lack a comprehensive picture of the settlement structure and pattern of the period immediately preceding the territorial expansion of the Neo-Assyrian kings.

Between the Middle Assyrian and the Neo-Assyrian period some sites, such as Tell Brak, were probably abandoned, while others, such as Tell Fekheriyeh, Tell Barri and Tell Hamidiye (all of which were significant settlements in the 2nd millennium BC), continued to be inhabited without substantial break.

The case of Tell Barri is especially indicative of this (D'Agostino 2009). Known as the ancient city of *Kahat*, the site, which comprises a 23 ha mound situated on the left bank of the Jaghjagh river, has revealed significant evidence of Late Bronze and Iron Age occupation from different areas of the settlement. Of these, the later phase is represented by extensive building activities dating to the time of Tukulti-Ninurta II (890–884 BC) in Area J and the contemporary re-planning of Area G with large residences. This new activity, together with the survival of the earlier settlement pattern from the 2nd millennium BC, suggests that Tell Barri resumed its position as a high status provincial town following its earlier importance in the Middle Assyrian period when Adad-nirari I (1305–1274 BC) probably constructed his palace. There are also strong indications that the site retained some sort of administrative function in addition to its role as the main regional settlement immediately following the transitional period. A continuous sequence of layers encompassing the transitional period has been recovered from a peripheral sector of the settlement primarily intended for domestic purposes. The fact that the function of this area appears not to have altered is significant not least because it would seem to reduce the scope for misinterpreting changes in the material assemblage at the turn of the 1st millennium. Excavations carried out in Area G have revealed a sequence of strata that are important for defining the events that characterised the site during the first half of 1st millennium BC. Here, the stratigraphy shows a progressive evolution in the occupation of the site with some change in the quality of buildings. Regarding pottery, the assemblage from Area G seems substantially homogeneous: proceeding upwards through the levels, it differentiates progressively in morphology and manufacturing technique with typical Late Bronze Age shapes of Middle Assyrian tradition decreasing in number from one stratum to the next. The typology of the ceramic material gradually assumes the characteristics of a typical Neo-Assyrian repertoire attested at other provincial and capital cities. We can interpret the evolution of the ceramic repertoire as a product of internal developments at the site arising from the peculiar social and economic dynamics affected by an Assyrian cultural environment. Evidence of products of external tradition is poor and limited to very few examples of hand-made ware but important for a series of considerations related to the existence of marginal manufactures next to the workshops producing standard Assyrian products.

The evidence that emerges from a site like Tell Halaf, ancient *Guzana*, is markedly different. Located at the western edge of the Khabur valley, the site was once the ancient capital city of the Aramaean kingdom of Bit-Bakhiani. Excavations on the citadel have revealed several layers dating prior to the Neo-Assyrian conquest. Here the ceramic types belonging to the later phase show influxes of the typical Neo-Assyrian repertoire, indicative of an alternative form of Iron Age pottery production from the kind of handmade production associated with the Early Iron Age phase of occupation (Novak & Becker 2012).

According to the evidence from Tell Barri and Tell Halaf it would seem, therefore, that two types of pottery production co-existed in the Upper Khabur valley (D'Agostino 2014; Novak & Becker 2012). Faint traces of a similar mix of traditions can also be observed at Barri where the presence of some hand-made grooved sherds has been detected within the Iron Age repertoire (D'Agostino 2014, 188–189; 2009, 27).

Work at other sites of Upper Tigris valley has thrown up further observations. At the beginning of 1990s the Upper Tigris course began to be extensively explored as part of the Ilısu Dam project. Following an intial reconnaissance survey, several mounds were selected for rescue excavation within the area destined to be flooded at the end of the works. The survey was neither intensive nor systematic; focusing exclusively on the banks of the river while ignoring the hills overlooking the bottom of the valley. Unfortunately, the sample of archaeological material dating to the first half of the 1st millennium BC is small though two main ceramic groups can be identified. These consist of local hand-made pots, often grooved in the upper portion of the rim or painted,[2] and Neo-Assyrian wheel-made vessels similar to those in use at Syrian and Iraqi sites. On the basis of the distribution of ceramic types identified by the survey, the sites scattered across the valley, which date from the Late Bronze Age to the Middle Iron Age, have been classified as Middle Assyrian, Neo-Assyrian, Assyrian oriented and local (Köroğlu 1998, 54–74; Parker 2003; Roaf & Schachner 2005). The hand-made painted and grooved ware, often found on the surface of sites disturbed by erosion, has been associated with temporary or small scale occupation. Alternatively, the wheel-made pottery usually comes from permanent dwellings, such as farmsteads or from the main quarters of large settlements and their satellite villages, and would have been produced within a central administrative setting.

At Ziyaret Tepe, identified with the city of *Tushan*, well known as a major settlement in the 2nd millennium and capital of the Assyrian province in the 1st millennium BC, extensive remains dating to the Iron Age period have been unearthed, both on the mound and in the lower town. Subsurface geophysical surveys and excavation revealed what appear to be substantial fortification walls and towers, large public buildings as well as quarters with domestic purposes. The sequence exposed in the step trench shows Middle Assyrian domestic structures directly below the surface cut by a pit that contained handmade grooved pottery (Matney *et al.* 2003, 178) that was in turn cut and covered by another pit and structures containing Neo-Assyrian pottery of the 7th century (Roaf 2005, 21; McDonald 2005, 23). Scant traces of eroded structures and hand-made sherds have also been found in a small area of the site located on top of an abandoned settlement of the Middle Assyrian period at Giricano (Schachner 2002; 2003).

Some sites, like Boztepe (Parker & Creekmore 2002) where a large house dated to the Neo-Assyrian period was uncovered, have revealed pottery closely related to the Assyrian repertoire of the imperial period with no evidence of hand-made herds while at others, such as Kenan Tepe, no Assyrian ceramics have been discovered, only large quantities of grooved pottery (Parker *et al.* 2002). Other sites, such as Salat Tepe, Hirbemerdon Tepe, Gre Dimse, Hakemi Use, Aşağı Salat, and Kavuşan Höyük have revealed layers with poorly preserved remains of dwellings, tombs, or pits containing hand-made pottery or Neo-Assyrian pottery, as well as simple scattering of these sherds. Evidence for the coexistence of both repertoires has been recorded at two sites. The first, Zeviya Tivilki, a single-period settlement north-east of Midyat, has revealed examples of hand-made and wheel-made pots in the same contexts (Ökse *et al.* 2010) while the excavations at Ziyaret Tepe show that hand-made grooved pottery continued to be part of the ceramic assemblage well into the Neo-Assyrian period (Middle Iron Age) alongside typical Late Assyrian forms (Matney 2008, 138; Matney *et al.* 2009, 54).[3] A similar situation is suggested by sites in the Upper Euphrates region where the coexistence of hand-made and wheel-made products of Hittite tradition is documented (Köroğlu 2003, 236).

The surveys identified a pattern of settlement dating to the Assyrian periods (Middle and Neo-) scattered mainly along the southern bank of the Tigris and in the area around Diyarbakır as well as mound sites with concentrations of hand-made grooved ware. While there does not appear to be any significant differences between these sites with regard to preferences for hilly or flat areas, all are concentrated on the land suitable for agricultural purposes.

Discussion

The purpose of this investigation is to get beyond a review of current interpretations of the profile of material culture for the northern territories and propose an alternative explanation. The tenet of our reasoning is the existence of two kinds of pottery production that, according to some scholars, are considered to be either contemporaneous or, as others have argued, represent two distinct chronological phases. In short, both these hypotheses bring alternative space and time differentiations into play as possible reasons for the existence of distinct assemblages.

Summarising the state of current research, it is clear that many single period sites are hard to place in chronological relation to nearby sites characterised by a different pottery repertoire. In other cases, there are a few sites that present a clear sequence of hand-made sherds sandwiched between layers containing Middle Assyrian and Neo-Assyrian artefacts; only the evidence from Zeviya Tivilki and the faint traces found in the lower city of Ziyaret Tepe reveal the coexistence of both repertoires in the same stratum.

Hand-made and wheel-made ceramics represent different ways of shaping vessels and could conceivably indicate two distinct methods of manufacture and organisation. This begs the question "to whom did these pots belong?" Is it possible that wheel-made pots were used by Assyrians and hand-made pots by indigenous peoples before the arrival of Assyrians and their assortment of mass-produced vessels? I think this reconstruction needs to be revised and investigated with respect to other factors rather than assume that particular types of pot corresponded exclusively to particular population groups, leaving aside here the issue about who introduced the hand-made pots.

The dating of the hand-made wares exclusively to the Early Iron Age period on the basis of limited evidence has in many cases been presupposed rather than demonstrated. More recently, however, it has been suggested that this repertoire was in use for a longer period, at least from the end of the Late Bronze Age onwards including the entire Neo-Assyrian period at which time it appears to have formed a complementary type of manufacture active in the Tigris valley.[4] It has long been accepted that changes in ceramic assemblages need not reflect changes in population in all cases but are perhaps better explained as the result of other socio-economic processes. This argument is strengthened, it seems, when we focus our attention on the domestic spaces of the main cities and villages rather than public buildings, or those farmsteads closely connected with the administrative centre or the estates of the Assyrian elite.

The arrival of the Assyrians did not result in the removal of established centres of local power. Instead existing structures were simply integrated into the new political system. The rural landscape, made up of small villages, formed a complex system (Liverani 1999). This is particularly true in the case of the Upper Tigris on the northern frontier of the Neo-Assyrian administrated area; a region that operated as an interface between the Anatolian and Mesopotamian worlds and where nomadic and tribal populations interacted with an urbanised Assyrian society (Matney 2010, 132). For this reason, the coexistence of villages gravitating towards alternative social and economic players does not conflict with what we already know from the historical and archaeological record. This is the region where Assyrians, Arameans, Mushki, Kasku, Urumu and other tribes confronted and met each other at the end of 2nd and later in the course of 1st millennium BC. The complete transformation of the pottery production in the valley at the time of Neo-Assyrian conquest is not a very plausible hypothesis. Although this theory has been put forth to strengthen the Early Iron Age date of the hand-made pottery, the relationship between ceramics and cultural history is often problematic, especially when we look at the chronological relationship between the different repertoires. While the diffusion of Assyrian wheel-made ceramic types is undeniable, it is confined to specific contexts. Nor can we suggest that the absence of handmade pots was a consequence of a deliberate policy pursued by Assyrians to dismantle the production facilities of the newly subjected Tigris valley because grooved and painted wares are not the products of centrally organised production centres, but of local workshops operating within the village economy. This would suggest that rural and local production facilities survived the introduction of centralised Assyrian workshops, a state of affairs that is supported by evidence from Giricano (Schachner 2003, 158).[5]

Studies of the relationship between ceramic change, on the one hand, and socio-economic developments documented in ethnographic and historical sources, on the other, indicate that no clear or consistent relationship exists between the two processes. The simpler modes of pottery production however are embedded in the basic economy of the population and a strong resistance by potters to technological change, in particular to new forming methods (which usually remain stable for a long period) is considered a critical indicator of socio-cultural change – a point that has been demonstrated for instance by D. Arnold's ethnographic studies (Henrickson 1989, 129–130). Innovation, or conservation, may be limited to only a portion of the ceramic assemblage and the introduction of the potter's wheel may result in the establishment of a separate industry that does not produce traditional shapes. The traditional local pottery, with production based in either the household or a simple workshop, may continue unchanged while a new mode of production, serving a wider market or specific segment or need of society, is added.

Differences in the material culture of both the Khabur and Tigris valleys during the Iron Age period appear to reflect dissimilar administrative strategies pursued by the Assyrians in response to the structural peculiarities of each subject territory and their social composition. In the central and eastern part of Upper Khabur, an area first colonised during the Late Bronze Age, the production of low status objects for daily use, such as ceramics, continued to be locally oriented well into the Early Iron Age; the appearance of new morphological traits in ceramics, for example, being explicable in terms of the normal development of a local pottery tradition. Some sites in the Khabur valley remained under Assyrian control or political influence, whereas other sites, particularly those situated in the western part of the valley, assumed a different political orientation and became seats of Aramaean administrated settlement. In sites like Tell Barri, where the Assyrian tradition remained stable for a long period, changes in the profile of the ceramic assemblage, involving a gradual movement away from Middle Assyrian toward Neo-Assyrian features, are the direct result of specialised production centres embedded in a dynamic economic environment continually transformed by the complex and varied demands of the community that used these pots.

From an archaeological point of view, the socio-economic and political reorientation of settlements can be observed in the new pottery repertoire and architecture of the Aramaean cities. Examples of this transformation are particularly evident in the material remains at Tell Halaf and Tell Fekheriye (Schwartz 1989, 278; Novak 2013).

A not dissimilar process can be seen in the settlements in the Tigris valley. Here the appearance of "Assyrian" traits in architecture and pottery are manifest signs of imperial impact, the absorption of existing populations into the provincial system and the introduction of a modified local administrative system. This reading, however, is complicated somewhat by the picture that emerges from the Upper Tigris where a stratigraphic and cultural break has been documented at several sites. In addition to the spread of hand-made grooved and painted ware, the archaeological data has revealed the appearance of impoverished domestic structures on top of or between strata containing architectural and ceramic features bearing a strong resemblance to those found in the southern regions under the political control of the Assyrians. We cannot be certain that the use of local ceramic traditions persisted because the sites in question lay outside the area of direct Assyrian control or whether the adoption of what could be described as centrally produced "imperial repertoires" was a feature of newly settled sites or Assyrian "colonies" (Parker & Creekmore 2002, 67–68). The evidence from Zeviya Tivilki and in the lower city of Ziyaret would certainly seem to caution against such assumptions. Both sites reveal zones of cultural interference in which local hand-made and non-local wheel-made vessels co-exist.

How can the articulated ceramic horizon of Upper Tigris be explained? The wheel-made ware may be a material-cultural indicator of the Assyrian sphere of economy activity. The appearance of this ware marks the introduction of an entirely new mode of ceramic production, a kind of workshop industry, alongside to the lasting local household economy. The gradual introduction and use of mass-produced ceramics, from carinated bowls to middle sized necked jars, suggests the existence of a few centralised production facilities employing specialist workers. Such workshops would have been indicative of a radical reorganisation of the existing local economy that may have arisen as a consequence of imperial integration. The production of hand-made ware, on the other hand, tells a different story. This method of manufacture was devoted primarily to producing shapes for cooking and serving food, activities that reflect the daily lives of ordinary people within the context of the household or village community. Since the manufacture of pots is a very conservative activity tied to the local tradition, people inhabiting the area would probably shape their ceramics according to past practices, techniques, forms, and decorative styles that in the case of hand-made pots emerged during the final phase of the Late Bronze Age (D'Agostino 2014, 188–189; Köroğlu 2003, 233–235).[6] This type of manufacturing would have retained a utilitarian function but one that also acquired and expressed social and cultural meaning, though not necessarily one associated with ethnicity (Matney 2010, 139; Roaf & Schachner 2005, 119–120). We can suggest that these products, mainly vessels of a utilitarian nature such as hole-mouth cooking pots and curved or sometime upper side carinated bowls, were employed by various people according to specific ways of preparing and consuming food. At the same time the other wheel-made vessels were adopted as Assyrian influence expanded and new forms of consumption, drinking habits and diet were introduced. In this case the limited array of hand-made types can be explained by culinary practices and the way food was served in rural domestic contexts. On closer inspection, it is also worth mentioning that cooking pots are rarely represented in the Neo-Assyrian style repertoire, a fact that argues in favour of the existence of local specialised potters producing sets of vessels for daily cooking activities, according to the local style. One can imagine these vessels being used for the preparation of traditional local dishes such as "shepherd's soup" or the "Upper Tigris potage". The networks producing and transmitting hand-made techniques remained active among local components of the population despite the introduction of wheel-made techniques associated with the new Assyrian workshops. Demand for these new products was probably generated by local elites involved in the provincial administration and closely tailored to their interests and aspirations. It seems likely for instance that objects of good quality such as wheel-made vessels acquired a special function and status on account of their association with the Assyrians, the new leading social group.

The persistence of hand-made pottery production suggests that Assyrian political control and the creation of a state economy did not result in the dismantling of local craft activities, although these activities formed part of the Assyrian economic system. This probably reflected the realities of a small rural economy typical of a frontier zone such as the Tigris valley where there was strong agro-pastoral component.

One of the goals of the Neo-Assyrian expansion, in addition to getting access to raw materials, was to make land more agriculturally productive (Parker 2001; Parpola 2008, 14). In short, the increased scale of the urban Assyrian capitals in the heartland and the expansion of imperial control required "associated incorporation of the countryside and rural settlement into the sphere of urban influence" (Wilkinson *et al.* 2005, 25). In this framework it makes sense that local villages and new urban foundations were united within an economic system that left room for marginal activities practiced by the rural elements of the society. According to the textual record (Parker 2003, 540–541) the imperial authorities maintained control over certain aspects of the regional economy. These were typically organised on a large scale and centrally administrated, monopolising certain strategic segments of the local economy such as the production and storage of agricultural surpluses and the herding of animals such as large state-owned flocks. Although land use became heavily influenced by large-scale economic forces rather than local social and political factors, Assyrian policy allowed villagers to maintain traditional activities where those activities were not in competition with the large estates or Assyrian interests.

Concluding remarks

Precisely how ancient populations reacted to Assyrian interference in the local economy is far from clear and any reconstruction must be treated as speculative. However, by studying the organisation of the production and distribution of pots a few points can be stressed. Firstly, there appears to be little interaction between the hand-made and wheel-made traditions in the Upper Tigris region. The hand-made and wheel turned vessels are morphologically distinct and show not shared attributes or mutual influence apart some exceptions.[7] This means that we have two parallel stabile systems of productions, the southern and the local Anatolian one. This clear difference in pottery traditions is substantial and can reflect either chronology or alternative productive standards. But as for the Upper Tigris concerns, some doubts arise that what we currently see might not be a reflection of a mere chronological differentiation.

Due to the limited nature of archaeological exploration in the area, the picture is obviously fragmentary. The Tur Abdin reliefs, for instance, have yet to be surveyed. Similarly, in the valley of the Upper Tigris only those areas in the proximity of the riverbed and limited portions of its hilly flanks have been investigated while the single period sites of the Jezirah have been rarely the target of dedicated projects. As a consequence a clear ceramic sequence for the region is lacking, especially for the early centuries of the Iron Age. Quite often it was assumed that there existed two ceramic horizons corresponding to the successive cultures that took control of the valley. The unconventional hypothesis proposed here envisages the coexistence of two different traditions distributed across the valley and appearing in separate contexts within the larger sites. This horizontal relationship became vertical and important in terms of chronological interrelation only in the case of settlements whose levels contained Assyrian pottery: where layers with hand-made potsherds are sandwiched between those containing Middle and Neo-Assyrian features. What emerges from the evaluation of the current state of the evidence is that the Iron Age ceramic cultures in Upper Tigris originated from foreign roots, the absence of earlier LBA precursors for the grooved hand-made and Assyrian wheel-made traditions being a case in point. Leaving aside the possible external origins for the Iron Age wares (D'Agostino 2012, 218–222), we need to think of these two distinct pottery forms as the products of two different yet complementary manufacturing techniques each serving different purposes (different value, different sphere of utilise as well as a different people's reach).

By referring to the data at hand I have attempted to read the current evidence and speculate on a possible interpretation of the archaeological and textual elements. In both the Upper Khabur and Tigris valleys, the local village economy was centred on animal husbandry and cereal cultivation; activities that continued in tandem with the exploitation of local resources by the Assyrian, namely sheep, cattle, horses, lumber, and metal, However, due to the changing socio-political situation the Assyrian approach to the region evolved over time. The development of new power groupings in the border regions as a result of Aramaean and nomadic ascendancy caused the Assyrian state to pursue a more aggressive policy of control over the rural areas; a policy that was characterised by military conquest and the direct management of those territories considered to be of strategic economic value. Urban sites in the Jezirah, such as Tell Barri, that had been under Assyrian control for a long time, became the centres of administrative power over the surrounding rural villages: a fact that is reflected by the enlargement of the settlements, its functional differentiation and the development of types of pottery manufacture involving a movement away from the standard Middle Assyrian forms towards the specialised production methods associated with Neo-Assyrian wares.

With regard to the Upper Tigris, a border region inhabited by various populations with distinct identities and traditions, the picture appears to be not dissimilar from the situation that existed in the Late Bronze Age. Only now there seems to be an expansion of Assyrian control over the economic activities of both Assyrian and local settlements. dependent but probably at a different degree from the town and subordinate to the Assyrian administration. The main production activities – including intensive farming of fertile fields along the rivers, breeding of large flocks of cattle and sheeps, exploitation of natural resources and control of trade routes – were monopolised by the state through local agents or under the auspices of large estates. The settlements where these activities were located show elements of the Assyrian material culture, expression of an evident state/centre organisation of productive facilities. Other marginal activities, marginal with respect to the Assyrian agricultural-based economy, such as small breeding and small farming, are managed by local communities, living in settlement interspersed over the territory and archaeologically characterised by a different material culture, that we can define local or Anatolian related or by the coexistence of elements coming from both socio-economic components. Conceivably local market and basic production facilities probably persisted.

Little is known about the characteristics of the pottery assemblage from the rural areas, though we can speculate that the communities on the border of the Assyrian Empire continued to manufacture their wares according to alternative traditions and this local production is bound to the sphere of tools used in the daily household activities. The preparation and consumption of food can be understood as one of the ways in which a colonised population expressed their own identity (Mills 1999, 253–254) but more simply is a dimension where traditional tools are preserved because functional and utilitarian for specific domestic purposes and are the most appropriate to obtain a certain local dish or drink.

Any inference based upon material culture is often largely arbitrary and the interpretative process depends on the significance given to the context. Only once wide stratigraphies and chronologies have been defined and once changes have been understood if gradual or rapid, that we can discuss the cultural change and the adherence between historical events and archaeological record, gaining new insight for the reconstruction of the ancient cultures of border regions. Obviously further readings and opposite interpretations are possible. The available fragmentary evidence may disguise a more complex entanglement of circumstances that has escaped current methods of archaeological investigation; only time and continued research will tell us what was really going on in the northern boundary regions of the Assyrian Empire at the turn of 1st millennium BC.

Notes

1. I am grateful to Juan Carlos Moreno Garcia for inviting me to join the workshop and for his kind hospitality at Lille. I also wish to thank the other participants for their discussion and their helpful comments. Themes of this chapter were first presented in workshops held in Rome, Klagenfurt and Berlin and published in a series of articles regarding the visibility of Assyrian impact on the archaeological record and the material changes resulting from their arrival in the Upper Mesopotamia (D'Agostino 2009; 2011; 2012; 2014).
2. These traits are recognisable from sites throughout Eastern Anatolia, from the Upper Euphrates to the Van region in north-west Iran and Armenia.
3. Also M. Roaf & A. Schachner 2005, 121 touched on the chronological range of the production of hand-made wares suggesting some types could have been still produced during the Neo-Assyrian period.
4. See D'Agostino 2012 for details on the debate and an updated bibliography.
5. Deposits on top of the Early Iron Age layer at Giricano reveal the existence of local hand-made grooved ware unrelated to Neo-Assyrian examples.
6. The differences observed in the repertoire of grooved pots (Konyar 2005) reveal the existence of more than one assemblage and suggest that these variations could be produced over space and time.
7. No attempts to produce for example Assyrian types with the hand-made techniques, except some specimens in Zeviya Tivilki, have been documented; and only limited cases of curved grooved bowls made on the wheel have been documented but outside the nuclear zone. I'm reporting the cases documented in the Tell Barri Late Bronze Age repertoire (see above for references) and the later specimens of grooved bowls from Urartean contexts (Konyar 2005).

Bibliography

Bartl, K. (1989) Zur Datierung der altmonochromen Ware von Tell Halaf. In O. M. C. Haex, H. H. Curvers & P. M. M. G. Akkermans (eds), *To the Euphrates and Beyond: Archaeological Studies in Honour of Maurits*, 257–274. *N. Van Loon*, Rotterdam.

D'Agostino, A. (2009) The Assyrian-Aramaean interaction in the Upper Khabur: the archaeological evidence from Tell Barri Iron Age levels, *Syria* 86: 15–40.

D'Agostino, A. (2011) The Upper Khabur and the Upper Tigris valleys between the end of the Late Bronze Age and the beginning of the Iron Age: an assessment of the archaeological evidence (settlement patterns and pottery). In K. Strobel (ed.), *Empires after Empire. Anatolia, Syrian and Assyria after Suppiluliuma II (ca. 1200–800/700 B.C.)* (Eothen 17), 87–136, *Firenze*.

D'Agostino, A. (2012) Tra le montagne anatoliche e le steppe siriane: problemi di archeologia nell'alta valle del fiume Tigri tra Bronzo Antico ed Età del Ferro. In S. Mazzoni (ed.), *Studi di Archeologia del Vicino Oriente. Scritti degli allievi fiorentini per Paolo Emilio Pecorella*, 185–240, pls 1–4, Firenze.

D'Agostino, A. (2014) The Upper Khabur and the Upper Tigris Valleys during the Late Bronze Age: settlements and ceramic horizons. In D. Bonatz (ed.), *The Archaeology of Political Spaces. The Upper Mesopotamian Piedmont in the Second Millennium BCE* (Topoi – Berliner Studien der Alten Welt 12), 169–199, Berlin.

Fales, F. M. (1990) The rural landscape of the Neo-Assyrian Empir: a survey. *State Archives of Assyria Bulletin* 4/2, 81–142.

Gaimster, D. & I. Freestone (eds) (1997) *Pottery in the Making. World Ceramic Traditions*, London.

Henrickson, R. C. (1989) The buff and the grey: ceramic assemblages and cultural process in the third millennium B.C. Central Zagros, Iran. In P. E. McGovern, M. D. Notis & W. D. Kingery (eds), *Cross-Craft and Cross-Cultural Interactions in Ceramics* (Ceramic and Civilization 4), 81–146, Westerville.

Konyar, E. (2005) Grooved pottery of the Van Lake Basin, *Colloquium Anatolicum* 4: 105–127.

Köroğlu, K. (1998) *Üçtepe I: Yeni Kazı ve Yüzey Bulguları Işığında Diyarbakır/Üçtepe ve Çevresinin Yeni ssur Dönemi Tarihi Coğrafyası*, Ankara.

Köroğlu, K. (2003) The Transition from Bronze Age to iron Age in eastern Anatolia. In B. Fischer, H. Genz, É. Jean & K. Köroğlu (eds), *Identifying Changes: The Transition from Bronze to Iron Ages in Anatolia and its Neighbouring Regions*, 232–244, Istanbul.

Liverani, M (1988) The growth of the Assyrian Empire in the Habur, *State Archives of Assyria Bulletin* 2/2, 81–98.

Liverani, M. (1999) The role of the village in shaping the ancient Near Eastern rural landscape. In L. Milano, S. de Martino, F. M. Fales & G. B. Lanfranchi (eds), *Landscapes. Territories, Frontiers and Horizons in the Ancient Near East, Papers presented to the XLIV Rencontre Assyriologique Internationale, Venezia, 7–11 July 1997, Part I, Invited Lectures*, 37–47, Padova.

Matney, T., J MacGinnis, H. McDonald, K. Nicoll, L. Rainville M. Roaf, M. L. Smith & D. Stein (2003) Archaeological Investigations at Ziyaret Tepe – 2002, *Anatolica* 29, 175–215.

Matney, T., B. Greenfield, A. Hartenberger, K. Keskin, K. Köroğlu, J. MacGinnis, W. Monroe, L. Rainville M. Shepperson, T. Vorderstrasse & D. Wicke (2009) Excavations at Ziyaret Tepe 2007–2008, *Anatolica* 35: 37–84.

Matney, T. (2010) Material culture and identity. Assyrian, Aramaeans, and the indigenous peoples of Iron Age southeastern Anatolia. In S. R. Steadman and J. C. Ross (eds), *Agency and Identity in the Ancient Near East. New Paths Forward*, 129–147, London.

Matthews, R. (2003) *The Archaeology of Mesopotamia. Theories and Approaches*. London and New York.

McDonald, H. (2005) Pottery from the Early Iron Age Pit (E-032). In T. Matney & L. Rainville (eds), Archaeological Investigations at Ziyaret Tepe, 2003–2004, *Anatolica* 31: 23–26

Mills, B. J. (1999) Ceramic and social contexts of food consumption. In J. M. Skibo & G. M. Feinman, *Pottery and People*, 99–114, Salt Lake City.

Novak, M. (2013) Between the Musku and the Arameans. The early history of Guzana/Tell Halaf. In A. Yener (ed.), *Across the Border: Late Bronze Age Relations between Syria and Anatolia*, (ANES Supplement 42), 293–309, Leuven–Paris–Walpole.
Novak, M & Becker, J. (2012) Zur Siedlungsgeschichte am 'Kopf der Quelle': Synchronisation der Stratigrafie auf dem Tell Halaf und eine Periodisierung in der Region von Ra's al-'Ain. In L. Martin, W. Orthmann & A. al-M. Baghdo (eds), *Tell Ḥalaf: Vorbericht über die dritte bis fünfte syrisch-deutsche Grabungskampagne. Vorderasiatische Forschungen der Max Freiherr von Oppenheim-Stiftung* Vol. 3:2, 221–269, Wiesbaden.
Ökse, A. T., A. Görmüş & E. Atay (2010) A rural Iron Age site at Zeviya Tivilki: in the construction zone of the Ilısu Dam, south-eastern Turkey. *Antiquity*, project gallery, Volume 084, Issue 323. http://www.antiquity.ac.uk/projgall/okse323/.
Parker, B. J. (2003) Archaeological manifestations of Empire: Assyria's imprint on Southeastern Anatolia, *American Journal of Archaeology* 103: 525–557.
Parker, B. J. & A. Creekmore (2002) The Upper Tigris Archaeological Research Project: a final report from the 1999 field season, *Anatolian Studies* 52: 19–74.
Parker, B. J., A. Creekmore, E. Moseman & R. Sasaki (2002) The Upper Tigris Archaeological Research Project (UTARP). A preliminary report from the year 2000 excavations at Kenan Tepe. In N. Tuna & J. Velibeyoğlu (eds), *Salvage Project of the Archaeological Heritage of the Ilısu and Carchemish Dam Reservoirs, Activities in 2000*, 631–643, Ankara.
Parpola, S. (2008) Cuneiform texts from Ziyaret Tepe (Tushan), 2002–2003, *SAAB* 17: 1–113.
Ponchia, S. (2004) Mountain routes in Assyrian royal inscriptions, *KASKAL* 1: 139–177.
Radner, K. (2006) Provinz. C. Assyrien. In M. P. Streck (ed.), *Reallexikon der Assyriologie und Vorderasiatischen Archäologie, Band 11, Lieferung 1/2: Prinz, Prinzessin - Qattara*, 42–68, Berlin.
Rice, P. (1987). *Pottery Analysis: A Sourcebook*, Chicago.
Roaf, M. (2005) Excavations in Operation E. In T. Matney & L. Rainville (eds), Archaeological Investigations at Ziyaret Tepe, 2003–2004, *Anatolica* 31: 21–23.
Roaf, M. & A. Schachner (2005) The Bronze Age to Iron Age transition in the Upper Tigris region: new information from Ziyaret Tepe and Giricano. In A. Çilingiroğlu & G. Darbyshire, *Anatolian Iron Ages 5. Proceedings of the Fifth Anatolian Iron Ages Colloquium held at Van, 6-10 August 2001*, 115–123, Ankara.
Roux, V. (2008) Evolutionary trajectories of technological traits and cultural transmission: a qualitative approach to the emergence and disappearance of the ceramic wheel-fashioning technique in the Southern Levant. In M. T. Stark, B. J. Bowser & L. Horne (eds), *Cultural Transmission and Material Culture. Breaking Down Boundaries*, 82–104, Tucson.
Schachner, A. (2002) Ausgrabungen in Giricano (2000–2001). Neue Forschungen an der Nordgrenze des Mesopotamischen Kulturraums, *Istanbuler Mitteilungen* 52: 9–57.
Schachner, A. (2003) From the Bronze Age to the Iron Age: identifying changes in the Upper Tigris region. The case of Giricano. In B. Fischer, H. Genz, É. Jean & K. Köroğlu (eds), *Identifying Changes: The Transition from Bronze to Iron Ages in Anatolia and its Neighbouring Regions*, 151–167, Istanbul.
Sinopoli, C. M. (1991) *Approaches to Archaeological Ceramics*, New York & London.
Wilkinson, T. J. (2002) The settlement transition of the second millennium BC in the western Khabur. In L. Al Gailani-Werr, J. Curtis, H. Martin, A. McMahon, J. Oates & J. Reade (eds), *Of Pots and Plans. Papers on the Archaeology and History of Mesopotamia and Syria presented to David Oates in Honour of his 75th Birthday*, 361–372, London.
Wilkinson, T. J. & E. Barbanes (2000) Settlement patterns in the Syrian Jazira during the Iron Age. In G. Bunnens (ed.), *Essays on Syria in the Iron Age* (Ancient Near Eastern Studies Supplement 7), 397–422, Louvain-Paris-Sterling.

Chapter 7

Silver circulation and the development of the private economy in the Assyrian Empire (9th–7th centuries BCE): considerations on private investments, prices and prosperity levels of the imperial *élite*

Salvatore Gaspa

Introduction

The role of silver as a value indicator in Mesopotamia is well known and the prices in silver represent an important perspective to evaluate economic performances of the societies of the 1st millennium BCE. In Assyria, it is clear that the wealth of many affluent persons and, consequently, the evolving socio-economic scenery which greatly resulted from the investments in land, people, and commodities that these individuals made throughout the imperial territory, originated from the benefits of the imperial policy. The first half of the 1st millennium BCE is a crucial phase in economic history of the Ancient Near East: with the establishment of the imperial power of Assyria and the eradication of various independent kingdoms, a vast region from Egypt and the Mediterranean Sea to Anatolia and western Iran became a unified network of economic exchanges of goods and people. The systematic exploitation of the conquered regions, now incorporated in a rigid provincial organisation, the new opportunity of work and social ascent offered by the creation of a large standing army and by the increasing demand for land, goods, slaves, and skilled craftsmen by the urban *élite*, particularly by the military officials and administrators of the state, had a great impact on the forms of settlement and the level of agricultural production in the rural areas as well as on the social composition of the Assyrian population. Groups of immigrants from regions touched by Assyrian imperialism settled in the main cities, where the opportunities of employment in the state apparatus and in the thriving trading activities allowed social ascent and profit prospects. However, it is also clear that the scarcity and the palatine/government-orientation of the sources are the main obstacle to the acquisition of a full understanding of the empire's economy and, consequently, to the definition of a model for its organisation and performance.[1] Thus, if compared with the vast documentation stemming from Babylonian archives of Neo-Babylonian, Persian, and Hellenistic period, the private sector of the Assyrian imperial economy is poorly represented in the available evidence, and the same can be stated about prices and currency (Postgate 1979, 195–197). With the progress in the publication of the legal texts corpus from the Neo-Assyrian archives the metals and their circulation in the economy of Assyria as well as the prices of the exchanged goods have been the subject of recent studies (Fales 1996; 2003; Radner 1999b). In the present contribution, the circulation of silver in the private sector will be reconsidered in order to provide an updated analysis of the quantitative data about the use of this metal as currency and a reference basis for future research on currency in Assyria. To this aim, the chronological, geographical, and transaction-related diffusion of the weight norms in use for silver will be discussed and displayed through a number of tables. Payments in silver in the investments made by various members of the Assyrian upper class enable us not only to know the volume of their spending and the possible interrelation of silver standard in use and prices of certain goods, but, more importantly, also to evaluate how the cost of goods vary and at which degree.

Prices of everyday commodities represent another important set of data which cannot be ignored, since they prove that silver was far from being a high-range money limited to large investments;[2] on the contrary, legal and administrative texts, as well as letters from the royal correspondence, show that it served in Assyrian cities as a means of payment in economic exchanges involving commodities of various type. This helps us to form an idea about the degree of monetisation of economic exchange in the Assyrian empire, an aspect that will also emerge in the Babylonian economy of the late centuries of the 1st millennium BCE. Finally, the discussion on the silver economy of the empire leads us to consider the wealth level of the urban property owners of Assyria: the consumption of certain household commodities in the evidence of marriage contracts may be taken as an important indicator of prosperity levels of a given social group, although the lack of comparative data from other Neo-Assyrian archival contexts and the difficulty to detect socio-economic differences among the individuals taken into consideration do not allow us to come to conclusive statements on the question.

Silver standards and their use in the imperial territory[3]

As known, the 1st millennium BCE is a crucial phase in the economic history of the Ancient Near East. It is clear that the electrum exemplars found at the beginning of 20th century at the Artemisium of Ephesus, in levels preceding the period of Croesus, place the origin of money in Lydia and also that the development phases in the transition from private money to state money take place in the Greek milieu (Bernareggi 1985,

26–31; Parise 2003, 134–136, 140–141); however, from the Assyriological point of view, it is also clear, too, that the millenary use of metals as currency in the cities of ancient Mesopotamia was behind these processes. In Mesopotamia of 3rd and 2nd millennia BCE, many of the functions which characterise (ancient and modern) money, such as its being reference of value, exchange means in transactions, and good of treasuring are played by silver, although in competition with other goods (barley), as witnessed, for example, by the Neo-Sumerian balance accounts, the pecuniary penalties and the compensations established in the Neo-Sumerian and Old Babylonian "codes", the Sumerian and Old Babylonian sale documents (Pomponio 2003, 59–108).

In a much-quoted passage of an Assyrian royal inscription describing the casting technique used to produce monumental statues, Sennacherib (705–681 BCE) compares the technique of casting metal in moulds to that used to produce objects weighing half a shekel each (Luckenbill 1924, 109, text E1 vii 18, and 123, text no. 2:29, now re-edited in RINAP 3/1, 17 vii 18). The interpretation of this passage has been much debated by scholars, since this could be taken as evidence for the existence of coinage in Assyria of the first millennium BCE. According to a different interpretation based on an alternative reading of the sign for "½" (*mišlu*), "half", the passage is not referring to the "half a shekel" (½ GÍN), but to the "shekel" (*ina*! 1! GÍN); in fact, the shekel (not the half-shekel), represents the basic unit of the Mesopotamian weight system. Accordingly, the passage in Sennacherib's inscription is actually showing the efficacy of the new casting method and the mastering of this technique by the Assyrian king; a technique through which casting bronze in large moulds for monumental statues was as easy as doing the same in small moulds for statues of only one shekel of weight (Vargyas 2002, 114–115). At present, there is no archaeological and textual evidence of coinage in Assyria of the 1st millennium BCE as well as in other regions of the Fertile Crescent. Moneylike objects have been discovered in different Near Eastern sites, but their exact function is still debated by scholars. Items such as the metal rings attested in Ur III and Old Babylonian texts could have served as means of storing and distributing metals in a convenient way (Snell 1995, 1488–1489). Also the little leaden roundels bearing a stamped decoration on one side from Middle Assyrian Assur could apparently be considered as precursors of coinage, but the complete lack of references to them in the contemporary written sources seems to suggest a different use, perhaps as decoration of some objects (Snell 1995, 1489). Other possible candidates are the *ḫušê*, "scraps, fragments", of silver and gold which are mentioned in an administrative list (SAA 7, 78:9) and in a letter of Sargon II's correspondence (SAA 1, 158:6) as part of the palace treasury stored in *tupninnu*-coffers.[4] It is known that when smaller amounts of silver were needed, the metal block was broken into smaller pieces which were then weighed. The same word for money, *kaspu*, literally meaning "the broken thing", derives from the verb *kasāpu*, "to break off, to chip".[5] But in the case of these Neo-Assyrian silver scraps, there are no proofs that they were a widespread means of exchange: these metal scraps could have been temporarily stored in order to be cast and reused. In any case, the lack of coinage does not mean absence of metal used as money, that is to say, as a *good* and a *technology* (Monroe 2005, 158) serving as a medium of exchange, a mode of payment, a standard of value, and a way of storing wealth (Snell 1995, 1487; Monroe 2005, 158). In fact, the legal documents from the Neo-Assyrian archives[6] attest that metals were largely used as currency in transactions of the Assyrian state of that period, and that this use was regulated by the state according to specific weight standards. Legal documents and letters of the Neo-Assyrian period attest the use of copper (*erû*), bronze (*siparru*), and silver (*ṣarpu*) as currency (*kaspu*; Radner 1999b, 128). This use, however, diversifies during the history of the Assyrian empire. If one extends the inquiry of circulation of these three metals also to the numerous references to acquirement of (raw and processed) metal through booty and tribute which can be found in the corpus of the Neo-Assyrian royal inscriptions, one may observe the progressive substitution of silver over bronze and copper. Bronze is especially used between the 10th and 8th centuries, but copper undermine its supremacy during the 8th century; on its turn, copper progressively loses of importance in the course of 7th century, when silver became the most used metal (Radner 1999b, 129). The earliest attestation of silver as currency refers to 790 BCE (ADW, ix). In any case, in the 8th and 7th centuries a coexistence of copper and silver as alternative means of payment cannot be denied. The change towards the use of silver as currency in payments is certainly to be connected to the events taking place in the reign of Sargon II (722–705 BCE): with the large income of goods deriving from the successful campaigns in the north-western sector, principally in Karkemiš (717 BCE), which change its status from foreign state paying tribute to Assyria to that of province of the Assyrian empire (Liverani 1997, 800; Fales 2001, 7), large amounts of this metal enter the treasury of the Assyrian state. As a consequence, silver begins to substitute bronze as primary currency metal (Radner 1999b, 129). In addition, the progressive decline of copper as a means of payment may also be considered as the result of a direct control and exploitation of the ore mines in Taurus by the Assyrians after Sargon's military exploits in the Syro-Anatolian region (Postgate 1979a, 199–200). As to the metals used as currency, exceptionally also iron could be used as money: in a purchase contract of the 7th century BCE, a certain Lū-balaṭ is said to have acquired an estate and an unknown number of persons for one talent of iron (SAA 14, 198 e.9' *ina* ŠÀ 1 GÚ.UN ⌜AN!.BAR!⌝).

Metals are regulated in the Assyrian empire according to weight standards: there are three standard units for silver, one for copper, and two for gold. Gold, however, was not used as currency in the Neo-Assyrian period (Radner 1999b, 132). In addition, these metals were used in transactions according to two different norms: a heavy norm (*dannu*) and a light norm (*qallu*; Powell 1987–90, 515–516; Fales 1996, 12–15; Radner 1999b, 130). In the sexagesimal system in use in Assyria, constituted by the talent (*biltu*), the mina (*manû*), and the shekel (*šiqlu*), the ratio between the heavy mina (*c.* 1.01 kg) and the light mina (*c.* 0.505 kg) corresponded to 1:2 (Radner 1999b, 130; Fales 2003, 113). From 15 sale contracts, principally coming from Assur (Qal'at Šerqāṭ), one may note that the value relation between copper and silver was of 60:1 (Fales 2003,

114), in other words, one talent of copper (= 60 copper minas) corresponded to one mina of silver. Silver was regulated according to three weight standards: the "king's mina" (*manû ša šarri*), the "mina of Karkemiš" (*manû ša Gargamis*), and the "merchant's mina" (*manû ša tamkāri*).[7] The first and the third standards are also attested with a different phraseology in two texts from Assur: in a loan document from the archive of the *ḫundurāiu* Aššur-erība (archive N10), dating to 614 BCE, a sum of *x* minas and 4 shekels of silver is said to be regulated "by the weight of the palace" (*ana šuqulti ša ēkalli*),[8] while in a receipt note from the dossier of Dād-aḫḫē, another member of the *ḫundurāiu* guild of the city (archive N9), half a mina of silver "according to the weight of the merchant" (*ina šuqulti ša tamkāri*) is mentioned.[9] The king's mina is documented in the archaeological evidence by a series of bronze lion-weights from Nimrud, inscribed in Assyrian and Aramaic with vertical strokes marking the weight; they date from the reign of Shalmaneser V to that of Sennacherib and represent the heavy mina of *c.* 1 kg (in the majority of the cases) and the light mina of half-kilo.[10] It is clear that the royal norm was also represented by stone weights: in a contract from Kalḫu of the reign of Aššur-dān III (772–755 BCE), the silver sum of the transaction is regulated according to "the royal stone (weight)" (*ina abni ša šarri*).[11] Stone duck-weights were also used in weighing operations and it is interesting to note that a duck-weight from Nimrud bears a lion-figure (Kwasman & Parpola 1991, xxxi fig. 6b), the Assyrian king's symbol.

Among these standards, the mina of Karkemiš represents the weight norm most used in the transactions. An important factor in the choice of this weight norm of western origin probably was the commercial scenario where the transaction took place. It is possible that the use of the Karkemiš mina, the dominant unit of currency in the western sector (North Syrian area), was in many cases due to the western location of the estate and of the commodities (included people) involved in the transaction conducted by members of the Assyrian ruling class. But a closer scrutiny of the Neo-Assyrian transactions reveals that this standard was also employed for properties located in areas of Assyria proper.[12] The *manû ša Gargamis* was presumably lighter than the Mesopotamian mina, and especially the king's mina, but the exact weight of this unit and its subdivision is still debated.[13] It has been assumed that this weight standard, which became popular in the reign of Sargon and especially during the successive reign periods until the end of the Assyrian empire (612 BCE), has to be connected with the appropriation by the state treasury of large quantities of silver which Sargon took as booty from Karkemiš; this amount, corresponding to 2100 talents and 24 minas of silver, was taken by Sargon after the victory over Pisiri, king of Karkemiš.[14] The treasury amassed by this ruler and carried off from Karkemiš by the Assyrian troops surpassed the much more celebrated booty later taken in Muṣāṣir and was probably the reason for the harsh treatment inflicted by the Assyrian king to this kingdom.[15] In such a perspective, the designations of the three weight standards for the silver used in payments would witness the sources of provenance of silver, that is to say, the state treasury for the king's mina, the booty from Karkemiš for the Karkemiš mina, and the riches resulting from overland trade for the merchant's mina (Radner 1999b, 131). Consequently, the royal mina would represent an official weight unit fully recognised by the Assyrian state, the mina of Karkemiš a regional weight norm of ancient attestation in the Euphratic area and in the Levant, although no Aramaic source makes mention of it (Fales 1996, 16 fn. 11), and the merchant's mina a norm used in the commercial practice, but confined to a very limited local dimension (Fales 1996, 15, 16–17, 32). According to Postgate, it is possible that this third silver norm was not a standard in its own right, that is to say a real weight in relationships with the other Assyrian standards, but a reference to the set of weights that were used in the specific transaction in question (Postgate 1976, 65).

The attestations regarding the use of these three weight norms for silver in Neo-Assyrian legal texts are displayed in the following list:

1. *Manû ša šarri*, "the king's mina"
   Attestations: BT 114 (*Iraq* 25, 93, pl. xxii); BT 115 (*Iraq* 25, 94, pl. xxiii); BT 124 (*Iraq* 25, 96, pl. xxii); BT 127 (*Iraq* 25, 98, pl. xvi); GPA 30; 31; 106; 107; ND 2080 (*Iraq* 16, 33, pl. v); SAA 6, 38; 42; 50; 51; 55; 65; 85; 115; 130; 138; 142; 143; 167; 180; 301; SAA 14, 3; 6; 67; 182; 188; 192; 274; 437–438; StAT 2, 140; 226; StAT 3, 106; TFS 47.

2. *Manû ša Gargamis*, "the mina of Karkemiš"
   Attestations: *Abr-Nahrain* 34, T 15;[16] Assur 2 (*Al-Rāfidān* 17, no. 2); Assur 4 (*Al-Rāfidān* 17, no. 4); Assur 6 (*Al-Rāfidān* 17, no. 5); GPA 1;[17] NATAPA 1, 18; 39; 61; NATAPA 2, 101; 129; ND 2093 (*Iraq* 16, pl. v); ND 2325 (*Iraq* 16, 42); ND 3424 (Ash 1954.737) (Radner 1999b, 151); ND 3426 (*Iraq* 15, 141, pl. xii); ND 3435 (*Iraq* 15, 142); SAA 6, 17;[18] 26; 34; 39; 40; 41; 45; 53; 54; 57; 81; 90; 91; 99; 103; 104; 107; 108; 110; 119; 158; 177; 183; 196; 202; 210; 219; 223; 224; 234; 235; 239; 245; 248; 250; 257; 262; 263; 269; 273; 274; 275; 284; 305; 306; 307; 311–313; 315; 316; 318; 323–324; 326; 329; 330; 333–335; 342–344; 346; 347; SAA 14, 8; 18; 21; 60–61; 63; 64; 69; 78; 94–95; 115; 126; 159; 264; 307; 359; 398; 425; 441; StAT 2, 119; 159–160; StAT 3, 42; 69; 70; 109; SU 51/43A (*Anatolian Studies* 7, 139); TH 113; VAT 5389 (VS 1, 86).

3. *Manû ša tamkāri*, "the merchant's mina"
   Attestations: BT 101 (*Iraq* 25, 89–90, pl. xix); GPA 248 (ADW 15); NATAPA 1, 37; ND 3479 (*Iraq* 15, 147); SAA 6, 27; 96; 97; StAT 2, 157.[19]

Considering the geographical distribution of the use of these weight norms for silver, one may observe a widespread diffusion of the attestations: in fact, the three different minas are documented both in the textual evidence of the archives of the main cities of the country, *i.e.* Assur (Qal'at Šerqāṭ), Kalḫu (Nimrud), and Nineveh (Qūyunǧiq), and in that coming from the minor centres, such as Imgur-Illil (Balawāt), Til Barsip (Tell Aḥmar), Ḫuzīrīna (Sultantepe), and Gūzāna (Tell Ḥalaf). The king's mina is documented in Assur (3 attestations),[20] Kalḫu (6 attestations),[21] Nineveh (23 attestations),[22] Imgur-Illil (4 attestations),[23] but not in Til Barsip, Ḫuzīrīna, and Gūzāna; the mina of Karkemiš in Assur (14 attestations),[24] Kalḫu (5 attestations),[25] Nineveh (84 attestations),[26] Til

Barsip (1 attestation),[27] Ḫuzīrīna (1 attestation),[28] and Gūzāna (1 attestation),[29] but not in Imgur-Illil; the merchant's mina in Assur (2 attestations),[30] Kalḫu (2 attestations),[31] Nineveh (3 attestations),[32] Imgur-Illil (1 attestation),[33] but not in Til Barsip, Ḫuzīrīna, and Gūzāna. In percentages, it follows that the attestations concerning the silver regulated according to the king's mina cover around the 24% of the Neo-Assyrian transactions, the mina of Karkemiš the 70%, the merchant's mina the 6% (Fig. 7.1).

Secondly, one may see that both the king's mina and the merchant's mina are completely absent from the commercial scenery of the western centres of Til Barsip, Ḫuzīrīna and Gūzāna, places where the documented transactions make use of the *manû ša Gargamis*. Finally, the majority of attestations for all the three weight standards concentrates in Nineveh, presumably as a reflex of the documentary situation of the archive of the empire's capital (and where many texts were presumably transferred after the change of the kingdom's capital to Nineveh in Sennacherib's reign), characterised by a large number of texts belonging to the period of the Sargonids (7th century BCE).

From a chronological point of view, one may observe that in the case of the dated texts (texts with a date and texts mentioning the name of the eponym),[34] from the archives of the main centres of the Assyrian empire, *i.e.* Nineveh,[35] Kalḫu,[36] and Assur[37] (Table 7.1), the bulk of attestations concerning the royal mina concentrates in the reign of Sennacherib (15 texts out of 22), while the mina of Karkemiš is documented especially during the reigns of the successors of Sargon II, principally in that of Assurbanipal (27 texts out of 79). The oldest attestation of this silver standard is probably in a sale contract written in 747 BCE, in the last phase of the reign of Aššur-nērārī V (754–745 BCE; Radner 1999b, 131). As to the *tamkāru*'s mina, the attestations in the dated texts are limited to three reign periods (Sargon, Sennacherib, and Esarhaddon), with the majority of the examples concentrating in the period of Sennacherib (three texts out

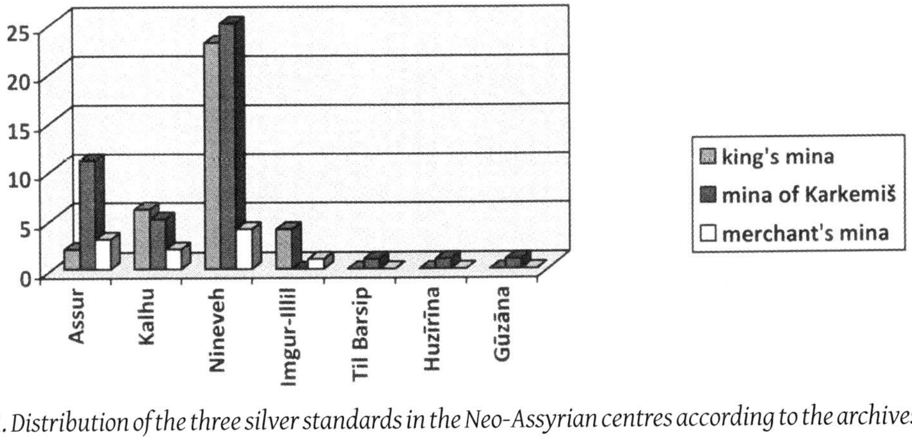

Fig. 7.1. Distribution of the three silver standards in the Neo-Assyrian centres according to the archives.

Table 7.1: Chronological distribution of the silver standards in the reigns of the Neo-Assyrian kings

	Types of mina		
KINGS[1]	*King's mina*	*Mina of Karkemiš*	*Merchant's mina*
AN V	–	SAA 6, 17.	–
TP III	GPA 106; 107.	–	–
SG II	–	SAA 6, 26; 34.	BT 101 (*Iraq* 25, pl. xix).
SN	SAA 6, 42; 65; 85; 115; 130; 138; 142; 143; 167; 180; BT 114 (*Iraq* 25, 93, pl. xxii); BT 115 (*Iraq* 25, 94, pl. xxiii); BT 124 (*Iraq* 25, 96, pl. xxii); BT 127 (*Iraq* 25, 98, pl. xvi); ND 2080 (*Iraq* 16, 33, pl. v).	*Abr-Nahrain* 34, T 15; NATAPA 2, 101; SAA 6, 39; 40; 41; 45; 81; 90; 91; 103; 104; 107; 108; 110; 119; 158; 177; 183; 196; StAT 2, 159–160; SU 51/43A (*Anatolian Studies* 7: 139).	SAA 6, 96; 97; StAT 2, 157.
ESH	SAA 6, 301.	SAA 6, 202; 210; 223; 224; 234; 235; 239; 245; 257; 262; 263; 269; 273; 274; 275; 284; 305; 306; SAA 14, 63; 64; StAT 3, 70.	ND 3479 (*Iraq* 15, 147).
ASB	SAA 14, 67; 437-438; StAT 3, 106.	NATAPA 2, 129; ND 3424 (Ash 1954.737); ND 3426 (*Iraq* 15, 141, pl. XII); ND 3435 (*Iraq* 15, 142); SAA 6, 307; 311; 312; 313; 315; 316; 318; 323-324; 329; 330; SAA 14, 8; 60-61; 69; 78; StAT 3, 109.	–
Ep. ASB	StAT 2, 140.	NATAPA 1, 18; 39; Assur 2 (*Al-Rāfidān* 17, no. 2); Assur 4 (*Al-Rāfidān* 17, no. 4); SAA 14, 94–95; 425; 441; StAT 3, 69.	–
Ep. AEI	–	ND 2093 (*Iraq* 16, pl. v); ND 2325 (*Iraq* 16, 42); SAA 14, 159.	–
Ep. SŠI	–	Assur 6 (*Al-Rāfidān* 17, no. 5); NATAPA 1, 61; VAT 5389 (VS 1, 86); StAT 3, 42.[2]	–

[1]*Abbreviations*: AN V = Aššur-nērārī V (754–745 BCE); TP III = Tiglath-pileser III (745–727 BCE); SG II = Sargon II (722–705 BCE); SN = Sennacherib (705–681 BCE); ESH = Esarhaddon (680–669 BCE); ASB = Assurbanipal (668–631? BCE); Ep. ASB = Eponyms of the reign of Assurbanipal; Ep. AEI = Eponyms of the reign of Aššur-etel-ilāni (630?–627? BCE); Ep. SŠI = Eponyms of the reign of Sîn-šarru-iškun (623?–612 BCE).
[2]Another possible occurrence of the Karkemiš mina in the Assur archive in the reign of Sîn-šarru-iškun is in NATAPA 2, 109, if we accept the restitution of the name of the mina given by Deller *et al.* in line 7: 3 MA.NA KUG.UD *ina* 1 MA.[NA-*e ša* URU.*gar-ga-mis*], '3 minas of silver by the mi[na of Karkemiš]'.

of five). That this silver standard was especially used during the Sargonid dynasty is confirmed by two undated texts, one attributed to the reign of Sargon,[38] the other to that of Esarhaddon or Assurbanipal.[39] Another undated document shows that this mina was already in use during the reign of Adad-nērārī III (810–783 BCE) or Shalmaneser IV (782–773 BCE).[40] Unfortunately, the lack of data for the period from the reign of Shalmaneser IV to that of Sargon prevents us from knowing the degree of diffusion of this standard in Assyria before the Sargonid period. Perhaps, the merchant's mina was re-introduced in Assyria during the reign of Sargon. Its use seems to have been ceased after the reign of Esarhaddon, when the Karkemiš standard became the most popular among the Assyrian minas.

Payments in silver and variation of prices in the investments of the "top spenders" of the imperial *élite*

In the transactions documented in the Neo-Assyrian legal texts, both in those involving private individuals and those involving the State and private individuals, the means of payment is silver (Radner 1999b, 134; Fales 2003, 109–110). This is not a novelty of the 1st millennium, since Old Assyrian documents from the commercial colony at Kaniš (Kültepe), in Eastern Anatolia, show that silver was used as a value reference model, means of payment, and means of indirect exchange already in the first half of the 2nd millennium BCE (Pomponio 2003, 104; Simonetti 2010, 388). In the 8th and 7th centuries BCE the international *scenario* of the Near East is changed: the policy of military and territorial expansion of imperial Assyria aims now at consolidating its dominion on the several political entities subjugated and also at establishing a more widespread exploitation of the economic systems of the conquered countries (Liverani 1997, 792–811). Large amounts of metal were already acquired by the state treasury in the Late Middle Assyrian age, especially in the reigns of Tukultī-Ninurta I (1233–1197 BCE) and Tiglath-pileser I (1114–1076 BCE), although we have to bear in mind that in the Middle Assyrian period the metal used as currency in the majority of the everyday transactions, at least at the local level, is lead (or tin), not silver (Rosa 2011, 111–129). Additional huge amounts of metal reached Assyria in the course of the 1st millennium BCE as the result of the territorial expansion of the Assyrian state on the level of the military and political dominion as well as on that of the broadening of the commercial networks.[41] These conditions promoted a wide circulation of currency metal both in the Assyrian homeland and in the provinces of the empire thanks to the trade of merchants, of landowners, and of profiteers more or less connected to the Palace and to powerful and influential individuals of the country.[42]

When used as currency, silver was subjected to two important operations: weighing and sealing. The amount of silver which passed from one person to another in the transactions was presumably weighed, as seems to be confirmed by the presence of supervisors in charge of this operation, called *bēl ḫiāṭi ša ṣarpi*, among the witnesses of some sale contracts from the area of Nabula (modern Girnavaz; Donbaz 1988,

7 text no. 1, 11 text no. 3). Since the checking of the weighing of the silver sum was a common operation in every transaction, it is reasonable to think that this operation had to be done by the witnesses involved in the transaction (Radner 1999b, 135). The weighing of silver in transactions is already attested before the 1st millennium BCE. Neo-Sumerian sale contracts mention the profession of the weigher of silver, an activity which could be done by smiths, merchants, or goldsmiths (Pomponio 2003, 71 and fn. 18).

If we now come from the private transactions to the sphere of the state central administration, one can observe that the weighing of metal is primarily under the responsibility and supervision of the treasurer (*masennu*). Some letters of the royal correspondence and administrative documents provide examples of the weighing activity, in which the *masennu* plays a major role.[43] The weighing of the metal by the State Treasury, represented by the figure of the *masennu*, was followed by the sealing of the different pieces weighed (Radner 1999b, 137). It is assumed that the metal used in commercial transactions, recorded in the legal documentation in relation to certain weight standards, is always metal that was weighed, sealed and turned into ingots (Radner 1999b, 137). Of weighing operations in Neo-Assyrian age we are informed both from texts and iconographical sources. Letters from the royal correspondence make clear that this operation required the collaboration of more individuals,[44] presumably due to the remarkable weight of the single metal ingots and of the size of the scale used to perform this operation. The act of weighing is represented in the Rassam Obelisk from Kalḫu, attributed to the reign of Aššurnaṣirpal II (Reade 1980, 12 and pl. iv), and in a wall panel of Sargon II's royal palace at Dūr-Šarrukēn (Khorsabad; Botta & Flandin 1849–50, pl. 140). In both illustrations a large balance with a tripartite structure for the weighing of metal ingots, presumably deriving from the raw and manufactured metal of the foreign tribute or booty, is represented. In the scene carved on the obelisk the two officials at the sides of the balance are depicted when performing two different operations: the bearded one is presumably loading one of the scale pans with two round makeweights, while the beardless one to the left of the balance was probably responsible for the weights and the regulation of the weighing tool. The blocks of metal are piled in two stocks, one for the weighed and the other for the not weighed. In the Khorsabad relief the Assyrian officials responsible for the weighing of the metal which originate from the sack of Muṣāṣir are both beardless and depicted in the act of weighing a large round-shaped ingot. The individual to the right of the scale is probably in charge of the makeweights, although the fragmentary image of the pan is not clear.

Prices of commodities are certainly an important source to know the role of silver as currency in the economic transactions documented in legal texts of the Neo-Assyrian period.[45] To this aim, we will take into consideration only the legal documents corpus stemming from the archives of Nineveh, which have recently been published in scientifically updated editions in two volumes of the series *State Archives of Assyria* (Kwasman & Parpola 1991; Mattila 2002). With the exception of few cases, all documents concentrate in the reign periods of Sennacherib, Esarhaddon, and Assurbanipal. As known, the transactions documented in the private archives generally concern the exchange of high-value goods. Very few data can be found, instead, on the use of silver in everyday transactions. Differently from the transactions attested in some Neo-Babylonian documents (*e.g.*, the Borsippean lists of silver payments), where utilitarian commodities for everyday consumption were acquired for very small sums of silver corresponding to fractions of a shekel (Jursa 2010, 629–641), in Assyria the purchase of utilitarian goods such as textiles, household utensils, and foodstuffs for silver is rarely documented, presumably because these were low-value goods in comparison with land and slaves. But it is also possible that there was no reason to record in legal documents transactions involving everyday goods and small sums of money.

The texts from the Nineveh archive shown in Table 7.2 belong to six categories: sale contracts, documents concerning loans and debts, documents concerning release

Table 7.2: Transactions in silver standards from the Ninevite archive (8th-7th century BCE)

A. Sale contracts

Text	*Date*	*Good*	*Price*
1. King's mina			
SAA 6, 115	702	4 hectares of land in the town of Dunnu	*x* minas
SAA 6, 130	696	17 slaves	8 ½ minas
SAA 6, 38	694?	*x* slaves	½ mina
SAA 6, 138	693	3 slaves	3 minas
SAA 6, 42	692	1 house	3 minas
SAA 6, 65	692	[*x* hectare]s of land and people	*x* minas
SAA 6, 85	692	2 slaves	1 mina
SAA 6, 142	692	1 house with a yard in Nineveh	1 mina
SAA 6, 50	*c.* 680	50 hectares of land, 10,000 vines, [1 house], 9 slaves in Ti'i	6 minas
SAA 6, 51	(duplicate of the preceding text)		
SAA 6, 55	*c.* 680	1 donkey-driver	1½ minas
SAA 6, 301	670	1 sash-weaver	1½ minas
SAA 14, 67	668	1 slave	½ mina
SAA 14, 3	–	10 slaves	*x* minas
SAA 14, 6	–	land and slaves	*x* minas
SAA 14, 182	–	1 hectare of land	12 minas
SAA 14, 188	–	1 house and 1 vacant lot	5½ minas
SAA 14, 192	–	land in Ṣibte	*x* minas
SAA 14, 274	–	[land and 1] well	*x* minas

(Continued)

Table 7.2: Transactions in silver standards from the Ninevite archive (8th-7th century BCE) (Continued)

Text	*Date*	*Good*	*Price*
2. Mina of Karkemiš			
SAA 6, 17	747	threshing floor of 90 square metres in Du'ūa	*x* minas
SAA 6, 34	709	3 slaves	3 minas
SAA 6, 119	699	5 hectares and 2 decares of land, 1 house, 1 threshing floor, 1 orchard, 1/6 of a well in Kiluḫte	1 mina
SAA 6, 39	694	*x* slaves	18 minas
SAA 6, 103	694	1 slave	2 minas
SAA 6, 40	693	15 slaves	*x* minas
SAA 6, 41	693	7 slaves	*x* minas
SAA 6, 177	684	10 slaves	6 minas
SAA 6, 90	683	17 slaves and 1 orchard in Nabur	*x* minas
SAA 6, 45	682	1 maid	1 mina
SAA 6, 54	–	5 slaves	*x* minas
SAA 6, 91	681	27 slaves with their properties (fields, houses, gardens, cattle, sheep, & kinsmen) in Dadi-ualla, province of Talmūsu	20 minas
SAA 6, 99	–	real estate	*x* minas
SAA 6, 110	681	7 slaves	2 minas
SAA 6, 196	681	*x* slaves	30 minas
SAA 6, 202	680	1 vineyard, 1 garden, 1 canal, the *foundation* of a well in Kipšūna	4 minas
SAA 6, 257	680	1 slave	1 mina
SAA 6, 53	*c.* 680	2 slaves	1 mina
SAA 6, 57	*c.* 680	20 slaves	10 minas
SAA 6, 219	*c.* 680	1 slave	1½ minas
SAA 6, 269	679	land and slaves	10 minas
SAA 6, 210	676	1 house and a half of a threshing floor in Zidada	*x* minas
SAA 6, 239	676	3 maids	*x* shekels
SAA 6, 274	676	1 slave	2 minas
SAA 6, 275	675	21 estates in various rural areas	3 ½ minas
SAA 6, 250	*c.* 675	3 slaves	2 minas
SAA 6, 245[1]	672	210 hectares of land, 4 towns (Til-raḫayāti, Bēt-Ramannu, Bēt-ša-muḫḫi-āli, Dūr-Nanāia), 6 slaves, 2 oxen	15 minas
SAA 6, 284	671	2 slaves	2 minas
SAA 6, 305	669	1 baker	1 mina

(Continued)

Table 7.2: Transactions in silver standards from the Ninevite archive (8th-7th century BCE) (Continued)

Text	Date	Good	Price
SAA 6, 306	(duplicate of the preceding text)		
SAA 14, 63	669	20 hectares of land in Ṭāb-pa[...]	15 shekels
SAA 14, 64	669	3 slaves	2 minas
SAA 14, 8	668	1 woman	½ mina
SAA 14, 18	–	1 slave	1 mina
SAA 14, 21	–	*x* slaves	*x* minas
SAA 6, 311	666	1 house in Bēt-Rība-ilu	4 minas
SAA 6, 312	666	5 slaves	[3 minas?]
SAA 6, 313	(duplicate of the preceding text)		
SAA 6, 315	666	60 hectares of land, 1 *barnyard*, 1 plot of 2 decares, 1 threshing floor, 5 slaves in Til-naḫīri	*x* minas
SAA 6, 316	(duplicate of the preceding text)		
SAA 6, 326	–	1 town (Musīna-aplu-iddina), land, [slaves], 1 vineyard with 1,500 vines, 1 vegetable garden, 6 slaves	17½ minas
SAA 6, 329	660	1 vineyard with 1,000 vines, 10 hectares of land, 1 grove of oak trees, 1 meadow, 2 houses, 1 garden, 1 pool, 1 gardener in Singāra	4 minas
SAA 6, 330	(duplicate of the preceding text)		
SAA 6, 343	*c.* 660	5 slaves	5 minas
SAA 6, 344	(duplicate of the preceding text)[2]		
SAA 6, 346	*c.* 660	1 slave	1 mina
SAA 6, 347	*c.* 660	1 slave	1 mina
SAA 6, 333	–	*x* hectares of land, [1 vineyard of *x* thousand vines], 1 house, 1 threshing floor, 1 grove, 8 slaves in the district of Ḫarrān	*x* minas
SAA 6, 334	–	4 estates, *x* slaves	*x* minas
SAA 6, 335	–	50 hectares of land, 1 house, 1 threshing floor, 2 vegetable gardens in the area of Qatna	10 minas
SAA 6, 342	–	10 slaves	*x* minas
SAA 14, 78	659	1 slave	1 mina
SAA 14, 115	–	1 woman	1 ½ minas
SAA 14, 264	–	*x* slaves	½ mina
SAA 14, 425	630	4 estates in Nabû-šimanni	1½ minas
3. Merchant's mina[3]			
SAA 6, 96	*c.* 680	4 slaves	3 minas
SAA 6, 27	–	23 hectares of land and 1 house in Ḫanūru	5¾ minas

(Continued)

Table 7.2: Transactions in silver standards from the Ninevite archive (8th-7th century BCE) (Continued)

B. Loan documents (LD) and debt-notes (DN)

Text	*Date*	*Amount of the loan*	*Interest*
1. King's mina			
SAA 6, 143 (DN)	692	1 mina	½ mina
SAA 6, 167 (DN)	686	1½ minas	¼ mina
SAA 6, 180 (DN)	683	½ mina	[...]
2. Mina of Karkemiš			
SAA 6, 26 (LD)	711	20 minas	⅓ (33.3%)
SAA 6, 81 (LD)	694	2 minas	Loan against a pledge; no interest
SAA 6, 104 (LD)	690	*x* shekels	2 shekels per mina per month
SAA 6, 107 (LD)	686	3 minas	6 shekels per month
SAA 6, 108 (LD)	683	½ mina	4 shekels per month
SAA 6, 183 (LD)	683	2 minas	[...]
SAA 6, 262 (LD)	680	1 mina	¼ (25%)
SAA 6, 263 (LD)	(duplicate of the preceding text)		
SAA 6, 223 (DN)	679	1 mina	In lieu of interest, usufruct of 6 hectares of land in Ḫatâ
SAA 6, 224 (DN)	(duplicate of the preceding text)		
SAA 6, 273 (LD)	676	5 minas minus 6 shekels	Unspecified
SAA 6, 234 (DN)	672	3 minas 30 shekels	50% per shekel
SAA 6, 235 (DN)	671	1 mina	2 shekels per mina per month
SAA 6, 307 (LD)	668	3 minas	Loan against a pledge; no interest
SAA 14, 69 (LD)	667	5 minas	5 shekels per month
SAA 6, 318 (LD)	665	10 minas	¼
SAA 6, 323 (LD)	664	10 minas	⅓
SAA 6, 324 (LD)	(duplicate of the preceding text)		
SAA 14, 60 (LD)	658	9 minas 15 shekels	¼
SAA 14, 61 (LD)	(duplicate of the preceding text)		
SAA 14, 137 (LD)[4]	657	15 minas	¼
SAA 14, 94 (LD)	646	1 mina	[¼]
SAA 14, 95 (LD)	(duplicate of the preceding text)		
SAA 14, 441 (LD)	634	1 mina	¼
SAA 14, 159 (LD)	625	*x* minas	Loan against a pledge; no interest
SAA 6, 248 (LD)	–	10 minas	¼
SAA 14, 359 (LD)[5]	–	2 minas	[...]

(Continued)

Table 7.2: Transactions in silver standards from the Ninevite archive (8th-7th century BCE) (Continued)

Text	*Date*	*Amount of the loan*	*Interest*
3. *Merchant's mina*			
SAA 6, 97 (LD)	693	17 minas	2 shekels per mina per month

C. Documents concerning release of slaves

Text	*Date*	*Price for the redeemed person*
1. *King's mina*		
SAA 14, 437	669	[1 min]a
SAA 14, 438	(duplicate of the preceding text)	

D. Leases

Text	*Date*	*Good*	*Price*
1. *Mina of Karkemiš*			
SAA 14, 126	–	50 hectares of land, [1] garden	8 minas

E. Futures contracts

Text	*Date*	*Object*	*Sum to be repayed*
1. *Mina of Karkemiš*			
SAA 6, 158	687	Repayment of a silver sum with 9 homers of wine	*x* shekels

F. Conveyance texts

Text	*Date*	*Good*	*Price*
1. *Mina of Karkemiš*			
SAA 14, 307	–	[...]	*x* minas
SAA 14, 398	–	[...]	2 minas

Notes:

[1]Pledge document.

[2]The place name 'Karkemiš' has been restituted in the text. See SAA 6, 344:8' ⌜*ina* ŠÀ⌝-*bi* 5 MA.NA KUG.⌜UD⌝ *ina*! *ša* ⌜URU⌝.[*gar-ga-mis*], 'for 5 minas of silver by the (mina) of [Karkemiš]'.

[3]Note that in Radner 1999 a or b, 152 the list of attestations of the merchant's mina also includes the text ADD 254 = SAA 14, 20. However, according to a new reading of the line 7' which is adopted in Mattila's recent edition of the document, the occurrence is to be interpreted as *ina* 1 MA.NA-*e* URUDU!.[MEŠ], 'according to the copp[er] mina'.

[4]The name of the type of mina is not restituted in Mattila's edition, perhaps the mina of Karkemiš is intended here: SAA 14, 137 15 MA.[NA *x x* KUG.UD]/*ina* 1 MA.N[A *ša gar-ga-mis*], '15 mi[nas ... of silver] by the min[a of Karkemiš?]'.

[5]This attestation is omitted in Radner 1999 a or b, 150–152, appendix 2, attestations of the mina of Karkemiš).

of slaves, leases, futures contracts, and conveyance texts. The mina of Karkemiš is the standard preferred in all these categories of texts, with the exception of release of slaves, where the royal mina is used. Its use in loans also occurs in peripheral areas such as Til Barsip[46] and Gūzāna.[47] The royal mina is attested for sale contracts, three debt-notes, and in releasing of slaves. The use of the *manû ša šarri* for sale contracts is documented in the archives of Assur[48] and Kalḫu,[49] while for loans it is also attested in Assur,[50] Kalḫu,[51] but especially at Imgur-Illil.[52] Finally, the merchant's mina is used in two sale contracts[53] and in a loan document.[54] If we enlarge the analysis to the texts of other Neo-Assyrian archives, we see that the *manû ša tamkāri* is employed in slave sales in Kalḫu[55] and in loans taking place both in Assur[56] and at Imgur-Illil.[57]

In order to evaluate the cost of some goods in Neo-Assyrian age, some case-studies can be taken into account. Of the prices of the goods listed above, we will consider the data concerning slaves, skilled labourers, and houses. Unless otherwise indicated, in the following examples the silver prices are intended as regulated by the standard of the mina of Karkemiš. In some texts the sum of silver paid for a slave is 1 mina;[58] this value of 1:1 can be postulated even in cases of sums paid for more slaves, as in the case of transactions involving two slaves for 2 minas[59] and five slaves for 5 minas.[60] The cost of 3 minas for three slaves is documented both in the case of silver normed according to the standard of Karkemiš[61] and in that following the king's standard.[62] The price of 1 mina is found also in the purchase of women, as in the case of a maid purchased by Šumma-ilāni in 682 BCE.[63] The same sum for a female slave is paid in a transaction from Kalḫu of eleven years later,[64] but in this case the weight norm of reference is the *tamkāru*'s mina. This price, although normed according to the royal mina, is also attested in a contract from Assur of 664 BCE.[65] Lower and higher sums per unit concern both male and female labourers. The deeds from the Nineveh archive witness purchases of two slaves at a cost of only 1 mina,[66] three slaves at the price of 2 minas,[67] and purchases of more slaves for sums of few shekels, as in the case of three female slaves in a document of Dannāya, an high official.[68] In addition, a number of slaves are paid half a mina in one of the unassigned contracts of the Ninevite archive;[69] for the same sum could be sold a woman.[70] A similar situation may be seen in a slave sale from Kalḫu, where six individuals (three men and three women) are sold for 2 *tamkāru*'s minas,[71] which means 0.33 minas per unit.[72] There are cases of prices which are slightly higher than 1 mina, as may be observed in some transactions in which a slave is traded for 1½ minas.[73] However, slaves bought for 2 minas[74] or 3 minas[75] each are also attested in this period. In particular, the value of 3 minas seems to be the highest sum in silver paid for a slave. As for the female personnel, a slave is bought for 1½ minas in a contract of Ṣalmu-aḫḫē.[76] The same price for a woman is attested in two contracts from Nineveh[77] and in two contracts from Assur,[78] but only in one of the Assur documents the silver norm is explicitly referred to the Karkemiš standard.[79] These data may be compared with those of an administrative document from Nineveh concerning women sold for silver sums; interestingly, the sum paid per individual is generally half a mina,[80] although some women were sold for 1/3 of a mina[81] or 1½ minas.[82] In many other transactions, however, more or less numerous groups of people are normally purchased along with land as slave labour; one may note that in this type of contracts the cost of slaves must have been ridiculously low, as witnessed by the total price of the purchased goods.[83]

The most interesting case is represented by the use of different silver standards for the purchase of slave labour in transactions conducted by the same buyer: in two contracts of the charioteer of the royal corps Šumma-ilāni, presumably dating back to the same year (*c.* 680 BCE), the amount of silver paid for a single individual is regulated in a case according to the mina di Karkemiš, with a price of half a mina per unit,[84] and in another case according to the king's mina, with a price equivalent to 1½ minas.[85] Differently, one may see that at a distance of about 1 year the price per unit could remain unchanged regardless of the type of weight norm in use. This may be observed in two contracts for the purchase of slaves, the first one (681 BCE) dealing with a transaction ruled according to the mina di Karkemiš,[86] the second one (*c.* 680 BCE?) the merchant's mina.[87] The price per unit is 0.75 minas of silver; this cost also characterises the purchase of slave families conducted by various individuals in different years by using different silver standards (king's mina, Karkemiš mina).[88]

Cases of fluctuation of prices per units in the same time inform us that, for example, in 681 BCE the price of a slave, calculated according to the Karkemiš norm, could be 0.75[89] or 0.3 minas.[90] In any case, in the same year the price could be raised even up to 1½ minas if the type of mina was not specified by the seller in the transaction.[91] The purchase of skilled labourers does not seem to know prices too different from those observed for the slaves. The price recorded in a contract of Rēmanni-Adad (670 BCE), chief charioteer of Assurbanipal,[92] for the purchase of a sash-weaver (*ušpār ṣiprāti*) is the same sum paid by the above-mentioned Šumma-ilāni for an individual of servile condition employed as a donkey-driver (*rādi imāri*) in a transaction of about ten years before,[93] namely, 1½ minas according to the royal norm. Many factors could influence the determination of the cost of a specialised weaver, but it seems that the usual price was around 1 mina: for instance, this is the price which the palace scribe Nabû-tuklatū'a paid to Nabû-šuma-iddina to acquire a weaver of multicoloured trim (*ušpār birmi*) in 765 BCE.[94] This is also the sum paid for a baker (*āpiu*) in another Rēmanni-Adad's contract; in this case the silver is normed according to the standard of Karkemiš.[95] Other skilled labourers were purchased by this chief charioteer, such as a camel driver[96] and a eunuch,[97] but the price paid for these professionals is not preserved in the documents.

In the context of transactions involving houses, there is a wide variety of prices. In the same year (692 BCE), for instance, houses both of 3 minas[98] and 1 mina are documented;[99] in both cases their price refers to the king's norm. In the first case, the purchased house is a building of unknown location that consists of different rooms (bedroom, yard, bathroom, servants' apartments, an upper floor, a storehouse, a wing with a tomb), while in the second one it is a building with a yard located in Nineveh. The cost of *c.* 3 minas, precisely 3 minas 30 shekels, is also that paid by Kakkullānu, cohort commander of the crown prince, for an outbuilding in Nineveh in 630 BCE.[100] Five years later, this individual bought another house in the city for 2 minas,[101] and in 617 BCE a house in the same city for half a mina is acquired by him from two individuals.[102] Prices inferior to 3 minas for houses constituted by various rooms are also attested. The one bought by an unknown individual in Nineveh for 2 minas and 30 shekels in 641 BCE, for example, was composed by a tool shed, a bedroom, a bathroom, a wedding pavilion(?), a storehouse, an upper story.[103] The price for a house, however, could also reach 4 minas in the standard of Karkemiš, as documented in the purchase by Rēmanni-Adad of a house in the village of Bēt-Rība-ilu, in the vicinity of the town of Ṣāb-Adad in 666 BCE.[104] Further information about the cost of Neo-Assyrian houses in the 7th cent. BCE may be found in deeds from Assur. We know, for example, that the price of a new house (É GIBIL), presumably located in Assur, was 2½ minas in 618 BCE,[105] a price not so far from the one attested in the above-mentioned Nineveh contract of 692 BCE. Of course, the determination of the cost largely depended, among various factors, also on the bigger or smaller internal articulation of the building. A house located in the same city, composed by a service room, a bedroom, an anteroom, a bathroom, two yards, two storerooms, a wing and an oven could cost up to 17(?) minas of the Karkemiš standard in 636 BCE.[106] But one wonders how small was the house with an upper story and an exit bought by Ḫala-šuri for just some shekels of silver in 642 BCE.[107] The cost of small building units, presumably constituting single components of a house or service buildings, are also documented in the Neo-Assyrian legal corpus. They give us further details on the picture of the prices for buildings in this period. A purchase document from the archive of the Arameans in Assur (archive N18) attests that a bath (*tuānu*) with a wall in Gūzāna was bought for 50 shekels of silver by a certain Qišeraya in 700 BCE,[108] while from a Ninevite contract we learn that three storehouses with a courtyard in Nineveh were bought for 30 shekels of silver in 687 BCE.[109] In other contracts the value in silver of the single building is difficult to determine, since the price includes not only the house, but also land and other immovables. To give some examples, a house and a plot of land are paid by a certain Bardî 5½ minas of the king's standard,[110] but with a "modest" sum of 1 mina of the Karkemiš standard it was possible to acquire a property located in the village of Kiluḫte including, in addition to the house, also 5 hectares and 2 decares of land, 1 threshing floor, 1 orchard and 1/6 of a well.[111] These price changes must not necessarily have been motivated by the objective conditions of the good that was exchanged (*e.g.*, physical condition and age of the slave, professional expertise of the skilled labourer, location of land and immovable properties, condition of the buildings and their internal structure, etc.). Speculation certainly played an important role in transactions. Clever speculative manoeuvrings were often facilitated by the use of different weight norms: this can be supposed in the case of buyers using different types of mina in their transactions (see above the case of Šumma-ilāni and that of Rēmanni-Adad; Fales 1996, 31–33; 2003, 122). The difference in weight of the above-described silver norms, all in mutual competition within the unregulated economic system of the Assyrian empire, in combination with the chronic instability of the exchange rate (*maḫīru*), were certainly at the basis of the fluctuations of prices per unit and of the consequent prospects of profit of many private entrepreneurs of the Assyrian *élite*. Some remarks should also be made about prices expressed in the *tamkāru*'s mina. As already observed, this standard had a circulation limited to the homeland. According to a purchase contract from Nineveh (reign of Sargon), a certain Zāzî, eunuch of the king, is said to have bought for 5¾ minas of the merchant's mina 23 hectares of land in the town of Ḫanūru.[112] Since no other land sale transactions are documented for this silver norm, it is difficult to determine the possible relationships with prices expressed in the other silver standards. However, it is interesting to note that another Ninevite land contract (reign of Assurbanipal) shows that 50 hectares of land under irrigation with a house, a threshing floor, and two vegetable gardens in the town of Burrim, in the environs of Qatna, were paid 10 Karkemiš minas by Rēmanni-Adad.[113] The size of the property bought by Rēmanni-Adad is around twice that purchased by Zāzî and the 1:2 ratio is mirrored by the price of the two estates (5 minas *vs.* 10 minas). This comparison seems to suggest a possible equivalence of price between the merchant's mina and the Karkemiš mina: following Postgate's interpretation, one is tempted to suppose that the merchant's mina used in the transaction of the above-mentioned 23 hectares of land were actually of the Karkemiš type. However, the fact that the documents belong to different reign periods and that many factors (*e.g.*, the location of the estates) could have determined the price of the two properties induce us to consider this just as a working hypothesis.

As regards to transactions related to individuals of servile condition, for example, a statistical analysis of prices for slaves of both sexes recorded in legal documents coming not only from Nineveh, but also from Kalḫu and Assur (Fales 2003, 121 table 4), partly confirms the picture provided by the Ninevite archive: while the price for a male slave is set usually between 1 and 1½ minas (46% of the cases), that for a female slave was between ¾ mina and ½ mina (45.5% of the cases). The purchase of land, immovable properties, and people are certainly the best context to evaluate the cost of goods and to have an idea of the economic conditions of the Neo-Assyrian imperial society. There are, however, other transactions which can give us useful insights into economic life of this period. As to the use of the three standards in silver loans, we may see that the use of the mina of the king and of that of the merchant is limited to few cases, while in the majority of the documents dealing with silver loans the standard in use is the Karkemiš mina. This is not surprising, since it has represented the most popular among the Assyrian silver norms until the end of the empire. As to the *tamkāru*'s mina, we may observe that the transactions involving this standard do not show elements explaining the choice of this silver norm instead of the royal and the Karkemiš minas; in fact, amounts of silver given as loans include small sums (*e.g.*, half a mina, one mina and half a shekel)[114] as well as remarkable amounts (*e.g.*, 17 minas). Also the interest rate does not show any significant deviation from the Neo-Assyrian practice documented in other loans; when documented, the sum of the interest is half a shekel,[115] 2 shekels,[116] or 3 shekels per month.[117] One wonders why the merchant's mina was used instead of the other standards. An answer to this question, however, cannot be made in light of the present evidence. Deeds concerning loans in personal dossiers do not allow us to understand the particular conditions determining this choice by the moneylender and the proportions in the use of the merchant's mina in the transactions of a given individual in comparison with other standards. In the dossier of the *ḫundurāiu* Dād-aḫḫē, for example, both a loan of silver expressed in the merchant's mina[118] and a loan of silver without any reference to the silver norm are documented.[119]

From a look at the dossiers of three individuals, one may see that there is no competition between silver standards in loans. According to three loan documents, Aplāya, "third man" of the crown prince Urdu-Mullissu (Sennacherib's son), is the owner of amounts of silver. The transactions take place in different years, namely in 690,[120] 686,[121] and 683 BCE.[122] In all these cases, the silver sum is always weighed following the Karkemiš standard with different rates of monthly interest. Another case is that of Silim-Aššur, an official from Nineveh who was grand vizier and second vizier during the reigns of Esarhaddon and Assurbanipal: he makes use of the Karkemiš mina in two debt-notes concerning two consecutive years (672–671). In the first note (672), 3 minas 30 shekels of silver are put at the disposal of a certain Marduk-erība and the interest is 50% per shekel in case this individual does not pay at the deadline.[123] In the second document (671), the sum, corresponding to 1 mina and qualified as "first fruits of Issār of Arbela", is provided to an individual called Zabinâ.[124] According to the contract, this man had to pay 1½ minas at the repayment deadline and in the event of nonpayment the sum would have increased by 2 shekels per mina each month. In the dossier of Silim-Aššur there are other documents attesting his activity as moneylender and as lender of other important goods (*e.g.*, barley, sheep, and wine). Interestingly, in a loan document written a year later the contract with Zabinâ the sum of silver given to Mīnu-aḫṭi-ana-ili is not specified as regards its weight norm[125] and the same can be observed in another contract written in the same year.[126] Since in this case too the sum of silver is qualified as "first fruits" of the goddess of Arbela, the only reason for the use of a different standard must have been for speculative reasons. Were the 12 minas of silver given by Silim-Aššur to Zārūtî in the Karkemiš or in another weight standard? The calculation of the interest of a fourth on this sum evidently changed according to the norm of reference. Analogously, Rēmanni-Adad prefers to use the Karkemiš standard for three silver loans in the years 668,[127] 665,[128] and 664.[129] In the first contract, the loan in question is a typical loan against a pledge: there is no interest and some individuals are placed as a pledge. However, one may see that in a loan document of the year 666 a sum of 1½ minas is placed against a pledge,[130] but in this case the mina used by Rēmanni-Adad for the silver sum is not specified, presumably on purpose. On the contrary, other loan transactions show that the activity as moneylenders of these "top spenders" of the Assyrian imperial *élite* was not always meant to bring profit (Kwasman & Parpola 1991, xxiii). In five documents where the Karkemiš standard is used sums of money are borrowed for no interest.[131] With the exception of one text concerning the loan of 5 minas minus 6 shekels (in other words, 4 minas 54 shekels),[132] all the deeds concern loans against a pledge.[133] We learn, for example, that in 668 Banî and Ṭusî owed a sum of 3 minas to Rēmanni-Adad without interest.[134] Perhaps, the fact that Banî, deputy of the chief physician at the royal court in Nineveh, acted as witness in some legal documents of Rēmanni-Adad's dossier (in the years 667, 664, 663, and [...]),[135] evidently as a result of his status of "friend" of the *mukīl-appāte*,[136] may explain the "preference treatment" of the king's chariot driver towards Banî.

Prices of commodities in administrative and legal texts: a look at the everyday transactions

The prices in silver treated above concern the high-value commodities (immovables and people) which are attested in transactions conducted by a number of palace-linked individuals. These prices exclusively come from legal documents. Further information on prices of commodities in Neo-Assyrian period can be found in other legal documents from private archives, as well as from administrative texts and letters. In this case, the prices refer to a different set of goods, namely utilitarian commodities (in form of both raw and processed items, staples, animals, etc.) which characterised the everyday trading activities in the Assyrian cities. In addition, other disbursements in silver document the practice to compensate the work of some professionals with sums of money amounting to one or more shekels in the private sphere. This evidence is presented and discussed here in detail.

A record of merchants' transactions from Nineveh dating to the 7th century BCE[137] gives us further insights into commodities and their values in the Neo-Assyrian period. This administrative document attests the private trading activities that some merchants of different provenance executed in the city of Ḫarrān. Their transactions, which are not controlled by the state, involve the purchase of various commodities for silver. In this case, the exchanged items were purchased by the merchants for remarkable sums of silver. These goods were normally part of the state income and these *tamkārus* were probably required to inform the central state administration about their illegal commercial activities. From this document, it seems that the interest of the Assyrian state was to hinder non-state-controlled commercial initiatives. The data provided by this text are of great interest, since they enable us to know the possible price per unit of certain commodities exchanged in private transactions (Table 7.3). The goods listed in the preserved lines of this tablet belong to various categories: iron, leather, stone, textiles, and unidentified items.

The above-mentioned transactions take place in the city of Ḫarrān and involve merchants coming from different places of the imperial territory as well as from abroad: among them, there is an ironsmith from Assur,[138] another individual from the same city which exported the purchased dyed skins from Kalḫu,[139] traders from the land of Kummuḫ,[140] a merchant from Babylon,[141] and an Aramaean.[142] Unfortunately, no details are given in the text about the silver standard(s) used in these purchases, but other transactions taking place in Ḫarrān and documented in the Nineveh archive[143] suggest that the Karkemiš mina was probably followed. These transactions also involved the purchase of a certain amount of coloured wool, exchanged for more than one mina. Another reference to wool price can be found in a note from Nebi Yunus regarding an unspecified quantity of shorn wool (evidently a huge amount of wool), whose cost is said to correspond to 20 talents 13 minas 18 1/3 shekels of silver. From the text SAA 11, 26 we learn about the foreign provenance of certain commodities. As regards to textiles, linen garments are said to have been acquired in the city from two foreign traders, namely the *kitûs* from an individual of Aramaean origin, while the *šaddīnus* from a Kummuḫaean. It is interesting to note that the price per unit of the *kitû* is higher than that of the second type of dress (41.5 *vs.* 6 shekels); perhaps, the linen garment in question consisted of a finely-executed luxury variety. Another Neo-Assyrian textile which

Table 7.3: Commodities and prices in private transactions of 7th century BCE Ḫarrān

Good: category	*Good: quantity*	*Price*	*Price per unit*
Iron	*x* talents	5 minas	–
	4 talents	1 mina	0.25 minas (= 15 shekels)
	Total: 75 talents	18 minas	0.24 minas (= 14.4 shekels)
Leather	301 dyed skins	10 2/3 minas	0.03 minas (= 2.12 shekels)
	3 dyed skins	6 ½ shekels	2.16 shekels
	Total: 304 dyed skins	(no total price)	–
	84 cured skins	2 minas 53? shekels	0.03 minas (= 2.05 shekels)
Other goods	8 boxes of [...][1]	2 minas 10 [shekels]	0.26 minas (= 16.2 shekels)
Stone	1 talent 6 minas blocks of genuine [...]-stone	1 mina 10 shekels	0.68 minas (= 43.7 shekels)
Textiles	2 linen garments	1 mina 23 shekels	0.61 minas (= 41.5 shekels)
	5 linen togas	½ mina	6 shekels
	4 5/6 minas of [black] wool and 1/3 mina of red wool	1 mina [*x* shekels?]	*c.* 0.19 minas per kilogram?
	Total: [...]	–	–

[1]In SAA 11, ad 26 e.16' Fales and Postgate suggest the reading *ṭi-ṭ*[*u*] for the content of the *quppu*-boxes. Another possibility is that the word in question is *ṭīṭu*, "fig", from which a variety of beer was produced in Assyria. Apparently, it is difficult to believe that a high amount of money was paid for fruits which were common in the Assyrian countryside, but from ND 2310 it is clear that fruits were exchanged in Assyrian cities: according to this text, the price for an unspecified amount of grapes corresponded to 4 shekels of silver.

could be purchased for a high sum of money was the *ṣipirtu*-sash: in fact, a letter from Kalḫu shows that such a textile was sold for half a mina (*i.e.*, 30 shekels).[144] Both these types of garments were commodities of high value in the palace-oriented economic system of Assyria: members of the royal court, the personnel linked to the palace household, and in general the urban *élites* in the main cities of the empire determined the demand for fine and luxury garments. Knotted *kitûs* for the palace are listed in an administrative document from Nineveh.[145] *Šaddīnus* were also highly appreciated in Assyria: this garment could be made of linen[146] or byssus.[147] These two textile products are also mentioned in a letter of Adda-ḫāti, governor of Hamath: the sender informs King Sargon about the collection of the tax imposed on the local population, corresponding to 2 talents and 18 minas of silver by the Karkemiš standard, as well as on the delivery of half a shekel of gold, 2 *šaddīnus*, and 3 *kitûs* to the king.[148] Linen garments received by the palace administration as tribute and audience gifts were then redistributed among the court members and the palace personnel: according to a letter, a number of *šaddīnus* and *kitûs* was assigned to the queen, the crown prince, the grand vizier, the commander-in-chief, the chief judge, the second vizier, the chief eunuch, and the palace superintendent,[149] while the overseer of the domestic quarters, the scribe of the palace, the chariot driver, and the "third man" of the chariot received one *šaddīnu* each.[150] In addition to the local production in Assyria, many textiles, both as raw materials and as processed products, were imported from abroad. The import of textiles from the land of Kummuḫ (classical Commagene) is also witnessed by a letter sent by the crown prince Sennacherib to Sargon which mentions red(?) wool brought by the emissaries of Kummuḫ to the Assyrian king as a tribute.[151] Linen garments were also integral part of household goods of women belonging to the Assyrian upper class, as we will see below. Concerning the price of textiles in the Neo-Assyrian period, a comparison may be made with other data concerning transactions of movable goods. Three documents from the archives of Assur shed

Table 7.4: Commodities and prices from documents from 7th century BCE Assur

Text	*Date*	*Good*	*Price*	*Price per unit*
NATAPA 2, 100	647	2 oxen	1 mina	0.5 minas (= 30 shekels)
		13 *urnutu*-garments	1 mina	0.07 minas (= 4.6 shekels)
NATAPA 2, 102	644?/629?	1 textile(?)[1]	8 shekels	8 shekels
NATAPA 2, 133	undated	1 ram	2½? shekels	2½? shekels
		1 haversack(?)/saddle bag(?)	1? shekel	1? shekel

[1] The reading of the occurrence is uncertain. The possibility that the commodity in question is the *maṣḫatu*-flour is suggested by Fales in NATAPA 2, ad 102:4.

light on the price of textiles as well as of livestock (Table 7.4). In this case too, the silver standard used in the purchases is not specified.

In a contract of 647 BCE, 13 *urnutu*-garments are purchased for 1 mina of silver;[152] accordingly, the price per unit of a single *urnutu* corresponded to 4.6 shekels, a sum slightly inferior to that of the five linen togas of the above-mentioned administrative text from Nineveh. In another document from Assur recording a silver loan of few years later, an unknown textile product(?) is paid 8 shekels.[153] Finally, a short note on expenditures for mixed commodities attests the cost of 1(?) shekel for one haversack(?) of goat hair.[154] The cost of an ox (30 shekels) and of a ram (2½? shekels) is also of particular interest, since the price of livestock is never explicitly expressed in land sale contracts,[155] where the cost of animals belonging to the purchased estate is generally included in the total price along with land, buildings, and slaves. The only comparable evidence is provided by a debt-note from Kalḫu, where the price of some rams is given: however, the money sum corresponds to 18½ minas of copper and the number of animals is not specified.[156] Additional information on the prices of animals in the Neo-Assyrian period seem to be exclusively concerned with beasts of burden, in all likelihood for their relevance as a means of transport of commodities in trading activities. A list from Nineveh records different prices paid for donkeys.[157] The price in silver changes according to the gender of the animals: while a male donkey could be purchased for 1½ minas 7 shekels (of silver),[158] the price for a female donkey could vary from a minimum of 32 shekels to a maximum of 1 mina.[159] Two female donkeys are exchanged for 1 mina, but in accordance with two different norms, *i.e.* the (regular? Karkemiš?) mina and the royal mina.[160] A contract of Bānītî substantially confirms the value of male donkeys of the administrative document; in fact, the buyer acquires two donkeys for 2½ minas 3 shekels:[161] this means that the price per unit was *c.* 1 mina 16 shekels. Instead, a lower price for a male donkey is given in a letter of possible commercial content from Kalḫu, according to which an *imāru* was sold to a certain Nergal-dān for half a mina of silver.[162] Higher prices may be found for mules. From a note concerning a good mule belonging to Mannu-kī-Arbail, for example, we learn that its value corresponded to 30(?) minas, but it is possible that this exceptional cost was due to the fact that the animal in question belonged to the royal property.[163] Camels represented another important transport means in the 1st millennium BCE. From a Babylonian letter dating to the reign of Sargon and dealing with disbursements of silver to various people we learn that one mina was the price of she-camels;[164] although the message does not specify the number of the animals, it is possible that the price of one *anaqātu* was not so different from that of a male camel. Another letter of the reign of Sargon, which comes from northern Babylonia, informs the king about business activities including sales of camels. From the words of the sender we know that the eunuch Nabû-ēpuš bought one camel for 1 2/3 mina of silver.[165] A different value is given in a note about two camels that Dannāya lent to three individuals in 674 BCE: according to the penalty clause, the price of one camel was 3 minas.[166] These prices may be compared with the one attested in Babylonia for the reign of Nabonidus (555–539 BCE), when the sum exchanged for one camel corresponded to 50 shekels (Jursa 2010, 550 and fn. 3015). In any case, all these values appear very far from the price of one shekel or half a shekel for a camel that Assurbanipal mentions in his prism inscriptions.[167]

Commodity prices are also listed in two documents found in Room ZT 16 of the north wing of the outer court of the North-West Palace at Kalḫu (Table 7.5); in all likelihood, this place housed part of the local *šakintu*'s archives (Postgate 1979b, 100). The listed expenses probably refer to the preparations for a wedding party. These expenditures concern not only foods and drinks, whose amounts are generally not specified, but also commodities presumably destined to be used during the ceremony (*i.e.*, the ring, the garments, etc.), the wages of skilled labourers employed for the

Table 7.5: Commodities and prices in lists of expenses from Kalḫu

Text	*Good: category*	*Good: description & quantity*	*Price*
ND 2310	Jewellery	1 signet ring	½ shekel
	Foodstuffs	loaves of bread for 10 days	7 shekels 5/6 mina
		meat	5/6 mina
		meat	½ shekel
		oil	1½ shekels
		wine	½ shekel
		wine	1 shekel
		grapes	4 shekels
	Working activities	'for butchering' (*i.e.*, the wages of a butcher?)	3 shekels
		wages of a goldsmith	1 shekel
ND 2312	Textiles & leather items	1 *kuzippu*-garment	4½ shekels
		1 wrapping-cloth(?)	2⅓ shekels
		1 *kāpilu*-object	1 shekel
	Drinks	6 *qû* of wine	6 shekels
		wine	1 shekel
	Foodstuffs	corn	1 shekel
	Journeys & relevant expenses	Nineveh	1 ¼ shekels
		Kalḫu	1 shekel
		Assur ('for the people in the city')	1 shekel
	Other expenses	'for yourself'	1 shekel
		'(for) the day the woman got well'	½ shekel
		to Šamaš-nādin-aḫi	2 shekels

butchering of the meat and for the production of the bride's gold jewellery, journeys in Nineveh, Kalḫu, and Assur, and additional outlays.

What is important to note is that these data constitute a vivid evidence of the cost of everyday commodities, especially foodstuffs. The purchases deal with relatively small amounts of silver, ranging from half a shekel to 5/6 mina. The text ND 2310 shows that only a part of the commodities was purchased; in fact, a large amount of corn (*i.e.*, 2 homers 5 seahs) was borrowed from two individuals.[168] To judge from the silver sum paid for corn in ND 2312, the amount of grain in question must have been small; this is also suggested from a letter from Kalḫu mentioning the purchase of a grain-heap(?) for 3 minas of silver.[169] Barley price was subject to a wide fluctuation in the Neo-Assyrian period. For instance, if we consider the information about the price of barley in the *Getreidekursangaben* formulae, 1 shekel could represent the price of 10 litres of barley, while 3 minas that of an amount equivalent to 1800 litres.[170] Additional commodities, presumably destined to the same wedding ceremony, are listed in another document from Room ZT 16, but in this case, the goods, which comprise textiles, foods for the banquet (wheat, flour, sheep), copper vessels and wooden tools, are not specified as regards to their cost, the only exception being two unspecified amounts of wool equivalent to 7 shekels of silver.[171] The prices of certain commodities substantially accord with those of the above-discussed texts. For five types of garments it is possible to know their value in shekels (*i.e.*, *kitû*: 41.5 shekels; *šaddīnu*: 6 shekels; *urnutu*: 4.6 shekels; *kuzippu*: 4½ shekels; wrapping-cloth: 2½ shekels).[172] Unfortunately, the lack of data about the specific quantities of foodstuffs (*e.g.*, number of loaves of bread and of meat cuts) prevents us from knowing the possible price per unit of these goods. The only exception is given by ND 2312, from which we learn that 6 *qû* of wine were purchased for 6 shekels: this means that 1 *qû* of wine was equivalent to 1 shekel. As a consequence, it is possible that the unspecified amounts of wine of half a shekel and of one shekel, which are listed in ND 2310 and ND 2312, corresponded to respectively half a *qû* and one *qû*. With regard to bread, if the sum of 7 shekels 5/6 mina (*i.e.*, 57 shekels) represents the total expense for ten days of consumption, it follows that the cost of bread for one day was equivalent to 5.7 shekels. As to jewels, no details are made about the material of the signet ring (*unqu*) of half a shekel. Signet rings were integral part of wealthy dowries, as we will see below: in the one of the woman called Ṣubētu, 16 silver signet rings are listed, but their value in shekels is not specified. On the basis of the price given in ND 2310, we may tentatively suggest a cost of 8 shekels for the 16 *unqu*s of this bride. Further information on prices of jewels may be found in a dowry list from Kalḫu: among the various goods, there is a gold earring of 5 shekels (of silver) according to the Karkemiš standard. This clearly shows that this silver norm was far from being used only in transactions of immovables and people involving large investments of money; on the contrary, it also served to determine the value of items of few shekels in marriage transactions. Nothing can be said, instead, about the prices of the everyday commodities given in ND 2310 and ND 2312, since the silver norm used to calculate them is not specified. Of particular interest are also the references to expenses for the compensation of the service of some professionals. The working activities which are covered by the expenses include the butchering activity (3 shekels), the work of a goldsmith (1 shekel), and that of an individual called Šamaš-nādin-aḫi (2 shekels), whose service, however, is not indicated in the text. Nothing can be said, instead, about the unnamed person receiving 1 shekel, who is mentioned in the text as "yourself". In Assyria, free persons of different professional sectors could be employed for hire (Postgate 1987, 261): in this case, however, only the work of the goldsmith is explicitly referred to as hired labour, as shown by the use of the word *igrē*, "wages (for hired labour)".[173] This goldsmith probably worked for the private sector to supplement the income he received as a full-time employee in the palace household.[174] To judge from the listed prices, the most expensive service was the work of the butcher, but his activity, which presumably required the slaughtering of the livestock destined to the wedding banquet, is not qualified as hired work. Analogous wages can be found in the legal documentation from the archives of the *ḫundurāius* in the *Außenhaken* area in Assur. These contracts are very instructive, since tell us that a sum of *c.* 3 shekels was the highest monthly pay for men working for hire in the 7th century BCE, while wages of around 1–2 shekels represent the majority of the cases (Radner 2007, 200, appendix A-c). This evidence induces us to conclude that 1) the wages of the professionals involved in the organisation of the ceremonial event in Kalḫu are in line with the standard wages of hired workers in Assur; and that 2) also the service of the *ṭābiḫu* and that of Šamaš-nādin-aḫi were probably hired work. That the activity of the *ṭābiḫu* was of great importance for the ceremonial event in preparation is suggested by the number of the sheep recorded in ND 2311, another text originating from the Room ZT 16 of the North-West Palace and probably connected to the same event: this text mentions 20 sheep with fleece and 2 sheep of the Qusaean variety.[175] The number of animals in ND 2311 as well as the references to the relationship between amount of bread and wine and days (of consumption?) in ND 2310, namely 10 days for bread and 12 days for 24 *qû* of wine,[176] may give us an idea of the proportions of this sumptuous banquet. Summing up, the disbursement for foodstuffs and drinks corresponded to 2 minas 2½ shekels, in other words to 86.5% of the total expenses for the ceremonial event.

Prices are certainly the best evidence to know the level of prosperity of the Assyrian upper class during the political and economic apogee of the empire under the Sargonids. Other important elements attesting the richness of the urban social *élites* are represented by the household goods which formed the dowries of women as well as the inheritance share of heirs. In the following table (Table 7.6) the goods composing the women's accoutrements in four marriage contracts are displayed. The data cover the textual evidence from Kalḫu and Assur of four different periods of the Neo-Assyrian age. Three out of the four texts can be assigned to the 7th century BCE.

Although the collected data from these marriage documents present a very limited evidence of the household material culture of the Neo-Assyrian age, they are of great interest for the knowledge of the main categories of commodities which composed the dowries and the relevant quantities of the single components. From the presence or absence of certain items (number of utilitarian goods *vs.* number of luxury items) we may see that the most represented groups of commodities are those of textiles and containers, followed by that of tools. The presence of all these goods in the texts is characterised by a marked irregularity. In fact, textiles are present in dowry lists of three texts (GPA 1; StAT 2, 164; ND 2307) and the same can be seen as regards to tools (StAT 2, 164; 184; ND 2307). Only the group of containers occurs in all the texts (GPA 1; StAT 2, 164; 184; ND 2307). Furniture items are included in two dowry lists of late 7th century BCE (StAT 2, 184; ND 2307), while jewellery is only mentioned in a contract of the 8th century (GPA 1) and in a document dating to the period following the reign of Assurbanipal (ND 2307). In addition, the dowries described in the Assur contracts also include silver in cash: one-third of mina of refined silver in the case of Mullissu-ḫammat's dowry (StAT 2, 164) and 2 minas in that of Šulmu-[...]-lumur (StAT 2, 184). The importance of the cash component in the dowries will progressively increase in

Table 7.6: Household commodities in four dowry lists of the 8th–7th century BCE

	GPA 1 Provenance: Kalḫu (date lost, 8th century BCE)	*StAT 2, 164 Provenance: Assur (reign of ESH, 675 BCE)*	*StAT 2, 184 Provenance: Assur (date lost, reign of ASB & later?)*	*ND 2307[1] Provenance: Kalḫu (after reign of ASB, 622 BCE)*
Textiles				
Wool	3[2]	1[3]		4[4]
Linen		4[5]		6[6]
Unspecified	9[7]	1[28]		35[9]
Containers				
Wood	1?[10]		2[11]	4[12]
Copper	1[13]	1[14]	2[15]	2[16]
Bronze	1[17]			
Unspecified				2[18]
Tools				
Wood		1[19]		3[20]
Iron			1[21]	1[22]
Stone				4[23]
Furniture				
Wood			4[24]	
Bronze				1[25]
Copper				7[26]
Iron			1[27]	

(Continued)

Table 7.6: Household commodities in four dowry lists of the 8th–7th century BCE (Continued)

	GPA 1 Provenance: Kalḫu (date lost, 8th century BCE)	StAT 2, 164 Provenance: Assur (reign of ESH, 675 BCE)	StAT 2, 184 Provenance: Assur (date lost, reign of ASB & later?)	ND 23071 Provenance: Kalḫu (after reign of ASB, 622 BCE)
Jewellery				
Copper	2[28]			
Gold	1[29]			2[30]
Silver				45[31]
Stone				
Cash component				
Silver		1/3 mina of refined silver	2 minas of silver	

[1]ND 2307 (*Iraq* 16, 37, pl. vi). [2]*x ša-ḫīli* of red wool, *x* pieces of purple wool together with a [...]-cloth, *x* pieces of purple wool together with a ditto cloth. [3]1 *urnutu*-garment. [4]2 *kuzippu*-garments of red wool of the port, 2 *urnutu*-garments of red wool of the port. [5]2 *urnutu*-garments, 1 *pazibdu*-dress, [1 ...]*rakatu*-dress. [6]5 *urnutu*-garments, 1 toga. [7]2 bedcovers, *x* TÚG.SI.LUḪ, *x* textile pieces of a palm wide, 1 [...]-cloth for the bridegroom, 6 ordinary coats, 2 *ša-ḫīli*, 2 *ḫulsu*-garments, 4 tunics, 2 *gammīdu*-garments. The text gives the total of 32 textiles. See GPA 1:12'. [8]4 *kandaraššu*-dresses, 2 house-quality *urnutu*-garments, 1 house-quality *maqaṭṭutu*-garment, 1 good-quality *maqaṭṭutu*-garment, 1 *naṣbutu*-garment, 2 *ḫuzūnu*-garments. [9]6[?] TÚG.UŠ-textiles, 6[?] *ḫuzūnu*-garments, 2 white(?) *kuzippu*-garments, 4 *urnutu*-garments, 1 roll of bedspreads, 2 bedcovers, 1 wrap, 1 tunic, 2 *gammīdu*-garments, 10 É.SAG-textiles for a pair of washed *kuzippu*-garments. [10]3 *sallu*-baskets(?). [11]2 *kappu*-bowls. [12]2 *kappu*-bowls for food, 2 *pursītu*-vessels of salt. [13]1 *saplu*-bowl. [14]1 *munaqqītu*-bowl. [15]2 *kappu*-bowls. [16]1 bucket, 1 *diqāru*-cooking pot. [17]1 *diqāru*-cooking pot. [18]2 *dannu*-containers of spices. [19]1 *kābu*-implement. [20]1 *ša*-KAR-tool, 2 ŠU.UN-implements. [21]1 shovel. [22]1 shovel. [23]2 implements of *ḫāltu*-stone, 1 (ditto of?) beryl, 1 kohl pen of stone(?). [24]1 bed, 1 table, 2 chairs with their [...]. [25]1 bed. [26]1 stool, 1 table, 2 chairs, [1 ...], 1 mirror(?), 1 pipe. [27]1 bed. [28]1 bracelet of 4 minas, [1 ...]. [29]1 earring of 5 shekels (of silver) by the (mina) of Karkemiš. [30]1 ... of stone and gold of 1 1/3 shekels, 1 *sabubu*-jewel of gold of half a shekel. [31]4 bracelets, 2 *daššu*-ornaments, 1 collar, 2 necklaces, 20 earrings, 16 signet rings.

the 1st millennium BCE, as evident from a look at the Neo-Babylonian sources, where the amount of silver could correspond to more than ten minas (Jursa 2010, 810–811).

From a look at the single components of these groups, we may see that the quantity, the material, and the typologies of the listed commodities differ from a text to another, although we may detect some common elements. For example, woollen and linen *urnutu*-garments were a very common element in Assyrian dowries (StAT 2, 164; ND 2307), as well as *ḫuzūnus* (StAT 2, 164; ND 2307), *gammīdus* (GPA 1; ND 2307), tunics (GPA 1; ND 2307), and bedcovers (GPA 1; ND 2307). Analogously, in the realm of household containers, *kappu*-bowls were amply used as vessels for eating (StAT 2, 184; ND 2307), while the *diqāru* represented the usual cooking utensil in the Assyrian domestic units (GPA 1; ND 2307). Other common items of dowries were iron shovels, tables, and chairs (StAT 2, 184; ND 2307). Socio-economic differences in the material culture of these dowries can be inferred from the presence of more varieties of the same item as well as of additional utensils. For example, in a contract from Assur (StAT 2, 184) both wooden and copper bowls are included. In a late document from Kalḫu (ND 2307), instead, the presence of containers specifically devoted to condiments (salt, spices) witness the high level of prosperity of the bride,[177] an aspect clearly visible also from the rich assortment of garments and other textile products (45 textiles) as well as from utensils which are not found in other dowry lists, such as *mušanniktu*-implements and kohl pens of (precious?) stone, and, last but not least, from the huge amount of jewels which accompanied these commodities (48 precious items).

The nature of some goods is strictly connected to the professional role of the woman involved in the transaction and the socio-economic *milieu* of her family. Mullissu-ḫammat, who is mentioned in the document dating to the reign of Esarhaddon, is the daughter of a horse keeper of Issār of Arbela.[178] The document also tells us that she was a votaress (*šēlūtu*) of the goddess.[179] The connection with the cultic sphere of this devotee is also shown by the presence of a copper libation bowl (*munaqqītu*) among the goods composing her dowry.[180] Interestingly, the same profession of Mullissu-ḫammat also characterises the social status of the woman called Šulmu-[...]-lumur, mentioned in another contract from the archive of the Egyptians in Assur.[181] The richest among these women is certainly Ṣubētu, daughter of Amat-Astārti, the harem manageress of the New Palace in Kalḫu.[182] Her dowry list also specifies the total cost of the items: the first group of jewels, consisting of two items, costs half a mina of silver (= 15 shekels each?);[183] the second group, which comprises 45 items, costs 2 minas 4 shekels of refined silver;[184] finally, the price of a set of 20 garments is 9½ minas 4 shekels.[185] It is not clear why only the value of this set of textiles is given in the texts, but it is reasonable to think that an analogous cost characterised also the other set of garments mentioned in the text. Nothing can be said, instead, of the woman involved in the marriage transaction of 8th century from Kalḫu, since the beginning of the text is lost. It is clear that the accoutrements of these women represent everyday items which were peculiar to the upper social stratum of the palace-linked property owners. Unfortunately, the lack of data concerning dowries from other Assyrian cities, archives, and periods of the Neo-Assyrian age[186] does not allow us to deduce whether certain everyday objects were diffusely present in domestic contexts or whether they were limited to certain periods or socio-economic contexts. In addition, Neo-Assyrian inheritance texts – other important sources for information on material culture of the household sector – contain few details about domestic objects[187] and, consequently, cannot be used for an in-depth analysis of living standards and their changes from a period to another. In any case, a certain wealth differentiation must have been existed within the Assyrian urban *élite*. Surprisingly, no one of these dowries include grinding stones, a characteristic implement of every Mesopotamian domestic unit. This aspect, which also characterises the Neo-Babylonian dowries, was probably due to the decrease of the value of this item in the 1st millennium BCE (Jursa 2010, 810). The above-described Assyrian dowries are composed by high-value items; in fact, no pottery vessels are included in them and the only stone objects are represented by three items of Ṣubētu's dowry. This can also be seen in a private letter concerning the adoption of a woman: the household items given to her only comprise a bed, three blankets, a bedspread, chairs, a table and two of the jewels which also characterise Ṣubētu's dowry, namely a silver bracelet and a silver *daššu*-ornament.[188] Also the absence or the restricted number of wooden implements and of pieces of furniture was evidently due to the low value of these items in comparison with their metal counterparts. Moreover, wooden items tend to be accompanied by metal typologies of the same object, as evident in the case of the wooden and copper bowls and in that of the wooden and iron beds,[189] with the metalware probably representing the "dinner service" for great occasions and the metal furniture the luxury items and status-symbols of the upper class.

In general, the 1st millennium BCE dowry lists seem to exclusively focus on high-value items, especially consisting of metal objects. This, of course, does not mean that wooden and stone items were absent from the houses of the Assyrian upper class: inventory lists recording private goods mention a variety of domestic implements of iron, wood, clay, and stone,[190] but, evidently, the low-value attributed to these commodities in the socio-economic context to which these women belong made these items unsuitable for a bride's dowry. This impression is also confirmed by a Middle Assyrian inheritance text which lists the commodities belonging to the personal property of Takla-šemāt: stone implements,[191] bronze vessels,[192] and wooden furniture[193] were common components of household movables of wealthy Assyrian families.

The most interesting comparison which may be made about the listed objects of these dowries concerns the two texts originating from Kalḫu, one dating to the 8th century and the other to the late 7th century BCE. Both the dowry lists show a rich variety of textiles which witness the strict connection of the two women with the palatine context. The number of garments at their disposal surpasses that of the textiles of the *šēlūtu* Mullissu-ḫammat, the daughter of a horse keeper of Egyptian origin. However, also the seventeen textiles of the votaress from Assur show a certain degree of internal differentiation as the ones of the above-mentioned women: in fact, both wool and linen garments are present in her dowry and of certain clothes different use-related qualities (*i.e.*, house-quality, good-quality) are listed. Her family belonged to the community of Egyptians of Assur, a part of which settled there before the Assyrian conquest of Memphis in 671 BCE. In light of the Assyrian name of this votaress, her dedication to the Assyrian goddess, and the social status of her father, it is likely that Pabba'u belonged to an Egyptian family of traders which had immigrated for business in Assyria many years before (Donbaz & Parpola 2001, xvi). Some of the garments (*kuzippu, ḫuzūnu, urnutu*)[194] and of the bed-clothes (*qarrāru, dappastu*)[195] of Ṣubētu's dowry are also mentioned in two Nimrud texts which originate from the North-West Palace at Kalḫu, the same place of provenance of the marriage contract of Ṣubētu, as observed above. It has been suggested that the disbursements for a possible wedding ceremony which are registered in these texts probably refer to Ṣubētu's marriage (Postgate 1979b, 102, 103). From one of these documents we learn that the cost of one *kuzippu* was 4½ shekels. Although the price per unit of Ṣubētu's garments is not specified, it is clear that the *kuzippus* which formed her dowry belonged to an expensive, and presumably high-quality, variety; in fact, to judge from the total price of 20 garments given in the marriage contract, that is 574 shekels, the medium price per unit is 28.7 shekels, which is more than six times the cost of the *kuzippu* (4.5 shekels) mentioned in ND 2312.

The study of the wealth level of the Assyrian upper class families may also be approached by considering the composition of private households. Household personnel belonging to the rich Assyrian businessmen comprised a variable number of servants and skilled labourers. As seen above, one of Rēmanni-Adad's business activities concerned the acquisition of skilled labourers such as specialised weavers, donkey and camel drivers, bakers as well as eunuchs. That these private households included various specialists may also be seen from an inheritance document, where the woman Ba'altī-yabâti gets a house and the relevant servants from her father:[196] the list of people includes two bakers, a fuller, and a fez-maker. Food-processing as well as the production of garments and other textile products for the members of the owner's family required the permanent presence of specialised workers. In this connection, it is reasonable to think that some of the women, especially girls, which were bought by these owners in their transactions, were employed in textile activities in their houses, presumably under the supervision of specialised weavers. Nothing can be said, instead, about the possible employment of these slaves in private workshops for commercial purposes (Postgate 1987, 266), although the possibility that many slaves employed in private households were trained in various crafts in order to raise their value and to develop the owner's private commercial activities cannot be ruled out.[197]

Conclusions

This overview on the private sector of the Neo-Assyrian empire economy and on the investments of members of the Assyrian urban *élite* has shown the central role of silver as currency both in large investments in immovable properties as well as in medium-to-small investments in everyday trading activities involving utilitarian commodities.

The analysis of the investments made by some affluent members of the Assyrian upper class has shown the high variability which characterises the use of the three standards and, consequently, of the prices of immovables and people. In this picture of such a marked variability, the Karkemiš norm emerges as the most versatile standard, for it was applied to different types of transactions. Moreover, the play on different silver norms by these businessmen over the years witnesses profit-aimed strategies which were probably motivated by the highly unstable exchange-rate of commodities in Assyria.

The information about the value in silver of everyday commodities that are not included in the high-range transactions completes the picture about the prices in Neo-Assyrian period, although the meagre evidence about the purchase of utilitarian goods prevents us from knowing the full range of prices for each of these movables, their development, and the relevant fluctuations in Assyria in the period under examination. From the available material, we may observe that the money value of utilitarian goods ranges between *c.* 40 shekels to half a shekel. Prices of such commodities corresponding to further subdivisions of the shekel are not attested in Assyria and will only emerge from Neo-Babylonian texts as a peculiarity of the Babylonian economy. In any case, it is worth noting that silver plays a significant role also in transactions concerning goods or services costing one or few shekels. The purchase of staples such as bread, meat, and fruit for small amounts of silver confirms that the use of this metal was widely diffused in the everyday transactions of Assyrian cities and that it functioned as value indicator also for common goods of everyday consumption. In this connection, we may suppose that the diffusion of the practice to compensate services with silver wages in the private sector of economy determined a wider diffusion of silver as a means of payment in those social strata of the Assyrian cities from which hired workers were taken by property owners.

As a consequence, also the access and the consumption of certain goods by individuals belonging to these social strata of the urban population probably changed, although the proportions of these socio-economic developments cannot be investigated in detail in the light of the present evidence. An amount equivalent to one shekel must have been the common price of many everyday goods and services which were available for silver in Assyria: this could also explain why the one-shekel sum was widely used by the royal propaganda to show the favorable price-rate and the high level of prosperity which the Assyrian king states to have established in the country.[198] The prices of common goods also give us an insight into cost of living in the Assyrian cities. For instance, the cost of some of the above-mentioned staples corresponded to the minimum monthly wage (1 shekel), while garments could be 4–40 times this pay.

Consumption of various commodities by the class of property owners represents another important perspective to evaluate economic performance and standards of living of the 1st millennium societies. However, the wealth level of the imperial upper class and its possible internal differentiation is difficult to determine, in light of the scarcity of sources about private households from the Neo-Assyrian period and of comparable data from the Middle Assyrian age. The above-presented analysis, focused on the domestic material culture of high-class Assyrian women, has shown how the data from dowry lists can be used to investigate the prosperity level and socio-economic differences within the class of the property owners of the 8th–7th centuries BCE. The tendency to include metal objects instead of stone and wood items in dowries is in line with what we know about the general situation of the 1st millennium BCE dowry lists as well as the presence of the cash component, two elements that are especially documented by the late Babylonian texts and that witness the increased degree of monetisation of the economy in Mesopotamia. Moreover, the data about prices of certain commodities in contemporary texts help us to have a more precise idea about the expenses that property owners met to prepare dowries, as we observed in the case of the possible cost of signet-rings and of *kuzippu*-garments. Also the evidence about small expenses gives us useful insights into role of silver in shaping the economic life of 1st millennium BCE Assyria: as seen in the case of the Nimrud texts, the smallest silver-based investments of everyday trading activity in the Assyrian urban context corresponded to one or few shekels and analogous amounts constituted the compensation which was paid for various services in the private sphere. It is hoped that new material as well as future and more in-depth research will further enrich the picture about the economic life of the private sector in the 1st millennium BC Assyria.

Acknowledgements
I would like to express my gratitude to Prof. Frederick Mario Fales (University of Udine) for reading and appreciating this paper and to Prof. Juan Carlos Moreno García (CNRS, Université Paris-Sorbonne Paris IV) for accepting and including it in the proceedings of the Lille conference. To both of them I am profoundly indebted.

Abbreviations

ADD = C. H. Johns, *Assyrian Deeds and Documents*, Cambridge 1898–1923.
ADW = A. Y. Ahmad & J. N. Postgate, *Archives from the Domestic Wing of the North-West Palace at Kalhu/ Nimrud* (Edubba 10), London, 2007.
Assur = field numbers of tablets excavated at Assur (Qal'at Šerqāṭ).
BT = *siglum* of texts published in B. Parker, Economic tablets from the Temple of Mamu at Balawat, *Iraq* 25 (1963): 86–103.
GPA = J. N. Postgate, *The Governor's Palace Archive* (Cuneiform Texts from Nimrud 2), London, 1973.
KAJ = E. Ebeling, *Keilschrifttexte aus Assur juristischen Inhalts* (Wissenschaftliche Veröffentlichung der Deutschen Orient-Gesellschaft 50), Leipzig, 1927.
KAN 4 = B. I. Faist, *Neuassyrische Rechtsurkunden*, IV (Wissenschaftliche Veröffentlichung der Deutschen Orient-Gesellschaft 132/Keilschrifttexte aus neuassyrischer Zeit 4), Wiesbaden, 2010.
MARV 3 = H. Freydank, *Mittelassyrische Rechtsurkunden und Verwaltungstexte*, III. (Wissenschaftliche Veröffentlichung der Deutschen Orient-Gesellschaft 92), Berlin, 1994.
NATAPA 1 = F. M. Fales & L. Jakob-Rost, Neo-Assyrian texts from Assur. Private archives in the Vorderasiatisches Museum of Berlin, Part I, *State Archives of Assyria Bulletin* 5 (1991).
NATAPA 2 = K. Deller, F. M. Fales & L. Jakob-Rost, Neo-Assyrian texts from Assur. Private archives in the Vorderasiatisches Museum of Berlin, Part II, *State Archives of Assyria Bulletin* 9 (1995).
ND = *siglum* of tablets excavated at Kalḫu (Nimrud). Edited in *Iraq* 15 (1953), 16 (1954), 23 (1961).
RINAP 1 = H. Tadmor & Sh. Yamada, *The Royal Inscriptions of Tiglath-pileser III (744–727 BC), and Shalmaneser V (726–722 BC), Kings of Assyria* (Royal Inscriptions of the Neo-Assyrian Period 1), Winona Lake, 2011.
RINAP 3/1 = A. K. Grayson & J. Novotny, *The Royal Inscriptions of Sennacherib, King of Assyria (704–681 BC), Part 1*, Winona Lake, 2012.
RINAP 4 = E. Leichty, *The Royal Inscriptions of Esarhaddon, King of Assyria (680–669 BC)* (Royal Inscriptions of the Neo-Assyrian Period 4), Winona Lake, 2011.
SAA 1 = S. Parpola, *The Correspondence of Sargon II, Part I: Letters from Assyria and the West* (State Archives of Assyria 1), Helsinki, 1987.
SAA 3 = A. Livingstone, *Court Poetry and Literary Miscellanea* (State Archives of Assyria 3), Helsinki, 1989.
SAA 5 = G. B. Lanfranchi & S. Parpola, *The Correspondence of Sargon II, Part II: Letters from the Northern and Northeastern Provinces* (State Archives of Assyria 5), Helsinki, 1990.

SAA 6 = Th. Kwasman & S. Parpola, *Legal Transactions of the Royal Court of Nineveh, Part I: Tiglath-Pileser III through Esarhaddon* (State Archives of Assyria 6), Helsinki, 1991.
SAA 7 = F. M. Fales & J. N. Postgate, *Imperial Administrative Records, Part I: Palace and Temple Administration* (State Archives of Assyria 7), Helsinki, 1992.
SAA 11 = F. M. Fales & J. N. Postgate, *Imperial Administrative Records, Part II: Provincial and Military Administration* (State Archives of Assyria 11), Helsinki, 1995.
SAA 14 = R. Mattila, *Legal Transactions of the Royal Court of Nineveh, Part II: Assurbanipal through Sin-šarru-iškun* (State Archives of Assyria 14), Helsinki, 2002.
SAA 15 = A. Fuchs & S. Parpola, *The Correspondence of Sargon II, Part III: Letters from Babylonia and the Eastern Provinces* (State Archives of Assyria 15), Helsinki, 2002.
SAA 16 = M. Luukko & G. Van Buylaere, *The Political Correspondence of Esarhaddon* (State Archives of Assyria 16), Helsinki, 2002.
SAA 17 = M. Dietrich, *The Babylonian Correspondence of Sargon and Sennacherib* (State Archives of Assyria 17), Helsinki, 2003.
StAT 2 = V. Donbaz & S. Parpola, *Neo-Assyrian Legal Texts in Istanbul* (Studien zu den Assur-Texten 2), Saarbrücken, 2001.
StAT 3 = B. Faist, *Alltagstexte aus neuassyrischen Archiven und Bibliotheken der Stadt Assur* (Studien zu den Assur-Texten 3), Wiesbaden, 2007.
SU = J. J. Finkelstein, Assyrian Contracts from Sultantepe, *Anatolian Studies* 7 (1957): 137–145.
TFS = S. Dalley & J. N. Postgate, *The Tablets from Fort Shalmaneser* (Cuneiform Texts from Nimrud 3), London, 1984.
TH = J. Friedrich *et al.*, *Die Inschriften vom Tell Halaf. Keilschrifttexte und aramäische Urkunden aus einer assyrischen Provinzhauptstadts* (Archiv für Orientforschung, Beiheft 6) Berlin, 1940. Reprint (1967).
VAT = *siglum* of tablets in the collections of the Vorderasiatisches Museum in Berlin (*Vorderasiatische Altertumskunde, Tontafel*).
VS = *Vorderasiatische Schriftdenkmäler der Staatlichen Museen zu Berlin.*

Notes

1. On the main difficulties to define a model for the economy of the 1st millennium BCE, see the discussion given in Bedford 2005, esp. 70–79.
2. The question about the high-range money value of silver is discussed in full in Jursa 2010, 472–473, 629–641, with previous bibliography.
3. Some of the observations contained in the paragraphs 1 and 2 have also appeared in my article 'Circolazione premonetale dell'argento: l'evidenza documentaria dell'Assiria del I millennio a.C.' *Rivista di Storia Economica* 27/1 (2011), 93–110.
4. A Middle Assyrian text from Assur mentions unweighed bronze scraps which were returned to the (treasury) box. See KAJ 310:62–63. On scraps of various metals see CAD Ḫ, 262b s.v. *ḫušû*.
5. This idea was present in many languages of precoinage societies, see Snell 1995, 1491.
6. For an analysis of the Neo-Assyrian legal documentation, see Radner 1997.
7. Other designations of the Assyrian mina existed, but their elucidation is beyond the scope of this paper. On these norms (*e.g.*, 'the mina of the land', 'the Assyrian mina', 'the mina of half a mina'), see Fales 1996, 15–17. Critical remarks on the supposed 'mina of Arbela' and 'Assyrian mina' are expressed in Radner 1999b, 130 fn. 21.
8. StAT 2, 28:1–2 [*x* M]A.NA 4 GÍN K[UG.UD]/⌜*ana*⌝ KI.LAL *šá* É.GAL.
9. NATAPA 1, 37 e.2–3½ MA.NA KUG.UD *ina* KI.LAL/*ša* LÚ*.DAM.GÀR.
10. Powell 1987–90, 516; Kwasman & Parpola 1991, xxiii and figs 3–4; Fales 1996, 13–14; 2003, 113 and fig. 4. The inscriptions on the lion-weights of Shalmaneser V have been re-edited in RINAP 1, 1–9, 1003.
11. ADW 30:11 1 MA.NA KUG.UD.MEŠ$^{?}$ *ina* NA$_4$ *ša* MAN.
12. See, *e.g.*, the contract SAA 6, 91, concerning the purchase of slaves and properties located in the province of Talmūsu (north of Nineveh, modern Jerahiya?). In the document SAA 6, 202,

the vineyard purchased is located in the city of Kipšūna (northern Assyrian city, modern Gefše). SAA 6, 275, a contract dealing with the purchase of land in various locations, mentions estates in Issēte (modern Šaqlāwa) and Ṭūba, two towns in north-eastern Assyria.

13. For a discussion on this norm and its possible value see Powell 1987–90, 516 and especially Vargyas 1996, 9–14. The mina of Karkemiš has been treated also in Zaccagnini 1999–2001, 39–56. According to Zaccagnini, the Karkemiš standard could be identified with the mina of 564 g, consisting of 60 shekels of 9.4 g each. The Assyrian conquest of the western region, where a mina of 470 g, lighter than the one used in Mesopotamia, was in use in the 2nd millennium BCE, brought about a generalised diffusion of the sexagesimal division of the weight units and the vitalisation of the sexagesimal multiple of the 9.4 g shekel. See Zaccagnini 1999–2001, 44.
14. Winckler 1889, 173, *Nimrud-inschrift*, 21.
15. See Baker 2002, 997a s.v. *Pisīri(s)*.
16. This attestation is omitted in the list given in Radner 1999b, 150–152, appendix 2 (attestations of the mina of Karkemiš).
17. Not included in the list given in Radner 1999b, 150–152, appendix 2 (attestations of the mina of Karkemiš).
18. An alternative reading of SAA 6, 17 e.13 could be *ina* 1 MA.NA *ša* LU[GAL], 'by the [ki]ng's mina'. See Radner 1999b, 131.
19. Note that in Radner 1999b, 152, appendix 2 (attestations of the merchant's mina) are erroneously included also the texts A 2650 (= StAT 2, 96) and ADD 254 (= SAA 14, 20).
20. StAT 2, 140; 226; StAT 3, 106.
21. GPA 30; 31; 106; 107; ND 2080 (*Iraq* 16, 33, pl. v); TFS 47.
22. SAA 6, 38; 42; 50; 51; 55; 65; 85; 115; 130; 138; 142; 143; 167; 180; 301; SAA 14, 3; 6; 67; 182; 188; 192; 274; 437–438.
23. BT 114 (*Iraq* 25, 93, pl. xxii); BT 115 (*Iraq* 25, 94, pl. xxiii); BT 124 (*Iraq* 25, 96, pl. xxii); BT 127 (*Iraq* 25, 98, pl. xvi).
24. Assur 2 (*Al-Rāfidān* 17, no. 2); Assur 4 (*Al-Rāfidān* 17, no. 4); Assur 6 (*Al-Rāfidān* 17, no. 5); NATAPA 1, 18; 39; 61; NATAPA 2, 101; 129; StAT 2, 119; StAT 3, 42; 69; 70; 109; VAT 5389 (VS 1, 86).
25. ND 2093 (*Iraq* 16, pl. v); ND 2325 (*Iraq* 16, 42); ND 3424 (Ash 1954.737); ND 3426 (*Iraq* 15, 141, pl. xii); ND 3435 (*Iraq* 15, 142).
26. SAA 6, 17; 26; 34; 39; 40; 41; 45; 53; 54; 57; 81; 90; 91; 99; 103; 104; 107; 108; 110; 119; 158; 177; 183; 196; 202; 210; 219; 223; 224; 234; 235; 239; 245; 248; 250; 257; 262; 263; 269; 273; 274; 275; 284; 305–307; 311–313; 315; 316; 318; 323–324; 326; 329; 330; 333–335; 342; 343; 346; 347; SAA 14, 8; 18; 21; 60–61; 63; 64; 69; 78; 94–95; 115; 126; 159; 264; 307; 359; 398; 425; 441.
27. *Abr-Nahrain* 34, T 15.
28. SU 51/43A (*Anatolian Studies* 7, 139).
29. TH 113.
30. NATAPA 1, 37; StAT 2, 157.
31. GPA 248 (ADW 15); ND 3479 (*Iraq* 15, 147).
32. SAA 6, 27; 96; 97.
33. BT 101 (*Iraq* 25, 89–90, pl. xix).
34. For a reconstruction of the list of the eponyms assignable to the reign of Assurbanipal and of his successors see Radner 1998, xviii–xx.
35. The texts of the Nineveh archive have been edited in Kwasman & Parpola 1991 and Mattila 2002.
36. For the legal documents from Kalḫu (Nimrud) see Postgate 1973 and Dalley & Postgate 1984.
37. A part of the legal text corpus stemming from the city of Assur (Qal'at Šerqāṭ) has been edited in NATAPA 1; NATAPA 2; StAT2; Faist 2007.
38. SAA 6, 27.
39. NATAPA 1, 37.
40. GPA 248 (ADW 15).
41. On the commercial system of the Neo-Assyrian state see Radner 2004, 152–168.

42. According to Lipiński, temples, especially the temple of Issār of Arbela, played a significant role in the introduction of silver as currency. See Lipiński 1979, 569–588. However, the hypothesis of a role of the temple institution as 'Banque de l'État' is difficult to support. See the criticism expressed in Parise 1989, 38 and Radner 1999b, 138 fn. 96. Also Lipiński's interpretation of terms indicating baked products, such as *aklu*, 'bread, loaf', and *ḫuḫḫuru* (a type of bread), as designations of silver ingots, respectively of 1 mina and half a mina, that were introduced by the temple of Issār of Arbela has to be rejected. See Lipiński 1979, 574–578. In fact, bread occurs in loan documents both as the object of the loan along with silver, as in SAA 14, 89 ('*ḫuḫḫuru*-bread ... and 6 shekels of silver belonging to the Sibitti'), and as qualification of silver sum given as a loan, as in SAA 6, 237 ('first fruits of Issār of Arbela, of/for the bread of the temple') and in TH 113 ('first fruits of Issār of Arbela, of/for the bread of the one who resides in the temple, bread, *ḫuḫḫuru*-bread, ...').
43. SAA 1, 51; 52; SAA 5, 287; SAA 7, 79.
44. See, *e.g.*, the letters SAA 13, 28:2'; 29:8; 61:17; 188:14, where the operation is indicated by a plural verbal form.
45. For prices in Neo-Assyrian period, see Fales 1996, 11–53; 2003, 109–131.
46. *Abr-Nahrain* 34, T 15.
47. TH 113.
48. StAT 2, 140 (archive N29).
49. GPA 30; 31; TFS 47.
50. StAT 2, 226 (archive N31).
51. GPA 106; 107; ND 2080 (*Iraq* 16, 33, pl. v).
52. BT 114 (*Iraq* 25, 93, pl. xxii); BT 115 (*Iraq* 25, 94, pl. xxiii); BT 124 (*Iraq* 25, 96, pl. xxii); BT 127 (*Iraq* 25, 98, pl. xvi).
53. SAA 6, 27; 96.
54. SAA 6, 97.
55. GPA 248 (ADW 15); ND 3479 (*Iraq* 15, 147).
56. NATAPA 1, 37 (archive N9); StAT 2, 157 (archive N30).
57. BT 101 (*Iraq* 25, 89–90, pl. xix).
58. SAA 6, 257; 346, 347; SAA 14, 18; 78. See also the letter SAA 5, 150 (reign of Sargon), which mentions bought slaves put for sale at one mina each. For this price see Fales 1996, 12* Chart IV.
59. SAA 6, 284.
60. SAA 6, 343.
61. SAA 6, 34.
62. SAA 6, 138.
63. SAA 6, 45.
64. ND 3479 (*Iraq* 15, 147).
65. StAT 3, 106 (archive N32).
66. SAA 6, 53.
67. SAA 6, 250.
68. SAA 6, 239.
69. SAA 14, 264. See also SAA 11, 175 r.5–6, about the selling of two people for half a mina of silver.
70. SAA 14, 8. Half a mina is the price for a woman also in other contracts from Nineveh, Kalḫu, and Assur, although the specific silver norm is not mentioned. See SAA 6, 88; 228; SAA 14, 34; 37; 38; 48; 443; ND 2344 (*Iraq* 16, 47); NATAPA 1, 41; StAT 3, 61. In StAT 3, 12 a woman is purchased for half a mina and one shekel. See also Fales 1996, 13* Chart V. The same sum is paid for two Elamite prisoners in a contract from Assur, see KAN 4, 20.
71. GPA 248 (ADW 15).
72. See Fales (1996, 13* Chart V) for other cases of slave women sold for 0.33 minas. See also KAN 4, 23.

73. SAA 6, 219.
74. SAA 6, 103; 274.
75. NATAPA 2, 109; StAT 3, 36.
76. SAA 14, 115. Note that this attestations is erroneously inserted in Fales 1996, 13* Chart V among the ones concerning the 0.5 price.
77. SAA 6, 197; SAA 14, 29.
78. NATAPA 1, 61; StAT 3, 59.
79. NATAPA 1, 61.
80. SAA 11, 175:2'–3', 6'–r.2. See also fn. 120.
81. SAA 11, 175:4'–5', r.3–4.
82. SAA 11, 175 r.7–8.
83. See, *e.g.*, SAA 6, 50; 91; 245; 326.
84. SAA 6, 53.
85. SAA 6, 55.
86. SAA 6, 91.
87. SAA 6, 96. But note that in Radner 1999a, 273a s.v. *Barsipītu* this document is dated to 695 BCE.
88. See Fales 1996, 10* Chart III.
89. SAA 6, 91.
90. SAA 6, 110.
91. SAA 6, 197. See Fales 2003, 122.
92. SAA 6, 301.
93. SAA 6, 55.
94. ADW 9. The silver standard is not indicated in the text.
95. SAA 6, 305.
96. SAA 6, 300.
97. SAA 6, 309
98. SAA 6, 42.
99. SAA 6, 142.
100. SAA 14, 35.
101. SAA 14, 40.
102. SAA 14, 47.
103. SAA 14, 149.
104. SAA 6, 311.
105. StAT 2, 207.
106. StAT 3, 69.
107. SAA 14, 102.
108. StAT 2, 53.
109. SAA 6, 154.
110. SAA 14, 188.
111. SAA 6, 119.
112. SAA 6, 27.
113. SAA 6, 335.
114. BT 101 (*Iraq* 25, 89–90, pl. xix); NATAPA 1, 37; StAT 2, 157.
115. BT 101 (*Iraq* 25, 89–90, pl. xix).
116. SAA 6, 97.
117. StAT 2, 157.
118. NATAPA 1, 37.
119. NATAPA 1, 38.
120. SAA 6, 104.
121. SAA 6, 107.
122. SAA 6, 108.
123. SAA 6, 234.

124. SAA 6, 235.
125. SAA 6, 236.
126. SAA 6, 237.
127. SAA 6, 307.
128. SAA 6, 318.
129. SAA 6, 323–324.
130. SAA 6, 317.
131. SAA 6, 81; 223; 273; 307; SAA 14, 159.
132. SAA 6, 273.
133. SAA 6, 81; 223; 307; SAA 14, 159.
134. SAA 6, 307.
135. SAA 6, 309 r.8; 320 r.5; 321 r.8' (duplicate of the previous text); 325 r.18'; 328 r.9; 339 r.8.
136. Banî is one of the court intellectuals which formed the circle of "friends" or "colleagues" of Rēmanni-Adad. See Fales 1987, 112.
137. SAA 11, 26.
138. SAA 11, 26:3'.
139. SAA 11, 26:7'–8'. For oxhides and relevant prices in bronze and lead in the Middle Assyrian period, see Freydank 1982, 65, text VAT 18062:19' (= MARV 3, 2).
140. SAA 11, 26:14', r.9.
141. SAA 11, 26 r.3.
142. SAA 11, 26 r.6.
143. SAA 6, 333 and 334 (both from Rēmanni-Adad's dossier).
144. Saggs 2001, 202–203, text ND 2757 r.19–20 TÚ[G].*ṣ*[*i*]*-pìr-a-ti/kam*[?]*-ra-te ina* ŠÀ ½ *m*[*a*][?]*-na-a-a*, 'piled up *ṣipirtu*-sashes for half a mina each'.
145. SAA 7, 109 r. iv 3'.
146. GPA 155 r. v 13'; ND 2307 r.2 (*Iraq* 16, 37, pl. vi).
147. RINAP 4, 103:21.
148. SAA 1, 176:4–9.
149. SAA 1, 34:14–r.17'.
150. SAA 1, 34 r.18'–21'.
151. SAA 1, 33:19–r.3.
152. NATAPA 2, 100:3–5 (archive N19).
153. NATAPA 2, 102:3–4 (archive N19).
154. NATAPA 2, 133 (archive N24). Goat hair for sacks is also mentioned in the Middle Babylonian text BaF 21, 343 (UM 29-13-944). See Faist 2001, 128.
155. For livestock purchased along with land, see SAA 6, 91; 245; SAA 14, 468. For the purchase of 30 hectares of land along with servants and fowl see SAA 6, 169.
156. GPA 104:1–2.
157. For a Middle Assyrian list of prices for horses, donkeys, and other commodities see Freydank 1982, 64–65, text VAT 18062:3', 7', 13', 16' (= MARV 3, 2). From this text we see, for example, that the price for a three-year horse was 15 minas 6 ½ shekels of tin (= 3 talents 46 minas 37 ½ shekels of lead), while that for a three-year mare was 18 minas 53 ½ shekel of bronze (= 3 talents 46 minas 42 shekels of lead). Bronze prices for horses are also attested in two texts from Tell Ṣabī Abyaḍ (T98-35, T98-73). See Faist 2001, 179.
158. SAA 11, 98:1–2.
159. SAA 11, 98:3–6. The listed prices are 32 shekels, 37 shekels, and 1 mina.
160. SAA 11, 98:4–5.
161. SAA 14, 187:6.
162. ADW 55:12–13.
163. SAA 6, 206:7. The penalty clause requires the payment of the 30 minas to the king.
164. SAA 17, 139 r.11.
165. SAA 15, 182:5'–6'.

166. SAA 6, 241 r.2.
167. Borger 1996, Prism A ix 48–49 *ina qa-bal-ti* KUR-*ia* ANŠE.A.AB.BA.MEŠ *ina* 1 GÍN ½ GÍN *kas-pi / i-šam-mu ina* KÁ *ma-ḫi-ri*, 'Inmitten meines Landes kauft man am Markttor Kamele für einen (oder) einen halben Sekel Silber'. See also *ibid*. Prism B viii 18–19.
168. ND 2310:13'–16' (*Iraq* 23, 20, pl. x). See also Postgate 1979b, 100–101.
169. ADW 55:14–e.16.
170. Calculated on the basis of the equivalence 1 *sūtu* of barley = 1 shekel (of silver). See Fales 1996, 22.
171. ND 2311:15–16 (*Iraq* 23, 20, pl. x). See also Postgate 1979b, 101.
172. Prices for garments are also attested in Middle Assyrian texts, although silver is not used as value indicator. From VAT 19544, for instance, we learn that the cost of a coat was 10 minas of lead. See Faist 2001, 179. Garments costing one or more shekels are documented in Middle Babylonian texts. The price for a *muḫtillû* was 4 shekels of silver (= 1 shekel of gold), while with an amount corresponding to 2 shekels of silver (= half a shekel of gold) it was possible to acquire a coat. See Müller 1982, 271.
173. ND 2310:22' (*Iraq* 23, 20, pl. x). See also Postgate 1979b, 101.
174. Working for hire outside the palace or the temple household could be due to financial difficulties, see Radner 2007, 192–193.
175. ND 2311:13–14 (*Iraq* 23, 20, pl. x).
176. ND 2310:2' (*Iraq* 23, 20, pl. x) 7? GÍN 5/6 MA.NA NINDA.MEŠ 10 U[D.MEŠ], ibidem 4' 24 *qa* GEŠTIN 12 UD.MES [*x x* (*x*)]*x*. See also Postgate 1979b, 100.
177. For a Neo-Babylonian dowry list of 491 BCE mentioning a spice box (*bīt riqqi*) and a salt cellar (*bīt ṭābti*), see Roth 1989–90, 24, text BM 74645:8–9.
178. StAT 2, 164:3–4.
179. StAT 2, 164 r.11.
180. StAT 2, 164:15.
181. STAT 2, 184:4'.
182. ND 2307:3 (*Iraq* 16, 37, pl. vi).
183. ND 2307:9 (*Iraq* 16, 37, pl. vi).
184. ND 2307:13 (*Iraq* 16, 37, pl. vi).
185. ND 2307:20 (*Iraq* 16, 37, pl. vi). On the authority of Parker, also in CAD K, 474b s.v. *kitû* 2b 4' the price is intended as corresponding to 34 shekels, although the sign of the number 9 is clearly visible on the tablet. See *Iraq* 16, pl. vi.
186. The small number of Neo-Assyrian marriage contracts and the wide variety which characterize them could be due to the fact that only unusual marriage transactions needed to be formally recorded in legal documents. See Postgate 1979b, 99.
187. Apart from the *kallu* and *siḫḫāru* vessels mentioned in the property division formula, very few household items are listed in these documents. See NATAPA 1, 28 (four wooden items, a chair); NATAPA 2, 71 (bracelets); StAT 2, 101 (a chariot, a chest); StAT 2, 235 (a copper bed).
188. SAA 16, 53:8–11, r.2–3.
189. StAT 2, 184.
190. See Deller & Finkel 1984, 78–79 for a 10th/9th century BCE inventory which lists movable items of a middle class household. The objects belong to different material-based categories: iron implements for various usages (shovels, axes, pegs, sickles, bellows with iron handles, thurible, etc.); wooden containers and other working tools (soaking vat, sieves, bowls, measuring vessels, spades, scales, etc.); wooden furniture (chairs, incense-stand, tripod, stools, boards, chest, racks for containers, plank-bed, etc.); pottery vessels for storing foods, beverages, and other goods (jars, pithoi, washbasins, cooling vessels, boxes, etc.); stone implements (millstones). Some of these objects also occur in VAT 9744 (unpubl., but cited in Deller & Finkel 1984, 86, 89), an inventory of household utensils of Rēmūt-ili, an individual from Assur: in his house there are pottery vessels (washbasins, pithoi, cooling vessels, storage jars) and wooden furniture (racks for containers, chairs, stools, table, etc.). See also StAT 2,

233 for an inventory of household objects from the same city listing wine jars of different capacities, as well as craters, a table, a cup, and a chair.
191. Postgate 1979b, 90, text TR 2037:26–27 (1 millstone with an upper stone and a *mušanniktu*-implement).
192. Postgate 1979b, 90, text TR 2037:28–31 (2 *diqāru*-cooking pots, 1 *saplu*-bowl, 1 *panušḫu*-vessel, 2 *kappu*-bowls, 1 *kamanitu*-implement, 1 censer).
193. Postgate 1979b, 90, text TR 2037:24–26, 34–37 (6 chairs, 3 beds, 1 small table for meals).
194. ND 2312:1 (*Iraq* 23, 21, pl. x).
195. ND 2311:4, 6–7 (*Iraq* 23, 20, pl. x).
196. SAA 14, 155.
197. This is documented in the Neo-Babylonian texts, see Jursa 2010, 235–237.
198. For this *topos*, see Borger 1996, Prism B i 36–38; Prism C i 128–131; SAA 3, 11:9–11. The shekel and the half-shekel also indicated a trifling amount in idiomatic use, see CAD Š/III, 98a s.v. *šiqlu* 1d.

Bibliography

Baker, H. D. (ed.) (2002) *The Prosopography of the Neo-Assyrian Empire, Volume 3, Part I: P-Ṣ*, Helsinki.

Bedford, P. R. (2005) The economy of the Near East in the first millennium BC. In J. G. Manning & I. Morris (eds), *The Ancient Economy: Evidence and Models*, Stanford.

Bernareggi, E. (1985), *Istituzioni di numismatica antica*, Bologna.

Borger, R. (1996) *Beiträge zum Inschriftenwerk Assurbanipals. Die Prismenklassen A, B, C = K, D, E, F, G, H, J und T sowie andere Inschriften*, Wiesbaden.

Botta, P. E. & E. Flandin (1849–50) *Monuments de Ninive, découvert et décrit par M. P. E. Botta, mesuré et dessiné par M. E. Flandin*, I–V, Paris.

Dalley, S. (1996–97) Neo-Assyrian tablets from Til Barsib, *Abr-Nahrain* 34: 66–99.

Deller, K. & I. L. Finkel (1984) A Neo-Assyrian inventory tablet of unknown provenance. *Zeitschrift für Assyriologie* 74: 76–91.

Donbaz, V. (1988) Some Neo-Assyrian contracts from Girnavaz and Vvcinity, *State Archives of Assyria Bulletin* 2: 3–30.

Faist, B. I. (2001) *Der Fernhandel des assyrischen Reiches zwischen dem 14. und 11. Jh. v. Chr* (Alter Orient und Altes Testament 265), Münster.

Fales, F.M. (1987) Prosopography of the Neo-Assyrian empire, 1: the archive of Rēmanni-Adad, *State Archives of Assyria Bulletin* 1: 93–114.

Fales, F. M. (1996) Prices in Neo-Assyrian sources, *State Archives of Assyria Bulletin* 10: 11–53.

Fales, F. M. (2001) *L'impero assiro. Storia e amministrazione (IX–VII secolo a.C.)*, Roma-Bari.

Fales, F. M. (2003) Prezzi e circolazione dell'argento nel I millennio a.C. In L. Milano & N. Parise (eds), *Il regolamento degli scambi nell'antichità (III–I millennio a.C.)*, 109–130, Roma-Bari.

Freydank, H. (1982) Fernhandel und Warenpreise nach einer mittelassyrischen Urkunden des 12. Jahrhunderts v.u.Z. In M. Dandamayev & R. McCormick Adams (eds), *Societies and Languages of the Ancient Near East. Studies in Honour of I. M. Diakonoff*, 64–75, Warminster.

Jursa, M. (2010) *Aspects of the Economic History of Babylonia in the First Millennium BC: Economic Geography, Economic Mentalities, Agriculture, the Use of Money, and the Problem of Economic Growth* (Veröffentlichungen zur Wirtschaftsgeschichte Babyloniens im 1. Jahrtausend v. Chr., Band 4/ Alter Orient und Altes Testament 377), Münster.

Lipiński, E. (1979) Les temples néo-assyriens et les origines du monnayage. In E. Lipiński (ed.), *State and Temple Economy in the Ancient Near East*. Proceedings of the International Conference organized by the Katholieke Universiteit Leuven from the 10th to the 14th of April 1978 (Orientalia Lovaniensia Analecta 5), 565–588, Leuven.

Liverani, M. (1997) *Antico Oriente. Storia società economia*, Roma-Bari.

Luckenbill, D. D. (1924) *The Annals of Sennacherib* (Oriental Institute Publications 2), Chicago.
Monroe, Ch. M. (2005) Money and trade. In D. C. Snell (ed.), *A Companion to the Ancient Near East*, 155–168, Oxford.
Müller, M. (1982) Gold, Silber und Blei als Wertmesser in Mesopotamien während der zweiten Hälfte des 2. Jahrtausends v.u.Z. In M. Dandamayev & R. McCormick Adams (eds), *Societies and Languages of the Ancient Near East. Studies in Honour of I. M. Diakonoff*, 270–278, Warminster.
Parise, N. (1987) Fra Assiri e Greci. Dall'argento di Ishtar alla moneta, *Dialoghi di archeologia* 5 (2): 37–39.
Parise, N. (2003) La nascita della moneta. In L. Milano & N. Parise (eds), *Il regolamento degli scambi nell'antichità (III-I millennio a.C.)*, 133–145, Roma-Bari.
Pomponio, F. (2003) Aspetti monetari e finanziari del periodo neosumerico e paleobabilonese. In L. Milano & N. Parise (eds), *Il regolamento degli scambi nell'antichità (III-I millennio a.C.)*, 59–108, Roma-Bari.
Postgate, J. N. (1976) *Fifty Neo-Assyrian Legal Documents*, Warminster.
Postgate, J. N. (1979a) The economic structure of the Assyrian empire. In M. T. Larsen (ed.), *Power and Propaganda. A Symposium on Ancient Empires* (Mesopotamia, Copenhagen Studies in Assyriology 7), 193–221, Copenhagen.
Postgate, J. N. (1979b) On some Assyrian ladies, *Iraq* 41: 89–103.
Postgate, J. N. (1987) Employer, employee and employment in the Neo-Assyrian empire. In M. A. Powell (ed.), *Labor in the Ancient Near East* (American Oriental Series 68), 257–270, New Haven.
Powell, M. A. (1987–90) Maße und Gewichte, *Reallexikon der Assyriologie* 7: 457–517.
Radner, K. (1997) *Die neuassyrischen Privatrechtsurkunden als Quelle für Mensch und Umwelt* (State Archives of Assyria Studies 6), Helsinki.
Radner, K. (ed.) (1998) *The Prosopography of the Neo-Assyrian Empire, Volume 1, Part I: A*, Helsinki.
Radner, K. (ed.) (1999a) *The Prosopography of the Neo-Assyrian Empire, Volume 1, Part II: B-G*, Helsinki.
Radner, K. (1999b) Money in the Neo-Assyrian empire. In J. G. Dercksen (ed.), *Trade and Finance in Ancient Mesopotamia (MOS Studies 1)* (PIHANS 84), 127–157, Leiden.
Radner, K. (2004) Assyrische Handelspolitik: Die Symbiose mit unhabhängigen Handelszentren und ihre Kontrolle durch Assyrien. In R. Rollinger & Ch. Ulf (eds), *Commerce and Monetary Systems in the Ancient World: Means of Transmission and Cultural Interaction* (Melammu Symposia 5/Oriens et Occidens, Studien zu antiken Kulturkontakten und ihrem Nachleben 6), 152–168, Wiesbaden.
Radner, K. (2007) Hired labour in the Neo-Assyrian empire, *State Archives of Assyria Bulletin* 16: 185–226.
Reade, J. E. (1980) The Rassam Obelisk, *Iraq* 42: 1–22.
Rosa, D. F. (2011) Argento, *annaku* e il problema della moneta e del denaro nel periodo Medio Assiro (XIV–XI sec. a.C.), *Rivista di Storia Economica* 27 (1), 111–129.
Roth, M. T. (1989–90) The material composition of the Neo-Babylonian dowry, *Archiv für Orientforschung* 36/37: 1–55.
Saggs, H. W. F. (2001) *The Nimrud Letters, 1952* (Cuneiform Texts from Nimrud 5), London.
Simonetti, C. (2010) La funzione dell'argento nella documentazione paleo-assira di Kaniš, *Rivista di Storia Economica* 26 (3): 377–385.
Snell, D. C. (1995) Methods of exchange and coinage in ancient western Asia. In J. M. Sasson *et al. other names please* (eds), *Civilizations of the Ancient Near East*, 1487–1497, I–IV, New York.
Vargyas, P. (1996) The Mina of Karkemiš in the Neo-Assyrian Sources, *State Archives of Assyria Bulletin* 10: 9–14.
Vargyas, P. (2002) Sennacherib's alleged half-shekel coins, *Journal of Near Eastern Studies* 61: 111–115.
Winckler, H. (1889) *Die Keilschrifttexte Sargons*, I, Leipzig.
Zaccagnini, C. (1999–2001) The mina of Karkemiš and other minas, *State Archives of Assyria Bulletin* 13: 39–56.

Chapter 8

Long-distance trade in Neo-Babylonian Mesopotamia: the effects of institutional changes

Laetitia Graslin-Thomé

The Neo-Babylonian period in Mesopotamia is characterised by important developments, of such importance that historians are led to analyse it as a time of organisation of a new kind of economy. This paper focuses on the way these developments may have influenced the exchanges of goods imported from outside Mesopotamia. It will first describe these exchanges, and the actors who are in charge of them. Secondly, it will focus on how the transformations which thoroughly changed the institutional and geographical background during the period may have influenced the overall organisation of long distance trade. We will especially try to explain the puzzling fact that Neo-Babylonian actors, who were so often involved in long-distance trade in former times, seem to withdraw nearly entirely from this activity, at the very moment when new and lucrative camel-transport trade appears in the Near East.

As usual in Assyriology, this research is heavily reliant upon ancient evidence, which, for our subject, comes mainly from institutional sources. The Neo-Babylonian age is one of the best documented periods of ancient Mesopotamian history, with thousands of texts from private and temple archives (Jursa 2005). Private texts belong to families of more or less well-established notables, involved in agricultural management, houses or field rentals. But their archives rarely mention trade, and very rarely long distance trade.[1] The most explicit references to the importation of exotic products are to be found in the numerous texts produced by the administration of the two main temples of Neo-Babylonian Mesopotamia: Eanna of Uruk, and Ebabbar of Sippar. Some of them regularly mention imported products, and give us some idea of how they were brought to Mesopotamia, and exchanged there.

The best known and most studied texts have already been gathered by Oppenheim in an article[2] which has been the authority on Neo-Babylonian long-distance trade for a long time. Oppenheim's article was based on a thorough analysis of two texts which take the form of a list of foreign goods, associated with a price in silver. One text, quoted above, YOS VI 168, dates from the 7th day of *tašritu*, in the 6th year of Nabonidus. Several foreign goods are associated with their value in silver. Some iron and dyed wool will be given as tithe[3] on behalf of two agents, whose names are given at the end of the text: Nādin-ahi and Šamaš-zēr-ibni. The second text, TCL XII, 84 (Oppenheim 1969, 236–237; Joannès 1997, 192–193; Graslin-Thomé 2009, 38–39), dated to 1 year and 2 days before the first[4] lists a consignment related to the sole Nādin-ahi, and does not give the silver value of the entries:

YOS VI 168
600 minas of copper from Yamana, at 3 minas 20 shekels of silver,
81 minas 20 shekels of **inzahurētu**-dye at 2 minas 2 shekels
37 minas of tin at 551/2 shekels of silver,
16 minas 15 shekels of **takiltu**-dyed wool at 2 minas 40 shekels,
all this: related to Šamaš-zēr-ibni, son of Nanaya-iddin.

295 minas of copper from Yamana, at 1 mina 38 1/3 shekels,
55 minas of lapis-lazuli, at 36 2/3 shekels
153 minas of **ṭumanu**-fibers at 1 mina 42 shekels,
233 minas 20 shekels of **inzahurētu**-dye at 48½ shekels,
130 minas of iron from Yamana at 32½ shekels,
257 minas of iron from Lebanon at 42 2/3 shekels
132 quarts of assorted honey, at 26 shekels,
20 jars of white wine at 1 mina,
120 minas of **hūratu**-dye, at 30 shekels
40 minas of **hashaltu**-spice (?) at 2 shekels
1 **kurru**-measure of **taturru**-spice (?) at 10 shekels
1 **kurru**-measur of juniper resin at 3 shekels
all this related to Nādin-ahi.

Date: *tašritu*, 7th day, year 6 of Nabonidus, king of Babylon. 3 minas 10 shekels of the **takiltu**-dyed wool are the tithe of Nādin-ahi, 5 minas of the **takiltu**-dyed wool and 40 minas of the iron ar the "tithe" of Šamaš-zēr-ibni.

Since the publication of Oppenheim's work, the knowledge on Neo-Babylonian economy improved significantly, thanks to the renewal of text publications, and the numerous scholar studies on Neo-Babylonian history completed in the last years.[5] According to Oppenheim's wish, expressed at the end of his article, a few texts have been added to the list of documents related to the long distance trade he managed to gather, some of them come from the administration of the Eanna temple in Uruk and one from Ebabbar, the temple of Sippar. Historians now deal with a small dossier of about ten texts, all of them produced by temple administration, whose content share strong similarities with the texts known by Oppenheim. Some consist of a list of imported products, linked to a quantity and a value in silver.[6] Others are contracts concluded between temples and middlemen employed by the sanctuaries to provide typical imported produces such as dyes and metals.[7] These texts are quite similar in format regardless of whether they originate in Eanna or in Ebabbar. In some cases,[8] it is recorded in the contract that the intermediaries had to travel to distant places to procure the exotic products, often called *mereštu*. Due to strong similarities between the texts, it is probably the case even when nothing is specified on this subject.

Contracts refer once to Chaldea[9] and more often to Eber-nari.[10] One text adds that the consignment had to be bought according to the price of the city of Thapsuhu, probably the city called Thapsacus in classical texts, located in northern Syria:[11]

BM 61088
[2]+1 ma-na KÙ-BABBAR NÍG-GA^{d}UTU a-na [KASKAL-II (?)]
*šá e-bi-*ÍD *ina muh-hi* ^{md}EN-M[U A-*šú šá*]
^{m}*Le-šir* A ^{m}DÙ-*eš*-DINGIR *u*$_{4}$*-mu šá*
*ul-tu e-bi-*ÍD *ir-ru-ub*
a-ki-i ma-hi-ir šá ^{uru} *Ta-ap-su-hu*
hi-ši-ih-tu$_{4}$ *šá* É-KUR *šá* KÙ-BABBAR-*a'* 3 *ma-na*
^{md}EN-MU *a-na* NÍG-GA ^{d}UTU *i-nam-din*
[*ina*] GUB-*zu šá* ^{md}EN-TIN-*iṭ* ^{lú}SANGA UD.KIB.NUN^{KI}

Three minas of silver, property of Šamaš for [the trade venture] of Transpotamia, is against the account of Bēl-iddin [son of] Lēširu of the Epeš-ili family. When he returns from Transpotamia, Bēl-iddin shall pay this 3 minas of silver, the temple's requirement, according to the rate of the city of Tapsuhu. In the presence of Bēl-Uballiṭ the šangû of Sippar. Witnesses. Date.

The different contracts have strong similarities. The temples provided one or two middlemen with capital, either in silver or in goods. Those middlemen had to deliver, in exchange, some goods which are often listed, after an unspecified timeframe. The temples and the intermediaries were bound by contracts, but do not appear to have shared long-term relations. In one example at least,[12] the contract was not honored by the middlemen, and was eventually ruled by a court decision. The middlemen enjoyed a relative liberty in decision making: the list of products was sometimes fixed, but neither prices nor timeframe were. This allowed a degree of freedom in order to be able to react to unexpected events, something necessary in the highly unpredictable context of long-distance trade. Remunerations are not mentioned either, but one text[13] stipulates that the travellers will have to pay the temple a tithe from their personal profits: the transaction negotiated with the temples is one of many arranged by the agent as part of this journey. It is impossible to know for certain who initiated these expeditions. The temples may have been the instigators, but more probably they contributed capital for an expedition organised independently by merchants who are not temple staff.

It is not clear either who exactly the agents traveling on behalf of the sanctuaries were. Their status is usually not mentioned. The text PTS 3068 (Kleber 2008, 327), that Oppenheim did not know, is the only exception:

PTS 3068
3 ma-na kù-babbar šám 12 gun síg$^{hi\text{-}a}$
níg-na ^{d}gašan *ša* unug^{ki} *u* ^{d}na-na-a
ina muh-hi ^{m}dingir-sag-*ia*-urù ^{lú}-sag-lugal
a-na hi-ših-tu$_{4}$ *šá* é-an-na kù-sig$_{17}$ zabar
ù me-reš-tu$_{4}$ *a-ki-i šá ina* kur *tam-tì*
i-mah-ha-ru a-na é-an-na *i-nam-dim*

ki-i mé-reš-tu$_4$ *pa-ni* [lú]*qí-i-pi*
u [lú] *šà-tam la ta-an-da-har*
kù-babbar a$_4$ 3 ma-na *a-na* é-an-na
i-nam-din e-lat ú-ìl-tì šá {ma}-mah-[ ]
šá ina muh-hi-šú
ina gub-zu *šá* [m]*mu-še-zib-*[d]amar-utu [lú]*qi-i-pi*
šá é-an-na [m]*ba-ni-ia* [lú]*šà-tam* é-an-n[a]
a-*šú šá* [m]*tab-né-e-a* a [lú]*šu-ha*
Scribe
Witnesses, date (22 *du'zū*, first year of Nabonid)
Three minas of silver, property of the lady of Uruk and Nanāja, price of twelve talents of wool, is against the account of Ilu-rēšia-uṣur, servant of the king. According to the temple's requirement, he will pay gold, bronze and other trade goods to Eanna, as he will find them in Meerland. In case the *qīpu* and the *šatammu* are not pleased with those trade goods, he will give 3 minas of silver to Eanna. This is in addition to the earlier deficit owed by him. Done on behalf of Mušezib-Marduk, *qīpu* of Eanna, Bānia, *šatammu* of Eanna, son of Tabnēa, of the Bā'iru family. Scribe, witnesses.

The clauses of this contract are similar to other texts referring to the delivery of exotic goods at Eanna temple, but it is the only one to record that the goods will be provided by a royal agent, Ilu-rēšia-uṣur, *ša reš šarri*. Ilu-rēšia-uṣur will receive wool in exchange. It is well known that, in some times of Mesopotamian history, royal agents played an important role for the importation of exotic products in Mesopotamia.[14] The mention of Ilu-rēšia-uṣur, *ša reš šarru*, in the above-mentioned text may seem to fit pretty well in this context. As the similarities between the texts are strong, it could sound tempting to argue that royal agents were usually involved in this context. However, despite similarities with the other texts dealing with the import of exotic goods, this example may not be particularly significant. The goods are to be found in Chaldea, and not in Transpotamia as in other texts. Furthermore, the final clause differs from the other texts: it mentions that the sanctuary may reject the exotic goods if they do not serve its needs. This could mean that the procedure and the intermediary are unusual, and that the temple administrators are not sure what to expect from them.[15]

This small "dossier" gives information on a specific form of supply of exotic goods to the main temples of Babylonia: they used long-distance expeditions led by travellers who did not seem to belong to regular staff of the sanctuaries. The kind of relation between the temple administration and external businessmen to whom the administrators entrust part of the temple activities is now well known, particularly since M. Jursa's studies on Neo-Babylonian administration (Jursa 1995; 2004): the central administration of Neo-Babylonian temples seem to mainly control the economic activities performed in the immediate vicinity of the central administration. They delegate numerous tasks to outsiders, especially when these tasks are not done in the immediate vicinity of the temple (Jursa 2010). In this way, goods entering or leaving the urban workshops and the main storehouses are accurately recorded, while land work or more generally any activities being carried out further from the central administration are only loosely accounted. The control on such activities, which is more difficult to operate for the central administration, is subcontracted to outsiders. The temple provides them with lands, tools, and seeds, and requires, in exchange, the delivery of a part of the crop. This way, temple administrators free themselves from the burden of controlling an unwieldy number of cultivators or herdsmen and remain in direct relationship with only a limited number of businessmen (Joannès 2000, 115; Jursa 2004a, 179). Purchases which relate to longer distance trade proceed in a similar way. The logistics of the organisation of the trade expedition are subcontracted to intermediaries, despite the fact that this choice limits the opportunity of profit, and even the possibility to directly choose the required goods.

However, in spite of the considerable quantities provided by these expeditions, they were not sufficient to cater for the day-to-day needs of the sanctuaries. One of the best documented examples[16] is the purple dyed clothes. The *takiltu* is the most common purple used in the temple, it is an imported good, coming from the West.[17] The amount of *takiltu*-dyed fabrics used in Neo-Babylonian temples cannot be evaluated accurately,[18] but partial data can be found in some documents. The *lubāru*, piece of fabric used during *lubuštu* celebration, requires half a mina of *takiltu* dyed wool (Zawadski 2006, 87). The quantities imported from Transpotamia in TCL XII 84, 11 minas 22 shekel, could seem to be enough to cover those needs. But a few texts[19] show that the temple administrators are looking for other sources of supply. Some texts mention silver delivery for *takiltu*: in *Nbn* 262, 37 shekels of silver remain from a silver delivery for *takiltu*, in *nbn* 1101 2 shekels ¾ of silver are delivered for 16 shekels of *takiltu*. These exemples show that there was a way to get *takiltu* against money, outside of the big commercial expeditions illustrated by Oppenheim's texts. This is confirmed by a letter cited by M. Jursa (BM 103491: Jursa 2006, 163). where a man called Nusku-hanania is exploring the country, looking for different products, among them purple.

Iron is an example of imported product whose need exceeds the amount listed in Oppenheim's texts. In YOS VI 168, 4 talents 17 minas of Lebanese iron are imported alongside with 2 talents 10 minas 8 shekels ½ of iron from Yamana. The volume is important, but less than the amount of iron (10 talents) given by Eanna to Šum-ukīn and Kalbā according to their agreement of rent farming (Cocquerillat 1968, 39). Even if iron is regularly imported by the trade expedition known through Oppenheims's texts, these expeditions cannot be enough to provide the iron required for the whole agricultural activities of the temples. The purchase of iron is, unsurprisingly, cited in several texts from the temples archives.[20]

Another way for the temples to get exotic goods is to be mentioned: royal gifts. Numerous texts record gifts from the king, mainly gold, but other commodities are mentioned as well.[21] Once again, a link is missing in the chain, and the texts do not mention how these products came in royal storehouses. One can think of tribute and other forced imports such as those well recorded in Neo-Assyrian evidence.[22] In one case, one can be more affirmative: most records of iron from Hume, in Cilicia, found in Ebabbar archives date from the reign of Nabonidus.[23] They are probably gifts given by the king from the booty taken during the military campaigns in the beginning of his reign. In this case, exceptionally, we are maybe able to answer to the often open question to know how exotic goods were imported.

To sum up, ancient evidence mainly records importations of exotic goods made by institutions, temples or palace. They organised military or pacific expeditions to bring back in Mesopotamia the *mereštu* required for their all-day use. But huge incertitudes remain to explain the import of exotic goods. Even if the quantities mentioned are important, they cannot cover more than a part of the needs. One has therefore the feeling that the importation of exotic goods best evidenced in our texts, whether big expeditions to Transpotamia or gifts made by the king on the tribute bought back from military campaigns, provide the main stocks of the temples, while punctual needs were bought otherwise.

Actually, scattered references in the texts show that part of the needs are provided through local or regional purchase. The main trading centre was Babylon, the political, religious, and economic centre of this period.[24] The highest administrators of the Babylonian temples regularly travel to the capital, for political, religious or economic reasons. Some of them even owned property there. Some senior administrators of the temples or craftsmen usually working for the sanctuary were, in this context, commissioned to buy some exotic goods there, on top of their usual task for the temples.[25] TBER 67 (Joannès 1982, 246–248, text no. 60) shows how Amurru-šar-uṣur, *qīpu*[26] *of* Eanna, took advantage of his travel to Babylon for unknown but probably extra-economic purposes to bring back some terebinth. The new year's and *akitu* feast required the travel of the highest administrators of Eanna to Babylon, as well as people from all over Babylonia. As usual, in Mesopotamia[27] and elsewhere, these religious feasts provided good opportunities for business. In other cases, the temples sent specialists to Babylon to buy commodities related to their craft: it was the best way to ensure of the quality of the purchased goods, to entrust to the specialists accustomed to use it the task to buy it. In Ebabbar, the master bronze craftsman, Libluṭ chose the tin necessary for his craft in Babylon (M 75281: Bongenaar 1997, 378). In Eanna, Bēl-ibni, the son of Nādin, and his son Hašdāia, are mentioned in several texts[28] related to the purchase of gold or other long distance trade products in Babylon. In these cases, the goods are purchased against silver, which, as M. Jursa showed recently turns to be more and more used for economic exchanges during the 6th century.[29]

There is no way of knowing how the commodities have been brought in Babylon, and no way, either, of knowing how they have been purchased. Our texts, written by local administrators, only care for the amount of products bought, record sometimes the name of sellers, but never explain how the sellers got the products they provide to the temple emissaries.

There is only one exception, but it may be very specific, as it concerns gold trade. Finding gold was apparently relatively easy in Babylonia: gold is never mentioned among commodities brought back from Transpotamia by the caravans described above. A reason of that is that there is no gold mine in the Levant (Moorey 1999, 220; Graslin-Thomé 2009, 238–240), gold seems to arrive from Egypt, India, maybe

Iran. The temples supply partly themselves in the South, through exchanges with the Sealand administration (Kleber 2008, 326–328; Jursa 2010, 93–94). But another part of the supply is bought in Babylon. Members of the temple staff bought it there in small quantities,[30] of a few shekels, from various merchants. TBER 67 or YOS VI 112 mention an amazing number of sellers. Each seller probably sold all the gold he could. One would not understand, otherwise, why the Eanna agents would have multiplied the suppliers without any reason. A royal merchant is listed among sellers, but there is no way of knowing if he is acting on his own or for the palace. Despite the fact that some merchants are related to the palace, the multiplicity of sellers does not advocate for a centralised trade organised by the state. It looks more like a decentralised trade in the hands of individuals who do not belong to an institution. They do not seem to be professional gold sellers either, the quantities of gold sold are too small, and one can think of travellers taking advantage of their stay in Babylon to do some business.[31] The opportunity to sell small quantities of gold also explains the cupidity of thieves, whose gold thefts are recorded in some legal texts:[32] they would not risk the huge penalties they faced if they had no way of exchanging the stolen gold.

The fact that agents from the sanctuaries are able to buy imported commodities in Babylon shows that these products circulated within Babylonia through other channels than those appearing in the texts from the temples. Babylon is the main economic centre, but some textual evidence confirms that some exotic goods are to be found in Uruk or Sippar. There are few of them, but enough to show that Ebabbar bought several exotic goods against silver such as dyed wool (Nbn 637), iron or dyes (Nbn 428) or gold (BM 74411). Such purchases are known in Eanna as well, where the sums involved are significant.[33]

In these cases, only the names of the sellers are known, neither their status nor the way they get the commodities are detailed. They deliver both exotic and local products. As an example Šula, during Nabonid reign, sold to Eanna both sheeps or wool and exotic products such as lead, wine and maybe the rare *kitinnu*-fabric.[34] He is one among the local sellers recorded in many texts in the process of selling or buying ordinary products to the main sanctuaries of Babylonia. He, for sure, did not import the exotic goods himself, and is only a local retailer. We have no clue of how the goods he is selling have been imported in Babylonia.

The positions of these sellers are many. Some sellers providing imported products such as gold, juniper, and possibly alum, are named *tamkarū*.[35] This denomination, which appears throughout Mesopotamian history, is often translated as merchant, but is acknowledged to represent a variety of functions. The *tamkāru*, depending on periods or places, can either be a merchant, a money lender, or a royal agent responsible for the importation of exotic goods (Joannès 1997, 177; Graslin-Thomé 2009, 281–282). Among the temple intermediaries, texts occasionally mention *tamkarū ša šarri*, which may be translated as "king merchants". Since both denominations, *tamkāru* and *tamkāru ša šarri*, may apparently be used one for another, M. Jursa (2010, 580–581 and n. 3157) suggests that both probably refer to professionals related to royal administration[36] or working at least partially for the king.[37] A lot of other sellers are not named by other means than their personal names, and are never labelled as *tamkarū*. They are probably independent sellers, acting on their own behalf, like those known through some private archives.[38] There are therefore, both for local and exotic goods, local sellers, sometimes linked to the palace, but sometimes not.

Very scarse evidence from private archives show traders travelling long-distance, apparently on their own purposes, which may include trade.[39] Donkeys used for travel, exotic goods or distant places are, very seldom, cited in private archives. In an unpublished letter, cited by M. Jursa, a certain Sin-Ili tells to Ṭabia that he did not manage to find the *mereštu* he was looking for in several cities from north Babylonia. But the evidence is very scarce, and there is not a single text to explicitly refer to direct importation from distant places. This fact explains why the historians usually think that the importations were mainly done by Neo-Babylonian traders (Oppeheim 1969; Jursa 2007; 2010, 224).

All in all the Neo-Babylonian sources shed light principally on institutional-related exchanges: the investment of temple capitals in expeditions of varying distances, royal bursaries and forcible importations. This is not surprising: temples and palaces were the main consumers of precious goods which account for the majority of imports. But this view is also distorted by the fact that our documentation generally comes from the temples: we can only look at the documentation from the end of the chain of supply which brought these supplies to the sanctuaries. The manner in which they were imported, the way they were distributed within Babylon is not documented: it does not matter much to the scribes who author the texts we are considering. The very fact that the sanctuary agents could buy from private middlemen attests to the reality that transactions existed outside the realm of the temples.

It is therefore quite difficult to quantify the proportion of both private and institutional involvement in this long-distance exchange. In fact, the very question is maybe not relevant: private and institutional trade is not clearly separated. Many people carry out private deals on the sidelines of missions for the palaces and temples, or, on the contrary, it is likely that the temples invested in expeditions whose initial purpose was private enterprise. We thus find a situation which is characteristic of the Neo-Babylonian – if not in general ancient – economy: the intimate link between private and institutional interests, with institutions relying upon the dynamism of businessmen who place themselves at the service of the palaces and sanctuaries.

Even if the picture of trade of exotic products remains incomplete, it is less puzzling than it was in Oppenheim's times, and allows some reflection on the place long distance trade had among the transformations which mark the beginning of the 1st millennium. The second part of this article will try to give some directions to answer this question. The methodological approach proposed here is to use the theoretical tools provided by the so-called New Economic History, initiated by D. C. North (1984, 1985, 1990 [2007]; North & Thomas 1973). This school of thought, developed by economists, had some impact on ancient historians, mainly on those working on ancient Greece.[40] It has been less influential in Assyriology. The purpose of this article is not to import by force in Assyriology a theoretical framework designed for another academic field,[41] but to use one of its theoretical tools to bring some light on transformations detected in first millennium economy.

One of the main theoretical tools proposed by North is the concept of institutions. North names as institutions all the rules, legal or informal, which enable exchange. How these institutions evolve is a considerable driving force for historical change in economy. Institutions are strongly related to transaction costs, defined by North as the entire costs associated with the exchange.[42] Costs of transport of course, but also costs of information, risk protection and more generally the total costs of arranging the set of contracts which contribute to making the exchange possible. These costs depend on external factors, like the state of the roads, the weather conditions, or the distance to mining area for example. But the institutional background is to be taken into account as well: costs to write contracts, to get state protection against risk, or tax costs for example. The evolution of these transaction costs, allowed or restrained by the institutions, is one of the motors of historical change: when transaction costs diminish, they sometimes allow new economic behaviour. Conversely, some institutional deadlocks which maintain high transaction costs can hinder necessary evolutions. In the case of long distance trade, the importance of transaction costs is certainly not to be neglected (North 1984; 1985).

When one uses the term "long-distance" one thinks especially of transport costs. These were notoriously high in antiquity, and often prevented the development of long distance trade, when the costs of the journey were greater than the dividend which could be expected from the goods brought back. During the first millennium, a number of factors changed the structuring of transport costs. The development of new routes and the upgrading of certain principal paths to service the needs of the empire[43] were favourable to exchanges. The integration of the region into a larger political framework is a favourable factor as well. However, the costs, recently estimated by Michaela Weszeli (in Jursa 2010, 151), for local commerce remain high, especially when taking into account the various local taxes that were applicable. For long-distance commerce, the extra cost associated with risk also needs to be considered. The expeditions had to be escorted by archers. Such is the case in Sippar when the temple sends a group of carpenters to supervise the supply of wood to a sanctuary, most likely in Lebanon.[44] This risk factor increases the cost of long distance trade.

Such high transport costs, as was the case during all antiquity, meant that only rare and expensive goods were imported at all. The lists of imported goods by the above-mentioned temples feature little more than those goods imported in earlier ages: the same metals, dyed fabrics, wine and woods are found in the shipments.[45] There appears to have been no significant development in transport costs which would have facilitated the importation of new items. Indeed, economists show that low transport costs lead to the development of regional specialisations (Krugman 1991; Graslin-Thomé 2009, 325–330). Cities or regions specialise themselves in the productions for which they have what economists[46] call a "relative advantage": the local supplies or specific skills allow them to product better and cheaper than other economic partners. But, in order to direct more of their production force to such goods, cities have to give up the production of other goods, for which they are not as productive. They have to import them. This mechanism works as soon as transport costs get low enough to allow imports for a reasonable cost. When transportation costs are too high, it remains more profitable to locally produce the goods required for the day-to-day running of a city or region locally. In Neo-Babylonian times, very few regions specialise in certain goods and choose to become dependent on the importation of others. It is maybe the case in Gibeon, where thousands of storage jars have been discovered, probably designed for exportations. The example of olive oil specialisation in Ekron (Tell Miqne) is more controversial.[47]

One significant factor in the development of transport costs during the 1st millennium is the domestication of the camel: its new found use over long distances may be interpreted in terms of transport costs in the desert.[48] This development is noticeable in some Neo-Assyrian documents, where camels are often associated with Arab tribes (Restö 2003, 119–266). The importance of transport by camels is well-known during the Roman era (Meyers 1997). However, camels are very rarely mentioned in Neo-Babylonian evidence. This is partly due to the fact that very few documents give concrete details about the way in which high-value goods found their way into Mesopotamia. When camels appear in Neo-Assyrian texts, it is in official or royal inscriptions, those which are precisely lacking in Neo-Babylonian evidence. But this cannot be enough to explain the total absence of transport by camel in Neo-Babylonian texts: when Babylonian businessmen practice trade with distant places, the animals mentioned in texts are always donkeys, never camels (Jursa 2010, 224–225). This gives the impression that this new means of transportation has not been adapted by Babylonians, despite the new opportunities it allows: a puzzling conclusion, which calls for an explanation. We will return to this question further down.

Another change of the modes of circulation which has an influence on long-distance exchanges is the population migrations which characterise this period. First millennium witnesses both forced movement of deportees (Bedford 2007), victims of Neo-Assyrian or Neo-Babylonian politics and voluntary migrations of Aramaic, Arab tribes or of other groups settled in Mesopotamia for various reasons. The letters of Nippur, which date from the middle of the 8th century, demonstrate how a system of exchange took place in the south of Mesopotamia between nomadic and settled groups (Cole 1996a; 1996b). While this exchange was local in nature, commodities involved are mainly agricultural staples, it springs from long-distance commerce, and exotic goods like purple dye are sometimes cited (Cole 1996a no. 1 and no. 45). It reflects the settlement in the course of the 8th century of Aramaic people from Syria in the lands between Nippur and Bit-Iakin. It is not implausible that certain members of these tribes continued to move around with their herds between Babylon and Habur region. Information exchanged between various correspondents refer to certain spoken and written linguistic characteristics which demonstrate[49] the long-lasting privileged relationship between Aramaics settled in the south of Nippur and those from certain regions of Syria. These relations were beneficial to commercial links, especially if some Aramaics maintained their nomadic lifestyle and moved between Syria and Babylon with their animals.[50] Links of this nature exist in the 8th century between the Nippur region and certain tribes settled at the foot of the Zagros in the Diyala region, thus aiding contact with Elam.[51] One may suggest a similar analysis concerning the Arab tribes[52] who settled increasingly in Babylon.[53]

The arrival of these populations results in reduced costs of transactions with the North's acceptance of the concept. It results in a relative cultural homogeneity, when Aramean becomes the *lingua franca* of the near East. It also contributes to reducing transport costs for goods if commodities are travelling with men and herds. This is confirmed indirectly by the relative wealth of western goods in Southern Babylon. Be it through Neo-Assyrian tributes or the acquisition of the Neo-Babylonian temples, this region supplied gold and even purple fabric similar to that produced in Phoenician cities.[54] While it is difficult to prove, one wonders if it is possible to identify these population migrations as the much-discussed vehicle of importation of exotic goods which is so absent in our archival sources[55].

This new place taken by nomad groups leads to the same direction as the domestication of the camel: a new kind of commerce for exotic goods, dealing over longer distance, much more flexible than before, and much more difficult to control by local authorities as well. This can lead to clashes between new groups involved in trade and local authorities which try to rule them.[56] But, in Neo-Babylonian times, this rather leads to a high involvement in long distance trade of people either coming from outside Mesopotamia, or recently settled there. This involvement has often been put forward to explain the scarcity of cuneiform evidence dealing with long-distance trade: this trade would nearly become the monopole of non-Akkadian people during Neo-Babylonian times (for example Oppenheim 1969; Dandamayev 1986; Jursa 2010, 224). Those new actors do not write in cuneiform. If they use some script, it is on perishable written medium, which explains why no written source remains for this period. But this point, often repeated, is not enough to explain why cuneiform-writing population withdrew from this economic activity. To answer this difficult and crucial question the kind of reasoning proposed by D C. North can prove to be helpful. North actually stresses the place of institutions and of transaction costs to explain economic change in history. A change in institutions can allow a lowering of transactions costs, which can, as a result, make some new economic behaviour possible. But, on the contrary, they can also prevent the appearance of new behaviours, or prevent some populations to take part to the economic change, when the institutional background does not change according to what would be necessary to allow a change in the economic system. The transaction costs remain to high, and the economic change is impossible. Following this idea, the aim of this paper is to propose the idea that there is, in Neo-Babylonian time, a standstill in institutional framework which prevents Babylonian businessmen from finding their place in the new long-distance trade network. Because of that, Babylonians do not take advantage of the new kind of trade which arises in the second part of the 1st millennium BC.

To understand where this institutional standstill comes from, let us review the changes, or lack thereof, in institutions, in the broad acceptance of the word advised by North, that could impact the Babylonians' involvement in long distance trade. The existence of a simplified system of weights and measures was a significant development. In Neo-Assyrian texts, the measurement of weight still lacks standardisation, leading to a great deal of difficulties and errors, be they intentional or not.[57] In Neo-Babylonian texts, the system is much simpler. We no longer find mention of the different terms which abound in Neo-Assyrian texts (Powell 1990). Nevertheless, heterogeneity remains a reality and the multiplicity of terms used to define the quality of silver (Joannès 1994; Vargyas 2000; Jursa 2010, 474–490) is significant: payment remains a complex transaction,[58] requiring the weighing of metal which did not protect against a quality of silver inferior to that expected. The costs linked to the weighing contribute to transaction costs remaining high, while the risks associated with the quality of the metal received were high enough to decisively encourage exchanges concluded with known and well-trusted partners. On the other hand, the establishment of a more monetary economy is favourable to the reduction of transaction costs and the development of exchanges. If we are to accept the conclusions of M. Jursa,[59] money becomes increasingly used in transactions in the sixth century. The proportion of money-based exchange will be a subject of debate among Assyriologists. It has, in any case, a significant influence on transaction costs: it simplifies exchanges and limits risks. M. Stolper has already demonstrated how the increasing reliance on money, mostly for fiscal reasons, has led to the development of entrepreneurial activity by private businessmen acting on behalf of the palace or the temples (Stolper 1985). Local commerce has benefited as a result. But we have seen that its effect is non-existent in the realm of long distance commerce which remains a secondary activity for the so-called "entrepreneurs".[60] It is as if the broadened use of money had opened them to a large set of local or regional economic activities, enough for the ambition of wealthy businessmen, who do not need to expand their activities into long-distance commerce. In this case, an institutional evolution leads to what could appear, from the Babylonian point of view, as a withdrawal from some activities.

An explanation for this blockage can also come from the dysfunction of other institutions, in the meaning given by North. The accounting procedures (Jursa 2004a; Graslin-Thomé 2015), or the slowness in adaptation to new economic behaviours (Jursa 2010; Graslin-Thomé 2014. See below) could be part of the answer. The contracts, another institution in the meaning given by North, probably played a role as well. Economic theory explains that contracts, be these formal or tacit in nature, are a way to reduce the risk involved by exchange. The purpose of these contracts was to limit the risks associated to transactions. In this matter, the long-distance commerce adhered to rules which were fundamentally different from local exchange. In the latter, in case of cheat, it is possible to plead to local authorities, even if dishonesty was discovered in retrospect. The parties are likely to know one another, or at least to be able to find one another, if they realise that the deal has not been carried out according to the rules. By contrast, long-distance trade occurs between parties who do not know one another and are likely never to meet again. It is, in this context, much more difficult to guarantee respect of the rules. Trade in gold is a good example of this difficulty. One text tells of agents from Eanna who bought gold in Babylon and hastened to verify its quality upon their return to Uruk.[61] Mesopotamian techniques governing the quality of gold consisted in melting down a portion of the metal and this could only be done once the agents return home (Joannès 1987; 1994). At this stage, it is a little late to think of returning to confront potential fraudsters. There is no legal way for the administration of the temple to react if the quality of the metal does not meet expectations. As such, no judicial framework exists to protect merchants and enable commerce on a large scale. It is understandable how, under these circumstances, the sanctuaries entrust the supply of primary materials to specialists: their weathered eye is the best means of guaranteeing the acceptable quality of the goods procured.

However, the juridical framework of long-distance trade is an unsolved problem in Neo-Babylonian times. It does not provide merchants with the protection they desire. The Neo-Babylonian era hardly sees any development in the protection and legal control of large-scale commerce. The contracts are well-known: the merchants use contracts known as *harrānu*-contrats, literally "contracts of the caravan". But, despite their name related to long-distance trade, those contracts are, in reality, a way of gathering capital for a variety of reasons (Lanz 1976; Joannès 1983; Jursa 2010, 206–214), usually on a very local scale. There is no specific formula for commercial transactions, let alone for long distance trade. There is therefore no specific clause precisely designed to respond to specific needs of long distance trade, most of all the difficult but essential protection against the risk.

Because of this lack of appropriate juridical framework, people involved in long distance trade have to look for other systems of protection against the risks specific to their activity (Graslin-Thomé 2014). One strategy may perhaps be revealed through YOS XIX 1. In this document a big house is given to Šamaš-zēr-ibni, against exotic goods, listed in the contract. To pay the capital in the form of a house ensures that the person entrusted with the money will not disappear without having delivered the merchandise. This measure has its limits, however, as is demonstrated in another text, AnOr VIII 70: in this text we learn that Eanna had to initiate legal proceedings to recuperate a house entrusted as capital for the commercial goods after ten years. On the whole, Neo-Babylonians involved in long distance trade seem to lack legal protection against risk. The need to find other means to protect themselves may explain that the temple prefers to deal with individuals whose reliability can be guaranteed in some way: agents of the king, or merchants they already know. It may also explain the dearth of evidence of exchanges with suppliers who have come from afar. In other words, long distance commerce, in the absence of any legal framework, appears too risky and it is preferable to deal with well-known partners. In any case there is no visible technical development during this period of contract law which might encourage the expansion of large-scale commerce.

This lack of legal background well adapted to long-distance trade may explain why Babylonian businessmen do not invest in this kind of economic activity: M. Jursa has shown that most Babylonian families that have enough money to invest in economy are for the most part of them "risk-averse": they prefer to invest their money in activities where investment return is predictable,[62] even if they are not as profitable as more hazardous ones. It is the case of the prebendary families labelled by Jursa as "rentiers": for these wealthy families, money is mainly used to secure or expand the family rural possessions. The "entrepreneurs", as Jursa calls another kind of wealthy businessmen, accept to run more risk, but there activities are mainly local: agricultural business, providing cash for the crown, or other profit-gathering activities. The temples administrators' behaviour is close to the rentiers': they avoid the risk and are not seeking the most profitable way to handle their possessions. That is how Ebabbar prefers to entrust outsiders to sell the bulk of its date production. This choice prevents the temple from getting the highest profit he could expect from his production, and makes it dependent on the main traders (Jursa 2010, 592). But it simplifies the task of the administrators, and lowers exposure to risk. This behavioural choice can explain that neither temples nor well-being temple families choose to involve in long-distance trade: the juridical framework is not designed to reduce the risk sufficiently to encourage them to invest their money. Local business suffices for the small part of businessmen eager to face more risk, for higher gains. They content themselves with local and regional business, especially as the institutional framework which does not change in the case of long-distance trade, is touched by several improvements as far as local business is concerned.

The result, even if institutional development is occurring, and that they could, in theory, benefit long-distance commerce, is that the effect of such transformations is not very significant. While it is true that archival sources are few, this lack of evidence shows that long-distance commerce is not a favored domain for entrepreneurs. Within the big institutions, commerce held in trust continues to be significant, while private operators stay in the background. The institutional framework, in the sense given by North, is definitely evolving but at too slow a pace and in too incomplete a way to inspire entrepreneurs to devote either energy or capital into it from other activities. As a result the distinction between local and long-distance commerce is significant. Major institutional changes, notably the growing move to a monetary economy, leads to the development of a dynamic business class. However the associated drawbacks appear to be a persistently poor adaptation by the institutions to long-distant commerce. This remains too prevalent to encourage entrepreneurs to invest in such projects. Babylonian businessmen choose to invest their capitals and energy in the enlarged local and regional activities permitted by economic change. This economic change has an opposite effect on long-distance trade: the changes exist, but are, from the Babylonian point of view, less interesting than the changes which impacted local and regional economic activities. Therefore, they are used by other populations, newcomers in Babylonia, who capture the changes ignored by Babylonians to their benefit.

Acknowledgement
I would like to thank C. Obranagain who helped me improve my English.

Notes

1. Several archives belong to private entrepreneurs dealing with trade. The most complete one, Iddin-Marduk's, is part of Egibi's archive. Iddin-Marduk is a medium scale businessman. He buys agricultural staples in the countryside around Babylon, to sell them in the city (Wunsch

1993; Jursa 2010, 214–224). Others smaller archives dealing with local trade are to be found in Neo-Babylonian evidence. Sîn-ilī's archiv, from Babylon, describes the business activities of Ṭābia. Unlike Iddin-Marduk, Ṭābia does not buy agricultural products, but takes control of agricultural land. Other archives shed light on the trade of agricultural staples: one of their distinguishing feature is the relatively high number of "*harrānu*" contracts they include: those partnership agreements are commonly used by businessmen to gather funds for their activities: they are to be found in Nippur, Uruk, Larsa, Sippar of Kiš (Jursa 2010, 218–219). But those businessmen usually limited their activities to their cities' hinterland, even if their area of influence depends of the actual size of the city: it is larger around Babylon than around a smaller city like Larsa. One would have expected to find texts related to long distance trade amoung the *harrānu* contracts, furthermore because the actual name of those contracts refers to caravan trade. But those contracts are used to gather capital for various reasons, and very few of them explicitly refer to trade. The only exception is the text GC II 84, where a special clause requires that the capital be divided once one of the contractors comes back from a specific journey. Most *harranu* contracts are cited by Lanz 1976.

2. Oppenheim 1969. On those textes, see more recently Joannès 1997; Graslin-Thomé 2009.
3. On tithe, see now Jursa 1998.
4. This date is probably mistaken, the two texts could be related to the same matter, Joannès 1997; Graslin-Thomé 2009, 41–42.
5. Jursa 2010 is an important overview on Neo-Babylonian economy which dramatically improved our general knowledge on babylonian economy. But very few pages are devoted to long distance trade (pp. 224–225).
6. YOS VI 168, PTS 2098, TCL XII 84.
7. YOS VII 63, Nbn 637, BM 61088 = Macginnis 2004, 30–31, McEwan 1984, GC II 111, PTS 3068 = Kleber 2008, 327–328, YOS VI 52, YOS VI 61. AnOr VIII 70 and YOS XIX 1 are related to long distance trade as well.
8. YOS VII 63, BM 61088 = Macginnis 2004, 30–31 and McEwan 1984, YOS VI, 62.
9. One text, PTS 3068 quoted below.
10. YOS VII 63, BM 61088, McEwan 1984, YOS VI 52, YOS VI 61.
11. BM 61088 = Macginnis 2004, 30–31. On the localisation of Thapsacus, see Graslin-Lemaire 2004.
12. AnOr VIII 70.
13. YOS VI 168.
14. Radner 1999 for neo-assyrian period. However, it it possible that, even in neo-assyrian period, private merchants were acting in regional and maybe long-distance trade as well. Merchants active in regional trade are known in Aššur (Radner 2008).
15. In contrast to other texts dealing with exotic goods, the main subject of PTS 3068 is the selling of wool by the temple. In this case, the implication of a royal agent is not unusual. Kleber 2008, 243–246 showed that the palace is the main buyer of Eanna's surpluses of wool. It is also not unfrequent that this wool was not exchanged against money, but against goods not produced in Eanna's household (Jursa 2010). Is the case of PTS 3068, the temple administrators seem to have taken the opportunity of their business relation with somebody who usually travels in Chaldea, a usual place to buy gold, to fill its stocks in this metal.
16. Thanks, mainly, to Zawadski 2006.
17. On *takiltu*, see Zawadski 2006, 23, Graslin-Thomé 2009, 196–204.
18. BM 101905, quoted by Zawadski 2006, 48, is unfortunately to badly preserved to even know if this "summary text" dating from the beginning of Darius' reign sums up the amount of *takiltu* wool used or left each year.
19. Nbn 262, 37 shekels of silver left from amount given for the purchase of *takiltu*. Nbn 1101, 2 shekels ¾ of silver given for 16 shekels of *takiltu*. For the prices of *takiltu*, Zawadski 2006, 109; Graslin-Thomé 2009, 203.
20. TBER 67, Iron bought at Babylon. Iron bought in Sippar amoung other local products in Nbn 428. Silver against iron in YOS XVII 229.
21. Kleber 2008, 265. Gold is by far the more common gift, but the king sometimes gives some gifts in kind, like grain, dates or cattle.

22. For Neo-Assyrian booties, see Jankowska 1969; Liverani 1992; Graslin-Thomé 2009. Neo-Babylonians booties are not as precisely described in royal inscriptions that they are in Neo-Assyrian times, but the building inscriptions, and the important building projects held in Neo-Babylonian Babylon are reliable witnesses of the amount to goods imported by Neo-Babylonian armies (Jursa 2010, 3).
23. CT 55 244 (Nab. 1), Nbn 571 (Nab. 9 and 10), YOS VI 210 (Nab. 12).
24. Jursa 2010, 63–79 underlines the importance of Babylon, where converges most human and economic wealth of Babylonia.
25. The list of goods, exotic or not, purchased in Babylon, are cited by Jursa 2010, 74–75: metal, silver, textiles, dyed wool, aromatics or precious stones are recorded.
26. Literally *qīpu* means "trustee", Beaulieu 1989 translates as "administrator", Bongenaar 1997 as "resident".
27. Biga 2002, for 2nd millennium ancient orient, Chandezon 2000 for ancient Greece.
28. TBER 68–69, YOS VI 115, TBER 67, YOS VI 112.
29. Jursa 2010, 772–780. In private archives, high-value commodities like animals or slaves are systematically bought against silver. In temples as well, use of money becomes common, contrary to the practices revealed by 8th century archives.
30. 1 shekels ¼ of gold in YOS VI 112, l. 5. Other quantities are much more important, like the more than 5 minas of gold bought against more than a talent of silver in YOS VI 115, l.6–7.
31. Jursa 2010, 64–89 lists the members of temple administration traveling to Babylon.
32. Joannès 2000, 214 mentions a small dossier of nine texts where several members of Eanna, among them at least two goldsmiths, are involved in a big network of gold misappropriation and resell.
33. Jursa 2010, 556–557. Dyes in GC I 170, aromatics (GC I 178), wine (GC I 395), dyed wool (YOS XIX 218) papyrus (GC I 92).
34. Nbn 439, but the text is badly damaged, only the *ki* of *kitinnu* remains.
35. GC II 39 a *tamkāru* provides gold to Eanna, maybe alum in TuM2/3 251 (Dandamayev 1971, 76).
36. Evidence of *tamkarū* is scarce in Neo-Babylonian times, in comparaison to Neo-Assyrian times. The word is to be found less than 30 times ine Neo-Babylonian evidence according to Dandamayev's account. But that does not mean necessarily that the function became less important: as we do not have royal archives, it is not surprising that we do not get the texts in which traders acting for the palace are mentioned.
37. Nothing in the evidence shows that all *tamkarū* are related to the palace, and directly depend from it. Part of their activity may be related to the palace, but they may very well acting on their owns behalf as well, for an other part of their activity (Joannès 1997).
38. Two small dossiers related to traders sometimes called *tamkarū* are known : the royal merchant Sin-ahu-iddin (Dandamaev 1995) and a family of merchants of Judean extraction (Jursa 2007).
39. Jursa 2010, 225 sums up the very few mentions, in private archives, which can be linked to long-distance trade. Arad-Gula, from Ea-eppēš-ilī's, sell a donkey in a syrian city (Nbk 360). Mušezib-marduk delivers 18 liters of good quality wine to Bel-Remanni, but it is probably only for his personnal use. In Ur, Sîn-uballitṭ ask for *musukkannu* wood for a writing board (UET IV, 185), on *musukannu*, see Graslin-Thomé 2009, 221–222. In Sippar, Iššar-tarībī kept in his archives several *harrānu* partnerships, and the geographical scope of his activities reaches as far as Humadešu in Iran. (Jursa 2005, 124).
40. See, for example, Bresson 2007.
41. The utility of theoretical models imported from other academic fields is not a new idea in Assyriology (Graslin-Thomé 2009, 99–131).
42. North 2007 [1990], 11: "If transaction costs were simply the costs of coordinating the increasingly complex interdependent parts of an economy they would be simply information costs or more specifically the costs of acquiring the information to measure the multiple dimensions of what is being exchanged. But they are also the costs of enforcing agreements and making credible commitments across time and space, necessary to realise the potential of this technology." Transaction cost are all the costs related to exchange.

43. For Neo-Assyrian times, see Favaro 2007; for main routes in Neo-Babylonian times, Graslin-Thomé 2009, 308–324 and Jursa 2010, 62–98.
44. Bongenaar 1997, 392–395. Some carpenters are, in Ebabbar, called LÚ NAGAR *šá* URU *labanānu*, "carpenters of Lebanon". When they are travelling abroad, the temple provides them travel rations, leather shoes and money to buy a donkey.
45. The commodities imported in 3rd millennium BC are the same than the goods recorded in Oppenheim's texts (Snell 1982, 118). Faist 2001, 53–55 lists the products imported in Mesopotamia by the end of 2nd millennium BC: metals, horses, cedar wood and some pieces of fabrics are the most common.
46. Following D. Ricardo.
47. Graslin-Thomé 2009, 368–369. But see Schloen 2001, 141–147.
48. Bibliography on the domestication of camel is abundant. See, for example, Groom 1981, 33–37; Restö 2003, 122–123; Graslin-Thomé 2009, 300.
49. According to Cole 1996a, 27. See also Fales 2009 [2007], 289.
50. About Arameans, see Brinkman 1968, 267–285; Frame 2007 [1992], 43–48; Lipiński 2000; Briquel-Chatonnet 2003; Fales 2009 [2007]. Evidence is scarce for Neo-Babylonian times, but it seems that Arameans are not as well integrated and settled than Chaldeans are. After the mass deportation from the end of Neo-Assyrian times Arameans mix up with the general population, are remain silent in our sources. Only the major tribes of Gambulu and Puqudu can still be clearly identified after the 7th century BC. Lipiński 2000, 429–437, 472–479; Radner 2006–2008; Fales 2009 [2007], 297.
51. Cole 1996a, 27–29; Graslin-Thomé 2009, 317.
52. Numerous cuneiform sources mention arrival of nomadic arabic tribes as soon as the beginning of 8th century (Eph'al 1978; Frame 2007 [1992], 50). Restö 2003, 190 finds mention of LÚ Arabāya in at least 20 texts from Nippur, Sippar and Uruk. Most of them date from from the time period 563–420 BC: Arab tribes are much more present in cuneiform sources during Neo-Babylonian and Achaemenid times than before. Those texts show Arabs involved in various economic activities, some possess slaves, other are slaves themselves, some of them works for temples in Sippar evidence. A specific Arabian organisation, *ālu ša arbāya* is known in Sippar: in those times, Arabic tribes seem to remain a distinct group, but pretty well integrated in Babylonian society.
53. Other strangers appear in cuneiform evidence. Egyptians appear in commercial background (Frame 2007 [1992], 49 and note 104; Eph'al 1978, 74–90), as well as Judeans (Jursa 2007).
54. For chaldeans tributes, see Jankowska 1969; Graslin-Thomé 2009, 317–319. In PTS 3068 quoted above, gold, bronze and trade goods are to be found in Chaldea. For the economic links with Sealands, see Kleber 2008, 326–329.
55. The question to know from where the trade goods present in Sealands are coming is still pending. Jursa 2010, 93 thinks that they come from a southern route, but Byrne 2003 questions the very existence of direct trade routes between Arabia and Babylonia before Persian times. In Neo-Babylonian texts, the Arab tribes always come from the west, and ride down the Euphrates. The entrance gate to Babylonia for caravans is, therefore, the middle Euphrates.
56. A well known example is the ambush set by Ninurta-Kudurri-Uşur, governor of Suhu in the middle Euphrates to a caravan of camels coming from the West (Liverani 1992).
57. Muller 2004 give several examples of additions of quantities expressed in minas who seems wrong to modern scholars. They have often been taken as a sign of the low calculation skills of the scribes, but may rather be the accurate result, incomprehensible for us because of the high complexity of the units of measure.
58. A text from the Nur-Sin archiv (Wunsch 1993, no. 65) deals with onions sold against a silver ingot. It foresees that the ingot will be cut by the buyer, not by the seller: M. Jursa 2010, 479 proposes that this clause can be due to the fact that the seller, a rural farmer does not know how to cut a large piece of silver, and prefers to trust the buyer, a businessman better accustomed to such a delicate task.
59. Conclusions presented in Jursa 2010.

60. The word "entrepreneur" has been advocated by van Driel 1999, and often taken over in following literature, with sometimes slightly different acceptances. See, for example, Graslin & Vivel 2005; Jursa 2010.
61. YOS VI 112, l. 23.
62. Iddin-Marduk is a good example of "risk-averse" entrepreneurs: he prefers to buy in advance the onions production that he will eventually sell in Babylon. In this way, he does not support the incertainty of a good or bad harvest. He reduces the risk of loss, but of unexpected gains as well (Graslin 2002; Graslin-Thomé in 2014).

List of Abbreviations

AnOr VIII: Pohl, A (1933) *Neubabylonische Rechtsurkunden aus den Berliner Staatlichen Museum 1*, Rome.
BM: tablets in the British Museum's Department of the Ancient Near East.
CT: Cuneiform Texts from Babylonian Tablets in the British Museum.
GC II: Dougherty R. P. (1933) *Archives from Erech Neo-babylonian and Persian Periods* (Goucher College Cuneiform Inscriptions 2), New Haven.
Nbk: Strassmaier J. N. (1889) *Inschriften von Nabuchodonosor, König von Babylon, Babylonische Texte*, V, Leipzig.
Nbn: Strassmaier J. N. (1889) *Inschriften von Nabonidus, König von Babylon, Babylonische Texte*, Leipzig.
PTS: Tablets in the Princeton Theological Seminary.
TBER: Durand J. M. (1981) *Textes babyloniens d'époque récente* (Recherche sur les grandes civilisations 6), Paris.
TCL XII: Contenau G. (1927) contrats néo-babyloniens 1: de Téglah-phalasar III à Nabonide (Textes cunéiformes du Louvre XII), Paris.
UET: Ur Excavations, Texts.
YOS VI: Dougherty R. Ph (1920) *Records from Erech. Time of Nabonidus* (Yale Oriental Studies, Babylonian Texts VI), New-Haven-London.
YOS XVII: Weisberg D. B. (1980) *Texts from the time of Nebuchadnezzar* (Yale Oriental Studies, Babylonian Texts XVII), New-Haven-London.
YOS XIX: Beaulieu P. A. (2000) *Legal and administratives texts from the time of Nabonidus* (Yale Oriental Series, Babylonian Texts XIX), New Haven-London.

Bibliography

Beaulieu, P.-A. (1989) *The Reign of Nabonidus, King of Babylon, 556–539 B. C.* (YNER 10), London.
Bedford, R. (2007) The Persian Near East. In W. Scheidel, I. Morris & R. Saller (eds), *The Cambridge Economic History of the Greco-Roman World*, 302–331, Cambridge.
Biga, M. G. (2002) Les foires d'après les textes d'Ebla. In D. Charpin & J.-M. Durand (eds), *Florilegium Marianum VI: Reccueil d'études à la mémoire d'André Parrot* (Mémoires de N.A.B.U. 7), 277–288, Antony.
Bongenaar, A C. V M. (1997) *The Neo-assyrian Ebabbar Temple at Sippar: its Administration and its Prosopography* (PIHANS 80), Leiden.
Bresson, A. (2007) *L'économie de la Grèce des cités. Les structures et la production*, Paris.
Briquel-Chatonnet, F. (2005) *Les Araméens et les premiers Arabes*, Aix en Provence.
Brinkman, J A. (1968) *A Political History of Post-Kassite Babylonia, 1158–722 BC* (AnOr 43), Rome.
Byrne, R. (2003) Early Assyrian contacts with Arabs and the impact on Levantine vassal tribute, *Bulletin of the American Society for Oriental Research* 331: 11–25.
Chandezon, C. (2000) Foires et panégyries dans le monde grec classique et hellénistique, *Revue des études grecques* 113: 70–100.
Cocquerillat, D. (1968) *Palmeraies et cultures de l'Eanna d'Uruk* (559–520) (ADFU 8), Berlin.
Cole, S W. (1996a) *The Early Neo-Babylonian Governor's Archive from Nippur* (Oriental Institute Publications 114), Chicago.
Cole, S W. (1996b). *Nippur in Late Assyrian Times 755–612 BC* (SAAS 4), Helsinki.

Dandamayev, M A. (1971) Die Rolle des Tamkārum in Babylonien im 2. und 1. Jahrtausend v. u. Z. In H. Klengel (ed.), *Beiträge zur socialen Struktur des alten Vorderasien* (Schriften zur Geschichte und Kultur des Alten Orients 1), 70–78, Berlin.

Dandamayev, M A. (1995) The neo-babylonian tamkāru. In Z. Zeitvit, S. Gitin & M. Sokoloffs (eds), *Solving Riddles and Untying Knots. Biblical, Epigraphic, and Semitic Studies in Honor of Jonas C. Greenfield*, 523–530, Winona Lake.

Dion, P E. (1997) *Les Araméens à l'âge du fer: histoire politique et structures sociales* (Études bibliques nouvelle série 34), Paris.

van Driel, G. (1999) Agricultural entrepreneurs in Mesopotamia. In H. Klengel & J. Renger (eds), *Landwirtschaft in alten Orient, ausgewählte Vorträge der XLI Rencontre assyriologique internationale, Berlin 4-8.7.1994* (BBVO 18), 213–223, Berlin.

Eph'al, I. (1978) The western minorities in Babylonia in the 6th–5th centuries BC: maintenance and cohesion. *Orientalia* ns 47: 74–90.

Eph'al, I. (1982) *The Ancient Arabs on the Borders of the Fertile Crescent 9th–5th Centuries BC*, Jérusalem.

Faist, B (2001) *Der Fernhandel des assyrischen Reiches zwischen dem 14. und 111 jh. v. Chr.* (AOAT 265), Münster.

Fales, F M. (2009) [2007] Arameans and Chaldeans. Environment and society. In G. Leick (ed.), *The Babylonian World*, 288–298, New York.

Favaro, S. (2007) Voyages et voyageurs à l'époque néo-assyrienne (SAAS 18), Helsinki.

Frame, G. (2007) [1992] *Babylonia 689-627 BC. A Political History* (PIHANS 69), Istanbul.

Graslin-Thomé, L. (2009) *Les échanges à longue distance en Mésopotamie au premier millénaire: une approche économique*, Paris.

Graslin-Thomé, L. (2014) Les marchands mésopotamiens et la théorie des jeux. In Z. Csabai, T. Grüll & G. Kalla (eds), *Economic History and Economic Theory in the Ancient Near East. Papers Dedicated to the Memory of Péter Vargyas* (Ancient Near Eastern and Mediterranean Studies 2), 603–628, Budapest.

Graslin-Thomé, L. (2015) La comptabilité dans la Mésopotamie de la seconde moitié du premier millénaire av. J.-C., *Comptabilité(s)* https://comptabilites.revues.org/1453.

Graslin, L. & A. Lemaire (2004) Tapsuhu-Thapsaque, *NABU*, 55–56.

Graslin, L. & C. Vivel (2005) Regards croisés sur la figure de l'entrepreneur: des Murašus aux théories de l'école autrichienne. In Ph. Clancier, F. Joannès, P. Rouillard & A. Tenu (eds), *Autour de Polanyi. Vocabulaire, théories et modalités des échanges*, 187–199, Paris.

Groom, N. (1981) *Frankincense and Myrrh, a Study of the Arabian Incense Trade*, New York.

Jankowska, N B. (1969) Some problems of the economy of the Assyrian Empire. In ?? Diakonoff (ed.), *Ancient Mesopotamia*, 253–276, Moscow.

Joannès, F. (1987) Méthodes de pesée néo-babyloniennes, *NABU* 2–3.

Joannès, F. (1994) Métaux précieux et moyens de paiement en Babylonie achéménide et hellénistique, *Transeuphratène* 9: 137–144.

Joannès, F. (1997) Structures et opérations commerciales en Babylonie. In J G. Dercksen (ed.), *Trade and Finance in Ancient Mesopotamia. Proceedings of the first MOS symposium (Leiden 1997)* (MOS Studies 1), 25–41, Istanbul.

Joannès, F. (ed.) (2000). *Rendre la justice en Mésopotamie* (Temps et espace), Saint Denis.

Jursa, M. (1995) *Die Landwirtschaft in neubabylonischen Sippar* (AfO Beiheift 25), Wien.

Jursa, M. (1998) *Tempelzehnt in Babylonien vom siebtenten bis zum dritten Jahrhundert v. Chr.* (AOAT 254), Münster.

Jursa, M. (2004a) Accounting in Neo-Babylonian institutional archives. In M. Hudson & C. Wunsch (eds), *Creating Economic Order: Record Keeping, Standarization and the Development of Accounting in the Ancient Near East*, 145–198, Bethesda.

Jursa, M. (2004b) Grundzüge der Wirtschaftsformen Babyloniens im ersten Jahrtausend v. Chr. In R. Rollinger & C. Ulf (eds), *Commerce and Monetary Systems in the Ancient World: Means of Transmission and Cultural Interaction*, 115–136, Stuttgart.

Jursa, M. (2006) Neubabylonische Briefe. In B. Janowski & G. Wilhem (eds), *Texte aus der Umwelt des Alten Testaments, Neue Folge Band 3, Briefe*, 158–172, Gütersloh.
Jursa, M. (2007) Eine Familie von konigskaufleuten judaischer Herkunft. *NABU*, 23–24.
Jursa, M. (2010) *Aspects of the Economic History of Babylonia in the First Millennium BC. Economic Geography, Economic Mentalities, Agriculture, the Use of Money and the Problem of Economic Growth* (Veröffentlichungen zur Wirtschaftsgeschichte Babyloniens im 1. Jahrtausend v. Chr. 4/ AOAT 377), Münster.
Kleber, K. (2008) *Tempel und Palast* (AOAT 358), Münster.
Krugman, P. (1991) *Geography and Trade*, Leuven.
Lanz, H. (1976) *Die Neubabylonischen harrânu-Geschäftsunternehmen* (Abhandlungen zur rechtswissenschaftlichen Grundlagenforschung 18), Berlin.
Lipiński, E. (2000) *The Aramaeans. Their Ancient History, Culture, Religion* (OLA 100), Leuven.
Liverani, M. (1992) *Studies in the Annals of Ashurnaşirpal II,2: Topological Analysis* (Quaderni di geographica storica), Rome.
Macginnis, J. (2004) Temple ventures across the river, *Transeuphratène* 27: 31–35.
McEwan, G. J P. (1984) Recall of a debt from the reign of Nabonidus, *OrAnt* 23: 49–52.
Meyers, E M. (1997) *The Oxford Encyclopedia of Archaeology in the Near East*, Oxford-New York.
Moorey, P R. S. (1999) *Ancient Mesopotamian Materials and Industries: the Archaeological Evidence*, Oxford.
Muller, G G. W. (2004) Zur Entwicklung von Preisen und Wirtschaft in Assyrien im 7th Jh v. Chr. In ?? Waetzoldt (ed.), *Von Sumer nach Ebla und zurück. Festschrift Giovanni Pettinato* (Heidelberger Studien zum alten Orient 9), 185–210, Heidelberg.
North, D C. (1981) *Structure and Change in Economic History*, New York.
North, D C. (1984) Transactions costs, institutions and economic history, *Journal of Institutional and Theoritical History* 140/1: 7–17.
North, D C. (1985). Transactions costs in history, *Journal of European Economic History* 14: 557–576.
North, D C. (2007) [1990] *Institutions, Institutional Change and Economic Performance*, Cambridge.
North, D C. & R P. Thomas (1973) *The Rise of Western World: a New Economic History*, Cambridge.
Oppenheim, A L. (1969) Essay on overland trade in the first millennium BC, *Journal of Cuneiform Studies* 21: 236–254.
Powell, M A. (1990) Masse und Gewichte. In D O. Edzard (ed.), *Reallexikon der Assyriologie und Vorderasiatischen Archäologie*, 457–517, Berlin.
Radner, K. (1999) Traders in the Neo-Assyrian Period. In J G. Dercksen (ed.), *Trade and Finance in Ancient Mesopotamia, proceedings of the first MOS Symposium (Leiden 1997)* (MOS series 1), 101–126, Leiden.
Radner, K. (2006–2008) Puqūdu. In M P. Streck (ed.), *Reallexikon der Assyriologie und Vorderasiatischen Archäologie* 11, 113–115, Berlin.
Radner, K. (2008) Lapis-lazuli, glas und gold. In R. Bohn, S. Conerman R. Kauz, K. Radner, F. Reichert, M.-C. Schöpfer-Pfaffen, M. Sommer *et al.* (eds), *Fernhandel in Antike und Mittelalter*, 9–24, Darmstadt.
Restö, J. (2003) *The Arabs in Antiquity. Their History from the Assyrian to the Umayyads*, New York.
Schloen, J D. (2001) *The House of the Father as fact and Symbol* (Studies in the Archaeology and History of the Levant 2), Winona Lake.
Snell, D C. (1982) *Ledgers and Prices. Early Mesopotamian Merchant Accounts* (YNER 8), New Haven.
Stolper, M W. (1985) *Entrepreneurs and Empire. The Murašu Firm and Persian Rule in Babylonia* (Uitgaben van het Nederlands Historisch-Archaeologisch Instituut te Istanbul 54), Istanbul.
Vargyas, P. (2000) Silver and money in Achaemenid and Hellenistic Babylonia. In J. Marzahn & H. Neumann (eds), *Assyriologica et Semitica, Festschrift für Joachim Oelsner* (AOAT 252), 513–521, Münster.
Wunsch, C. (1993) *Die Urkunden des babylonischen Geschäftsmannes Iddin-Marduk, Zum Handel mit Naturalien im 6. Jahrhundert v. Chr.* (Cuneiform Monographs 3), Groningen.
Zawadski, S. (2006) *Garments of the Gods. Studies on the Textile Industry and the Pantheon of Sippar according to the Texts from the Ebabbar Archive* (Orbis Biblicus et Orientalis 218), Fribourg.

Chapter 9

The empire of trade and the empires of force: Tyre in the Neo-Assyrian and Neo-Babylonian periods

Caroline van der Brugge & Kristin Kleber

The wealthy city of Tyre and its extensive trading network fostered the imagination and envy of people in antiquity, as much as it has spurred the interest of modern researchers. Many popular and scientific treatments of Phoenician history emphasise either the extensive commercial network in the Mediterranean or the well-documented relationship between Tyre and the Neo-Assyrian Empire. Assyria's regained strength is often depicted as a motor for colonisation of the Mediterranean, either in a positive sense that the Phoenicians served Assyria in return for the commercial benefits of a *pax Assyriaca*,[1] or in a negative sense, that systematic search for raw materials like silver was caused by Assyria's needs from the 9th century onwards.[2] In the following, we shall re-evaluate this claim and discuss the interrelatedness between the economic and political situation of a trade city in the changing historical circumstances from the Early to the Middle Iron Age. Tyre's history in the Neo-Babylonian period is less known due to the scarcity of textual sources. The re-evaluation of a file of cuneiform texts mentioning Tyre, and the identification of new texts now help to reconstruct the otherwise enigmatic political events around the famous 13-year siege of Tyre, thereby yielding new evidence on Neo-Babylonian policy in the west. While the Neo-Assyrian and Neo-Babylonian periods are the main focus, we begin with a brief outline of Tyre's situation in the Late Bronze Age, as it is important to realise that it was mainly continuity in Tyre's disposition combined with technological change that triggered major developments in the Iron Age.

The geopolitical situation of Tyre in the Late Bronze Age

Tyre's present configuration is very different from that of the ancient city. Today Tyre is a peninsula joined to the mainland, but in antiquity it was an island approximately 1 km off the coast.[3] This topographical situation allowed the city to turn into an island fortress that was almost impregnable for enemies. Yet, a major downside was the lack of wells on the rocky island.[4] Rainwater stored in cisterns often proved insufficient to meet the requirements of the island's population. Opposite the island, the city of Usu was situated on the mainland from where drinking water, straw, clay and firewood were brought to Tyre by boats. The mainland also served as a cemetery. The sensitive supply situation was utilised by attackers: they occupied Usu first in order to cut off the delivery of essential goods to the island.[5]

Cities like Byblos or Sidon that were located onshore suffered from different issues. Their geographical situation favoured the traditional pattern of an urban centre with an agricultural hinterland. Enemies could harm the cities by devastating fields or despoiling the harvest. This was indeed a dreaded reality in the Late Bronze Age, as letters of Rīb-Hadda, king of Byblos, demonstrate. He saw his peasantry migrating to other cities after the small state of Amurru had repeatedly robbed the entire yield.[6]

By contrast, in the Amarna letters written by the king of Tyre neither a peasantry nor a food shortage is ever mentioned; the city even sold provisions to Byblos in exchange for ivory.[7] This difference is important: the area of Usu, Tyre's immediate hinterland, did obviously not serve as an agricultural belt on whose food production the city's livelihood depended. Unlike Byblos, Tyre must have had a material infrastructure and a network of contacts that enabled it to exchange merchandise for grain and other necessities. For some time it could even supply itself with drinking water and firewood from further away, but this entailed skyrocketing transportation costs which made a long-term provisioning from farther distances highly unprofitable.[8] Firewood was needed in large quantities for Tyre's industries, namely glass fabrication[9] and production of purple dye.[10]

The Amarna correspondence illustrates Tyre's disposition as a city dedicated to and entirely living off trade and commercial production, already in the Late Bronze Age. The merchandise consisted mainly of products from Cyprus[11] and manufactured luxury goods. Unlike other Levantine cities, Tyre did not yet trade in timber in this period, because its merchants had no direct access to the hardwood of the Lebanese cedar forests.[12]

The Egyptian elite were one of the major purchasers of Tyre's luxury items. This explains the city's remarkable loyalty to its overlord in a time when other Levantine cities tried to wrench their independence from Egypt. But other trading partners were also treated with the respectful, yet calculated generosity that regulated international trade in the Late Bronze Age.[13] A sufficient defence against aggressors, a functioning infrastructure, as well as friendly and loyal relations with customers are all characteristics of good salesmanship. But even a good merchant cannot take end-to-end precautions against the vicissitudes of history.

The period of crisis

During the crisis at the end of the Late Bronze Age, the island city suffered a severe setback. Egypt, one of its main trading partners, faced internal problems: severe draught and a succession of weak rulers forced Egypt to retreat from the Levant. The Hittite kingdom disappeared entirely, as did the city of Ugarit. Cyprus suffered from invasions of the Sea Peoples who also appeared on the Levantine coast south of Tyre and conquered cities like Gaza, Ashkelon, Ashdod and Dor. It seems that the Phoenician coastal towns were not attacked. But Tyre's trading network declined quickly and substantially. Bikai's excavation at Tyre demonstrates a sharp decrease in Cypriot pottery around 1200 BC, indicating (temporarily) diminished contacts with the copper island. Archaeological evidence suggests continuing habitation, but with a short period of serious depopulation.[14] A brief abandonment of the city is also implied by the account of the Roman historian Justin, who wrote in the 2nd century AD. According to him, Tyre was (re-)founded by Sidonian refugees.[15]

When the Egyptian official Wenamun travelled to Byblos around 1080 BC to buy cedar wood, Tyre had become a city with a functioning harbour again.[16] Hiram I, who reigned over Tyre in the 10th century, initiated many building projects on the island, including the elevation of parts of the city, the enlargement of the city itself, and the rebuilding of temples.[17] These are signs of a renewed period of blossom at a time when the former territorial states Egypt, Assyria and Babylonia were still struggling with the aftermath of the collapse.

The formation of a new commercial network[18]

Aramaean and Neo-Hittite kingdoms appeared in northern Syria. This created new outlet markets for Tyre's own beautifully manufactured items and stimulated merchants to act as middlemen in a transit trade of foreign merchandise. Tyre's trading network, described in a poetical text that Ezekiel included in his prophecy on Tyre,[19] left traces in the material record.[20] Expansion of the Phoenician commercial network into the Neo-Hittite states, for example, is shown by a Phoenician inscription in Sam'al, a Phoenician harbour installation at Myriandros on the gulf of Alexandretta, as well as Phoenician influences on material culture at Carchemish.[21] Furthermore, Tyre developed friendly and close contacts with Israel and Aram-Damascus.[22] Excavations in the southern Levantine coastal area have detected Phoenician presence in this area from the 11th century onwards.[23] In the Philistine city of Dor a heavy destruction layer from the middle of this century has been uncovered; the excavators linked it to the process of Phoenician expansion.[24] After the destruction, Phoenicians comprised the majority of the city's population, while pottery finds confirm trade with Cyprus.[25] In the 9th century the term "Sidonians" became common as a *pars pro toto* for "Phoenicians".[26] This does not imply a strong position of Sidon. On the contrary, the fact that Ittô-baʿal I, who is mentioned in the Tyrian king list, was called "King of the Tyrians and Sidonians"[27] suggests Tyrian dominance over Sidon.

Phoenician maritime trade expanded further westwards. From the 10th century onwards, Phoenician merchants sailed across the Mediterranean Sea. 10th-century contacts with the Aegean world[28] as well as late 10th- or early 9th-century trade contacts with southern Spain[29] have been demonstrated archaeologically. On Sardinia, a Phoenician inscription from the second half of the 9th century (the "Nora-stone") has been found. It mentions a king Pummay who probably corresponds to the Greek Pygmalion in the Tyrian king list.[30] This king is said to have founded the colony of Kition on Cyprus.[31] Tyre's contacts with Cyprus had continued through the period of decline in the 12th century[32] but a Tyrian colony is not attested before the end of the 8th century, when Lulî suppressed a revolt in Kition,[33] despite the existence of a late 9th-century Phoenician temple of Astarte in Kition.[34]

When by the end of the 9th century the Phoenicians had reached many shores of the Mediterranean Sea, they entered a new phase of trade: colonisation. For the foundation of Carthage, two different years circulate in Greek historiographical sources: 814 and 825 BC.[35] Archaeological data confirm that these dates are realistic: the first signs of Phoenician settlement appear in the period between 835 and 800 BC.[36] From the same period are the Phoenician finds excavated in Onuba (modern day Huelva[37]) and in Gadir (modern day Cadiz) that suggest the start of Phoenician settlements in this area on the southern Spanish coast beyond the Pillars of Hercules. The hinterland of this coastal area was rich in silver and other metals. In addition, the first Phoenician settlements in the region around Malaga were established in the same period.[38]

Before elaborating on this phase of colonisation, let us first turn to Tyrian contacts with Assyria. In the 11th century, Tiglath-pileser I went on campaign to the Levant, but in contrast to Byblos, Sidon and Arwad, Tyre is not mentioned among the tribute paying cities.[39] The first contact between Tyre and Assyria is recorded when Assurnasirpal II turned up in the Levant around 870 BC. This time Tyre paid tribute.[40] Tyre and Sidon were the only two Levantine city states (if Sidon had not already been part of Tyre's kingdom) that were invited to the inauguration of Assurnaṣirpal's new palace.[41] Shalmaneser III received tribute from Tyre four times,[42]Adad-nārārī III only once.[43]

Six attested payments of tribute in a period of almost 100 years do not speak in favour of a severe Assyrian pressure on Tyre. It was a new situation for the Tyrian merchants, and they may have seen the expanding Assyrian Empire with its growing elite and its need of building materials, crafted goods and craftsmen as a business opportunity, and the tribute not only as a burden, but also as an investment in relations with Assyria. It is not unlikely that Tyrian agents in Carchemish coordinated trade with the Assyrians who had their regional commercial centre in nearby Kār-Shalmaneser.[44]

In this period, Assyrian domination or demand was not vigorous enough to trigger or force Tyrian exploration of and colonisation in the west. We see the process of colonisation as a consequential step in the development of Tyre's maritime trade,[45] comparable to the situation in Europe in the 15th century AD, when Portugal (via the east) and Spain (via the west) were both eager to explore sea routes to the Far East for the purpose of direct trade. Developments in ships, navigation and cartography made these voyages possible, as well as investments in infrastructure. In contrast to Spain, Portugal had developed a form of royal capitalism in which the state had created commercial institutions, such as the factory (*feitoria* in Portuguese). These self-contained communities or enclaves, representing Portuguese royal commercial interests abroad, first arose in the European trading centres. When the Portuguese ships sailed around Africa or to the Far East, a number of *feitorias* were established along the route, in order to foster local trade.[46] At the beginning of the 1st millennium BC, the Phoenicians were able to make significant progress in naval technology, which enabled the construction of larger and stronger ships, especially cargo vessels called "ships of Tarshish".[47] It is very likely that these and other nautical developments had made voyaging to and colonisation in the western part of the Mediterranean Sea possible, and, at the same time, the wish to trade with the western Mediterranean had encouraged these developments.

But even then the voyages were hazardous; many attempts must have failed. According to Strabo (*Geography* 3.5.5), three attempts were made to establish Gadir. Expeditions were expensive and required cooperation, planning, preparation and a reason. In this respect it is not surprising that the founding of Carthage and the colonisation of the southern Spanish coast happened around the same time. When the Phoenicians gained a foothold in southern Spain, they created and organised efficient logistics for obtaining silver and other metals. They also introduced new mining techniques to the indigenous people, who then processed the metal and transported it to the coast where it was sold to Phoenician traders.[48] Being the most wealthy and powerful city of the Levantine coast it is very likely that Tyre had had the lead in these developments, as classical sources confirm.[49] Furthermore, we have to assume that within Tyre a leading authority, probably the king, directed the creation and exploitation of the western Mediterranean network, comparable to the founding of the Portuguese *feitorias* along the sea route to the Far East.

The world of the Tyrian merchants in the 9th and first half of the 8th centuries was characterised by growing trade with Greece, Assyria, Egypt[50] and the Neo-Hittite states as well as participation in the copper trade with Cyprus. The merchants also explored the western Mediterranean Sea and found new business opportunities. Colonisation was the next step in this expansion and at the same time a transition to another phase of maritime trade. But around 740 BC, when this network was functioning and increasingly created wealth for Tyre, circumstances were about to change again for the Tyrian merchants.

The clash with the Neo-Assyrian empire

When in 745 BC Tiglath-pileser III ascended the Assyrian throne, he began to expand the empire at once. First he subdued parts of Urartu and the northern Syrian states, including the city of Arpad to which he laid siege for three years. Immediately thereafter he turned his attention to the Levantine regions south of Arpad, where several kings paid him tribute as they had done to his predecessors. However, unlike his predecessors, this Assyrian king did not campaign to collect a one-off payment but strove to stay in control of the subjected regions. Right from the beginning he installed Assyrian trading stations (*kārānu*), where trade performed by local merchants was taxed. This is shown by a letter from the Assyrian governor of Simirra, Qurdi-Aššur-lāmur, to the Assyrian king.[51] The letter also indicates that the Assyrians imposed restrictions on trade: the Tyrians were not permitted to sell timber to Egypt and the Philistine cities.[52]

Most important was that *kārānu* facilitated direct trade with Assyria.[53] It is clear that by installing these trading stations the Assyrians were able to redirect the flow of goods and profits. In consequence, the local commercial structures changed. This policy was not limited to the Lebanon region. Tiglath-pileser subdued Arab tribes near the border with Egypt and let them control the Arabian long distance trade from Edom to the west. He conquered Gaza and made it a "*bīt kāri* of Assyria".[54] Thus, Assyria gained control over, or even took over, Philistine trade with Egypt and Arabia. There is no proof yet but it is reasonable to assume that *kārānu* were also established in the Neo-Hittite states. On the Assyrian side, this trade was coordinated by royal merchants (*tamkārū*) who provided the king with slaves, horses, metals and luxury goods of any kind. Direct Assyrian trade with local merchants intensified.[55]

The effects of this Assyrian policy on Tyrian trade were considerable. Until around 740 BC, Tyrian merchants functioned as middlemen, transporting merchandise from all regions that local tradesmen had carried to the seaports. Tyrian ships circulated the Mediterranean Sea and thereby brought these products to other ports where local traders took over and transported the merchandise further inland.[56] The appearance of Tyrian agents in cities as far inland as Carchemish shows that some of them were active in land trade as well. But now, after a permanent infrastructure for the flow of goods to Assyria had been established in the Levant and the Neo-Hittite states, a large portion of it was transported directly from the subdued states to Assyria, partly in the form of tribute, and partly via trade. We lack quantitative information about the size of this drain towards the centre, but the empire certainly aimed at maximising resources for its core.[57] Therefore less merchandise reached the eastern harbours where the Tyrian ships were waiting; consequently the position of the Tyrian merchants as middlemen weakened.

Like the Philistines who intensified the production of olive oil in the 7th century,[58] the Tyrians could have tried to increase the production of their own manufactured items in order to compensate for the decreased trade volume. Crafted goods had made the merchants wealthy in the Late Bronze Age, but by the middle of the 8th century they had become a relatively small part of the total Tyrian trade volume.[59] In addition, the eastern markets for luxury goods had declined. Assyrian conquest and deportation of local elites led to the emigration of artisans from the Neo-Hittite states to Greece, Italy and Scythia.[60] In the Phoenician area the ivory-carving industry declined in the late 8th century, and Syrian and Phoenician ivory carvers left for Greece.[61]

As a consequence, the most realistic strategy for Tyre was to focus on trade with overseas regions like Cyprus, Greece and Egypt, and to further explore Tyre's own Mediterranean network of trade posts and colonies. These markets were unreachable for the Assyrians and, evenly important, they could be expanded within the infrastructure that the Tyrians already had built. The process of realignment of their commercial policies took no more than 15–20 years. In order to understand how they implemented it, we have to return briefly to the early days of Assyrian domination.

When at the beginning of his reign Tiglath-pileser undertook campaigns to subdue Neo-Hittite and Aramaean states, the Tyrians tried to gratify the king by bringing him tribute in Arpad.[62] In addition to the effect that this kept the Assyrian army away, they may have hoped to give Tyrian trade with Assyria a new impulse. If so, their hopes were certainly disappointed after the new Assyrian economic policy to control the northern Levantine trade was implemented. Shortly thereafter, Tyre and a number of other Levantine kingdoms revolted, but after the arrival of Tiglath-pileser Hiram II submitted immediately.[63] This inconsistent policy most likely reflects internal disputes about how to deal with the problem. Mattan II, who paid an enormous sum to the Assyrians shortly after his enthronement, did not reign very long. Katzenstein has suggested that he was murdered by Tyrian merchants who did not agree with his strategy.[64]

For almost 10 years Tyre's policy had alternated between cooperating with the Assyrians and resisting them, but under king Lulî, the city eventually chose opposition. When Tiglath-pileser died in 727 BC, Tyre revolted again and did not surrender when his successor Shalmaneser V arrived. Tyre was besieged and cut off from the mainland for 5 years.[65] It must have been a well-considered and well-prepared revolt. Within a period of little more than 10 years Tyre's attitude towards Assyria had changed from obliging to hostile. This change was only possible because of the city's flourishing western trade network and colonies, and because of its position on the fortified island.

The economic strategy under Lulî

At the beginning of his reign, Sargon II ended the siege of Tyre. Violent repression was not an adequate strategy to benefit from Tyre's trade. Tyre on the other hand, needed access to the mainland and control over its hinterland. Therefore, probably, a treaty was conducted, in which Sargon demanded loyalty and tribute on a yearly basis. On account of the position of Tyre, the city was able to ask for something in return. We know that the city regained its hinterland including Sidon.[66] In the Levant, Sargon further changed commercial structures by deporting the Israelites, subduing Gaza, taking over control in Carchemish and conquering Ashdod. He also stimulated direct trade between Assyria and Egypt.[67] Tyre continued expanding its western network: In Carthage considerable demographic, economic and urban growth took place during the latter part of the 8th and the whole of the 7th centuries; and in southern Spain the output of the mines grew until it reached industrial proportions in the 7th century.[68]

Due to their complete dependence on trade, the Tyrians had been forced and succeeded to find new markets. The Assyrians, on the other hand, never installed a *kāru* on the island, as they did in the port of Arwad, the other Phoenician island city.[69]

This situation reflects a certain balance in the relationship, in which Tyre, although a vassal state, had obtained privileges.

The history behind Sargon's Cyprus stele possibly mirrors this balance. The stele, found in AD 1844 in the debris of medieval ruins at Kition, was interpreted as a boundary marker for the western edge of the Assyrian Empire. In addition to general phrases, it mentions seven Cypriot kings who brought tribute to Sargon in Babylon. What adds to its mystery is the fact that the stele is the only archaeological evidence of Assyrian presence on Cyprus.[70] Its text has been linked to a part of Sargon's annals that relate to Cyprus, and for which Na'aman[71] has suggested a new transliteration and translation:

> "Šilṭa [of] Tyre [pays? tax? ... to] Assyr[ia. (And) seven kin]gs of the {land} of Ia', a district [of the land of Adnana], who are situated a journey of seven days away in the middle of the sea of the setting sun [and their locations are dista]nt, who since old days, to his? [...] together s[topped the[ir presents (and)] withheld [their tributes. And Šilṭa bro]ught his heavy tribute, and to suppress the ho[lst? of ...] he ap[plied to me for military aid]. I sent my officer, who is fearless in battle, with my royal guard, to avenge him, [and ... they cros]sed?. When they saw the strong troops of Ashur, at the mention of my name they became afraid and their arms collapsed. They brought to Babylon, into my presence, gold, silver, ut[ensils of ebony and boxwood, the manufacture] of their land, and [to ...] I entrusted [them]."

Josephus mentions a revolt of Kition, the suppression of which he ascribes to Lulî.[72] It is uncertain whether the revolts mentioned by Josephus and by the annals are one and the same, but if we assume that they are, a hypothesis can be formulated to explain the events. Lulî may have asked Sargon for assistance[73] in a Tyrian mission to Cyprus in order to end the revolt through negotiations.[74] The royal guard (it was not an army!) served only to impress the Cypriots. Afterwards the seven kings that had revolted went to Sargon in Babylon to pay their respect and an Assyrian stele was installed at the island, in or near Kition. The success of the negotiations must have lasted for a long time, because in the following decades Phoenician influence on Cyprus continued unabated, as archaeological finds demonstrate.[75] Moreover, Lulî's flight to Cyprus after Sargon's death, only six years after the stele had been erected, shows that he must have felt safe there. Tyre certainly did not dominate Cyprus as a whole. Texts from the time of Esarhaddon and Assurbanipal list ten Cypriot kings, thereby implying the existence of ten independent political entities, whereas the absence of Kition and Lapithos in these lists indicates that these two were under some sort of political control, perhaps from Tyre.[76]

At the time of Lulî's flight to Cyprus, Tyre was certainly not left behind without adequate defence. The king's escape was a planned move, possibly to safeguard Tyre's relationship with its large western network. Sennacherib punished Tyre for its disloyalty by depriving it of the mainland territory.[77] It is unclear how long the tense situation for Tyre that resulted from Sennacherib's reorganisation of the

Levant lasted. As far as we know, Sennacherib never returned to the region.[78] During his reign, Tyre may have regained part of its mainland possessions, although Sidon stayed independent. The Mediterranean trade network and the colonies blossomed, other parts of the Levant recovered as well. The Phoenicians were able to set up a trade structure at least in some parts of the Levant again.[79] And at the end of Sennacherib's reign, Egypt's political and economic influence in the southern Levant increased substantially.[80]

Cooperation between Tyre and the Assyrians under Esarhaddon

The relative freedom ended under Esarhaddon. In 677 BC he destroyed Sidon in order to restore Assyrian control. Regarding Tyre, however, he chose to effect a treaty[81] which is known to us, although the first two of the originally four columns are almost unreadable.[82] The third column contains an important negotiation result for the Tyrian merchants, who were given free entrance to the Levantine mainland in Assyrian hands, with its area and cities accurately described.[83] In addition, Tyre was given part of the Sidonian hinterland.[84] Tyre, in turn, had to endure the presence of an Assyrian deputy (*qēpu*) and was forbidden to have any contacts with the pharaoh when this Assyrian official was not present.[85] The date of the contract is uncertain, possible moments are the destruction of Sidon in 677 BC and Esarhaddon's conquest of Egypt followed by Tyre's submission in 671 BC. We tend to favour the earlier date, because in 671 BC Tyre's position was much weaker: the Tyrian king Baʿal submitted to Esarhaddon and delivered his daughters together with all the outstanding tribute. In 670 BC, Esarhaddon stayed in Assyria facing a revolt of his aristocracy, and in 669 BC the Assyrian king died on his way to Egypt.[86] Hence, 677 BC is the most probable date for the conclusion of the pact.

In the absence of direct evidence we can only try to deduce the reason for the treaty by observing what happened before and after its conclusion. In 701 BC Sennacherib had expelled Tyre from its Levantine mainland possessions and transferred these territories to the newly installed king in Sidon. We can assume that he also had taken away Tyre's permission to trade with the Levantine cities and regions under Assyrian control.

For the period after the treaty three observations can be made. The first observation is the erection of a new Assyrian trading post, Kār-Esarhaddon, near the ruins of Sidon. Surely, it was a prestige project for the Assyrian king, but even such a project needed a practical purpose. Assyria did not possess a fleet with which it could participate in maritime trade. Most likely, Kār-Esarhaddon was built for Assyria to participate in direct trade with Tyre on a large scale in order to obtain Tyre's merchandise produced or purchased in the colonies. There is indirect support for this purpose of Kār-Esarhaddon, although the text is from a slightly later period, around 671 BC, after Esarhaddon had ended the Tyrian revolt:

> "I conquered Tyre, which is in the midst of the sea, (and) took away all of the cities (and) possessions of Baʿalu, its king, who had trusted in Taharqa, king of Kush; (and) I conquered (Lower) Egypt, Upper Egypt, and Kush, struck Taharqa, its king, five times with arrows, and ruled his entire land.
>
> I wrote to all of the kings who are in the midst of the sea, from Iadnana (Cyprus) (and) Ionia to KUR*tar-si-si*, (and) they bowed down at my feet. I received their heavy tribute."[87]

What the king describes is Tyre's western trade network, which was obviously not under Esarhaddon's direct command, but to which Assyria finally had gained entrance. It stretched from Cyprus and Ionia to Tartessos beyond the Pillars of Hercules. By ending Tyre's revolt in 671 BC Esarhaddon had restored his access to Tyre's Mediterranean trade that he had lost in 674 BC when Tyre revolted. The alleged payment of tribute by the kings of this network may simply refer to the fact that Assyria received items from overseas in Tyre's tribute; then it may be one of the twists of the truth, typical for the genre, to inflate the king's accomplishments without excogitating. Should there be more truth to it, it possibly resembled the payment of the seven Cypriot kings almost forty years earlier: the Mediterranean kings were not under direct control of Assyria, but they paid him respect and brought him gifts.

The second observation is that Esarhaddon refers to the "22 kings of Hatti, the seashore and the islands" on three occasions (and Assurbanipal once). It is clear that Esarhaddon sees these kings as a group in some way. They are mentioned in an Assyrian text from around 676 BC describing their participation in the building of Kār-Esarhaddon and in a text about building projects in Nineveh. The context of the third text is unclear.[88] Thirdly, a unanimous policy of the Levantine states may also be reflected by the fact that Esarhaddon had a free passage through the Levant in 674 BC on his way to Egypt. He went straight through again in 671 and 669 BC, as did Assurbanipal in 667 BC.

These observations lead to the following reconstruction of Tyre's motives for the treaty. Whether or not the trading restriction from 701 BC had been reversed already during Sennacherib's reign remains unclear, but either way, Tyre wanted to formally effect this arrangement with the new Assyrian king. The merchants had something to offer to Assyria in return, namely access to their overseas network. Together with the 21 other kings (from Cyprus and the Levant) Baʿal formed an alliance that supported Assyria in its building projects as well as its effort to conquer Egypt.[89] Perhaps they even accompanied Esarhaddon on his first campaign to Egypt as they did under Assurbanipal. For Assyria, the advantage was the connection to the Mediterranean network, especially the western part (Tartessos) which was under control of Tyre, not Sidon, and where silver and tin came from.

The treaty, however, does not seem to have constituted a firm basis for long-term cooperation with the Assyrians. In 674 BC Esarhaddon lost the battle against Egypt: The Tyrians probably considered this failure an opportunity to break the treaty and withhold payment. Therefore, three years later, when Esarhaddon returned to defeat the Egyptians, he laid siege to Tyre and the city surrendered.

When in 667 BC Assurbanipal entered Egypt, the 22 kings were involved in his campaign.[90] But when Egypt revolted four years later, Tyre did too. Assurbanipal besieged Tyre from the land and the sea, laying a complete blockade around the island city that forced it to surrender. This time Baʿal had to hand over the crown-prince as a hostage and Tyre's coastal area was turned into an Assyrian province.[91] However, in the almost 35 years thereafter Assurbanipal returned to the Levant only once,[92] with the result that the Assyrian grip on the Levant loosened again. When the Assyrian Empire declined, its administrative structures in the periphery started to dissolve.[93] In an economic perspective the weakness of Assyria meant for Tyre and the other Phoenician cities that they could mind their business relatively undisturbed by imperial demands. Sidon was revived in this period, and Tyre established a trading quarter in Memphis in return for an Egyptian royal domain in the cedar forest.[94]

Tyre in the early Neo-Babylonian period

From 610 BC on, Syria and the southern Levant became a battleground in the struggle between the remnants of the Assyrian Empire with its Egyptian ally and the rising Neo-Babylonian Empire. At the end of Nabopolassar's reign Babylonia had positioned itself as the new dominant power in the area. After the final defeat of the Egyptian troops at Carchemish,[95] Nebuchadnezzar devoted several campaigns to securing the submission of the Levantine states. The Chronicle states that "all the kings of Hatti" (a catch-all phrase for the west) paid tribute to Nebuchadnezzar in his 1st year (604/3 BC).[96] In the *Hofkalender*, an inscription that mentions Nebuchadnezzar's 7th year (598/7 BC), Tyre is listed next to Gaza, Sidon, Arwad and Ashdod[97] as having contributed to the building of the South Palace in Babylon. Thus, the Phoenician cities had accepted vassalage and did not participate in Judah's revolt in 601–597 BC. Their business possibly profited from the fact that Ashkelon was destroyed in 603 BC. The foremost Babylonian goals were to secure the area and to receive tribute; any further interference with the Levantine trade network or with its administrative structures is unlikely in these early years. However, the dominance of the new empire was not yet confirmed. The Phoenicians paid tribute as long as the Babylonians appeared powerful, but after Nebuchadnezzar faced an internal revolt in Babylonia in 594 BC, the western vassal states considered defecting.[98]

The reconstruction of historical events thereafter is more difficult, as the Babylonian Chronicle breaks after mentioning another campaign to Syria in the 11th year of Nebuchadnezzar (593 BC). There is a gap of 37 years before the sixth tablet resumes with the reign of Neriglissar. With the necessary caution, secondary and tertiary sources such as Flavius Josephus, Herodotus and the Bible can be turned to account to fill the gap. In addition, we can now also use Babylonian archival tablets issued at Tyre. Previously most of them were thought to refer to a small village of deportees, called Ṣūru (Tyre), near Nippur in Babylonia. In Kleber (2008) this file was re-evaluated, new documents added and an earlier dossier of texts mentioning

Tyre was identified.[99] As a result, we can now be sure that Tyre at the Mediterranean coast is meant, not a village in Babylonia. In the following we shall elaborate on the consequences that the information gained from Babylonian material has on the reconstruction of Tyre's history in the Neo-Babylonian period.

From Nebuchadnezzar's *Hofkalender* Tyre's status as a vassal state of Babylonia is virtually certain for 598/7 BC.[100] From the 14th year of Nebuchadnezzar (591 BC) we have the first Babylonian archival documents that attest to the presence of a crew of Babylonian workers at Tyre.[101] Only four documents belong to this file; they all mention iron tools or silver that were sent to Tyre to be received there by an official of the Eanna temple (the *qīpu*) whose task it was to organise the temple's corvée service owed to the king. We do not know what was built. It may have been a trading post or a military facility. Since we have strong indications that a garrison was placed onto Tyre after the siege, it is possible that a building for this military unit had been built already by then. This garrison may have served to guard Tyre's loyalty after an attempt to defect from Babylonia's political line. But it is possible that other military facilities had been necessary. After all, a stronghold in one of the Phoenician seaports was particularly important because, unlike Babylonia, Egypt possessed a navy, and would therefore always be able to challenge Babylonian domination of the coastal area. Without the support of the coastal vassals and their ships, Babylonia would also not be able to conquer Egypt, something that was certainly still on Nebuchadnezzar's political agenda. The cuneiform tablets from Uruk are significant because the building activities – whether they reflect the erection of a trading post or a garrison – would in any case constitute a severe drawback, the former for Tyre's mercantile interests, the latter for its status and independence. Tyre had to bear it, as Babylonia was undisputedly the dominant power in these years.

This situation changed when Apries ascended the Egyptian throne in 589 BC and immediately challenged Babylonian dominance in the Syro-Palestinian area. Judah and Ammon defected from Babylonian rule probably in the same year.[102] According to the date in 2 Kings 25, Nebuchadnezzar's punitive campaigns began shortly thereafter, near the end of his 16th year. Biblical sources tell us that the siege of Jerusalem was lifted in 588/7 BC because Egyptian troops advanced,[103] but resumed after Apries' army retreated. The Babylonian king directed the campaign from his headquarters, the fortress Riblah in the Hamath area. Clearly, much more was going on in Greater Syria than the subjugation of Judah. The Babylonian army seems to have been in great distress, even after the fall of Jerusalem. A document from Uruk relates additional subscriptions of Babylonian foot soldiers ("archers") who had to "come to the help of Bēl and the king" in September/October 586 BC.[104] This unusual phrase and the fact that the solders had to be at the collection point Upia within 10 days – they could hardly travel faster – betrays urgency. After Jerusalem was taken, Judah was turned into a Babylonian province but the Biblical report about the assassination of Gedaliah by order of the Ammonite king[105] indicates that the west was everything but secured for the Babylonians. There are hints that campaigns against Ammon, Moab and the Lebanon area took place in the years after the fall of Jerusalem, or more precisely between Nebuchadnezzar's 23rd year (582/1 BC), and his invasion of Egypt at the beginning of 567 BC.[106] Lipschits (2004) has adduced archaeological evidence to underpin the suggestion that Ammon was turned into a Babylonian province in this period.

Tyre may have been part of a larger Syro-Palestinian coalition against Babylonia that arose after the accession of Apries, or it joined this coalition shortly later in view of Apries' display of power in the Levant. Herodotus (II, 161) claims that Apries "attacked Sidon and fought a battle with the Tyrians by sea". Diodorus Siculus (I, 68, 1) adds that Apries "made a campaign with strong land and sea forces against Cyprus and Phoenicia, took Sidon by storm, and so terrified the other cities of Phoenicia that he secured their submission". No date is given, but it is likely that these events took place within the context of an Egyptian thrust into the Levant after Apries' accession. This demonstration of renewed Egyptian power may have convinced Tyre (and perhaps also Sidon) to switch sides.[107] The Egyptians had a well-maintained fleet and cooperated with the Greeks. This challenged Tyre's position in its Mediterranean network and was perhaps seen as potentially more damaging than yet another land siege, in which no Western Asian empire had succeeded before. Whatever the reasoning was, Tyre decided to close its gates to the Babylonians.

The siege of Tyre and its aftermath

In his prophecy concerning the fate of Tyre from 587 BC, Ezekiel (Ez. 26) speaks of "many nations" that will be hurled up against Tyre "like the sea hurls up its waves" while the Babylonian army would arrive from the north "with horses, chariots, cavalry and a great army". Obviously Ezekiel envisaged a land siege in combination with military assistance by the coastal states with their fleets.[108] However, had a sea blockade been effective, Tyre could not have held out that long. An effective sea blockade did not come to pass, perhaps due to a superiority of Tyre and its allies in sea battles. Nevertheless, even a land siege that lasted for 13 years was hard to sustain for Tyre, and not possible without Cypriot and perhaps also Egyptian help. The city may even have received clandestine support of other Phoenician and/or Philistine towns. We do not know what happened, perhaps its naval support system weakened, or Ittô-baʿal died, or the Tyrians realised that the situation was no longer sustainable. Eventually Tyre capitulated and negotiated the turnover of the city into Nebuchadnezzar's hands, perhaps against the right to remain a (vassal) state with its own king.[109] Ittô-baʿal III was succeeded by king Baʿal II. The city seems not to have been plundered, if this is how we should understand Ezekiel's prophecy (Ez. 29: 17–20) that "neither he (Nebuchadnezzar) nor his army got anything from Tyre to pay for the labour that he had performed against her". We believe that the negotiated capitulation stipulated the preservation of Tyre's kingship, but the agreement was overridden ten years later. From then on, Tyre was administered by "judges" according to Josephus. It seems that Tyre became part of a province.

The chronology of the siege of Tyre was until recently dependent on a passage in Josephus' *De antiquitate* (= *Contra Apionem*) in which Josephus relates a list of Tyrian rulers. On this basis, Katzenstein (1973, 325f.) reconstructed the chronology and came to the conclusion that the siege began in Nebuchadnezzar's 20th year, 585 BC. With few exceptions all subsequent treatments of the history of Tyre followed Katzenstein's reconstruction. However, we now believe that Katzenstein's chronology stands on feet of clay. In the appendix below we shall review the arguments anew and argue that an emendation of Josephus' text making Nebuchadnezzar's 17th year (588/7 BC) to the year in which the siege began, cannot be excluded. If the siege began in 588/7, it would have ended in 575/4, the 30th year of Nebuchadnezzar's reign.

We can now add more than a dozen dated Babylonian documents from Sippar, Nippur and Uruk that contribute to a reconstruction of the events after the end of the siege. Most of them were drawn up at Tyre and therefore date from after the siege.[110] Particularly interesting is the text Ni 361 because it was drafted at Tyre in the 31st year of Nebuchadnezzar's reign (574/3 BC).[111] This is two years *prior* to the end of the siege according to Katzenstein's chronology, but one year after the end of the siege according to a chronology that dates the siege from 588/7–575/4. If the date of the text can be confirmed by collation, this text would be a very strong argument in favour of a beginning of the siege in the 17th year of Nebuchadnezzar. Thereafter, the earliest securely dated texts that mention Tyre were drawn up after the end of the siege regardless which chronology is followed.

The Babylonian archival material is evidence for a heavy Babylonian presence at Tyre after the siege. The texts frequently mention soldiers and military equipment such as armour, tents and leather shoes. Some tablets document business transactions between the temple and private individuals, perhaps merchants, who supplied the temple with silver necessary to pay for rations of the temple's workers and soldiers. The file reflects the military occupation of the island by Babylonian troops, something that Assyria had never done. Occasionally "work" (*dullu*) is mentioned.[112] One text records wheat rations for Babylonian workers. Its subscript refers to an agricultural rental payment (*šibšu*) of a "Town of the New Canal" (Āl-nāri-eššil). If the wheat and the rental payment are connected, the new settlement may have been an agricultural holding of Babylonians somewhere in the fertile plains of the Levantine coast which may have sustained the garrison.[113]

The dossier contains documents dating from the 31st, 35th, and 38th–42nd years of Nebuchadnezzar and from the accession year of Amēl-Marduk (thus, from the period 574/3–562 BC). That points to a long-term and most likely continuous presence of Babylonian troops at Tyre from the end of the siege onwards. We believe that the city of Tyre was occupied, and a garrison of Babylonian troops was stationed in it. It may even have served as a collection point for Babylonian soldiers on campaigns in the west. Zawadzki (2003, 279) proposed that Nebuchadnezzar may have faced another Tyrian revolt between the month Abu of the 41st and the month Tašrītu of the 42nd year of Nebuchadnezzar as an explanation for the loss of Tyre's native kingship. However, in view of the file that proves a continuous Babylonian military presence from at least year 38 Nebuchadnezzar on (and probably already from the end of the siege on) to the accession year of Amēl-Marduk, a new insurrection is unlikely. An alternative explanation why Tyre's kingship was discontinued may be that Baʿal II had died which freed Nebuchadnezzar from respecting the treaty effected on occasion of Tyre's submission. There was no reason to continue Tyre's special status as all attempts to conquer Egypt had not brought the expected success.[114] Egypt remained strong under Amasis while the Babylonian king was nearing the end of his life.

Tyre's kingship was reintroduced in 558/7.[115] No source informs us about the reasons for this decision. One could speculate that there may have been a connection to the preparations for Neriglissar's campaign against Pirindu in 557/6 BC. In addition to the royal cities Ura and Kirši – reached over land – the Babylonians also took Pitusu, an island off the coast of Asia Minor, by boats. The help of Phoenician cities, perhaps including Tyre, is likely, and the restoration of Tyre's kingship may have been the reward for Tyre's promise to help.[116] The royal house of Tyre was in Babylonian captivity: Josephus relates that when king Balatorus died, his successor Merbalos (Mahar-baʿal) was brought from Babylon. When he died four years later, his brother Hiram III was fetched again from Babylon.[117]

In spite of its renewed status as a vassal state, Tyre could never regain its former splendour. The long siege and the loss of independence had severe consequences for the city and its trade. It is likely that families that could afford it had brought their wealth and family members who would not actively fight to the colonies on Cyprus and to Carthage already during the early years of the siege. Nevertheless, the defenders and the remaining population had to be supplied with the necessities of life from far away. Instead of merchandise, ships carried water, food, straw and firewood. The usual trade ventures across the Mediterranean were curtailed or seized altogether, and producers waited in vain to trade their products against merchandise that previously arrived on Tyrian ships. Katzenstein connected the story about Arganthonius, the king of Tartessos, about whom Herodotus relates that he invited Phocaeans to settle in his realm, to the years of the siege.[118] The Greeks had started to compete already before the Neo-Babylonian period commenced, but Tyre's nadir and the close Greek cooperation with Egypt helped to strengthen Greek maritime trade. In the period between 580 and 550 BC several Tyrian colonies in Spain were abandoned.[119] At the same time Carthage became more important and eventually independent from Tyre.[120] The reasons were interconnected: a shifting power balance in the central and western Mediterranean Sea due to pressure from Greek colonists, and the loss of Tyre as the administrative centre and seat of the king as a result of Babylonian conquest. Tyre had irretrievably lost its function as the political and economic hub in the Mediterranean trade network.

Summary

In this contribution we presented Tyre's relationship with the Neo-Assyrian and Neo-Babylonian Empires from a Tyrian vantage point, connecting the political and economic situation at home with the developments in the overseas trade network. After a relatively fast recovery following the Late Bronze Age collapse, Tyre had begun to explore the coastal areas of the Mediterranean Sea in search of new products as well as trading partners. In the 9th century, trading colonies were founded on the North African and Spanish shores. The long voyages were made possible by technological innovations in shipbuilding and navigation, and were not triggered by Assyrian pressure. Assyria's domination of the Neo-Hittite states and the Levant began in the middle of the 8th century and entailed severe disruptions of the flourishing eastern Mediterranean mercantile network. In this period Tyre did not profit from trade with the Assyrians. On the contrary, Assyrian appropriations of Syrian and Levantine produce and merchandise curtailed opportunities for Phoenician trade. Furthermore, the destruction of Neo-Hittite and Aramaean kingdoms led to a loss of partners and the decline of, for example, the ivory carving industry. Tyre's reaction was a shift of emphasis by further developing the western Mediterranean part of the network, visible by the increase in number and size of trading posts and colonies there.

Tyre's naval superiority, its location on an island offshore, and its support system that allowed the city to withstand land blockades gave Tyre a special position in comparison with other Phoenician cities vis-à-vis the Assyrian and Babylonian Empires. Tyre was hard to control and had, by virtue of its naval technology, expertise and extensive contacts, much to offer. In the reign of Sargon Assyrian policy regarding Tyre changed. Instead of the previous attempts to force the city into submission, the Assyrians cooperated with Tyre, culminating in Sargon's claim that Cyprus was part of the Assyrian realm. After a brief return to force under Sennacherib, this cooperation continued in the reign of Esarhaddon. Assyria participated in the thriving business by the erection of Kār-Esarhaddon, while the Tyrians formally regained their trading opportunities with the Levantine coastal area dominated by Assyria, as the remains of the treaty show. A major change in the political scene was the growing influence of Egypt that started to challenge Assyrian dominance in the Levant. Tyre and other coastal cities changed loyalties depending on how they assessed the outcome of the confrontation between the two great powers. When Assyria incorporated Egypt into its realm, it also pacified the west. The strong position of Egypt was a major cause for Nebuchadnezzar's policy concerning Tyre and the Levant. His destructions of Ashkelon and of the strongholds of Judah were not only punishments for subversive behaviour but also a strategy to keep Egypt out of Western Asia. In the face of Tyre's naval power, the Babylonians considered it essential to control the city in order to pacify the Levant. The long siege and the following military occupation of the island have to be seen in this light. This, as well as the loss of kingship had severe consequences for Tyre's economic position. In combination with Greek rivalry in trade these events led to a definitive decline of Tyre's role as the centre of the Mediterranean network it had created during the first half of the 1st millennium BC.

Appendix: the debate about the chronology of the siege of Tyre

The traditional reconstruction of the chronology of the siege of Tyre depends on a passage in Flavius Josephus' *De antiquitate* (= *Contra Apionem*) that makes the impression to be corrupted by transmission. In this appendix, we want to discuss the evidence anew and emphasise that the reconstruction by Katzenstein (1973, 325–336) who dates the siege between *c.* 585/4 and 572 BC should not be considered as the final word. We believe that a reconstruction to the effect that the siege began in the 17th year of Nebuchadnezzar, thereby dating the siege to 588/7–575/4, is a textual and historical possibility. However, until we have definite proof from Babylonian texts, the exact chronology remains uncertain.

The context of the passage on Tyre

In an attempt to reconstruct the original text, it is important to be aware of the context of the passages on Tyrian history within Josephus' work. The author's intention is clear: he tries to corroborate the Biblical account that the temple in Jerusalem was destroyed in the 18th year of Nebuchadnezzar and that its rebuilding began in the 2nd year of Cyrus (*Contra Apionem* I, 145). In order to enable his reader to calculate the temporal distance between Nebuchadnezzar's reign and that of Cyrus, Josephus relates Berossos' list of Neo-Babylonian kings (*Contra Apionem* I, 145–153). Thereafter, he wants to present additional proof by citing "Phoenician records" that contained a list of rulers of Tyre, and a date of the siege of Tyre. This independent Tyrian chronology serves Josephus as confirmation for the Babylonian chronology derived from Berossos and thereby for his own statement that the temple lay waste for 50 years.

The pertinent passage from *Contra Apionem* I, 155–160 runs as follows:[121]

> [155]"I shall add the Phoenician records as well – for one must not pass over the abundance of proofs. The calculation of dates goes like this. [156]In the reign of king Ithobalos, Naboukodrosoros besieged Tyre for 13 years. After him Baal reigned for 10 years. [157]Thereafter judges were appointed: Ednibalos, son of Baslechos, was judge for 2 months, Chelbes, son of Abdaeos, for 10 months, Abbalos, the high-priest, for 3 months; Myttynos and Gerastartos, son of Abdelimos, were judges for 6 years, after whom Balatoros was king for 1 year. [158]When he died they sent for Merbalos and summoned him from Babylon, and he reigned for 4 years; when he died they summoned his brother Eiromos, who reigned for 20 years. It was during his reign that Cyrus became ruler of the Persians. [159]So the whole period is 54 years, with 3 months in addition; for it was in the seventh year of the reign of Naboukodrosoros that he began to besiege Tyre, and in the fourteenth year of the reign of Eiromos that Cyrus the Persian seized power.[160] The Chaldean and Tyrian materials are in agreement with our writings on the subject of the sanctuary, and my evidence from these statements for the antiquity of our people is consistent and incontestable. Thus I think that what I have now said is sufficient for any who are not excessively contentious."

The passage contains a calculation error: the sum of the years in the Tyrian chronology is 55 years and 3 months instead of 54 years and 3 months.[122]

Furthermore, two conjectures with relevance to the chronology have been suggested: one that "seventh" was an error for "seventeenth" (Gutschmid 1893, 552–556), and the other that it was Ittô-baʿal's "seventh year" not Nebuchadnezzar's (Niese 1887, 30). Before we discuss these suggestions, we must first look at a more recent alternative reconstruction that does away with the conjectures.

No conjecture

In 2008 Schaudig proposed that it was indeed the 7th year of Nebuchadnezzar (598/97) when the siege began, but that the passage "in the fourteenth year of the reign of Eiromos that Cyrus the Persian seized power" refers not to Cyrus' accession as emperor but to his accession in Persia after his defeat of Astyages. This event most likely took place in 550 BC.[123] The 20th year of Eiromos (Hiram) would then be 544 BC. 54 years prior to this date was the 7th year of Nebuchadnezzar (598 BC). Zawadzki (in press) contains a comprehensive overview of the status questionis, including a detailed critique of this suggestion. Therefore it suffices here to summarize the most important arguments that speak against this reconstruction, which we share with Zawadzki:

1. In the *Hofkalender* which mentions Nebuchadnezzar's 7th year, the king of Tyre is listed as a contributor to the inaugurated South-Palace in Babylon. The positive connotation excludes the interpretation that he was a hostage.
2. The Babylonian Chronicle does not mention the beginning of the siege of Tyre for the 7th year – an unlikely omission in view of the fact that the siege turned out to be a major undertaking.
3. It is questionable whether anybody in Josephus' time was able to date Cyrus' accession in Persia. In order to link the Biblical chronology with that of Tyre, Josephus needed a date that recurs in the Bible – that can only be Cyrus' accession in Babylon when he conquered the Neo-Babylonian Empire and thereby gained rule over the Levant.
4. The "early" Eanna dossier on Tyre that dates to 591 BC would, according to Schaudig's calculation date from the time of the ongoing siege. This is not plausible as these documents were issued at Tyre.[124]

Niese's conjecture (the 7th year of Ittô-baʿal)

The "Standard" text[125] of the pertinent passage is: ἑβδόμῳ μὲν γὰρ᾽ἔτει τῆς Ναβουχοδονοςόρου βασιλείας᾽ἤρξατο πολιορκεῖν Τύρον – "For (it was) in the 7th year of Nebuchadnezzar's kingship that he began to besiege Tyre". In Niese's critical apparatus we find a reference to the Latin version that puts Nebuchadnezzar in the nominative.[126] Furthermore, Niese adds that, based on reason, one must reconstruct the text ("rationi conueniens est ita haec refingere") as follows: "ἑβδόμῳ μὲν γὰρ ἔτει τῆς Ιθωβάλου βασιλείας Ναβουχοδονόσορος ἤρξατο ..."

Siegert (2008) accepted Niese's conjecture on the basis of manuscript M (which Niese had not known) because it has, just like the Latin translation, Nebuchadnezzar in the nominative as direct subject of the verb.[127] However, this does not automatically prove Niese's assumption that Ittô-baʿal's kingship was meant in the original.[128] This assumption finds no clear argument in the text itself because Ittô-baʿal's name is not mentioned immediately before this phrase, but only in *Contra Apionem* I, 156 – three sections away from this anaphora. If Ittô-baʿal's kingship was intended, his name had to be mentioned again.

Also the logic of the text flow speaks against Niese's assumption that Ittô-baʿal's 7th year is meant. As stated above, the Tyrian list of kings and judges serves Josephus to establish a second chronology which is independent from the Bible and from the Babylonian king list.[129] The only way to achieve this is to give two anchor dates that link the Biblical and Babylonian data with the data derived from his Tyrian sources. The undisputed lower anchor is Cyrus' accession.[130] The upper anchor should therefore be a date in Nebuchadnezzar's reign that can be linked with the Tyrian king list, that is, the beginning of the siege of Tyre.

If we assume that Josephus gave his reader only one anchor date, namely the accession of Cyrus, the reader needs to use the Babylonian king list to find out which year of the reign of Nebuchadnezzar corresponds to the 7th year of Ittô-baʿal. In this case, Josephus would have failed to establish an independent chronology that corroborates the Biblical and the Babylonian chronology presented before: the whole passage would become senseless if seen from the perspective of Josephus' aim.

Gutschmid's conjecture (the 17th year of Nebuchadnezzar)

Gutschmid (1893, 552f.) proposed to emend the passage to "seventeenth" and based his reasoning on the fact that manuscripts L, E and S write επὶ instead of ἔτει.[131] The way how Gutschmid emended the text: "ἑβδόμῳ μὲν γὰρ επὶ ί N. β." is certainly not acceptable from a philological point of view, and consequently did not find much acceptance by editors and commenters of *Contra Apionem*. Nevertheless, we believe that "seventh" as an error from an original "seventeenth" is possible. Early manuscripts frequently vary in the writing of numbers between the word for the number and the numeral. A copyist may have written 17th as numeral ιζ′. Subsequently the jota may have gotten lost (ζ′), and in a next step a copyist wrote ἑβδόμῳ "seventh" in this passage. Naturally, this remains a conjecture, as all manuscripts, including the Latin version, have "seventh" here.

The context speaks in favour of this emendation: If we subtract the 55 years (and three months, the sum of all Tyrian reigns + 13 years of the siege) from year 533/2 BC (the 20th year of Hiram) we arrive at 588/7 BC, which is the 17th year of Nebuchadnezzar.[132]

We emphasise that although this supports the emendation of "7" to "17" in the text, it is not automatically proof of historical reality.

Katzenstein's historical reconstruction of the chronology of the siege of Tyre

Katzenstein (1973, 328) followed Niese's assumption and translated "it was in the seventh year of his (Ethbaal's) reign that Nabuchodonosor began the siege of Tyre". However, he dates the beginning of the siege in Nebuchadnezzar's 20th year, that is 585/4 BC. He considers all dates approximate, but gives slightly contradictory statements concerning the end of the siege. On page 326 he lets the siege end in 573/2, the 32nd year of Nebuchadnezzar, while on page 328 he writes that the siege "came to an end ca. 572 B.C.E (=Nebuchadnezzar's 33rd year)". Since the "lower anchor", Cyrus' accession year (538/7 BC according to him), remains the same, Katzenstein thereby shrinks the length of the whole period between the beginning of the siege (585/4 BC according to him) and the 14th year of Hiram (538/7 BC according to him) to 47 years instead of the 49 years and 3 months attributed to it in Josephus' text. How does he come to this conclusion? Where are the remaining 3 years that have "disappeared" in comparison to the timeframe in Josephus' text? The clue lies in Katzenstein's implicit refusal to accept the total time span that Josephus gives as correct. According to the table of the approximate absolute dates (Katzenstein 1973, 327f.), Baʿal II reigned from *c.* 573/72 to *c.* 564 BC. This is 8–9 years, instead of the 10 years that Josephus' Tyrian king list reserved for him. The same table squeezes the 15 months of the reigns of the judges Ednibalos (2 months), Chelbes (10 months) and Abbalos (3 months) in the time between 564 (which is, according to Katzenstein, also the last year of Baʿal II) and 563 BC.[133] Furthermore, he considers 538 instead of 539 BC as the year when "Cyrus, the Persian, seized power".

Naturally, it is difficult to attribute accurate dates to reigns that lasted shorter than one year. Josephus only relates the duration of each rule. Josephus' text is an uneasy source – his calculation error (54 instead of 55 years) and the necessary emendation for the year in which the siege began, make it hard to feel certain.

Historical arguments

We shall finally have a look at the historical arguments. We have mentioned the Nippur Archive text Ni 361 which dates to 31 Nebuchadnezzar (574/3 BC) and was drafted at Tyre. Because its date is at some distance from the chronologically next text from 35 Nebuchadnezzar, it would be necessary to collate the date of this text, to make sure that it is indeed 31 and not 41 Nebuchadnezzar. If the date is correct, the siege must have ended by 574/3 at the latest, and consequently must have begun in either the 17th or 18th year of Nebuchadnezzar.

Zawadzki (2008 and in press) connects two Sippar texts that date to 31 Nebuchadnezzar and mention a military camp (*madāktu*) with the siege of Tyre. Can these documents serve as certain counter-arguments against Nebuchadnezzar's 30th year as the year in which the siege ended? First of all, it is not unthinkable that the military camp would remain in place until structures for a more permanent Babylonian garrison at Tyre are established. Furthermore, both documents (BM 63820 and 74919) do not explicitly mention Tyre. Therefore it remains uncertain which camp is meant. The same is true for the undated letter YOS 21, 133 that mentions a military camp (*madāktu*).[134] These texts are therefore inconclusive.

We also have to consider the dates of Ezekiel's prophecies, although they naturally do not have the same argumentative power as dates from Babylonian texts. According to Ez. 24, 1–2 the revelation that Nebuchadnezzar had just started to lay siege to Jerusalem occurred on 10.X.9 Exile (January 588).[135] This may be a post-factum date, made to correspond the date given in 2 Kings 25, 1. In the following year, on 10.X.10 Exile, Ezekiel predicted that also Egypt would be devastated – most likely a reaction on the information (which we know from Jer. 37) that Apries' troops came to help the besieged Jerusalem but then had to retreat. On 1.I.11 Exile, which is the beginning of Nebuchadnezzar's 18th year (spring 587 BC) Ezekiel "prophesied" the siege and destruction of Tyre (Ez. 26). If the siege of Tyre had begun in 588/7 BC (17 Nebuchadnezzar), the "prophecy" would date very shortly after the beginning of the siege. Perhaps the news that also Tyre would be/was besieged, had just reached Ezekiel's circles of information, unless the prophecy's date was added or changed post-factum by someone who had exact information.

Finally, on 1.I.27 Exile which is the spring of 571 BC (34 Nbk), Ezekiel (Ez. 29, 17–Ez. 30) refers to the outcome of the siege of Tyre in connection with his prophecy that Nebuchadnezzar would conquer Egypt. This is in any case sometime after the end of the siege (either 4 years, if the siege ended in 575/4 (30 Nbk), or 2 years according to Katzenstein's dates of 573 or 572 as the end of the siege). The prophecy mentions Tyre in passing but is directed against Egypt. It may reflect the preparations for a major attack.[136] The dates in Ezekiel do not contradict a reconstruction that the siege started in the 17th, or latest in the 18th year, but they alone can naturally not be taken as proof of historical reality.

Conclusion of the chronology debate

The chronology of the siege of Tyre is to a large extent based on a passage in Josephus' *Contra Apionem* which poses substantial philological and historical problems. The reconstruction of the chronology by Katzenstein, who dates the siege from *c.* 585/4 to 573/2 BC stands on feet of clay. An alternative date of 588/7–575/4 is possible on the basis of an emendation of year "7" to year "17" in Josephus' text. On the basis of Josephus' text alone (because of the calculation error), we cannot exclude that the siege began slightly (one year) later. Furthermore, we do not know whether the information that Josephus gives is correct at all and how we must interpret and solve the other obvious difficulties that this text presents.

The siege of Tyre should most likely be interpreted in the light of a great insurrection of Levantine states shortly after Apries' accession in Egypt which makes 589 BC a likely terminus post quem for the beginning of the siege. On the basis of the information from Babylonian sources that attest to Babylonian military presence at Tyre, the siege of Tyre must have ended in any case before the 35th year. If the date 31 Nebuchadnezzar of the Nippur text Ni 361 is correct, the *terminus ante quem* for the end of the siege 574/3 BC, which means that the (13-year) siege began in the 17th or 18th year of Nebuchadnezzar's reign.

If we add Ezekiel's dated prophecies to the overall picture, the likelihood of the latter reconstruction rises further.

From a text-critical point of view, the emendation to 17th in *Contra Apionem* 1, 159 is possible, and from a historical point of view, 588/7 BC is possible as well. We therefore believe that a chronology that dates the siege to 588/7–575/4 deserves consideration, but until Babylonian dates help us to prove or disprove it, we must keep in mind that all dates derived from Josephus are uncertain.

Acknowledgements

We wish to express our gratitude to several people who have helped to improve this article: Eleftheria Pappa for helpful comments concerning radiocarbon dating of archaeological evidence from Phoenician colonies; Gerard Boter and Rutger Allan who answered questions on Greek syntax and manuscripts; Jaap-Jan Flinterman who first suggested that the error 7 for 17 in Josephus' *Contra Apionem* may be based on the writing in numerals, Michael Jursa for general comments on the manuscript, and Stefan Zawadzki who placed a draft of his new article (Zawadzki in press) at our disposal before publication.

Notes

1. For instance Fales 2008; Lipiński 2006, 189. Radner 2004, 157 does not mention the term *pax Assyriaca* but speaks of a symbiosis between Assyria and independent trading cities. Sommer (2009, 101) mentions a symbiotic balance between Assyria and Phoenicia. See also Kestemont 1983, 77f.
2. For instance Bondi 1988, 41f.; Frankenstein 1979, 273. Aubet 2001, 70 mentions several scholars who have supported this theory.
3. For the ancient configuration of Tyre before and after the construction of the causeway by Alexander the Great, see Marriner *et al.* 2008.
4. Submarine freshwater springs further north were known in antiquity. According to Strabo (*Geography* 16.2.13) they were used to acquire drinkable water in times of war (described for the island of Arwad). However, it is questionable how well the technique of covering the submarine well with a vessel connected to a leather pipe really worked. Without modern technical equipment, present day attempts to bring undiluted freshwater to the surface have failed.
5. The Amarna archive contains ten letters (EA 146–EA 155, see Moran 1992) from Abī-Milki, king of Tyre, to the pharaoh that all concern the same problem, namely that the Sidonian king Zimredda had conquered Usu. In eight letters Abī-Milki requested help from Egypt to reconquer Usu because Tyre suffered from a severe shortage of water and firewood.
6. See, for instance, EA 85 and EA 125.

7. EA 77.
8. The transport of both goods required a lot of ships and manpower that, as a consequence, were not available for the transport of merchandise. See also Morley 1996, 59–62 on Von Thünen's isolated state. This is why the Tyrian king in his letters did not ask the pharaoh for wood or water like the king of Byblos asked for grain; he asked for support to reconquer Usu instead.
9. Glass from Tyre was once a desired good in Egypt (see, for instance, EA 148). For a history of glassmaking, see Oppenheim 1973 and Engle 1980.
10. Production of purple dye requires the heating of the hypobranchial gland of *Murex* snails over a long period. According to Pliny the Elder (*Naturalis Historia* IX.62), the mass was heated at a moderate temperature for at least nine days.
11. According to Bikai 1978, 54, table 13A, see p. 68 for the dates of the strata, 24% of the excavated pottery from the period between 1600 and 1370 BC and 10% in the following 170 years appeared to be Cypriot. This implies extensive trade with the copper island throughout the entire Late Bronze Age.
12. Markoe 2000, 19.
13. For rules of conduct in the international circulation of goods and people, see Liverani 2001, 57–65. A letter from Ugarit from around 1190 BC illustrates an incident involving maritime trade: an official had taken the cargo of a shipwrecked Ugaritic vessel in the vicinity of Tyre. The king of Tyre ordered the cargo to be returned to the sailors (RS 18.031, Pardee 2003, 448). It was also a royal task to defend the interests of the merchants on an international level: in another letter (Arnaud 1982), the Tyrian king urged the king of Ugarit to collect the money owed to a merchant by an inhabitant of Ugarit who had ordered two big doors but had taken them without payment.
14. Bikai 1978, 54 (table 13.A), 56, 73–74.
15. Justin, *Epitoma Historiarum Philippicarum* XVIII, 3; see also Katzenstein 1973, 59; Markoe 2000, 25. Justin dates the establishment of Tyre one year before the fall of Troy, which was dated by Eratosthenes to the year 1183 BC. The date for the foundation of Tyre is more or less supported by Flavius Josephus (*Antiquitates Judaicae* VIII, 62) from whose data one can calculate a foundation of Tyre around 1200 BC: he mentions the number of years from the foundation of Tyre to the start of the building of the Judean temple in Jerusalem in Hiram I's 11th year (240), while Josephus, *Contra Apionem* I, 18 informs us about the number of years from the beginning of Hiram's reign to the foundation of Carthage. Unfortunately this last number is ambiguous: Josephus' counting mistake, combined with the uncertain founding date of Carthage leads to different outcomes. Dochhorn (2001, 81 and 86) gives a good overview of the text editions and the calculations, as well as the interpretation of these dates by four modern scholars. Calculating the earliest possible solution, taking 814 BC as the founding year for Carthage plus 136 years between this date and the beginning of the reign of Hiram I, leads to 950 BC as the accession year of Hiram (Lipiński 1970, 64 and 2006, 174). If we add this date to the number of years before Hiram became king (240–10), we get 1180 BC as date for the (re)foundation of Tyre. Other combinations lead to earlier dates up to 1210 BC. Although Josephus lived slightly before Justin, it is not likely that Justin depended on him as a source for his dates because Josephus' information refers to different events.
16. Pritchard 1969, 25–29 contains the narrative of Wenamun; for the date see Katzenstein 1973, 70.
17. Josephus, *Antiquitates Judaicae* VIII, 144–147. In addition to the Bible (see, for instance, II Samuel 5:11 and I Kings 5:15), there is another, most likely independent source that confirmed the existence of Hiram. This is Menander of Ephesus whose list of Tyrian kings was cited by Josephus (*Contra Apionem* I.18). The existence of two kings on this list is possibly affirmed by other sources: the first is the Nora stone, found on Sardinia in 1773. Its Phoenician inscription contains the name of a king Pummay, which is very likely the Greek name Pygmalion. For an elaborate discussion on this name, see Dochhorn 2005, 95–99. On palaeographical grounds this inscription has been dated to the 9th century BC, preferably to its second half (Cross

1972b) or perhaps even to the early 8th century (Lipiński 2004, 236). The date is in line with what the Tyrian king list says about Pygmalion: he came to power around 831 BC or 820 BC (Dochhorn 2001, 86; Lipiński 2006, 174) and ruled for 47 years. According to Josephus, quoting Menander (*Contra Apionem* I.18), his sister Elissa founded Carthage (Cross, 1972b). The second source are the annals of Shalmaneser III, where a certain "^{m}*Ba-a'-li-ma-an-zer*, the Tyrian" paid tribute to the Assyrian king in 841 BC (Barnes 1991, 35). The name may correspond to a king Badezorus on the king list. Other variants of the name have also survived (see Barnes 1991, 38–39 (table 1), Lipiński 1970, 60–62; nuanced by Dochhorn 2005). There is some uncertainty about the period and length of his kingship. Lipiński 2006, 170–174 is convinced that both names concern the same king.

18. The conventional chronology between the 11th and late 8th centuries for the Ancient Near East, Greece and Iberia has been deduced from pottery sequences which suffer from a lack of absolute dates. Recent radiocarbon dating has shed new light on absolute dates for Phoenician presence in Iberia and Carthage. For the discussion on this topic see, for instance, Pappa 2012; Nijboer & Van der Plicht 2006 and Torres Ortiz 2008. In this article the radiocarbon dates are used for the founding of colonies in southern Spain and Carthage. Unfortunately, no new absolute dates are available yet for archaeological evidence from other places. Due to this incertitude, this article does not use conventional dates that have been deducted from the pottery sequence for direct evidence on the timeline of events concerning specific Tyrian colonies.
19. Ez. 27 and 28.
20. Archaeology cannot distinguish between different Phoenician cities. When texts cannot help to specify, the designation "Phoenician" is used.
21. Aubet 2001, 49–50.
22. Contacts with Israel are supported by I Kings 16: 31–33, as well as by excavations in Samaria where Phoenician pottery and ivories have been found (see Liverani 2005, 121). Good relationships with Damascus may be inferred from the fact that the crown prince of Damascus erected a stele dedicated to Melqart, the city-god of Tyre, in the vicinity of Aleppo, perhaps in memory of a victory of Aram-Damascus over Assyria (Cross 1972a, 42). It is possible that Tyre had supported its neighbouring state financially in this war.
23. Stern (1990, 29–30) mentions Achzib, Akko, Tell Keisan, Tell Abu Hawam, Cabul and Dor. With the exception of Dor, all excavated cities in the coastal area belonged to the strip of mainland that was in Tyrian hands at least from the 9th century onwards, therefore it is possible that this had already been the case in the 10th or even late 11th century.
24. Stern 1990. Gilboa *et al.* 2008, 133–134 incline to a later date of destruction, the late 11th or early 10th century. Although no explicit offensive violence of Tyre against other cities or states is known, by analogy with Josephus' information about Hiram I suppressing a rebellion in a city overseas, Tyrian participation or even initiative cannot be ruled out.
25. Stern 1990, 32.
26. Katzenstein 1973, 130.
27. Josephus, *Antiquitates Judaicae* VIII, 317, IX, 138: "King of the Tyrians and Sidonians", VIII, 324: "king of the Tyrians"; I Kings 16:31: "King of the Sidonians". For the Tyrian king list, see Josephus, *Contra Apionem* I.18.
28. Aubet 2001, 54 mentions a 10th-century Phoenician inscription from Knossos. For an overview of all Phoenician imports on Crete, see Hoffman 1997. Bikai 1978, 75 states that Greek pottery in Tyre shows expansion of the trading sphere into Greece.
29. Dates have been based on the radiocarbon method. These contacts only concerned trading activities; there was no Phoenician settlement; see Torres Ortiz 2008. For problems regarding the dating of the earliest settlement in Iberia, see Pappa 2012.
30. See footnote 17 above.
31. This suggestion has not been generally accepted. Aubet 2001, 51–52 proposes that Kition was founded around 820 BC; Smith 2008, 264 sees a change from trade to Phoenician administrative

control in the second half of the 8th century; Lipiński 2004, 50 states that Kition's relation with the Phoenician city states remains unclear through the 9th–6th centuries. Josephus, *Antiquitates Judaicae* VIII, 146 reports that Hiram I suppressed a revolt overseas, but it is far from certain that this was Kition (Bikai 1978, 74). Lipiński's suggestion (2004, 42 with footnote 23) that it may have been Akko fits best into the overall framework of the development of the Tyrian trading network.

32. For finds of Cypriot pottery in Tyre, see Bikai 1978, 54, table 13.A. During the Iron Age, the percentage of Cypriot pottery declined to 4% or less. Although Cypriot pottery has been found in all strata, an interruption in trade in the period of stratum 14 (1200–1070/1050 BC) is a possibility. For Phoenician pottery from the 11th century near Amathos and Paleopaphos (Cyprus), see Aubet 2008, 250 and Lipiński 2004, 47–49. For a Phoenician tomb dated to the early 9th century, see Lipiński 2004, 42–43. He sees this burial as proof of Phoenician settlement, contra Smith 2008, 265.
33. For an interpretation of the suppression of this revolt, mentioned by Josephus (*Antiquitates Judaicae* IX, 284), see p. 194.
34. For the temple, see Karageorghis 1976, 97–100. Phoenician sanctuaries were often linked to commercial activities (see Pappa 2012, 23), therefore this temple does not imply political dominance.
35. For 814 BC, see Timaeus in Dionysius of Halicarnassus *Roman Antiquities* I, 74; for 825 BC, see Justin, *Epitoma Historiarum Philippicarum* XVIII, 6.
36. Aubet 2008, 247. Dates have been based on the radiocarbon method.
37. Alhough for some time Huelva was seen as the ancient city named Tartessos, this is not proven. It is not even known whether Tartessos was a city, a region or a polity. What is certain, however, is that it was situated in southern Spain in the region near Cadiz and Huelva.
38. Pappa 2012, 23; Torres Ortiz 2008, 140–142. Dates have been based on the radiocarbon method.
39. Grayson 1991, 37, text A.0.87.3, lines 16–25, where only Byblos, Sidon and Arwad are mentioned.
40. Grayson 1991, 219, text A.0.101.1, line 86.
41. Katzenstein (1973, 133) states that Sidon may already have been under Tyrian influence. The inauguration of the palace at Kalhu was celebrated around 863 BC, hence most likely in the reign of Ittô-baʿal I of Tyre, who came to power in 878 or 867 BC (Josephus, *Contra Apionem* I, 18; Lipiński 1970, 64; Dochhorn 2001, 86).
42. In 858, 856, 841 and 838 BC; see Grayson 1996, 11, 17, 19, text A.0.102.2 (Kurkh stele) col. ii lines 7 and 39; 54, text A.0.102.8 lines 25''–27''; 79 text A.0.102.16 lines 161'–162'.
43. Grayson 1996, 213, text A.0.104.8 line 12.
44. Aubet 2008, 252; Radner 2004, 157. Aubet 2001, 50 points out to Phoenician presence in Carchemish still in the reign of Tiglath-pileser III.
45. Instead of Phoenician trade, Tyrian trade is mentioned here. Tyre is said to have founded many colonies, of which Carthage and Gadir were the most famous. Both cities had a temple dedicated to Melqart. See also footnote 47 for the Tyrian "ships of Tarshish" and their relation with southern Spain. Katzenstein (1973, 115) states that Tyre was the only Phoenician city with colonies. Although there is a silence on other Phoenician mother cities, one cannot exclude that cities like Arwad, Byblos or Ashkelon had also founded colonies or at least established footholds overseas. The question why there are many Phoenician colonies in southern Spain at very short distances from each other has not been answered yet.
46. Bateman 2012, 25–26; Diffie & Winius 1977, 312–316.
47. See the literature cited in Marriner *et al.* 2008, 1291. The "ships of Tarshish" are mentioned in the Bible. They are specifically linked to Tyre. The name Tarshish can refer to Tarsus in Cilicia near the gulf of Alexandretta or to Tartessos in southern Spain. The Bible suggests the second option, because the Tarshish fleet needed three years to return (I Kings 10:22; II Chronicles 9:21). The biblical narratives about Hiram and Solomon which refer to Tarshsish date almost certainly from a later period: contemporaneous circumstances were transposed to the 10th century. See also Jamieson-Drake (1991), who concludes on the basis of archaeological

information that Judah was a very small kingdom or even chiefdom in the 10th century. In Jonah 1:3 God sends the prophet to Nineveh, but instead Jonah embarks for Tarshish. Jonah wanted to flee from God as far away as possible, thus certainly Spain is meant, not Cilicia (see also footnote 87 for Cilicia subdued by Assyrians). Isaiah 23: 10 refers to Tarshish as a daughter (=colony) of Tyre. This new type of cargo vessel made voyages across the whole length of the Mediterranean Sea possible. Aubet (2001, 174–175) describes these merchant ships, but does not call them ships of Tarshish, because she explains the name Tarshish differently. For Tarshish in a text of Esarhaddon see footnote 87. For an elaborate discussion on Tarshish see Lipiński 2004, 225–265 and Aubet 2001, 204–206.

48. Aubet 2001, 281–284.
49. Justin, *Epitoma Historiarum Philippicarum* XVIII, 4–6 for Carthage; Strabo, *Geography* 3.5.5 for Gadir.
50. Redford 1992, 334–335 states that at the beginning of the 8th century a burst of Phoenician art with Egyptian influences can be observed. Due to the recent discussions on absolute dating this development probably must be placed in the 9th century.
51. See Luukko 2012, 28–29 for the text of the letter and Tadmor & Yamada 2011, XVII for Qurdi-Aššur-lāmur as governor of Simirrra.
52. Yamada 2008, 302 states that the letter must be dated between 734 and 732 BC, because by then Tyre was subjugated. We, however, agree with Tammuz 2011, 191 who points out that it must have been earlier, between 738 and 734 BC because of the restriction on trade with Philistine cities and Egypt which obviously were Tiglath-pileser's enemies at the time of the letter, whilst from 734 BC on the Philistine cities were his vassals. The fact that the governor had just installed tax collectors makes it even probable that the letter dates from 737 or 736 BC, not long after the installation of Qurdi-Aššur-lāmur as governor in 738 BC.
53. This can be inferred from an inscription of Sargon II: *Den versiegelten Hafen des Landes Muṣur öffnete ich, vermengte die Einwohner von Assyrien und Ägypten miteinander und ließ sie Handel treiben* (Fuchs 1994, 314).
54. Tadmor & Yamada 2011, 122 (47 rev. lines 3'–6'); 127 (48 lines 14–19); Tadmor 1966, 89–90; Elat 1978, 26. This article was written in 2013. Now, in 2016, an article suggesting a different policy of Tiglath-pileser II, Sargon and Sennacherib in the southern Levant is in preparation.
55. Radner 1999, 103ff collected important evidence that Assyrian and foreign merchants brought merchandise directly to Assyria. From 717 BC on, private financers of trade (*bēl harrāni*) are attested in Assyria (Radner 1999, 109f).
56. The functioning of the trading network has been described in the poem used by Ezekiel (Ez. 27: 12–25). The same structure (i.e. locals carry out the inland trade, while Tyrian merchants are at the ports) is reflected in I Kings 5: 23: Tyre arranges the transport of beams over sea, while Solomon transports them over land. Aubet 2001, 281 states that indigenous Iberian people brought their metals to the coast. Herodotus IV, 196 gives a description of the manner how Carthagenians traded with indigenous people along the coast of modern day Morocco: the merchandise is not transported beyond the beach, but tidily arranged on the sand.
57. Some, though not much, quantitative information on tribute is available but without knowing the aggregate size of the economy it does not help much.
58. Gitin & Golani 2001, 40–41.
59. Ez. 27: 12–24 describes Tyre's merchandise. Most of these goods were not produced in Tyre itself.
60. Van Loon 1974.
61. Barnett 1982, 48 and 57.
62. Tadmor & Yamada 2011, 38–39 (11 line 1–12 line 2').
63. Tadmor & Yamada 2011, 70 and 77 (27 line 3 and 32 line 2). At this time Egypt still was a divided state, the Kushite pharaohs did not control the Nile Delta yet. As a result, Egypt did not play a role in the Levantine revolt. See also Redford 1992, 343–345.
64. Katzenstein 1973, 218–219. For the payment, see Tadmor & Yamada 2011, 123 (47 rev. line16'): 150 talents of gold are mentioned before a lacuna. In Tadmor & Yamada 2011, 133 (49 rev. line 26) 50 talents of gold and 2000 talents of silver are mentioned.

65. Josephus, *Antiquitates Judaicae* IX, 287; he writes that only the drinking water was made inaccessible to the Tyrians for 5 years.
66. Katzenstein 1973, 244.
67. See footnote 53. For the first time, the Assyrians also faced problems with Egypt. A king from the Nile Delta sent his official to the aid of Gaza, but then he retreated to Egypt. There is discussion about the identity of this king. For a king from Sais, see Redford 1992, 346–347, for a king from Tanis, see Ahlström 1993, 674.
68. Aubet 2001, 226 states that the start of the period of growth for Carthage was around 730 BC. For mining on an industrial level, see Aubet 2001, 283. On p. 352, she further states that around 720 a period of remarkable growth of the western colonies started. This conclusion is debated now for two reasons, the first one being the new dates generated through radiocarbon dating, which has influenced the period from the 11th century to the end of the 8th century (Pappa 2012, 4–5). In addition to that, it is difficult to link such a change to a decade or a few years. Nevertheless, her conclusion has been supported by the first appearance of Phoenician silver bowls and bronze jugs on Cyprus and in the west in large quantities at the end of the 8th century (Falsone 1988, 239). The Assyrian economic policy in the Levant and the Neo-Hittite states may have triggered accelerated growth of the western network from *c.* 730 BC on.
69. Elat 1978, 27.
70. Radner 2010, 429–434, 440; Na'aman 2001, 358.
71. Na'aman 2001, 359–360.
72. Josephus, *Antiquitates Judaicae* IX, 284: "and Eloulai, who was surnamed Puas, reigned as king for 36 years. When the Kitieis revolted, he sailed there and made them subject again." Na'aman 2001, 360 believes that Šilṭa and Lulî are not the same king, unlike Lipiński 2004, 53f. who translated the name Lulî (*Halūlay) as "the splendid one" and Šilṭa as "potentate". In Greek Lulî is called Eloulaios. It is possible that one or both names were nicknames.
73. Already in 715 BC Lulî had asked Sargon for assistance against Ionian pirates; see Fuchs 1994, 319–320: Khorsabad Annals lines 117–119; Radner 2010, 438. Both requests and the fact that they were granted suggest an Assyrian interest in Tyre's trade, either because of tribute or because of Assyrian participation (investment) in this trade, for which unfortunately no further evidence exists.
74. Since Tyre did not strive for territorial expansion, it is unlikely that the seven kings were vassals of Tyre. It is possible that a situation comparable to that in southern Spain had been created, in the sense that these small Cypriot kingdoms were bound by contract to mine and process copper and sell it exclusively to Tyrian traders. A crisis would arise when they did not stand by the agreements. This would also explain that the kings had gone to Babylon themselves, after they had come to an agreement with Lulî. However, see also Radner 2010, 439 who suggests that this visit was followed by a direct and more permanent link between the kings of Cyprus and the Assyrian king.
75. Lipiński 2004, 55. Examples of archaeological finds: in Kition and its sphere of political control, from the late 8th century on, the Phoenician alphabet came into use for inscriptions; 7th-century Phoenician inscriptions further appeared in Salamis, Kourion, and Chytroi (Smith 2008, 270, 275, 278); in the 8th and 7th centuries Kourion hosted Phoenician craftsmen, while in inland Golgoi a 7th-century Phoenician amphora indicates Phoenician contacts, as well as do archaeological finds of Phoenician inscriptions in royal tombs from this period in Chytroi (Lipiński 2004, 55, 59, 65).
76. Smith 2008, 276–277. Of course there can also be other reasons for the absence of these cities.
77. Grayson & Novotny 2012, 63–64 (4 lines 32–35); the territory included Sidon, where Sennacherib installed a new king.
78. There are several sources which describe the end of this campaign of Sennacherib. His annals (Grayson & Novotny 2012, 65–66 (4 lines 55–58)) reveal his sudden retreat to Assyria without having conquered Jerusalem. II Kings 19, 35–36 describes the surprising event in terms of an angel who killed the Assyrian soldiers at night. Herodotus II, 141 relates a story in which field-mice gnawed away Assyrian leather gear which forced Sennacherib to give up the plan

to invade Egypt. What really happened remains unknown, perhaps a pestilence occurred, or a political emergency related to Assyria's problems with the Cimmerians, Scythians and Chaldeans.

79. The reign of Manasseh (first half of the 7th century) was a peaceful time in Judah (Ahlström 1993, 730). Near Jerusalem a royal "summer palace" was built, containing Phoenician architectural features and ornamentation (Lipiński 2004, 512). After its submission to Sargon and Sennacherib, Ekron developed into the largest ancient olive oil production centre yet uncovered, and had its temple complex built in the first quarter of the 7th century. Phoenician contacts with the Philistine city in this time are visible in inscriptions and silver jewellery (Gitin & Golani 2001, 40–43).
80. Redford 1992, 354–355.
81. Most Assyrian kings had done the same: the letter of Qurdi-Aššur-lāmur (Luukko 2012, 28–29) shows that arrangements had been made between Tiglat-pileser III and Tyre; Sargon II undoubtedly had ended the siege by making arrangements with the Tyrians. The king who did not (successfully) negotiate with Tyre was Shalmaneser V, and he had to pay for it with a fruitless siege.
82. Parpola & Watanabe 1988, 24–27.
83. In practice this meant that Esarhaddon granted Tyre undisturbed trade in the Levant. Assyria was certainly still engaging in this trade.
84. Leichty 2011, 17 (1 iii lines 15–17): Esarhaddon gave the cities Ma'rubbu and Sarepta to Tyre. The remaining parts of the treaty do not speak of cities that Esarhaddon gave to Baʿal of Tyre but the name of the Sidonian god Eshmun, right after Melqart, indicates that Tyre regained control over at least part of Sidonian land. Therefore the contract must have been concluded after the destruction of Sidon. See also Katzenstein 1973, 265–266.
85. As Katzenstein 1973, 270–271 convincingly argues.
86. Katzenstein 1973 is erratic on this issue. On pp. 267–268 he mentions a feeling which he shares with Olmstead and Weidner that the treaty must originate from *c.* 676 BC. On p. 271, however, he states that if the person whose letters cannot be opened without the presence of the *qēpu* is the pharaoh, then the date of the treaty must be after 674 or shortly after 671 BC. The first of these two dates, however, is not likely, because that was the moment when Tyre started its revolt that ended in 671 BC. On p. 277 he favoures 671 BC with the argument that the treaty curtailed Tyrian trade, and would therefore fit to Tyre's submission. But the curtailing of Tyrian trade is an interpretation, not a fact, and, moreover, the pharaoh had fled to the south when Esarhaddon conquered Memphis (Redford 1992, 360–361). It is clear that Katzenstein has struggled with the date as he himself suggests on p. 277.
87. Leichty 2011, 135 (60, lines 7'– 11'). The name KUR*tar-si-si* was translated as Tarsus, but we have reason to believe that Tarshish (Tartessos, see footnote 47) is meant here. In the annals of Sennacherib Tarsus is written as URU.*tar-zi* and URU.*ta-ar-zu* (Grayson, Novotny 2012, 135–136: 17 I lines 66 and 75). Furthermore, a description of the region "from Cyprus and Ionia to Tarsus" is not logical, neither in a geographical, nor in a political sense. Sennacherib had subdued a revolt in Cilicia and conquered Tarsus in 696 BC. Thereafter he rebuilt the city (Dalley 1999, 73). It can be assumed that in the time of Esarhaddon the city had still been in Assyrian hands. Therefore, a reason to mention this city in relation to Tyre does not come up easily. In a geographical description one would expect "from Cyprus and Tarsus to Ionia", although it is possible that the region around Tarsus itself was called Ionia by the Assyrians (Aubet 2001, 123). The translation "from Cyprus and Ionia to Tartessos" makes sense in both ways: it is Tyre's Mediterranean trade network and it describes the northern sea route from the Levant to Spain.
88. Leichty 2011, 16 (1 ii line 80), where the kings build Kār-Esarhaddon; Leichty 2011, 23 (1 v lines 54–73a), where the 22 kings deliver materials for building activities in Nineveh; Leichty 2011, 193 (103 line 34) is almost unreadable and translated as "32 kings", but Katzenstein 1973, 280 uses the translation "22 kings". For Assurbanipal, see Streck 1916, 9: Rassam Cylinder

i lines 68–74. In addition to Tyre and ten kings from Cyprus, the following kingdoms are mentioned: the Phoenican cities of Byblos, Arwad and Samsimuruna, the Philistine cities of Gaza, Ashkelon, Ashdod and Ekron, and the more inland kingdoms of Judah, Edom, Moab and Ammon. The treaty mentions the entire district of the Philistines, all the cities within Assyrian territory on the seacoast and Byblos, the Lebanon, all the cities in the mountains – an area that includes the twelve Levantine kingdoms in the group of 22.

89. Although several of the ten Cypriot kings among the 22 kings have Greek names, Lipiński 2004, 62 states that the spelling of their names reveals a Phoenician intermediate agent. It is illustrative of the cooperation, although certainly no evidence.
90. Pritchard 1969, 294: "During my march (to Egypt) 22 kings from the seashore, the islands and the mainlands, servants who belong to me, brought heavy gifts to me and kissed my feet. I made these kings accompany my army over the land – as well as (over) the sea-route with their armed forces and their ships (respectively)". See also Streck 1916, 9 Rassam Cylinder i lines 68–74.
91. Streck 1916, 17–19: Rassam Cylinder ii lines 49–62.
92. Katzenstein 1973, 293–294.
93. Vanderhooft 2003, 235–242.
94. Katzenstein 1973, 299f.
95. In 605 BC, see Grayson 2000, 99. According to Josephus (*Antiquitates Judaicae* X, 220; *Contra Apionem* I, 136) Nebuchadnezzar took not only Egyptians, but also Judeans, Phoenicians and Syrians captive. Perhaps some of them were the Phoenicians mentioned on ration lists from the palace at Babylon, see Katzenstein 1973, 307.
96. Grayson 2000, 100, lines 15–17 (Chronicle 5). The most comprehensive overview of Neo-Babylonian history is Von Voigtlander 1963. See also Vanderhooft 1999, 69–89; da Riva 2008, 2–18.
97. As the list is not in topographical order, it may reflect a sequence of power and influence. Tyre as the most important Phoenician city was mentioned first. Na'aman 2000, 41 interpreted the broken entry ^{kur}*mir*-[x-x] as Samsimurūna.
98. This is indicated by the visit of envoys from Edom, Moab, Ammon, Tyre and Sidon to Jerusalem according to Jer. 27: 3. Hopes that Nebuchadnezzar's rule would end soon were expressed by the prophet Hananja (Jer. 28). In the same year the Judean king Zedekiah may have been summoned to Babylon (Jer. 51: 59).
99. Kleber 2008, 141–154. N. Czechowicz (cited in Kleber 2008) had already proposed in 2002 that Phoenician Tyre, not a Babylonian village was meant. Zawadzki 2003 thought likewise that some of the texts must refer to Tyre.
100. See Jursa 2007, 67f. The "Hofkalender" (edited in Unger 1931, 282–294, a new edition is being prepared by R. da Riva for Zeitschrift für Assyriologie. Addendum: In the meanwhile this article has been published: R. da Riva, "Nebuchadnezzar II's Prism (EŞ 7834): A New Edition", Zeitschrift für Assyriologie 103 (2013), 196–229.) is a building inscription that mentions palace officials, governors of cities and tribal areas in the Babylonian core, and rulers of vassal states who contributed (by sending workers and/or tribute) to the building of the South palace in Babylon. These rulers are given the title "king" (LUGAL); also the positive context excludes that they are hostages or deportees, as Lipiński 2006, 199 and Schaudig 2008, 536 suggested.
101. Kleber 2008, 144f.
102. Ez. 21: 23–28 contains a prophecy that the king of Babylon would perform divination at a road crossing to determine whether he would first lay siege to Jerusalem or to Rabba (Rabbat-Ammon).
103. Jer. 37: 5; Von Voigtlander 1963, 112.
104. Kleber 2008, nr. 20 (translation on pp. 214ff.).
105. The Biblical passage only says that Gedaliah was "installed" but does not give him a specific title (Cogan & Tadmor 1988, 327). We follow those scholars who believe that Gedaliah was installed as governor (see Na'aman 2000). Vanderhooft 2003, 244 disagrees but does not suggest that Judah continued as a kingdom. He believes that Judah was left without any effective

administration after the murder of Gedaliah. The assassination of Gedaliah is described in II Kings 25: 22–25; Jer. 40–41.

106. Josephus (*Antiquitates Judaicae* X, 181f.) gives the following abstruse statement to prove that Jeremiah's prophecy against Egypt came true: "for on the fifth year after the destruction of Jerusalem, which was the twenty-third of the reign of Nebuchadnezzar, he made an expedition against Celesyria; and when he had possessed himself of it, he made war against the Ammonites and Moabites; and when he had brought all these nations under subjection, he fell upon Egypt, in order to overthrow it; and he slew the king that then reigned and set up another; and he took those Jews that were there captives, and led them away to Babylon." Several events were telescoped, and the information about Nebuchadnezzar's invasion of Egypt that took place after Amasis' coup d'état, is clearly distorted. The first part (campaigns against Lebanon (Celesyria), Moab, Ammon and Egypt) probably came from another source that summarized Babylonian achievements. The information about a third deportation in Nebuchadnezzar's 23rd year may have come from Jer. 52:30, although Jeremiah explicitly says that the 745 persons were led away from Judah by "Nebusaradan".

107. According to Katzenstein 1973, 329f., see also p. 319, the siege was brought about by the refusal of some Babylonian demands that Tyre did not want to fulfil, such as "a free flank, and perhaps even a fleet and a base for its ultimate aim: to make Egypt submissive to Babylon". We think that this incident happened earlier but agree with Katzenstein insofar as Egypt's military pressure, the deliberation of the results of choosing one of the two sides, and Babylonian demands will certainly all have played a role. Tyre's position, just like that of the southern Levant, was between a rock and a hard place. They could not please both sides and were pushed into a choice that would in either case harm them.

108. The details of how Ezekiel pictures Tyre's end are surprising. He describes it as if the Babylonians were able to take Tyre by means of ordinary siege equipment: They would first conquer Tyre's mainland territory and then "set up a siege wall ... build a ramp up to" the "walls and raise a roof of shields" against Tyre, after which Nebuchadnezzar would break the city walls and towers with battering rams. The passage is best interpreted as a stereotypical description of a siege, disregarding the island location (Greenberg 1997, 542). Marriner *et al.* 2007, 9220 proposed that Nebuchadnezzar attempted to build a causeway in the shallow waters between Tyre and the coast like Alexander the Great later did, but we do not have any evidence that would support this assumption.

109. Katzenstein 1973, 331 interprets Ezekiel's words in such a way that "there was no capitulation of Tyre" but rather that "both parties came to an understanding". The subsequent military occupation of the city, however, compels to assume a negotiated end of the siege that resulted in a weak position of Tyre under Babylonian rule.

110. A paraphrase of the documents can be found in tables 8 and 9 on pages 145–149 in Kleber 2008; see pp. 142–144 for the identification of their place of issue (Ṣūru) with Tyre on the Mediterranean coast. We must now add BM 73237 (28.VI. accession year of Amēl-Marduk), edited by S. Zawadzki (in press). The text was not drafted at Tyre but mentions provisions, most likely (the text is rather damaged) for soldiers who will be stationed at Tyre in the following year(s). The date of some other texts is uncertain: the Uruk-text GC 1, 151 records rations for two men who deliver sacrificial remains to the king. They were sent with soldiers to Tyre. The date of this text is broken, yet it was hitherto taken as proof that Nebuchadnezzar was personally in charge of the siege (Katzenstein 1973, 332 with older literature). This is not excluded, but the text may also belong to the after-siege file. Zawadzki 2008 proposed a connection of several other texts from the Ebabbar archive that date from the years 28–31 Nebuchadnezzar with the siege of Tyre because these texts mention military equipment and a camp. Because Tyre is not mentioned explicitly, they may relate to Tyre or other military campaigns in these years.

111. The text itself is still unpublished but a summary of its content and its date (16 [..].31 Nebuchadnezzar) was given by Joannès 1987, 147. Because the chronologically next text dates from 35 Nebuchadnezzar, it is desirable to collate the text to verify its date.
112. Only one text (PTS 3181, published in Joannès 1987, 155–157) is more specific about the "work", but the passage is broken. Before *-pi-ti* in line 6 there is space for two signs (maximal three very small signs), the first one must be *šá*. *Ṣāpītu* "siege tower" (with *ṣubbû* "to inspect") is tempting, but the siege had ended several years prior to the drafting of this text. Perhaps the passage can be interpreted as ^{lú}RIG$_{7}$ [*ša ṣu*]*-pi-ti ana muh-hi* ^{uru}*ṣur-ru* [*ú*]*-ṣap-pu-ú* "the temple dependents who soak/dye on Tyre" if one thinks of purple dye/wool production, but the preposition *ana muhhi* instead of *ina* would be unusual. The Eanna temple paid high sums for imported dyed wool from the west, so it makes sense to engage temple workers in this industry as long as they were stationed at Tyre. A possible hint that the temple's foreign trade balance profited from Eanna's engagement in the west comes from VS 20, 90. The text mentions the 35th year of Nebuchadnezzar and lists the arrival of a small quantity of either cedar wood (as an aromatic) or a type of wool (the latter part of the sign is unclear) "of the city of Tyre" at the Eanna temple.
113. The text is the aforementioned PTS 3181. Colonies of Babylonian settlers are also attested in the Hābūr region in the time of Nabonidus (the file is treated by Jursa and Wagensonner 2014). The king (probably Nabonidus) had given land grants to temples; the Ebabbar temple then sent farmers to cultivate grapes in order to produce wine and raisins for use in the cult. The purpose of the settlement in the Levant was most likely the sustenance of the garrison.
114. In later historiography Nebuchadnezzar is credited with the conquest of Egypt. A Babylonian attack on Egypt is described in a fragmentary cuneiform text (Nbk 48 in Langdon 1912, 206f.) that mentions Amasis and the year 37 Nebuchadnezzar. In 571/0 Apries suffered the devastating defeat against Cyrene which led to Amasis' *coup d'état*. According to Edel 1978, Apries asked for Nebuchadnezzar's help which led to a combined invasion of land and naval forces in 567 BC (37 Nbk). The Amasis-stele dates the battle to the 8th of Athyr 4 Amasis (20 March 567 BC), see Edel 1978, 15. However, the attempts to conquer Egypt failed. Josephus (*Contra Apionem* 1, 144) relates in a context where he mentions the siege of Tyre, that Megasthenes credited Nebuchadnezzar with the subjection of "most of Libya and Iberia" – most likely a reflection of Nebuchadnezzar's conquest of Tyre, similarly to Esarhaddon's claim that all the kings from Cyprus and Greece to Tarsisi (Tartessos) submitted to him (see above).
115. On the basis of Josephus' information that the accession year of Cyrus (539 BC) is the 14th year of Hiram (Eiromos): 14 years of Eiromos + 4 years of Merbalos + 1 year of Balatorus.
116. Also Katzenstein 1973, 342 weighed three possibilities for the reinstallation of a Tyrian king: either active Tyrian help in Neriglissar's campaign against Pirindu, a decision of Nabonidus after the latter's *coup d'état*, or an alleged campaign of the Median king Astyages against Harran.
117. Josephus, *Contra Apionem* I, 158; see also Katzenstein 1973, 343f.
118. Herodotus I, 163; see Katzenstein 1973, 337.
119. Toscanos and other settlements at the coast near Malaga, Granada and Almería (Aubet 2001, 307, 321), the dating is based on Greek pottery.
120. The exact date of independence cannot be ascertained.
121. Translation of the PACE project: http://pace.mcmaster.ca/york/york/showText?text=apion).
122. Some interpreters tried to solve this discrepancy by assuming that the single year of Balatoros (Ba'al-'ator) happened while Mattan and Ger-ʿaštart were still judges (see the appendix by J. Dochhorn in Siegert 2008, 51f.).
123. It is mentioned in the Babylonian Chronicle but the date is not preserved. The entry stands after the 3rd (553/2 BC) and immediately before the entry for the 7th year of Nabonidus' reign (549/8 BC). Thus, the most likely date is the 6th year (550/49 BC).

124. For the "early" dossier see Kleber 2008, 144f. and for the reasoning that all these texts come from Tyre in the Levant, and that no village called Ṣūru existed in Babylonia, see Kleber 2008, 141–154. Schaudig 2008 was not aware of this new interpretation of the Tyre dossier when writing his paper.
125. This is the "Standard" text in Niese 1887 and Siegert 2008, vol. 2, 150 based on Codici L (Laurentianus), E (Eliensis) and S (Schleusingenisis). It contains a conjecture as all three manuscripts have an erroneous' ἐπὶ instead of' ἔτει; M omits this word altogether (Siegert 2008, 130).' ἔτει is the most logical correction and is based on the Latin version of the Eusebius Chronicle (Siegert 2008, 130).
126. Niese 1887, 30: "*septimo siquidem anno regni sui nabuchodonosor coepit* Lat, h.e. τῆς βασιλείας Ναβουχοδονόσορος".
127. Siegert 2008, 131 fn. 54 assumed that the Greek manuscripts L, E and S "corrected" their *Vorlage* by changing the word order and the grammatical ending on the name of Nebuchadnezzar ("*falsche Renominalisierung*"). Thereby the passage in L, E and S received its present form, which displays not an entirely wrong but an unusual syntax.
128. Lipiński 2006, 197 noted that, if not Nebuchadnezzar's but somebody else's kingship was intended, the text would have *regni eius* instead of *regni sui*. One may argue that the failure to differentiate between *eius* and *suus* is an early attestation of a feature typical in later Latin. Yet, neither from the Latin, nor from the Greek text one is obliged to infer that somebody else's kingship was meant. The redactors of the Greek manuscript M who inserted αὐ τοῦ "his" after the word βασιλείας "kingship" may have wanted to clarify that it was Nebuchadnezzar's kingship. Generally, M is a rather late manuscript from the 16th century and is not better in quality than L, E and S (Siegert 2008, vol. 2, p. 35). Siegert quotes only two passages where M has "better" readings than the other manuscripts, but one of these two passages is this one. It is unlikely that manuscript M has the original text here, as Ittô-baʿal's name is not mentioned in the sentence before. A parallel where αὐ τοῦ refers to someone else's rule is *Contra Apionem* I, 150. But in this passage Nabonidus is mentioned immediately before. Therefore no logical problem occurs there.
129. Josephus' Babylonian king list gives, just like the Tyrian king list, the total duration of reigns without taking the overlap for accession years into consideration which gives an almost correct duration. The only error that occurred is that nine instead of two months were attributed to the reign of Lâbâši-Marduk.
130. Josephus refers to 539 BC (not 538 BC), otherwise the temporal distance between the 18th year of Nebuchadnezzar (587/6) and the 2nd year of Cyrus (537/6 BC) would not be 50 years.
131. Lipiński 2006, 197f. has the same argumentation, therefore obviously follows Gutschmid.
132. The calculation may vary slightly since it is uncertain how we should deal with the calculation error (Josephus says that the period is 54 years and three months). Furthermore, variants in the manuscripts attribute six months to either Ednibalos (instead of two months) or Abbalos (instead of three months), see Siegert 2008, vol. 1, 130. However, we would in any case be in the vicinity of 588 BC. Although they agree on the 17th year for the text, Gutschmid 1893, 553 and Lipiński 2006, 169 regarded Nebuchadnezzar's 18th year as the time when the siege began for historical reasons.
133. We disagree with Katzenstein in another detail, one that does not influence the chronology of the siege, but the overall reconstruction of the chronology. Katzenstein adds the remaining 6 years – that is, the 6 years that form the difference between the 49 years and three months of the rules and the final statement "the whole period is 54 [55!] years and three months", to the reign of Ittô-baʿal, attributing the absolute dates of *c*. 591/0–*c*. 574/3 to his reign. This is a rather strange interpretation of what Josephus' phrase "the whole period" refers to. Josephus ends the king list with the full reign of Hiram which is 20 years, not with his 14th that is equated with Cyrus' accession year. From the point of view of text logic, these six years are the last six years of Hiram's reign. We do not know when Ittô-baʿal ruled apart from the fact that he ruled when the siege began.

134. The letter is likely although not certainly part of the Tyre dossier. Prosopography places it between 578 and 560 BC (see Kleber 2008, 148 and 221f.).
135. We assume that Ezekiel was deported at the end of the 7th year of Nebuchadnezzar (597 BC) and that 597/6 BC was the first year of the exile.
136. We believe that the conquest of Egypt was Nebuchadnezzar's final aim, and that Tyre first had to fall. In 570 BC Egypt was shaken by a crisis that began with the devastating loss of the contingent of Apries' army that had been sent against Cyrene.

Bibliography

Ahlström, G. W. (1993) *The History of Ancient Palestine from the Palaeolithic Period to Alexander's Conquest*, Sheffield.

Arnaud, D. (1982) Une lettre du roi de Tyr au roi d'Ugarit: milieux d'affaires et de culture en Syrie à la fin de l'âge du bronze récent, *Syria, revue d'art oriental et d'archéologie* 59: 101–107.

Aubet, M. E. (2001) *The Phoenicians and the West. Politics, Colonies and Trade* (2nd ed.), Cambridge.

Aubet, M. E. (2008) Political and economic implications of the new Phoenician chronologies. In C. Sagona (ed.), *Beyond the Homeland: Markers in Phoenician Chronology*, 247–259, Leuven.

Barnes, W. H. (1991) *Studies in the Chronology of the Divided Monarchy of Israel*, Atlanta.

Barnett, R. D. (1982) *Ancient Ivories in the Middle East*, Jerusalem.

Bateman, V. N. (2012) *Markets and Growth in Early Modern Europe*, London.

Bikai, P. (1978) *The Pottery of Tyre*, Warminster.

Bondi, S. F. (1988) The course of history. In S. Moscati (ed.), *The Phoenicians*, 38–45, Milano.

Cogan, M. & H. Tadmor (1988) *II Kings. A New Translation with Introduction and Commentary*, New Haven.

Cross, F. M. (1972a) The stele dedicated to Melcarth by Ben adad of Damascus, *Bulletin of the American Schools of Oriental Research* 205: 36–42.

Cross, F. M. (1972b) An Interpretation of the Nora Stone. *Bulletin of the American Schools of Oriental Research* 208: 13–19.

Da Riva, R. (2008) *The Neo-Babylonian Royal Inscriptions*, Guides to the Mesopotamian Textual Record 4, Münster.

Dalley, S. (1999) Sennacherib and Tarsus. *Anatolian Studies* 49: 73–80.

Diffie, B. W. & G. D. Winius (1977) *Foundations of the Portuguese Empire, 1415-1580*, Minneapolis.

Dochhorn, J. (2001) Die auf Menander von Ephesus zurückgehende Liste der Könige von Tyrus. In J. U. Kalms (ed.), *Internationales Josephus-Kolloquium Amsterdam 2000*, 77–102, Münster.

Dochhorn, J. (2005) Die phönizischen Personennamen in den bei Josephus überlieferten Quellen zur Geschichte von Tyrus, *Welt des Orients* 35: 67–117.

Edel, E. (1978) Amasis und Nebukadrezar II. *Göttinger Miszellen* 29: 13–20.

Elat, M. (1978) The economic relations of the Neo-Assyrian Empire with Egypt. *Journal of the American Oriental Society* 98: 20–34.

Engle, A. (1980) *The Sidonian Glassmakers and their Market* (Readings in Glass History 11), Jerusalem.

Fales, F. M. (2008) On Pax Assyriaca in the eighth-seventh centuries BCE and its implications. In R. Cohen & R. Westbrook (eds), *Isaiah's Vision of Peace in Biblical and Modern International Relations*, 17–35, Houndmills.

Falsone, G. (1988) Phoenicia as a bronzeworking centre in the Iron Age. In J. Curtis (ed.), *Bronzeworking centres of western Asia c. 1000-539 B.C.*, 227–350, London and New York.

Frankenstein, S. (1979) The Phoenicians in the far west: a function of Neo-Assyrian imperialism. In M. T. Larsen (ed.), *Power and Propaganda*, 263–294, Copenhagen.

Fuchs, A. (1994) *Die Inschriften Sargons II aus Khorsabad*, Göttingen.

Gilboa, A., L. Sharon & E. Boaretto (2008) Tel Dor and the chronology of Phoenician "pre-colonisation" stages. In C. Sagona (ed.), *Beyond the Homeland: Markers in Phoenician Chronology*, 113–204, Leuven.

Gitin, S. & A. Golani (2001) The Tel Miqne silver hoards: the Assyrian and Phoenician connections. In M. S. Balmuth (ed.), *Hacksilber to Coinage: New Insights into the Monetary History of the Near East and Greece*, 27–48, New York.
Grayson, A. K. (1991) *Assyrian Rulers of the Early first Millennium BC I (1114-859 BC)*, Toronto, Buffalo and London.
Grayson, A. K. (1996) *Assyrian Rulers of the Early first Millennium BC II (858-745 BC)*, Toronto, Buffalo and London.
Grayson, A. K. (2000) *Assyrian and Babylonian Chronicles*, Winona Lake.
Grayson, A. K. & J. Novotny (2012) *The Royal Inscriptions of Sennacherib, King of Assyria (704-681 BC) part 1.* Royal Inscriptions of the Neo-Assyrian Period 3 (1), Winona Lake.
Greenberg, M. (1997) *Ezekiel 21-37. A New Translation with Introduction and commentary. Anchor Bible*, New York.
Gutschmid, A. von (1893) *Kleine Schriften, Band IV. Schriften zur Griechischen Geschichte und Literatur*, Leipzig.
Hoffman, G. L. (1997) *Imports and Immigrants. Near Eastern Contacts with Iron Age Crete*, Ann Arbor.
Jamieson-Drake, D. W. (1991) *Scribes and Schools in Monarchic Judah*, Sheffield.
Joannès, F. (1987) Trois textes de Ṣurru a l'époque néo-babylonienne. *Revue d'Assyriologie* 81: 147–158.
Jursa, M. (2007) Der neubabylonische Hof. In B. Jacobs & R. Rollinger (eds), *Der Achämenidenhof*, 67–106, Wiesbaden.
Jursa, M. & K. Wagensonner (2014) The estates of Šamaš on the Habur. In M. Kozuh *et al.* M. Kozuh, W.F.M. Henkelman, Ch.E. Jones, Ch. Woods (eds), *Extraction and Control. Studies in Honor of Matthew W. Stolper*, 109–130, Chicago.
Karageorghis, V. (1976) *Kition. Mycenaean and Phoenician Discoveries in Cyprus*, London.
Katzenstein, H. J. (1973) *The History of Tyre. From the Beginning of the Second Millennium B.C.E. until the Fall of the Neo-Babylonian Empire in 538 B.C.E*, Jerusalem.
Kestemont, G. (1983) Tyr et les Assyriens. In E. Gubel, E. Lipiński & B. Servais-Soyez, *Redt Tyrus/ Sauvons Tyr*, 53–78, Leuven.
Kleber, K. (2008) *Tempel und Palast. Die Beziehungen zwischen dem König und dem Eanna-Tempel im spätbabylonischen Uruk* (Alter Orient und Altes Testament 358), Münster.
Langdon, S. (1912) *Die neubabylonischen Königsinschriften*, Leipzig.
Leichty, E. (2011) *The Royal Inscriptions of Esarhaddon, King of Assyria (680-669 BC)*. Royal Inscriptions of the Neo-Assyrian Period 4, Winona Lake.
Lipiński, E. (1970) Ba'li-Ma'zer II and the chronology of Tyre. *Rivista degli Studi Orientali* 45: 59–65.
Lipiński, E. (2004) *Itineraria Phoenicia*, Leuven.
Lipiński, E. (2006) *On the Skirts of Canaan in the Iron Age*, Leuven, Paris and Dudley.
Lipschits, O. (2004) Ammon in transition from vassal kingdom to Babylonian province. *Bulletin of the American Schools of Oriental Research* 335: 37–52.
Liverani, M. (2001) *International Relations in the Ancient Near East, 1600-1100 BC*. Houndmills, Basingstoke and New York.
Liverani, M. (2005) *Israel's History and the History of Israel*, London.
Loon, M. van (1974) *Oude lering, nieuwe nering. Het uitzwermen der Noord-Syrische ambachtslieden in de late 8e eeuw v. Chr*, Amsterdam.
Luukko, M. (2012) *The Correspondence of Tiglath-Pileser III and Sargon II from Calah/Nimrud* (State Archives of Assyria 19), Helsinki.
Markoe, G. E. (2000) *Phoenicians*, London.
Marriner, N., C. Morhange & S. Meulé (2007) Holocene morphogenesis of Alexander the Great's isthmus at Tyre in Lebanon, *Proceedings of the National Academy of Science* 104: 9218–9223.
Marriner, N., C. Morhange & N. Carayon (2008) Ancient Tyre and its harbours: 5000 years of human-environment interactions, *Journal of Archaeological Science* 35: 1281–1310.

Moran, W. L. (1992) *The Amarna Letters*, Baltimore.
Morley, N. (1996) *Metropolis and Hinterland. The City of Rome and the Italian Economy 200 B.C A.D. 200*, Cambridge.
Na'aman, N. (2000) Royal vassals or governors? On the status of Sheshbazzar and Zerubbabel in the Persian empire. *Henoch* 22, 35–44.
Na'aman, N. (2001) The conquest of Yadnana according to the Inscriptions of Sargon II. In T. Abusch *et al*. P. Beaulieu, J. Huehnergard, P. Machinist, P. Steinkeller, C. Noyes (eds), *Historiography in the Cuneiform World*, 357–363, Bethesda.
Niese, B. (1887) *Flavii Josephi Opera*, 2a ed., 1986 (reprint), Hildesheim.
Nijboer, A. J. & J. van der Plicht (2006) An interpretation of the radioncarbon determinations of the oldest indigenous-Phoenician stratum thus far, excavated at Huelva, Tartessos (south-west Spain), (formerly Bulletin Antieke Beschaving) 81: 31–36.
Oppenheim, A. L. (1973) Towards a History of Glass in the Ancient Near East, *Journal of the American Oriental Society* 93: 259–266.
Pappa, E. (2012) Framing some aspects of the Early Iron Age "chronological mess". Aegean synchronisms with the West and their significance for the Greek Geometric Series, *Kubaba* 3: 1–38.
Pardee, D. (2003) Une formule épistolaire en ougaritique et accadien. In P. Marrassini (ed.), *Semitic and Assyriological Studies Presented to Pelio Fronzaroli by Pupils and Colleagues*, 446–475, Wiesbaden.
Parpola, S. & K. Watanabe (1988) *Neo-Assyrian Treaties and Loyalty Oaths*, State Archives of Assyria, Helsinki.
Pritchard, J. B. (1969) *Ancient Near Eastern Texts Relating to the Old Testament* (3rd edition), Princeton.
Radner, K. (1999) Traders in the Neo-Assyrian period. In J. G Dercksen (ed.), *Trade and Finance in Ancient Mesopotamia*, 127–157, Leiden.
Radner, K. (2004) Assyrische Handelspolitik: Die Symbiose mit Unabhängigen Handelszentren und ihre Kontrolle durch Assyrien. In R. Rollinger & C. Ulf (eds), *Commerce and Monetary Systems in the Ancient World: Means of Transmission and Cultural Interaction*, 152–169, Wiesbaden.
Radner, K. (2010) The stele of Sargon II of Assyria: a focus for an emerging Cypriot identity at Kition? In R. Rollinger, B. Gufler, M. Lang & I. Madreiter (eds), *Interkulturalität in der Alten Welt. Vorderasien, Hellas, Ägypten und die vielfältigen Ebenen des Kontakts*, 429–449, Wiesbaden.
Redford, D. B. (1992) *Egypt, Canaan, and Israel in Ancient Times*, Princeton.
Schaudig, H. (2008) A Tanit-Sign from Babylon and the conquest of Tyre by Nebuchadrezzar II, *Ugarit-Forschungen* 40: 533–546.
Siegert, F. (2008) *Flavius Josephus: Über die Ursprünglichkeit des Judentums (Contra Apionem)*, Göttingen.
Smith, J. S. (2008) Cyprus, the Phoenicians and Kition. In C. Sagona (ed.), *Beyond the Homeland: Markers in Phoenician Chronology*, 261–303, Leuven.
Sommer, M. (2009) Networks of commerce and knowledge in the Iron Age: The case of the Phoenicians. In Malkin, I., C. Constantakopoulou & K. Panagopoulou (eds), *Greek and Roman Networks in the Mediterranean*, 94–108, London-New York.
Stern, E. (1990) New evidence from Dor for the first appearance of the Phoenicians along the northern coast of Israel, *Bulletin of the American Schools of Oriental Research* 279: 27–34.
Streck, M. (1916) *Assurbanipal und die Letzten Assyrischen Könige bis zum Untergang Niniveh's*, II Teil, Leipzig.
Tadmor, H. (1966) Philistia under Assyrian rule, *Biblical Archaeologist* 29: 86–102.
Tadmor, H. & S. Yamada (2011) *The Royal Inscriptions of Tiglath-Pileser III (744–727 BC) and Shalmaneser V (727–722 BC), Kings of Assyria*, Royal Inscriptions of the Neo-Assyrian Period 1, Winona Lake.
Tammuz, O. (2009–2010 [2011]) The expansion of the kingdom of Damascus under Rezin and its aftermath, *State Archives of Assyria Bulletin* 18: 187–203.
Torres Ortiz, M. (2008) The chronology of the Late Bronze Age in western Iberia and the beginning of the Phoenician colonization in the western Mediterranean. In D. Brandherm & M. Trachsel

(eds), *A new Dawn for the Dark Age? Shifting Paradigms in Mediterranean Iron Age Chronology*. British Archaeological Report S187, 135–147, Oxford.
Unger, E. (1931) *Babylon. Die heilige Stadt nach der Beschreibung der Babylonier*, Berlin-Leipzig.
Vanderhooft, D. S. (1999) *The Neo-Babylonian Empire and Babylon in the Latter Prophets*. HSM 59 Harvard Semitic Studies, Atlanta.
Vanderhooft, D. S. (2003) Babylonian strategies of imperial control in the west: royal practise and rhetoric. In O. Lipschits & J. Blenkinsopp (eds), *Judah and the Judeans in the Neo-Babylonian Period*, 235–262, Winona Lake.
Voigtlander, E. von (1963) *A Survey of Neo-Babylonian History*, Ann Arbor.
Yamada, S. (2008) Qurdi-Assur-lamur: His letters and career. In M. Cogan & D. Kahn (eds), *Treasures on Camels' Humps. Historical and Literary Studies from the Ancient Near East, Presented to Israel Eph'al*, 296–311, Jerusalem.
Zawadzki, S. (2003) Nebuchadnezzar and Tyre in the light of new texts from the Ebabbar Archives in Sippar (Festschrift Hayim and Miriam Tadmor), *Eretz-Israel* 27: 276–281.
Zawadzki, S. (2008) Nebuchadnezzar's campaign in the 30th year (575 B.C.): a conflict with Tyre? In M. Cogan & D. Kahn (eds), *Treasures on Camel's Humps. Historical and Literary Studies from the Ancient Near East Presented to Israel Eph'al*, 331–336, Jerusalem.
Zawadzki, S. (in press) *Chronology of the Tyrian history in the Neo-Babylonian period*.

Chapter 10

Temples and agricultural labour in Egypt, from the Late New Kingdom to the Saite Period*

Juan Carlos Moreno García

Introduction

The New Kingdom witnessed important changes in the role played by the temples in the agricultural economy of the country. For the first time the sources concerning their economic and agricultural activities are relatively abundant; they include not only inscriptions inscribed in the monuments of individuals and in the temples themselves, but also royal decrees and many administrative documents produced by the sanctuaries. As for the archaeological record, the impressive remains of several New Kingdom temples (Ramesseum, Karnak, Luxor, Abu-Simbel) confirm their importance as crucial institutions in the agricultural organization of the country during the second half of the 2nd millennium BC. Older interpretations that considered temples (and their personnel, usually described as "clergy") as potential menaces or, at beast, counterweights to the power of the king, have been abandoned. Instead, more balanced views now see them as part of the structure of the state, not as rival entities, while their personnel, especially at the highest level, cannot be reduced to the rather limited category of clergy. Rather they combined both "religious" and "civil" titles and, consequently, cannot strictly be regarded simply as priests. However, a crucial question still remains unsolved: why did temples become such important economic institutions during the New Kingdom?

In previous periods, the main institutional elements of the Egyptian agricultural landscape were a mix of agricultural and work centres of the crown and temples. Thus, for instance, during the last centuries of the 3rd millennium BC, agricultural centres of the crown (*ḥwt*) and provincial temples formed networks of installations which produced, stocked and distributed provisions and other goods to the agents of the king in mission (officials, armies, teams of workers, etc.), under the supervision of the pharaonic administration. Temples also obtained substantial land donations, as well as working personnel, granted by the crown, especially in the provinces, and the role of these local sanctuaries appears quite important in the cultivation of otherwise untilled land and pasture areas. But from the beginning of the 2nd millennium the *ḥwt* centres disappeared (except in some epigraphic formulae) while a new crown institution emerged, the *ẖnrt*, apparently a work camp. In any case, both during the Old and Middle Kingdoms the pharaoh granted substantial land endowments to provincial temples, ranging between half a hectare to about a hundred hectares, in some cases provided with workers and prisoners of war. In all, local temples appear as relatively modest institutions, both in architectural and economic terms, but their role was crucial for the integration of the provincial elites into the pharaonic administration.

However, the end of the Middle Kingdom and the troubled period that followed, marked by internal political division and the emergence of several competing powers (including the Hyksos kingdom in the north and the Theban monarchy in the south), brought together new changes. In the south, the Theban kingdom seems to have followed a policy of endowment as well as of reorganisation of the agricultural domains of the temples under its control. Perhaps more importantly, the old agricultural centres of the crown (like the *ẖnrt* work camps) seem to have vanished or, at least, to have lost their former importance as economic units as well as nodal points of territorial organization (Moreno García 2006). The advent of the New Kingdom, when the Theban kings finally imposed their authority all over Egypt, witnessed the emergence of temples as the most powerful economic institutions of the country, but subject to the control of the king. So much so that temples also became the main centres of economic and political integration in newly conquered areas abroad, such as Nubia, as well as managerial agencies, frequently in charge of the cultivation of the fields belonging to other institutions, like the crown. The imperial expansion into Nubia and Asia provided a flow of prisoners and deportees that were often granted to temples as workforce and who made it possible to put potentially agricultural land into cultivation, as in some areas of Middle Egypt.

Temples thus took up some of the economic, organizational and managerial functions previously fulfilled by the centres of the crown and, in so doing, the latter became superfluous. Furthermore, they also provided a more decentralized managerial organization that enabled the crown to save costs. Finally, they also appear as partial regulators of the flows of wealth crossing Egypt during the New Kingdom, from trade to mining and exports, playing an important role (still to be determined) in the transformation of agricultural produce into precious metals and promoting some market transactions. The taxes paid, among other goods, in silver and gold to the crown reveal that temples were able to accumulate these precious metals through their economic activities, independently of the donations of the king. And, in the case of silver, a metal which was not produced within Egyptian borders, payments made in this metal (sometimes quite substantial) to the royal treasury point to some kind of commercialization of the produce of temples. Thus, for instance, it is quite noteworthy that a merchant and "overseer of the carriers of gold" called Khnumnakht, managed to be appointed as boat captain and profited from his newly acquired position to steal substantial amounts of gold but also of grain (more than 6000 sacks of grain) destined for the temple of Khnum in Elephantine, in collusion with the personnel of this institution (scribes, inspectors, cultivators). As in other cases of robbery of temple property, merchants were essential mediators in order to launder the stolen goods (Vernus 1993, 124–139). As for their agricultural assets, temples not only cultivated their own land but also the fields of other institutions (the crown, the royal "Harem", other temples, etc.) in exchange for a share of the crops. The Wilbour papyrus, an important contemporary land record at the time of the robberies committed by Khnumnakht, also reveals that fields belonging to temples and to the crown were grouped together in domains (*rmnyt*) of several hundreds *aruras* each (1 arura = 0.27 ha), frequently scattered along the Nile Valley. Such domains were usually administered by or were under the control of temples and cultivated by true "agricultural entrepreneurs", according to an administrative structure whereby an official or a priest was responsible for a given domain which, in turn, was cultivated by an "agricultural entrepreneur" while peasants, prisoners of war and modest cultivators actually worked the land (Moreno García 2008 and 2010b).

However, it would be erroneous to consider temples as independent entities, opposed to the king and in a position to contest or at least to limit his authority. Their assets, in fact, were partly at the disposal of the crown, which could use temple facilities and goods to its own advantage. Thus, for instance, the papyrus Harris I records the grants made by Ramesses III of more than 100,000 workers and more than a million aruras (about 2700 km^2) to the main temples of Egypt, especially to his own funerary temple at Medinet Habu. To put it another way, these donations represented about 5% of the Egyptian population and almost 15% of the total agricultural area of the country. However, the slightly later Wilbour papyrus records very few traces of such donations, thus showing that land grants were far from perennial and that, in fact, the same domains were transferred and re-transferred between institutions from one reign to the next. Moreover, the Wilbour papyrus and other contemporary administrative documents also reveal that part of the temple land was also distributed among soldiers, officers, priests and wealthy peasants, probably as recompense or in exchange for some services. Also a small amount of temple land consisted of "donation fields" granted by the king to provide for the cult of a royal statue; the fields were exploited by an individual within the framework of the temple administration and they represented in fact a reward providing the recipient with considerable income. Finally, temple land was cultivated by a combination of different systems: temple permanent agricultural personnel (*jḥwtjw*), compulsory workers through *corvée*, "agricultural entrepreneurs" in exchange for part of the harvest, land leases and, finally, dignitaries or people granted with temple fields by the king. The balance between all these modalities of cultivation changed over time. Consequently, the land in the hands of the temples was not only an economic asset; it also enabled these institutions to maintain a dense network of economic and social relations linking together the temples, the crown, the dignitaries, the local elite and provincial society, even at its humbler level.

By the end of the 2nd millennium this organization experienced many changes. The collapse of the Egyptian empire in Nubia and the Levant interrupted the flow of deportees and prisoners employed in the cultivation of temple land. Consequently, other modalities of work gained in importance, such as *corvée* and, later on, land leases. Another consequence of the end of the empire was a certain "ruralization" of the elites of the country, at least in Upper Egypt, and the reinforcement of their links with temples, as land now became their main source of income when imperial service, the army, even the administration (because of the division of the country in several polities), could no longer provide so many paths for wealth and promotion as in New Kingdom times. In the following pages I shall analyze all these changes.

Before the Iron Age: temples and labour in New Kingdom Egypt

The advent of the New Kingdom (1550–1069 BC) reinforced the economic role of temples in Egypt. In previous decades, temples benefited from administrative measures taken by the Theban kings and by local rulers under their authority in order to endow and reorganize the landed assets of several provincial temples in Upper Egypt. In one case, Sobeknakht, governor of Elkab and overseer of priests of the local temple, boasted about his reorganization of the land in the town of Ageny:

> "one who counters the Office of the fields, who petitions to the king concerning the fields of this god in (the locality of) Ageni that were established by boundary-stones bearing the big name of the perfect god Sobekhotep [III], deceased, beloved of (goddess) Nekhbet. Amount of low-lying fields: 200 aruras lying in the high fields and 1200 aruras of khato land. Total: 1400 aruras." (Helck 1975, 16)

Another inscription celebrates the endowment of the temple of Medamud by Theban pharaoh Sobekemsaf I and the establishment of boundary-stelae in order to mark its limits; however, the fields were already occupied by tenants who should be compensated "plot for plot, threshing-floor for threshing-floor, with respect to this endowment of (god) Montu in Medamud." Another passage of this inscription gives the dimensions of the endowment, about 396 ha or 1675 aruras (Helck 1975, 62). As for the decree of Theban pharaoh Intef V in the temple of Coptos, he formally deposed a certain Teti from the temple of god Min and removed his revenue from the sanctuary, a punishment extended to his descendants; as for any supporter who might help him, he would also lose his position in the sanctuary and his fields would be seized and given to the temple of Min (Helck 1975, 73–74). Also a new stela of the Theban pharaoh Kamose, recently discovered at Ermant by Christophe Thiers, mentions the delivery of offerings, as well as building works and ceremonies accomplished in the temple of Karnak (Biston-Moulin 2011). Finally, the inscription of Sataimau of Edfu, dated from the very beginning of the New Kingdom (around 1550 BCE), provides an excellent example of the patronage provided by the king to provincial temples as well as of the rewards bestowed on the local elite, especially in a period of war and reunification and reorganization of the country, when its collaboration and support were crucial:

> "Favours from the king concerning the temple of (god) Horus Behdety. (My) Lord [=king Ahmose] gave (me) a favour: his causing that I be appointed to be second lector-priest of Horus Behdety. (My) Lord repeated for me a favour: he enjoined to (me) his statue which is in its hall, which is in this temple, its income having been fixed, (it) being settled and enduring. Bread: 180 portions; beer: 6 jars; pure meat, flesh, haunch; back; spine; kidney fat; 'lower' fields: 6+x arouras; 'high' fields: 30 arouras – preserved as an eternal ordinance and as a permanent record in a decree of king Nebpehtyre, justified, strong ruler who seized the two lands [=Egypt], in the house of his father, Horus Behdety, the great god." (Davies, 2012, 54–55 and 76)

Similar documents, such us the contemporary stele of Iwf, also from Edfu (Sethe 1927, 29–31), reveal that such rewards, whereby officials were appointed as priests and became beneficiaries of substantial land income, served to enhance the links between the monarchy and selected members of the local elite through the mediation of provincial temples. Furthermore, important economic transactions between members of the elite, even between members of the royal family, were recorded in stelae placed in the temple of Karnak just prior to the beginning of the New Kingdom (Lacau 1933; Harari 1959).

Temples appear then as crucial instruments of power and of integration of the local elites in the hands of the Theban kings during the late Second Intermediate Period, and this organizational model was later extended all over Egypt following the Theban conquest of the country. Temples thus became huge economic institutions, to the point that they made it apparently unnecessary to reintroduce, or simply preserve, older agricultural centres of the crown as now they managed their own, increasingly large, land as well as the fields of the king and other institutions. The cultivation of these fields was possible thanks to the combination of several forms of work. In this respect, a royal inscription, the Nauri decree of pharaoh Seti I (1294–1279 BC), evokes different modalities of *compulsory work* used in the tenures of temples, including the requisition of workers, the transfer of people from one district to another and some forms of *corvée* designated by the terms *brt* (a Semitic loan) and *bḥ*. Another passage of the same inscription mentions *mrt*-workers, the traditional term employed to designate the seasonal *corvée* workforce (Kitchen 1968a, 45–58, 60). In fact, many New Kingdom inscriptions boast about the prisoners captured by the pharaonic armies in the course of victorious campaigns abroad and later granted by the king to temples as *mrt*-workers. However, while the transfer of people and the use of *corvée*-work had been used for centuries in the cultivation of temple fields (Moreno García 1998; 2001; 2006b; 2007; 2008; 2014b), it is quite surprising that the Nauri decree fails to mention a well-known category of workers who tilled the tenures of temples, dignitaries and the crown during the New Kingdom, the cultivators-*jḥwtj*. Their rapid expansion during this period was inseparable from the Egyptian conquests abroad and the flow of prisoners, deportees and slaves that followed, to the point that the end of the Egyptian empire in the 12th century BC gradually brought down this form of agricultural workforce with it and opened a period of considerable transformations in the organization of the institutional agriculture (Moreno García 2006a).

The jḥwtj*-system*

While in previous periods of Egyptian history the main source of manpower employed in institutional agriculture was, according to the available sources, *corvée* workers such as the *mrt*, *nswty* and *ḥm(-nswt)* (lit. king serf), the advent of the New Kingdom was characterized by two new phenomena that were quite probably related to each other: on the one hand the arrival of considerable numbers of prisoners of war, deportees, people sent as tribute, etc., who were transferred by the king to temples and to other institutions as workforce; on the other hand, a change in the balance between the different forms of labour employed until then in institutional agriculture, leading to the expansion of the *jḥwtj*-system, although *jḥwtj* workers were well documented prior to the New Kingdom but quite probably on a less important scale (Moreno García 2008; 2010b). However, while the influx of prisoners of war, deportees and slaves to temples was celebrated in contemporary sources as proof of royal largesse, other documents also reveal the importance of other modalities of cultivation of the temple land, from *corvées* to agricultural "entrepreneurs". In other words, *jḥwtj* cultivators only represented a fraction of the agricultural manpower available in Egypt, and their importance was furthermore limited to very specific periods in Egyptian history, the New Kingdom being just one of them. But when the number of military campaigns decreased, when foreign conquests were lost and, consequently, the flow of foreign manpower into Egypt diminished or simply stopped altogether (as happened at the end of the New Kingdom), the *jḥwtj*-system was seriously affected and began to gradually disappear while other forms of rural labour, some traditional (like *corvées*) and others new (such as land leases or agricultural workers like *nmḥ* and *mnḥ*), thrived.

The *jḥwtjw* (pl. of *jḥwtj*) were a special category of agricultural workers, and their name derives from a particular category of land, *ʿḥt*. The interpretation of this term is not without difficulties, but in any case *ʿḥt*-land was characterized by the use of some kind of compulsory work according to the oldest sources, from the 3rd millennium BC. Nevertheless it seems that *jḥwtj*-work cannot be assimilated to a special form of *corvée* and, in fact, its role prior to the New Kingdom seems rather reduced. Administrative and literary texts then become more precise and reveal that *jḥwtjw* were cultivators forced to till standardized plots of 20 aruras each (about 5.4 ha) and to deliver standard quotas of grain (200 sacks, one sack being equivalent to 76.8 liters). The expected yield, from an administrative and accounting point of view was then of 10 sacks/arura (actual yields would be more variable, probably somewhat higher; Moreno García

2010b). However the social and economic condition of *jḥwtjw* was quite diversified. While literary texts depict *jḥwtjw* as miserable, subject to every possible abuse by unscrupulous and greedy agents of the king, administrative texts reveal that the term *jḥwtj* encompassed in fact different social categories, from modest cultivators to truly agricultural entrepreneurs able to deliver thousands of sacks of grain from several localities to the institutions which owned the land, and who were thus in possession of considerable means and enjoying a certain social position. So the *jḥwtj*-system was not based on the labour of seasonal *corvée* workers but on cultivators permanently attached to institutions, forced to work their fields according to a system of quotas and provided with ploughs and draught animals by these institutions (temples, royal palace, even the domains of the elite; Gardiner 1937, 105 and 122–123).

The origins of *jḥwtj* cultivators were quite diverse, but war captives and deportees seem to have been the main sources of provisioning. For instance, a passage of the annals of pharaoh Tuthmosis III states that some of the prisoners of war captured during a military campaign were intended to become *mrt*-workers occupied in the production of textiles; others instead would become *jḥwtj* workers and put in charge of the cultivation of *ʿḥt* fields (Sethe 1927, 742). Another text evokes the case of a Syrian, presumably a prisoner of war, who was part of a group of *ḥmw* (serfs, slaves) led by a chief of a fortress and settled as a *jḥwtj* in the fields of a temple (Kitchen 1968c, 79). As for papyrus Louvre E 3228c, it mentions the case of a foreign *jḥwtj* who was sold by some individuals (Malinine 1951). However there is also evidence of other sources for procuring *jḥwtjw*. New Kingdom inscriptions, for instance, often testify that scribes and dignitaries found guilty of some crime, as well as criminals, could be reduced to the condition of *jḥwtj* (Kitchen 1968a, 54, 55 and 58; 1968c, 266).[1] Aged veterans could also be forced to become *jḥwtj* while soldiers in prison were transformed into *jḥwtj*, assigned to dignitaries and made to till the land (Gardiner 1937, 11). Perhaps the most eloquent proof of the compulsory nature of the activities carried out by *jḥwtj* cultivators is the fact that they were sometimes assessed in silver as well as bought and sold, as in the cases of the *jḥwtj* mentioned in papyrus Louvre E 3228c and sold for 6 *deben* of silver (about 540 g), the *jḥwtj* in the stele of Shoshenq assessed at 4⅓ *kite* (about 39 g: Blackman 1941, 85, 91) or the *jḥwtj* recorded in papyrus Rylands V and sold as a slave (Griffith 1909, 53–54). Another document, a stela of the reign of Osorkon II found in the temple of Khnum at Elephantine, declares about a *jḥwtj* who had succeeded in (illegally) becoming a priest in the temple: "he is now (again) a *jḥwtj* among the people of poor condition" (Jansen-Winkeln 2007a, 120–121).

However other categories of *jḥwtj* were rather well-off, particularly those able to deliver huge quantities of grain, much larger than the standard 200 sacks, not just in one but in several different localities (Gardiner 1941, 56–58). Quite probably they must be considered as true agricultural "entrepreneurs", certainly in charge of *ʿḥt* fields but able nevertheless to exploit large domains owned by institutions such as temples and the crown and, consequently, able to produce a high income for them. This work system is particularly evident in the Wilbour papyrus (about 1140 BC). On the one hand, because the area of many of the domains exploited by *jḥwtjw*, as well as the quantities of grain expected from them, exceeded the work and productive possibilities of a simple peasant, not to speak of a "normal" *jḥwtj*. This means that the *jḥwtjw* in charge of the large domains recorded in the Wilbour papyrus had at their disposal considerable resources in terms of workforce and agricultural implements in order to cultivate dozens if not hundreds of aruras. On the other hand, because about 9% of the nearly 2400 tenants of temple land recorded in this document by their names and titles were *jḥwtjw*, while the rest belonged to well-off members of local society, from priests and "ladies", to officers, dignitaries and military personnel; so these particular *jḥwtjw* enjoyed a condition similar to the other prominent people listed in the papyrus, thus revealing that, quite probably, they were also relatively well-off and considered as part of the small local elite. Other documents provide further evidence about well-off *jḥwtj*, to be distinguished from the mass of modest cultivators also called *jḥwtj*, such as when they borrowed grain at 50% interest to do business with it, as any other individual would do (Černy & Parker 1971; to be compared with papyrus Louvre E 9293: Malinine 1953, 20–24).

A very tentative and purely "impressionist" evaluation of the number of modest *jḥwtjw* in Ramesside times suggests that there would have been around 25,000, in charge of the cultivation of 500,000 aruras (135,000 ha) and who delivered 5 million sacks of grain (their value would be 10 million *deben* of copper or 100,000 *deben* of silver, roughly 9 tons). These figures are only based on a very limited set of data and, therefore, only pretend to give a very approximate idea of the weight of the *jḥwtj*-system within the institutional agriculture. Nevertheless they also suggest that only a fraction of the land owned by temples and other institutions (such as the crown) was cultivated through this system. The rest (in fact, the greater part of their landed assets) was probably worked through a mixture of other modalities of work, from agricultural "entrepreneurs" (including well-off *jḥwtjw*) to *corvée*, from dignitaries granted temple land to individuals who leased fields from these institutions and paid rent for them, as in the case of the tenants who cultivated crown land near Kom Ombo and paid gold into the pharaoh's treasury (Gardiner 1950). Despite the relevance of *jḥwtj* cultivators in official New Kingdom inscriptions, therefore, they only represented a fraction of the agricultural workforce employed by the temples. However, it is also quite possible that their importance might be explained by their strategic contribution to the exploitation of the landed assets of temples and crown fields. In this respect, 25,000 modest *jḥwtj* would then represent the permanent workforce that could be profitably employed by temples; beyond this limit, their upkeep would no longer be so productive and other forms of occasional work or indirect exploitation of land could then be considered, such as *corvées*, hired workers, "entrepreneurs", etc. The *jḥwtj*-system probably supplied the institutions with their basic requirements in grain and workforce in order to provide for their needs and remain economically operative. This system is comparable to those prevailing in other regions of the ancient Near East. First millennium Mesopotamian temples, for instance, cultivated their land either directly, by means of agricultural workers (*ikkâru*), or indirectly, leasing their fields to cultivators (*errešu*) (Joannès 2004).

However, the socio-economic changes that occurred at the end of the 2nd millennium had a deep impact on the organization of agriculture based on the *jḥwtj*-system. Papyrus Reinhardt, for instance, is an administrative document of the 10th century BC which registers the agricultural domains of the God Amun in the region of Akhmim as well as the personnel who tilled them and paid the respective taxes (Vleeming 1993). While the information recorded is quite similar to that contained in the Wilbour papyrus (12th century BC), some noticeable differences appear, most notably the use of *corvée* (*bḥ*) in the cultivation of *ʿḥt*-land and the very scarce references to *jḥwtjw*. Other contemporary documents confirm the rarity of *jḥwtj* workers, but also evoke for the first time in this type of administrative register a special category of fields called *nmḥ*-land, usually translated as "free-tenant land", which was absent in the Wilbour papyrus (Gasse 1988). A papyrus of the first half of the 8th century BC gives a list of several *jḥwtjw*, but the rest of the document, as well as contemporary papyri with similar contents, only mention *mnḥ*-tenants (Vittmann 2015b, 396–397). Later on, *jḥwtj*-workers were even rarer in the administrative documents, until the term *jḥwtj* finally became synonymous with peasant (Moreno García 2010b, 343–344). It thus seems quite probable that the gradual disappearance of the *jḥwtjw* in the Egyptian sources from the end of the 2nd millennium BC was the result of several circumstances: the end of the Egyptian empire in Nubia and the Levant; the subsequent scarcity of deportees and prisoners of war flowing into Egypt, depriving temples of a strategic source of agricultural manpower; the gradual return to traditional forms of exploitation of institutional land (like *corvées*); the emergence of new categories of agricultural workforce; the expansion of land leases dealing with institutional land; and, finally, the growing role played by wages and the circulation of silver in an economy that was increasingly integrated in the international networks of exchanges of the Iron Age (Muhs 2005, 3–5).

It might be observed, nevertheless, that the close association between the *jḥwtj*-system, military campaigns launched into foreign territories and the arrival of potential workers into Egypt (deportees, prisoners of war, slaves), reappeared briefly during the period that followed the Kushite expansion into Egypt and its subsequent interventions in the Levant. Several texts from the reigns of kings Piye (747–716 BC) and Taharqa (690–664 BC) record the sale of slaves designated by the expression "northerner, man of the north" (Malinine 1951; 1953, 35–49; 1982, 94–95; Vleeming 1980, 1–17), a reference already found in texts from the very beginning of the 9th century BC (Jansen-Winkeln 2007, 77–80; Ritner 2009b, 271–278) and which was still present in documents from the reign of the first Saite pharaoh, Psamtik I (664–610 BC; Malinine 1946). In any case the transactions dealing with "northerner" slaves in Kushite times also involved the personnel of the temple of Amun, thus implying that the slaves had been previously granted to the temple. This interpretation is supported by the triumphal inscription of Piye (which explicitly mentions deportees from the region of Memphis: Eide *et al.* 1994, 97), as well as by the inscription Kawa no. 6 from the reign of Taharqa, which celebrates the endowment of a sanctuary with gardeners who were also "northerners" (Eide *et al.* 1994, 171). In this context, a reference in papyrus Louvre E 3228c is quite relevant, as it concerns the sale of a "northerner" who was also a *jḥwtj* (Malinie 1951). Another inscription also dated from the reign of Taharqa mentions the endowment of a cultic foundation for Osiris with several goods, including a field of about 2.5 ha and a *jḥwtj* (Graefe & Wassef 1979). Finally, the endowment of Taharqa's temple at Sanam, in Nubia, also included *jḥwtjw* (Pope 2014). Taken together, all this evidence shows that the frequent military actions waged by Kushite kings in Lower Egypt and the Levant revived the flow of prisoners of war into Egypt; their subsequent endowment to temples made possible the reappearance of *jḥwtjw* working the fields of temples. This movement was ephemeral, however, as documents from the reign of Taharqa also mention *nmḥ*-tenants as well as the first known Egyptian land lease documents, thus pointing to the existence of other forms of agricultural work. The transition was completed under the Ptolemies. Papyrus Brookly 37.1647E, for instance, mention cultivators who tilled fields of 20 aruras each, as their *jḥwtjw* forerunners, but in exchange of wages, not as compulsory workers (Vinson 2004).

Changes at the end of the 2nd and the beginning of the 1st millennium BC

The frequent mentions of *jḥwtjw* in the inscriptions and literary and administrative documents of the New Kingdom suggest an agricultural predominance of this category of workers that, quite probably, should nevertheless be qualified, especially when considering their relatively small number as well as their real weight in the organization of the pharaonic institutional agriculture. Their decline was concomitant with the end of the Ramesside Empire but, at the same time, new categories of tenants and rural workers began to appear in the sources of the late 2nd millennium. However, it is quite improbable that the latter represented, in fact, completely new forms of work and land tenure; more likely, the new terminology corresponds to traditional forms of cultivation of temple land, whose associated terms were now obsolete and which had been replaced by new ones. Two categories are especially relevant in this respect, the *nmḥ* and the *mnḥ*.

The nmḥw: "free/independent" tenants

The term *nmḥ* (pl. *nmḥw*) designated originally the orphan, but its semantic field became gradually enlarged and encompassed further meanings, from people whose means of living and possessions were independent from service to the temples and the king (especially at the beginning of the 2nd millennium BC: Kótahy 2006) to "free" tenants, independent from big landholders, temples and great institutions but subject, nevertheless, to state taxes (from the beginning of the New Kingdom). Hence the frequency of the expression "*nmḥ* of the land of Pharaoh." While their social status was often opposed to that of dignitaries (*sr*) in Egyptian sources, it was nevertheless also different from that of serfs (*b3k*) and slaves (*ḥm*). That is why papyri from the first half of the 1st millennium make a sharp contrast between the concepts of "acting like a serf (*b3k*)" and "acting like a freeman (*nmḥ*)" (Malinine 1953, 50–55; Griffith 1909a, pls xvii–xix; 1909b, pls xvii–xviii; 1909c, 54–55, 213–215; Malinine & Pirenne 1950, 73–74). In fact, New Kingdom inscriptions frequently evoke *nmḥw* as beneficiaries of the protection of the king and his agents (Kruchten 1981, 31–33 and 93; Gnirs 1989, 104–110; Römer 1994, 412–451; David 2011). By the end of the New Kingdom a new expression appeared, "field of *nmḥ*", both in administrative texts and in documents dealing with the management of the fields belonging to temples, the royal family and the members of the elite.

The expression "field of *nmḥ*" appeared for the first time around 1280 BC (19th Dynasty), not in Egypt but in Nubia, then under Egyptian control (Meeks 1979, 622–623, 663–664; Römer 1994, 412–451). It was not until two centuries later that it began to be attested in stelae and administrative papyri from Upper Egypt, but it is entirely absent from the rich corpus of donation stelae and inscriptions of Lower Egypt. Another important aspect is that donation stelae are much more scarce in Upper Egypt (only four) than in Lower Egypt (about 120, mainly from the very end of the 2nd to the middle of the 1st millennium BC); however three out of the four Upper Egyptian donation stelae deal, significantly, with "fields of *nmḥ*". As for the Nubian stelae, the combination of chronological precocity, geographical "marginality" and relative quantitative importance (three out of eight Nubian donation stelae refer to "fields of *nmḥ*") deserves close scrutiny.

All three Nubian stelae reveal that the "fields of *nmḥ*" bordered the fields of the king or those of a dignitary (Kitchen 1968b, 75; perhaps also Gauthier 1913, 196). Three other Nubian donation stelae that are not mainly concerned with "fields of *nmḥ*" nevertheless show a similar pattern, as they celebrate land grants to a local chief (Kitchen 1968b, 72) and to royal statues (Kitchen 1968b; 1968d, 350–353); these fields also bordered those belonging to the king, to some members of his family or to high dignitaries, as well as fields defined as "fields with no heir", the land of a herder and, finally, "fields of *nmḥ*". The contents of the latter group of stelae suggest that the endowments were intended to strengthen the links between the Pharaoh and some high dignitaries and local potentates through the mediation of temples, the institutions that accumulated prestige, authority and wealth in Nubian territory during the New Kingdom (Kemp 1972a; 1972b; 1978). Thus the early references to Nubian "fields of *nmḥ*" in this context might provide some clues as to their role, as they are mentioned together with local institutions and eminent members of Nubian society. In this light, "fields of *nmḥ*" were probably held by local potentates, bearing no rank or function title, but enjoying a certain wealth and status, similar to those of their elite neighbours. Two elements might confirm this hypothesis. On the one hand, certain types of tenures enjoying a somewhat privileged status, such as donation fields (*ḥnk*) and "fields of *nmḥ*", are quite scarce in Ramesside and later land registers. This circumstance confirms that the "fields of *nmḥ*" were a special kind of tenure used by the king as a selective tool for honouring and co-opting certain individuals by way of social and/or symbolic elevation. On the other hand, all Nubian donation stelae recording "fields of *nmḥ*" are dated from Ramesside times, a period when Nubian elites left their towns (that had remained separate from Egyptian settlements until then) and settled within Egyptian localities in that region. Temples were then the most important foci of institutional power and wealth in the Nubian territory (O'Connor 1993, 61).

As for the first mention of a "field of *nmḥ*" in Egypt, it appears for the first time in a letter from Elephantine (a town bordering Nubia) dated from the 11th century BC (Gardiner 1950, 115–124, 128–131). According to this document, the mayor of Elephantine informed his superiors of a "field of *nmḥ*" regularly tilled by some *nmḥw* who paid a rent or tax in gold to the treasury of the Pharaoh; he also stresses the differences between the way in which he cultivated some temple land near Kom Ombo and that used by these same *nmḥw*, as he should deliver 100 sacks of grain to the scribe of the temple. The fact that these *nmḥw* owned gold and paid their taxes or rent in this metal is another fact that points to their well-off condition. It has been argued that "fields of *nmḥ*" might have appeared earlier in Egypt. Thus A. H. Gardiner suggests in his study of the Wilbour papyrus that the status of a special category of land mentioned there, the so-called *apportioning domains*, was comparable to that of "fields of *nmḥ*" (Gardiner 1948b, 206). However this term never appears in this land register. Only later comparable documents, dated from the 11th century BC, such as the aforementioned letter from Elephantine, introduce for the first time this expression (Gasse 1988, 13, 37–38, 97, 105, 213–214). But even in these texts the references to "fields of *nmḥ*" are so rare when compared with other categories of plots that the identification proposed by Gardiner appears quite improbable. Papyrus Louvre AF 6345, for instance, confirms the scarcity of "fields of *nmḥ*". Only three plots are so defined in this land register and, moreover, they only represent a small fraction of the agricultural domains where each was located: 1+x aruras out of 800 in the first case, 40.5 aruras out of 667 in the second and, finally, 10 aruras out of 1800 in the third, respectively. It should be noticed that these fields were also recorded as being *khato* land (a particular type of crown land), that their geographical location was very precise, between the towns of Inmut and Iatity, to the north of Akhmim, and that they were attached to the Pharaoh's warehouses (Gasse 1988, 59).

From the beginning of the 1st millennium BC references to "fields of *nmḥ*" become more frequent in the Egyptian documents, especially the transactions passed on between some members of the royal family and individuals. This is the case, for instance, of the funerary endowment established by Sheshonq I (945–924 BC) for the statue of his father in the temple of Osiris at Abydos, and which included 100 aruras of "fields of *nmḥ*" managed by a *jḥwtj* (Blackman 1941; Ritner 2009b, 166–172).

Henuttawy, sister and wife of Smendes II, great priest of Amun, declared that she had bought some land, including "fields of *nmḥ*" (Winand 2003, 603–672; Muhs 2009; Ritner 2009b, 138–143). As for princess Maatkare, she obtained, when she was just a child, some property that she had bought as well as "anything of any sort that the people of the land sold to her" and which was recorded as goods of *nmḥw* (Winand 2003, 672–690; Ritner 2009b, 163–165). As for Iuwelot, great priest of Amun and son of king Osorkon I (924–889 BC), he acquired a domain measuring 556 aruras that he bequeathed to his son; the land, located in the domain of Amun but also considered to be depending on the royal domain, was considered collectively as "fields of *nmḥ*" (lines 3, 6, 8), a heading followed by the description of the actual plots that formed the domain and which were exploited by a special category of tenants called *mnḥ* (different from *nmḥ*; Jansen-Winkeln 2007a, 77–80; Ritner 2009b, 271–278). Another high priest of Amun, Menkheperre, bought a field from about two dozen individuals ("the *nmḥw* of the town"; Weeks & The Epigraphic Survey 1981, 17–20; Römer 1994, 571–577; Ritner 2009b, 130–135). Finally, princess Karo(m)ama, daughter of Takelot II (850–825 BC), obtained by inheritance a field of 35 aruras formed by riverine land and "fields of *nmḥ*" (Jansen-Winkeln 2007a, 161; Ritner 2009b, 379–380).

Other documents concerning "fields of *nmḥ*" record instead transactions between ordinary individuals. This is the case of a stela dated from 655 BC, found near Karnak, concerning the sale or donation between a scribe and a priestess of a "high field of *nmḥ*" of 10 aruras, located in the domain of Amun (Legrain 1906; Meeks 1979, 612 n. 22 and 673). As for papyrus Turin 2118-2121, it describes in detail several transactions that occurred over a period of fifteen years, around 650 BC, related to a "field of *nmḥ*" of about 2.5 ha located in the domain of Amun, in the Theban region. The field had originally been bequeathed to the children and later to the grandchildren of the original owners until it was finally sold to another person (Pernigotti 1975). Papyrus Louvre E 10935 also makes it possible to follow the ups and downs of a "high field of *nmḥ*" of about 5.5 ha over an extensive period of time (628–556 BC). Located in the domain of Amun in the region of Coptos, it was successively passed on to different members of the clergy and the royal household, until it was finally transferred to the pious endowment established for the mother of the ultimate buyer (Pestman 1994, 35–42). As for British Museum papyrus 10117, dated from 542 BC, it deals with the sale of a "high field of *nmḥ*" of about 8 ha located in the domain of Amun and which had remained in the hands of the same family for four generations, including its sale to a third party and its later purchase by this family again (Malinine & Pirenne 1950, 25–28). Finally, papyrus Loeb 68 confirms the sale of a "field of *nmḥ*" of one arura in 502 BC, but the precise location of the plot is not known due to the poor state of preservation of this document (Malinine & Pirenne 1950, 30–32). As in the case of the epigraphical inscriptions dealing with "fields of *nmḥ*", the papyrological evidence also shows that this category of land was only attested in Upper Egypt, thus suggesting that it was an agricultural phenomenon that was very restricted from a geographical point of view.

From all these references it is possible to draw three main conclusions. First, "fields of *nmḥ*" were part of the landed assets of temples but they were exploited by individuals entitled to make free use of their rights over this category of land, such as selling or leasing it to a third party or bequeathing it to their heirs. Secondly, members of the royal family and of the highest elite of the country did not hesitate to buy this kind of fields from ordinary individuals in order to create private agricultural domains within a cult institution. This characteristic reminds us of another more ancient term, *s3ḥ*, which had the basic meaning of "endowment", "being beneficiary of an endowment"; their holders were usually dignitaries rewarded by the crown with a field (also located in a temple domain) and who could also hold priestly functions (van den Boorn 1988, 187–188).[2] Finally, the scarce references to "fields of *nmḥ*" in the donation stelae and in the late 2nd and early 1st millennium BC land registers, as well as their (usually) relatively modest dimensions, suggest that their importance was quite limited within the pharaonic land tenure system. However, their dimensions were in many cases larger than the average tenure needed to feed a peasant family (about 5 aruras or 1.25 ha). Furthermore, the rarity of the "fields of *nmḥ*" is also evident from the analysis of the land leases dated from the Kushite, Saite and Achaemenid periods (Hughes 1952; Donker van Heel 1996; 1997; 1998c; 1999). Only one plot in the entire corpus was explicitly defined as being a "field of *nmḥ*" (Donker van Heel 1997).

Other documents relative to the exploitation of temple land (Cruz-Uribe 2000; 2004) and the fields of individuals (Parker 1962, 49–52; Porten & Szubin 1995; Vleeming 1991, 72–93) also lack any mention of this type of tenure. It may then be concluded that transactions concerning "fields of *nmḥ*" only involved, on the one hand, the rural elite and small but relatively well-off landholders and, on the other hand, temples and members of the royalty and the high priesthood of Amun. Unfortunately there are few clues as to the origins of the "fields of *nmḥ*" held by temples (purchase? Cession by individuals? Royal dispositions?). Nevertheless, 1) the fact that members of the highest levels of Egyptian society (including the royal family) bought this kind of plot from, say, the "*nmḥw* of the town"; 2) that holders of "fields of *nmḥ*" could buy, sell and dispose of them at will, and 3) that they could pay their taxes/rent directly to the royal treasury, probably point to the original sale, cession or donation of private tenures to temples, thus formally transformed into temple land but subject nevertheless to some restrictions. Thanks to these transactions it may be posited that the original owner of a field put himself under the protection of a sanctuary, established useful connections with a powerful institution (and its influential rulers) and assured the transmission of the land in the hands of his direct descendants, ideally "from son to son, and from heir to heir", while avoiding any intrusion or claim from collateral branches of his own extended family, as stated in the famous Apanage stela (Jansen-Winkeln 2007a, 77–80; Ritner 2009b, 271–278).

As for the temple, it also profited from the transaction. The land thus acquired enabled the sanctuaries to expand their sphere of influence thanks to the incorporation of certain eminent members of the local society and their property; certainly the rights over the land thus obtained could be sold or transferred to a third party, but the fields nevertheless remained part of the domain (*pr* lit. house) of the God. To sum up, these transactions may be interpreted more as strategies aimed at preserving the property of wealthy individuals as well as instruments of social promotion than a particular modality of cultivation of institutional land. In the period of political division and internal turmoil that followed the loss of the Egyptian empire (and the sources of income with went with it), the domain of Amun became the most powerful and stable institution in Upper Egypt, the only region where "fields of *nmḥ*" are attested after the end of the New Kingdom. Holding temple land tenures, priestly positions and establishing some kind of relation with temples appeared to be attractive if not indispensable sources of wealth, power and social position for both higher and lower elites in an otherwise uncertain world (Moreno García 2013a; 2013b). All these facts could explain the importance acquired by "fields of *nmḥ*" in 1st millennium Upper Egypt; also the quest for legitimacy through lengthy genealogies evoking priestly positions and contacts with temples held by single families for many generations, a practice that was to expand considerably in private monuments during the first half of the 1st millennium BC (Jansen-Winkeln 2005; 2006; Bierbrier 2006). In this vein, papyrus Louvre E 10935, quoted *supra*, provides a further argument as "fields of *nmḥ*" were used there by individuals in order to create a pious foundation.

If this interpretation of "fields of *nmḥ*" is correct, it would be possible to better understand the parallel expansion of the "fields of *nmḥ*" in Upper Egypt and of the donation stelae in Lower Egypt from the very end of the 2nd millennium BC. Two different but contemporary developments that point in both cases to temples as centres of institutional stability, of agricultural wealth and of reorganization of the local elites around them. Both phenomena would then reveal a particular modality of integration of the local elites within the economic and social networks dominated by temples. Temples became not only centres of economic activity and political authority, but also of institutional stability in a context marked by political fragmentation following the end of the New Kingdom. Hence they could guarantee the consolidation and transmission of the landed assets of certain sectors of the elite within their own families. As quoted before, the domain of Amun was the uncontested dominant power in Upper Egypt, and "fields of *nmḥ*" provided local elites with a privileged tool (among others) for obtaining security, income and power. Thus, for example, the demotic literature presents the notables of the villages as the main local authorities, and their ties to the local temples as essential in order to strengthen their authority, as in the case of a demotic literary text where a local potentate (lit. a "great man") was also a priest in the local temple, a profitable source of income, as he obtained part of the agricultural income of the sanctuary because of his condition of priest and, in addition, he also exploited some fields of the temple as a cultivator in exchange for a part of the harvest; the considerable wealth thus amassed allowed him to pay wages to the personnel of the temple, who were thus considered his clients (the text states that he had "acquired" them) and he could even marry his sons and daughters to priests and potentates (lit. "great men") of another town. As in other periods of Egyptian history, access to temple land was crucial for the social and economic reproduction of the pharaonic elite (Tait 2008–2009, 115–124).

Lower Egypt, by contrast, witnessed the gradual vanishing of the last remnants of the monarchy that had once ruled all over Egypt. In its place emerged a multitude of principalities subject to foreign influence and, eventually, to conflictual relations between them (Libyans, Kushites, Assyrians). Under these conditions, Lower Egyptian temples played a role that was very similar to that of the Domain of Amun in Upper Egypt, only on a more local scale. In fact, the chronology and geographical location of the numerous donation stelae from this period closely follows the emergence and consolidation of the principalities of the Delta (Meeks 1979, 614–619). It comes as no surprise therefore that donation stelae were rare where and when a unified monarchy governed all Egypt, even if nominally in some areas of the country, as happened during the 21st dynasty (1069–945 BC). This situation changed during the following dynasty, when the royal authority gradually vanished even in Lower Egypt, its main stronghold; a noteworthy sign being the modest royal donations to the temples in this region (Bickel *et al.* 1998) compared to the exponential increase in the number of donation stelae that occurred at the same time. Finally, the absence of any mention of "fields of *nmḥ*" in Lower Egypt, even after the reunification of the country under the Saite kings, and the continuity of donation stelae there probably obeys local particularities perhaps linked to the importance of tribal property or the weight of Libyan traditions and rulers in this part of the country during the first centuries of the 1st millennium BC (Ritner 2009a, 337). Furthermore, the abundant donation stelae in Lower Egypt could be taken to be expressions of a particular form of visibility and social elevation developed by the local elite in a dynamic and fluid society, well integrated in the vibrant exchange networks of the Mediterranean. Upper Egypt, by contrast, appears more rigid and isolated, far from the Mediterranean and dominated by a powerful single institution heir to the political structures in place during the New Kingdom.

Mnḥ: *a controversial category of tenants*

From the very end of the New Kingdom a new category of tenant appears in the written record, the *mnḥw* (sing. *mnḥ*) (Moreno García 2011). The basic meaning of this term is "youngster", but its occasional mention in contexts referring to military personnel led to the idea that *mnḥ* also meant "recruit" and that in peace time *mnḥw* also cultivated the land either for soldiers or for landowners (Gardiner 1947, 214; Vleeming 1993, 58; Allam 1994). However their social condition seems to have been more complex. The *Apanage* stela, for instance, shows that the owners of "fields of *nmḥ*" were military men (shield bearers), "ladies" (*ʿnḫ(t) n n(j)wt* lit. the living one of the town) and *mnḥw*. Having in mind that lady Nesi held a "field of *nmḥ*" of five aruras and was also considered a *mnḥ*, it may be concluded that *mnḥw* were not necessarily military personnel as the term also included women. Other *mnḥw* recorded in this document held quite extensive agricultural domains, of 71, 45 and 37 aruras (about 18, 11 and 9 ha respectively: Jansen-Winkeln 2007a, 77–80; Ritner 2009b, 271–278). They appear to have been quite well-off when compared to ordinary peasants (at least in some cases, as in this document) and their social condition, once again, was not directly linked to the exercise of military functions. Furthermore, the fact that they could also hold "fields of *nmḥ*" points to an economic independence which, simply, did not correspond to their stereotypical depiction as dependants in some texts. Quite the contrary, the *mnḥw* mentioned in the *Apanage* stela reminds us of the well-off *jḥwtjw* of the Wilbour papyrus, as much for the (sometimes considerable) size of their tenures as for their recording together with eminent members of the local society, like "ladies" and officers. A passage from an early 9th century BC fragmentary inscription found at Elephantine seems precisely to consider both social categories as similar (Seidlmayer 1982, 329–334; Jansen-Winkeln 2007a, 120–121), while a middle 8th century BC unpublished papyrus from Vienna contains a column with a list of *mnḥw* and another column with a list of *jḥwtjw* (papyrus Vienna D 12011b: Vittmann 2015b, 396). Contemporary documents contain either a long list of *mnḥw* (papyrus Vienna D 12013, II: Vittmann 2015b, 396 n. 58) or a list of *mnḥw* with Libyan names (papyrus Vienna D 12011 c II: Vittmann 2015b, 396-397), while some also appear in the archive of El-Hibeh, from the late 11th–early 10th century BC (Lefèvre 2012 and pers. comm.). Be that as it may, the condition of *mnḥw* as landholders is corroborated by other land registers where they appear in this role, as in papyrus Reinhardt (Vleeming 1993, 33 and 35). In any case it is quite difficult to get a more precise idea of the characteristics of this social group for lack of sources. But judging from the extant evidence it appears quite reductive to equate *mnḥw* to military personnel. Their emergence in texts from the very end of the 2nd millennium and the early 1st millennium BC points once more to substantial changes in the social organization of pharaonic agriculture during this period of transition (Moreno García 2011).

The emergence of land leases (7th–6th centuries BC)

A real novelty?

The crisis of the Near Eastern palatial systems at the end of the Late Bronze Age was followed by the emergence of new land and maritime trade routes, the increasing role of private networks of exchange, the appearance of written contracts in areas where they were absent (Lüddeckens 1960; Donker van Heel 1990; Martin 1995; Ritner 2002) and the consolidation of small polities apparently linked to trade activities and the control of caravan routes (Phoenician and South Arabian city-states, Aramaean kingdoms, Moab, Edom, Ammon, etc.). The increasing participation of Egypt in these circuits of exchange during the 1st millennium BC involved the development of contracts in current economic and legal activities, especially marriage contracts (Lüddeckens 1960), divisions of property and land leases (Martin 1995). Here, an individual or an institution leased some land to an individual tenant (or a collective group of tenants) in exchange for a rent, usually a percentage of the harvest. The expansion of this practice appears then to have been concomitant with the increasingly limited role played by the *jḥwtjw* from the end of the New Kingdom and, consequently, with the development of other forms of exploitation of temple land involving the participation of free tenants (*nmḥw, mnḥw*). In this vein, the analysis of the Kushite (747–656 BC) and Saite (664–525 BC) land leases is particularly relevant (Hughes 1952; Donker van Heel 1996; 1997; 1998a; 1998c; 1998d; 1999; 2014b), especially when considering their impact on agricultural practices and the social relations built upon them (Eyre 1997; 2004).

The well known corpus of land leases, mainly from the Saite period, has recently been enriched with a new and earlier group of texts dating from the Kushite period. Nevertheless the expression "Kushite and Saite land leases" is somewhat misleading, as Table 10.1 reveals.

The data from this table indeed shows that the known land leases were not uniformly distributed during the period considered. In fact, all of them are dated from the reigns of Taharqa and Amasis (those written during the Achaemenid rule over Egypt or later are not considered in this study). It would be tempting to ascribe this particularity simply to the random nature of discoveries, especially when considering that these reigns were also the best documented ones of the entire Kushite-Saite period from a papyrological point of view, while papyri from other reigns were much scarcer. However, this possibility might be ruled out because of the absence of land leases dated from Psamtik I and Darius I in spite of the relative abundance of demotic and abnormal hieratic documents produced under their reigns.

Table 10.1: Land leases (7th–6th centuries BC)

King	*Documents*[1]	*Documents by regnal year*	*Land leases*	*Leases/documents*
Piye (747–716)	2	0.06	0	0
Shabaka (716–702)	2	0.14	0	0
Taharqa (690–664)	21	0.80	5	23.80%
Psamtik I (664–610)	14	0.26	0	0
Necho II (610–595)	1	0.06	0	0
Psamtik II (595–589)	3	0.50	0	0
Apries (589–570)	4	0.21	0	0
Amasis (570–526)	48	1.06	9	18.75%
Cambyses (525–522)	5	1.66	0	0
Darius I (522–486)	82[2]	2.15	3[3]	3.66%

[1]Papyrus in abnormal hieratic and demotic (Depauw 2008 [Version 1.0, February 2007]);
[2]Four written in Aramaic; [3]One written in Aramaic and another one, in demotic, still unpublished (papyrus Moscou I.1.δ.424)

Another element suggests that very particular circumstances affected the reigns of Taharqa and Amasis and influenced the production of abundant land leases. It can be observed that a special category of ritual personnel played a dominant role in these documents, the funerary priests of relatively modest condition known as *choachytes*, present in 11 out of the 14 land leases from the reigns of Taharqa and Amasis. The sources relative to *choachytes* are abundant and concern above all the Theban *choachytes*, though some documents attest their presence at Memphis as well (Thompson 1988, 170–174, 180; Donker van Heel 1998b; Andrews 2004). Many Theban papyri from the 7th and 6th centuries BC record their private transactions, such as the acquisition of slaves and cultivators (Malinine 1951; 1982, 94–95), the division of houses (Malinine 1982, 96–97), loans, purchases and the sale of diverse sources of income (Malinine 1953, 102–116; Cruz-Uribe 1980), etc., thus making it possible to follow the careers and economic strategies of some of the best documented individual cases (Donker van Heel 2012; 2014). But what is really striking is the abundance of land leases during the reigns of Taharqa and Amasis and their importance in the economic choices and strategies of *choachytes*, in sharp contrast to later periods. Thus, for instance, while land leases are frequently attested in Ptolemaic documents (Felber 1997), *choachytes* are nevertheless almost entirely absent from them. What is more, the rich corpus of papyri dealing with the affairs of the Theban *choachytes* in the 2nd century BC (84 documents) contain mainly letters and the records of diverse types of transactions, but only one land lease (Pestman 1993). This fact has led several authors to think that the material conditions of Ptolemaic *choachytes* were more modest than those of other categories of priests and ritual personnel, such as lector-priests, usually recorded as holders of land tenures (Vleeming 1995, 245). Against this observation it might be argued that the social condition of *choachytes* was always relatively modest and, therefore, what is actually surprising is not their almost complete absence from Ptolemaic land leases but, on the contrary, their predominance in similar Kushite and Saite documents. To put it another way, the real questions to be answered are why Kushite and Saite land leases were restricted to the reigns of Taharqa and Amasis, why modest ritual personnel such as *choachytes* and others played so eminent a role in these agrarian transactions and, finally, why *choachytes* from later periods showed so little interest in (or had so limited access to) the possession of arable holdings.

The term "arable" may cast some light on these questions, especially because of the apparent similarity between the economic choices and strategies of Kushite and Saite *choachytes* and those of former Upper Egyptian tenants such as the *nmḥw*. It should be remembered that the bulk of the documentary evidence at our disposal concerns Upper Egyptian *choachytes*, with the only exception being some scattered references to their Memphite colleagues. After the end of the New Kingdom, when temples (most notably the Domain of Amun) were the dominant institutions in Upper Egypt, the fact of establishing ties with them was apparently indispensable in order to gain access to influential centres of power, wealth and decision-making. At the same time, the demise of the pharaonic empire in Nubia and the Levant deprived the highest elite of important sources of income. This further strengthened the role of temple land in Upper Egypt as an essential source of income for the local elites in a context of increasing ruralisation, faced with an independent Nubia, far from a Mediterranean area in full economic expansion and confronted with a Lower Egypt experiencing deep changes, from urbanization to agricultural development and integration in the trade networks of the Eastern Mediterranean and the Near East. Under these conditions, the productive choices and economic strategies of Upper Egyptian landholders such as the *nmḥw* of the late 2nd and early 1st millennium BC may be interpreted as a trend towards ruralization, in the wider context of a "return to the land" developed by the local elites now deprived of other sources of wealth, prestige and promotion after the loss of the imperial conquests. This trend might have been further boosted by the scarcity of the traditional sources of workforce that sustained the *jḥwtj*-system and the subsequent increasing participation of individuals in order to exploit the land owned by the temples. The spread of contractual practices in the agricultural domain is but an illustration of the influence and the weight of private economic transactions in the economies of the Iron Age.

In the light of these considerations it may be posited that the land leases involving the Theban *choachytes* confirm the importance of temple land given the local economic conditions, where alternative opportunities for personal enrichment were rare for modest local elites. Hence the activities of the female Theban *choachyte* Tsenhor, of the *choachyte* Djekhy and his son, and of some temple goose farmers from the beginning of the 5th century BC are in all probability quite representative of the economic possibilities open to this social sector linked to the temples of Upper Egypt: loans, purchase of cattle and slaves, transactions with building plots, lease of temple land, etc. (Vleeming 1991; Pestman 1994; Donker van Heel 1996; 2012; 2014a). Later on, the conquest and subsequent integration of Egypt as part of the great empires that encompassed much of the Eastern Mediterranean and the Near East (Assyrian, Achaemenid and Macedonian empires) opened new venues for economic diversity at the disposal of these modest elites. Thus loans, small trading activities, investment in building plots, "traffic" of priestly positions, etc., probably became more lucrative than the uncertainties associated with agriculture. This would explain why the Theban *choachytes* from the Ptolemaic Period turned away from land leases and, like other modest ritual and priestly personnel, involved themselves in other lucrative activities such as small trade (Agut-Labordère 2011a; 2011b; 2011c; Chankowski 2001). However, the sources reveal that in previous centuries they regarded access to temple land as an attractive option. One example is a set of papyri which describe the story of a plot of land between 539 and 497 BC. It was a "field of *nmḥ*" of 33 aruras (about 8.9 ha) held by a family of priests for several generations until its final sale to an individual bearing no titles called Ankhsematawy (Malinine & Pirenne 1950, 25–28). But in 497 BC a *choachyte* turned to the authorities and twice claimed before them in order to be authorized to work on this plot, and to this effect he showed a document on behalf of Ankhsematawy (Cruz-Uribe 2000).

Whether the ruralisation of Upper Egyptian elites and their "return to land" may partly explain why Kushite and Saite *choachytes* leased institutional land, other circumstances may also help understand why they did so during the reigns of Taharqa and Amasis, when Egyptian foreign policy became deeply involved in the affairs of the Levant. The recent discovery of an inscription referring to the wars between Amasis and the Babylonians around 582 BC is but another proof of the pharaonic involvement in the politics of the Eastern Mediterranean during the first half of the 1st millennium BC (Abd el-Maksoud & Valbelle 2013). The wars of the Kushite and Saite kings against the Assyrian and the Neo-Babylonian empires, the extended use of mercenaries in the Saite armies and, finally, the Saite diplomatic gifts to the Greek sanctuaries in search of allies (particularly in Amasis times), must have been a heavy burden on Egyptian resources and the royal treasury. Amasis, in fact, allegedly introduced a sort of income tax whereby each Egyptian should declare the amount of his wealth and revenue. Another king, Teos/Tachos, second pharaoh of the 30th dynasty, borrowed from the priests "until the end of the war against the Persians" (Dunand 1973, 30). It is then quite possible that such fiscal pressure on the resources of the country, that also reached the temples, induced these cult institutions to increase their agricultural production. An abnormal hieratic tablet from the reign of Amasis reveals the zeal of his agents when collecting the grain tax due to the king in the localities of Dendera and Elephantine. From a reference on the verso of the document we learn that the tax was paid by the temples (Černy 1932), and its amount (about 10% of the harvest according to other sources) was 825 artabas/month at Dendera, which corresponds to a yearly estimated production of 99,000 artabas and to a temple agricultural domain of about 5000 aruras (1350 ha). These figures are very similar to those known from other provincial temples (Moreno García 2006b, 123–124).

If *choachytes* were tempted (or more or less forced) to till temple land in a context of increasing fiscal pressure, this would explain another characteristic of the land leases in which they appear. In seven out of eleven land leases related to them the lessee was not a single individual but a collective formed by two, five and, in one case, fifteen people. This circumstance raises many questions about the profitability of such agricultural ventures, unless the plots cultivated were quite substantial. Two other land leases whose protagonists were herders of the God Montu present similar characteristics, as the lessees were also a group of people. In one case a herder leased a cow together with the land, thus increasing the rent to be paid. Unfortunately, the extension of the fields involved in these transactions is very rarely evoked, and the available references range between 1.25 ha (papyrus Louvre E 7844) to x+2 ha (papyrus Louvre E 7852) and 9.25 ha (cf. *supra*). These data remind us of later references, as in the case of a field of about 2,25 ha cultivated by several members of the same family of *choachytes* (Pestman 1994, 4 and 13). When considering the modest social status of *choachytes* and the relatively reduced extension of their tenures, it is possible that their collective exploitation of a plot leased from a temple obeyed an economic strategy seeking two possible goals: either to perform fiscal duties otherwise too heavy for a single cultivator or to profit from exceptional possibilities to do business and make some additional income. In any case the connections with powerful institutions and influential people obtained through these agricultural contracts also enabled the lessees to integrate themselves within the main foci of local power, the temples. In any case the first of these goals was apparently closer to reality. The harvest tax receipts indeed show the modest income obtained from the plots they exploited and later on, during the centuries that followed the Macedonian conquest of Egypt, *choachytes* were much less eager to cultivate temple land.

The land leases dating from the reign of Amasis were part of the private archive of a family of Theban *choachytes* that also included, among other documents, some harvest tax receipts (Donker van Heel 1996, documents 3, 12, 14–16; 2012). These receipts complete the information provided by the land leases and, furthermore, also make it possible to calculate the extension of the plots leased from the owning institutions. The tax paid oscillated between five and six sacks (Donker van Heel 1996, documents 12, 14–15), thus pointing to a harvest of about 50–60 sacks (the harvest tax was 10%) and, consequently, to plots of 5–6 aruras (1.25–1.50 ha); the tax quoted in document 16 was larger, 37 sacks (which corresponds to a field of about 37 aruras or 10 ha), but it was cultivated by three people, including a *choachyte* and a herder of the domain of the God Montu. Bearing in mind that a field of 5 aruras (1.25 ha) was considered sufficient to provide for the needs of a peasant family, and that Ramesside and later papyri such as the Wilbour papyrus show that many standard plots granted by temples also measured five aruras (Katary 1999, 75–77; Vleeming 1991, 46–59), the socio-economic status of *choachytes* seems to have been a modest one. However, when harvest tax receipts became really abundant, in the Ptolemaic period, *choachytes* were conspicuously absent from the personnel who exploited the land of the temples (Kaplony-Heckel 2000; 2001a; 2001b; 2004), a fact in accordance with the conclusions reached from the analysis of the Ptolemaic land leases: after the Kushite and Saite periods *choachytes* seem to have not been interested at all in the exploitation of temple land. Thus, their predominance in the Kushite and Saite land leases and harvest tax points to very precise and exceptional conditions occurring during the reigns of Taharqa and Amasis.

To sum up, it appears that the production of Kushite and Saite land leases obeys, precisely, very particular circumstances linked to the policies followed by kings Taharqa and Amasis. Their wars against Assyrians and Neo-Babylonians, not to speak of internal challenges to their authority, demanded the increasing mobilization of the resources of the country, including those in the hands of temples. The temple endowments granted by Taharqa both in Egypt and Nubia, the references to the fiscal measures taken by Amasis, as well as the restoration and endowment of numerous temples under his reign, could be partly justified by the needs of their war efforts, such as the recruitment of tens of thousands of mercenaries by the Saite kings (Agut-Labordère 2012a; 2012b; Iancu 2014). In any case, the use of contracts in agricultural ventures and the use of traditional forms of work to cultivate temple land (including *corvée*) reveal that Egypt did not escape the economic transformations that affected other areas of the Mediterranean and the Near East during the early Iron Age. What is more, these changes also reached a region and an economy marked by their rural nature, like Upper Egypt, and their main institutions (temples). To put it another way, although the production of land leases might obey very particular political and social circumstances, their use is also concomitant with long-term economic trends, such as the gradual disappearance of the *jḥwtj*-system and the increasing participation of individuals and free tenants in the exploitation of temple land. Finally, the close relationship between wars, the arrival of prisoners and deportees and the *jḥwtj*-system seems to have briefly flourished again under the reigns of Kushite pharaohs Piyi (747–716 BC) and Taharqa (690–664 BC), when some texts refer to slaves designated by the term "northerner", delivered to sanctuaries and called, in some instances, *jḥwtjw* (Malinine 1951). However, the importance of these late *jḥwtjw* was rather ephemeral due, among other circumstances, to the emergence of the first agrarian contracts during the reign of Taharqa. It must also be noted that the flow of prisoners also existed in the opposite direction, when Egyptians were captured and settled in Mesopotamia (Wiseman 1966; Bongenaar & Haring 1994; Stolper 1998).

Agrarian contracts and rural workforce

Most of the Kushite and Saite land leases concern fields located in the Domain of Amun and leased by the mediation of a priest to an individual or to a group who would pay a percentage of the harvest in return (usually ¼ or ⅓). In two cases the lessor of the field was a *choachyte* (Donker van Heel 1996, documents 17 and 21), but the circumstances surrounding both transactions appear to have been rather atypical. In one case he receives the whole harvest once the harvest tax had been deducted (perhaps the lease actually conceals the reimbursement of a debt: Donker van Heel 1996, document 21). In the other case, he and the lessee pay the harvest tax together and they share the rest on equal terms (Donker van Heel 1996, document 17); as the *choachyte* receives then ½ of the harvest instead of the customary ¼ or ⅓ (he should have also paid the totality of the harvest tax), it is also possible that these advantageous conditions also conceal the reimbursement of a debt or of a service. In fact, loans figure among the economic activities usually developed by *choachytes*. Furthermore, in both cases the *choachytes* obtained the fields as remuneration in exchange for their funerary services, and this could lead to rather complex situations: according to papyrus Louvre E 7836 a field belonging to the Domain of Amun was granted to a priest who, subsequently, transferred it to a *choachyte* as payment in order to carry out funerary ceremonies; the field thus became the "endowment field" of the *choachyte*. However the latter did not exploit the land himself, so he leased it to a collective group of lessees including a herder and his partners (Donker van Heel 1996, document 17). Although *choachytes* were usually remunerated with diverse goods and foodstuff for their ritual services, there are actually some instances in which they were paid with fields (Donker van

Heel 1996, documents 17 and 21; Pestman 1994, documents 1 and 14). Hence, in these two cases a collective group of lessees ensured the actual cultivation of the field, while in two other similar known cases, both of them dating from the first Persian domination over Egypt (reign of Darius I), the fields were apparently exploited on a familial basis (Pestman 1994, 4). The generally modest extension of the fields exploited or in the hands of *choachytes* suggests that the tenants usually exploited the land on their own, unless very favourable conditions convinced them to lease the land to a third party in order to have a debt or a service reimbursed.

Some land leases include an indemnifying provision in case the lessee damaged the fields leased out. This was expressed by a standardized formula in which the lessee was defined as being a *jḥwtj* (Donker van Heel 1996, 208–209 and documents 6, 19 and 20), while other dispositions make it clear that he should cultivate the land in the way *jḥwtjw* customarily did (Donker van Heel 1996, document 19); moreover, if he was to rent a yoke of oxen, it was called "a *jḥwtj*'s yoke". These examples reveal the semantic changes that affected the basic meaning of the term *jḥwtj* from the early 1st millennium BC, to the point that in later times it became synonymous with peasant. This change is explicitly quoted in the *Demotic Chronicle* (a prophetic text going back to the early Ptolemaic period), where in a passage including the term *jḥwtj* ("the *jḥwtj* cries ...") this was translated as *wjʿ* "peasant" in the comment that accompanies the text ("this means: the peasant will go to the field crying over the wheat": *Demotic Chronicle* XII:8; Spiegelberg 1914, 13 and 21). Another example appears in a late literary text known as *The Brooklyn Teaching*: "the *jḥwtj* is chief of every occupation. For him do they work. His hands are their breath of life" (Jasnow 1992, 114). A similar meaning occurs in the triumphal stela of Piyi: "capture its people, its herds, its ships upon the river! Do not allow the *jḥwtjw* to go forth to the fields! Do not allow the plowmen to plow!" (line 9: Grimal 1981, 22–23; Jansen-Winkeln 2007b, 338; Ritner 2009b, 478).

Finally, the first "juridical manuals" attested in Egypt further confirm the importance of contracts in the agricultural sphere, as they evoke for the first time the work of peasants (*wjʿ*) in the context of potential conflicts that arose between lessors and lessees. In fact these manuals reveal the importance and normal use of contracts in Egyptian society, not only in agriculture but in such diverse fields as renting houses and fields, silver loans and the division of family property (Donker van Heel 1990; Lippert 2004).

Beyond *nmḥw* and agrarian contracts: other modalities of rural workforce (first half of the 1st millennium BC)

As stated in previous pages, the gradual disappearance of the *jḥwtj*-system in the exploitation of land held by institutions such as temples was concomitant, not only with the emergence of new modalities of work, but also with the expansion of traditional ones. The partial use of *corvée* work (*bḥ*) in the cultivation of *ʿḥt*-land, instead of *jḥwtjw*, is an excellent case in view of this transformation. Another one is the possible mention of seasonal *corvée* workers, designated by the old term *mrt* (the reading is not certain), in a papyrus evoking the delivery of grain under the supervision of the scribes of some temples (Fischer-Elfert 1989). Other documents record the endowments granted by some pharaohs to several temples, but the fact that they only mention a *jḥwtj* in each case further confirms that this category of cultivators was becoming increasingly rare (Blackman 1941; Graefe & Wassef 1979; Perdu 2002, 17–29). In general, these texts celebrate the endowments of fields, cattle and people granted by the king to a sanctuary, usually with no further precision about the status of the personnel involved in the donations (Hughes & The Epigraphic Survey 1954, pl. 16; Caminos 1958, 54 §40; Jansen-Winkeln 2007a, 166). However, inspiration from artistic and epigraphic models of the past (the so-called archaism of the Late Period: Der Manuelian 1994; Morkot 2003; Payraudeau 2007), apparent in the inscriptions and works of art of the first half of the 1st millennium BC, also left their mark with the reintroduction of older terms fallen into disuse, such as *mrt*-workers or *ʿḥt*-land. This circumstance explains why both terms appear in the Memphis decree of Apries, which reproduced the vocabulary and formulae of the royal decrees of the 3rd millennium BC (Der Manuelian 1994, 373–380).

The rare *jḥwtjw* still referred to in the sources of the first half of the 1st millennium frequently reveal a social condition quite close to slavery: they were valued in silver and could be bought and sold, as in the case of the prisoner of war mentioned in the papyrus Louvre E 3228c who was also a *jḥwtj* and who was sold for six *deben* of silver (Malinine 1951); or the *jḥwtj* evoked in the stela of Sheshonq I (945–924 BC) and valued at one *deben* and 4⅓ *qite* (Blackman 1941, 85 and 91; Ritner 2009b, 166–172); or the *jḥwtj* of the papyrus Rylands V, a contract whereby he sold himself as a slave for another person. Further papyri concerning this same *jḥwtj* (papyri Rylands III, IV, VI and VII) reveal that he renewed his slave contract several years later (Griffith 1909c, 53–54). As for the stela of the reign of Osorkon II in the temple of Khnum at Elephantine, it declares about a *jḥwtj* who had become a priest illegally that "he is now (again) a *jḥwtj* among the people of poor condition" (Jansen-Winkeln 2007a, 120–121). However, there are also some references to moderately well-off *jḥwtjw*, such as the one who borrowed some grain on the condition of returning it at an interest of 50% (Černy & Parker 1971) or another one at the service of the God Horus of Edfu who bought a cow (Cruz-Uribe 1985, 17–19). These examples are a good illustration of the internal stratification of the Egyptian peasantry in a period when the term *jḥwtj* designated, precisely, the peasant. As in the case of the *jḥwtj* who sold himself as a slave, other documents confirm the social inequalities within peasantry, to the point that in hard times some people were forced to sell not only their land but also themselves to another person, thus becoming their clients or serfs. In return they received some basic goods (grain, cloths, oil, etc.) and were allowed to continue cultivating their former fields (Bakir 1952, 85–86). In other cases, fictive adoptions concealed in fact what represented the enslavement of the person designated by the term *šrj* "son" (Malinine & Pirenne 1950, 76–77; Bakir 1952, pl. 17; Pestman 1994, 37 and 41). Finally, in some cases these transactions enabled the purchaser to consolidate his landed patrimony and to acquire highly-valued tenures, such as plots around a well (an excellent example in Parker 1962, 49–52).

With the conquest and integration of Egypt in the Achaemenid Empire the sources contain scattered references to a certain reorganization (or granting) of some landed tenures, especially at the beginning of the Persian domination (Cruz-Uribe 2004; Vittmann 2015a). Yet the evidence is too scarce to infer fundamental changes in the organization and status of the workforce employed there. It seems then that the modalities of exploitation of institutional land continued unchanged and, in fact, it is possible to detect Egyptians who tilled the land of the foreigners who arrived in the Nile Valley, as in the case of the agricultural domains granted to Achaemenid princes or the field given to a Philistine (Driver 1957, 30–31, 33–34; Kemp 2006[2], 363–364, 371; Porten & Szubin 1994). In the later case, the use of a contract only continued a practice well rooted in Egypt by then, confirmed by some texts of the 5th and 4th centuries BC, including the occasional mention of a Mede (Devauchelle 2002, 135; Vleeming 1991, 72–93; Spiegelberg 1932, 72–75, pls 43–45).

Conclusion

An important change took place in Egypt from the late Ramesside period on, according to crucial evidence provided by documents such as the Wilbour papyrus (12th century BC) and other administrative texts of the late 2nd and early 1st millennium BC (Gardiner 1948a; 1948b; Janssen 1991; 2004; Demarée 2006). During this period the Egyptian sources record for the first time *nmḥw* as holders of crown and temple land and paying their taxes directly to the royal treasury. Contrary to the standard agricultural exploitations and quotas of grain typical of the *jḥwtj*-system, *nmḥw* worked on a different basis, as independent individuals and free tenants who also tilled a special category of temple land (the "fields of *nmḥ*") and who disposed freely of these tenures, selling them to members of the elite, including the royal family itself. The sources also echo other transformations that occurred between the late 2nd and the early 1st millennium BC. The contents of papyrus Reinhardt (10th century BC), for instance, are quite similar to those of the Wilbour papyrus but they nevertheless reveal some significant differences, such as the use of *corvée* work (*bḥ*) in the cultivation of *ꜥḥt*-land instead of *jḥwtjw*, or the rarity of *jḥwtjw* altogether (Vleeming 1993). Similar contemporary documents, such as the Griffith papyri, the Louvre fragments, papyrus Berlin 23252, papyrus Prachov and others, further confirm the scarcity of *jḥwtjw*, but they mention for the first time the "fields of *nmḥ*" in this type of land register (they are conspicuously absent in the Wilbour papyrus as well as in related Ramesside registers: Gasse 1988). Later on, *jḥwtjw* became even rarer in the administrative sources and, in the case of land leases dealing with temple land, they appear only as peasants, not subject to the standardized quotas and tenures typical of the former *jḥwtj*-system.

So the gradual disappearance of the exploitation of institutional land through the *jḥwtj*-system promoted the emergence of new forms of labour, the extended use of traditional ones such as *corvée* work and, especially, the increasing participation of independent cultivators in these agrarian ventures. Among them *nmḥw* figure conspicuously in Upper Egyptian sources, thus pointing to a probable "ruralization" of certain sectors of the local elites in this region: the end of the Egyptian empire in Nubia and the Levant, and of the opportunities for gaining income, prestige and social promotion that went with it, encouraged the rapprochement of this social sector to the temples, the most important source of economic, political and symbolic power in the South. Strategies such as the donations of land to these institutions enabled the local elites to protect part of their landed assets by transferring them to a powerful institution; also to continue to manage these fields even if through the mediation of the temple sphere. By doing so, these potentates could consolidate and secure their patrimonies, benefit from the institutional stability provided by the temples and, finally, integrate themselves into the patronage networks dominated by these centres, the royal family and the Domain of Amun. As for Upper Egyptian sub-elites, such as the *choachytes*, their overwhelming prominence in the preserved land leases from the Kushite and Saite period probably points to a similar strategy, without excluding other circumstantial reasons, such as an increasing tax burden in the context of frequent wars abroad or simply good opportunities for doing business by cultivating temple land. In any case, the increasing importance of land leases reveals the emergence of new forms of economic organization, more decentralised and influenced by the integration of Egypt in the commercial and economic networks of the Mediterranean, the Near East and North-eastern Africa. This also explains the increasing use of contracts in other areas of Egyptian economic and social life, such as marriages, wills, sales, etc.

The particular circumstances of Lower Egypt are more complex and difficult to understand because of the scarcity of administrative sources. However, the expansion of the grants of land to the local temples, in a context of political fragmentation, the emergence of petty polities and the better integration of this region than Upper Egypt into the international networks of exchange, reveals that deep local changes were taking place there. Some social groups were becoming rich and, eager for social promotion, they sought prestige, recognition and social visibility. Temples could provide that. In fact, Lower Egypt became four centuries later the cradle of the monarchy that reunified the country, under the rule of the Saite kings, who established close links with, among others, Cypriot and Greek merchants. We can only guess the reasons underlying a prosperity manifest in urban growth, the building of new temples and the agricultural expansion experienced by this region. It is quite probable that its economic basis was the export of cereals, textiles, horses and luxuries, as well as customs revenue, as attested for later periods (an example in Briant & Descat 1998). In any case, the scarcity of administrative documents makes it quite difficult to know what the characteristics of the agricultural workforce employed in Lower Egyptian temples were. Certainly the *jḥwtj*-system is not attested there after the end of the New Kingdom. But the lack of references to the *nmḥw* suggests the existence of some differences with the South. Perhaps the use of land leases in order to exploit both institutional and private land played a major role in this area, thus explaining the importance of these agreements in the first "juridical manuals", apparently compiled for the first time under the Saite kings in this area and in demotic (the administrative language of the North, in contrast with Abnormal hieratic, prevailing in the South: Martin 2007). Finally, the use of clients, serfs and hired workers in the cultivation of private tenures should not be underestimated, as people in hard times sold both their land and themselves to others in return for staple items and the right to continue cultivating their former fields.

Notes

* This article is a modified version of my article "L'évolution des statuts de la main-d'œuvre rurale en Égypte de la fin du Nouvel Empire à l'époque Saïte (ca. 1150–525 av. J.-C.)", in J. Zurbach (ed.), *La main-d'œuvre agricole en Méditerranée archaïque. Statuts et dynamiques économiques* (Scripta Antiqua 73), 15–48, Bordeaux-Athènes, 2015.

1. As for criminals, cf. Middle Kingdom papyrus Brooklyn 35.1446 as well as Ramesside papyrus Baldwin r° III, 6–8+papyrus Amiens r° IV, 5, 12 and V, 3 (Janssen 2004). Papyrus CGC 58053-58055 also mentions the assignation of criminals and convicts to hard works and their displacement to the islands of the Nile (Kitchen 1968a, 322–325), a practice already in use during the Middle Kingdom, as stated in papyrus Cairo JE 71583, x+38: "bring (here) the conscripts who belong to the rabble" (Luft 2006, 119–128, 166–167).
2. Several inscriptions evoke such royal rewards ranging from 5 to 40 aruras according to the available evidence (Sethe 1927, 1637 and 2078), and which could subsequently be transferred to oher people. That is the case of the transaction recorded in the stela CGC 34507, whereby the "endowment field" (*3ḥt s3ḥ)* of a priest but in the hands of a lady was sold to an overseer of a granary in exchange for seven *qite* of silver (Kitchen 1968b, 155). On the other hand, the endowment decree of king Sobekemsaf I celebrates the reorganisation of the agricultural domain of (God) Montu cultivated until then by *s3ḥ*-people, who should be compensated *"plot for plot, threshing-floor for threshing-floor"* for dropping their rights to the temple land they had held (Helck 1975, 62).

Bibliography

Abd el-Maksoud, M. & D. Valbelle (2013) Une stèle de l'an 7 d'Apriès découverte sur le site de Tell Défenneh, *Revue d'Égyptologie* 64: 1–14.

Agut-Labordère, D. (2011a) L'oracle et l'hoplite. Les élites sacerdotales et l'effort de guerre sous les dynasties égyptiennes indigènes, *Journal of the Economic and Social History of the Orient* 54: 627–645.

Agut-Labordère, D. (2011b) "La vache et les policiers": pratique de l'investissement commercial dans l'Égypte tardive. In B. Legras (ed.), *Transferts culturels et droits dans le monde grec et hellénistique: actes du colloque international (Reims, 14-17 mai 2008)* 269–281, Paris.

Agut-Labordère, D. (2011c) La ΠΑΡΑΘΗΚΗ au Serapeum: les (petites) affaires de Ptolémaios. In A. Jördens & J. F. Quack (eds), *Ägypten zwischen innerem Zwist und äußerem Druck: die Zeit Ptolemaios' VI. bis VIII. Internationales Symposion Heidelberg 16.-19.9.2007*, 276–291, Wiesbaden.

Agut-Labordère, D. (2012a) Plus que des mercenaires! L'intégration des hommes de guerre grecs au service de la monarchie Saïte, *Pallas* 89: 293–306.

Agut-Labordère, D. (2012b) Approche cartographique des relations des pharaons saïtes (664–526) et indépendants (404–342) avec les cités grecques. In L. Capdetrey & J. Zurbach (eds), *Mobilités grecques. Mouvements, réseaux, contacts en Méditerranée de l'époque archaïque à l'époque hellénistique*, 219–234 Bordeaux.

Allam, S. (1994) Implications in the hieratic P. Berlin 8523 registration of land holdings. In B. M. Bryan & D. Lorton (eds), *Essays in Egyptology in Honor of Hans Goedicke*, 1–7 San Antonio.

Andrews, C. A. R. (2004) Papyrus BM 10381: An inheritance of the Memphite choachytes. In F. Hoffmann & H. J. Thissen (eds), *Res severa verum gaudium: Festschrift für Karl-Theodor Zauzich zum 65. Geburtstag am 8. Juni 2004*, 27–32, pl. 1, Leuven.

Bakir, A. M. (1952) *Slavery in Pharaonic Egypt*, Cairo.

Bickel, S., M. Gabolde & P. Tallet (1998) Des annales héliopolitaines de la Troisième Période intermédiaire, *Bulletin de l'Institut Français d'Archéologie Orientale* 98: 31–56.

Bierbrier, M. L. (2006) Genealogy and chronology. In E. Hornung, R. Krauss & D. A. Warburton (eds), *Ancient Egyptian Chronology*, 37–44, Leiden-Boston.

Biston-Moulin, S. (2011) De Sésostris Ier à Kamosis. Note sur un remploi de Karnak, *ENIM* 4: 81–90.

Blackman, A. M. (1941) The stela of Shoshenk, Great Chief of the Meshwesh, *Journal of Egyptian Archaeology* 27: 83–95.

Bongenaar, A. & B. Haring (1994) Egyptians in neo-Babylonian Sippar, *Journal of Cuneiform Studies* 46: 59–72.

Briant, P. & R. Descat (1998) Un registre douanier de la satrapie d'Égypte à l'époque achéménide (TAD C3,7). In N. Grimal & B. Menu (eds), *Le commerce en Égypte ancienne*, 59–104, Cairo.

Caminos, R. A. (1958) *The Chronicle of Prince Osorkon*, Rome.

Černy, J. (1932) The abnormal-hieratic tablet Leiden I 431. In S. Glanville & N. MacDonald Griffith (eds), *Studies Presented to Francis Llewellyn Griffith*, 45–56, pls 2–7, London.

Černy, J. & R. A. Parker (1971) An abnormal hieratic tablet, *Journal of Egyptian Archaeology* 57: 127–131, pl. 35.

Chankowski, V. (ed.) (2001) Les dieux manieurs d'argent: activités bancaires et formes de gestion dans les sanctuaires, *Topoi* 12–13: 9–132.

Cruz-Uribe, E. (1980) A sale of inherited property from the reign of Darius I, *Journal of Egyptian Archaeology* 66: 120–126, pl. 14.

Cruz-Uribe, E. (1985) *Saite and Persian Demotic Cattle Documents. A Study in Legal Forms and Principles in Ancient Egypt*, Chico.

Cruz-Uribe, E. (2000) Two early demotic letters from Thebes (P. dém. Louvre E 3231c and 3231b), *Revue d'Égyptologie* 51: 9–19, pls 1–2.

Cruz-Uribe, E. (2004) Early demotic texts from Heracleopolis. In F. Hoffmann & H. J. Thissen (eds), *Res severa verum gaudium: Festschrift für Karl-Theodor Zauzich zum 65. Geburtstag am 8. Juni 2004*, 59–66, pls 8–9, Leuven.

David, A. (2011) The *nmḥ* and the paradox of the voiceless in the Eloquent Peasant, *Journal of Egyptian Archaeology* 97: 73–85.

Davies, W. V. (2012) The tomb of Sataimau at Hagr Edfu: an overview, *British Museum Studies in Ancient Egypt and Sudan* 20: 47–80.

Demarée, R. J. (2006) *The Bankes Late Ramesside Papyri*, London.

Depauw, M. (2008) *A Chronological Survey of Precisely Dated Demotic and Abnormal Hieratic Sources*, Cologne.

Der Manuelian, P. (1994) *Living in the Past. Studies in Archaism of the Egyptian Twenty-Sixth Dynasty*, London-New York.

Devauchelle, D. (2002) Les archives Michel Malinine conservées au Cabinet d'Égyptologie du Collège de France (Paris). In K. Ryholt, K. (ed.), *Acts of the Seventh International Congress of Demotic Studies*, 131–137, Copenhague.

Donker van Heel, K. (1990) *The Legal Manual of Hermopolis (P. Mattha). Text and Translation*, Leiden.

Donker van Heel, K. (1996) *Abnormal Hieratic and Early Demotic Texts Collected by the Theban Choachytes in the Reign of Amasis: Papyrus from the Louvre Eisenlohr Lot*, Leiden.

Donker van Heel, K. (1997) Papyrus Louvre E 7852: a land lease from the reign of Taharka, *Revue d'Égyptologie* 48: 81–93, pl. 8.

Donker van Heel, K. (1998a) Kushite abnormal hieratic land leases. In Chr. Eyre (ed.), *Proceedings of the Seventh International Congress of Egyptologists*, 339–343.

Donker van Heel, K. (1998b) Papyrus Leiden I 379: The inheritance of the Memphite choachyte Imouthes, *Oudheidkundige Mededeelingen uit het Rijksmuseum van Oudheden te Leiden* 78: 33–57.

Donker van Heel, K. (1998c) Papyrus Louvre E 7856 verso and recto : leasing land in the reign of Taharka, *Revue d'Égyptologie* 49: 91–105, pls 12–13.

Donker van Heel, K. (1998d) Use of land in the Kushite and Saite periods (Egypt, 747–656 and 664–525 B. C.). In B. Haring & R. de Maaijer (eds), *Landless and Hungry? Access to Land in Early and Traditional Societies*, 90–102, Leiden.

Donker van Heel, K. (1999) Papyrus Louvre E 7851 recto and verso : two more land leases from the reign of Taharka, *Revue d'Égyptologie* 50: 135–147, pls 13–14.

Donker van Heel, K. (2004) A day in the life of the ancient Egyptian goatherd Ityaa: abnormal hieratic P. Michaelides 1 and 2 (P. BM EA 10907 and 10906), *Journal of Egyptian Archaeology* 90, 153–166.

Donker van Heel, K. (2012) *Djekhy & Son: Doing Business in Ancient Egypt*, Cairo-New York.

Donker van Heel, K. (2014a) *Mrs Tsenhor: A Female Entrepreneur in Ancient Egypt*, Cairo-New York.

Donker van Heel, K. (2014b) P. Louvre E 7858: another abnormal hieratic puzzle. In B. J. J. Haring, O. E. Kaper & R. van Walsem (eds), *The Workman's Progress: Studies in the Village of Deir el-Medina and Other Documents from Western Thebes in Honour of Rob Demarée* (Egyptologische Uitgaven 28), 43–55, Leiden.

Driver, G. R. (1957) *Aramaic Documents of the Fifth Century B.C.*, Oxford.

Dunand, F. (1973) *Le culte d'Isis dans le Bassin Oriental de la Méditerranée, I, Le culte d'Isis et les Ptolémées*, Leiden.

Eide, T., T. Hägg, R. H. Pierce & L. Török (1994) *Fontes Historiae Nubiorum, vol. I : From the Eighth to the Mid-Fifth Century BC*, Bergen.

Eyre, C. J. (1997) Peasants and "modern" leasing strategies in ancient Egypt, *Journal of the Economic and Social History of the Orient* 40: 367–390.

Eyre, C. J. (2004) How relevant was personal status to the functioning of the rural economy in Pharaonic Egypt ? In B. Menu (ed.), *La dépendance rurale dans l'antiquité égyptienne et proche-orientale*, 157–186, Cairo.

Felber, H. (1997) *Demotische Ackerpachtverträge der Ptolemäerzeit: Untersuchungen zu Aufbau, Entwicklung und inhaltlichen Aspekten einer Gruppe von demotischen Urkunden*, Wiesbaden.

Fischer-Elfert, H.-W. (1989) Zwei Akten aus der Getreideverwaltung der XXI. Dynastie (P. Berlin 14.384 und P. Berlin 23098). In H. Altenmüller & R. Germer (eds), *Miscellanea aegyptologica: Wolfgang Helck zum 75. Geburtstag*, 39–65, pls I–III.

Gardiner, A. H. (1937) *Late-Egyptian Miscellanies*, Brussels.

Gardiner, A H. (1941) Ramesside texts relating to the taxation and transport of corn, *Journal of Egyptian Archaeology* 27: 19–73.

Gardiner, A. H. (1947) *Ancient Egyptian Onomastica*, Oxford.

Gardiner, A. H. (1948a) *Ramesside Administrative Documents*, London-Oxford.

Gardiner, A. H. (1948b) *The Wilbour Papyrus, vol. II: Commentary*, London-Oxford.

Gardiner, A. H. (1950) A protest against unjustified tax-demands, *Revue d'Égyptologie* 6: 115–133.

Gasse, A. (1988) *Données nouvelles administratives et sacerdotales sur l'organisation du domaine d'Amon (XXe–XXIe dynasties) à la lumière des papyrus Prachov, Reinhardt et Grundbuch [avec édition princeps des papyrus Louvre AF 6345 et 6346-6347]*, Cairo.

Gauthier, H. (1913) *Les temples immergés de la Nubie. Le temple d'Amada*. Cairo.

Gnirs, A. M. (1989) Haremhab – ein Staatsreformator ? Neue Betrachtungen zum Haremhab Dekret, *Studien zur altägyptischen Kultur* 16: 83–110.

Graefe, E. & M. Wassef (1979) Eine fromme Stiftung für den Gott Osiris-der-seinen-Anhänger-in-der-Unterwelt-rettet aus dem Jahre 21 des Taharqa (670 v. Chr.), *Mitteilungen des Deutschen Archäologischen Instituts, Abteilung Kairo* 35: 103–118, pl. 17.
Griffith, F. L. (1909a) *Catalogue of the Demotic Papyri in the John Rylands Library*, vol. I, Manchester.
Griffith, F. L. (1909b) *Catalogue of the Demotic Papyri in the John Rylands Library*, vol. II, Manchester.
Griffith, F. L. (1909c) *Catalogue of the Demotic Papyri in the John Rylands Library*, vol. III, Manchester.
Grimal, N.-C. (1981) *La stèle triomphale de Pi('ankh)y au Musée du Caire*, Cairo.
Harari, I (1959) Nature de la stèle de donation de fonction du roi Ahmôsis à la reine Ahmès-Nefertari, *Annales du Service des Antiquités de l'Égypte* 56: 139–201.
Helck, W. (1975) *Historisch-biographische Texte der 2. Zwischenzeit und neue Texte der 18. Dynastie*, Wiesbaden.
Hughes, G. R. (1952) *Saite Demotic Land Leases*, Chicago.
Hughes, G. R. & The Epigraphic Survey (1954) *Reliefs and Inscriptions at Karnak*, vol. III, Chicago.
Iancu, L.-M. (2014) World-systems based on reciprocity. Eastern empires, Aegean polities and Greek mercenaries in the Archaic age, *Romanian Journal of History and International Studies* 1: 53–70.
Jansen-Winkeln, K. (2005) Die Entwicklung der genealogischen Informationen nach dem Neuen Reich. In M. Fitzenreiter (ed.), *Genealogie: Realität und Fiktion von Identität*, 137–145, London.
Jansen-Winkeln, K. (2006) The relevance of genealogical information for Egyptian chronology, *Ägypten und Levant* 16: 257–273.
Jansen-Winkeln, K. (2007a) *Inschriften der Spätzeit, vol. I : Die 21. Dynastie*, Wiesbaden.
Jansen-Winkeln, K. (2007b) *Inschriften der Spätzeit, vol. II : Die 22.-24. Dynastie*, Wiesbaden.
Janssen, J. J. (1991) *Late Ramesside Letters and Communications*, London.
Janssen, J. J. (2004) *Grain Transport in the Ramesside Period : Papyrus Baldwin (BM EA 10061) and Papyrus Amiens*, London.
Jasnow, R. (1992) *A Late Period Hieratic Wisdom Text (P. Brooklyn 47.218.135)*, Chicago.
Jasnow, R. (2001) Pre-demotic Pharaonic sources. In R. Westbrook & R. Jasnow (eds), *Security for Debt in Ancient Near Eastern Law*, 35–45, Leiden-Boston.
Joannès, F. (2004) La dépendance rurale en Babylonie VIIe–IVe siècles av. J.-C. In B. Menu (ed.), *La dépendance rurale dans l'antiquité égyptienne et proche-orientale*, 239–251, Cairo.
Kaplony-Heckel, U. (2000) Demotic ostraca from Thebes: percentages and relations between Pharaoh and the temple, *Journal of the American Research Centre in Egypt* 37: 75–80.
Kaplony-Heckel, U. (2001a) Theben-Ost III: Die r-rx=w-Tempel-Quittungen und ähnliche Texte. Erster Teil: Allgemeiner Teil und Texte Nr. 18-25. *Zeitschrift für Ägyptische Sprache und Altertumskunde* 128: 24–40.
Kaplony-Heckel, U. (2001b) Zur Landwirtschaftsverwaltung in Oberägypten. In B. Palme (ed.), *Wiener Papyri: als Festgabe zum 60. Geburtstag von Hermann Harrauer (P. Harrauer)*, 35–54, Vienna.
Kaplony-Heckel, U. (2004) Rund um die thebanischen Tempel (demotische Ostraka zur Pfründen-Wirtschaft). In F. Hoffmann & H. J. Thissen (ed.), *Res severa verum gaudium: Festschrift für Karl-Theodor Zauzich zum 65. Geburtstag am 8. Juni 2004*, 283–337, Leuven.
Katary, S. L. D. (1999) Land-tenure in the New Kingdom: The role of women smallholders and the military. In A. K. Bowman & E. Rogan (eds), *Agriculture in Egypt: from Pharaonic to Modern Times*, 61–82, Oxford.
Kemp, B. J. (1972a) Fortified towns in Nubia. In P. J. Ucko, R. Tringham & G. W. Dimbleby (eds), *Man, Settlement and Urbanism*, 651–656, London.
Kemp, B. J. (1972b) Temple and town in ancient Egypt. In P. J. Ucko, R. Tringham & G. W. Dimbleby (eds), *Man, Settlement and Urbanism*, 657–680, London.
Kemp, B. J. (1978) Imperialism and empire in New Kingdom Egypt (*c.* 1575–1087 B. C.). In P. Garnsey & C. R. Whittaker (eds), *Imperialism in the Ancient World*, 7–57, Cambridge.
Kemp, B. J. (2006) *Ancient Egypt: Anatomy of a Civilization*, London-New York.
Kitchen, K. A. (1968a) *Ramesside Inscriptions, Historical and Biographical*, vol. I, Oxford.
Kitchen, K. A. (1968b) *Ramesside Inscriptions, Historical and Biographical*, vol. III, Oxford.

Kitchen, K. A. (1968c) *Ramesside Inscriptions, Historical and Biographical*, vol. IV, Oxford.
Kitchen, K. A. (1968d) *Ramesside Inscriptions, Historical and Biographical*, vol. VI, Oxford.
Kitchen, K. A. (1986) *The Third Intermediate Period in Egypt (1100-650 B.C.)*, Warminster.
Kitchen, K. A. (2001) Economics in ancient Arabia. From Alexander to the Augustans. In Z. H. Archibald, J. K. Davies, V. Gabrielsen & G. J. Oliver (eds), *Hellenistic Economies*, 157–173, London.
Kóthay, K. A. (2006) The Widow and Orphan in Egypt before the New Kingdom, *Acta Antiqua Academiae Scientiarum Hungaricae* 46: 151–164.
Kruchten, J.-M. (1981) *Le decret d'Horemheb. Traduction, commentaire épigraphique, philologique et institutionnel*, Brussels.
Lacau, P. (1933) *Une stèle juridique de Karnak*, Cairo.
Lefèvre, D. (2012) Archives et diplomatique à la XXIe dynastie. À propos d'un papyrus «d'el-Hibeh», *EDAL* 3: 25–47, pl. VII.
Legrain, G. (1906) Deux stèles inédites, *Annales du Service des Antiquités de l'Égypte* 7: 226–227.
Lippert, S. L. (2004) *Ein demotisches juristisches Lehrbuch. Untersuchungen zu Papyrus Berlin P 23757 rto*, Wiesbaden.
Lüddeckens, E. (1960) *Ägyptische Eheverträge*, Wiesbaden.
Lüddeckens, E. (2006) *Urkunden zur Chronologie der späten 12. Dynastie: Briefe aus Illahun*, Vienna.
Malinine, M. (1946) Une vente d'esclave à l'époque de Psammétique Ier (Papyrus du Vatican 10574, en hiératique 'anormal'), *Revue d'Égyptologie* 5: 119–131.
Malinine, M. (1951) Un jugement rendu à Thèbes sous la XXVe Dynastie (Pap. Louvre E 3228c), *Revue d'Égyptologie* 6: 157–178, pls 4–6.
Malinine, M. (1953) *Choix de textes juridiques en hiératique "anormal" et en démotique (XXVe-XXVIIe dynasties)*, Paris.
Malinine, M. (1982) Transcriptions hiéroglyphiques de quatre textes du Musée du Louvre écrits en hiératique anormal, *Revue d'Égyptologie* 34: 93–100.
Malinine, M. & J. Pirenne (1950) Documents juridiques égyptiens (Deuxième série), *Archive d'histoire du droit oriental* 2: 11–91.
Martin, C. J. (1995) Marriages, wills and leases of land : some notes on the formulae of demotic contracts. In M. J. Geller & H. Maehler (ed.), *Legal Documents of the Hellenistic World*, 58–78, London.
Martin, C. J. (2007) The Saite 'demoticisation' of southern Egypt. In K. R. Lomas, R. D. Whitehouse & J. B. Wilkins (eds), *Literacy and the State in the Ancient Mediterranean*, 25–38, London.
Meeks, D. (1979) Les donations aux temples dans l'Égypte du Ier millénaire avant J.-C. In É. Lipiński (ed.), *State and Temple Economy in the Ancient Near East*, vol. II, 605–687, Leuven.
Moreno García, J. C. (1998) La population *mrt*: une approche du problème de la servitude en Egypte au IIIe millénaire (I). *Journal of Egyptian Archaeology* 84: 71–83.
Moreno García, J. C. (2001) L'organisation sociale de l'agriculture dans l'Egypte pharaonique pendant l'ancien empire (2650–2150 avant J.-C.), *Journal of the Economic and Social History of the Orient* 44: 411–450.
Moreno García, J. C. (2006) Les temples provinciaux et leur rôle dans l'agriculture institutionnelle de l'Ancien et du Moyen Empire. In J. C. Moreno García (ed.), *L'agriculture institutionnelle en Égypte ancienne: état de la question et perspectives interdisciplinaires*, 89–120, Villeneuve d'Ascq.
Moreno García, J. C. (2007) The state and the organization of the rural landscape in 3rd millennium BC pharaonic Egypt. In M. Bollig, O. Bubenzer, R. Vogelsang & H.-P. Wotzka (eds), *Aridity, Change and Conflict in Africa*, 313–330, Cologne.
Moreno García, J. C. (2008) La dépendance rurale en Égypte ancienne, *Journal of the Economic and Social History of the Orient* 51: 99–150.
Moreno García, J. C. (2010b) Les *jḥwtjw* et leur rôle socio-économique au IIIe et IIe millénaires avant J.-C. In J. C. Moreno García (ed.), *Élites et pouvoir en Egypte ancienne*, 321–351, Villeneuve d'Ascq.

Moreno García, J. C. (2011) Les *mnḥw*: société et transformations agraires en Égypte entre la fin du IIe et le début du Ier millénaire, *Revue d'Égyptologie* 62: 105–114.
Moreno García, J. C. (2013a) Land donations. In E. Frood & W. Wendrich (ed.), *UCLA Encyclopedia of Egyptology*, Los Angeles: http://digital2.library.ucla.edu/viewItem.do?ark=21198/zz002hgp07
Moreno García, J. C. (2013b) Conflicting interests over the possession and transfer of institutional land: individual *versus* family strategies. In E. Frood & A. McDonald (eds), *Decorum and Experience: Essays in Ancient Culture for John Baines*, 258–263, Oxford.
Moreno García, J. C. (2014) Penser l'économie pharaonique. *Annales, Histoire, Sciences Sociales* 69: 7–38.
Morkot, R. (2003) Archaism and innovation in art from the New Kingdom to the Twenty-sixth Dynasty. In J. Tait (ed.), *"Never Had the Like Occurred": Egypt's View of Its Past*, 79–99, London.
Muhs, B. P. (2005) *Tax Receipts, Taxpayers, and Taxes in Early Ptolemaic Thebes*, Chicago.
Muhs, B. P. (2009) Oracular property decrees in their historical and chronological context. In G. P. F. Broekman, R. J. Demarée & O. E. Kaper (eds), *The Libyan Period in Egypt. Historical and Cultural Studies into the 21st-24th Dynasties*, 265–275, Leiden-Louvain.
O'Connor, D. (1993) *Ancient Nubia: Egypt's Rival in Africa*, Philadelphia.
Parker, R. A. (1962) *A Saite Oracle Papyrus from Thebes in the Brooklyn Museum (Papyrus Brooklyn 47.218.3)*, Providence.
Payraudeau, F. (2007) Les prémices du mouvement archaïsant à Thèbes et la statue Caire JE 37382 du quatrième prophètte Djedkhonsouiouefânkh, *Bulletin de l'Institut Français d'Archéologie Orientale* 107: 141–156.
Perdu, O. (2002) *Recueil des inscriptions royales Saïtes, vol. I : Psammétique Ier*, Paris.
Pernigotti, S. (1975) Un nuovo testo giuridico in ieratico 'anormale', *Bulletin de l'Institut Français d'Archéologie Orientale* 75: 73–95, pls XI–XII.
Pestman, P. W. (1993) *The Archive of the Theban Choachytes (Second Century B. C.). A Survey of the Demotic and Greek Papyri Contained in the Archive*, Leuven.
Pestman, P. W. (1994) *Les papyrus démotiques de Tsenhor (P. Tsenhor). Les archives privées d'une femme égyptienne du temps de Darius Ier* (Studia Demotica 4), Leuven.
Pope, J. W. (2014) *The Double Kingdom under Taharqo. Studies in the History of Kush and Egypt, c. 690–664 BC*, Leiden-Boston.
Porten, B. & H. Z. Szubin (1994) An aramaic joint venture agreement (a new interpretation of the Bauer-Meissner Papyrus). In S. Allam (ed.), *Grund und Boden in Altägypten (Rechtliche und sozio-ökonomische Verhältnisse)*, 65–95, Tübingen.
Ritner, R. K. (2002) Third Intermediate Period antecedents of demotic legal terminology. In K. Ryholt (ed.), *Acts of the Seventh International Congress of Demotic Studies*, 343–360, Copenhague.
Ritner, R. K. (2009a) Fragmentation and reintegration in the Third Intermediate Period. In G. P. F. Broekman, R. J. Demarée & O. E. Kaper (eds) *The Libyan Period in Egypt. Historical and Cultural Studies into the 21st-24th Dynasties*, 327–340, Leiden-Leuven.
Ritner, R. K. (2009b) *The Libyan Anarchy. Inscriptions from Egypt's Third Intermediate Period*, Atlanta.
Römer, M. (1994) *Gottes- und Priesterherrschaft in Ägypten am Ende des Neuen Reiches* (Ägypten und Altes Testament 21), Wiesbaden.
Seidlmayer, S. J. (1982) Stadt und Tempel von Elephantine: Neunter/Zehnter Grabungsbericht, *Mitteilungen des Deutschen Archäologischen Instituts, Abteilung Kairo* 38: 271–344.
Sethe, K. (1927) *Urkunden der 18. Dynastie*, Leipzig.
Spiegelberg, W. (1914) *Die sogenannte demotische Chronik des Pap. 215 der Bibliothèque Nationale zu Paris*, Leipzig.
Spiegelberg, W. (1932) *Die demotischen Denkmäler, III : Demotische Inschriften und Papyri (CGC 50023-50165)*, Leipzig.
Stolper, M. W. (1998) Inscribed in Egyptian. In M. Brosius & A. Kuhrt (eds), *Studies in Persian History. Essays in Memory of David M. Lewis*, 133–143, Leiden.

Tait, J. (2008–2009) Pa-di-pep Tells Pharaoh the Story of the Condemnation of Djed-her: Fragments of Demotic Narrative in the British Museum, *Enchoria* 31: 113–43, pl. 13.

Thareani-Sussely, Y. (2007) Ancient caravanserai: an archaeological view from 'Aroer, *Levant* 39: 123–141.

Thompson, D. J. (1988) *Memphis under the Ptolemies*, Princeton.

Van den Boorn, G. P. F. (1988) *The duties of the vizier: civil administration in the Early New Kingdom*, London.

Vernus, P. (1993) *Affaires et scandales sous les Ramsès. La crise des valeurs dans l'Égypte du Nouvel Empire*, Paris.

Vinson, S. (2004) P. Brooklyn 37.1647^{E}, D(1)/2. An early Ptolemaic agricultural account. In F. Hoffmann & H. J. Thissen (eds), *Res severa verum gaudium: Festschrift für Karl-Theodor Zauzich zum 65. Geburtstag am 8. Juni 2004*, 695–611, pl. 55, Leuven.

Vittmann, G. (2015a) Two administrative letters from Meidum (P. Ashmolean 1984.87 and 1984.89). In F. Haikal (ed.), *Mélanges offerts à Ola el-Aguizy*, 433–450, Cairo.

Vittmann, G. (2015b) Der Stand der Erforschung des Kursivhieratischen (und neue Texte). In U. Verhoeven (ed.), *Ägyptologische "Binsen"-Weisheiten I-II. Neue Forschungen und Methoden der Hieratistik*, 383–433, Mainz-Stuttgart.

Vleeming, S. P. (1980) The sale of a slave in the time of Pharaoh Py, *Oudheidkundige Mededeelingen uit het Rijksmuseum van Oudheden te Leiden* 61: 1–17.

Vleeming, S. P. (1991) *The Gooseherds of Hou (Pap. Hou): A Dossier Relating to Various Agricultural Affairs from Provincial Egypt of the Early Fifth Century B. C.*, Leuven.

Vleeming, S. P. (1993) *Papyrus Reinhardt. An Egyptian Land List from the Tenth Century B.C.*, Berlin.

Vleeming, S. P. (1995) The office of a choachyte in the Theban area. In S. P. Vleeming (ed.), *Hundred-gated Thebes*, 241–255, Leiden-New York.

Weeks, K. R. & The Epigraphic Survey (1981) *The Temple of Khonsu*, vol. II, Chicago.

Winand, J. (2003) Les décrets oraculaires pris en l'honneur d'Henouttaouy et de Maâtkarê (X^{e} et VIIe pylones), *Cahiers de Karnak* 11: 603–707.

Wiseman, D. J. (1966) Some Egyptians in Babylonia, *Iraq* 28: 154–158.

Chapter 11

North-east Africa and trade at the crossroads of the Nile Valley, the Mediterranean and the Red Sea

Robert G. Morkot

In writing a doctoral dissertation addressing the relationship between the Egyptian empire in Nubia during the New Kingdom (*c*. 1550–1070 BC) and the emergence of the Kushite state, economic factors were central.[1] At the time of writing (1984–1990), the literature on the Egyptian economy was limited, with many of the older interpretations still accepted; challenge was largely from scholars influenced by the works of Karl Polanyi.[2] Yet there was consensus that Egypt suffered economic decline in the late New Kingdom. Even those who questioned the interpretation that presented Egyptian activities in Nubia as purely exploitative acknowledged that the "colonial" centres ceased to function, that gold production effectively stopped, and that the Egyptians withdrew from Nubia in the late 20th Dynasty (Trigger 1976). The Egyptian economy during the Third Intermediate Period is almost totally without discussion: an obsession with aspects of material culture (notably coffin development), and with genealogical and prosopographical minutiae has seen broader issues neglected.[3] Similarly, the discussions, such as they were, of the emergence of an independent and powerful Kushite state, had little to say on the economic factors that contributed.[4]

The basic problem was an academic failure to treat the period 1100–700 BC as a continuation, development, and metamorphosis from the New Kingdom phase. This occurred for a number of reasons, and *appeared* to be supported by the archaeology. Egyptologists were more concerned with the loss of empire and the Libyan domination, leading to what they regarded as a very long decline throughout the 1st millennium BCE. From the Nubian/Kushite perspective, the "Dark Age" also made a convenient chapter break, or end/start for a book, leaving the questions it raised unanswered.[5]

The accepted characterisation of the "end" of the Late Bronze Age argued for the decline of Egypt's power and influence internationally, the collapse of its empire, and internal economic crisis (Černý 1965). Certainly the disintegration of the other major power of the region, the Hittite empire, had repercussions for Egypt. These problems began in the reign of Ramesses II, increasing through those of his successors with the major threats posed by the invasions of Egyptian territory by the Libyans and "Sea Peoples". It was not a process of continuous decline, as both Merneptah and Ramesses III successfully reasserted Egyptian authority in parts of Palestine; but by the reign of Ramesses VI the Egyptian empire in Western Asia was gone. The well-known, and frequently cited, *Report of Wenamun* – whether an actual "report" or a piece of literary fiction – is used to show how far Egypt's prestige and influence had fallen in Byblos, a major trading partner for many hundreds of years (Goedicke 1975). There were economic problems within Egypt, but the view epitomised by Černý (1965), which dominated Egyptology for a long time, generalised from a particularly rich set of documents with economic relevance but only of Upper Egyptian provenance. Although these documents reveal administrative corruption and theft, they also show that the perpetrators were found out and dealt with. Similarly, in cases of grain shortage, the controlling officials brought food supplies from stores elsewhere. The evidence from Middle and Lower Egypt is lacking, so we have no way of comparing the different regions.

This is not the place to examine the complexities of the archaeology or the numerous different, and opposing, theories about the collapse of the Late Bronze Age states.[6] From the perspective of Egypt and its neighbours in north-east Africa, there is a serious disparity in the textual and archaeological material. The following narrative aims to highlight some of the key issues and questions over the broad period from *c.* 1300–700 BC. In some areas it is clear that recent excavation is providing new material for understanding this period.

The West: Libya

There is remarkably little evidence for Libya and Libyans in the earlier part of the Egyptian New Kingdom (*c.* 1550–1070 BC), but by the reign of Amenhotep III (*c.* 1390–1352 BC) there were close contacts, and the names of "tribal" groups are recorded (notably the Libu and the Meshwesh) replacing the more generalised and "archaic" terms Tjehenu and Tjemeh. There is also archaeological material from sites at Marsa Matruh, and Zawiyet Umm el-Rakham.

The repeated waves of Libyan invasion and migration that began in the reign of Sety I (*c.* 1294–1279 BC) led to a pragmatic Egyptian accommodation of the situation: settling Libyans in certain parts of Egypt (especially the Delta), and employing significant numbers in the army (Kitchen 1990; O'Connor 1990; Snape 2003). This eventually led to the rise of Libyan rulers as both pharaohs and local "princes". The documentary evidence of the reign of Merneptah (*c.* 1213–1203 BC) is quite explicit that the movements of Libyans were caused by famine in their own country. Precisely *where* they were coming from is not specified: O'Connor suggested that Cyrenaica was probably the homeland of some groups, and this has generally been favoured. However, the more easterly region of Marmarica might be more likely. Marmarica, a large region stretching from the Gulf of Bomba in the west almost to Alexandria in the east, is effectively a unit in terms of landscape and environment. It has numerous coastal wadis and potentially could support agriculture and pasturing; but it is also a more fragile ecological system than Cyrenaica, and if there was climatic change and desiccation this may have caused a significant disruption to traditional ways of life (Hulin 2009).

Eastern "Libya" had been a part of the trade network of the Late Bronze Age (LBA), certainly from the time of Amenhotep III and Akhenaten. The sea routes around the eastern Mediterranean would have required ships to sail across from Crete and follow the coast in order to get supplies of fresh water. The evidence from Marsa Matruh shows direct exchange between such traders and the local population (White 2002). The slightly later material from Zawiyet Umm el-Rakham reflects a change, with Egyptian intervention and control, albeit briefly and ultimately unsuccessfully (Snape & Wilson 2007). The presence of "Libyans" at the Egyptian court is particularly well documented from the reign of Akhenaten (*c.* 1352–1336 BC), which would have increased political and diplomatic contacts with other Western Asiatic powers. The temple scenes depicting the conflicts between Egyptians and Libyan groups (now specified with "tribal" names) from the reigns of Sety I and Ramesses III (*c.* 1184–1153 BC) show that the Libyans acquired Western Asiatic type swords, and significantly, horses and chariots: they thus became integrated, albeit rather late, into the LBA world. What the Libyans provided in return is less certain. The standard "tribute" depicted comprises ostrich eggs and ostrich feathers: but the Egyptian preference for showing "luxuries" may cloud the actuality (Richardson 1999).

The introduction of chariots and horses to Libya is a typically Late Bronze Age phenomenon, but occurs quite late when compared with Egypt and the wider East Mediterranean worlds. The battle reliefs of Sety I on the exterior north wall of the Hypostyle Hall at Karnak, imply that the king's Libyan campaign was regarded as of equal significance to his Asiatic conflicts. The scenes show that the Libyans were using the imported types of sword, but they are not shown with horses and chariots. The records of the reign of Merneptah state that chariots and horses form part of the Libyan army, although the numbers appear to be small. The Libyan conflicts of the reign of Ramesses III also include chariots and horses.

From Libya itself rock drawings of chariots, some drawn by four horses, are well known. However, as with all rock art they are difficult to date and interpret: some appear in areas in which it would have been nigh impossible to use chariots. By the 5th century BC Herodotus wrote about the Libyan horses and four-horse chariots of the Asbystae inland from Cyrene, and of the Garamantes.

The Merneptah inscriptions indicate famine and presumably therefore some phase of significantly serious desiccation, presumably due to lack of winter rain. There are other changes identifiable within Libya: the seasonal trading of Phoenicians in the west (and perhaps also in Cyrenaica), was followed by the foundation of permanent centres, most notably Utica (traditionally around 1100 BC, although the archaeology is

8th–7th centuries) and Carthage (traditionally around 800 BC). Later Greek settlement in the east (although perhaps following earlier Mycenaean explorations) was the prelude to the foundation of Cyrene in the period around 600 BC (James 2005).

The questions that emerge, and which cannot be answered as there is no evidence, as yet, are:

- Was there an extended period of desiccation? Or was it short-term?
- What were the connections between Libyan pharaohs and Libya? There is no evidence whatsoever from Egyptian sources.
- Phoenician and "Greek" trading and settlement. These certainly have their origins in the period under discussion even if the historical narratives and archaeology are at variance.

The current work of a number of projects should go some way to resolving issues around the emergence of the Garamantes in the west of Libya and how they can be related to events further east.[7]

The South: Kush, Punt, Ethiopia and the Red Sea

The evidence for the economy of "Nubia" during the LBA (Egyptian New Kingdom) is extensive and thoroughly discussed (Morkot 1995a). Within the territories controlled directly by the Egyptians (Wawat and the province of Kush), land holding and internal production appears to have been reorganised along Egyptian lines. This applies not only to agriculture where the evidence shows that temples, statue cults and administrative offices had fields assigned to them, as in Egypt; but also to production of sculpture, funerary goods, and pottery. The decline of indigenous pottery production, once associated with a decline in population, is now generally ascribed to "acculturation" – by which we should perhaps understand economic centralisation. Other indigenous cultural features remained, revealing a complex mixing of Egyptian with "Nubian".

Egypt was certainly reliant on the region to the south for gold and the other "luxury" commodities with which it maintained its dominant position in the LBA world. The relationship was not, however, purely exploitative. Egypt invested heavily in town and temple building in its Nubian territories and, in addition to the gold exploitation and cross-frontier trade, a range of more "lowly" agricultural products was shipped to Egypt on a significant scale. Large numbers of cattle were imported from the Dongola Reach of Upper Nubia, which probably lay outside direct Egyptian control. Conversely, horses and chariots were introduced into Nubia, and horses appear to have been bred there as early as the late 18th Dynasty (Morkot 2007). The result of this close economic relationship over a period of four centuries was undoubtedly a complex mixture of economic zones and interactions, with a range of systems.

The evidence for the process of Egyptian abandonment of its Nubian territories is less clear than in Asia, but "rebellions", notably by the kingdom of Irem, threatened the far south of Egyptian control from early in the 19th Dynasty. The old idea of total depopulation of Nubia from the later New Kingdom has now been fairy conclusively disproven, and a far more complex model of change can be assumed – but not yet detailed (Morkot 1994; 2000). The first excavations at Amara West suggested that the town site, which served as the Egyptian administrative centre in Kush, was closed down sometime in the reigns of Ramesses IX–XI (*c.* 1126–1070 BC). The recent excavations at the site have now shown that there was occupation during the succeeding period. These are not, of course, mutually exclusive: the Egyptian administration may well have abandoned the southern province and the town and redrawn the frontier in the face of expanding indigenous power from further south. This raises the issue of the rise of the indigenous Kushite kingdom that by the mid-eighth century was able to invade and conquer Egypt. There is still limited evidence, and the interpretation of that evidence divides scholarship.[8]

One of the key products of Nubia was gold (Vercoutter 1959). The records from the Theban region listing donations to the temple of Amun show a decline from the reign of Thutmose III (who gave 15 tonnes of gold over a period of about 30 years) to that of Ramesses III. Gold was produced in the Eastern Desert, and also along the Nile Valley south of the Second Cataract. Vercoutter assessed the evidence, and the scenes in the tomb of Tutankhamun's Viceroy Huy show that gold production was directly under the control of the Viceroy. The evidence identified by Spence at Sesebi substantiates Vercoutter's analysis, and suggests a significant production of gold in the Abri-Delgo reach of the Nile during the late 18th dynasty.[9] Given the technologies and extraction methods of the period, this may have been of short duration. The Egyptian documentary evidence suggests that gold production in the earlier 20th Dynasty was small, and possibly no longer economically viable. Despite this, there appears to have been no abandonment of Nubia, and the withdrawal from the region south of the Second Cataract was only very late in the 20th Dynasty, and may have been as much due to changing power structures in Upper Nubia as to economic factors.

Egyptian economic activities in Nubia appear to show direct involvement with gold production, but there was probably a reliance on local power holders for other "luxuries", particularly those which were the product of longer-distance networks. With the working-out of the gold available allied with rising local power and internal dynastic problems in Egypt, abandonment of the region may have seemed a sensible response. Indeed, the situation and influencing factors may have been parallel to those at the end of the Middle Kingdom.

The agricultural situation is also a controversial subject. It has been argued that Lower Nubia suffered from a decline in productivity caused by a series of low Niles, resulting in emigration.[10] This need not have been the case, as Helen Jacquet-Gordon long ago observed: lower floods in Nubia do not have the same impact as in Egypt, as water remains available, and with increased exposure of land in a narrow flood plain (Jacquet-Gordon 1982). In any case, Egypt during the Third Intermediate Period was a time of high Nile inundations, amply recorded by the Quay inscriptions at Karnak.

One reference from the late 20th Dynasty implying a low inundation with consequent shortages does not indicate a long term problem. In Upper Nubia, the situation may have been different, with increased desiccation: this could have had a serious impact on nomadic or desert populations, causing movements into the river valley. Further east, in Ethiopia, Fattovich has suggested that the recession amongst the Gash cultures was caused by climatic change, and this may have resulted in population movements, but if so they are undocumented (Fattovich 1989; 1990). All of these issues remain somewhat speculative, but should certainly be considered in the broader analysis. Elsewhere, there certainly were agricultural and climatic problems in the later phases of the LBA. However, "climate change" brings a range of different issues in different regions (as we now know, all too well): one region may have drought whilst another has prolonged rain and flood.

However the Kushite state expanded and developed (which is not the direct subject of this paper), its rulers – whether it was one or more chiefdom – must have had control of substantial economic resources. There are enormous problems in trying to understand the economy of Nubia during the "Napatan" period (broadly 1000–300 BC), and the lack of material forces us to supplement the data by comparison with other phases. Lower Nubia, even if not totally depopulated, is unlikely to have been much more than a subsistence economy, with the major productive regions further south in the Abri-Delgo and Dongola Reaches of Upper Nubia, and the savannah of the central Sudan. In Medieval times Nubia was largely self-sufficient in foodstuffs from agriculture and it is likely that local craftsmen supplied most of the manufactured articles (Shinnie 1978). Trade was, therefore, *mainly* luxury orientated. A very similar situation seems to have prevailed in Meroitic times. Under the Viceregal administration a local, largely self-sufficient agricultural economy was established that was very similar to that in Egypt, with exports of a wide-range of locally acquired mineral and agricultural products, exploitation of gold resources both in the Nile Valley and Eastern Desert and export of cattle from the Kerma-Dongola reaches (Morkot 1995a; 2001). Morkot argued that the main luxury trade was carried out between the local rulers of southern Kush and their counterparts further south (Morkot 1991a; 1995a; 2001).

The question must arise of why an increasingly centralised political entity with a self-sufficient agricultural base expanded in the way that the Kushite state apparently did (Zibelius-Chen 1989). Was international trade an important factor? Was Kush already involved in international trade?

It has been argued that the collapse of the palace-based states of the LBA saw a change in the main axes of trade in western Asia and the east Mediterranean, although it should be noted that many features of the internal economies of, for example, Egypt and Assyria, appear to have continued functioning in very much the same way as they had in the LBA.[11] In this model, the new powers controlling trade were those at the centre, rather than the edges: the Levantine or Phoenician cities, and the states of Syria-Palestine, notably Israel, Judah, and Aram-Damascus. The history of the tenth to eighth centuries is dominated by the rivalries and expansions of these various states. This period of change saw the fragmentation of the old empires of Egypt and the Hittites and the emergence of the Aramaic and Neo-Hittite successor states in north Syria and along the fringes of the Fertile Crescent and, it is argued, the appearance of nomadic Arab tribes from the south. Israel under Solomon dominated the trade routes for some time, exploiting the Red Sea ports and exacting dues from the Arabian tribes. Later attempts to re-open the Red Sea routes apparently failed. In this characterisation of trade, Egypt's importance is dramatically reduced, and Nubia and the Middle Nile cease to be considered.

Liverani has discussed the economic implications of the "end" of the LBA and argued that the growth of nomadic and semi-nomadic groups may have been a *result* rather than a cause of the crisis (Liverani 1987; 1990). This was also the period of camel-oasis-desert expansion, which saw the rise of the Aramaean states and of the Arabians (Liverani 1987, 70). Trade was no longer entirely palace-centred and gift exchange gradually gave way to commerce (Liverani 1987, 72). Significantly, there was a shift in the gold routes from the LBA to Iron I (Liverani 1987, 73). The decline, or cessation, of significant gold production meant that Egypt no longer had the monopoly. There was also a change in the trade axis to the east of the Red Sea and an Assyrian desire to control these land routes that had a major impact on the political situation in Syria-Palestine during the 9th–7th centuries. Frankenstein suggested that the problems encountered by Wenamun at Byblos may already reflect this new regional configuration, and the first major expansion of Assyria into western Asia under Tiglathpileser I (*c.* 1115–1077 BC).[12]

Although it is widely accepted that the north–south trade axis moved from the control of Egypt to the eastern side of the Red Sea, coming under the power of the emergent Arabian states, the development of these Arabian trade routes is still a matter of considerable obscurity. The direct archaeological evidence from south Arabia does not indicate the formation of major states there until the 6th and 5th centuries BC. These centuries were also the time of Arabian activity in Ethiopia which was significant in the emergence of the Aksumite state. There is a little evidence from around 600 BC for Egyptian contacts with Arabia, although it is uncertain whether these were direct or not. Fattovich, in commenting on the Sudanese coastal site of Aqiq, argues for a network of contacts and exchanges during the ime of the Gash Group (*c.* 2700–1400 BC) connecting Egypt and Nubia, the Upper Nile, Horn of Africa and South Arabia (Fattovich 2006–2007).

There is evidence for the increased use of the domesticated camel for carriage and transport in the 10th–8th centuries BC (Bulliet 1975), and this would certainly have made the west Arabian routes easier to use. The biblical record has usually been cited as evidence that these routes began to function during the reign of Solomon,[13] but Groom questioned this, arguing that the biblical Queen of Sheba was not a south, but a north Arabian ruler (Groom 1981, 42–54). As such she would have been leader of another people called Sabaeans who lived in northern Arabia and who are mentioned in a number of sources. Groom identified It'amra the Sabaean, of the reign of Sargon II, as ruler of the same people and not of the south Arabian state. Solomon's visitor would thus have been an earlier representative of the Arabian female rulers attested by the Assyrian texts of the late 8th century (Groom 1981, 44–45). Groom points out that the commodities brought by the queen – gold, spices and precious stones – were more typically northern than southern Arabian and contests the assumption that the Arabian incense trade was itself highly developed so early.[14] Incense *may* have been included in the commodities brought to Solomon, and small quantities exchanged through networks to the south, but there is insufficient evidence to support the idea that it was being exploited on a large scale until the first two centuries AD. Indeed, incense is central to arguments about the trade routes, and the assumption that the region of "Punt" was the major supplier of frankincense and myrrh is actually without solid archaeological evidence. The Egyptian sources certainly indicate importation of the trees and the resin from Punt and through the Middle Nile routes, but quantifying this is impossible. Other sources of aromatic resins were available in Egypt and south-western Asia, and these may have been more significant in the Bronze Age (Serpico 2000).

Although it seems likely that there was an increasing use of the Arabian land routes, there were also sporadic attempts to re-open trade along the Red Sea. The biblical texts name the intended destination as Ophir, which is argued by some to be Oman, India, or even Malaysia. Others, more realistically, prefer to see Ophir as the same as Punt,[15] or possibly somewhere on the Red Sea coast of Arabia that itself had contacts with East Africa. Punt had been a trading partner of Egypt from very early times, and although the geographical region was probably roughly the same (although even that is questionable) it was a variable polity. Current opinion suggests that the "Punt" of the LBA (Egyptian New Kingdom) was in eastern Africa and possibly located in the Gash delta region of Ethiopia.[16]

Fattovich relates the end of Egyptian trade contact with Punt to the sudden dryness in North-eastern Africa and the socio-political weakness of Egypt during the Third Intermediate Period (Fattovich 1990, 266). Fattovich notes the disappearance of large villages in the Atbara-Gash region (which he suggests to be the archaeological equivalent of part of LBA Punt) at this time, which is suggestive of a local breakdown. The collapse of the Egyptian trade with Punt also seems to be correlated with the rise of the South Arabian trade routes.[17] Although there is evidence for activity by peoples from south Arabia in Ethiopia during the 6th–5th centuries BC, there are no archaeological indications, so far, that the Arabs of south Arabia were beginning to exploit the resources of the Ethiopian highland at this early date. Fattovich sees a Meroitic expansion toward the highlands in the later 1st millennium BC (4th–1st centuries), but is it possible that the emergent Kushite state in the central Sudan was exploiting, directly or indirectly, the resources of east Sudan and the Ethiopian highland and establishing contacts with the western Asiatic powers via the Red Sea avoiding Egypt?

Whilst the exact nature of Arabia's role in international trade remains unclear, that of the coastal cities of the Levant is much better documented. The Phoenician cities came to specialise in the production of luxury goods, or the acquisition of luxury raw materials.[18] Amongst the tribute of the "Sea Coast" received by Assurnasirpal II (883–859 BC) were large and small monkeys, ebony, and ivory.[19] That received by Tiglathpileser III (745–727 BC) was very similar, specifying in addition iron, ivory and elephant-hides (ANET 282–284). Some of the imports listed, notably the linen, would have originated in Egypt, but others – such as the ebony, ivory, and elephant hides – certainly had an East African origin. The inclusion of iron raises the issue of whether iron working was already being practised in Kush.[20]

Unfortunately, there is remarkably little evidence to illuminate what the role of Egypt in the international trade of the 9th–7th centuries BC was. There is equally little evidence as to what commodities were imported and exported.

In LBA Egypt the trade in "luxury" raw materials and manufactures was controlled through the palace. Nubian commodities such as ivory, ebony, incense, and gold figured largely in this. If, as is usually accepted, the Nubian "luxury" trade was severed at the end of the 20th Dynasty, Egypt must have been forced to export different commodities – or rely on its own products. One of the problems in discussing Egypt's international economic activity is the documentary evidence (e.g. in the Amarna Letters) for luxuries, many of them from the south. The archaeological evidence, for example from the royal tombs at Byblos and Ugarit, shows the significance of stone vessels (and probably their contents). For the earlier 1st millennium, Egyptian artefacts have been excavated in graves throughout the Mediterranean, from Spain and Carthage, Etruria and the Aegean islands, suggesting that these were goods traded with the Phoenicians and then traded on by them (Culican 1970; Parcerisa 1985). Notable amongst these objects were alabaster vessels and faience amulets. Neither of these manufactures was new in Egypt's international exchange.[21] Even if there was disruption to the luxury trade, which is doubtful, there were other products which were royal monopolies: fine cloth and papyrus. These are documented as exports at the end of the 20th Dynasty.[22]

Based upon assumptions about the relationship between the temples of Amun at Thebes and at Gebel Barkal, it has been assumed by Török and Kendall that such trade contacts as might have existed between Kush and Egypt during the pre-25th Dynasty would have been with Thebes rather than the Delta (Kendall 1999; Török 1995). The presence of Upper Egyptian marl wares at el-Kurru certainly supports a direct contact with Thebes, but this does not exclude connections with the Delta rulers. There are two possibilities raised by the Assyrian record of commodities which must be of Nubian origin: that they were reaching the Phoenician cities either directly via the Red Sea routes, or indirectly through the Egyptian rulers.

The exports of the Pharaonic period – gold, ivory, ebony, skins, feathers, and humans – were also those of later times. The scanty evidence available from the Achaemenid period suggests that ivory, and perhaps ebony, continued to be important.

Humans were sent as soldiers and as slaves at all periods, some no-doubt from within Kushite terrirories, and others captured in cross-frontier expeditions. There was probably an increase in the slave-trade during the Roman period, and later the *Baqt* refers only to slaves, although it is possible that gold and ivory were also exported.[23]

One document not usually cited as evidence of Egyptian-Kushite trade contacts is the inscription of Crown Prince Osorkon at Karnak (Caminos 1958; see also Kendall 1999). Prince Osorkon served as High Priest of Amun at Karnak during the reign of his father, Takeloth II, and probably eventually ascended the throne as Osorkon III. In some sections listing Osorkon's benefactions to Amun during the reign of Takeloth II are products specified as Nubian. These include gold, or "fine gold" of Khent-hen-nefer, and dry myrrh "of the best of Nehes-land" (Caminos 1958, 125–126, 166). It may be significant that both geographical designations are "archaic" rather than contemporary political terms. Fresh incense and dry myrrh are listed elsewhere, but not specifically as from Nubia. It is possible that the gold was acquired directly from Lower Nubia, but incense must have been of more southerly origin.

Further indication of the continuance of the "luxury" trade is provided by the Assyrian sources. An Assyrian document records the receipt of elephant hides, rolls of papyrus, and garments made of *byssos* (the finest linen) from Ashdod and another kingdom, probably Gaza or Ashkelon.[24] The papyrus and *byssos* were certainly Egyptian manufactures (and probably a royal monopoly) but the elephant hides must be of Kushite origin. If elephant hides were being exported, then it is reasonable to assume that ivory was as well. The ivory working of the 9th–7th centuries BC is one of the most notable productions of western Asia. It is generally accepted that the Syrian elephant was, by this time, extinct, and although some of the ivory worked in Assyria probably came from India via Babylonia, it is certain that some of the ivory excavated at Nimrud was African.[25] The origin of many worked pieces in the Phoenician workshops again suggests that the ivory was imported, probably from Africa, and of course, ivory had long been one of the most notable of the Nubian exports. Nubia must be the most likely source of this ivory, the size of some of the pieces indicating that it came from the Bush elephant.[26] Although elephants were hunted in north-west Africa, it has been assumed that they were of the Forest type, with smaller tusks. It is unlikely that the Phoenician expansion into the western Mediterranean actually brought large quantities of ivory, at least early enough to coincide with the major periods of Phoenician and Syrian ivory carving.[27]

Rather surprisingly, ivory working is almost completely unattested in Egypt during the Third Intermediate Period, but this may be due to accident of survival and changes in burial custom. The iconography of the western Asiatic ivories shows strong Egyptian influence, some of which is certainly of the Third Intermediate Period (rather than being a New Kingdom residue), and it seems possible that faience amulets served as the model for some of the designs.[28]

There are enormous problems in attempting to understand the economy of the Kushite kingdom, but there is sufficient evidence to *suggest* that "trade" continued.

This would doubtless have been elite controlled and in the form of gift-exchange. Indeed, the evidence from the period following the 25th Dynasty, another phase in which relations between Kush and Egypt are generally suggested to have been severely restricted, show that there was considerable "trade". There were contacts between the rulers buried at el-Kurru and the Red Sea coast, as shells from the cemetery indicate. How direct, or frequent, any contact between the Nile and coast was is much more difficult to assess. Equally, any contact with Arabia or the Phoenicians is undocumented, but perhaps worthy of consideration: probably most exports continued by the Nile route.

The obvious evidence relates to the "luxuries" which had always been Kushite exports, and which can be certainly said to have a Sudanese origin. The possibility of breeding and export of horses has already been discussed. The control of such northward trade would probably have been as it was in the heyday of the Kerma kingdom, based in the Dongola-Napata Reach. Ultimately, the Kurru chiefs came to control this trade, although they were not necessarily the original power. One explanation of the emergence of the Kushite kingdom would be that the Dongola/Kurru chiefs expanded their power southwards into the central Sudan in order to gain control of the source, as well as the transmission of such commodities. Again, the question of iron-working may be significant. It has always been assumed that the Kerma kings acted as middlemen in the trade with Egypt, rather than dominating the central Sudan. This may have been the case, but now, in the 8th century BC, the Kushites created a large kingdom covering both the Butana and the Nubian Nile Valley.

In return for these luxury materials, the Kushites probably received grain and cloth, which are not preserved in the archaeological record. It is more certain that pottery was being imported from Upper Egypt (probably Thebes), presumably for its contents. Likewise the Levantine storage jars from el-Kurru and Hillat el-Arab were probably acquired through Egypt, either for their original contents, or, as more widely assumed, refilled (Heidorn 1994; Vincentelli 2006). In the later, Meroitic, period wine was imported from and through Egypt, and is also documented during the Viceregal period and was doubtless important in all historical phases. The archaeological evidence inevitably emphasises luxury manufactures: jewellery, faience and stone vessels, amulets and the like. However, there is still no firm agreement on the dating of the calcite and faience vessels from el-Kurru, and whether they should be considered as contemporary (requiring a redating of the cemetery's chronology), as "attractive 'antiques' of types no longer produced" in Egypt, or as pillage from New Kingdom burials rather than contemporary imports (Kendall 1999).

It has often been assumed that the trade in luxury commodities ended with the collapse of the viceregal administration, and the apparent breaking of contacts with the Middle Nile in the Libyan period. Since most of the commodities originated in the central Sudan, it is reasonable to ask whether the controllers of the source would have attempted to establish contact with Egypt, to ensure the continuing supply of Egyptian commodities. The Egyptians themselves would have still required, or desired, many of the products. If, as argued here, a successor-state immediately appeared in Lower Nubia, the continuance of trade is even more likely, if on a much-reduced scale.

The consensus is that the "end" of the LBA saw changes in the control of trade and trade-routes: Egypt was far less important than it had been, whilst the Western Asiatic powers – the Phoenician cities, Israel and Damascus – became dominant. The increasing use of the camel opened up the Arabian land routes, although there was some continued use (or attempted use) of the Red Sea routes by Israel, at times in alliance with Tyre. There is some evidence for the continued transmission of commodities from Nubia to Egypt, and it is unlikely that it would have completely ceased, even if there was political hostility. It is unclear what effect the rise of the Arabian trade routes may have had on the trade in prestige commodities from Nubia. It is possible, although there is no supporting evidence, that much of the ivory used in western Asia at this time came from the eastern Sudan, but via the Red Sea/Arabian routes rather than the Nile Valley.

Within the broader context, the rise of Kush should be examined against the background of the collapse of the LBA states and the eventual ascendancy of the Assyrian empire in the mid-8th century BC. Other factors in the region of North-eastern Africa, the Red Sea and Arabia may have been significant but are currently undocumented. It is also uncertain when the Arabians began to cross the Red Sea; although the middle of the 1st millennium has been suggested, it may have been as early as the 8th century BC and there is some evidence for trade across the Red Sea in the 2nd millennium. Jacqueline Pirenne proposed that the earliest wave of Arabian migration was caused by the Assyrians in the 8th–7th centuries. Fattovich suggested that the Gash Delta cultures ceased about the same time as the end of the Egyptian New Kingdom. He has also suggested the possible influence of Nubia on the pre-Aksumite cultures and detailed finds of Kushite material in pre-Aksumite contexts. While our knowledge of the archaeology of western Arabia, Ethiopia and the Eastern Sudan is still limited for this period, knowledge has considerably increased in recent years, and it is important to consider the *possibilities* of contact and influence, insubstantial though the evidence may be.

There is some evidence that the commodities of Kush continued to pass to western Asia, either through Egypt, or by the Red Sea-Arabian routes. In addition to the more usual products, the Assyrian evidence suggests that horses may have been brought from Kush and that there were Kushites in Assyria from the mid-8th century (Dalley 1985; Heidorn 1997; Morkot 1995a, 237–238; 1999, 144). Although not in itself necessarily indicative of Kushite political expansion, it shows that Kush was not entirely cut off from the western Asiatic world and that individuals were still going to Egypt and farther afield. Even if the Kushite state was the result of the coalescence of already existing political units, there must have been political, economic, or other factors which caused this.

Population movement has been noted as a prime factor in the process of state formation elsewhere. It is possible that some movement took place following the end of the Viceregal period, but there is no indication that, for example, there were large numbers of people forced into the Nile Valley or central Sudan by climatic changes. There is evidence for populations continuing in the Eastern Desert through the 1st millennium into Roman times. There *may* have been political events elsewhere – the Ethiopian highlands, Darfur-Kordofan, southern Sudan – which forced people into the Butana and Dongola Reach. Climatic change may have caused the recession amongst the Gash cultures, as Fattovich has suggested, and may have caused population movements. While population movements *may* have been a factor in state formation, they are without evidence, and other factors might have been more important. Since it has been argued here that states already existed throughout the region, the emergence of a more centralised and coherent power may have been the result of conflict within Kush itself. All of these factors are significant in considering the changing economic situation of the early 1st millennium.

The exhaustion of the gold supply by the later 20th Dynasty (*c.* 1150–1070 BC) is probably something about which we can be reasonably confident. The use, reuse, and possible decline in supply of other metals at the end of the LBA, and the increasing use of silver and iron are certainly significant economic factors (Sherratt 2000; 2003). The control of long distance trade in the nascent Kushite "state" is doubtless another major issue. The southern contacts of the rulers are shown by material naming Shabaqo and Taharqo from Gebel Moya.[29] Whether direct or indirect, this traded material travelled a considerable distance. Recent survey and excavation in the Wadi Howar have revealed the existence of a 25th Dynasty fortress, raising questions about Kushite activities westward, and potential trade links, population movements, and neighbouring polities (Lange 2005; Jesse 2004; Jesse *et al.* 2006).

In conclusion: there are many complex issues around the internal and external economies of Libya, Egypt, Nubia-Kush and the Red Sea region from the late New Kingdom through the Third Intermediate Period to around 600 BC. Broadly, we can say that the emerging Kushite state(s) engaged in trading activities with the states of south-western Asia, and that that trade began (directly or indirectly) before it came to dominate Egypt as the "25th Dynasty" (*c.* 750–656 BC). How, or whether, trade was a determining factor in Kushite expansion remains speculative. There do seem to be connections between the Kushite state and the Red Sea, but there is no substantial evidence that the older Nile route for export of African commodities was replaced by the Red Sea routes until later, perhaps not even until the Ptolemaic or Roman periods: the more important factor may have been who controlled the Nile routes. Some commodities (such as incense) *may* have been sourced more directly from southern Arabia, and East African supplies may have been affected by climatic change – but this is impossible to assess at present. There are no indications that hunting had a major effect on elephant populations, either in numbers or location, although a gradual eastward movement can perhaps be noted later, leading to Aksumite domination of the ivory trade in 3rd–4th centuries AD.

Notes

1. Morkot 1994. An outline of Part 1 appeared as Morkot 1987; other elements (some revised) as Morkot 1991a; 1995a; 1995b; 1999 and 2001.
2. Janssen 1975; for Nubia, Kemp 1972a; 1972b; 1978; Frandsen 1979.
3. See most recently, for example, Dodson 2012, a fine example of the genre: the index contains no reference to the economy or to trade.
4. An exception being Zibelius-Chen 1989.
5. For example Adams 1977; Shinnie 1967; Trigger 1976.
6. Drews 1993; cf. the radical proposals of James *et al.* 1991.
7. On the Garamantes see also Liverani 2000.
8. For the alternative discussions at the Meroitic Conference Berlin-Gösen 1992 and the Nubian Conference at Lille 1994: Kendall 1999; Morkot 1999; Török 1995.
9. Spence & Rose 2009; Spence *et al.* 2011; and the recent work of Klemm & Klemm 2013.
10. Adams 1977, 244 following the interpretation of Cecil Firth.
11. Postgate 1979. The gradual move towards a silver and eventually coinage-based economy was discussed by other contributors.
12. Frankenstein 1979, 266. See Fletcher 2012 for a critique.
13. Kitchen 1993, 606 suggests the possibility that the rise of the Levantine and Arabian incense routes were important for the decline of Punt: one could also argue that any climatic or political changes in the region of East Africa understood to be Punt, may have stimulated a search for other sources.
14. Groom 1981, 52–53, in contrast to Mitchell 1982, 494 and 495.
15. See discussion of Groom 1981, 48–54, Mitchell 1982, 480.
16. Kitchen 1971; 1993; 1999 for the extensive discussions on the location, and the evidence. Fattovich 1990 for archaeological possibilities, also Fattovich 1982; 1989; 1991.
17. A possibility also noted by Kitchen 1993, 606; Fattovich 1998.
18. Frankenstein 1979, 268 with critique of Fletcher 2012.
19. Annals from the temple of Ninurta at Nimrud: ANET 275–76. The translation by Oppenheim gives "ivory from walrus tusk" which is clearly impossible.
20. Trigger 1969 dispelled the older myths around Kushite iron working and lists examples of iron from the royal cemeteries. Current projects are re-examining iron working at Meroe itself.
21. However one should note differing interpretations of the 6th Dynasty alabaster vessels from Byblos and Kerma – whether contemporary imports or later reuse: Lacovara 1991 and Kemp in Trigger *et al.* 1983, 129. Kendall 1999 similarly regards all later New Kingdom stone vessels from el-Kurru as reuse. Ramesside alabaster vessels, certainly near contemporary, were excavated at Ugarit. See also Sparks 2003; Bevan 2003.
22. On the *Report of Wenamun* see discussion of varying translations in Goedicke 1975.
23. Morkot 1991b, 325. The rock inscription of Shorkaror (1st century AD) at Gebel Qeili clearly indicates such a cross-frontier capture. For the *Baqt* see Shinnie 1978.
24. Postgate 1974, 283–284; 111.1.1 a letter of Sennacherib as Crown Prince to Sargon II listing contributions received from Azu[ri] of Ashdod and another nearby city-state, by the palace at Nineveh.
25. On the ivories generally see Barnett 1975, and the detailed volumes of Georgina Herrmann. The size of some furniture elements and unworked tusks from the Nimrud excavations are suggestive of African rather than Indian origin.
26. There has been considerable confusion in the literature caused by assumptions over the type of elephant see Morkot 1998; Krzyszkowska & Morkot 2000.
27. As suggested by Barnett 1975, 166–168 who also postulated Phoenico-Israelite trade with India, which he identified as Ophir.
28. The designs and techniques are reminiscent of faience amulets, which would have been easy to transport.
29. Gerharz 1994: some of Gerharz's re-assessment is now being challenged, but it remains the only significant published re-examination of the original excavations.

Bibliography

Adams, W. Y. (1977) *Nubia: Corridor to Africa*, Princeton.

Barnett, R. D. (1982) *Ancient Ivories in Middle East Qedem* 14), Jerusalem.

Bevan, A. (2003) Reconstructing the role of Egyptian culture in the value regimes of the Bronze Age Aegean: stone vessels and their social contexts. In R. Matthews & C. Roemer (eds), *Ancient Prespectives on Egypt*, 57–73. London.

Bulliet, R. W. (1975) *The Camel and the Wheel*, Cambridge MA.

Caminos, R. A. (1958) *The Chronicle of Prince Osorkon* (Analecta Orientalia 37), Rome.

Černý, J. (1965) Egypt from the death of Ramesses III to the end of the twenty-first Dynasty. *In Cambridge Ancient History* rev. ed. Vol. II, Chapter 35 (fascicle), Cambridge.

Culican, W. (1970) Almuñecar, Assur and Phoenician penetration of the western Mediterranean, *Levant* 2: 28–36.

Dalley, S. (1985) Foreign chariotry and cavalry in the armies of Tiglath-pileser III and Sargon II, *Iraq* 47: 31–48.

Davies, N. & A. H. Gardiner (1926) *The Tomb of Huy, Viceroy of Nubia in the Reign of Tut'ankhamun (No. 40)*, London.

Drews, R. (1993) *The End of the Bronze Age. Changes in Warfare and the Catastrophe ca. 1200 B.C.*, Princeton.

Dodson, A. (2012) *Afterglow of Empire: Egypt from the Fall of the New Kingdom to the Saite Renaissance*, Cairo-NewYork.

Drews, R. (1993) *The End of the Bronze Age. Changes in Warfare and the Catastrophe ca. 1200 B.C.*, Princeton.

Fattovich, R. (1982) The problem of Sudanese-Ethiopian contacts in antiquity. In J. M. Plumley (ed.), *Nubian Studies. Proceedings of the Symposium for Nubian studies*, 76–86, Warminster.

Fattovich, R. (1989) The Gash Delta between 1000 B.C. and A.D. 1000. *Studia Meroitica 1984* (*Meroitica* 10), 797–816, Berlin.

Fattovich, R. (1990) The problem of Punt in the light of the recent field work in the Eastern Sudan. In. S. Schöske (ed.), *Akten des Vierten Internationalen Ägyptologen-Kongresses. Bd. 4: Geschichte, Verwaltungs- und Wirtschaftsgeschichte, Rechtsgeschichte, Nachbarkulturen* (*Studien zur Altägyptischen Kultur* 4), 257–272, Hamburg.

Fattovich, R. (1991) At the periphery of the empire: the Gash Delta (Eastern Sudan). In W.V. Davies (ed.), *Egypt and Africa. Nubia from Prehistory to Islam*, 40–48, London.

Fattovich, R. (2006–2007) Aqiq: a coastal site in the red Sea, Sudan. In B. Gratien (ed.), *Mélanges offerts à Francis Geus* (*Cahiers de Recherches de l'Institut de Papyrologie et d'Égyptologie de Lille* 26), 87–97, Villeneuve d'Ascq.

Fattovich, R., A. Manzo & K.A. Bard (1998) Méroé et Axoum: nouveaux éléments de comparaison, *Archéologie du Nil Moyen* 8: 43–53.

Fletcher, R. N. (2012) Opening the Mediterranean: Assyria, the Levant and the transformation of Early Iron Age trade, *Antiquity* 86: 211–220.

Frandsen, P. J. (1979) Egyptian imperialism. In M. T. Larsen (ed.), *Power and Propaganda. A Symposium on Ancient Empires* (Mesopotamia 7), 167–190, Copenhagen.

Frankenstein, S. (1979) The Phoenicians in the far west: a function of Neo-Assyrian imperialism. In M. T. Larsen (ed.), *Power and Propaganda. A Symposium on Ancient Empires* (Mesopotamia 7), 263–294, Copenhagen.

Gerharz, R. (1994) *Jebel Moya* (Meroitica 14), Berlin.

Goedicke, H. (1975) *The Report of Wenamun*, Baltimore-London.

Groom, N. (1981) *Frankincense and Myrrh. A Study of the Arabian Incense Trade*, London-New York-Beirut.

Heidorn, L. (1994) Historical implications of the pottery from the earliest tombs at El Kurru, *Journal of the American Research Center in Egypt* 31: 115–131.

Heidorn, L. (1997) The horses of Kush, *Journal of Near Eastern Studies* 56: 105–114.

Hulin, L. (2009) The Western Marmarica Coastal Survey 2009: preliminary report, *Libyan Studies* 40: 95–103.

Jacquet-Gordon, H. (1982) Review of W. Y. Adams, *Meroitic North and South* (*Meroitica* 2), *Orientalistische Literaturzeitung* 77: 451–454.
James, P. (2005) Archaic Greek colonies in Libya: historical *vs.* archaeological chronologies? *Libyan Studies* 36: 1–20.
James, P. J., I. J. Thorpe, N. Kokkinos, R. G. Morkot & J. A. Frankish (1991) *Centuries of Darkness*, London.
Janssen, J. (1975) Prolegomena to the study of Egypt's economic history during the New Kingdom, *Studien zur Altägyptischen Kultur* 3: 127–185.
Jesse, F. (2004) The Wadi Howar. In D. A. Welsby & J. R. Anderson, *Sudan: Ancient Treasures*, 53–60, London.
Jesse, F. & R. Kuper (2006) Napata in the west? – the Gala Abu Ahmed fortress in lower Wadi Howar (NW-Sudan), *Archéologie du Nil Moyen* 10: 135–159.
Kemp, B. J. (1972a) Fortified towns in Nubia. In P. J. Ucko, R. Tringham & G. W. Dimbleby (eds), *Man, Settlement and Urbanism*, 651–656, London.
Kemp. B. J. (1972b) Temple and town in ancient Egypt. In P. J. Ucko, R. Tringham & G. W. Dimbleby (eds), *Man, Settlement and Urbanism*, 657–680, London.
Kemp, B. J. (1978) Imperialism and empire in New Kingdom Egypt (*c.* 1575–1087 BC). In P. D. A. Garnsey & C. R. Whittaker (eds), *Imperialism in the Ancient World*, 7–57, Cambridge.
Kendall, T. (1999) The origin of the Napatan state: El Kurru and the evidence for the royal ancestors, *Studien zum Antiken Sudan. Akten der 7.Internationalen Tagung für meroitistische Forschungen vom 14. bis 19. September 1992 in Gosen/bei Berlin* (Meroitica 15), 3–117, Berlin.
Kitchen, K.A. (1971) Punt and how to get there, *Orientalia* 40: 184–207.
Kitchen, K. A. (1990) The arrival of the Libyans in Late New Kingdom Egypt. In A. Leahy (ed.), *Libya and Egypt c 1300-750 B.C.*, 15–27, London.
Kitchen, K. A. (1993) The land of Punt. In T. Shaw, P. Sinclair, B. Andah & A. Okpoko (eds), *The Archaeology of Africa: Food, Metals and Towns*, 587–608, London-New York.
Kitchen, K. A. (1999) Further thoughts on Punt and its neighbours. In A. Leahy & J. Tait (eds), *Studies on Ancient Egypt in Honour of H.S. Smith*, 173–178, London.
Klemm, R. & D. Klemm (2013) *Gold and Gold Mining in Ancient Egypt and Nubia. Geoarchaeology of the Ancient Gold Mining Sites in the Egyptian and Sudanese Eastern Deserts*, Heidelberg-New York-London.
Krzyszkowska, O. & R. G. Morkot (2000) Ivory and related materials. In P. T. Nicholson & I. Shaw (eds), *Ancient Egyptian Materials and Technology*, 320–331, Cambridge.
Lacovara, P. (1991) The stone vase deposit at Kerma. In W. V. Davies (ed.), *Egypt and Africa. Nubia from Prehistory to Islam*, 118–128, London.
Lange, M. (2005) More archaeological work in Lower Wadi Howar (northern Sudan) – a preliminary report on the 2003 field season, *Nyame Akuma* 63: 15–19.
Liverani, M. (1987) The collapse of the Near Eastern regional system at the end of the Bronze Age: the case of Syria. In M. Rowlands, M. Larsen & K. Kristiansen (eds), *Centre and Periphery in the Ancient World*, 66–73, Cambridge.
Liverani, M. (1990) *Prestige and Interest. International Relations in the Near East ca 1600-1100 B.C.*, Padova.
Liverani, M. (2000) The Garamantes: a fresh approach, *Libyan Studies* 31: 17–28.
Mitchell, T. C. (1982) Israel and Judah until the revolt of Jehu (931–841 B.C.) and Israel and Judah from Jehu until the period of Assyian domination. *Cambridge Ancient History* III.1, 442–510, Cambridge.
Morkot, R. G. (1987) Studies in New Kingdom Nubia 1. Politics, economics and ideology: Egyptian imperialism in Nubia, *Wepwawet* 3: 29–49.
Morkot, R. G. (1991a) Nubia in the New Kingdom: the limits of Egyptian control. In W. V. Davies (ed.), *Egypt and Africa. Nubia from Prehistory to Islam*, 294–301, London.
Morkot, R. G. (1991b) Nubia and Achaemenid Persia. In H. Sancisi-Weerdenberg & A. Kuhrt (eds), *Asia Minor and Egypt: Old Cultures in a New Empire* (Achaemenid History VI), 321–336, Leiden.
Morkot, R. G. (1994) The Nubian Dark Age. In Ch. Bonnet (ed.), *Etudes Nubiennes (Genève)* 2, 45–47.

Morkot, R. G. (1994) *Economic and Cultural Exchange between Kush and Egypt*. PhD Dissertation, London University.

Morkot, R. G. (1995a) The economy of Nubia in the New Kingdom. In B. Gratien (ed.), *Actes de la VIIIe conférence internationale des études nubiennes 1 - Communications Principales* (*Cahiers de Recherches de l'Institut de Papyrologie et d'Égyptologie de Lille* 17), 175–187, Villeneuve d'Ascq.

Morkot, R. G. (1995b) The foundations of the Kushite state. A response to the paper of László Török. In B. Gratien (ed.), *Actes de la VIIIe conférence internationale des études nubiennes 1 - Communications Principales* (*Cahiers de Recherches de l'Institut de Papyrologie et d'Égyptologie de Lille* 17), 229–242, Villeneuve d'Ascq.

Morkot, R. G. (1998) "There are no elephants in Dongola"; notes on Nubian ivory. In B. Gratien (ed.), *Actes de la VIIIe conférence internationale des études nubiennes 1 - Communications Principales* (*Cahiers de Recherches de l'Institut de Papyrologie et d'Égyptologie de Lille* 17), 147–154, Villeneuve d'Ascq.

Morkot, R. G. (1999) The origin of the "Napatan" state. A contribution to T. Kendall's main paper. *Studien zum Antiken Sudan. Akten der 7. Internationalen Tagung für meroitistische Forschungen vom 14. bis 19. September 1992 in Gosen/bei Berlin* (Meroitica 15), 139–148, Berlin.

Morkot, R. G. (2000) *The Black Pharaohs: Egypt's Nubian Rulers*, London.

Morkot, R. G. (2001) Egypt and Nubia. In S. E. Alcock, T. N. D'Altroy, K. D. Morrison & C. M. Sinopoli (eds), *Empires. Perspectives from Archaeology and History*, 227–251, Cambridge.

Morkot, R. G. (2007) War and the economy: the international "arms trade" in the Late Bronze Age and after. In Th. Schneider & K. Szpakowska (eds), *Egyptian Stories. A British Egyptological Tribute to Alan B. Lloyd on the Occasion of his Retirement. Alter Orient und Altes Testament* (Veröffentlichungen zur Kultur und Geschichte des Alten Orients und des Altes Testaments 347), 169–195, Münster.

O'Connor, D. (1990) The nature of Tjemhu (Libyan) society in the later New Kingdom. In A. Leahy (ed.), *Libya and Egypt c 1300–750 B.C.*, 29–113, London.

Parcerisa, J. & I. Padro (1985) *Egyptian-type Documents from the Mediterranean Littoral of the Iberian Peninsula before the Roman Conquest. III. Study of the Material*, Leiden.

Postgate, N. J. (1974) *Taxation and Conscription in the Assyrian Empire* (Studia Pohl: Series maior 3), Roma.

Postgate, N. J. (1979) The economic structure of the Assyrian empire. In M. T. Larsen (ed.), *Power and Propaganda. A Symposium on Ancient Empires* (Mesopotamia 7), 193–221, Copenhagen.

Richardson, S. (1999) Libya domestica: Libyan trade and society on the eve of the invasion of Egypt, *Journal of the American Research Center in Egypt* 36: 149–164.

Serpico, M. (2000) Resins, amber and bitumen. In P. Nicholson & I. Shaw (eds), *Ancient Egyptian Materials and Technology*, 430–474, Cambridge.

Sherratt, S. (2000) Circulation of metals at the end of the Bronze Age in the Eastern Mediterranean. In C. F. E. Pare (ed.), *Metals Make the World Go Round: the Supply and Circulation of Metals in Bronze Age Europe*, 82–98, Oxford.

Sherratt, S. (2003) The Mediterranean economy: "globalization" at the end of the second millennium B.C.E. In W. G. Dever & S. Gitin (eds), *Symbiosis, Symbolism, and the Power of the Past. Canaan, Ancient Israel, and Their Neighbors from the Late Bronze Age through Roman Palaestina*, 37–62, Winona Lake.

Shinnie, P. L. (1967) *Meroe: a Civilization of the Sudan*, London.

Shinnie, P. L. (1978) Trade in medieval Nubia. *In Études Nubiennes. Colloque de Chantilly* (Institut française d'Archéologie orientale Bibliothèque d'Étude 77), 253–263, Cairo.

Snape, S. (2003) The emergence of Libya on the horizon of Egypt. In D. O'Connor & S. Quirke (eds), *Mysterious Lands*, 93–106, London.

Snape, S. & P. Wilson (2007) *Zawiyet Umm el-Rakham I: The Temple and Chapels*, Bolton.

Sparks, R. S. (2003) Egyptian stone vessels and the politics of exchange. In R. Matthews & C. Roemer (eds), *Ancient Perspectives on Egypt*, 39–56, London.

Spence, K. & P. Rose (2009) Fieldwork at Sesebi, *Sudan & Nubia* 13: 38–46.

Spence, K., Rose, P. J., Bradshaw, R., Collet, P., Hassan, A., MacGinnis, J., Masson, A. & van Pelt, P. (2011) Sesebi 2011, *Sudan & Nubia* 15: 34–39.

Török, L. (1995) The emergence of the kingdom of Kush and her myth of the state in the first millennium BC. In B. Gratien (ed.), *Actes de la VIIIe conférence internationale des études nubiennes 1 - Communications Principales* (*Cahiers de Recherches de l'Institut de Papyrologie et d'Égyptologie de Lille* 17), 203–228, Villeneuve d'Ascq.

Török, L. (1999) The origin of the Napatan state: the long chronology of the el-Kurru cemetery. A contribution to T. Kendall's main paper. *Studien zum Antiken Sudan. Akten der 7. Internationalen Tagung für meroitistische Forschungen vom 14. bis 19. September 1992 in Gosen/bei Berlin.* Meroitica 15, Berlin, 149–159.

Trigger, B.G. (1969) The Myth of Meroe and the African Iron Age, *African Historical Studies* 2/1, 23–50.

Trigger, B. G. (1976) *Nubia under the Pharaohs*, London.

Trigger, B. G., B. J. Kemp, D. O'Connor & A. B. Lloyd (1983) *Ancient Egypt, a Social History*, Cambridge.

Vercoutter, J. (1959) The gold of Kush, *Kush* 7: 120–153.

Vincentelli, I. (2006) *Hillat el-Arab: the joint Sudanese-Italian expedition in the Napata Region. Sudan*, Oxford.

White, D. (2002) *Marsa Matruh I. The Excavation. II. The Objects. The University of Pennsylvania Museum of Archaeology and Anthropology's Excavations on Bates's Island, Marsa Matruh, Egypt 1985–1989*, Philadelphia.

Zibelius-Chen, K. (1989) Uberlegungen zur Ägyptischen Nubienpolitik in der Dritten Zwischenzeit, *Studien zur Altägyptischen Kultur* 16: 329–345.

Chapter 12

Temples, trade and money in Egypt in the 1st millennium BC

Renate Müller-Wollermann

This paper will focus on the relationship between temples and the state, their income and the expenditure of the state and especially between temples and the evolution of money and coined money in particular. An emphasis on temple treasuries will clip these issues together.

It should be taken into consideration that a rupture in the time axis of the 1st millennium BC might be the Persian conquest of the country in 525 BC, although one should also have in mind the laissez-faire attitude of the Persians toward the culture of conquered regions.

Temples

The evidence for the economic situation of temples in the first millennium is meagre, to say the least. In comparison with the preceding New Kingdom it is next to nothing. We have nearly no idea about the income of temples and of their expenditures. Nevertheless, some Egyptologists claim that temples are the second most important economic power in the country and that the state lost power to the temples from about 1000 BC onwards. The main reason for the loss of power was the dissolution of the centralised state around 1080 until about 700 BC, a period called the Third Intermediate Period. For the following Late Period prosperity of the temples was claimed as well (Redford 2001, 155–157). Moreover, there is no archaeological evidence for temple treasuries during this time. Therefore, we have to rely on texts.

At least we do have some texts from the first half of the 1st millennium which show that kings equipped temples to some extent.

For example, we have a text of Sheshonq I, who reigned from 931 until 910 BC, which specifies the annual levy to a temple in Herakleopolis at the Fayyūm entrance. Every year 365 oxen must be handed over to the temple by a number of officials and villages in the region (Ritner 2009, 180–186). Sheshonq's aim was to reinstall the cult that had been neglected in the troubled time before.

In the first 3¼ years of his reign his son and successor Osorkon I (910–896 BC) carved the endowments to temples on a well of the temple of Bubastis in the delta. They comprised more than 27,000 kg of gold and more than 180,000 kg of silver (Ritner 2009, 249–258). It may have been much more, as the text is partly destroyed and therefore the information not complete. These riches may have been acquired by his father on his campaign against Palestine.

Other texts stem from the beginning of the reign of king Taharqa, who sat on the throne from 690 until 664 BC. They contain very detailed lists of gifts presented by the king to the Amun temple of Kawa in Nubia. The lists contain gold, silver and copper utensils, but also basic materials such as incense, wax, linen, and timber. He also refurbished the temple and equipped it with huge numbers of staff and craftsmen (Ritner 2009, 527–539, 545–555). The exact amount of what was endowed to the temple is not known, because in many passages the king speaks only of "incalculable numbers". In the first years, the gifts seem to stem from his own resources, but from his 8th year onwards, the wealth seems to result from war profits (Redford 1992, 354–355).

A decree of Amasis (569–526 BC) in the 26th Dynasty says that serfs, cattle and the product of the surrounding land shall be given to the temple of Ptah in Memphis (Gunn 1927). Other royal donation texts are of minor economic importance; they disappear after the 26th Dynasty and reappear in the 30th Dynasty (Meeks 1979).

As we have only a few texts from different kings and different places, we cannot say for sure whether these texts are symptomatic or not. One should like to mention, however, that such texts are known from earlier time periods as well, but not from later. In the Late Period, there is only archaeological evidence for building and enlarging temples, especially under the last Pharaonic king Nectanebo II (360–343 BC).

On the other hand, we have some evidence that shows that the state squeezed the temples by shortening their income or increasing the levies in favour of the state. This was made necessary by an increased expenditure of the state for military activities, especially for paying mercenaries and building up a navy.

State expenditure: mercenaries

In Egypt mercenaries were even more useful than in other countries. During the inundation one could neither fight wars, because the expanse of water hindered the movement of troops, nor till the fields. In the rest of the year, ordinary soldiers, and this means peasants, had to cultivate their fields besides taking part in the expeditions. Mercenaries were more flexible, but their employment and the use of a navy required additional resources and the income and possessions of temples were used to acquire these resources. The introduction of coined money was a way to ease these measures.

Greek settlers, not necessarily mercenaries, can be found in Egypt from the middle of the 7th century BC. The foundation of the Greek emporion in Naucratis will have taken place in the first decade of the reign of Psammetichus I, around 660. The first settlers, however, may have been merchants, not mercenaries. The original Egyptian settlement can be dated back to the Libyan Period, i.e. the end of the 10th century (Yoyotte 1993–1994, 679–680). Moreover, Herodotus records the settlement of Greeks and Carians in the eastern delta, who were later resettled in the Memphite region. He says: "The Ionians and Carians who had helped him to conquer were given by Psammetichus places to dwell in called The Camps, opposite to each other on either side of the Nile; and besides this he paid them all he had promised" and further on "Long afterwards, king Amasis removed them thence and settled them at Memphis, to be his guard against the Egyptians" (Herodotus II 154). "The Camps" may have been situated in the region between Faqus and Qantir (Carrez-Maratray 2000, 163) and the change of place will have occurred in the beginning of Amasis's reign, i.e. in the 60s of the 6th century at the latest. It does not mean that mercenaries were remunerated with land, but that they were given land to settle during their employment.

Greek mercenaries remained in Egypt even after 525 BC, that is the Persian conquest (Carrez-Maratray 2000). They are further attested in the Achaemenid empire during the campaign of Cyrus the Younger in 401/400 BC, during the satrapial rebellions after 370 BC and, of course, during the wars concerning Egypt (Seibt 1977). They fought on both sides, on the Egyptian one and the Persian.

We are relatively well informed about the number of Greek mercenaries in Egypt. Herodotus tells us that the king Apries, who reigned from 589 until 570 BC, had 30,000 Carian and Ionian mercenaries (Herodotus II 163). According to Thucydides, a soldier earned a drachme per day (Thucydides VII 27, 2). A drachme weighed a little more than 3 g of silver. This means that Apries had to pay 100 kg of silver per day to his foreign mercenaries, if Herodotus is right. Tachos (362–360 BC) had 10,000 Greek mercenaries in addition to his Egyptian soldiers, and Nectanebo II, who reigned from 360 until 342 BC, employed 20,000 Greek mercenaries, about the same number of Libyans, and 60,000 Egyptians (Diodorus XVI 47, 6), which means that he had to pay the largest sum to finance his army. Moreover, according to Diodorus (XV 29, 1), the payment of mercenaries in Egypt was high compared to the payment in other countries.

State expenditure: navy

The second major item of expenditure was the navy. As is well known, Egypt was no famous sea-faring nation and, therefore, had no important navy before the time of Necho (610–593 BC), at least not a navy equipped for sea-battles, i.e. for ramming, rather than one just for transporting troops. On the other hand, Egypt learned during the Greco-Persian conflict, as well as Greece and Persia, that the role of navies was crucial. Indeed the building of the Persian navy was provoked by the existence of the Egyptian fleet. In 480, according to Herodotus, 200 Egyptian ships took part in the battle of Salamis on the side of the Persians and under Persian leadership (Herodotus VII 89). These ships may have been triremes, as they were "invented" in the end in Egypt shortly after 535 BC. As a trireme was manned by 170 rowers, 34,000 shipmen were involved, a number quite close to that of Apries's navy, mentioned above. Whether the rowmen of Salamis were mercenaries or Egyptians, who had been trained in the meantime, is not known. Moreover, it is not known how many ships could be rescued after the battle. In 459 BC the Athenian navy sailed from Cyprus to Egypt and brought the delta and parts of Memphis under their control. Further, the Persian navy under Megabyzos defeated the Athenians and Egyptians in the years 456–454 BC. Here, for sure, a large part of the navy was lost and had to be rebuilt.

State income: temples

In order to cope with these demands, the Egyptians had to introduce several measures; one was to acquire additional income, especially from the temples, the other to ease these measures, namely in the form of money and especially coined money.

Cambyses was the first Persian king who reduced the direct income of the Egyptian temples, at least to some extent. Instead of direct revenues, temples were given places in Egypt from which they could obtain necessities. According to a text on the verso of the Demotic Chronicle, a text perhaps dating to the Ptolemaic period, all temples were affected with the exception of three, the Ptah temple in Memphis, the temple of *Wn-ḫm*, probably north of Memphis, and the temple of *Pr-Ḥʿpj* near Heliopolis (Spiegelberg 1914, 32–33). Although the last two temples cannot be located precisely, it is clear that temples in the region of Memphis were exempted, and Memphis, of course, was the seat of the Persian satrap and had to be looked after. Agut-Labordère even interpreted this text in such a way that Egyptian temples should be self-sufficient (Agut-Labordère 2005). Another remarkable phenomenon is the shift of the textile industry from state institutions in the New Kingdom to temples in the Late Period (Tata 1986, 241–244), which means that temples held a grip on an important export product. Darius I, as is generally assumed, supported again the Egyptian temples and even continued work in the famous temple in the Kharga oasis; at least this was done in his name (Lloyd 2007, 107–108). But matters changed again in the 30th Dynasty, this time not in favour of the Persians, but against them. The Athenian politician Chabrias advised king Tachos to finance his war in Palestine against the Persians with additional assessments put on the temples. This has been handed down to us by Pseudo-Aristotle in his Oikonomikos:

> "When Taos, king of Egypt, needed funds for an expedition he was making, Chabrias of Athens advised him to inform the priests that to save expense it was necessary to

> suppress some of the temples together with the majority of the attendant priests. On hearing this, each priesthood, being anxious to retain their own temple, offered him money from their private possessions (as well as from the temple funds). When the king had thus received money from them all, Chabrias bade him tell the priests to spend on the temple-service and on their own maintenance one-tenth of what they formerly spent and lend him the remainder until he had made peace with the king of Persia." (Aristotle, Oeconomica II, 25)

So, according to political circumstances, Egyptian temples were squeezed in favour of the Persians or in favour of the Greeks.

Another measure taken by the state in order to have a firm grip on the temples, especially on the temple of Amun in Karnak, was the institution of the God's wife of Amun at the beginning of the New Kingdom. This institution should have limited the omnipotence of the temple in Thebes and was also equipped with a treasury (Graefe 1981, 19–20, 75). Shortly after the Persian conquest, the office disappeared never to re-emerge. On the one hand, it was too powerful to leave it in Egyptian hands, on the other, it was not appropriate to send Persian royal daughters abroad (Ayad 2001). In general, the families of priests in Upper Egypt did not simply die out during the Persian Period, but they lacked possibilities of self-presentation (Vittmann 2009, 109–114).

Trade

Let us go back to the beginning of the 1st millennium BC and to trade at that time and the beginning of the use of money.

The evidence for foreign trade in the 1st millennium is meagre. This is connected with the fact that most trade items were made of perishable material, but also with the fact that Egyptian texts are more or less silent. Greek sources provide far more information. From Greek texts we learn that the main item exported from Egypt into the Greek world was grain, other items were linen and papyrus (Austin 1970, 35–36). Another exported article traded into the Levant was fish, which was found in many sites (Lernau 2006, 483), such as Dor, Megiddo and Lachish. The imported goods consisted mainly of wine and olive oil (Austin 1970, 36–37). Further information is provided by an Aramaic papyrus from Elephantine dated to 475 or 454 BC which lists custom duties. Imported goods from Ionia[1] and Phoenicia were gold, silver, bronze, tin, iron, wood, wool, wine and oil, the only exported good mentioned is natron (Porten & Yardeni 1993). Wine and oil are more visible in the archaeological material (Wilson 2011, 166), because they were transported in amphorae. Other items wrapped in perishable material, or not at all, were less noticeable; therefore, trade in textiles especially is highly under-estimated.

In the 21st Dynasty we see an increase of the number of silver objects in the royal necropolis of Tanis in the delta. Where this silver is coming from is not clear, but definitely not from Egypt. It can only have been come into Egypt by trade, not by tribute, because Egypt was not in a position to demand tribute at that time.

In the 22nd Dynasty Sheshonq I (931–910 BC) conducted a military campaign in Palestine, but not in order to conquer these areas, but to control the trade routes. Partners in trade activities were the Phoenician cities at the coast and, in the first line, Tyre. The trade between Phoenicia and Egypt was not only for the economic benefit of both, but created an inflow of silver into Egypt.

One can find silver, however, not only in the royal necropolis or in texts written by kings, but also in ordinary payment documents. In the preceding time, the New Kingdom, one can find silver only as a measure of value, not of payment, recognisable by text passages saying that silver was given in objects (which were not necessarily made of silver). In the 21st Dynasty texts mention real silver instead of objects. In the 22nd Dynasty one can find silver of the treasury of the god Harsaphes in the texts. In later times silver as a measure of payment is always defined as silver of a certain treasury. From the 22nd Dynasty until Psammetichus, the first king of the 26th Dynasty, it is always silver of the treasury of the god Harsaphes, from then on until the Persian conquest in 525 BC it is silver of the treasury of the town, i.e. Thebes, afterwards silver of the treasury of the god Ptah, i.e. Ptah in Memphis. The terminology is applied in such a consequent way that one can use the designation of treasuries as a criterium for dating the documents. This implies that temple treasuries guaranteed the weight and probably also the pureness of the silver pieces which were handed out.

In the 26th Dynasty Naukratis was the only place in Egypt which handled the trade with Greece and was a "port of trade" in the tradition of the Polanyi school (Möller 2000 and this volume). Later, other towns took over this role such as Heracleion/Thonis at the Mediterranean coast and Egypt was much more open to international trade (Pfeiffer 2010, 18–20).

Treasuries

The evidence for treasuries, temple treasuries and state treasuries, is next to nothing. The only treasury of the 1st millennium which is known archaeologically and designated as such, is the treasury of Shabaqa, who reigned from 712 until 698 BC, in the Karnak temple (Leclant 1965, 19–23). Other constructions made of brick were interpreted as magazines for temple offerings (Traunecker 1987), but not as treasuries in the precise sense of the word. Texts again provide more information, especially in the form of titles of their overseers and other personnel. The exact function of these officials, is, however, hard to determine, the more so as one text indicates that the post of an overseer of a temple treasury could be a part-time job (Vittmann 1998, 428–429).

In the 27th Dynasty an overseer of the treasury, obviously in Memphis, is known, who equipped the temple of Ptah (Jansen-Winkeln 1998, 163–168, pl. x). There is evidence for officials of the temple treasury of Amun in Karnak in the 25th Dynasty (Jansen-Winkeln 2001, 16, 19, 334–335, pls 5–6) and the treasury of the God's Wife of Amun in Karnak in the 22nd Dynasty (Graefe 1981, 75). At least one overseer of the treasury in Sais is known in the 26th Dynasty, another official praises himself for having filled the temple of Neith in Sais anew (Heise 2007, 225ff., 234ff.). Further, but indirect, evidence is given for the treasury of the Neith temple in Sais by the Naukratis stela of Nectanebo I (380–363 BC; Lichtheim 1980, 86–89) which says that a part of the duties collected should go to this temple; therefore, it must have been endowed with a treasury. A parallel of this text was found in Thonis/Herakleion at the Mediterranean coast (Yoyotte 2001). Other temples may have gained by customs duties as well such as those at the southern frontier (Posener 1947, 126).

Our knowledge of state treasuries, apart from the Persian Period, is limited to one official who bears the title of Overseer of the State Treasury at the time of Apries/Amasis in the 6th century BC, but his location is unknown (Pressl 1998, 31, 231–233). Apart from this title, we have only the indirect evidence provided by the Naukratis stela. If a small part of the revenues went to the temple treasury in Sais, the rest must have gone to the state treasury. In the Persian 27th Dynasty the situation is different – to no-one's surprise, because the Persian leaders wanted to control the income. So, the "house of the king" collected the customs duties listed on the Aramaic Elephantine papyrus mentioned above. Aramaic letters found in Saqqara were sent by the satrap Arsames to the chief of the treasury, who bore an Egyptian name and moved between Persia and Egypt (Driver 1954). In the case of Ptah-hotep, an overseer of the treasury buried in Saqqara, it is unknown whether he was the overseer of the state treasury or the treasury of the temple of Ptah (Pressl 1998, 31, 305).

This reveals a major problem concerning the exact definition and use of treasuries. Even if some evidence exists for state treasuries in the Persian Period, it is well known that Persian satraps, not only in Egypt, used temple treasuries for their purposes (Klinkott 2005, 402). That the official silver pieces were given out by the temple of Ptah is a further indication to this policy. It may have been even more the case during the indigenous Egyptian dynasties. Therefore, the distinction between temple treasuries and state treasuries becomes more and more blurred.

Money

In order to make use of mercenaries, Egypt had to comply with their needs. Most mercenaries were Greek and used to coined money. Therefore, they expected coins as payment, the more so, as coins could be easily transported back to their homelands when they returned after their employment. It is, however, unclear how many of them returned home after their service and how long their conscription lasted; Wallinga tentatively assumes a period of 4 years (Wallinga 1991, 185–186). Those who lived in the country or remained there after the end of their contract may have used the coins to buy Greek products such as wine or oil (Wilson & Gilbert 2007, 260). Those who settled will have used them to start a new life.

The first coins mentioned in Egyptian texts were staters, i.e. Athenian tetradrachms, at the end of the 5th century BC; sometimes they are specified as *sttr n Wjnn*, Ionian staters. For the first time they appear on a Demotic ostracon from the year 13 of Darius II, that is 412 BC, from ᶜAin Manāwir near Dūš in the south of Kharga oasis (Chauveau 2012). In ostraca from the same place from the year 414 BC, the stater is still absent, however, it appears quite often in the years after 410 BC. Moreover, it is converted according to the scheme whereby so and so many staters are so and so many silver *dbn* (an Egyptian weight of 91 g), are so and so many staters again. Therefore, the reference point and the means of payment was the stater and not the silver *dbn*. No-one, however, will claim that the remote village of ᶜAin Manāwir was a centre of foreign mercenaries or merchants, even if trade routes into the desert went via this place, which was guarded by a fortification (Cruz-Uribe 2003, 37, 42). Herodotus (III 26) mentions Samians dwelling in the Oasis, which should be identified with Kharga, and they may well be mercenaries. One should assume, therefore, that Greek tetradrachms were used in the Nile valley even earlier. Indeed, they can be found nearly contemporaneously in Aramaic texts from Elephantine. At the same time, however, Demotic documents from all regions mention the silver from the treasury of Ptah as a point of reference and means of payment. The stater, therefore, was in use, but not as an exclusive medium of payment.

Further evidence for the use of coins as coins are the late hoards of the 4th century BC. In this period more and more hoards exclusively contain Athenian tetradrachms, in fact they number in the thousands. A good proportion of these coins are newly struck and show no signs of wear, much less cuts made in order to test the quality of the silver. The best known hoards of this kind are those from Tell el-Maskhuta in north-east Egypt, with more than 6000 coins (Robinson 1947) deposited as a dedication to a temple, and one from the Fayyūm, today in Michigan, with 347 coins (unpublished). The mass of identical pieces is puzzling and, even more so are two other facts; the first is that Athenian tetradrachms imitated in Palestine, Syria and Phoenicia are well known and the second, of particular interest, is that in Egypt several coin dies have been found which show the image of Athenian tetradrachms (Meadows 2011). As it seems highly unlikely that these coin dies were unintentionally carried off from Athens to Egypt, the unavoidable conclusion is that Athenian tetradrachms were recoined in Egypt. Moreover, this must have been done to a considerable extent, because the coins of the Fayyūm hoard indicate several slightly different coin dies. A problem, however, is dating these recoined pieces. While, until quite recently, the general opinion was that the real Athenian tetradrachms showing Athene with a frontal eye date from the 5th century BC and that those with a profile eye date from the 4th century, it remains unclear whether the imitations follow the same pattern. At the present time, it is still uncertain which among this enormous number of Athenian tetradrachms found in the Mediterranean area or lying in museums without any find spot known are original Athenian tetradrachms and which are recoined.

One assumes that the Egyptian recoined pieces, the imitations, date from the 30th Dynasty. In any case, they seem to have been struck before the coins that are discussed below. The dating of all these coins is unclear – with the exception of the first one.

1. An Athenian imitation made of gold from the reign of Tachos (Hill 1926, 130–132, pl. VI.23). Again one can see the owl, but instead of Alpha, Theta, Epsilon one sees Tau, Alpha, Omega, designating Tachos, and instead of the olive spray a papyrus plant. Its weight of 8.30 g corresponds to the Persian gold daric. One might add that this coin is unique and was found in Memphis.
2. Much more numerous, however, is the following coin that is known in about 80 specimens, but with slight differences in its stamps and a weight of 8–9 g. It is a gold coin with the inscription *nb.w nfr* "good gold". This coinage also seems to have been struck in the 30th Dynasty, probably under Nectanebo II just before Alexander the Great (Dumke 2011, 59–61). For the first time, however, Egyptians freed themselves from Greek stamps and created something entirely new.
3. More than a dozen imitations of tetradrachms were found in Iraq and Syria struck by Artaxerxes III (343–338) probably in Memphis (Vleeming 2001, 1–4); they bear demotic inscriptions.
4. The very last independent coinage was struck by the last Persian king Darius III (335–332 BC) or his satraps Sabakes and Mazakes respectively in the 2nd Persian Period (Nicolet-Pierre 1979). These coins bear inscriptions in Aramaic and were mainly discovered in hoards in Syria.
5. An Athenian imitation made of silver weighing 0.64 g; the Athenian ethnic Alpha, Theta, Epsilon, however, is replaced by Nun, Alpha, Ypsilon, designating Naukratis (Newell 1938, 60–62, pl. IV.35). Only one specimen is known, and this is probably the only city coinage in Egypt before the reign of Alexander the Great, because the bronze coins of Naukratis may be still later.
6. A silver coin found in Xois in the Delta, a tritemorion; its weight is 0.56 g, that is the 32nd part of a tetradrachm (Goyon 1987). One can see the owl and the inscription Alpha, Theta, Epsilon, the acronym designating Athens, but instead of the olive spray the sign *nb.w ḥḏ*, i.e. silver.
7. Two silver coins with the head of Athena on the obverse; the reverse shows two eagles framing the hieroglyphs *nfr* and *nb* (van Alfen 2002, 23–24; Dumke 2011,

87–88). Whether these signs are hieroglyphs at all seems to be highly problematic. Both coins are tritemoria and their find spot is unclear.

8. Silver fractions of Athenian type, but with the hieroglyphic symbol *w3ḥ*. Five specimens are known and they all may come from a hoard in Sicily. Their weight is 0.40–0.50 g, that is between an Athenian obol and hemiobol (van Alfen 2002, 20).

On the one hand, the indigenous coin inscriptions weaken the hypothesis that coins were invented in order to pay mercenaries; on the other, the find spots outside Egypt may speak in favour of it. The coins nos 5–8 presented above, however, are by far too small to have been used as payment for mercenaries. They may rather have served as small change and been used for other purposes and in other economic circles than the tetradrachms. This fact also weakens the hypothesis of Kienitz that the Egyptian coins were struck earlier than the imitations of Athenian tetradrachms (Kienitz 1953, 118); one must, however, admit that he was not yet aware of the coin finds outside Egypt. Small change may even have been struck later than great nominals. In any case, all these developments were brought to a halt by Alexander and the Ptolemies and their coinage.

These are the phenomena of foreign and indigenous coins of Pharaonic Egypt. Let us now go back and consider how foreign coins came into the country and what they evoked. It has been assumed for a long time that they arrived in Egypt by means of trade. Their places of origin were direct and indirect trade partners of Egypt. Athens as a buyer of Egyptian grain is well known, other places, however, are less known such as Phaselis in southern Lycia, which also was in need of grain, because it had no hinterland that could be used for agriculture (Schäfer 1981, Faltplan; Heipp-Tamer 1993, 32–33). Moreover, it was situated on the route from Greece to Egypt, and the same holds true for Cyprus. If one looks at the nominals in the hoards, it becomes very obvious that the coins were definitely used for the payment of large deliveries of goods; they were not the small change of sailors or merchants. In addition, they were used for the payment of mercenaries. These foreign soldiers had indeed flooded the country since the 26th Dynasty, and some even settled down with their families (Kaplan 2003). They can be found throughout the country, in the south as far as Nubia, whereas the early coin hoards are concentrated in the delta. Ordinary mercenaries, however, would have left the country and taken the coins with them. This means that the mass of coins in the north of Egypt results from trade.

The next point at issue relates to the question who put these coin hoards together. Was it Greek merchants who brought the hoards with them, Greek mercenaries who piled them up or was it Egyptians who collected the coins over time? The answer is not easy to give and probably depends on the function of each hoard. In the case of the hoard of Tell el-Maskhuta, a votive gift to a Canaanite temple, it may have been accumulated by pious people. In the case of a relatively small hoard found in the sarcophagus of a Phoenician, it may have been put together by this person – if the find spot is conveyed correctly at all (Buttrey 1994, 71–72).

Leaving aside these votive hoards, the question arises as to what the Egyptians did with these coins. During the First Persian Period they may have been used to pay the tribute to the Persian king that had to be paid in silver. According to Herodotus it amounted to 700 talents (Herodotus III 91). The sum of this tribute, however, seems to be much less than the profit generated by the export of grain. Others may have been melted down and moulded into silver plates or statues which were dedicated to Egyptian temples. In any case, the mass of silver coins will have been in the hands of the state, not in the hands of private individuals. Large hoards are in any case far too rich to have belonged to private persons; in that case, it would have made them multi-millionaires. Only occasionally do individuals appear to have had the chance to obtain single coins. The demotic texts provide evidence for that. The light Egyptian coins, however, show that small change was available.

A different explanation is required for the imitations of tetradrachms struck in Egypt. They were probably minted with the clear aim to guarantee payments. The text of Pseudo-Aristotle speaks about warfare in Palestine in the 30th Dynasty under Tachos and the need for silver to finance the war; the passage has been quoted above. Due to the fact that his troops were multinationals, an international currency such as Athenian tetradrachms offered itself a good choice. In the course of time, they paved the way for striking similar-looking, but Egyptian-type coins. Taking the slightly different coin dies into consideration, the minting must have run into millions of coins. This mass of money cannot have been used only for mercenaries or merchants; it must have been in local use as well.

Conclusion

To sum up, the role of the temples in comparison with that of the state is not easy to determine. It depends on the fact – and this means the time – whether the state is strong or not. The role of the temples in trade is even more complicated to determine, because the evidence is meagre. The role of the temples in the evolution of coined money, however, is a strong one, as they paved the way to a money economy, even if a real money economy was still far away. On the whole, it seems that there was a switch from state-run to temple-run economic institutions in the Late Period.

Note

1. All the captains come from Phaselis; the cautious reservations made by Briant and Descat 1998, 63, are superfluous, because in general erroneous formulations are not rare.

Bibliography

Agut-Labordère, D. (2005) Le sens du Décret de Cambyse, *Transeuphratène* 29: 9–16.

Aristotle = Tredennick, H. & G. C. Armstrong (1962) *Oeconomica and Magna Moralia*, London.

Austin, M. M. (1970) *Greece and Egypt in the Archaic Age* (Proceedings of the Cambridge Philological Society Supplement 2), Cambridge.

Ayad, M. (2001) Some thoughts on the disappearance of the office of the God's Wife of Amun, *Journal of the Society for the Study of Egyptian Antiquities* 28: 1–14.

Briant, P. & R. Descat (1998) Un registre douanier de la satrapie d'Égypte à l'époque achéménide (TAD C3,7). In N. Grimal & B. Menu (eds), *Le commerce en Égypte ancienne* (Bibliothèque d'Étude 121), 59–104, Cairo.

Buttrey, T. V. (1994) CH VIII, 57. In U. Wartenberg, M. Jessop Price & K. A. McGregor, *Coin Hoards Volume VIII. Greek Hoards*, 71–72, London.

Carrez-Maratray, J.-Y. (2000) Le "monopole de Naucratis" et la "bataille de Péluse": ruptures ou continuités de la présence grecque en Égypte des Saïtes aux Perses, *Transeuphratène* 19: 159–172.

Chauveau, M. (2012) Démotique, *Annuaire de l'École pratique des hautes études (EPHE), Section des sciences historiques et philologiques* 143. http://ashp.revues.org/index1246.html.

Cruz-Uribe, E. (2003) The invasion of Egypt by Cambyses, *Transeuphratène* 25: 9–60.

Diodorus = Sherman, C. L. (1952) *Diodorus of Sicily VII*, London.

Driver, G. R. (1954) *Aramaic Documents of the Fifth Century B.C.*, Oxford.

Dumke, G. (2011) Gutes Gold. Überlegungen zum Sinnhorizont der *nbw nfr*-Prägungen des Nektanebos II. In B. Eckhardt & K. Martin (eds), *Geld als Medium in der Antike*, 59–92, Berlin.

Goyon, G. (1987) La plus ancienne(?) monnaie frappée en Égypte: un *tritemorion*, *Bulletin de l'Institut Français d'Archéologie Orientale* 87: 219–223, pls. XLIII–XLIV.

Graefe, E. (1981) *Untersuchungen zur Verwaltung und Geschichte der Institution der Gottesgemahlin des Amun vom Beginn des Neuen Reiches bis zur Spätzeit. Band II: Analyse und Indices*, Wiesbaden.

Gunn, B. (1927) The stela of Apries at Mîtrahîna, *Annales du Service de l'Antiquités de l'Égypte* 27: 211–237.

Heipp-Tamer, C. (1993) *Die Münzprägung der lykischen Stadt Phaselis in griechischer Zeit*, Saarbrücken.

Heise, J. (2007). *Erinnern und Gedenken. Aspekte der biographischen Inschriften der ägyptischen Spätzeit* (Orbis Biblicus et Orientalis 226, Fribourg/Göttingen.

Herodotus = Godley, A. D. (1960–1963) *Herodotus I-III*, London.

Hill, G. F. (1926) Greek Coins Acquired by the British Museum in 1925, *The Numismatic Chronicle and Journal of the Royal Numismatic Society* 5. ser. 6: 117–136, pls. V–VI.

Jansen-Winkeln, K. (1998) Drei Denkmäler mit archaisierender Orthographie, *Orientalia* 67: 155–172, pls VIII–X.

Jansen-Winkeln, K. (2001) *Biographische und religiöse Inschriften der Spätzeit aus dem Ägyptischen Museum Kairo*, Wiesbaden.

Kaplan, P. (2003) Cross-cultural contacts among mercenary communities in Saite and Persian Egypt, *Mediterranean Historical Review* 18: 1–31.

Kienitz, F. K. (1953) *Die politische Geschichte Ägyptens vom 7. bis zum 4. Jahrhundert vor der Zeitwende*, Berlin.

Klinkott, H. (2005) *Der Satrap. Ein achaimenidischer Amtsträger und seine Handlungsspielräume*, Frankfurt.

Leclant, J. (1965) *Recherches sur les monuments thébains de la XXVe dynastie dite éthiopienne*, Cairo.

Lernau, O. (2006) Fish remains. In I. Finkelstein, D. Ussishkin & B. Halpern (eds), *Megiddo IV. The 1998–2002 Seasons*, 474–496, Tel Aviv.

Lichtheim, M. (1980) *Ancient Egyptian Literature. A Book of Readings. Volume III: The Late Period*, Berkeley-Los Angeles-London.

Lloyd, A. B. (2007) Darius I in Egypt: Suez and Hibis. In C. Tuplin (ed.), *Persian Responses. Political and Cultural Interaction With(in) the Achaemenid Empire*, 99–115, Swansea.

Meadows, A. (2011) Athenian coin dies from Egypt: the new discovery at Herakleion, *Revue belge de numismatique et de sigillographie* 157: 95–116.
Meeks, D. (1979) Les donations aux temples dans l'Égypte du Ier millénaire avant J.-C. In E. Lipinski (ed.), *State and Temple Economy in the Ancient Near East* II (Orientalia Lovaniensia Analecta 6), 605–687, Leuven.
Möller, A. (2000) *Trade in Archaic Greece*, Oxford.
Newell, E. T. (1938) *Miscellanea Numismatica: Cyrene to India*, New York, The American Numismatic Society.
Nicolet-Pierre, H. (1979) Les monnaies des deux derniers satrapes d'Égypte avant la conquête d'Alexandre. In O. Mørkholm & N. M. Waggoner (eds), *Greek Numismatics and Archaeology. Essays in Honor of Margaret Thompson*, 221–230, pls 25–26, Wetteren.
Pfeiffer, S. (2010) Naukratis, Heracleion-Thonis and Alexandria – remarks on the presence and trade activities of Greeks in the north-west delta from the seventh century BC to the end of the fourth century BC. In D. Robinson & A. Wilson (eds), *Alexandria and the North-Western Delta. Joint Conference Proceedings of Alexandria: City and Harbour (Oxford 2004) and The Trade and Topography of Egypt's North-West Delta, 8th century BC to 8th century AD (Berlin 2006)* (Oxford Centre for Maritime Archaeology 5), 15–24, Oxford.
Porten, B. & A. Yardeni (1993) *Textbook of Aramaic Documents from Ancient Egypt. 3. Literature · Accounts · Lists*, Winona Lake.
Posener, G. (1947) Les douanes de la Méditerranée dans l'Éypte saite, *Revue de philologie, de littérature et d'histoire anciennes* 3rd Série 21 = 73: 117–131.
Pressl, D. A. (1998) *Beamte und Soldaten. Die Verwaltung in der 26. Dynastie in Ägypten (664–525 v. Chr.)* (Europäische Hochschulschriften III 779), Frankfurt.
Redford, D. B. (1992) *Egypt, Canaan, and Israel in Ancient Times*, Princeton.
Redford, D. B. (2001) The so-called "codification" of Egyptian law under Darius I. In J W. Watts (ed.), *Persia and Torah. The Theory of Imperial Authorization of the Pentateuch*, 135–159, Atlanta.
Ritner, R. K. (2009) *The Libyan Anarchy. Inscriptions from Egypt's Third Intermediate Period*, Atlanta.
Robinson, E. S. G. (1947) The Tell el-Maskhuta Hoard of Athenian Tetradrachms, *Numismatic Chronicle* 6 Ser. 7: 115–121.
Schäfer, J. (ed.) (1981). *Phaselis. Beiträge zur Topographie und Geschichte der Stadt und ihrer Häfen*, Tübingen.
Seibt, G. F. (1977) *Griechische Söldner im Achaimenidenreich*, Bonn.
Spiegelberg, W. (1914) *Die sogenannte demotische Chronik des Pap. 215 der Bibliothèque Nationale zu Paris nebst den auf der Rückseite des Papyrus stehenden Texten* (Demotische Studien 7), Leipzig.
Tata, G. (1986) *The Development of the Egyptian Textile Industry*. Dissertation, University of Utah.
Thucydides = Smith, C. F. (1958) *Thucydides IV*, London.
Traunecker, C. (1987) Les "temples hauts" de Basse Époque: un aspect du fonctionnement économique des temples, *Revue d'Égyptologie* 38: 147–162.
van Alfen, P. G. (2002) The "Owls" from the 1989 Syria Hoard, with a review of pre-Macedonian coinage in Egypt, *American Journal of Numismatics*, 2nd Series 14: 1–57.
Vittmann, G. (1998) *Der demotische Papyrus Rylands 9* (Ägypten und Altes Testament 38), Wiesbaden.
Vittmann, G. (2009) Rupture and continuity. On priests and officials in Egypt during the Persian Period. In P. Briant & M. Chauveau (eds), *Organisation des pouvoirs et contacts culturels dans les pays de l'empire achéménide*, 89–121, Paris.
Vleeming, S. P. (2001) *Some coins of Artaxerxes and other short texts in the demotic script found on various objects and gathered from many publications* (Studia Demotica 5), Leuven-Paris-Sterling.
Wallinga, H. T. (1991) Polycrates and Egypt: the testimony of the *Samaina*. In H. Sancisi-Weerdenburg & A. Kuhrt (eds), *Asia Minor and Egypt: Old Cultures in a New Empire. Proceedings of the Groningen 1988 Achaemenid History Workshop* (Achaemenid History VI), 179–197, Leiden.

Wilson, P. (2011) Pots, people and the plural community: a case study of the Greeks in Egypt at Sais. In K. Duistermaat & I. Regulski (eds), *Intercultural Contacts in the Ancient Mediterranean. Proceedings of the International Conference at the Netherlands-Flemish Institute in Cairo, 25th to 29th October 2008* (Orientalia Lovaniensia Analecta 202), 159–170, Leuven-Paris-Dudley MA.

Wilson, P. & G. Gilbert (2007) Sais and its trading relations with the eastern Mediterranean. In P. Kousoulis & K. Magliveras (eds), *Moving Across Borders. Foreign Relations, Religion and Cultural Interactions in the Ancient Mediterranean* (Orientalia Lovaniensia Analecta 159), 251–265, Leuven-Paris-Dudley MA.

Yoyotte, J. (1993–1994) Égyptologie, *Annuaire du Collège de France* 94: 667–698.

Yoyotte, J. (2001) Le second affichage du décret de l'an 2 de Nekhtnebef et la découverte de Thônis-Héracléion, *Égypte Afrique & Orient* 24: 25–34.

Chapter 13

From “institutional” to “private”: traders, routes and commerce from the Late Bronze Age to the Iron Age[1]

Susan Sherratt

“Institutional” and “private” trade in the 2nd millennium BC

A little over 10 years ago, Maria Eugenia Aubet observed that the situation in the Iron Age in the eastern Mediterranean with regard to systems of international trade was more reminiscent of the 3rd millennium and the first half of the 2nd millennium than of the Late Bronze Age (Aubet 2000, 78). In this she was following Mario Liverani, who a decade or so earlier had characterised the Late Bronze Age, particularly in the Syro-Palestinian region, as a time when the royal palaces, in one way or another, were the basic and almost exclusive agents in long-distance exchange. This arose from, and in its turn also contributed to maintaining, a social and political system based on a convergence of the interests of “great” and “little” kings and their surrounding classes of palace-based elites, such as the *maryannu*, scribes and administrative personnel, merchants and so on, who were ultimately all dependent on the rather crude exploitation of village communities within their kingdoms (Liverani 1987, 66–69).

By comparison, the conventional picture for the early 2nd millennium – for instance in the case of the Old Assyrian merchants involved in the karum at Kültepe-Kanesh and the Anatolian trading network (Garelli 1963; Sagona & Zimanski 2009, 227–233), or of the Old Babylonian merchants and traders operating out of Ur and down the Gulf in the Isin-Larsa period (Potts 1990, 219–226) – is generally one of such early 2nd millennium merchants as predominantly independent private citizens, with their own family dynasties and networks of partnerships, who remained relatively free of any centralised bureaucratic control, even though the rulers of the states to which they belonged undoubtedly had a direct interest in their activities (Garelli 1963, 198–204; Potts 1990, 224; Postgate 1992, 219–221). In this respect, it seems to me that there is a difference mainly only of emphasis along a spectrum between these and characters like Abdihaqab and Sinaranu in the Late Bronze Age

Ugarit texts, who may have been very closely connected with the palace and also responsible for trading on its behalf, but had their own commercial enterprises some or even much of the time (Heltzer 1988; Knapp 1991, 47–49).

Nevertheless, there is a general impression afforded by a number of Late Bronze Age (late 2nd millennium) texts, including a number of the Ugarit documents and much of the Amarna correspondence, that, ideologically at least, there was an aspiration towards keeping the exchange and circulation of items which were of particular importance to the positions and status of rulers and their associated elite circles as far as possible under their own control (Liverani 1997, 108, fig. 4). This is perhaps most vividly exemplified in the case of bronze (which one might regard as the petroleum oil of the Late Bronze Age) by the separate exchange and circulation in standardised ingot form of its constituents, copper and tin, which would only be united at their destinations, presumably in the hands of "palace-approved" smiths. The late 14th century Uluburun wreck (Bass 1986; Bass *et al.* 1989), which sank off the southern Anatolian coast with its 354 copper ingots (around 10 tons) and over 120 tin ingots (about 1 ton) – incidentally the ideal ratio for bronze with a 10% tin content – and with its cargo of other goods which would not seem out of place in tribute or booty lists or among the gifts exchanged by rulers in the Amarna letters, is probably a good (if unfortunate) archaeological illustration of this, even though we do not know either the sender (or senders) of this cargo or to whom it was being sent. While this might be seen as a case of one (or maybe several) rulers putting too many eggs in one basket, this was perhaps paradoxically the safest thing to do if control was the principal aim. Another illustration, if perhaps only symbolically, is the ceremonial stone ingot mould found in Ahat-Milkou's palace at Ras ibn Hani, one of the ports of the kingdom of Ugarit (Lagarce *et al.* 1983; Craddock *et al.* 1997). At the very least, it emphasises the close relationship between the standardised ingot form and royal ideology at a time when the palace was still functioning. But what about the ships' crews who actually transported these valuable goods and raw materials from palace to palace or ruler to ruler? Some of them, at least, seem to have been doing a little trading on the side on their own account as they went along, to judge by the three large pithoi stacked full of brand new Cypriot pots on the Uluburun ship (Bass 1986, 274). And indeed Michal Artzy (1997) has argued that it was precisely in the private, purely commercial activities of seaborne carriers and their crews that the seeds were first sown which led to the fatal undermining of palatially administered trade and exchange in important goods and materials by the end of the 13th century.

Questions of scale and diversification: controlling the uncontrollable

Before I go any further, there are a number of very general points that I would like to make about the shift of balance from institutional to private (and indeed *vice-versa*) and from Bronze Age to Iron Age. The first is that what happens in both the Late Bronze Age *and* the Early Iron Age, different though they may appear in outcome, really comes down to issues of scale (both geographical scale and scale of numbers of people involved), and the effects of increasing scale on the strategies of various interested parties who may find themselves in conflict or competition with one another. The second, which goes together with scale, is the issue of greater diversification, an aspect which has some particularly far-reaching implications towards the end of the 2nd millennium. The third concerns the nature of the economic base and, in particular, the relationships between political and social and economic power, which (like democracy) are easier to cope with on a small scale and in conditions in which interests and activities are generally relatively uniform. The fourth is that, while ancient texts may take us some way, in order to achieve a fully rounded picture of what was going on at any point in time we also need the testimony of archaeology, which can tell us about activities that the texts never mention, and which lay beneath or beyond the radar of literate elites, perhaps fatally for many of them.

There can be no doubt that the growth in scale of exchange and trade in the east Mediterranean as between the earlier and later 2nd millennium – in geographical scale (particularly in a westward and overseas direction), in the numbers and variety of people or groups of people involved, and to some extent in the diversity of goods and materials exchanged – led to an increasing determination on the part of the already socially and politically powerful to monopolise as far as possible the production and circulation of materials or goods on which their social status or their practical power depended, including materials with what might be regarded as "prime" or convertible value within the system in which they operated. Bronze has already been mentioned, but attempts to control other particularly desirable materials include the circumscription of iron circulation, by which gifts and possession of highly prized iron objects, on which great decorative care was often lavished, were confined to the realms of the divine and the royal (Snodgrass 1980; 1982; Waldbaum 1980; Muhly 1980; Gurney 1990, 67). They also include the royal monopolisation of the manufacture of glass in Egypt, from the reign of Tuthmosis III onwards (Shortland *et al.* 2001). In both these cases, control was assisted by a certain amount of "hype" or propaganda: for instance, the invention of terms for iron – such as "precious metal of the sky" (Limet 1984) or "iron of heaven" (Waldbaum 1980, 79) – which appeared only relatively late in the texts, and which fenced it firmly within the province of theocratic rulers and elites who were thus more able to claim a monopoly on its use and circulation; or the designation of blue glass as "royal" lapis lazuli, implying that it was superior to natural lapis and/or the particular province of royalty (Shortland 2001, 213–214). In such cases, in which either the natural rarity of raw materials (such as tin) or the limited dissemination of techniques (such as glass ingot or iron manufacture) made control easier, this array of strategies seems to have been relatively successful.

It is perhaps possible to go further, and suggest that the imperial aspirations of Liverani's Mitannian, Egyptian and Hittite "great kings", from roughly the middle of the 2nd millennium in western Asia, and the nature of these "empires", were largely driven by similar considerations of control over the circulation of status-enhancing and otherwise powerful goods and materials. At any rate, the clashes between these expanding powers in the crossroad of the Levant often seem less strictly territorial than focused on long-distance route networks along which resources travelled and on intersection points along these networks. Coastal centres, at which overland and maritime routes articulated, were perhaps of particular importance, as Egypt had already recognised in the case of Byblos as far back as the Old Kingdom; and it is no coincidence that Ugarit, in particular, was forced to change its allegiance more than once, and that both Egyptians and Hittites saw overwhelming advantages in allowing it a free hand to continue its maritime business without undue interference. Similarly, the Hittite concern with their western and south-western borders, which caused them endless trouble and which they never succeeded in pacifying properly, can probably best be explained by their desire to keep an eye on maritime traffic on the Aegean and southern Mediterranean coasts. So, too, can the wishful thinking which led them to aspire to conquer (or claim they had conquered) the island of Cyprus (Hellbing 1979, 58; Knapp 2008, 314, 324–335). Neither Hittites nor Egyptians were ever terribly comfortable on the open sea and were inherently suspicious of anyone who was, and as a result preferred to have friendly (or vassal) centres transact their overseas exchanges for them and act as a filter against undesirable or unknown elements, just as, much later in the 7th century, on the principle that "better the devil you know than the devil you don't", the Egyptian authorities encouraged a collection of Greek traders to establish a trading post at Naukratis on the Canopic branch of the Nile through which all foreign maritime trade was to pass (Herodotus 2. 178–179).

Sea traffic, which expanded greatly in the later part of the 2nd millennium, was indeed the vulnerable under-belly of any system which sought to maintain a modicum of control, since although it is relatively easy to monitor overland routes by means of customs-posts, military garrisons and roadblocks, sea routes are a quite different proposition, particularly given the unpredictability of landfalls and the ability of (at least smaller) ships to make use of isolated creeks or river estuaries or simply pull up on a beach. Indeed, one need only look at the plethora of potential (and probably actual) Bronze Age harbours around the east Mediterranean coasts, as compiled by Lucy Blue (1995), to see how essentially uncontrollable sea trade might be. As we shall see, it was the scale, diversity and geographical range of sea traffic and trade which eventually led to the undermining of Late Bronze Age institutions and, incidentally, to the Iron Age in the eastern Mediterranean. And, indeed, one of the characteristics of the later 13th century was the springing up of new short-lived coastal settlements, such as Tel Nami on the Carmel coast or Pyla-Kokkinokremos and Maa on Cyprus, some of which articulated with minor routes into the interiors and seem designed to bypass existing controls at longer-established ports (Artzy 1994; Karageorghis & Demas 1984; 1988; South 1984, 17; Brown 2013).

The seeds of a shifting balance

I shall return to diversity and diversification, but I would like first briefly to consider the question of the relationship between political and economic power. There is a frequent assumption that the ultimate sources of political power were chiefly agrarian and based on holding or control over land. This may well have been true of many Near Eastern kingdoms, but there are also centres in which it seems likely to me that political power resided at least as much in mercantile activity as in agrarian control. One of these is Ugarit, where the close relationships between merchants and palace can be seen in two ways: from one point of view, as palatial involvement in important mercantile activities, and from the opposite point of view as mercantile involvement in the affairs of the palace. At the very least, it seems likely that mercantile activity provided much of the revenue of the palace, and Bounni's suggestion of the way in which Ugarit's second port at Ras ibn Hani may have been set up in the 13th century by a member of the Ugaritic royal family as a rival trading establishment to Minet el-Beida after a family quarrel (Bounni 1991, 107) would merely underline the probability that much of the power of the Ugaritic aristocracy depended on such activity. Although we know pitifully little about them in the later second millennium, it also seems likely that other coastal city-states, such as Tyre, Sidon and Byblos, already operated in a similar way. The locations of these, on offshore or estuarine islands or promontories, are hardly conducive to economies dependent primarily on agricultural hinterlands, and there is no particular reason to suppose that the "merchant princes" or "princes of the sea" of later Biblical texts were any less mercantile in their power base in the later second millennium than they were in the first, particularly since, from the time of the stalemate resulting from the Battle of Kadesh in the early 13th century BC, these cities may well effectively have fallen into a relative no-man's land, uninterfered with by Egyptians and Hittites alike. Above all, however, it is on Cyprus that, particularly in the 13th century, one can plausibly conjecture that the greatest political power resided firmly in the hands of maritime mercantile elites. The spectacular growth of coastal urban centres during this period, at Enkomi, Kition, Hala Sultan Tekke and Palaepaphos among others, and the beautification of these by means of urban grid-planning, ashlar masonry and urban sanctuaries (what Ora Negbi (1986) once termed "the climax of urbanisation on Cyprus") cannot be divorced from the evidence for increasing overseas trade and increasingly diverse internal manufacturing capacity within these centres at this time.

Diversification: from pots to iron, and from Bronze Age to Iron Age

In order to finish off the established, institutionalised powers of the Late Bronze Age and usher in the more privatised agents of the Early Iron Age, we need to turn our attention both to the purely archaeological record and to areas further to the west. There is little that can be more purely archaeological than pottery, which rarely if ever figures in ancient texts or iconography, but which is pervasive and ubiquitous in the archaeological record, to the point where all sorts of improbable interpretations, from ethnic identity-markers to evidence of gift-exchange at a high social level, are regularly hung upon it. Precisely because pottery does not figure in elite considerations and is essentially of little intrinsic value, its production and distribution in most cases did not need to be controlled, and an informal commercial trade in pottery (and here I mean especially pottery which was transported for its own sake, rather than as packaging for something else) was a relatively innocuous activity from the point of view of palaces and rulers, and as such could be allowed to continue relatively unhindered. In the Late Bronze Age, two regions in particular produced pottery in relatively large quantities for overseas trade during the 14th and 13th centuries: Cyprus, whose Base Ring and White Slip bowls and jugs, over and above its Base Ring and White Shaved juglets, arrived in the Levant in truly stupendous quantities (Artzy 2001); and the Aegean, above all the Argolid, where there is evidence of production of special shapes designed specifically for an east Mediterranean market (Gjerstad 1926, 218–220; Stubbings 1951, 42–43; van Wijngaarden 2002, 10–13). The observations that Cypriot and Aegean pottery end up in the same contexts in the Levant, where the Aegean is usually heavily outnumbered by the Cypriot (Hankey 1981, 44–45), and that a fair amount of the Aegean pottery found in the east Mediterranean is marked after firing with signs that can be related to the Cypriot Bronze Age script (Hirschfeld 1992), suggest that Cypriot traders were mainly responsible for the carriage and exchange of this pottery (van Wijngaarden 2002, 275–277). Interestingly, two regions where both Aegean and Cypriot pottery of a non-packaging type is noticeably rare, are Egypt (especially after the uncharacteristic burst of Aegean open shapes which reached it in the Amarna period (Hankey 1973; Merrillees 1968)) and the Hittite imperial territories. It is difficult to imagine that either the Egyptian or Hittite authorities had any real objection to Aegean or Cypriot bowls, cups and so on, but it is possible that, particularly in the 13th century, they were already aware of the risks these Cypriot maritime traders posed to their own control of the circulation of more valuable goods and materials (Sherratt 1999, 171–172).

Pottery may not be worth much in itself, but on the kind of scale it was moving it must have been of considerable economic value to the producers, and particularly to the Cypriot carriers and traders who were transporting and trading it. They made such a virtue of pottery because it was something from the informal marketing of which they themselves could profit directly. By contrast, the Cypriot copper, which may also have travelled with it, seems more likely to have been dispatched as official consignments directly from sender to recipient (cf. e.g. EA 33-37, EA 40: Moran 1992, 104–111, 113). From the point of view of established institutions like palaces all this was fine, as long as this informal trade in pottery did not diversify into other more valuable or powerfully important items.

However, it did. During the course of the 13th century production of a wheelmade painted pottery of roughly Aegean type gradually got underway in the Cypriot coastal cities as a form of import substitution, and the products of this manufacture made their way to the Levant (and in the case of some "packaging" types, like stirrup jars, to Egypt; Knapp 2008, 257; Sherratt 2013, 637–638). There was also a thriving industry in ready-made Cypriot bronze objects, such as tripod stands (Matthäus 1982). In addition to this, particularly in the later 13th century we can glimpse relatively small-scale Cypriot maritime traders operating further and further west, in the western Aegean and in southern Italy, Sicily and Sardinia (Vagnetti & Lo Schiavo 1989; Phelps *et al.* 1999). This coincided with the beginning of a steady influx of selected "Urnfield" bronze types, including novel types of weapons and other forms of personal ornaments, which were initially produced mainly in areas around the Alps, into the Aegean and east Mediterranean. The numbers of these deposited and the quite frequent combination of Cypriot and "Urnfield" bronzes in the same contexts (as on the Gelidonya wreck) suggest that Cypriot ships were closely involved in their carriage and distribution, and that they were being distributed informally along the routes to anyone with the means and desire to acquire them (Sherratt 2000).

So far, then, it is possible to see Cypriot small scale traders, acting on their own account, making a living from an informal trade in pottery (both their own and that of some Aegean regions), then diversifying into "Aegean" pottery produced in their own cities, and into finished bronze goods, again both their own and "novel" bronze types brought in from the central Mediterranean and Adriatic. To this, by the end of the 13th century, they had added an informal trade in bronze in highly commoditised form in weighted units of scrap, as seen for instance at Tel Nami (Artzy 1994), in the numerous scrap hoards dotted around the East Mediterranean and Aegean (Knapp *et al.* 1988) and, for example, on the Gelidonya wreck (Bass 1967). At the same time, there is further evidence of "privatisation" in some of the Cypriot cities, such as Kition and Enkomi, in the widespread recycling of bronze, some of it possibly liberated from earlier tombs in another manifestation of entrepreneurism (Karageorghis & Kassianidou 1999; cf. also Sherratt 2012). On the basis of this, and of some quite radical architectural modifications in the so-called "Fortress" building at Enkomi (associated since the beginning of the Late Bronze Age with copper processing), Sidney Pickles and Eddie Peltenburg (1998) have concluded that signficant changes took place in Enkomi's metalworking organisation in the 13th century, to create out of what had been a single integrated industrial entity a number of quite separate and independent residential units-cum-workshops, which they attribute to small, probably family-based enterprises. They go on to argue that such family enterprises would no longer have depended on assured, "official" supplies of copper from the Cypriot mines, or of tin delivered as centrally organised consignments, but instead were operating in a small-scale essentially competitive environment in which they would have to get hold of their raw materials by whatever means they could.

This leads me on to the final stage in Cypriot entrepreneurial diversification, and indeed into the Iron Age, in the sense that, although other prolific bronzeworking regions such as Luristan and the Caucasus may also have been relatively quick off the mark in turning their attention to producing increasing numbers of iron cutting implements at roughly around this time (and the south-west Caucasus, in particular, may have been producing iron for Hittite royal consumption for several centuries: Khakhutaishvili 2009), in the East Mediterranean it is first and foremost on Cyprus that we see the effects, both short-term and long-term, of a more regular and sustained production of iron objects of a kind which had the potential to alter cultural perceptions and eventually to transform iron from the ultimate in precious metals to a base metal, so that by the end of the 8th century some 160 tons of iron could be left lying around in a storeroom at Khorsabad when the capital was abandoned (Pleiner & Bjorkman 1974, 293). Essentially, this was just yet another form of diversification. Late Bronze Age Cypriot copper processors, like others, seem occasionally to have produced, quite adventitiously, small usable pieces of iron (just the right size for a knife or dagger blade) as a result of smelting copper sulphide ores with the help of iron-rich fluxes (cf. Gale *et al.* 1990). But presumably, because it happened only rarely, they were not quite sure how they did it and were thus unable to do so on any sort of predictable or regular basis. Pickles and Peltenburg (1998) have convincingly shown how, under conditions in which every scrap of copper was valuable to small-scale private workers who could not depend on "official" consignments of copper, they seem, quite accidentally, to have developed processes of copper extraction which would have ensured a usable piece of iron (already carburised and quenched as an incidental part of the process) on virtually every occasion. At any rate, from around 1200 BC onwards, there are increasing numbers of iron objects, including knives and daggers, on Cyprus, not merely in tombs but also apparently just left lying around or lost and not retrieved in urban settlements (Sherratt 1994, 61). Such objects, which include types also represented among the newly "fashionable" Urnfield bronzes, have the ability to bridge the divide between Bronze and Iron Age attitudes to iron very effectively, since they are both personal ornaments *and* useful cutting implements, and thus allow the practical advantages of well-processed iron to be appreciated in use. If we consider that it was precisely these sorts of ultra-valuable iron objects – knives and daggers in particular – which kings used to give each other as gifts, it is easy to see how attractive a now regular supply of such objects might be both to Cypriot traders and to their less than royal customers. In any case, it is not long before we see such items, especially knives and other objects of almost certain Cypriot manufacture, turning up in the Levant, the Aegean and even in the Central Mediterranean, long before the beginning of anything that might conventionally be called an Iron Age, particularly to the west of the east Mediterranean.

Silver and the effects of scale

It is perhaps unnecessary to point out that, once sufficient numbers of copperworkers had cracked the technology of regularly producing good iron suitable for practical bladed objects, then the acquisition and circulation of iron, unlike bronze (in which at least the tin was rare in the ground), could not easily be controlled by centralised administrations; and this is quite possibly why Egypt south of the Delta, which was particularly reluctant to abandon the idea of control over such ideologically charged materials, resisted full iron adoption until over half a millennium later (Snodgrass 1982, fig. 2). Already by the beginning of the 12th century, however, much of the control of bronze had been lost in the east Mediterranean by the informal maritime trading of ready-made objects brought in from Italy and the Alpine region, and by the trading and recycling of bronze in commoditised scrap form. Silver, which had provided a standard of exchange (and, in a growing number of circumstances, a medium of exchange) in the Near East since at least the end of the 3rd millennium, was also subject to a net increase in circulation as silver sources in the central and western Mediterranean fed into the system, possibly mainly through the activities of Cypriots, towards the end of the Bronze Age, and it, too, began to circulate informally in small weighted units, foreshadowing the introduction of stamped coinage in the earlier 1st millennium. There are indications of the cupellation of silver, for instance, at Maa-Palaeokastro in western Cyprus (Karageorghis & Demas 1988, 65), while a cached hoard of two small silver ingots and scraps from a silver bowl from late 13th century Pyla-Kokkinokremos (Karageorghis & Demas 1984, 64–65) could be regarded as an immediate forerunner of an impressive number of what have been convincingly identified as hack-silver hoards deposited in the Levant and elsewhere in the East Mediterranean from the 12th century onwards (Thompson 2003), with some of the silver in these suggested, as a result of lead isotope analysis, to be of Sardinian origin (Thompson 2007). These, too, may be seen as both symptom and result of a thriving entrepreneurial commercial trade, which flourished outside the control of palatial or state institutions.

It was this final undermining of an inherently precarious and relatively short-term control, which came about as a result of dramatic increases in geographical scale (especially by sea) and scale of involvement and as a result of steady diversification on the part of relatively free agents in interstitial niches of the system which were not (or no longer) subject to the control of Liverani's "great kings", which virtually ensured an arguably irrevocable shift in balance from the administered to the commercial or, in a less exact and somewhat over-simplified shorthand, from "institutional" to "private". The symptoms of this increase in scale and diversification are well illustrated, for instance, by the varieties of goods and their highly varied origins listed in the 6th century Lamentation for Tyre, "merchant of the people for many isles", in *Ezekiel* 27 (Liverani 1991). This is not to say that in many places the private did not merge with or *become* the institutional, as, of course, it had many times in the past and as may well have continued to be the case in the Phoenician cities of the early 1st millennium (Bondi 1978; 2001; Aubet 1993, 91–96), but with ever-expanding scale and diversity it simply became harder for anyone to control the *status quo ante*. In the 1st millennium, attempts were made to compensate for this in various ways: the expansion of territorial empires and of direct tribute, the development of industrial slavery, and the elaboration of ideologies (such as those encapsulated in Moses Finley's *Ancient Economy* of 1973) which disparaged those who gained their livings from trading and commerce or, for example at Athens, excluded metics, many of whom were engaged in such activities, from citizenship and political involvement. All the same, the rise and prosperity of many of the most powerful first millennium centres, from Nineveh and Persepolis, to Rome and Carthage, were based ultimately, either directly or indirectly, on growing networks of commercial traders and proliferating routes which, in the last resort, made lasting and effective institutional control of circulating goods and materials virtually impossible.

Concluding remarks

In this brief overview there has been little scope for delicate shading, for delineating the subtleties and caveats which are necessary to qualify any broad-brush account like the one presented above. Nevertheless, such qualifications cannot be glossed over entirely. A transition from "institutional" to "private" is a very crude way of expressing what is better seen as a gradual, uneven and in many ways organic shift of emphasis along an existing spectrum of individual (or "private") entrepreneurial and state (or palatial) organised exchange, both of which existed in some form or another in various regions throughout the 2nd millennium BC. More importantly, perhaps, in the face of the increasing scale and diversity of a geographically expanding system, it involved the forced abandonment of an ideal of state or institutionalised elite control over the exchange and circulation of economically crucial and ideologically powerful materials, such as bronze and its constituents, which was only ever precariously maintained, and which was constantly at risk of erosion as more regions and greater numbers of people became involved, and as some of these seized opportunities to diversify into less restricted commercial roles. In short, it was above all the relentlessly increasing scale and diversity of geographical and actor involvement, together with a rapid entrepreneurial diversification in some regions, such as Cyprus, which led to the loss of control, and which ensured that, by the middle of the first millennium, the eastern Mediterranean and Near Eastern world looked in several ways quite different from how it had looked less than a millennium earlier.

Acknowledgements

I should like to record my gratitude to Juan Carlos Moreno García and the organisers of the ESF Workshop, as well as to its participants, for a most stimulating occasion, during which I learned a great deal and which will undoubtedly have done much to draw attention to a number of fundamental questions concerning economic developments in the early first millennium over a wide but interconnected area.

Note

1. This cannot claim to be a research paper. Rather, it is designed to present a brief overview, as I see them, of the changes in economic environment in the eastern Mediterranean in the closing centuries of the second and the early centuries of the 1st millennium BC, in order to stimulate further discussion and exploration in accordance with the aims of the ESF Exploratory Workshop at which it was originally presented. More detailed and sustained arguments in support of most of the views put forward here can be found in the various items listed in the bibliography.

Bibliography

Artzy, M. (1994) Incense, camels and collared rim jars: desert trade routes and maritime outlets in the second millennium, *Oxford Journal of Archaeology* 13/2: 121–147.
Artzy, M. (1997) Nomads of the sea. In S. Swiny, R. L. Hohlfelder & H. W. Swiny (eds), *Res Maritimae: Cyprus and the Eastern Mediterranean from Prehistory to Late Antiquity*, 1–16, Atlanta.
Artzy, M. (2001) White Slip ware for export? The economics of production. In V. Karageorghis (ed.), *The White Slip Ware of Late Bronze Age Cyprus*, 107–115, Wien.
Aubet, M. E. (1993) *The Phoenicians and the West: Politics, Colonies and Trade*, Cambridge.
Aubet, M. E. (2000) Aspects of Tyrian trade and colonization in the eastern Mediterranean, *Münstersche Beiträge zur Antiken Handelsgeschichte* 19/1: 70–120.
Bass, G. F. (1967) *Cape Gelidonya: a Bronze Age Shipwreck, Transactions of the American Philosophical Society* 57/8, Philadelphia.
Bass, G. F. (1986) A Bronze Age shipwreck at Ulu Burun (Kaş): 1984 campaign, *American Journal of Archaeology* 90: 269–296.
Bass, G. F., C. Pulak, D. Collon & J. Weinstein (1989) The Bronze Age shipwreck at Ulu Burun: 1986 campaign, *American Journal of Archaeology* 93: 1–29.
Blue, L. K. (1995) *A topographical analysis of the location of harbours and anchorages of the eastern Mediterranean in the Middle and Late Bronze Age*. Unpublished DPhil thesis, University of Oxford.
Bondi, S. F. (1978). Note sull'economia fenicia I: impresa privata e ruolo dello stato, *Egitto e Vicino Oriente* 1: 139–149.
Bondi, S. F. (2001) Political and administrative organization. In S. Moscati (ed.), *The Phoenicians*, 153–159, London.
Bounni, A. (1991) La Syrie, Chypre et l'Egée d'après les fouilles de Ras ibn Hani. In V. Karageorghis (ed.), *Proceedings of an International Symposium, The Civilizations of the Aegean and their Diffusion in Cyprus and the Eastern Mediterranean, 2000–600 B.C.*, 105–110, Larnaca.
Brown, M. (2013) Waterways and the political geography of south-east Cyprus in the second millennium BC, *Annual of the British School at Athens* 108: 121–136.
Craddock, P. T., I. C. Freestone & C. D. Dawe (1997) Casting metals in limestone moulds, *Historical Metallurgy* 31/1: 1–7.
Finley, M. I. (1973) *The Ancient Economy*, London.
Gale, N. H., H. G. Bachmann, B. Rothenberg, Z. A. Stos-Gale & R. F. Tylecore (1990) The adventitious production of iron in the smelting of copper. In B. Rothenberg (ed.), *The Ancient Metallurgy of Copper*, 182–191, London.
Garelli, P. (1963) *Les Assyriens en Cappadoce*, Paris.
Gjerstad, E. (1926) *Studies on Prehistoric Cyprus*, Uppsala.
Gurney, O. R. (1990) *The Hittites* (2nd edition), Harmondsworth.
Hankey, V. (1973) The Aegean deposit at El Amarna. *In The Mycenaeans in the Eastern Mediterranean. Acts of the International Archaeological Symposium, Nicosia, March-April 1972*, 128–136, Nicosia.
Hankey, V. (1981) The Aegean interest in El Amarna, *Journal of Mediterranean Anthropology and Archaeology* 1: 3–49.
Hellbing, L. (1979) *Alasia Problems* (Studies in Mediterranean Archaeology 57), Göteborg.
Heltzer, M. (1988) Sinaranu, son of Siginu, and the trade relations between Ugarit and Crete, *Minos* 23: 7–11.
Hirschfeld, N. (1992) Cypriot marks on Mycenaean pottery. In J.-P. Olivier (ed.), *Mykenaïka* (Bulletin de Correspondance Hellénique supplement 25), 315–319 Athens.
Karageorghis, V. & M. Demas (1984) *Pyla-Kokkinokremos. A Late 13th-century B.C. Fortified Settlement in Cyprus*, Nicosia.
Karageorghis, V. & M. Demas (1988) *Excavations at Maa-Palaeokastro 1979–1986*, Nicosia.

Karageorghis, V. & V. Kassianidou (1999) Metalworking and recycling in Late Bronze Age Cyprus – the evidence from Kition, *Oxford Journal of Archaeology* 18:2: 171–188.
Khakhutaishvili, D. A. (2009) *The Manufacture of Iron in Ancient Colchis* (British Archaeological Report S1905), Oxford.
Knapp, A. B. (1991) Spice, drugs, grain and grog: organic goods in Bronze Age east Mediterranean trade. In N. H. Gale (ed.), *Bronze Age Trade in the Mediterranean* (Studies in Mediterranean Archaeology 90), 21–68, Jonsered.
Knapp, A. B. (2008). *Prehistoric and Protohistoric Cyprus. Identity, Insularity, and Connectivity*, Oxford.
Knapp, A. B., J. D. Muhly & P. Muhly (1988) To hoard is human: Late Bronze Age metal deposits in Cyprus and the Aegean, *Report of the Department of Antiquities, Cyprus* 1988/1: 233–262.
Lagarce, J., E. Lagarce, N. Saliby & A. Bounni (1983) Les fouilles à Ras Ibn Hani en Syrie (campagnes de 1980, 1981 et 1982), *Comptes-Rendus de l'Académie des Inscriptions et Belles Lettres* 1983: 249–290.
Limet, H. (1984) Documents relatifs au fer à Mari, *Mari: Annales de Recherche Interdisciplinaire* 3: 191–196.
Liverani, M. (1987) The collapse of the Near Eastern regional system at the end of the Bronze Age: the case of Syria. In M. Rowlands, M. Larsen & K. Kristiansen (eds), *Centre and Periphery in the Ancient World*, 66–73, Cambridge.
Liverani, M. (1991) The trade network of Tyre according to Ezek. 27. In M. Cogan & I. Eph'al (eds), *Ah, Assyria: Studies in Assyrian History and Ancient Near Eastern Historiography presented to Hayim Tadmor* (Scripta Hierosalymitana 33), 65–79 Jerusalem.
Liverani, M. (1997) Ramesside Egypt in a changing world: an institutional approach. *In L'Impero Ramesside. Convegno Internazionale in Onore di Sergio Donadoni*, 101–115, Roma.
Matthäus, H. (1982) Die zyprische Metallindustrie in der ausgehenden Bronzezeit: einheimische, ägäische und nahöstliche Elemente. In J. D. Muhly, R. Maddin & V. Karageorghis (eds), *Early Metallurgy in Cyprus*, 185–199, Nicosia.
Merrillees, R. (1968) *The Cypriote Bronze Age Pottery found in Egypt* (Studies in Mediterranean Archaeology 18), Lund.
Moran, W. L. (ed. and transl.) (1992) *The Amarna Letters*, Baltimore.
Muhly, J. D. (1980) The Bronze Age setting. In T. A. Wertime & J. D. Muhly (eds), *The Coming of the Age of Iron*, 25–67, New Haven.
Negbi, O. (1986) The climax of urban development in Bronze Age Cyprus, *Report of the Department of Antiquities, Cyprus* 1986: 97–121.
Phelps, W., Y. Lolos & Y. Vichos (eds) (1999) *The Point Iria Wreck: Interconnections in the Mediterranean ca. 1200 BC*, Athens.
Pickles, S. & E. Peltenburg (1998) Metallurgy, society and the bronze/iron transition in the east Mediterranean and the Near East, *Report of the Department of Antiquities, Cyprus* 1998: 67–100.
Pleiner, R. & J. K. Bjorkman (1974) The Assyrian Iron Age: the history of iron in the Assyrian civilization, *Proceedings of the American Philosophical Society* 118/3: 283–313.
Postgate, J. N. (1992) *Early Mesopotamia: Society and Economy at the Dawn of History*, London.
Potts, D. T. (1990) *The Arabian Gulf in Antiquity*, vol. 1, Oxford.
Sagona, A. & P. Zimanski (2009) *Ancient Turkey*, London.
Sherratt, S. (1994) Commerce, iron and ideology: metallurgical innovation in 12th-11th century Cyprus. In V. Karageorghis (ed.), *Cyprus in the 11th Century B.C.*, 59–107, Nicosia.
Sherratt, S. (1999). *E pur si muove*: pots, markets and values in the second millennium Mediterranean. In J. P. Crielaard, V. Stissi & G. J. van Wijngaarden (eds), *The Complex Past of Pottery. Production, Circulation and Consumption of Mycenaean and Greek Pottery (Sixteenth to Early Fifth Centuries BC)*, 163–211, Amsterdam.

Sherratt, S. (2000) Circulation of metals and the end of the Bronze Age in the eastern Mediterranean. In C. F. E. Pare (ed.), *Metals Make the World Go Round. The Supply and Circulation of Metals in Bronze Age Europe*, 82–98, Oxford.

Sherratt, S. (2012) The intercultural transformative capacities of irregularly appropriated goods. In J. Maran & P. W. Stockhammer (eds.), *Materiality and Social Practice: Transformative Capacities of Intercultural Encounters*, 152–172, Oxford.

Sherratt, S. (2013) The ceramic phenomenon of the "Sea Peoples": an overview. In A. E. Killebrew & G. Lehmann (eds), *The Philistines and Other "Sea Peoples" in Texts and Archaeology* (Archaeology and Biblical Studies 15), 619–644, Atlanta.

Shortland, A. J. (2001) Social influences on the development and spread of glass. In A. J. Shortland (ed.), *The Social Context of Technological Change: Egypt and the Near East, 1650–1550 BC*, 211–222, Oxford.

Shortland, A. J., P. T. Nicholson & C. M. Jackson (2001) Glass and faience at Amarna: different methods of both supply for production, and subsequent distribution. In A. J. Shortland (ed.), *The Social Context of Technological Change: Egypt and the Near East, 1650–1550 BC*, 147–160, Oxford.

Snodgrass, A. M. (1980) Iron and early metallurgy in the Mediterranean. In T. A. Wertime & J. D. Muhly (eds), *The Coming of the Age of Iron*, 335–374, New Haven.

Snodgrass, A. M. (1982) Cyprus and the beginnings of iron technology in the eastern Mediterranean. In J. D. Muhly, R. Maddin & V. Karageorghis (eds), *Early Metallurgy in Cyprus*, 285–295, Nicosia.

South, A. (1984) Kalavasos-Ayios Dhimitrios and the Late Bronze Age of Cyprus. In V. Karageorghis & J. D. Muhly (eds), *Cyprus at the Close of the Late Bronze Age*, 11–17, Nicosia.

Stubbings, F. H. (1951) *Mycenaean Pottery from the Levant*,. Cambridge.

Thompson, C. M. (2003) Sealed silver in Iron Age Cisjordan and the "invention" of coinage, *Oxford Journal of Archaeology* 22/1: 67–107.

Thompson, C. M. (2007) Silver in the Age of Iron and the orientalizing economies of Archaic Greece, *American Schools of Oriental Research Newsletter* 58/4: 18–19.

Vagnetti, L. & F. Lo Schiavo (1989) Late Bronze Age long distance trade in the Mediterranean: the role of the Cypriots. In E. Peltenburg (ed.), *Early Society in Cyprus*, 217–243, Edinburgh.

Waldbaum, J. (1980) The first archaeological appearance of iron and the transition to the Iron Age. In T. A. Wertime & J. D. Muhly (eds), *The Coming of the Age of Iron*, 60–98, New Haven.

Wijngaarden, G. J. van (2002) *Use and Appreciation of Mycenaean pottery in the Levant, Cyprus and Italy (ca. 1600–1200 BC)*, Amsterdam.

Chapter 14

Intercultural contacts between Egypt and the Arabian Peninsula at the turn of the 2nd to the 1st millennium BCE

Gunnar Sperveslage

Introduction

The Arabian Peninsula, and South Arabia in particular, has been one of the most important sources for aromatics such as frankincense, myrrh, gums and resins, fragrant woods and also spices, which arrived in South Arabia from India and south-east Asia. These goods were traded via long distance networks, connecting South Arabia to north-east Africa, the Mediterranean, Mesopotamia and India (Groom 1981; Peacock & Williams 2007). Therefore it seems surprising that little is known from the ancient Egyptian or, respectively, an Egyptological perspective. But it has to be borne in mind, first, that the Arabian trade goods are materials that normally do not survive in the archaeological record and, secondly, that the archaeology of the Arabian Peninsula is a rather young discipline. Archaeological research in Saudi Arabia in particular has intensified only recently, within the last decade.

Connectivity, mobility, communication and hybridisation are but a few key words for describing cross-cultural networks which contributed to the formation of identities in ancient societies. As a matter of fact, intercultural contacts between two regions and the cultural impact of one civilisation or society on the other are always bilateral phenomena, whether determined by economic interests, political domination, colonisation, or peer polity interaction (see e.g. van Dommelen & Knapp 2010). The Arabian Peninsula, and in particular north-west Arabia, is located on the periphery of the Egyptian empire (Fig. 14.1). Egyptian cultural impact can be observed within the material remains on various occasions. Object mobility not only reflects trade and exchange, but also interest in and curiosity about a foreign culture. Adoption of foreign elements, such as motifs and probably also ideas, could be used to improve culture and lifestyle (see e.g. Wengrow 2010). This tendency is no less true for the Arabian Peninsula than for all other regions and societies in the Egyptian sphere of influence.

In this contribution, the Egyptian impact on the Arabian Peninsula is scrutinised during the Iron Age. This period followed a dramatic decline of Egyptian political influence in the Levant and the abandonment of the Sinai copper mines. The socio-political situation in the ancient Near East had changed and the city states which were formerly dominated by the great powers of Egypt, Mesopotamia and the Fertile Crescent, had become independent nation states. The new conditions provided an excellent opportunity for the north Arabian oasis settlements to establish themselves within international trade networks.

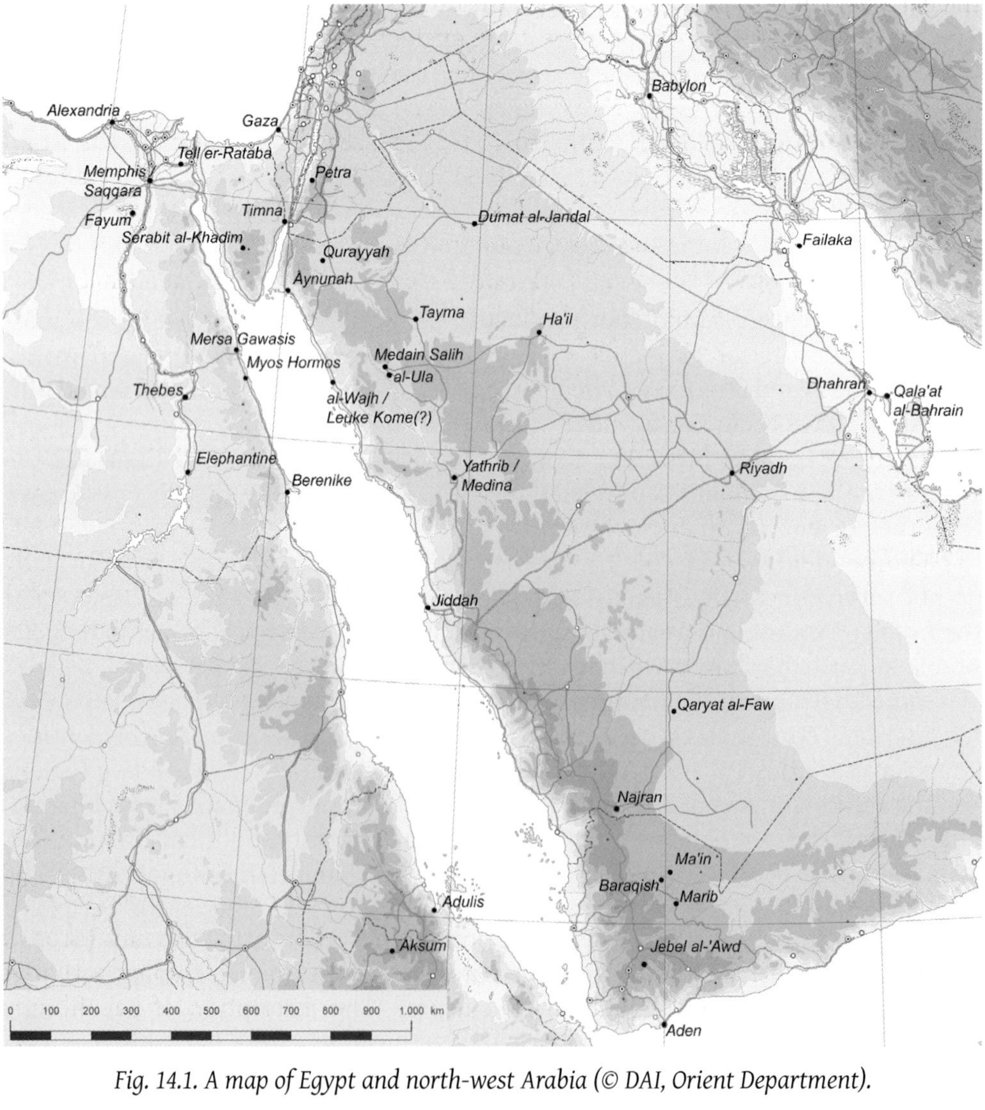

Fig. 14.1. A map of Egypt and north-west Arabia (© DAI, Orient Department).

A general outline of the ancient trade in frankincense

At the end of the 2nd millennium BCE the camel was domesticated on the Arabian Peninsula (Uerpmann & Uerpmann 2002; Heide 2010) and it replaced the donkey as a pack animal on long distance trade routes. The ability of the camel to get along without water for days increased the efficiency of trade in desert regions. Although watering holes and wells occur frequently, only the large oases, which are not less than a few days' ride apart, were capable of supplying large caravans with enough water. The overland trade of aromatics, and especially of frankincense, was the most important source of revenue for South Arabia, resulting in prosperity and wealth. In the early 1st century BCE, not long after the domestication of the camel, the ancient South Arabian Kingdom of Saba arose as an ancient civilisation of high culture.

Assyrian texts document the appearance of South Arabia in world history. In 853 BCE the first occurrence of the term "Arab" is attested in the annals of King Shalmaneser III (Eph'al 1982, 21; Retsö 2003, 124–128), when "Gindibu, the Arab" together with 1000 camels joined a coalition against the Assyrian king in the battle at Qarqar. Another cuneiform text tells us that in the first half of the 8th century BCE the governor of Suhu and Mari assaulted a caravan of merchants from Tayma and Saba, capturing 200 camels and all trade goods (Cavigneaux & Khalil Ismail 1990, 351). Other Assyrian documents of the 8th and 7th centuries BCE report further conflicts between the Assyrian Empire and the Arabian Kingdoms as well as "tribute" paid by the Arabs to Assyrian kings (Eph'al 1982, 81–100), which should certainly be interpreted as diplomatic gifts (Potts 2010, 74–76).

There was a high demand for South Arabian aromatics in Assyria which provided an incentive for the Assyrian kings to try to control the trade routes and the caravan cities in the oases of north Arabia, through which goods and cargo were distributed (Byrne 2003). Success in this endeavour was assured to the last king of the Babylonian Empire, Nabonidus, in the mid-6th century BCE (Beaulieu 1989; Schaudig 2001, 9–23). He took control of the oases in north-west Arabia and built a palace at Tayma, where he himself resided for a decade. The Babylonian presence in the oasis has now been confirmed by cuneiform texts from the excavations at the ancient site of Tayma (Eichmann *et al.* 2006; Hausleiter 2011, 114–115) and several rock inscriptions from the hinterland of Tayma, which refer to this Babylonian king (Müller & al-Said 2002; al-Said 2009; Fig. 14.2).

Interactions between South Arabia, the Ancient Near East and the Mediterranean, were not necessarily hostile, as might be inferred from the forgoing remarks. An altar from Delos with a Greek-Minaean bilingual text (Clermont-Ganneau 1908) and a recently published bronze inscription of the Sabaean Sabahhumu (Bron & Lemaire 2009) clearly indicate the wide extent of South Arabian trading activities and interaction between neighbouring cultures. The inscription of Sabahhumu which is dated to *c.* 600 BCE includes his biographical details. He not only took part in several successful military campaigns within South Arabia; he also led caravans

Fig. 14.2. Rock inscription of Ramesses III at Tayma (Photo: Sebastiano Lora, © DAI, Orient Department).

on the frankincense route. His mercantile expeditions took him as far as Gaza and Cyprus. The inscription therefore documents how broad the range of a single person's mobility might be (see also Eichmann in press).

Documentation of Arabia in Egyptian sources of the Ptolemaic and Roman Periods

While contacts between Arabia and the Ancient Near East, Assyria and Babylonia, are well attested and have been the subject of several studies, evidence from Egypt is scarce. The first of the few occurrences of the term "Arabia" in Egyptian sources is as late as the 3rd century BCE. The demotic list of toponyms in a papyrus from Saqqara mentions *p3-t3-3lbj* (Spiegelberg 1908, 273; Saleh 1978, 69; Winnicki 2009, 310) along with *p3-t3-Ḫr* "Syria" and *p3-t3-Nḥs* "Nubia" as references to the neighbouring countries. Evidence in hieroglyphic script for "Arabia" has survived on the statue of Darius I from Susa (Roaf 1974; Calmeyer 1991), where the term *Hgr* is found. In demotic sources, the term *Hgr* refers either to Syria or north Arabia and describes inhabitants of a desert region (Stadler 2004, 131–134; Winnicki 2009, 340–348). The list of names on the base of the Darius statue follows the Achaemenid formulary. *Hgr* is substituted for the term *arabāya* (Retsö 2003, 237–240) and therefore should be interpreted as an Achaemenid, rather than an Egyptian attestation.

In fact, the late occurrence of the term "Arabia" in demotic texts from the Ptolemaic and Roman Periods coincides with archaeological and epigraphic evidence for Egyptian contacts to the Arabian Peninsula (for an overview, see also Vittmann 2003, 180–193). The import of the Arabian aromatics calamus and myrrh is explicitly mentioned in the inscription on the sarcophagus of the Minaean merchant Zayd'il (Robin 1994, 295–296; Vittmann 1998, 1241–1243). The sarcophagus, now in the Egyptian Museum, Cairo, dates to the Ptolemaic Period. It probably originated from Saqqara, where, according to the inscription, Zayd'il's burial was in the vicinity of the Serapeum. Not only was Zayd'il interred in Egypt; Egyptian loanwords in the Minaean inscription indicate that Zayd'il was an acculturated member of Egyptian society.

Inscriptions of the first half of the 4th century BCE from ancient Yemen contain information on South Arabian trade with Egypt as well. Four Minaean inscriptions report of trading expeditions to Egypt, the Levant and Mesopotamia (Robin 1994, 286-290). These expeditions were conducted on land routes along the frankincense road, leading from the Yemeni highlands north to Petra and Gaza. The use of maritime routes is attested as well; several pottery sherds of southern Arabian origin were found at the Roman ports of Myos Hormos and Berenike, some of them incised with South Arabian inscriptions (Tomber 2008, 50–51; Sidebotham 2011, 72–74, 224). These finds are evidence for contacts across the Red Sea, but they alone do not provide an answer to the question of whether people from South Arabia travelled to the Egyptian Red Sea harbours. That they did, however, is attested by several rock inscriptions and graffiti along the routes through Egypt's Eastern Desert (Colin 1988; Robin 1994, 296–297; Bülow-Jacobsen *et al.* 1995, 112–115; Tokunaga 2003).

Early contacts and Egyptian naval activities on the Red Sea

These few examples clearly show that trade connections between Egypt and the Arabian Peninsula were already well established in the late pharaonic period and in Ptolemaic and Roman times. According to recent archaeological fieldwork, the time span of intercultural contacts can be projected back at least as far as the late Old Kingdom. Contacts may have been initiated even as early as prehistoric times, as the source of Egyptian obsidian may lie in the Yemeni highlands (Zarins 1989; 1990; Aston *et al.* 2000), although it has still to be proven, whether the provenance is Yemen or Ethiopia (for new prospects see Khalidi *et al.* 2010; 2012). Direct contacts to South Arabia, however, existed at least since the late Old Kingdom. The Italo-American excavations at Mersa Gawasis on the Egyptian Red Sea coast exposed detailed information on the ancient harbour site and its use from the late Old Kingdom to the early New Kingdom (Bard & Fattovich 2007; Bard *et al.* 2007). Ship timbers and naval equipment, such as blades of steering oars, ropes, anchors and cargo boxes have been found, as well as some fragments of exotic pottery, indicating the wide network of naval activities around 2000 BCE. A few pottery sherds occurred that originated from the Yemeni Tihama and the Aden region. They were found in assemblages dating from the late Old to the late Middle Kingdom (Bard & Fattovich 2007, 130–131; Bard *et al.* 2007, 147). Surprisingly, most of the sherds belong to closed bowls, which were cooking vessels, used for domestic purposes rather than containers for transporting commodities (Bard *et al.* 2007, 147). There are far too few sherds and too little information on which to base a reliable interpretation of their occurrence. Apparently, the vessels did not contain anything like frankincense and myrrh imported from South Arabia. It is tempting to suppose that the vessels were brought to Mersa Gawasis by people from South Arabia – either on their own boats or as passengers on Egyptian ships – where they stayed for a while and perhaps even established some kind of commercial settlement. The domestic character of the pottery would seem to support this hypothesis, but still it remains conjectural. However, the presence of South Arabian pottery in Middle Kingdom Egypt illustrates beyond doubt aspects of long distance trade and exchange of goods conducted by people from ancient Yemen long before the rise of the Sabaean Kingdom.

Recent epigraphic evidence suggests Ramesside interest in north-west Arabia (Fig. 2). In 2010, Saudi Arabian archaeologists discovered a hieroglyphic rock inscription mentioning cartouches with the names of King Ramesses III (al-Ansary 2011; Sperveslage & Eichmann 2012; recently also discussed by Somaglino & Tallet 2011; 2013).

Right column: *nzw-bjt nb-t3.wj Wsr-M3ʿ.t-Rʿ mr Jmn*
The King of Upper and Lower Egypt, Lord of the Two Lands, User-Maat-Ra, beloved of Amun

Left column: *z3-Rʿ nb-ḫ3.w Rʿ-ms-sw ḥq3 Jwnw*
The Son of Ra, Lord of Crowns, Ramesses, Ruler of Heliopolis

Horizontal line: *mr.y ḥq3 ʿ3 t3 nb*
Beloved of the "Great Ruler of All Lands"

The inscription, carved in sunk relief, is situated above the flank of a wadi about 60 km to the north-west of Tayma. In antiquity, the region served as a resting place for caravans and travellers; there is a well and several rock drawings and inscriptions from different eras. Unfortunately, the inscription does not contain any additional information. It mentions the names of Ramesses III followed by a *mr.y*-formula containing the epithet "Great Ruler of All Lands", which reasonably refers to the god Amun (Sperveslage & Eichmann 2012) rather than to the king himself (Somaglino & Tallet 2011, 363; 2013, 512). There is no hint of the purpose of the Egyptian presence near Tayma. The inscription is very well carved with standard hieroglyphs and hence should have been made by an official expedition, with economic, military and/or political intentions. Neighbouring regions had been frequented by Egyptians from the Early Dynastic Period to acquire commodities, goods and raw materials, either by their own expeditions or by trade (Seidlmayer 2007, 52–59), but to argue for the exact purpose of the Tayma expedition is a difficult matter. During Ramesses III's reign, Egypt had to face the "Sea peoples", a term which describes a powerful force attacking Egypt from the north (Sandars 1985; Oren 2010). Confrontation with the "Sea Peoples" weakened Egyptian military power, and as a result, Egypt's political domination over the Levant had declined (Higginbotham 2000, 52–56; Morris 2005, 691–710), making it less probable that Ramesses III sent a military force to north-west Arabia to take over control of the trading routes and oases. It is more likely to assume that Ramesses III was interested in the supply of raw materials. During his reign several expeditions were undertaken, among them two expeditions to the Sinai copper mines at Serabit al-Khadim and Timna, as recorded in the historical section of pHarris I (Grandet 1994, I 338–339). The war with the "Sea Peoples" resulted in a high demand for copper to manufacture weapons (Hikade 2001: 201–203), providing a likely impetus for a large-scale expedition to Timna. As has been argued elsewhere (Sperveslage & Eichmann 2012), the Ramesside expedition to the oasis of Tayma can be understood in relation to the expedition to Timna. Just possibly a division of the Timna expedition was sent to north-west Arabia to prospect for further promising deposits of raw material. However, there are no deposits of copper and gold in the region of Tayma, although such deposits, as well as turquoise, are found in the costal regions of the western Hejaz (Roberts *et al.* 1975; de Jesus *et al.* 1982; Kisnawi, de Jesus & Rihani 1983; Hauptmann 2004, 73). A copper-prospecting expedition can thus be ruled out.

Yet another incentive could have been to secure access to the supply in aromatics. Along the frankincense route, Tayma was the last major caravan stop before entering the Levant. To purchase aromatics such as frankincense and myrrh directly at Tayma would have lowered the costs for the Egyptians, in particular if the expedition to Tayma was conducted within the context of a mining expedition to Timna. The efforts and logistic costs for the expedition would have been reduced. But a literal reading of of pHarris I, which includes no mention of acquiring aromatics does not support such an interpretation.

Copper miners, Midianites and painted pottery groups

The cartouches of Ramesses III witness the temporary presence of Egyptians in north-west Arabia and can be interpreted as expressing either economic or political interest in that region. The rock inscription confirms direct contact between Egypt and Tayma in the Late Bronze Age. Egyptian impact on north-west Arabia has been argued by Peter J. Parr (1988; 1989; 1996) and Beno Rothenberg (1998) based on the distribution of a certain type of painted pottery (Fig. 14.3). In the Late Bronze Age, pottery with a diagnostic polychrome decoration is found at many sites on the Sinai Peninsula, in the Levant and in north-west Arabia (Rothenberg & Glass 1983; Parr 1988; Hausleiter, 2014). This pottery was known as "Midianite pottery". But since no archaeological remains can yet be ascribed to the Midianite tribes and as the term "Midianite pottery" suggests unproved ethnic implications, the pottery is today called "Qurayyah Painted Ware" after the main find spot of these ceramics, the site of Qurayyah (the term "Hejaz Ware" can also be found). Information about the producers of this ware is scarce, due in particular to the lack of archaeological exploration at the ancient site of Qurayyah itself. Large amounts of Qurayyah Painted Ware have been found during the excavations of the copper mining site at Timna (Rothenberg 1988, 92-94; 1998), suggesting that those who produced it were specialists in copper mining and thus had been engaged by the Egyptians to exploit the copper mines at Timna on their behalf (Rothenberg 1998).

According to Parr (1988; 1996), the producers of Qurayyah Painted Ware dominated the Hejaz and controlled the incense trade. They attained such a position as a result of Egyptian influence. The producers of the Qurayyah Painted Ware are either to be equated with the Shasu Bedouins (so Parr 1988) or a subgroup of the "Sea Peoples" (subsequently, Parr 1996), who had been settled in the southern Levant and north-west Arabia by the Egyptian government. The affiliation of these people to the "Sea Peoples" cannot be ruled out, since the decorative patterns of the Qurayyah Painted Ware are comparable to those of Philistine Ware (Parr 1996; Rothenberg 1998), although recent analysis has shown that Qurayyah Painted Ware was produced locally (Hausleiter 2011, 111; 2014). Regardless, the idea that the Egyptians had established settlements of these people is not confirmed by Egyptian sources (as has been argued elsewhere; see Sperveslage 2011; 2013). The general political situation in the Levant and the loss of Egyptian influence make it less probable that the Egyptians were responsible for settling and protecting a population group in that region (see also Higginbotham 2000, 55–56). The decline of Egyptian domination resulted in a political power vacuum in the Levant and the adjoining regions that was filled by nomadic and semi-nomadic local tribes. They controlled the oases and water resources and

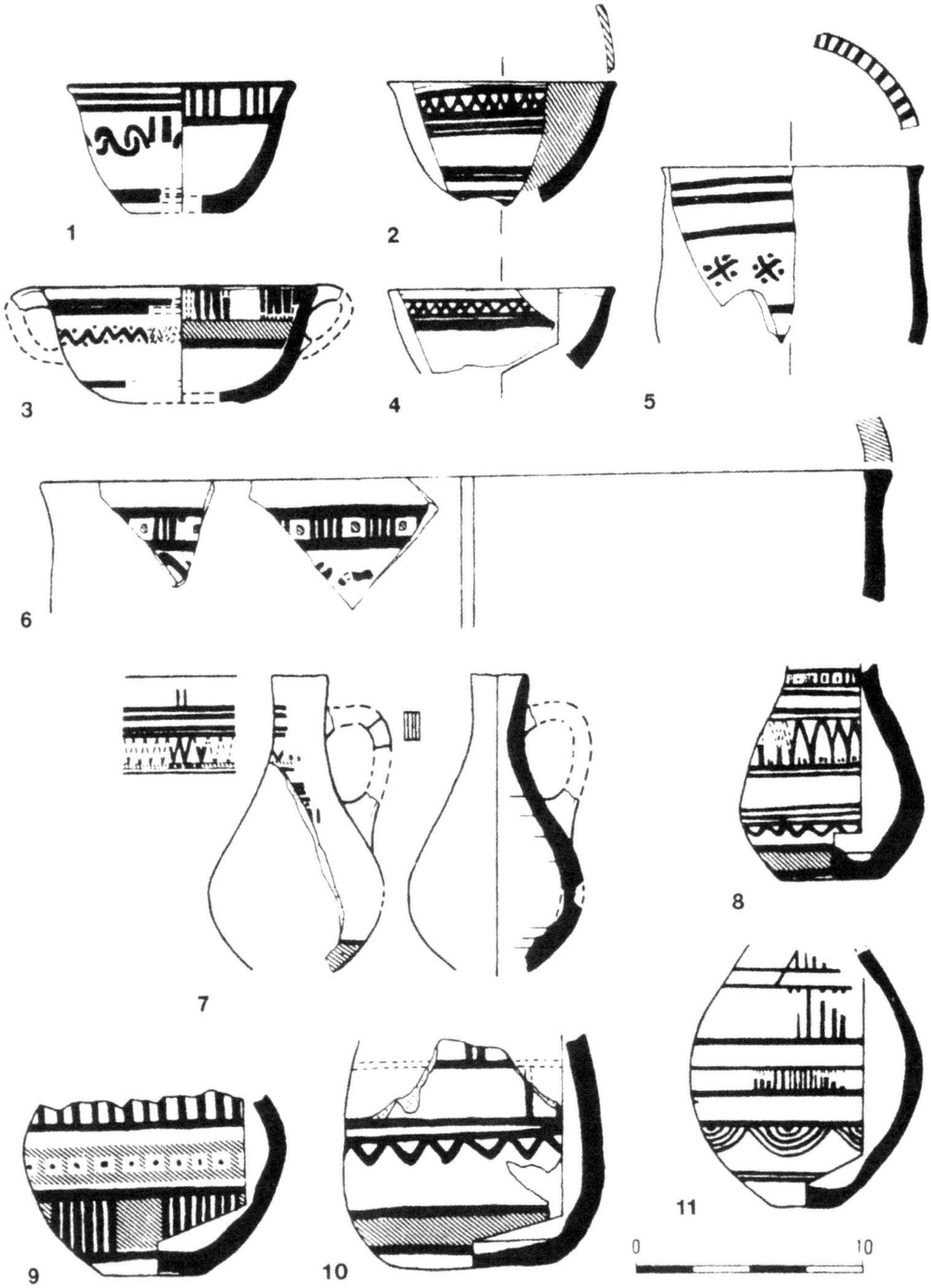

Fig. 14.3. Qurayyah Painted Ware from Timna (after Rothenberg 1998, 198 fig. 1).

thus were in charge of trading routes and goods. Control over the trade in aromatics brought wealth and prosperity as well as socio-economic and socio-political changes. People gave up their nomadic lifestyle and became sedentary, initiating a process of urbanisation (Finkelstein 1988).

The producers of the Qurayyah Painted Ware might have extended their influence into the southern Levant and northern Hejaz because of the power vacuum. Distribution of Qurayyah Painted Ware reveals that – to the south – their influence reached as far as Tayma and al-Ula. Although only a few sherds of Qurayyah Painted Ware were found at Tayma, a later imitation of this ware in a local tradition during the Iron Age indicates a clear impact (Hausleiter 2011, 111–113). In the absence of direct archaeological evidence, it can only be supposed that these people played an active part as middlemen for the Arabian contacts to the Nile Valley (see also Sperveslage, 2013).

The Iron Age: Egyptian amulets in Arabian temples and tombs

For the Iron Age, archaeological remains from three different regions contribute to our knowledge of cultural networks linking Egypt and the Arabian Peninsula. The first of these regions comprises the oasis of Tayma in north-west Arabia, where excavations were initiated in the late 1970s by an American team from Harvard University (Bawden *et al.* 1980) and resumed by Saudi Arabian archaeologists in the 1980s (Abu Duruk 1986; 1989; 1990). Since 2004 a German-Saudi Arabian cooperation has been conducted archaeological fieldwork at Tayma which includes environmental studies (Eichmann *et al.* 2006a; 2006b; 2010; 2011; Eichmann & Hausleiter in press). The second region is the ancient land of Dilmun, extending from Kuwait to eastern Saudi Arabia and Bahrain. Settlements on the island of Failaka (Kuwait) and on Bahrain, as well as a field of tumuli at Dhahran in Saudi Arabia excavated in the 1980s (Zarins *et al.* 1984), are of particular importance for relations with Egypt. A third region is found in Yemen. The Sabaean cemetery associated with the Awām Temple at Marib was investigated by the German Archaeological Institute between 1997 and 2000 (Hitgen 1998; Gerlach 2002). All these sites have revealed Egyptian or Egyptian-style artefacts from funerary and sacral contexts.

North-west Arabia: The oasis of Tayma

The oasis of Tayma is located in north-west Arabia (Fig. 14.4). Along with the neighbouring oases of al-Ula and Dumat al-Jandal, Tayma constitutes one of the most prominent cities on the ancient frankincense route. The prosperity of the oasis is a result of topography and the natural resources of the region. The ancient settlement of Tayma is situated at the edge of a topographic depression, which extends over an area of *c.* 1.5 km^2 and which, according to hydrological investigation, was a permanent lake until the mid-5th millennium BCE. Today, the depression forms a *sabkha* and retains water only after seasonal rainfall. Artesian ground water is available at a

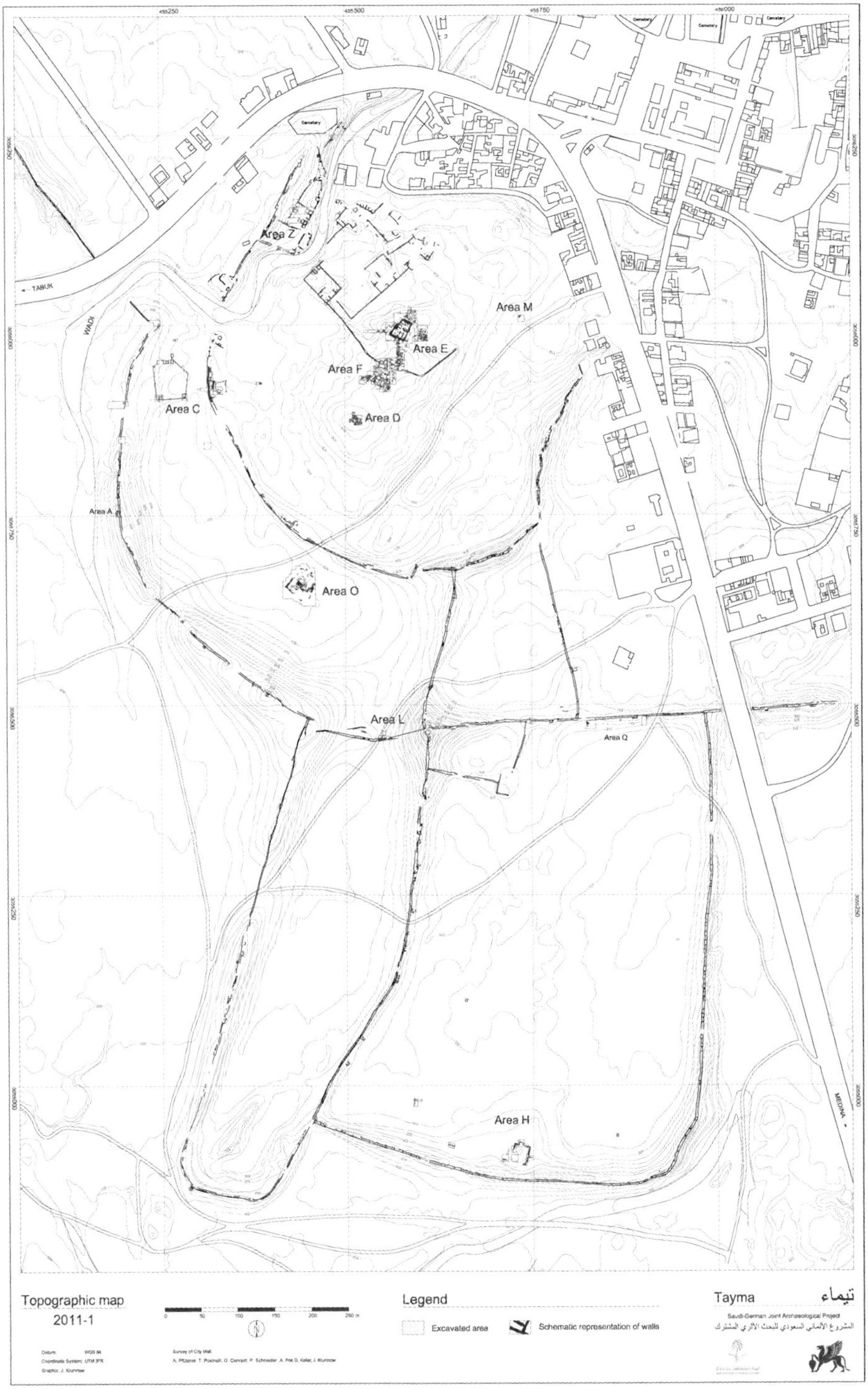

Fig. 14.4. The excavation site at Tayma (Graphic: Jan Krumnow, © DAI, Orient Department).

depth of only a few meters – about 1 m in the *sabkha* and about 4 m in the palm grooves. These conditions allowed occupation throughout the year and encouraged the development of a permanent settlement (Eichmann *et al.* 2006a, 165; Hausleiter 2010, 223–226). Rock drawings and flint tools indicate that the oasis was already inhabited in the Chalcolithic Period and was continuously occupied. In the Middle Bronze Age, a substantial wall system, surrounding the palm grooves and parts of the *sabkha*, was built with a total length of *c.* 18.2 km (P. Schneider 2010; Hausleiter 2011, 107). Despite of the wall system, however, only minimal evidence can be ascribed to a Middle or Late Bronze Age settlement so far. The earliest excavated architectural remains belong to the Early Iron Age and are dated to the 12th–9th centuries BCE by radiocarbon (Hausleiter 2010, 230–231; 2011, 111–113; Eichmann *et al.* 2011). Early Iron Age evidence is found in excavation Area A at the outer wall and in Area O, which is situated between the inner and outer enclosure.

In Area O, an edifice built of stone, designated O-b1, was exposed (Fig. 14.5). It is surrounded by pillars and encircled by a substantial temenos wall 2 m in width. The core of building O-b1 measures *c.* 11 × 7 m; the temenos encloses an area of more than 1300 m². The characteristic architecture, as well as a substantial amount of finds which can be described as prestigious objects, and the absence of artefacts related to a domestic setting are suggestive of a temple or sanctuary. The building was destroyed by fire, while still in use, as carbonised plant remains were found in the debris. After the conflagration the building and its site remained abandoned until about half a millennium later. During the second occupational period graves were cut into the bedrock and into the architectural remains, distorting the primary contexts of artefacts within the temple site (Lora *et al.* 2010, 238–239).

Among the finds related to temple O-b1 were painted ceramics and elaborate artefacts made of wood decorated with intarsia of bone and ivory, as well as wooden boxes and figural items (Hausleiter 2010, 230–231; 2011, 111–113). Some artefacts have close parallels in the Levant and hence reveal contacts to and influences from the northern regions. Even more distinctive are the connections to Egypt, which are reflected by several Egyptian faience objects. Amulets depicting Egyptian gods such as Isis and Sakhmet/Bastet have been recovered, as well as protective figurines such as a nude female with a guenon resting on her arm (Fig. 14.7), and a guenon playing a harp (Fig. 14.6), fragments of a crocodile and a bull figurine. Other tiny fragments of faience probably also derive from figurines. Furthermore, sherds and fragments of more than a dozen different faience vessels, some with black painted decoration, were found. Among them are fragments of a compartmentalized box with a rounded base and of a bowl with lotus ornament (Fig. 14.8). All these faience items were found within the temenos of building O-b1, and most originate from inside the core of the edifice. Although only the figurine of a crocodile found in room 2 and the guenon with a harp found in room 7 were discovered in their primary context, the association of all the other finds with building O-b1 is beyond any doubt, since all items can

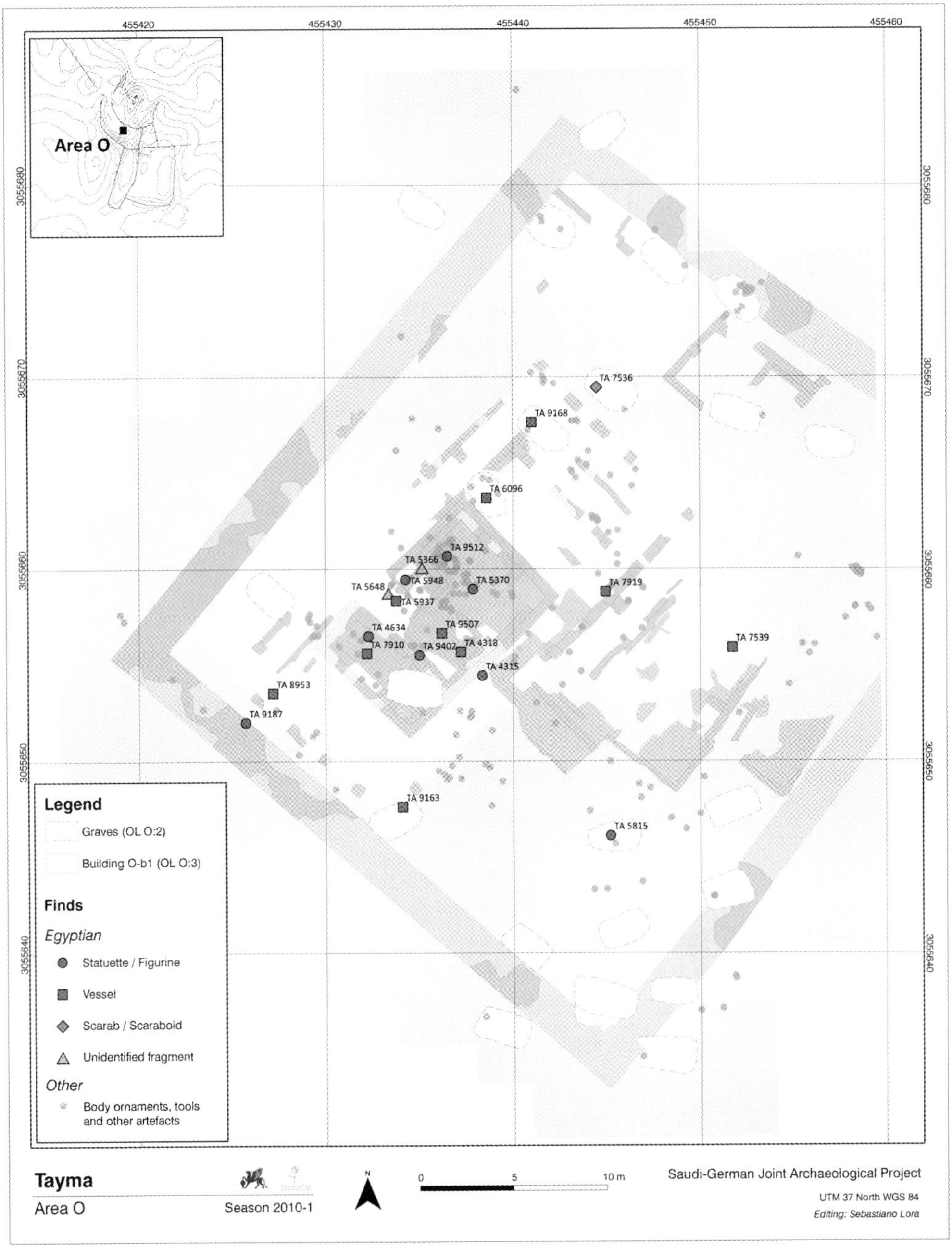

Fig. 14.5. The temple O-b1 in Area O at Tayma (Graphic: Jan Krumnow, © DAI, Orient Department).

be dated to the Third Intermediate Period (Sperveslage in press a). Thus it is very unlikely that they should belong to the burials of the second occupational period 500 years later.

Similar objects and close parallels from Egypt proper can be found for many of the Egyptian artefacts (see Sperveslage in press a). And as can be judged from the fabric, the faience material is of Egyptian origin (Annie Caubet, pers. comm.). Therefore, the amulets, figurines and vessels should have been produced in an Egyptian workshop. They were neither manufactured in the Levant nor locally, but imported from Egypt to Tayma. Whether as a result of direct contact or via intermediaries is unclear, as there is a lack of information especially from epigraphic sources. If contact was made through intermediaries they were presumably the nomadic and semi-nomadic tribes of the north-west Arabian desert steppe, like the producers of the Qurayyah Painted Ware and their successors, who played a major role in the distribution of goods and ideas.

The context of the Early Iron Age Egyptian finds is a temple, but in later times, Egyptian amulets have also been found in tombs. In the late 1980s a team of Saudi Arabian archaeologists conducted excavations on the so-called "Industrial Site", a large cemetery area at Sana'iye directly south of the settlement of Tayma. The tombs date to the first half or the middle of the 1st millennium BCE (Abu Duruk 1989; 1990; Hausleiter 2010, 231); the dead were provided with painted pottery vessels, beads and amulets as grave goods. Two scarabs and two Udjat-amulets among the items found (Abu Duruk 1989, 15, pl. 9; 1990, 15) have parallels dating to Dynasty 26 (Fig. 14.9). These Egyptian artefacts from the cemetery of Sana'iye are imports from the Nile Valley.

Until now, no occupational level within the ancient settlement of Tayma has been found that correlates with the Sana'iye cemetery. Thus no further archaeological evidence for the quality of contacts to Egypt in this period can be cited, but support for direct connections derives from a rock inscription in the environment of the oasis. At Gebel Ghuneim, the highest peak of a mountain ridge about 10 km south-west of Tayma, an inscription in Thamudic script mentions an Egyptian woman (Winnett & Reed 1970, 106, no. 37). Gebel Ghuneim was sacred to the god Salm; inscriptions and graffiti which mainly date to the mid-6th century BCE are frequent there (Müller 1985, 666; Winnett & Reed 1970). The reading of the inscription naming the Egyptian woman, however, is controversial. Winnett and Reed (1970, 106) translate it "lay with an Egyptian woman", whereas al-Said (2003, 59–60) supposes instead that a personal name is mentioned and reads "Bi, the Egyptian woman". Regardless, the inscription clearly documents an Egyptian woman in the region of Tayma. It is tempting to suggest that this woman was brought to Tayma as the wife of an Arabian tradesman after an expedition to Egypt. In South Arabia, the marriage of Minaeans with foreign women is documented in the so called "*Hierodulenlisten*", epigraphic texts from the temple of Ma'in, dating to the 5th or 4th century BCE (Robin 1994, 297–301; Bron 1998, 102–121). In these lists eight women from Egypt are recorded (Müller & Vittmann 1993), as well as several others from elsewhere – such as Gaza or Dedan. Some scholars propose that Minaean merchants met these women on their journeys and took them home to Ma'in (Robin 1994, 297). Viewing the mention of an Egyptian woman at Gebel Ghuneim in the same light, is speculative, but nonetheless an option.

Fig. 14.6. Faience figurine of a naked woman with a guenon resting on her arm (TA 4315) (Photo: Irmgard Wagner, © DAI, Orient Department).

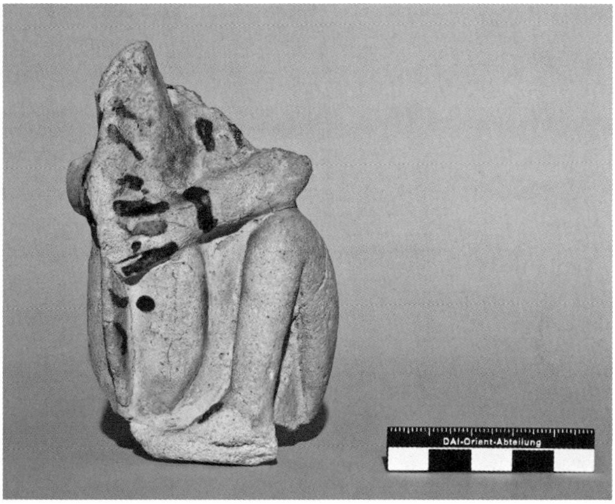

Fig. 14.7. Faience figurine of a guenon playing a harp (TA 9512) (Photo: Johannes Kramer, © DAI, Orient Department).

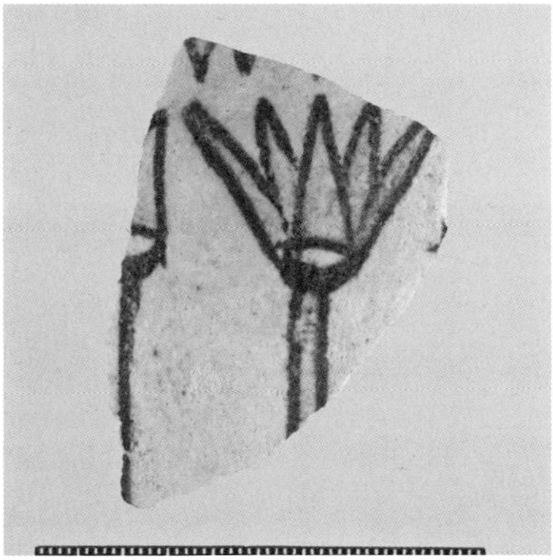

Fig. 14.8. Fragment of a faience vessel with lotus ornament (TA 7919###) (Photo: Irmgard Wagner, © DAI, Orient Department).

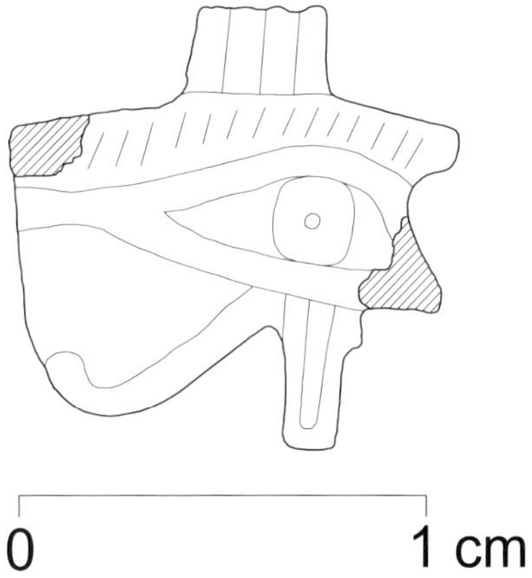

Fig. 14.9. Udjat amulet from Sana'iye cemetery (drawing: © G. Sperveslage).

The Gulf region: Failaka, Bahrain and Dhahran

The Gulf region was governed by the land of Dilmun, located on the islands of Bahrain and Tarut and the adjoining Arabian littoral (Potts 1990; 2010), which epigraphically appears first in Sumerian cuneiform texts from the end of the 4th millennium BCE.

Dilmun was incorporated in trade networks between ancient Mesopotamia and the civilisation of the Indus Valley. Timber and wood, metals and luxury goods were imported from Dilmun to Mesopotamia. The land and its prosperity also benefited from artesian aquifers. Therefore, in Sumerian mythology Dilmun became a synonym for paradise. Archaeological research initiated in the 1950s by a Danish team, directed by P. V. Glob and G. Bibby (see Bibby 1969 for a summarising account), established the Gulf region as an important constituent in pre-Iron Age intercultural networks.

Besides the islands of Bahrain and Tarut, Dilmun covered wide parts of the eastern Arabian mainland and extended northward as far as Kuwait and the island of Failaka. On Failaka a representative complex (building F6) was excavated which is datable to the 2nd millennium BCE and which has been interpreted as a palace (Højlund 1987, 138–149). Within this edifice, a scarab and a scaraboid were found, both made of steatite with antelopes depicted on the undersides (Kjærum 1983, 128–129, no. 315–316). Both items show clearly the influence of local glyptic and are comparable to other seals from the Dilmun region. They were produced locally, adopting the shape of an Egyptian prototype but using indigenous decorative motifs. Whether the presence of these two seals on Failaka reflects contacts between Egypt and Dilmun remains doubtful. Egyptian scarabs might well have reached Failaka by trade through Mesopotamia. However, the fact that they adopted the Egyptian scarab indicates that Egyptian forms and motifs attracted the locals; probably they knew of the distant and exotic origin.

Egyptian artefacts in the Gulf region are not limited to the Bronze Age. At Qala'at al-Bahrain a silver hoard was discovered during excavations in the occupational levels of the neo-Babylonian period ("City IV") (Bibby 1964). The hoard contained a silver signet ring with Egyptian hieroglyphs. It can be compared to Egyptian signet rings from the Saite Period (Dynasty 26) and is either Egyptianising Phoenician work or was produced locally in the 7th century BCE (Krauss *et al.* 1983). More scarabs and scarab-shaped seals were found during the excavation of a tumuli field at Dhahran near modern Dammam (Fig. 14.10). They were discovered together with other seals, which according to their decoration and style are clearly of Mesopotamian or Canaanite origin (Zarins *et al.* 1984; 40–41, pl. 52). The motifs on the undersides are of non-Egyptian origin as well and appear to be Phoenician.

The cited examples from the Gulf region indicate that a deep interest in Egyptian amulets also existed in the far east of the Arabian Peninsula. But as all the scarabs and scaraboids appear to be non-Egyptian products, they provide no evidence for direct contact. Instead, they reveal networks to the Levant. The Gulf region was involved in the incense trade, but its main objective was the distribution of goods which came from South Arabia via central Arabia to Mesopotamia, and probably also goods, such as ivory, that were brought from central Africa via South Arabia to the Gulf. Thus there was little impetus for contact with far western regions like Egypt, while Egypt, too, might have had less interest, since exports obtainable via the Gulf region were available from much closer sources – Nubia (ivory), Cyprus (copper), the Levant (timber) and north-west Arabia (aromatics).

South Arabia: The Sabaean Kingdom at Marib

In north-eastern Yemen, about 135 km east of Sana'a near to the fringe of the Rub al-Khali desert, the extensive oasis of Marib, capital of the kingdom of Saba, is located. The ancient settlement had a substantial fortification wall surrounding administrative centres, as well as sacral and domestic spaces. Smaller settlements lay outside the city wall in the wide region of the oasis, including the Awām Temple, dedicated to Almaqah. A Sabaean cemetery extends to the south of the temple. The so-called mausoleum east of the temenos and some other tombs to the south of the cemetery were excavated in the early 1950s (Albright 1958). Systematic excavations within the cemetery were then conducted by the Sana'a branch of the German Archaeological Institute (Hitgen 1998; Gerlach 2002). The cemetery was in use since the early 1st millennium BCE, although its main phase of occupation dates from the 6th–3rd centuries BCE, according to epigraphic finds (Gerlach 2002, 35). The tombs are constructed of stone, but they differ greatly in architectural design and in the quality of the stone working, suggesting that individuals of varying social status were buried in the cemetery of Awām (Gerlach 2002, 51–54).

Many objects were recovered from the burials documenting the diversity of Sabaean grave goods. Unfortunately, the cemetery had suffered much from looting in antiquity, as well as in recent times. Almost all finds are without any stratigraphic context and can hardly be ascribed to a specific burial (Gerlach 2002, 45, 54–56). This is a great loss, since several Egyptian or Egyptian-style artefacts were found during the excavations. It is impossible to reconstruct neither the number of burials to which these artefacts belonged, nor to evaluate the social status of their owners. But since Egyptian finds occurred in three different sectors of the excavation (Area A, B and D), they should at least derive from different burials. There was not just one single "Egyptianised" person, but rather a more or less even distribution of Egyptian and Egyptian-style objects within the cemetery.

Ahmed Fakhry published six Egyptian amulets (Fig. 14.11), which he purchased during his visit to Yemen in 1947 and which are said to be from Marib (Fakhry 1951/1952, I 136–138). Fakhry also visited Marib and was told by the local inhabitants that they regularly plundered the ancient cemetery for artefacts to sell at Sana'a (Fakhry 1951/1952, I 88). It is thus highly probable that Fakhry's Egyptian amulets originate from the cemetery of the Awām Temple at Marib; together with the amulets from the German excavations they provide an impression of Sabaean elite emulation of the Egyptians.

The Egyptian finds from Marib are either imports from Egypt or Egyptian-style objects manufactured in the Levant. Determining their origin is problematic, especially since Fakhry published only drawings. They are small amulets and scarabs which had probably been brought to Marib by Sabaean trading activities to the north, in Egypt and the Levant. Fakhry (1951/1952, I 136–138) published two scarabs with Egyptian hieroglyphs, two rectangular plaques, an amulet in the shape of a flower and an amulet depicting the god Bes. All these objects are datable to the Late Period, probably to Dynasty 26.

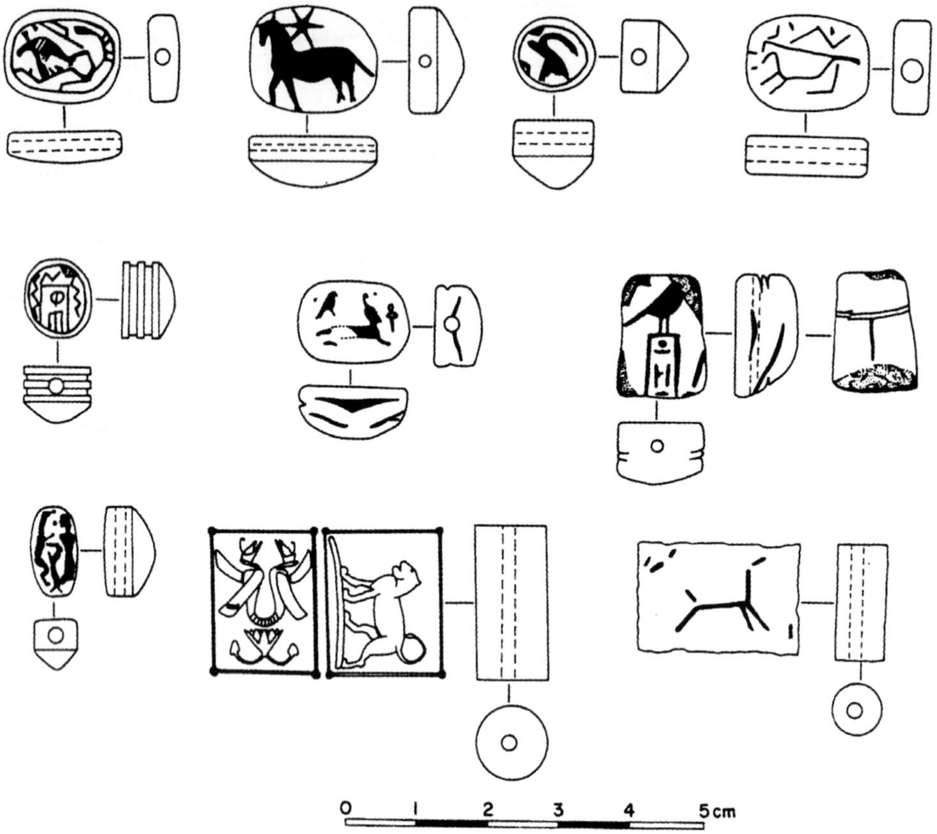

Fig. 14.10. Scarabs and seals from the Dhahran tumuli field (after Zarins et al. *1984, pl. 52).*

The excavations of the German Archaeological Institute added a few scarabs (Gerlach 2002, pl. 22), which almost certainly can be dated to the Third Intermediate or Late Period. The decoration on the underside shows some Levantine influences, so these scarabs were produced in a Levantine, rather than in an Egyptian workshop. Another amulet in the shape of a female figure might have been manufactured in the Levant as well. Furthermore, two seals with early Hebrew inscriptions were found that indicate once more contacts to the Levantine region.

A small limestone statuette (ht. 7.5 cm) was also found (Hitgen 1988, 122; Gerlach 2002, 55, pl. 23). It represents a sphinx and preserves traces of red and black painting; the head is missing, but there are remains of a distinctive coiffure on the shoulders. A similar sphinx with the same coiffure originates from Addi-Keramaten in Ethiopia (Anfray 1990, 44) and is datable to the Preaksumite Period (6th–5th century BCE). Although the general sphinx type is Egyptian in origin, the statuette from Marib was most likely produced in the Ethiopian highlands and thus would serve as an indicator for contact and exchange between Yemen and Ethiopia in the mid-1st millennium

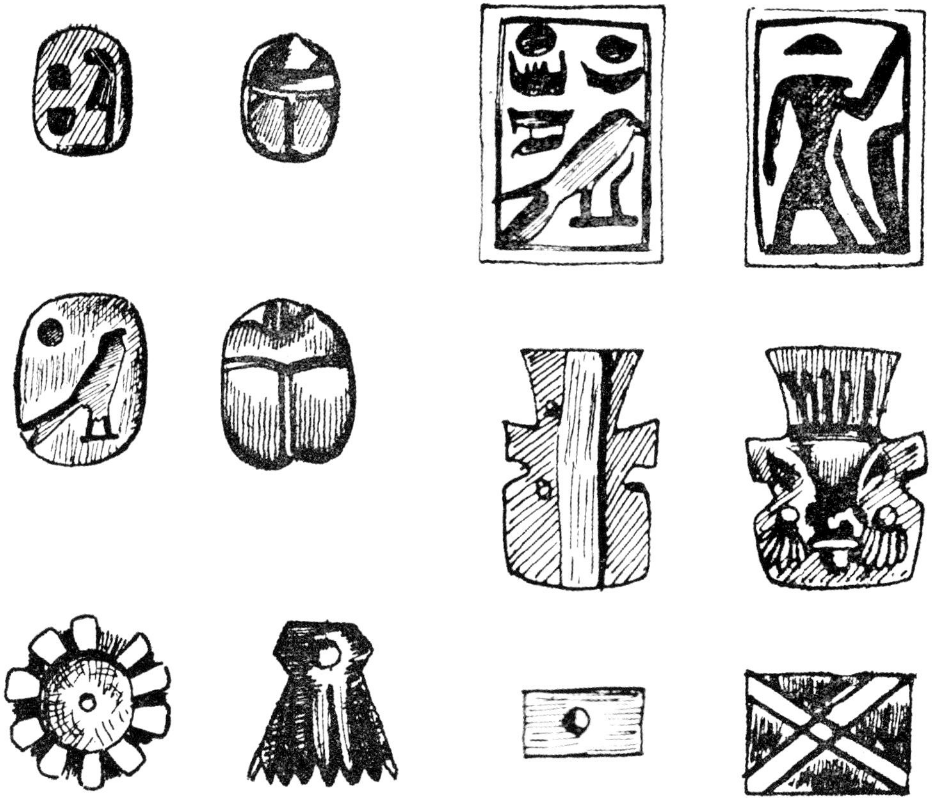

Fig. 14.11. Egyptian amulets, probably originating from Marib (after Fakhry 1951/1952, I fig. 96).

BCE (see e.g. Japp *et al.* 2011). By contrast, the other objects related to Egypt most probably came to Marib within the context of trading activities along the frankincense route. In the first half of the 1st millennium BCE the Sabaean network of trade and communication extended north to Egypt, Assur and the Levant. As the inscription of Sabahhumu mentioned above (Bron & Lemaire 2009) indicates, caravans – at least occasionally – travelled the entire route from South Arabia to Gaza without selling their goods to intermediaries. Thus Sabaean merchants like Sabahhumu maintained direct contact with Egypt and the Levant.

Egyptian artefacts on the Arabian Peninsula in the context of mobility and identity

The brief discussion of the three different sites or regions in north-west Arabia, the Gulf region and South Arabia is by no means exhaustive. There are other sites within the Arabian Peninsula that reveal Egyptian influence as well (see Sperveslage 2014).

But as case studies, the three examples cited give an impression of the intercultural contacts between Egypt and Arabia. They contribute to our understanding of communication and trading networks in the Iron Age and clearly show that the Arabian Peninsula was on no account an unknown region. It was inhabited by different communities, which were not very powerful politically, but connected through their own activities to the neighbouring civilisations in Mesopotamia, the Indus Valley and, not least, to Egypt.

As the Arabian Peninsula was not a single entity, neither politically, culturally, nor ethnically, the Egyptian impact varies at the different sites. Egyptian cultural influence cannot be described in general terms, but site by site. The case studies of north-west, eastern and southern Arabia reveal general differences in the Egyptian material remains. The Egyptian finds from north-west Arabia, i.e. from Tayma, were produced in Egypt and are imports from the Nile Valley, while the finds from eastern Arabia, as well as from Marib in South Arabia, are Levantine products. Distance has a certain effect on the intensity of contacts and influence. North-west Arabia and the oasis of Tayma are much closer to the Nile Valley than the Gulf Region and South Arabia, where middlemen will have been involved. This might explain why Egyptian objects are found at Tayma, while Egyptian-style amulets of local or Levantine origin were discovered in the more distant regions. Direct contacts between the Gulf region and Egypt were less important for both regions and might have been intentional only in a few instances, because the main products of both regions involved in exchange were available to the other from much closer sources and through different networks, in particular through South Arabia. On the other hand, this does not rule out direct contacts, which might have existed to some extent, without leaving any evidence.

Direct or indirect contacts need not necessarily be reflected by the presence of Egyptian and Egyptian-style objects. Several South Arabian inscriptions clearly indicate direct trading connections of the Sabaean and Minaean Kingdoms with Egypt at least since the late 7th century BCE. The evidence for the first half of the 4th century is clear, since expeditions to Egypt are explicitly mentioned in Minaean texts (Robin 1994, 286–290). And as the Sabaean Sabahhumu, whose inscription has been cited above, travelled as far as Cyprus, it can be expected that at the same time Sabaean caravans would have reached Egypt as well. Even though direct contacts apparently existed, the Egyptian artefacts from the Awām cemetery were mainly produced in Levantine workshops. However, the evaluation of the amulets published by Ahmed Fakhry, based on drawings alone, is difficult and some of them might be Egyptian work. Thus, by contrast to the Gulf region where only Egyptian-style objects are attested, the direct contacts of the Sabaeans involved both Egyptian and Egyptian-style objects.

Despite all differences in the character of finds between the three regions there are also similarities. Beginning in the Early Iron Age, Egyptian and Egyptian-style objects are found on the Arabian Peninsula. Bronze Age contexts – like the palace on the island of Failaka – are rare. But caution is called for when interpreting this observation. Although it might be related to the general shift which affected the Mediterranean and the Ancient Near East at the end of the Late Bronze Age, it has to be remembered that at present few archaeological remains from the Bronze Age are known on the Arabian Peninsula. Future fieldwork may well change the overall picture.

Remarkably, all Egyptian and Egyptian-style objects were unearthed in sacral or funerary contexts (as grave goods). Those found in sanctuaries or temples probably had been donated as votives. By contrast, no such artefacts have been discovered within domestic contexts. According to general models of interpreting intercultural relations, this reveals an adoption of Egyptian culture and ideas in the Arabian communities and an emulation of elites (Whitehouse & Wilkins 1989; Higginbotham 2000, 10–16; Sperveslage, 2013; see also Wengrow 2010). Emulation and acquisition of prestigious items are usually characteristic of local elites seeking to enhance their social standing. But as objects of prestige do not necessarily reflect social status and hence can also be found within the lower classes (Seidlmayer 2009), caution must be exercised in ascribing them to social elites and a culture of court life. But it will not be inaccurate to suppose that the owners of Egyptian and Egyptian-style objects were primarily merchants and traders who acquired these objects on their expeditions. These were people belonging to the social elites, who kept such items to enhance their own prestige, while selling others within the local elites.

The material remains indicate trading networks and elite emulation, but it is noteworthy that information on the contacts between Egypt and the Arabian Peninsula is derived almost exclusively from Arabia. Evidence from within the Nile Valley is hard to find. For the Bronze Age there are the South Arabian pottery sherds at Mersa Gawasis and again pottery evidence from the Roman ports at Myos Hormos and Berenike (Tomber 2008, 50–51; Sidebotham 2011, 72–74, 224). There are two possible reasons for the lack of evidence from Iron Age Egypt. Firstly, trading goods reaching Egypt from the Arabian Peninsula could have been made of materials that did not survive in archaeological contexts. Frankincense, myrrh, other resins and aromatics – and probably agricultural products and livestock as well – which are mentioned in papyri of the Ptolemaic to Byzantine Period (Harrauer 1983), leave little or no traces at all. And secondly, as mentioned above, the Arabian Peninsula was neither a great empire nor a single entity. Therefore the Arabian oasis settlements are not referred to in historical records. Such a discrepancy between records from Egypt and Arabia is not exceptional. A similar phenomenon has been noticed, for example, in the case of Late Bronze Age Sardinia (Russell 2010). Although on Sardinia itself emulation of and influences from mainland Italy can be recognized in the Late Bronze Age Nuragic material culture, no correlating Nuragic finds have been found on the Italian mainland. Contact certainly existed, but the material remains in Italy do not reflect it, because Nuragic people exported short-lived goods to the mainland like agricultural products and probably unworked copper (Russell 2010, 122). A comparable explanation may well account for the lack of evidence in Egypt much better than the presumption that

Egyptians considered Arabia an unfathomable, desolate region, interesting only as far as strategic concerns with the border to the Sinai Peninsula (so Saleh 1978, 70). The latter scenario derives from the way the Romans thought of Arabia as reflected in the Latin names for northern and central Arabia (*arabia deserta*) and South Arabia, which was known as *arabia felix* due to its wealth.

However, a few indirect indications from Egypt proper do exist. Some hitherto unidentified Semitic toponyms and names of tribes possibly refer to north-west Arabia (see also Saleh 1978). Another much more rewarding source is provided by personal names. From the New Kingdom, more than 500 personal names of Semitic origin are known (T. Schneider 1993). Although it is difficult to associate these names with specific attestations within Semitic onomastica, since similar names and roots can be found in several Semitic languages, some names are very probably derived from Early Arabian languages (T. Schneider 1993, 359). In total, 46 personal names are almost certainly of Arabian origin and belong to the north Arabian dialects (Thamudic, Safaitic and Lihyanite language) rather than to ancient South Arabian dialects (Sabaean, Minaean, Qatabanian and Hadramautic language), revealing a stronger connection to northern than to southern Arabia. If the identification of the names is correct, it can be concluded that several people of Arabian origin lived in the Nile Valley during the New Kingdom and, furthermore, that they were not all peasants nor labourers, since their names are recorded on stelae, belonging to higher social classes, and in administrative documents. Then, if this was true in the Late Bronze Age, a similar state may well have obtained during the Iron Age, i.e. the Third Intermediate and the Late Period. Migration is one aspect of mobility in ancient societies and an indication of trade and communication networks. For the Ptolemaic and Roman period, Arabian communities are well attested in Egypt, especially in the Fayum region. Arabians constituted the fourth largest group of foreigners in Hellenistic Egypt, after Greeks, Persians and Jews (Clarysse & Thompson 2006, II 159–160). Once again, the Minaean Zayd'il, whose sarcophagus was mentioned above, has to be taken in account; he supplied Egyptian temples with aromatics and when he died, he was buried at Saqqara. He adapted to Egyptian culture; the use of Egyptian loanwords in the sarcophagus inscription suggests that he probably spoke Egyptian, and certainly he made his home in Egypt. But Zayd'il is the only Arabian person of the Ptolemaic period attested in the archaeological record rather than exclusively by inscriptions and textual evidence. Nothing is known of the material culture of the Arabian community in the Fayum, although according to tax receipts, at least 800 Arabians lived there (Clarysse & Thompson 2006, II 159–160). Arabic personal names in New Kingdom documents and large-scale Arabian communities in the Ptolemaic Period are no evidence for the Iron Age, but on analogy – as contacts are assured by evidence from the Arabian Peninsula – may give an impression of what might have been.

The interaction between Egypt and the Arabian Peninsula was primarily motivated by economic interests. Egyptian demand for incense and related commodities, which were essential in domestic as well as sacral contexts, was considerable. They were used for fumigation in the cult and for rituals, when worshipping the gods and honouring the dead. Furthermore, they were ingredients in medication and unguents (Germer 2008, 117–122), but also to scent interiors and clothing. Since incense products were put to a variety of purposes, they can hardly be described as luxury goods. Rather, they were indispensable in everyday life; hence much effort was expended to import these products. Expeditions to the mysterious land of Punt began during the Old Kingdom, and resins of lesser quality, such as obtained from terebinth trees, were introduced from the Levant. To meet demand, Egypt developed a strong economic interest in the Arabian Peninsula and its resources. The rock inscription of Ramesses III at Tayma attests an Egyptian expedition to the region. The need for incense products and their high cost might well have inspired a wish to control the north Arabian routes and centres. A more powerful position of the Egyptian Empire during the Iron Age could have led to an attempt at military occupation to control the trading network. But due to the political situation, such efforts proved successful only for the Assyrian and Babylonian kings.

The evidence and artefacts presented here derive primarily from on-going excavations and thus reflect the current state of research. New finds and new evidence may well necessitate a shift of emphasis and lead to new interpretations. At present, the artefacts from the Arabian Peninsula provide insights into the intercultural contacts between Egypt and Arabia. The inhabitants of the oasis settlements dominated the trading networks as active parties. Forming their own identities within the framework of these networks, they developed a taste for prestigious objects of the nearby high cultures, integrating foreign elements into new contexts. In this respect, Egyptian influence seems to have been a prevalent factor – among the elites, and probably also among people of lower social classes.

Acknowledgements

First of all I would like to thank Juan Carlos Moreno García for the invitation to contribute to this volume. The subject of this paper is based on my doctoral dissertation which I defended at the Free University of Berlin in 2014, with research generously funded by the Gerda Henkel Foundation. I am much indebted to my supervisors, Stephan J. Seidlmayer and Ricardo Eichmann for their unflagging support. I am also very grateful to Arnulf Hausleiter and the Tayma project of the German Archaeological Institute for discussion and support.

Bibliography

Abu Duruk, H. I. (1986) *Introduction to the Archaeology of Tayma*, Riyadh.

Abu Duruk, H. I. (1989) A preliminary report on the industrial site excavation at Tayma, first season 1408 H/1987 A.D, *ATLAL* 12: 9–19.

Abu Duruk, H. I. (1990) A preliminary report on the industrial site excavation at Tayma, second season 1410 H/1989 A.D., *ATLAL* 13: 9–19.

al-Ansary, A. R. (2011) Editorial, *Adumatu* 23: 4–6.

Albright, F. P. (1958) Excavations at Marib in Yemen. In R. L. Bowen & F. P. Albright (eds), *Archaeological Discoveries in South Arabia* (Publications of the American Foundation for the Study of Men 2), 215–268, Baltimore.

al-Said, S. F. (2003) *Al-'alāqāt al-ḥaḍāriyyah bayna "l-ǧazīrah al-'arabiyyah wa-Miṣr fī ḍaw' an-nuqūš al-'arabiyyah al-qadīmah*, Riyadh.

al-Said, S. F. (2009) Eine neu entdeckte Erwähnung des Königs Nabonid in den thamudischen Inschriften, *Zeitschrift für Orientarchäologie* 2: 258–263.

Anfray, F. (1990) *Les anciens ethiopiens. Siècles d'histoire*, Paris.

Aston, B. G., J. A. Harrel & I. Shaw (2000) Stone. In P. T. Nicholson & I. Shaw (eds), *Ancient Egyptian Materials and Technology*, 5–77, Cambridge.

Bard, K. A. & R. Fattovich (eds) (2007) *Harbor of the Pharaohs to the Land of Punt. Archaeological Investigations at Mersa/Wadi Gawasis, Egypt, 2001–2005*, Naples.

Bard, K. A., R. Fattovich & C. Ward (2007) Sea Port to Punt: new evidence from Mersā Gawāsīs, Red Sea (Egypt). In J. Starkey, P. Starkey & T. Wilkinson (eds), *Natural Recources and Cultural Connections of the Red Sea* (British Archaeological Report S1661/Society for Arabian Studies Monographs 5), 143–148, Oxford.

Bawden, G., C. Edens & R. Miller (1980) Preliminary archaeological investigations at Taymā, *ATLAL* 4: 69–106.

Beaulieu, P.-A. (1989) *The Reign of Nabonidus, King of Babylon 556–539 BC* (Yale Near Eastern Researches 10), New Haven.

Bibby, T. G. (1964) Arabiens Arkæologi. Dansk arkæologisk ekspeditions 8. kampagne, 1961/2. Dansk arkæologisk ekspeditions 9. kampagne, 1962/3, *Kuml* 1964: 86–111.

Bibby, T. G. (1969) *Looking for Dilmun*, New York.

Bron, F. (1998) *Inventaire des inscriptions sudarabiques 3: Ma'īn*, Paris-Rome.

Bron, F. & A. Lemaire (2009) Nouvelle inscription sabéenne et le commerce en Transeuphratène, *Transeuphratène* 38: 11–29.

Bülow-Jacobsen, A., H. Cuvigny, J.-L. Fournet, M. Gabolde & Chr. Robin (1995) Les inscriptions d'Al-Muwayh, *Bulletin de l'Institut Français d'Archéologie Orientale* 95: 103–124.

Byrne, R. (2003) Early Assyrian contacts with Arabs and the impact on Levantine vassal tribute, *Bulletin of the American Schools of Oriental Research* 331: 11–25.

Calmeyer, P. (1991) Ägyptischer Stil und reichsachaimenidische Inhalte auf dem Sockel der Dareios-Statue aus Susa/Heliopolis. In H. Sancisi-Weerdenburg & A. Kuhrt (eds), *Achaemenid History VI. Asia Minor and Egypt: Old Cultures in a new Empire. Proceedings of the Groningen 1988 Achaemenid History Workshop*, 285–303, Leiden.

Cavigneaux, A. & B. Khalil Ismael (1990) Die Statthalter von Suhu und Mari im 8. Jh. v.Chr, *Baghdader Mitteilungen* 21: 321–456.

Clarysse, W. & D. J. Thompson (2006) *Counting the People in Hellenistic Egypt*, Cambridge.

Clermont-Ganneau, C. (1908) Inscription bilingue minéo-grecque découverte a Délos, *Comptes-rendus des séances de l'Académie des Inscriptions et Belles-Lettres* 52: 546–560.

Colin, G. (1988) A propos des graffites sud-arabiques du Ouādi Hammāmāt, *Bulletin de l'Institut Français d'Archéologie Orientale* 88: 33–36.

de Jesus, P. S., S. Al-Sugiran, B. Rihani, A. Kesnawi, M. Toplyn & J. Incagnoli (1982) Preliminary report of the ancient mining survey 1981 (1401), *ATLAL* 6: 63–79.

Eichmann, R. (in press) Die Oasensiedlung von Tayma (NW-Arabien) im Kontext überregionaler Netzwerke. In R. G. Stiegner (ed.), *Ancient South Arabia: A Much Neglected Crossroad of Civilizations* (Wiener Offene Orientalistik 11), Vienna.

Eichmann, R. & A. Hausleiter (eds) (in press). *Tayma I. Reports on the SCTA-DAI excavations*, Riyadh.

Eichmann, R., H. Schaudig & A. Hausleiter (2006a) Archaeology and epigraphy at Tayma (Saudi Arabia), *Arabian Archaeology and Epigraphy* 17: 163–176.

Eichmann, R., A. Hausleiter, M. H. al-Najem & S. F. al-Said (2006b) Tayma – Spring 2004. Report on the joint Saudi-Arabian-German archaeological project, *ATLAL* 19: 91–116.

Eichmann, R., A. Hausleiter, M. H. al-Najem & S. F. al-Said (2010) Tayma – Autumn 2004 and Spring 2005, 2nd report on the joint Saudi-Arabian-German archaeological project, *ATLAL* 20: 101–147.

Eichmann, R., A. Hausleiter, M. H. al-Najem & S. F. al-Said (2011) Tayma – Autumn 2005 and 2006 (Spring and Autumn, 3rd report on the joint Saudi-Arabian-German archaeological project, *ATLAL* 21: 64–118.

Eph'al, I. (1982) *The Ancient Arabs. Nomads on the Borders of the Fertile Crescent. 9th–5th Centuries B.C.*, Jerusalem.

Fakhry, A. (1951/52) *An Archaeological Journey to Yemen (March–May, 1947)*, Cairo.

Finkelstein, I. (1988) Arabian trade and socio-political conditions in the Negev in the twelfth–eleventh century B.C.E, *Journal of Near Eastern Studies* 47: 241–252.

Gerlach, I. (2002) Der Friedhof des Awām-Tempels in Marib. Bericht der Ausgrabungen von 1997 bis 2000, *Archäologische Berichte aus dem Yemen* 9: 41–91.

Germer, R. (2008) *Handbuch der altägyptischen Heilpflanzen* (Philippika 21) Wiesbaden.

Grandet, P. (1994) *Le Papyrus Harris I (BM 9999)*, 2 vols. Bibliothèque d'Étude 109. Cairo.

Groom, N. (1981) *Frankincense and Myrrh. A Study of the Arabian Incense Trade*, London.

Harrauer, H. (1983) Ausländische Waren in Ägyptens Papyri. *In Araber in Ägypten. Freundesgabe für Helene Loebenstein zum 65. Geburtstag*, 51–64, Wien.

Hauptmann, A. (2004) "Greenstones" from Basta. Their mineralogical composition and possible provenance. In H. J. Nissen, M. Muheisen & H. G. Gebel (eds), *Basta 1. The Human Ecology* (Monograph of the Faculty of Archaeology and Anthropology/Yarmouk University 4), 169–176 Berlin.

Hausleiter, A. (2010) L'oasis de Taymâ'. In A. I. al-Ghabban, B. André-Salvini, F. Demange, C. Juvin & M. Cotty (eds), *Routes d'Arabie. Archéologie et histoire du Royaume d'Arabie Saoudite*, 218–239, Paris.

Hausleiter, A. (2011) Das antike Tayma': Eine Oase im Kontaktbereich der Kulturen. In U. Franke & J. Gierlichs (eds), *Roads of Arabia. Archäologische Schätze aus Saudi-Arabien*, 100–123, Tübingen/Berlin.

Hausleiter, A. (2014) Pottery groups of the late 2nd/early 1st millennia B.C. in northwest Arabia and new evidence from the excavations at Tayma. In M. Luciani & A. Hausleiter (eds), *Recent Trends in the Study of Late Bronze Age Ceramics in Syro-Mesopotamia and Neighbouring Regions* (Orient-Archäologie 32), 399–434, Rahden/Westfalen.

Heide, M. (2010) The domestication of the camel: biological, archaeological and inscriptional evidence from Mesopotamia, Egypt, Israel and Arabia, and traditional evidence from the Hebrew Bible, *Ugarit-Forschungen* 42: 331–382.

Higginbotham, C. R. (2000) *Egyptianization and Elite Emulation in Ramesside Palestine. Governance and Accommodation on the Imperial Periphery* (Culture & History of the Ancient Near East 2) Leiden-Boston-Cologne.

Hikade, T. (2001) *Das Expeditionswesen im ägyptischen Neuen Reich. Ein Beitrag zu Rohstoffversorgung und Außenhandel* (Studien zur Archäologie und Geschichte Altägyptens 21), Heidelberg.

Hitgen, H. (1998) The 1997 excavations of the German Institute of Archaeology at the cemetery of Awām in Marib, *Proceedings of the Seminar for Arabian Studies* 28: 117–124.

Højlund, F. (1987) *The Bronze Age Pottery, Failaka/Dilmun: The Second Millennium Settlements* Vol. 2 (Jutland Archaeological Society Publications 17/2), Aarhus.

Japp, S., I. Gerlach, H. Hitgen & M. Schnelle (2011) Yeha and Hawelti: cultural contacts between Saba' and D'MT. New research by the German Archaeological Institute in Ethiopia, *Proceedings of the Seminar for Arabian Studies* 41: 145–160.

Khalidi, L., K. Lewis & B. Gratuze (2012) New perspectives on regional and interregional obsidian circulation in prehistoric and early historic Arabia, *Proceedings of the Seminar for Arabian Studies* 42: 143–164.

Khalidi, L., C. Oppenheimer, B. Gratuze, S. Boucetta, A. Sanabani & A. Al-Mosabi (2010) Obsidian sources in Highland Yemen and their Relevance to Archaeological Research in the Red Sea Region. *Journal of Archaeological Science* 37, 2332–2345.

Kisnawi, A., P. S. de Jesus & B. Rihani (1983) Preliminary report on the mining survey, northwest Hijaz, 1982, *ATLAL* 7: 76–83.

Kjærum, P. (1983) *The Stamp and Cylinder Seals 1:1, Failaka/Dilmun: The Second Millennium Settlements* (Jutland Archaeological Society Publications 17/1), Aarhus.

Krauss, R., P. Lombard & D. T. Potts (1983) The silver hoard from City IV Qala'at al-Bahrain. In D. Potts (ed.), *Dilmun. New Studies in the Archaeology and Early History of Bahrain* (Berliner Beiträge zum Vorderen Orient 2), 161–166, Berlin.

Lora, S., E. Petiti & A. Hausleiter (2010) Burial contexts at Tayma, NW Arabia: archaeological and anthropological data. In L. Weeks (ed.), *Death and Burial in Arabia and Beyond* (Society for Arabian Studies Monographs 10/British Archaeological Reports S2107), 237–247, Oxford.

Morris, E. F. (2005) *The Architecture of Imperialism. Military Bases and the Evolution of Foreign Policy in Egypt's New Kingdom* (Probleme der Ägyptologie 22), Leiden-Boston-Cologne.

Müller, W. W. (1985) Felsinschriften aus der nordarabischen Oase Taima', in welchen Kriege gegen die Nabayot, die Massa' und gegen Dedan erwähnt werden. In O. Kaiser (ed.), *Texte aus der Umwelt des Alten Testaments I.6: Historisch-chronologische Texte III*, 666–668, Gütersloh.

Müller, W. W. & S. F. al-Said (2002) Der babylonische König Nabonid in den taymanischen Inschriften. In N. Nebes (ed.), *Neue Beiträge zur Semitistik*, 105–122, Wiesbaden.

Müller, W. W. & G. Vittmann (1993) Zu den Personennamen der aus Ägypten stammenden Frauen in den sogenannten "Hierodulenlisten" von Ma'īn, *Orientalia* 62: 1–10.

Oren, E. D. (ed.) (2000) *The Sea Peoples and Their World: A Reassessment*, Philadelphia.

Parr, P. J. (1988) Pottery of the late second millennium BC from north-west Arabia and its historical implications. In D. T. Potts (ed.), *Araby the Blest. Studies in Arabian Archaeology* (Carsten Niebuhr Institute Publications 7), 73–90, Copenhagen.

Parr, P. J. (1989) Aspects of the archaeology of north-west Arabia in the first millennium BC. In T. Fahd (ed.), *L'Arabie préislamique et son environnement historique et culturel* (Travaux du Centre de Recherche sur le Proche-Orient et la Grèce Antiques 10), 39–66, Leiden.

Parr, P. J. (1996) Further reflections on late second millennium settlement in north-west Arabia. In J. D. Seeger (ed.), *Retrieving the Past. Essays on Archaeological Research and Methodology in Honor of Gus W. Van Beek*, 213–218, Winona Lake.

Peacock, D. P. S. & D. Williams (eds) (2007) *Food for the Gods. New Light on the Ancient Incense Trade*, Oxford.

Potts, D. T. (1990) *The Arabian Gulf in Antiquity*, Oxford.

Potts, D. T. (2010) L'histoire des origines. In A. I. al-Ghabban, B. André-Salvini, F. Demange, C. Juvin & M. Cotty (eds), *Routes d'Arabie. Archéologie et histoire du Royaume d'Arabie Saoudite*, 70–79, Paris.

Retsö, J. (2003) *The Arabs in Antiquity. Their History from the Assyrians to the Umayyads*, London-New York.

Roaf, M. (1974) The subject peoples on the base of the statue of Darius, *Cahiers de la Délégation Archéologique Française en Iran* 4: 73–160.

Roberts, R. J., W. R. Greenwood, R. G. Worl, F. C. W. Dodge & T. H. Kiilsgaard (1975) *Mineral Deposits in Western Saudi Arabia. A Preliminary Report* (revised 1977) (U.S. Geological Survey. Saudi Arabian Project Report 201), Jiddah.

Robin, C. (1994) L'Égypte dans les inscriptions de l'Arabie méridionale préislamique. In C. Berger, G. Cleric & N. Grimal (eds), *Hommages à Jean Leclant. Vol. 4: Varia* (Bibliothèque d'Étude 104/4), 285–301, Cairo.

Rothenberg, B. (1988) *The Egyptian Mining Temple at Timna*, London.

Rothenberg, B. (1998) Who were the "Midianite" copper miners of the Arabah? About the "Midianite Enigma". In T. Rheren, A. Hauptmann & J. D. Muhly (eds), *Metallurgica Antiqua. In Honour of Hans-Gert Bachmann and Robert Maddin* (Veröffentlichungen aus dem Deutschen Bergbau-Museum 72/ Der Anschnitt, Beiheft 8), 197–212, Bochum.

Rothenberg, B. & J. Glass (1983) The Midianite pottery. In J. F. A. Sawyer & D. J. A. Clines (eds), *Midian, Moab and Edom. The History and Archaeology of Late Bronze and Iron Age Jordan and North-West Arabia* (Journal for the Study of the Old Testament, Supplement 24), 65–124, Sheffield.

Russell, A. (2010) Foreign materials, islander mobility and elite identity in Late Bronze Age Sardinia. In P. van Dommelen & A. B. Knapp (eds), *Material Connections in the Ancient Mediterranean. Mobility, Materiality and Identity*, 106–126, London-New York.

Saleh, A.-A. (1978) Arabia and the northern Arabs in Ancient Egyptian records. *In Book of the 50th Anniversary of Archaeological Studies in Cairo University, Part III (Journal of the Faculty of Archaeology, Special Issue)*, 69–77, Cairo.

Sandars, N. K. (1985[2]) *The Sea Peoples. Warriors of the Ancient Mediterranean*, London.

Schaudig, H. (2001) *Die Inschriften Nabonids von Babylon und Kyros' des Großen samt den in ihrem Umfeld entstandenen Tendenzschriften. Textausgabe und Grammatik* (Alter Orient und Altes Testament 256), Münster.

Schneider, P. I. (2010) Die Mauern von Tayma. In J. Lorentzen, F. Pirson, P. Schneider & U. Wulf-Rheidt (eds), *Aktuelle Forschungen zur Konstruktion, Funktion und Semantik antiker Stadtbefestigungen* (Byzas 10), 1–25, Istanbul.

Schneider, T. (1993) *Asiatische Personennamen in ägyptischen Quellen des Neuen Reiches* (Orbis Biblicus et Orientalis 114), Fribourg-Göttingen.

Seidlmayer, S. J. (2007) Gaben und Abgaben im Ägypten des Alten Reiches. In H. Klinkott, S. Kubisch & R. Müller-Wollermann (eds.): *Geschenke und Steuern, Zölle und Tribute. Antike Abgabeformen in Anspruch und Wirklichkeit*. Culture & History of the Ancient Near East 29. Leiden-Boston, 31–63.

Seidlmayer, S. J. (2009) Prestigegüter im Kontext der Breitenkultur im Ägypten des 3. und 2. Jahrtausends v.Chr. In B. Hildebrandt & C. Veit (eds.), *Der Wert der Dinge. Güter im Prestigediskurs*. Münchner Studien zur Alten Welt 6. München, 309–333.

Sidebotham, S. E. (2011) *Berenike and the Ancient Maritime Spice Route*, Berkeley-Los Angeles-London.

Somaglino, C. & P. Tallet (2011) Une mystérieuse route sud-orientale sous le règne de Ramsès III, *Bulletin de l'Institut Français d'Archéologie Orientale* 111: 361–369.

Somaglino, C. & P. Tallet (2013) A Road to the Arabian Peninsula in the Reign of Ramesses III. In F. Förster & H. Riemer (eds), *Desert Road Archaeology in Ancient Egypt and Beyond. Towards Establishing a New Field of Archaeological Research* (Africa Praehistorica 26), 511–528, Köln.

Sperveslage, G. (2011) Die Stele Ramses' II. von Tell er-Rataba und die vermeintlichen Städte der Shasu, *Journal of Egyptian History* 4: 118–128.

Sperveslage, G. (2013) Ägyptische Einflüsse auf der Arabischen Halbinsel in vorislamischer Zeit am Beispiel der Oase von Tayma, *Zeitschrift für Orientarchäologie* 6: 234–252.

Sperveslage, G. (2014) *Ägypten und Arabien. Ein Beitrag zu den interkulturellen Beziehungen Altägyptens*, PhD dissertation Free University of Berlin (to be published as Alter Orient und Altes Testament 420).

Sperveslage, G. (in press a) Ägyptische und ägyptisierende Funde der Kampagnen 2006 bis 2010 aus Tayma. In R. Eichmann & A. Hausleiter (eds), *Tayma I. Reports on the SCTA-DAI excavations*, Riyadh.

Sperveslage, G. (in press b) Ägypten und Arabien. In R. Eichmann & A. Hausleiter (eds), *Tayma I. Reports on the SCTA-DAI excavations*, Riyadh.

Sperveslage, G. & R. Eichmann (2012) Egyptian cultural impact on north-west Arabia in the second and first millennium BC, *Proceedings of the Seminar for Arabian Studies* 42: 371–383.

Spiegelberg, W. (1908) *Die demotischen Denkmäler II: Die demotischen Papyrus, CG 30601–31270, 50001–50022*, Straßburg.

Stadler, M. A. (2004) *Isis, das göttliche Kind und die Weltordnung. Neue Religiöse Texte aus dem Fayum nach dem Papyrus Wien D. 12006 recto* (Mitteilungen aus der Papyrussammlung der Österreichischen Nationalbibliothek 28), Wien.

Tokunaga, R. (2003) South Arabic graffiti in the Eastern Desert (Wadi Hammamat and Wadi Manih), *Annales du Service des antiquités de l'Égypte* 77: 181–188.

Tomber, R. (2008) *Indo-Roman Trade. From Pots to Pepper*, London.

Uerpmann, H.-P. & M. Uerpmann (2002) The appearance of the domestic camel in south-east Arabia, *Journal of Oman Studies* 12: 235–260.

van Dommelen, P. & A. B. Knapp (eds) (2010) *Material Connections in the Ancient Mediterranean. Mobility, Materiality and Identity*, London-New York.

Vittmann, G. (1998) Beobachtungen und Überlegungen zu Fremden und hellenisierten Ägyptern im Dienste einheimischer Kulte. In W. Clarysse, A. Schoors & H. Willems (eds), *Egyptian Religion. The Last Thousand Years. Studies Dedicated to the Memory of Jan Quaegebeur*, Vol. 2 (Orientalia Lovaniensia Analecta 85), 1231–1250. Leuven.

Vittmann, G. (2003) *Ägypten und die Fremden im ersten vorchristlichen Jahrtausend* (Kulturgeschichte der antiken Welt 97), Mainz.

Wengrow, D. (2010) *What Makes Civilization? The Ancient Near East and he Future of the West*, Oxford.

Whitehouse, R. D. & J. B. Wilkins (1989) Greeks and natives in south-east Italy: approaches to the archaeological evidence. In T. C. Champion (ed.), *Centre and Periphery. Comparative Studies in Archaeology* (One World Archaeology 11), 102–126 London.

Winnett, F. V & W. L. Reed (1970) *Ancient Records from North Arabia* (Near and Middle East Series 6), Toronto.

Winnicki, J. K. (2009) *Late Egypt and Her Neighbours. Foreign Population in Egypt in the First Millennium BC* (*Journal of Juristic Papyrology* Supplement 22), Warsaw.

Zarins, J. (1989) Ancient Egypt and the Red Sea trade: the case for obsidian in the Predynastic and Archaic Periods. In A. Leonard & B. Beyer Williams (eds), *Essays in Ancient Civilization presented to Helene J. Kantor* (Studies in Ancient Oriental Civilisation 47), 339–368, Chicago.

Zarins, J. (1990) Obsidian and the Red Sea trade. Prehistoric aspects. In M. Taddei & P. Calliero (eds), *South Asian Archaeology 1987, Part I* (Serie Orientale Roma 66/1), 507–541, Rome.

Zarins, J., A. S. Mughannum & M. Kamal (1984) Excavations at Dhahran South – the Tumuli Field (208–292) 1403 A.H. 1983. A preliminary report, *ATLAL* 8: 25–54.

Chapter 15

Interactions between temple, king and local elites: the *hanšû* land schemes in Babylonia (8th–6th centuries BC)

John P. Nielsen & Caroline Waerzeggers

Introduction

One of the most striking changes that happened in Babylonian society in the first half of the 1st millennium BC was the widespread adoption of family names by affluent segments of Babylonian society. The antecedents of the practice had appeared in the Kassite period, perhaps even before the 15th century BC (Wunsch 2014, 289–290; Lambert 1957; Nielsen 2011), but it was only in the 8th century BC that family names became more common in cuneiform documents. "Ahhēšāya, son of Hašdiya, descendant of the Šangû-Ninurta family" is just one of thousands of examples of the three-part filiation (name, patronymic, family name) that gained currency as a result of this trend.[1]

The origins and significance of this naming practice remain poorly understood. There is certainly a measure of continuity with the family names recorded in texts from the 2nd millennium BC (Lambert 1957; Brinkman 2006; Nielsen 2011; Wunsch 2014), but the sudden and widespread increase in the adoption and use of family names by large sections of the urban population between the 8th and 7th centuries BC – to the point that they are nearly ubiquitous in documents from the sixth century BC – rather reflects a new dynamic in Babylonian society (Brinkman 1989; Nielsen 2011).

It is difficult to appraise the significance of this dynamic, for several reasons. First, the dearth of cuneiform texts from the early centuries of the 1st millennium BC obscures its earliest manifestations. By the time the documentation picks up again in the 7th century BC, the use of family names was already widespread in northern cities, chiefly at Borsippa, Babylon, Dilbat, and Sippar (Beaulieu 2000, 1; Nielsen 2011). In the south, in Uruk and Ur, at least some members of the urban elites conceived of themselves as belonging to ancestral groups, even if it had not yet become common practice to note family affiliation on tablets there.[2] Second, while family names became widespread, their use remained restricted; many, indeed perhaps most, families living in 1st millennium BC Babylonia never adopted any family names at all. It was a particular segment of elite society which used (mostly male; on metronyms, see Wunsch 2006) ancestry or occupational titles as a means of self-identification and family names to mark such adherence. How this segment may be defined, however, and how it related to other groups in society are questions that need further study. Populations who adopted family names upheld Babylonian religious and cultural values, were often closely associated with civic and religious institutions, and owned property portfolios that included houses, land, movables and, not uncommonly, priestly offices (prebends). Those without family names seem to constitute a more heterogenous group, composed of immigrants, pastoralists, artisans, sharecroppers, soldiers, slaves, and others.[3] In this paper, we want to make a contribution towards understanding the emergence and anchoring of the former group.

Between the reigns of king Nabopolassar and Xerxes, from *c.* 620–484 BC, Babylonia experienced a golden era as a number of beneficial factors came together that enabled economic growth and raised the standard of living (Jursa 2004; 2005b; 2010). In recent scholarship, this thriving period of Babylonian history has become known as the "long 6th century BC," a periodisation that is based on the extreme wealth of cuneiform documentation that survives from this duration of time. One of the beneficial factors that spurred the economy was the existence of a vigorous urban elite. Michael Jursa has recently identified urban landowners as being among the first to bring about the crucial transformation of the Babylonian countryside, by turning their barley fields into more intensively cultivated date palm gardens (Jursa 2010, 767–768). These landowners are the family name bearing elites that first make their appearance in cuneiform sources of the 8th and 7th centuries BC. As agents of economic change, these families made an important impact on the history of Babylonia.

This paper examines the emergence of these elites in the first half of the 1st millennium BC. In view of the scarcity of sources, only a few avenues of research can be explored. One of these is the history of land acquisition by the families in question. A quick look at the evidence reveals a connection, albeit perhaps an indirect one, between the acquisition of land and the adoption of family names in the 8th century BC. It was in this period that we begin to find family names with some frequency in the written record (Nielsen 2011). Their number then grows exponentially until by the mid-7th century BC there are 137 different family names recorded in Babylon alone (Nielsen 2011, 26), a number that continued to rise to 190 by the fifth century BC (Wunsch 2014). In Borsippa, the second most important city in Babylonia, an even bigger explosion of family names is recorded. At the beginning of the Neo-Babylonian Empire – at the end of the 7th century BC – 70 family names were in use in Borsippa, a number that tripled by the 5th century, exceeding even the example of Babylon (Wunsch 2014). When we look at the history of the practice, it would seem therefore that the 8th century BC was the crucial, transformative period. At that time, family names were used in two distinct contexts: (1) to identify kin membership of individuals (that is, for identification purposes of persons) and (2) to identify ownership of estates that figured in the land allotment schemes (*hanšû*, "fifty") of Chaldean kings (that is, for identification purposes of land). The dual application of ancestral names to members of the emergent elite and to their landed estates, suggests that there was a connection between the two. The nature of this connection is the topic of this paper.

Hanšû land

Our knowledge about the origins of *hanšû* land is limited and dependent on a few mentions of royal divisions (*zu'uztu*) performed by various kings, acts which apparently organised land as *hanšû* ("fifty").[4] These divisions were carried out during two broad phases as a response to historical circumstances. The first phase of royal divisions occurred over the duration of the 8th century BC as monarchs attempted to address the instability attributed in large part by the influx of Aramean tribal groups during the previous centuries, and the second phase of divisions were performed in the latter half of the 7th century BC in the wake of the two major conflicts for Babylonian independence: the failed Šamaš-šuma-ukīn revolt and the successful uprising led by Nabopolassar. Although royal motivations for performing *zu'uztu* are not spelled out in inscriptions, the common thread linking both phases of land divisions was likely the monarch's desire to re-establish urban control of the agricultural hinterland after periods of upheaval and, by doing so, to ensure support in cities benefiting from the scheme. Whereas the creation of *hanšû* land in the 8th century BC represented an innovation, the later seventh century BC divisions were a continuation or expansion of the system as it had come to function by the mid-7th century BC.

The land divisions of Erība-Marduk, Merodach-Baladan II and Sargon II

Tablets recording mid-7th century BC transfers of *hanšû* land occasionally reference royal divisions carried out during the 8th century BC by Erība-Marduk at Babylon,[5] by Merodach-Baladan II (721–710, 704) at Kish,[6] and by Sargon II (709–705) at Babylon.[7] The evidence points to Erība-Marduk, whose reign lasted for at least 9 years and ended prior to 760 BC, as the first king to implement the *zu'uztu* in Babylonia.[8] As a Chaldean from the Bīt-Yakīn tribe in southern Babylonia, Erība-Marduk was probably keen to win the support of the cities in the north of the realm after claiming the Babylonian throne. The previous decades had been particularly unsettled and for several years in the early 8th century BC the throne of Babylon had been vacant (Cole 1994, 223–227). No royal inscriptions of significant length survive from his reign, but a later chronicle from the 6th century BC commemorates his service to the people of Babylon and Borsippa, stating that:

> "Erība-Marduk ... slew with the sword the Arameans who had taken by murder and insurrection the fields of the inhabitants of Babylon and Borsippa and brought about their defeat. He took the fields and orchards away from them and gave (them) to the Babylonians and the Borsippeans." (Grayson 1975 no. 24 rev. 9–13)

Having wrested these fields and orchards from the Arameans, the *zu'uztu* was probably Erība-Marduk's solution to the problem of restoring land that had been under tribal control to an urban population for whom private ownership was the norm.[9] Who the chief beneficiaries of this royal division were was unstated in the chronicle, but there are two points that support the belief that at its inception, *hanšû* land was intended chiefly to support the leading figures in the temple hierarchy: the political interests that both the Assyrian and Chaldean rulers who claimed the Babylonian throne had in cultivating the support of the temple community at the time when *zu'uztu* was first enacted and the manner in which these land allotments were regarded by later descendants of this group.

That the temple elites were a group whose loyalty was worth cultivating becomes evident when we place Erība-Marduk's reign within the context of preceding events. The Assyrian kings who were active in northern Babylonia during the 9th and early 8th centuries BC, while stopping short of claiming the Babylonian throne for themselves, did strive to establish a favorable environment for Assyrian interests in Babylonia. In particular, the claims made by Shalmaneser III (858–824) and Adad-nīrārī III (810–783) that they subdued the Chaldeans and made sacrifices at or received the remnants of sacrificial meals from Babylon, Borsippa, and Cutha reflect an Assyrian strategy to gain influence in northern Babylonia through ties to the temple elite (Brinkman 1968; Galter 2007; Frame 2008; Siddall 2013, 75–79). With Assyrian power declining under Adad-nīrārī, Erība-Marduk's seizure of the Babylonian throne probably represents a Chaldean counter to Assyrian aims. As a non-Babylonian, it stands to reason that he would have appropriated aspects of the Assyrian policy by courting the support of the temple elite in northern Babylonia; his enactment of the *zu'uztu* was likely a major pillar of this effort, and we will adduce documentary evidence in section "The beneficiaries of the land schemes" below in support of this suggestion. Moreover, a recently published cylinder of Erība-Marduk attests to his pious patronage of the temple cult of Uruk (George 2011, no. 77).

Erība-Marduk's act was not soon forgotten. The only textual reference to the *zu'uztu* of Erība-Marduk dates from BM 36479, an exchange of property concluded at Babylon in 655 BC, more than a century after the end of his reign (BM 36479, see Wunsch 2014). The principals in the exchange were Nabû-nāṣir, an *ērib-bīti* ("temple-enterer") of Marduk from the Balīhu family, and Bēl-rēmanni of the Rē'i-sisê family. Nabû-nāṣir received land in the *hanšû* of Bēl-mudammiq descendant of Bēl-eṭēru in return for land that included two shares (*zittu*) in a field in the division of Erība-Marduk, terminology that suggests that the latter field was also part of a *hanšû*. Both principals belonged to prominent urban families: by the mid-7th century BC the Balīhu family had established a presence among the temple enterers of Marduk at Babylon and the Rē'i-sisê family may have obtained the governorship of Dilbat.[10] Moreover, both possessed some knowledge of the previous owners of the land being exchanged and were able to recall that some of it had been part of the *zu'uztu* of Erība-Marduk (BM 36479: 17–18). The impression one takes from this single record is that even though the land had changed hands over the previous century, it had remained in the property of individuals from prominent families, and that it had retained its special status based on the initial system established by Erība-Marduk.

It is also significant that Erība-Marduk's actions were recalled favorably by the Borsippean chronicler whose work we have cited earlier. The extant copy of this so-called "Eclectic Chronicle" dates to the 6th century BC and was produced in Borsippa (for the provenance of this chronicle, see Waerzeggers 2012). It gives a selective account of Babylonian history from the 11th to the 8th century BC, focusing on certain noteworthy events while omitting many others. The choice of topics was motivated by the compiler's interest in the local history of his city. He was particularly keen to show the privileged treatment enjoyed by Borsippa's citizens under earlier kings, a topos into which the episode describing Erība-Marduk's exploits clearly fits.

The evidence from the 7th century land exchange deed (BM 36479) and from the 6th century chronicle (Grayson 1975 no. 24) bears witness to a living memory of Erība-Marduk's endowment among those who identified themselves as heirs of the initial beneficiaries. Individual families as well as larger urban communities looked back on the royal grants as a significant episode in their existence, that was worth telling and recording. The land division acts of Merodach-Baladan II and Sargon II were similarly remembered (see notes 4 and 5).

The land divisions of Kandalānu and Nabopolassar

The second phase of royal divisions of land occurred in the latter half of the 7th century BC. Two kings in particular acted as patrons of these schemes: Kandalānu (647–627) and Nabopolassar (625–605). As puppet-king of Ashurbanipal and as liberator of Babylonia, these kings played distinctly different roles within the narrative of Babylonia's monarchical history; but, marking crucial developments in Assyrian-Babylonian relations, their reigns were also exposed to similar challenges.

Kandalānu, Ashurbanipal's co-regent after the revolt of Šamaš-šuma-ukīn,[11] issued two divisions of land in the area of Uruk in his 8th and 15th regnal year.[12] The historical context of these schemes is comparable to that of Erība-Marduk's in the eighth century. Kandalānu's reign ushered in a period of restoration after the intense struggles that accompanied Šamaš-šuma-ukīn's revolt. The city of Uruk had been closely associated with the Sealand where members of the Chaldean Bīt-Yakīn tribe waged fierce opposition against Ashurbanipal.[13] In the aftermath of the revolt, Ashurbanipal entrusted the Sealand to the Governor of Uruk (Frame 1992, 179; Jursa 2007, 130), in an attempt to strengthen the authority and support of Uruk's city-based elites and further quell the political ambitions of Chaldean tribes nearby. The land divisions of Kandalānu may have served a similar aim, though Bojana Janković, who recently studied the evidence from Uruk, concluded that the beneficiaries of this scheme belonged to a lower social stratum, connected in an uncertain manner to the local temple (Eanna), where documentation about the division was kept (Janković in Jursa 2010, 421–422). An interesting detail of this dossier is its conscious emulation of a land grant by Kandalānu's 8th century BC predecessor, Merodach-Baladan II. A local scribe opened up Eanna's archives, retrieved materials pertaining to the earlier grant, and used these to document the current exercise (Janković in Jursa 2010, n. 2410). The maintenance of the archive as well as its consultation and completion at the time of Kandalānu bear witness to a tradition of conservation and remembrance, comparable to what we have observed in Erība-Marduk's land grant above.

Nabopolassar reorganised land holdings of the Ebabbar temple of Sippar by means of a *hanšû* scheme late in the 7th century.[14] The region of Sippar had been the scene of heavy fighting throughout Nabopolassar's long struggle for independence (Da Riva 2001), and the allocation of land may have served the purpose of stabilising the ravaged countryside after these perils. As observed by G. van Driel, the social profile of the beneficiaries of this scheme was mixed. Some persons belonged to the local urban elite: being "temple enterers," they observed priestly charges in the Ebabbar temple and they wielded family names as a marker of their status. Other beneficiaries enjoyed a less elevated social position: undistinguished by family names, they were identified only by patronymics (van Driel 2002, 300).

Finally, mention should be made of two references to royal divisions near Nippur: one in a purchase of a share of an inheritance that was concluded at Nippur in 633 (*ina zu-ú-uz-ti* lugal [TuM 2/3 132: 2–3]) and one in a purchase of a share of a field and orchard that occurred during the reign of Sîn-šarra-iškun ([*ina zu-ú*]-*uz-ti* lugal [TuM 2/3 280: 3]). In these two texts, the name of the king who oversaw the division was not specified.

The beneficiaries of the land schemes

We have seen that the land schemes presented a flexible tool for rulers in unstable periods to enter into a process of negotiation with local groups. As a flexible instrument, the schemes did not serve one purpose, but could be applied in different contexts and with different target groups in mind. The grant schemes of the eighth century kings seem to have been the precedent that inspired later initiatives, and it is therefore worthwhile to have a closer look at the social dynamics that resulted from them.

Beyond their immediate political use to the grantor-kings, the land schemes presented social and economic benefits to the grantees and their descendants. *Hanšû* land meant income from rents and a stable basis of existence; it also meant the prospect of hereditary wealth and the promise of a patrimonial future. In the previous section, we have seen that some heirs invoked the moment of endowment by royal grant more than a century after the initial act. Name-giving practice was a second mechanism through which the link between land and grantee was maintained from one generation to the next. Parcels of *hanšû* land were known, if not in the wider community, then at least among members of the literate elite, by reference to the name of the grantholder. Initially, the name used for this purpose was mostly a combination of the grantee's personal name and his family name. For instance, in the region of Dilbat, we find a *hanšû* named after a certain "Uraš-iddin, descendant of the Saggillu family" (OECT 10 399 [645 BC]); in Kish, there was a *hanšû* named after one "Nabû-lē'i, descendant of the Amēlāya family" (OECT 10 7 [648 BC]). Over time, as the generation of original grantholders receded into the past, only the family name was retained as a toponymic tag. As an example we may refer to the naming history of a particular parcel of *hanšû* land in the Borsippa area: seventh century texts refer to the parcel as the *hanšû ša bīt Illûa//Ea-ilūta-bani*, "*hanšû* of the house of Illûa, descendant of Ea-ilūta-bani". By the 6th century, the name had become *hanšû ša bīt Ilūta-bani* "*hanšû* of the house of Ilūta-bani", Ilūta-bani being a short version of the family name Ea-ilūta-bani.[15] Not all *hanšû* names developed in this way; some estates continued to be named after individuals and some estates were not named after grantholders at all. However, the majority of *hanšû* names refer – if not solely, then at least partly – to the family name of the grantee.

The existence of strong ties between the city-based families and their estates in the countryside is also evidenced by the fact that families, who had been forced to sell *hanšû* land in periods of hardship, tried to buy back and reconstitute their lost patrimonies. Such restoration efforts are documented well into the Achaemenid period, nearly 300 years after the land schemes came into existence.[16] The 8th century land schemes, and later schemes inspired by them, can therefore be considered a major force in shaping and maintaining a self-conscious social elite in Iron Age Babylonia.

Who were the beneficiaries of the *hanšû* land schemes? Obviously, the grantees were powerful enough in eighth century society to be courted by ambitious Chaldean leaders like Erība-Marduk and Merodach-Baladan II, but beyond this bare fact, we hardly know anything about them. The much later *Eclectic Chronicle*, cited earlier, situates the beneficiaries in the cities of Babylon and Borsippa, while locating their need for protection in the countryside where their interests were threatened by Aramean murderers and squatters. A roughly similar point of view is espoused by a contemporary source. VS 1 37 is a monumental stela of Merodach-Baladan II that describes his efforts to expel intruders from the estates of inhabitants of Babylon and Borsippa:

> "The estates of the Babylonians of old, that an invading army unlawfully seized, and that foreigners grazed off unguarded – their boundaries forgotten, their division marks gone, their boundary stones removed and not standing upright – Marduk-apla-iddin restored the parcels and returned them to the privileged citizens of Babylon and Borsippa." (VS 1 37: iii 15-25)[17]

Like the *Eclectic Chronicle*, this text sets up a dichotomy between city and countryside, and between local/urban/cultivated elites and foreign/roaming/uncultivated intruders. The urban background of the grantees was clearly felt to be relevant. Is it possible to gain a more specific understanding of the particular segment(s) of urban society to which the grantees belonged?

The stele identifies the grantees collectively as "privileged citizens" (*ṣābē kidinni*) of Babylon and Borsippa, a status that refers to the enjoyment of tax and corvée exemptions of various kinds.[18] The text does not explicitly identify this allocation of land as a division (*zu'uztu*) nor as the creation of a *hanšû*. It is mentioned as the backdrop of an individual donation by the king to the governor of Babylon. Beyond this, it is difficult to gain a more specific understanding of the identity of the grantees from contemporary sources. There is, however, a set of data from a later epoch (i.e. the long 6th century BC) that indirectly sheds light on this matter. This dataset consists of *hanšû* names attested in the rich corpus of cuneiform archives from Borsippa.[19] The corpus dates to the period between the late 7th and early 5th centuries BC; that is, between *c.* 150 and 280 years after the land schemes in this area came into being. Despite its late date, the dataset of *hanšû* names is relevant because toponymic tags – with their social referents – were transmitted from one generation to the next, even if the referent or his heirs were no longer *de facto* owners of the land. In this way, it was possible for a member of the Kidin-Sîn family, for instance, to own a parcel of land in the *hanšû* of the Basia family. At the time of recording, the Basia family was no longer in charge of the land but their status as original grantees was commemorated in the *hanšû*'s name. Naming practices thus offer a reflection of Borsippean society in the 8th century – or rather of that part of this society that was singled out by royal favor – at a much later point in time.

An in-depth study of these *hanšû* names cannot be presented in the context of this article, but certain patterns are relevant for our discussion. First, although there is significant overlap between the set of family names used as (fossilised) name tags of *hanšû* estates and the set of family names that were in active use during the long 6th century, there is no one-on-one match. On the one hand, the number of family names increased. This is in keeping with the general trend observed throughout Babylonia at that time (Nielsen 2011); it is also in keeping with what may be expected of the divergent sizes of the earlier and later samples. On the other hand, and this is more interesting, two earlier names are absent from the later sample (Lahašu, Lāsimu). This may be explained in several ways. Conceivably, these lineages became extinct or impoverished, disappearing from literate society. More likely, however, a source bias is at play. Most archives from Borsippa in the long 6th century BC pertain to priestly families associated with the Ezida temple (Waerzeggers 2010). The sample thus favors a single segment of urban society, leaving us largely in the dark about families with artisanal, military and entrepreneurial backgrounds. Some of the family names recorded in the *hanšû* sample may pertain to clans with such socio-economic profiles.

hanšû ša ... ([20])
bīt **Abunāya**; Nabû-remēni//Abunāya; Apkallu//**Aqar-Nabû**;[21] *bīt* **Ašgandu** (or Šukandu); *bīt* **Atkuppu**; *bīt mār* **Bā'iru**; *bīt* **Banê-ša-ilia**; Šumā//Banê-ša-ilia; Nabû-šuma-iškun//**Bārû**; *bīt* **Basia**;[22] *bīt* **Bēlāya**; *bīt* **Bibbê**; *bīt* **Bitahhi**; Kāṣir//**Eda-ēṭir**; *bīt* **Esagil-mansum**; *bīt*

Gallābu; Ahu-ēreš//**Huršanāya**; *bīt* **Huṣābu**; *bīt* **Iddin-Papsukkal**; Saggillu//Iddin-Papsukkal; *bīt* **(Ea-)ilūta-bani**; Nādin-ahi//(Ea-)Ilūta-bani; Suppê-Bēl//Ilūta-bani; Illû'a//Ea-ilūta-bani; *bīt* **Iššakku**; *bīt* **Kidin-Sîn**; Nabû-šuma-ukīn//Kidin-Sîn; [PN]//Kidin-Sîn; *bīt* Kudurru *u bīt* fLē'ītu; *bīt* **Lahašu**; *bīt mār* **Lāsimu**; *bīt* **Mubannû**;[23] *bīt* **Naggāru**; Nummuru//Naggāru; *apil* **Nappāhu**; *bīt* **Nikkāya**; *bīt* **Pahhāru**;[24] Nabû-ēṭir//**Purattāya**; *bīt* **Rē'i-alpi**; Nabû-zēra-ibni/Nabû-apla-iddin/Rē'i-alpi; *bīt* **Rē'i-sisê**; *bīt* **Rīšāya**; *bīt* **Ṣillāya**; *bīt* **Ṭābihu**.

Second, of the family names that were still in vogue in the 6th century, 60% (20 out of 33) belonged to families who were affiliated to the Ezida temple, mostly as priests or administrators. Although this strongly suggests that the land schemes were especially designed to benefit members of the temple community, we must first consider the possibility that these families only began to exercise temple functions *after* they had become protégés of the 8th century kings. The bulk of the Borsippa corpus dates after the reign of Esarhaddon,[25] and it can therefore not assist us in the task of tracing the history of Ezida's priestly community beyond the 7th century BC. There is, however, one older text that we may consult for this purpose.[26] It is preserved on a monumental stele that was presumably found in the Ezida temple district, separate from the remainder of the Borsippa corpus, which derives from a residential area.[27] The text records the endowment of a priest of Ezida in the reign of Nabu-šuma-iškun, a king who ruled between Erība-Marduk and Merodach-Baladan II in the mid-8th century BC.[28] The persons who were called upon to act as witnesses of the transaction are listed towards the end of the document, as required by cuneiform legal practice. This list offers a glimpse of the prominent members of Ezida's temple community, roughly at the time of the land division schemes.

Nabû-šuma-imbu, descendant of **Ēda-ēṭir**, temple enterer of Nabû and Governor of Borsippa; Nabû-ēṭir, descendant of **Arad-Ea**, temple enterer of Nabû and *šatammu* of the temples; Nabû-ušebši, descendant of Ēda-ēṭir, temple enterer of Nabû; Nādin, descendant of **Arkât-ilāni-damqā**, temple enterer of Nabû; Nabû-usippi, descendant of Ēda-ēṭir, *šangû* of Adad; Nabû-ahhē-erība, descendant of **Ahhiya'ūtu**, temple enterer of Nabû; Marduk-šuma-ukīn, descendant of **Ilūta-bani**, temple enterer of Nabû; Nabû-zēra-iddin, descendant of **Ilī-bāni**, temple enterer of Nabû; Nabû-šuma-iškun, descendant of Ēda-ēṭir, temple enterer of Nabû; Zēria, descendant of **Kidin-Nanāya**, temple enterer of Nabû; Marduk, descendant of **Nūr-Papsukkal**, temple enterer of Nabû; Ahhēa, descendant of Arkât-ilāni-damqā, temple enterer of Nanāya; Dummuqu, descendant of **Iddin-Papsukkal**, temple enterer of Nanāya; Zērūtu, descendant of Iddin-Papsukkal, temple enterer of Nanāya; Bēl-ēreš, descendant of **Naggāru**, temple enterer of Mār-bīti; Nabû-šuma-iškun, descendant of Arkât-ilāni-damqā, temple enterer of Sutītu; Pir'û, descendant of **Kidin-Sîn**, overseer of the bakers; Nabû-lē'i, descendant of **Ilšu-abūšu**, overseer of the brewers; (scribe) Nabû-lē'i, descendant of Iddin-Papsukkal, *šangû* of Sutītu, lamentation singer of Nabû, scribe of Ezida.

Five out of 12 families represented at this transaction feature in the toponymic corpus of *hanšû* names from the long 6th century. This supports our earlier suggestion that the land schemes were directed towards members of the temple communities who resided in Babylonian towns. Although it is certainly possible that the schemes were socially more inclusive than our temple-based corpus bears out, for the time being we may conclude that temple affiliates were a particularly visible and successful target group of royal favor in the 8th century BC. These grantees stood at the helm of long and imposing priestly genealogies that persisted until the reign of the Persian king Xerxes, nearly 300 years later. The history of these priestly lineages is captured in the text corpus from the long 6th century BC (Waerzeggers 2010).

Finally, let us return to the *Eclectic Chronicle*, that we discussed earlier as a source on Erība-Marduk's expulsion of Arameans and subsequent restoration of land rights to Borsippa's citizens. The copy of this chronicle is part of a larger set of similar historiographic writings preserved in the archives of priests attached to the Ezida temple in the long 6th century BC. Little is known about the authorship and function of these texts, but the name of one chronicler has been preserved: Nabû-kāṣir of the Ea-ilūta-bani family (Millard 1964; Grayson 1975, no. 15; Waerzeggers 2012, 295). The Ea-ilūta-bani family was among the beneficiaries of the land grants of Erība-Marduk and Merodach-Baladan II. In Nabû-kāṣir's time the family was still in control of its original estate, which was named after the family in customary fashion. The *hanšû ša bīt-(Ea-)Ilūtu-bani* ("Fifty of the house of Ea-ilūta-bani") is documented without interruption from the mid-7th to the mid-6th century BC in numerous archival texts from Borsippa.[29] The episode in the chronicle thus contains the foundation story of the very milieu in which the chronicle was compiled. This milieu was affiliated to the temple institution, and tied to the land by its estates, awarded by kings of long ago.

Conclusion

The land allotment schemes that we discussed in this paper were used in different historical contexts and its beneficiaries were of diverse social backgrounds. The earlier phase seems to have favored urban families with close links to the temple, while the later phase was directed towards temple households and lower social, perhaps rural, population groups. All kings who acted as initiators of such schemes reigned in politically troubled times, during or shortly after major power struggles, and it is therefore reasonable to conclude that land allotment schemes were used as a political tool, to raise support from temple institutions and their communities.[30] In the long run, these schemes outgrew their political urgency. The hereditary property rights attached to these estates enabled the longevity of the grantees' lineages. Moreover, the schemes proved to be vital for the economic growth in the sixth century BC, as it was on the reclaimed parcels of land that the agricultural transformation of the Babylonian countryside from barley to date cultivation was first accomplished (Jursa 2010, 767–768).

Acknowledgements
Research on this article was carried out within the framework of ERC StG project BABYLON (211148). We are grateful to the trustees of the British Museum for allowing us to cite from unpublished cuneiform tablets in their care.

Abbreviations

AOAT = Alter Orient und Altes Testament.
BM = *siglum* of tablets in the British Museum.
MAH = *siglum* of tablets in the Musée d'Art et d'Histoire in Geneva.
NABU = *Nouvelles Assyriologiques Brèves et Utilitaires.*
OECT = Oxford Editions of Cuneiform Texts.
TuM 2/3 = Krückman, O. *Texte und Materialien der Frau Professor Hilprecht Collection of Babylonian Antiquities im eigentum der Universität Jena*, vol. II/III: *Neubabylonische Rechts- und Verwaltungs-Texte*, Leipzig 1933.
VS 1 = Hinrichs, J. C. *Vorderasiatische Schriftdenkmäler*, vol. 1, Leipzig 1907.

Notes

1. This particular example is taken from BM 118968: 3–4 (660 BC; cf. Nielsen 2011, 187 n. 32).
2. At Nippur, by contrast, there appears to have been a conscious rejection of the practice by the leading citizens, cf. Nielsen 2011.
3. Though there were exceptional individuals such as Lâbâši and his father Nādinu who came from a city – in this case, Dilbat – where family name usage was well established among the elite and who were engaged in building a real-estate portfolio that included *hanšû* land but who eschewed the use of a family name in all documentation of their activities, see Nielsen 2016.
4. See on the early Neo-Babylonian land divisions and on the term *zu'uztu*, literally "division," Brinkman 1995, 25–26 and van Driel 2002, 297–305. For *hanšû* land, see also Peat 1983 and Brinkman 1964.
5. *ina zu-ú-uz-ti šá eri-ba-*^{d}amar.utu lugal (BM 36479: 17–18; Babylon, transaction dated in the 13th year of Šamaš-šuma-ukīn, i.e. 655 BC; cf. Brinkman & Kennedy 1983, 30 and Nielsen 2011, 40 n. 89–90). A land division (*zu'uztu*) by Erība-Marduk is also mentioned in a *kudurru* of Merodach-Baladan II (VS 1 37 iii 51).
6. *ina zu-ú-uz-tu šá* ^{Id}amar.utu-[ibila-sum^{na}] lugal tin.tir^{ki} (BM 46799+: 2; Kish, transaction dated in the 12th year of Šamaš-šuma-ukīn, i.e. 656 BC; cf. Nielsen 2010, 98–100).
7. *ina zu-ú-uz-ti šá* ^{I}lugal-gin (BM 60118A: 4–5; Babylon, transaction dated to the 18th year of Šamaš-šuma-ukīn, i.e. 650 BC; cf. Brinkman & Kennedy 1983, 34 and Nielsen 2011, 46 n. 121).
8. For this king, see Brinkman 1964; 1968, 221–224; George 2011, 171–174.
9. On the interactions between Chaldeans, Arameans, and Babylonians in the 8th century BC, see Frame 2013.
10. On the Balīhu family of Babylon, see Nielsen 2011, 40–41; on the Rē'i-sisê family possibly holding the governorship of Dilbat in the mid-7th century BC, see Nielsen 2011, 108–109.
11. The identity of this "shadowy" (Jursa 2014, 124) royal figure remains obscure; cf. Frame 1992, 191–213.
12. These are discussed by Janković in Jursa 2010, 421–422; see also van Driel 2002, 304–305.
13. For the association between Uruk and the Sealand see Beaulieu 2002 and Janković 2007; for the role of the Sealand in the revolt of Šamaš-šuma-ukīn, see Frame 1992, 175–182.
14. The earliest reference dates to the end of his reign, see Da Riva 2002, 85–88; note that it does not explicitly mention Nabopolassar as patron of this scheme. See also van Driel 2002, 300, 304.
15. TuM 2/3 135: 3 (read *ina muh-hi* 50$^{!}$-*e*$^{!}$ instead of *ina muh-hi* numun).
16. E.g. BM 29379 (Camb 07; property in the *hanšû* of the Esagil-mansum family in Borsippa is kept within the eponymous family after a brief alienation through a dowry transfer).
17. The text and its historical context are discussed by Leemans 1948, 444–448; Brinkman 1964, 15–17.
18. See for recent discussions of *kidinnu*, Pongratz-Leisten 1997; Holloway 2002, 296–302; Paulus 2010, 197–198 n. 28 with literature.

19. The evidence pertaining to *hanšû* is presented by Zadok 2006, 420–447. For the Borsippa archives, see Jursa 2005a, Waerzeggers 2005; 2010, Zadok 2009.
20. Text references are to be found in Zadok 2006, 422–447 unless otherwise specified. Only *hanšûs* named after individuals and families are mentioned here. A minority of *hanšû* names is based on non-personal referents. The following *hanšû* names, listed by Zadok 2006, are based on misreadings of the passages concerned: *hanšû ša* Nabû-ahhē-iddin/Nabû-šuma-iškun/Ša-haṭṭi-ēreš (p. 436; to be read *bu-un* še.numun instead of 50*e* še.numun), Nabû-šuma-iškun/Nabû-iqbi/Adad-nāṣir (p. 435) is not the name of a *hanšû*; the "estate of the cultic performers" (*bīt-kurgarrê*) is not identified as a *hanšû* in the pertinent texts (p. 442).
21. OECT 12 A 83; cf. Nielsen 2011, 94.
22. This *hanšû* is attested in the Bēliya'u archive, see a.o. BM 28961 (Camb 07), BM 28952 (Dar 10?), BM 96280 (Dar [x]).
23. References to this *hanšû* are to be found on p. 429 and p. 445 in Zadok 2006; note that BM 101980 and duplicate Roth 1990, 53 are wrongly said to contain a reference to the *hanšû ša bīt Rē'i-alpi* by Zadok 2006, 426, instead of to the *hanšû ša bīt Mubannû* (as in Zadok 2005; collation B. Still).
24. MAH 16232 and duplicate TuM 2/3 23; note the corrections of Joannès 1989, 174 by Nielsen 2011, 92 n. 310.
25. There are only very few exceptions, e.g. BM 26528 from the reign of Nabû-šuma-iškun (*c.* 760–748 BC; cf. Zadok 1997; Brinkman 2005).
26. VS 1 36 (*c.* 750 BC); Thureau-Dangin 1919.
27. On the discovery and dispersal of the Borsippa archives, see Waerzeggers 2005; 2010.
28. On this king, see Cole 1994, Frame 1995, 117–126; 1998, Waerzeggers 2011, 739–740, 743–744.
29. The dossier is part of the Ea–ilūta-bani archive, see Joannès 1989, 65–72 and Nielsen 2011, 91–94.
30. A particularly vivid picture of the threat experienced at the time of the first phase of land allotments is contained in an inscription dated to the reign of the mid-8th century BC king Nabû-šuma-iškun, whom we have met above (see n. 25 and n. 28): "Babylonians, Borsippeans, the people of Duteti on the bank of the Euphrates, all the Chaldeans and Arameans and the people of Dilbat for many days hurled their weapons against each other and slaughtered each other; they also engaged in hostilities with the Borsippeans over their fields" (Lambert 1968, 128).

Bibliography

Beaulieu, P.-A. (2000) The descendants of Sîn-lēqi-unninni. In J. Marzahn & H. Neumann (eds), *Assyriologica et Semitica: Festschrift für Joachim Oelsner* (AOAT 252), 1–16, Münster.

Beaulieu, P.-A. (2002) Ea-dayān, governor of the Sealand, and other dignitaries of the Neo-Babylonian Empire, *Journal of Cuneiform Studies* 54: 99–123.

Brinkman, J. A. (1964) Merodach-Baladan II. In R. D. Biggs and J. A. Brinkman (eds), *Studies Presented to A. Leo Oppenheim*, 6–53, Chicago.

Brinkman, J. A. (1968) *A Policital History of Post-Kassite Babylonia, 1158–722 B.C.* (Analecta Orientalia 43), Rome.

Brinkman, J. A. (1989) A legal text from the Reign of Erība-Marduk (*c.* 775 BC). In H. Behrens & M. T. Roth (eds), *Dumu-e2-dub-ba-a: Studies in Honor of Ake W. Sjöberg* (Occasional Publication of the Samuel Noah Kramer Fund 11), 37–47, Philadelphia.

Brinkman, J. A. (1995) Reflections on the geography of Babylonia (1000–600 BC). In M. Liverani (ed.), *Neo-Assyrian Geography*, 19–29, Rome.

Brinkman, J. A. (2005) Notes on two early Neo-Babylonian legal texts (BM 26528 and BM 114720), *NABU* 2005/49.

Brinkman, J. A. (2006) The use of occupation names as patronyms in the Kassite Period: a forerunner of Neo-Babylonian ancestral names? In A. K. Guinan M. deJong Ellis, F. Ferrara, S. Freedman, M. Rutz, L. Sassmannshausen, S. Tinney, & M. Waters (eds), *If A Man Builds a Joyful House: Assyriological Studies in Honor of Erle Verdun Leichty* (Cuneiform Monographs 31), 23–43, Leiden.

Brinkman, J. A. & D. A. Kennedy (1983) Documentary evidence for the economic base of early Neo-Babylonian society: a survey of dated Babylonian economic texts, 721–626 B.C., *Journal of Cuneiform Studies* 35: 1–90.

Cole, S. W. (1994) The crimes and sacrileges of Nabû-šuma-iškun, *Zeitschrift für Assyriologie und Vorderasiatische Archäologie* 84: 220–252.

Da Riva, R. (2001) Sippar in the Reign of Sîn-šum-līšir (626 BC), *Altorientalische Forschungen* 28: 40–64.

Da Riva, R. (2002) *Der Ebabbar-Tempel von Sippar in frühneubabylonischer Zeit (640–580 v. Chr.)* (AOAT 291), Münster.

Driel, G. van (2002) *Elusive Silver: In Search of a Role for a Market in an Agrarian Environment: Aspects of Mesopotamia's Society*, Leiden.

Frame, G. (1992) *Babylonia 689–627 B.C.: A Political History*, Istanbul.

Frame, G. (1995) *Rulers of Babylonia. From the Second Dynasty of Isin to the End of Assyrian Domination (1157–612 BC)* (Royal Inscriptions of Mesopotamia, Babylonian Periods Vol. 2), Toronto.

Frame, G. (1998) Nabû-šuma-iškun, *Reallexikon der Assyriologie* 9: 33.

Frame, G. (2008) Babylon: Assyria's problem and Assyria's prize, *Journal of the Canadian Society for Mesopotamian Studies* 3: 21–31.

Frame, G. (2013) The political history and historical geography of the Aramean, Chaldean, and Arab tribes in Babylonia in the Neo-Assyrian Period. In A. Berlejung & M. P. Streck (eds), *Arameans, Chaldeans, and Arabs in Babylonia and Palestine in the First Millennium B.C.* (Leipziger Altorientalische Studien 3), 87–121, Wiesbaden.

Galter, H. D. (2007) Looking down the Tigris: the interrelations between Assyria and Babylonia. In G. Leick (ed.), *The Babylonian World*, 527–540, New York-London.

George, A. R. (2011) Other Neo-Babylonian royal inscriptions. In A. R. George (ed), *Cuneiform Royal Inscriptions and Related Texts in the Schøyen Collection* (Cornell University Studies in Assyriology and Sumerology 17), 171–186, Bethesda.

Grayson, A. K. (1975) *Assyrian and Babylonian Chronicles*, Locust Valley.

Holloway, S. W. (2002) *Aššur is King! Aššur is King! Religion in the Exercise of Power in the Neo-Assyrian Empire* (Culture and History of the Ancient Near East 10), Leiden.

Janković, B. (2007) Von *gugallus*, Überschwemmungen und Kronland, *Wiener Zeitschrift für die Kunde des Morgenlandes* 97: 219–242.

Joannès, F. (1989) *Archives de Borsippa: La famille Ea-ilûta-bani: Étude d'un lot d'archives familiales en Babylonie du VIIIe au Ve siècle av. J.-C.*, Genève.

Jursa, M. (2004) Grundzüge der Wirtschaftsformen Babyloniens im ersten Jahrtausend v. Chr. In R. Rollinger & C. Ulf (eds), *Commerce and Monetary Systems in the Ancient World: Means of Transmission and Cultural Interaction*, 115–136, Wiesbaden.

Jursa, M. (2005a) *Neo-Babylonian Legal and Administrative Documents: Typology, Contents and Archives* (Guides to the Mesopotamian Textual Record 1), Münster.

Jursa, M. (2005b) Money-based exchange and redistribution: the transformation of the institutional economy in first millennium Babylonia. In P. Clancier, F. Joannès, P. Rouillard, & A. Tenu (eds), *Autour de Polanyi: Vocabulaires, théories et modalités des échanges*, 171–186, Paris.

Jursa, M. (2007) Die Söhne Kudurrus und die Herkunft der neubabylonischen Dynastie, *Revue d'assyriologie et d'archéologie orientale* 101: 125–136.

Jursa, M. (2010) *Aspects of the Economic History of Babylonia in the First Millennium BC: Economic Geography, Economic Mentalities, Agriculture, the Use of Money and the Problem of Economic Growth* (AOAT 377), Münster.

Jursa, M. (2014) The Neo-Babylonian empire. In M. Gehler & R. Rollinger (eds), *Imperien und Reiche in der Weltgeschichte: Epochenübergreifende und globalhistorische Vergleiche*, 121–148, Wiesbaden.

Lambert, W. G. (1957) Ancestors, authors, and canonicity, *Journal of Cuneiform Studies* 11: 1–14, 112.

Lambert, W. G. (1968) Literary style in first millennium Mesopotamia, *Journal of the American Oriental Society* 88: 128.

Leemans, W. F. (1948) Marduk-apal-iddina II, zijn tijd en zijn geslacht, *Jaarbericht van het Vooraziatisch-Egyptisch Genootschap Ex Oriente Lux* 10: 432–455.

Millard, A. R. (1964) Another Babylonian chronicle text, *Iraq* 26: 14–35.

Nielsen, J. P. (2010) Three early Neo-Babylonian tablets belonging to Bēl-ēṭir of the Miṣirāya Kin Group, *Journal of Cuneiform Studies* 62: 95–104.

Nielsen, J. P. (2011) *Sons and Descendants: A Social History of Kin Groups and Family Names in the Early Neo-Babylonian Period, 747-626 BC* (Culture and History of the Ancient Near East 43), Leiden.

Nielsen, J. P. (2016) Taking refuge at Borsippa: the archive of Lâbâši son of Nādinu, *Archiv für Orientforschung* 53: 93–109.

Peat, J. A. (1983) *Hanšû Land and the rab hanšî, Iraq* 45: 124–127.

Pongratz-Leisten, B. (1997) Das "negative Sündenbekenntnis" des Königs anläßlich des babylonischen Neujahrsfestes und die kiddinūtu von Babylon. In A. Assmann & T. Sundermeier (eds), *Schuld, Gewissen und Person: Studien zur Geschichte des inneren Menschen* (Studien zum Verstehen fremder Religionen 9), 83–101, Gütersloh.

Roth, M. T. (1990) The material composition of the Neo-Babylonian dowry, *Archiv für Orientforschung* 36/37: 1–55.

Siddall, L. R. (2013) *The Reign of Adad-nīrārī III: An Historical and Ideological Analysis of An Assyrian King and His Times* (Cuneiform Monographs 45), Leiden-Boston.

Thureau-Dangin, F. (1919) Une acte de donation de Marduk-zākir-šumi, *Revue d'Assyriologie* 16: 117–156.

Waerzeggers, C. (2005) The dispersal history of the Borsippa archives. In H. D. Baker & M. Jursa (eds), *Approaching the Babylonian Economy* (AOAT 330), 343–363, Münster.

Waerzeggers, C. (2010) *The Ezida Temple of Borsippa: Priesthood, Cult, Archives* (Achaemenid History 15), Leiden.

Waerzeggers, C. (2012) The Babylonian chronicles: classification and provenance, *Journal of Near Eastern Studies* 71: 285–298.

Wunsch, C. (2006) Metronymika in Babylonien: Frauen als Ahnherrin der Familie. In G. del Olmo Lete, L. Feliu, & A. Albà (eds), *Šapal tibnim mû ilakkū. Studies Presented to Joaquín Sanmartín* (Aula Orientalis Supplementa, 22), 459–469, Sabadell.

Wunsch, C. (2014), Familiennamen in Babylonien. In M. Krebernik & H. Neumann (eds), *Babylonien und seine Nachbarn in neu- und spätbabylonischer Zeit* (AOAT 369), 289–314, Münster.

Zadok, R. (1997) Two N/LB documents from the British Museum, *NABU* 1997/11.

Zadok, R. (2005) Borsippean notes (suite). *NABU* 2005/51.

Zadok, R. (2006) The geography of the Borsippa region. In Y. Amit, E. Ben Zvi, I. Finkelstein, & O. Lipschits (eds), *Essays on Ancient Israel in Its Near Eastern Context: A Tribute to Nadav Na'aman*, 389–453, Winona Lake.

Zadok, R. (2009) *Catalogue of Documents from Borsippa or Related to Borsippa in the British Museum I* (Nisaba 21), Messina.

Chapter 16

Organisation and financing of trade and caravans in the Near East

Jean-Baptiste Yon

As some are better qualified than me for earlier periods, I will deal here with the subject only from the Hellenistic period. This paper is to be seen as an outsider attempt, with elements which may be used to better understand the first half of the 1st millennium BC. Of all the possible points of view, I will focus mainly on what I know best, the organisers of trade themselves. Who were the people who organised the trade? Who funded it? How was a caravan, in the rare cases for which we have information, organised, by whom and how?

I shall not present here an overall picture, rather a set of dossiers. It is a fragmented picture, which likely reflects reality. To transport an item from China to Rome, one had to face many stages of unloading and reloading and the interconnection of multiple networks. The documentation provides information on some of these networks, at different times, but it is difficult to relate them to each other.[1]

The Hellenistic period

Zenon Papyri

The Zenon archive is very important for the administration of Egypt, but a smaller part regards Palestine between autumn 260 and spring 258 BC.[2] The direct role of Ptolemaic government is surely significant but impossible to assess. The archive has more to show for the Egyptian economy than for Syria, a smaller part of Apollonios's interest. However, it is fairly characteristic as it gives information on a small part of a network which connects the Aegean, Egypt and Arabian Peninsula, even though we have only fragmentary evidence. Rather than dealing at length on the matter, I would like to draw attention to the variety of transactions involved.

Palestine was apparently at the centre of a network: trade was conducted between Asia Minor and Egypt, via Syria. In that region there is clear evidence of caravan trade, within the territories under Ptolemaic control: straw with a caravan of mules going to Hauran (Southern Syria). Or most importantly, camel caravans were travelling between Phoenicia, Galilee, Gaza and Egypt, with connections with South Arabia.

As shown by some documents (*P. Cairo Zen.* 4, *Addenda et Corrigenda* 59009), incense and perfumes found in Gaza may be the product of trade with the Minaeans (Libanos Minaios), but another possible origin was Gerrha, which meant trade in the direction of the Gulf.[3] Another point to underline is the great diversity of the people with whom Apollonios was trading. Thus, in the document just mentioned, Malichos Moabite could well be a Nabatean, which would mean the first appearance of Nabatene as an actor of trade.

To sum up, one has to underscore the fairly large number of players in trade, and the apparent complexity of organisation: definitely State was not the driving force, as far as Zenon archives could be used in that context.

Delos and the Mediterranean

The same diversity of stakeholders is very clear in Mediterranean trade of the Hellenistic period and the position of Oriental traders in this context deserves a few words. This is well-known from the classical period, and has been developing until Roman times; one telling example is that of the Nabateans expansion as seen on the map. But the clearest example is Delos, with impressive lists of individuals from every corner of the Eastern world (Phoenician coast, Seleucid Syria, Arabia). It could be supplemented by the evidence from other Aegean islands.[4]

Most of these men were merchants, as can be seen by the names of their associations "*naukleroi* and merchants." By extension, one can surmise that others are also there for the same thing, but even though it is generally true, details may be different. Some individuals, such as the banker Philostratos of Ascalon, belonged to a social elite and, obviously, those communities were socially stratified. The actual status and purpose of those associations are subject to debate. Were they built only on a religious basis or mutual professional support, or were they an early form of companies? That we do not know and those hypotheses are not mutually exclusive.[5]

Another example is the wheat trade, sometimes in the hands of merchants from Tyre and Sidon, as in the case of an inscription from Oropos: Dionysios, son of Ariston, from Tyre, and Heliodoros, son of Mousaios, from Sidon, were importing wheat (*sitos*: *IG* VII, 4262) there. There is nothing typically oriental of course. This was again a commerce of redistribution, as we have seen for the case of Zenon. In the same way, the gift of ivory by a Tyrian at Delos does not account for the origin of ivory and it cannot be concluded that it had been directly imported by this Basiliskos (*IG*, XI 2, 203 A71, dated 270 BC).

One must add that similarly, in a later period, eastern communities such as the Nabateans or Tyrians at Pozzuoli were presumably there for trade and maintained close links with their cities. It may have had a real importance in financing: sales at Delos or at Pozzuoli probably funded purchases in the Middle East for re-exportation to the West. Too little documentation on the products prevents further conclusion.[6]

Documents from the early Imperial period can partially compensate for this lack of direct evidence on trade and the products of the Eastern trade. Interestingly, it comes from the same milieu, that of traders.

Periplus Maris Erythraei and Indian trade at the beginning of our era

The Periplus Maris Erythraei

The work known as *Periplus Maris Erythraei* (Περίπλους τὴς Ἐρυθράς Θαλάσσης) is a guide for trade routes from Egypt all the way down the west coast of India. Definitely written by an hellenophone merchant from Egypt (Casson 1989, 15), it confirms that "in the first century A.D. there was an established pattern of seaborne trade from the Roman Empire to India" (Millar 1998a, 530). As Fergus Millar puts it in an influential paper on the caravan trade: "It provides just what we do not know, or hardly know, of land trade with Asia: the various different routes of exchange, the political relations involved, and above all detailed account of the objects of trade" (Millar 1998b, 120).

One particular point of interest is that it provides information about a business that theoretically could have existed in the Hellenistic period and even before (without the participation of the Greeks of course) on some segments.

Local powers and trade

The *Periplus Maris Erythraei* documents only part of the trade, but allows insights into the operations, in particular the role of kings and local rulers.[7] As a matter of fact, all this discussion depends on the interpretation of difficult phrases in the Greek text (Casson 1989, appx 1), such as ὅρμος ἀποδεδείγμενος, ἐμπόριον ἔνθεσμον, ἐμπόριον νόμιμον. One thing which may be taken for granted is that, in those places, some sort of institutionalised trade took place, but I do not think that a clear and definitive solution has yet been reached.[8]

That those sovereigns had an interest in trade is evidenced for South Arabia, both by the *Periplus* and by inscriptions (the *Mercantile Code of Qataban*: Beeston 1959; Avanzini 2004). According to Seland, certain products (especially horses) were imported especially for the king at Kanè and Muza (*PME* 24 and 28), but it is not clear if those commodities were really given to the king and the governor (τῷ τε βασιλεῖ καὶ τῷ τυράννῳ δίδονται ἵπποι τε καὶ ἡμίονοι νωτηγοὶ ...) or if the text is referring "to what could be offered for sale to the court as against ordinary buyers" as convincingly stated by Casson (1989, 154).[9]

It is not clear either if the king really had a monopoly over the exportation of local goods, except for a few products. Thus at Mosca Limèn (in the so-called "frankincense-bearing land" χώρα λιβανωτοφόρος), the king and its men had control over the markets (centralisation of business in fixed markets) for all trade in frankincense,[10] as it is shown as well by Pliny in his *Natural History*, with a Roman perspective.[11] But the *Periplus* does not make clear if taxes were raised; frankincense was sold for the king's profit, which may be enough. With Pliny's text, the focus is on taxes paid to the king, the priests and dignitaries, then to the Roman tax collector (one-quarter of the value of the goods). It also details some parts of the organisation of caravans. But the big difference is that Thomna the capital city of the *Gebbanitae* was not part of the "frankincense-bearing land", but belonged to their western neighbour, where trade (and taxes) was conducted on the way to the Roman Empire.[12]

The same conclusion on the monopoly of trade detained by the king has been drawn from what is said of Scythia in the *Periplus*.[13] Barbarikon (designated as a παραθαλάσσιον ἐμπόριον) is the only unequivocal example. There, all the cargoes are sent up the river to the king at the metropolis (*PME* 39: τὰ δὲ φορτία πάντα εἰς τὴν μητρόπολιν ἀναφέρεται διὰ τοῦ ποταμοῦ τῷ βασιλεῖ). Evidence is less clear-cut for other places. The difference with South Arabia is, it seems, that the king had a monopoly on all importations, not on product for export.

Muziris and colonies abroad

By contrast, documents on trade conducted by Greeks point to individual initiatives. A well-known and often studied document is a papyrus document drawn probably at Alexandria (Casson 1990, on *P. Vindob. G* 40822). It is an "agreement between two shippers (...), for a cargo (...) that, having originated in Muziris, had apparently just arrived in some Red Sea port" (Casson 1989, 14). There is no evidence of governmental connections (but for taxes paid in Egypt to a collector of customs, taxes amounting to a quarter of the value of what was brought from India; Young 2001, 214). If we go one step further, a look at the personality of these merchants shows that they were wealthy: the investment was not small and risk was involved. In the end, the adventure was rewarding, provided that the merchants had the money to purchase the goods exported from India. That real colonies of traders were permanently established in several ports of India is made clear by the references to Westerners serving as middlemen between their countrymen who arrived with cargoes and local merchants. Though, as we saw, at Barygaza, trade was in the hands of local merchants, at Muziris/Nelkynda there is evidence for a foreign colony. On the *Tabula Peutingeriana* (section 5, segment XI), a building is identified as *Templ(um) Augusti* not far from Muziris. It could only have been built by individuals originating from the Roman Empire. Clear evidence is provided as well by discoveries in Egypt. One of the two merchants involved in the Vienna papyrus refered to above was very probably resident at Muziris. On the other hand, recent excavations in Egypt have provided information on Indian and Arabian individuals, probably traders, established on the Red Sea coast (Tomber 2008; Sidebotham & Zych 2012).

Trade in Mesene

The same conclusion is true for other regions such as Mesene, in the southern Mesopotamian area, designated in a Syriac text as the meeting place of the merchants of the East, where colonies of resident traders have very clearly existed as well. Whereas it deserves little more than a cursory mention in the *Periplus*, documents such as incriptions from Palmyra, a well-known Manichean codex or literary texts are very revealing of the importance of this little kingdom.

At the beginning of our era, the conversion of some women of the entourage of king Izates of Adiabene, during his sojourn in Mesene, shows the variety of population concerned by trade in this area. This Jewish merchant was, no doubt, resident at Spasinou Charax.[14] In that particular case, we have here another network, that of Jewish merchants, but not only. At the same time, the Jewish population of Mesopotamia had strong ties to Palestine, for religious motives, but surprisingly few documents give information on the subject.

Another text is the so-called *Song of the Soul* (or *Hymn of the Pearl*), a Syriac apocryphal text of the 2nd century AD, translated into Greek. It is a highly symbolic description of the hero's expulsion from paradise and his return to his heavenly home. One prince declares "I quitted the East and went down ... I passed through the borders of Maishan, the meeting place of the merchants of the East, and I reached the land of Babylonia" (l.16-1.18; he then "descended to Egypt"). On his return to the East, the prince's route was the same "(he) came to the great Maishan, to the haven of merchants which sits on the shore of the sea" (l.70–1.71).[15] Reference here is made to the kingdom, not directly to its ports, even if Spasinou Charax itself, without being a port, may have been an *emporion.*

Several Palmyrene inscriptions make mention of Charax, as if trade stopped there. It is true that Palmyrenes, merchants or others, seem to have had a special relation to Mesene and its king.

Functioning of trade

The best known example of those men of influence is Iaraios, a Palmyrene, satrape in Bahrain (*IGLS* XVII, 245) for the king of Mesene Meeradates (σατρά[π]ης Θιλουανων Μεεραδατου βασιλέως Σπασίνου Χάρακος). It is clear that the island was under Mesene domination and was part of the whole network of exchange controlled by Mesene. The real function of Iaraios and its links with trade are not obvious, but we have many examples of men of foreign extraction who lead the administration for small sovereigns. Their independence from local societies was surely a great advantage for the king. Another Palmyrene, of a family well-known for its trading connections, may have been archont of Mesene (*SEG* 20, 385 = *IGLS* XVII, 246): the interpretation depends on a restoration, which is very tempting, but still remains hypothetical.

Another trader, maybe of foreign origin, had a leading role in the same kingdom. Mani, in AD 240, came with his father to Phorat in Mesene, and met there a merchant named Ôg- (name lost), who a great influence on his fellow traders, "... in Pharat, Ôg[...] by name, remarkable by his power and his influence on other men ... I watched as the merchants, who were preparing to ship up to Persia and India, sealed his goods, but stood still until he came on board."[16] The name Ôg- could be restored as Ôgga, a well-known name at Palmyra. Thus, he could be Palmyrene, although it is far from assured. But it leads to further glimpses on the way trade was really functioning, nonetheless because for once we can see the social differentiation at work.

Caravan trade in the Rome Empire: the case of Palmyra

Palmyra and caravans

At Palmyra, the evidence is much richer on trade. What was going on can be described with greater details than almost anywhere else in the Roman East. Despite this, the actual extent of our knowledge is rather limited. Even goods that were transported are to a large extent unknown. We can easily make some assumptions, but except for textiles (silk) discovered in the excavations, only a few documents explicitly confirm these hypotheses (Matthews 1984; Gawlikowski 1994).

The routes

Euphrates

The fortune of Palmyrenes was due to their control of a short-cut across the desert (as opposed to a more northern route from Antioch to Zeugma and then following the Euphrates). For the Palmyrenes, the Euphrates was used only on the last part of the way, probably from Hit (on this route, see especially Gawlikowski 1988). A famous inscription has been interpreted as a proof of the use of boats on the Euphrates which means that camels and other packing animals were left grazing on the bank of the river, waiting for the traders return (*IGLS* XVII, 59). For the same period, we know almost nothing for the northern (land-)route and even less for the Silk Road through Central Asia.[17] Change may have happened later in early proto-Byzantine period, but again our knowledge is rather limited. In this context, it is difficult to assess the role of Antioch, capital city of the Seleucids and one of the biggest cities of the empire in the Roman period. The Syrian tetrapolis was build as a new focus for trade, thus replacing Aleppo. It was certainly one of the places where goods brought by Palmyrene caravans were sold, as was Tyre, but, to the exception of one Antiochene citizen, tax-collector at Palmyra, evidence is rather scarce on relations between the two cities (*IGLS* XVII, 196).

The development of Palmyra was due to a phenomenon well explained by Strabo's testimony on the difficulties of traders following the Euphrates (at the end of the Hellenistic period): they were forced to use a more inland route to escape the phylarchs who were ransoming travellers on the banks of the Euphrates. One reason for the success of the desert shortcut was the close connections of Palmyrene leaders with the tribes of the steppes. Thus, they could arrange a safe passage for the caravans, with guides, good relays, and packing animals as well. The route was protected as well by military units, as is evidenced by several inscriptions for *stratègoi* and troups in the steppe, all obviously part of a Palmyrene militia (Yon 2002, 112–118).

Scythia and Mesene

From Mesene, Palmyrene traders like their Mesopotamian partners could go further by way of sea (see above for Mani and Og...). Two bilingual inscriptions from Palmyra give evidence on the return from Scythia (North-Western India) by ships owned by

Palmyrenes, dating to the mid-2nd century AD.[18] The relief of a ship found in the necropolis of the same city is another document that can be explained in the same way (Colledge 1976, pl. 103).

Egypt and the Red Sea

There are signs of new development during the 3rd century, with clear proofs of Palmyrene involvment in Egypt and on the Red Sea coast. Clearly Egypt was playing a major role for Palmyrene traders. One of the reasons may be that roads previously used were now blocked. Other itineraries had to be considered as well. Two individuals, obviously Palmyrenes themselves (because of their names), were honoured at Coptos by Palmyrene wool merchants, under the name of *Palmyrene naukleroi of the Erythrean sea* (*SEG* 34, 1593): Ζαβδάλα Σαλμάνου καὶ Ἀνεῖνα Ἁδριανῶν Παλμυρηνῶν ναυκλήρων Ἐρυθραικῶν; [Ἁ]δριανοὶ Παλμυρηνοὶ ἐριέμποροι. This document is very important as it gives information on the existence of companies of merchants: it does not seem the case even in Palmyra, as we shall see. There is no doubt that they were following local model, that of Egyptian companies. Incidently, one can add that the importance of Egypt for Palmyra is a reason that may explain the strategy of Zenobia later in the century. But it is another story.

Soqotra

Clearly, Palmyrenes were developing other routes and it can be further substantiated by recent discoveries of Palmyrene inscriptions at Qani (Briquel Chatonnet 2010), or of South Arabian inscriptions in the Hadramawt where Indians, Chaldeans (most probably people from Mesene) and Palmyrene met (Bron 1986). The most eloquent document is indeed the so-called Abgar inscription, discovered in a grotto on the Soqotra island. The evidence points here plainly to a date around the middle of 3rd century (Robin & Gorea 2002). As a matter of fact, the text is only a dedication and Abgar did not make clear the reason of his stay in Soqotra, except if the term *šmmr* is to be interpreted as "batelier". One has to remember as well that, according to the *Periplus*, the king of Hadramawt had farmed out the island (called Dioscouridès) and put it under guard. At the time, it was not open to Greek traders, but it is difficult to know the situation in the days of Abgar. This recent discovery may illuminate the changes in the routes. If the great itineraries were still used, in detail they were subject to change.

This possible new type of organisation of trade at that time has an impact on the image we have of Palmyrene caravans. In the following, I will mostly focus not on the organisation of caravans, a subject in itself, but on the involvement of individuals in trade as opposed to civic authorities.[19]

The organisation of the caravans

The term συνοδία (or *šyrt'* in Aramaic) appears only by the end of the first third of the 2nd century (Starcky 1949, no. 81 of 135 pC). Before, and even quite often after, it is only merchants: οἱ ἀναβάν[τε]ς [ἀπ]ὸ [Χ]ου[μ]ανων ἔνποροι *tgry' dy slq 'mhwn*. One good example is an inscription (*CIS*, II, 3916 (142 pC)) made for a synodiarch (συνοδιάρχης) by οἱ συναναβάντες μετ' αὐτοῦ ἔμποροι, suggesting that we are not dealing with a caravan. But the Aramaic text is more precise, and the expression *bny šyrt' dy slq 'mh* means "members of the caravan that went up with him." This fact may point to differences in the organisation of expeditions. But the difference between the designations may mean that the text is not made on behalf of the caravan, but by a group within it. The complexity of these designations is further increased by the fact that two languages are not always consistent.

The most striking designation is "caravan of all the Palmyrenes."[20] It is clearly an official term, as is the term synodiarch, a function recognised by civil authorities, as evidenced by some of the decrees. This designation should at least hint to a possible differentiation between normal caravans and official caravans. But the opposition may lie in the difference between caravans led by synodiarchs, as an expression of civic institutions, and groups of merchants (*emporoi*) who were going with the caravans independently. Synodiarchs (συνοδιάρχης) were professionals responsible for conducting expeditions safely, while also taking care of organisational tasks. On top of the structure nevertheless, but apparently outside civic institutions, were the great notables who allowed the existence of the caravans by their wealth and power in the nomadic tribes of the region.[21] They have no special title in the text, but nevertheless were thanked as benefactors without whom the caravans would not be possible. That says nothing about their functions or their effective participation in caravans, because reasons for gratitude were so obvious that details were unnecessary. Their role may not have been only financial and they also had to protect merchants against the nomads. Relations in the desert and in the cities of Mesopotamia and elsewhere were implicitly recognised by members of the caravan when they thanked the great notables. Young is highly sceptical on the existence of this class of "patrons" or "protectors", as distinct from the synodiarchs.[22] However, the fact that the same individuals (Šo'adû or Marcus Ulpius Iarḥaî) appear over and over is in itself a sign of their particular status. The restriction of their "patronage" or "protection" to trade may be an error of perspective, as they were doubtless dominant figures in other domains as well and, indeed, belonged to the same class of the local elite, and obviously were related by family links. However, given the position of caravans in the society of Palmyra, they had to be involved in caravan trade, as amply shown by the inscriptions concerning Šo'adû, over 15 years (AD 132–147). We have in fact a twofold structure with caravans more or less related to civic organisation (without financial support?), and on the other side, great notables acting on their own. It is true for trade, as it was certainly in other realms of the public life of Palmyra. As often no imperial intervention was needed, but only civic power and social relations inside the city were at work.

All the examples listed here can be seen as a way of tackling the issue of state involvement in trade, with conflicting results. More important, it seems, was the segmentation of trade in itself. It is impossible to follow goods from China to Britain, except on a few parts of the track, and it may be indicative on the international trade as it functioned during the Hellenistic and Roman periods. Only the *Periplus Maris Erythraei* and related documents (the "Muziris" papyrus) give an actual grasp on the two ends of trade itineraries, from Egypt to India. Everywhere else, almost only the part that ran through the Roman Empire (and the Mediterranean for the Hellenistic period) is clearly evidenced. In a sense, the structure of our documentation reflects closely what trade was really like, with exchanges made through different intermediaries, in an ever changing pattern (in details, if not on the whole); the different itineraries of the Palmyrenes, from Rome to Scythia, via Egypt, Syria, Mesopotamia Mesene, Arabia and Soqotra is the most telling example. As a matter of fact, one cannot expect a static situation for a period extending for more than six centuries, from the conquest of Alexander to the Protobyzantine epoch.

Notes

1. For a different point of view, that of the Roman Empire, see Young 2001.
2. As evidenced by the compilation of Durand 1997.
3. To quote the Greek text, admittedly very fragmentary: κασί[ας]/σουσίνου/λιβάνου Μ[ιναίου/ ζμύρνης /παρὰ Μαλιχου Μωβίτου/λιβάνου Γερ(ραίου) (τάλαντα) λ/ζμύρνης (τάλαντα) λ.
4. See Yon 2007, 57. On Philostratos of Ascalon, see e.g. Baslez 1987, 87.
5. On this question, see Ameling 1990, 195–199.
6. For Tyrians at Pozzuoli, see most recently Aliquot 2011, 80–91. For the Nabateans, Roche 1996 and Schmid 2007.
7. For the following, I draw heavily on Seland 2010.
8. See for example the essays collected in Boussac *et al.* 2012.
9. The meaning of the verb δίδοναι "to give" in *PME* 24 is not easily explained. See as well *PME* 6 and 49.
10. Seland 2010, 24–25. See *PME* 32: (about λίβανον) οὔτε γὰρ λάθρα οὔτε φανερῶς χωρὶς βασιλικῆς δόσεως εἰς πλοῖον ἐμβληθῆναι δύναται "For neither covertly nor overtly can frankincense be loaded aboard a ship without royal permission."
11. Pliny, *Natural History* XII, 63–65 "*evehi non potest nisi per Gebbanitas, itaque et horum regi penditur vectigal. caput eorum Thomna abest a Gaza, nostri litoris in Iudaea oppido, XXXVII D p., quod dividitur in mansiones camelorum LXV. sunt et quae sacerdotibus dantur portiones scribisque regum certae. sed praeter hos et custodes satellitesque et ostiarii et ministri populantur. iam quacumque iter est aliubi pro aqua, aliubi pro pabulo aut pro mansionibus variisque portoriis pendunt..., iterumque imperii nostri publicanis penditur.*" "(Frankincense) can only be exported through the country of the Gebbanitae, and accordingly a tax is paid on it to the king of that people as well. Their capital is Thomna, which is 1487½ miles distant from the town of Gaza in Judaea on the Mediterranean coast; the journey is divided into 65 stages with halts for camels. Fixed portion of the frankincense are also given to the priests and the king's secretaries, but beside these the guards and their attendants and the gate-keepers and servants also have their pickings; indeed all along the route they keep on paying, at one place for water, at another for fodder, or the charges for lodging at the halts, and the various tolls; and then again payment is made to the customs officers of our Empire."
12. I leave aside here the important role of the Nabateans, for which see Young 2001, 90–117. After the end of the Nabatean kingdom, documentation is sparse on the overland incense traffic.
13. Seland 2010, 50: "Barbarikon and Minnagar offer perhaps the clearest example of administered trade. Not only was trade centered at one city and some goods reserved for the king, as was frequently the case, but in Scythia trade took place at the capital rather than at the port city,

and the king is explicitly mentioned in connection with 'all the cargoes' rather than for certain goods only."

14. Flavius Josephus, *Ant. Iud.* XX (34–35) καθ' ὃν χρόνον ὁ Ἰζάτης ἐν τῷ Σπασίνου χάρακι διέτριβεν Ἰουδαῖός τις ἔμπορος Ἀνανίας ὄνομα πρὸς τὰς γυναῖκας εἰσιὼν τοῦ βασιλέως ἐδίδασκεν αὐτὰς τὸν θεὸν σέβειν, ὡς Ἰουδαίοις πάτριον ἦν. ("Now, during the time Izates abode at Spasinou Charax, a certain Jewish merchant, whose name was Ananias, got among the women that belonged to the king, and taught them to worship God according to the Jewish religion.")
15. In the Greek version of the *Acta Thomae*, l. 18–19 and 68–71: "παρελθὼν δὲ καὶ τὰ τῶν Μοσάνων μεθόρια ἔνθα ἐστὶν τὸ καταγώγιον τῶν ἀνατολικῶν ἐμπόρων ἀφικόμην εἰς τὴν τῶν Βαβυλωνίων χώραν ... καὶ καταλείψας ἐπ' ἀριστερὰ τὴν Βαβυλῶνα εἰς τὴν Μέσον ἀφικόμην τὴν μεγάλην οὖσαν παραλίαν". (See P.-H. Poirier, *L'hymne de la perle des actes de Thomas* [*Homo religiosus* 8. Louvain: Université de Louvain, 1981], 352–356).
16. *Kölner Mani-Codex* 144: [..... . ἐ]ν Φαρὰτ' Ὠγ [... τὸ ὄν]ομα, ἄν(θρωπ)ος ἐπί[σημος ἐ]πὶ τῆι αὐτοῦ [δυνάμει] κ̣αὶ ἐξουσίαι ων [..... ..].γ. ἀνδρῶν. [εἶδον δὲ] τ̣οὺς ἐμπόρους [ὡς ἐπὶ τῶν] πλοίων εἰς Πέρ[σας καὶ ε]ἰ̣ς Ἴνδους πε[ριπλεύσο]ν̣τες ἐσφρά[γισαν τὰ ὤνι]α̣ αὐτοῦ οὐ[κ αἴροντες ἕ]ως ἀνήει.
17. Maes Titianos according to Ptolemy (1, 11, 6) had travelled to these remote areas: Μάην γάρ φησί τινα τὸν καὶ Τιτιανὸν, ἄνδρα Μακεδόνα καὶ ἐκ πατρὸς ἔμπορον, συγγράψασθαι τὴν ἀναμέτρησιν οὐδ' αὐτὸν ἐπελθόντα, διαπεμψάμενον δέ τινας πρὸς τοὺς Σῆρας.
18. *IGLS* XVII, 26 and 250: I cite from the later text [ἔ]μποροι οἱ ἀν[αχ]θέντες ἀπὸ Σκυθ[ίας] [ἐν] πλύῳ Ονα[ιν]ου Αδδουδανου "traders brought back from Scythia in the ship of Onainos son of Addoudanes."
19. For what follows see Yon 2002 and 2007 with previous bibliography.
20. *IGLS* XVII, 127: ἡ ἀναβᾶσα συνοδία πάντων Παλμυρηνῶν *[šyrt' dy] tdmr klh.*
21. See Will 1957; Yon 2002, 112-118.
22. On the whole, it does not seem probable that synodiarchs were on the same level than "patrons". The "classic" point of view is exponed by Will 1957 (see as well Yon 2002, 100-118); *contra*, Young 2001, 154-156, who remarks that in one case (*Inv* X, 111, in AD 156), Marcus Ulpius Iarḥaî is refered to as "the synodiarch himself". But the actual wording of the Aramaic text (no Greek text) *qm w'drnn*, translated by Starcky as "parce qu'il s'est tenu (à sa tête) et qu'il les a aidées en toute chose", could mean as well "because he set about to help them in every manner", with an inchoative sense for the verb *qm* (see *IGLS* XVII, 124, "notes critiques" for that meaning).

Bibliography

Aliquot, J. (2011) Les Tyriens dans le monde romain d'Auguste à Dioclétien. In P.-L. Gatier, J. Aliquot & L. Nordiguian (eds), *Sources de l'histoire de Tyr. Textes de l'Antiquité et du Moyen-Âge*, 73–115, Beirut.

Ameling, W. (1990) Κοινὸν τῶν Σιδωνίων, Zeitschrift für Papyrologie und Epigraphik 81: 189–199.

Avanzini, A. (2004) *Corpus of South Arabian Inscriptions I-III: Qatabanic, Marginal Qatabanic, Awsanite inscriptions* (Arabia Antica 2), Pisa.

Baslez, M.-Fr. (1987) Le rôle et la place des Phéniciens dans la vie économique des ports de l'Égée. In E. Lipiński (ed.), *Studia Phoenicia V: Phoenicia and the East Mediterranean in the first Millennium BC* (Orientalia Lovanensia Analecta 22), 267–285, Leuven.

Beeston, A. F. L. (1959) *The Mercantile Code of Qataban* (Qahtan, Studies in Old South Arabian Epigraphy, 1), London.

Boussac, M.-F., J.-F. Salles & J.-B. Yon (2012) *Autour du* Périple de la mer Érythrée (*Topoi* Supplement 11), Lyon.

Briquel Chatonnet, F. (2010) Les graffiti en langues nord-sémitiques de Bir 'Alī (Qāni'). In J.-Fr. Salles & A. Sedov (eds), *Qāni'. Le port antique du Ḥaḍramawt entre la Méditerranée, l'Afrique et l'Inde. Fouilles russes 1972, 1985–1989, 1991, 1993–1994* (Indicopleustoi 6), 387 and pls 130–131, 542–543, Turnhout.

Bron, Fr. (1986) Palmyréniens et Chaldéens en Arabie du Sud, *Studi Epigrafici e Linguistici* 3: 95–98.

Casson, L. (1990) New Light on Maritime Loans: P.Vindob G 40822, *Zeitschrift für Papyrologie und Epigraphik* 84: 195–206.
Colledge, M. A. R. (1976) *The Art of Palmyra*, London.
Durand, X. (1997) *Des Grecs en Palestine au* III*e siècle avant Jésus-Christ: le dossier syrien des archives de Zénon de Caunos (261-252)* (Cahiers de la Revue biblique 38), Paris.
Gawlikowski, M. (1988) Le commerce de Palmyre sur terre et sur eau. In J.-Fr. Salles (ed.), *L'Arabie et ses mers bordières I, Itinéraires et voisinages* (Travaux de la Maison de l'Orient 16), 163–172, Lyon.
Gawlikowski, M. (1994) Palmyra as a trading centre, *Iraq* 56: 27–33.
Matthews, J. F. (1984) The tax-law of Palmyra, *Journal of Roman Studies* 74: 157–180.
Millar, F. (1998a) Looking east from the Classical World: colonialism, culture, and trade from Alexander the Great to Shapur I, *International History Review* 20: 507–531 (= *Rome, the Greek World, and the East. Volume 3: The Greek World, the Jews, and the East*, Chapel Hill 2006, 300–327).
Millar, F. (1998b) Caravan cities: the Roman Near East and long-distance trade by land. In M. Austin, J. Harries & C. Smith (eds), Modus operandi. *Essays in Honour of Geoffrey Rickman* (*Bulletin of the Institute of Classical Studies* Supplement 71), 119–137, London (= *Rome, the Greek World, and the East. Volume 3: The Greek World, the Jews, and the East*, Chapel Hill 2006, 275–299).
Robin, Chr. & M. Gorea (2002) Les vestiges antiques de la grotte de Ḥôq (Suquṭra, Yémen), *Comptes rendus de l'Académie des Inscriptions et Belles Lettres:* 409–445.
Roche, M.-J. (1996) Remarques sur les Nabatéens en Méditerranée, *Semitica* 45: 73–99.
Schmid, S. G. (2007) La distribution de la céramique nabatéenne et l'organisation du commerce nabatéen de longue distance. In M. Sartre (ed.), *Productions et échanges dans la Syrie grecque et romaine* (*Topoi* Supplement 8), 61–91, Lyon.
Seland, E. (2010) *Ports and Political Power in the Periplus: Complex Societies and Maritime Trade on the Indian Ocean in the First Century AD*, Oxford.
Sidebotham, S. E. & I. Zych (2012) Results of fieldwork at Berenike: a Ptolemaic-Roman port on the Red Sea coast of Egypt, 2008–2010. In M.-Fr. Boussac, J.-Fr. Salles & J.-B. Yon (eds), Autour du *Périple de la mer Érythrée* (*Topoi* Supplement 110), 133–157, Lyon.
Tomber, R. (2008) *Indo-Roman Trade. From Pots to Pepper*, London.
Will, Er. (1957) Marchands et chefs de caravane à Palmyre, *Syria* 34: 262–277 (= *De l'Euphrate au Rhin. Aspects de l'hellénisation et de la romanisation du Proche-Orient*. Bibliothèque Archéologique et Historique 135. Beirut 1995, 541–556).
Yon, J.-B. (2002) *Les notables de Palmyre* (Bibliothèque Archéologique et Historique 163), Beirut.
Yon, J.-B. (2007) Les commerçants du Proche-Orient: désignation et vocabulaire. In J. Andreau & V. Chankowski (eds), *Vocabulaire et expression de l'économie dans le monde antique* (Ausonius Études 19), 51–87, Bordeaux.
Young, G. K. (2001) *Rome's Eastern Trade. International Commerce and Imperial Policy, 31 BC–AD 305*, where. London-New York.

Chapter 17

Aegean economies from Bronze Age to Iron Age: some lines of development, 13th–7th centuries BC

Julien Zurbach

Introduction

To try to present a synthesis of the development of Greece from the Late Bronze Age to the end of the Archaic period, from the age of the Mycenaean palaces to that of the Archaic city-states, is obviously not a simple task, because of the quantity of data and complexity of analysis involved, but also because such a synthesis would perhaps not be expected in a volume on "dynamics of production and economic interaction" centred on the Near East and Egypt. There is indeed a double problem here: the quite vast chronological frame, and the problem of continuity or discontinuity, is linked to the development of different themes and inquiries among historians and archaeologists working on different periods and areas. It appears quite normal, since a long time, to draw comparisons between Aegean and Near Eastern or Anatolian palaces of the Late Bronze Age, and economic problems are a fundamental area of Mycenaean studies, in philology as well as archaeology. The situation is quite different after the fall of the palaces *c.* 1190–1185 and even more after the end of the Bronze Age *c.* 1070–1050. Themes of economic history have been quite neglected, in fact, in the reconstructions of the early stages of Greek society. There are two main reasons for this.

The first is the current chronological division between protohistory and historical times, with the transition being placed somewhere in Protogeometric times around the 11th century BC. In fact, in most analysis this is not even considered a transition but a complete *tabula rasa* followed by a radical new beginning. The "revolution of the 8th century" as constructed in the 1980s, as a new beginning in all sectors, from religious life to economy and demography, has been rightly criticised in favour of more complex scenarii of evolution from the 10th century onwards (on the whole see Dickinson 2006, with bibliography). But the profound rupture between the end of Mycenaean civilisation and the beginning of the world of city-states remains a quite undisputed horizon for any historical work. This means that the evolutions between Late Bronze Age societies and the Archaic city-states has usually been reduced to binary questions under the heading "continuity or discontinuity", this last option being the most favoured in the last decades. The role of Mycenaean foundations in socio-economic structures has simply not been a theme, with some very isolated exceptions (most notably Foxhall 1995). The *Cambridge Economic History of the Greco-Roman World* has a chapter on the Bronze Age Aegean but does not really try to present a detailed understanding of the transition period (Saller *et al.* 2007).

The question of continuity, furthermore, has usually been studied from non-economic perspectives, particularly the religious system or the nature of politics. This is a sign of the dominance of questions elaborated in the framework of cultural studies. In the 1980s and 1990s the dominant question in the history of Archaic and Classical Greece has been centered on the ultimate foundations of the *poleis*, on "what makes a community". The answers were stressing cultural and symbolic means of building collective identities, religious bounds and commensality being the first and most important (De Polignac 1984/1995; Schmitt-Pantel 1992). This question has been the first on the agenda, particularly in France: every single historical question, from the evolution of marriage until that of slavery, was supposed to have a link to the formation of the *polis*. Since then there has been a new tendency to underline the role of prestige and individual strategies in early Greek societies in a context of mobility and connectivity (Zurbach 2013). The connection of these lines of research with the global ideological context of our societies has already been underlined (Manning & Morris 2005).

One justification of the cultural framework was the need to integrate other kinds of sources than the literary and epigraphic texts, which are very rare before the 5th century and indeed completely absent in Greece from the beginning of the 12th century BC to the middle of the 8th. But, as evident and legitimate this would appear, it has not been so easy nor did it go without problems. In fact, the archaeology of the Archaic and Classical Greek world remains for a good part in a state of underdevelopment as compared to that of other periods and regions. Bioarchaeology for instance has been the subject of a recent book covering all periods of archaeology in Greece, where it appears that most of the available data are protohistoric, Roman or medieval, with a clear lack from the Classical periods (Schepartz, Fox & Bourbou 2009; with Buikstra & Lagia 2009). The same could be said on the situation of archaeobotanical and archaeozoological studies. There are notable exceptions (for instance Margaritis 2014) and the situation may be rapidly changing. But on the whole it is clear that the cultural framework has not been an incentive to innovations on the ground, focusing on traditional categories of sites and material like rich tombs and sanctuaries, where the most important processes are supposed to take place. It could even be argued that it has been disconnected from the mass of data constructed by the evolution of survey methods from the 1970s onwards, even if it produced a good deal of rhetorical constructs on the importance of the "spatial turn".

On the whole the situation of sources for the period between the end of the Bronze Age and the beginning of the Hellenistic Age is quite unsatisfying. Between the data elaborated by protohistoric archaeology and the tradition of technological studies on Hellenistic and Roman societies, studies on the technological systems of Archaic and Classical Greece are rare and concentrate in areas connected with the tradition of Classical archaeology, leaving aside for instance agricultural and pastoral systems (exceptions: Forbes 1995; Foxhall 1995; Amouretti 1976). The same is true of environmental reconstruction, diet and skeletal analysis, the architecture of everyday life as opposed to that of temples, etc. This is partly a problem of the elaboration of data, the earlier periods being for instance quite difficult to identify in survey material. But it has certainly to do with the general conceptions of these societies and the reluctance by dominant theories to examine any problem of socio-economic nature unless it can be easily integrated in a cultural perspective, like the much-used and overused gift giving or maussian gift.

I would like to argue here that taking into account the characteristics of Late Bronze Age Greek societies as they appear in a more precise way in recent years leads to a new evaluation of the kinds of historical evolution we can isolate in Greece, and that this can be done without taking side in a too clear-cut "continuity *vs* discontinuity" debate. This will be done by examining three fundamental areas of the economic structure: land, labour, and money.

Land

In no other field than the land economy has the contrast appeared so clearly between the supposedly state-organised and palace-controlled Mycenaean society and the world of city-states. That the palace or the king could have been considered the ultimate and real proprietary of all immovable, or at least all the land, is an old idea with a history as long as the "Asiatic mode of production" and further. But there is not the least allusion in Mycenaean texts to (a) the fact that the palace or king detains a kind of eminent property rights, or (b) the fact that, if such a thing ever existed, it had any consequence on the property rights from an economic perspective, imposing a control on alienations *vel sim*. In short, even if it had existed, we could not be sure that this was something more than an ideological motive with political motivations. Some land of course is controlled and/or detained by the palace and the king; but a general property on all land is a hypothesis that has to be recognised for what it is: a phantasm. The palace, nevertheless, was an important actor of the agrarian economy of the Aegean at the time of the Linear B archives (14th–13th century BC): the dignitaries had a more or less formal access to land, the palace gave plots of land to craftsmen and soldiers, land was a source of fiscal revenue, and it is probable that the palace had some land, which was rented out or perhaps also directly exploited.

On the other hand, the city-state from the 8th century onwards is clearly founded on the private appropriation of land. Even the hints at collective appropriation or exploitation of the land which have been recognised in Homeric texts are unconvincing. The large family or clan, which has long been a pregnant motive of Archaic history, does not appear as having any kind of land property in any source; its very existence is now doubtful (Bourriot 1976). The patriarchal nuclear family seems to be the only institution having a kind of private property. Public land is not well attested before the 5th century, and must have been a quite complicated category, with land belonging to civic subdivisions or associations next to civic land, where this category existed (see Papazarkadas 2011 and Migeotte 2014, chap. III/1). The existence of a *compascuum* land as collective land belonging to the community, open to the exploitation of wood, wild plants and animals, and animal grazing by all members of the community, has to be supposed on the basis of Homeric and Hesiodic evidence and the use of *eschatia* in later times. But this does not alter the fact that the free family was the basis of the exploitation of land.

This contrast seems so strong that one is tempted to abandon any idea of a link between the agrarian structures of the LBA and those of the Archaic period, a tendency reinforced by the fact that information on the so-called Dark Age (11th–9th centuries BC) is very scanty on this point. The only apparent link between Mycenaean and Archaic agrarian structures has been recognised long ago: it is the very word *damos*, written *da-mo* in the Linear B syllabary, and equivalent to the Attic *demos*, meaning the whole of the civic group but also a local community being the base of the territorial organisation of Attica. There is a tendency to eliminate this last point of continuity. Morris for instance refuses any link between the Mycenaean and Classical terms, but without clear arguments (Morris 2000, 101, 162). He echoes a tendency to underline the palatial context of this institution in the Linear B texts, therefore considering it an element of palatial administration. It is much more interesting to see here a degree of continuity revealed by the very word meaning "community". The Mycenaean *damoi* are in fact not part of the palace but an institution external to it, local communities with access to resources and land, slaves of their own, and a capacity to speak collectively in court. They are most probably an ancestor to Dark Age and Archaic communities, which explains the use of the term in the frame of the city-states.

This equation of course does not signify that there was no historical process and evolution between the 13th and 6th centuries. But some other facts seem to indicate that some parts of the agrarian economy, and not the least important, have been transmitted in the *damoi* communities from the LBA until the time of the city-states.

The first is the very method of land allocation. Allocation of land on a geometric basis, tending towards equality of all plots, has long been seen as a characteristic of the egalitarian practice of Greek city-states and linked to the inalienability of land, both being considered by ancient writers and some modern historians as going back to an original distribution of land, at the time of the *Landnahme* by Dorians, of the foundation of the colony, or else (Asheri 1966). This idea has been criticised on internal grounds: complete inalienability is impossible, and the equality of land distribution is an idea of the 4th century BC. Survey at Metaponto and work on urban plans like that of Megara Hyblaea (founded *c.* 730 BC) or Himera (founded *c.* 648 BC) have underlined the importance of practical considerations (Carter 2006; Broise *et al.* 2005; Allegro 1999). There may have been, and there has certainly been, a connection with egalitarian concerns. But these concerns are not a component of the very essence of the city-state; they are much more the products of particular historical situations where social problems, organised as an episode of class struggle or less crystallised, lead to the appearance of such ideas. Before Solon at Athens the modest people asked for a general redistribution of land on an egalitarian basis; and in the 4th century it is probable that such problems were the explanation to the almost egalitarian distribution, for instance, at Corcyra Nigra (Lombardo 1993). Whatever that may be, it is clear that the technique of land distribution in an orthogonal pattern existed before its use by the city-state; and this has been confirmed by the Mycenean evidence, which points to orthogonal distributions already at the end of the 13th century (Zurbach 2008).

On an even more fundamental point, but slightly more hypothetical, the historical processes of Mycenaean times could have laid the foundations of the private property characteristic of later times. It is in fact a well-known process of the history of palaces that the grant of land for services becomes with time a mean of access to a quasi-private property for the people to which this land was given. This is well-known in the Near East at different periods. Mycenaean texts give some indications on conditional land tenure, but nothing about its evolution, since they do not have any chronological depth, and date to the last year of the palaces' existence. It is not certain that the introduction of practices linked to private property, like inheritance, always goes against the interests of the institution paying services with land (for instance Bingen 1983). But in the case of Mycenaean Greece, the plots mentioned as attributed to soldiers or craftsmen can be supposed to have still existed one year after our texts were written, when the palace had disappeared; and not every soldier or craftsman will have been killed or have migrated. In addition, one can legitimately suppose that service land would have demonstrated the same kind of evolution as in other places, leading progressively to private appropriation. Liverani (1984; 2005, 50) has supposed that the Late Bronze Age in the Levant was a crucial period in the definition of a kind of private property – a bundle of rights where the individual has more rights than any institution or group, not necessarily the private property *per se* – against institutions like the family, the palace or the temple. This could well have been the case in the Aegean as well. It can be noted in this perspective that the clearest case of quasi-private appropriation of land is the *temenos* of the king (*wanax*). It is clearly a plot linked to the function, but that function can be supposed to be hereditary, and the palace has very little rights on it, if any: the *temenos* is not subject to fiscal payments. This Mycenaean *temenos* is the probable ancestor to the *temenos* of the Cyrenaean kings and the special land of the Spartan kings (see Carlier 1984). In that case the *temenos* would be the only case of inherited terminology, when the entire complicated Mycenaean terminology for categories of land and tenure had otherwise disappeared without leaving any traces; it would in fact be significant that the survival is on the side of the quasi-private property.

The technological side of the agrarian economy is even more obscure than its institutional side. Seen from the *longue durée* defined by major technological shifts, the whole period from the Middle Bronze Age to the end of the Classical period seems to be one of stability, based at least in the Aegean regions on a predominantly agricultural system with animals on the margins, transfer of vegetal biomass through grazing on the *eschatia* and regular stays on agricultural land, the simple ard with much use of hand work, and a diversified production concentrating not so much on the "mediterranean triad" than on different kinds of pulses, barley, and fruits. The introduction of the ard dates back probably to the Early Bronze Age, whereas innovations in the transformation of goods, like the diversification of millstones, begin in the 4th century BC (Amouretti 1976; 1985). The introduction of iron in agricultural systems is not evident before the end of the 6th century BC, too late to have played any major role in Archaic developments. Among the innovations usually dated to the "Dark Ages" or the Geometric and Early Archaic periods are the agricultural terraces, but their chronology is still obscure and the technique at least, if not its wide use, must date back to the Bronze Age. The only point of evolution is the introduction of the chicken, which may have had a major effect on diets and on the accessibility of meat; but data remain too scanty to elaborate on this.

Labour

When one turns to labour conditions and statuses of the workforce it seems that here as well the contrast is strong between the world of the palaces and that of the city-states. The current conception of that opposition is in some way parallel to the conceptions on agrarian systems. On one side the city-state has developed a system of slave economy based on a clear contrast between liberty and political participation as opposed to the complete exclusion of slaves (Finley 1960; 1964; Garlan 1995). The Mycenaean palatial societies were allegedly characterized by a diversity of statuses, ignoring complete slavery or avoiding giving it any significant place because everyone was anyway a subject of the king and palace, a type of generalised servitude which would be the basis for the system of obligations towards king and palace. Even if it is normally accepted that the polarity of statuses, the neat opposition between absolute slavery and complete liberty, is a quite late development dating to the second part of the Archaic period, it is generally accepted that the statuses and conditions of the workforce have to be radically different in the Late Bronze Age and in the civic societies of Archaic times.

Control of production by the Mycenaean palaces appears to have taken many different forms and to have been quite different from sector to sector. The clearest instance of control of an integrated chain of production is the textile production in the territory of Cnossos during the 14th century BC. Here the palace has accounts of the number of sheep, the location of each flock, the amounts of wool delivered, the state of workers' groups and their objectives of production. But other systems exist as well. Bronzesmiths at Pylos (De Fidio 1989) appear to have received quantities of bronze from the palace and to have been subject to an obligation to deliver finished products, in a system called *ta-ra-si-ja*, known as well in the frame of the Cnossian textile industry, where it is opposed to another, probably named *ke-ri-mi-ja*, on which we are completely ignorant. The potters were probably organised without relation to the palace: there is only one potter in a text from Pylos, and pottery production appears to have taken place in specialised communities where some families, or even each family, had a kiln. This echoes the geographical distribution of bronze-smiths, who, even if subject to obligations, were organised according to principles external to the palace. Does the existence of these different kinds of economic control mean that personal statuses were different as well? It seems that bronze-smiths were free, and some of them had slaves. The potter known from Pylos has a plot of land, as do some other categories, most notably those attached to the house of the king or of the vizir (the *wa-na-ka-te-ro* and *ra-wa-ke-si-jo* people). On the other side it is not surprising to find groups of servile status in the much more controlled textile production. The best example is the groups of women in Pylos, amounting to more than 750 women registered together with their children, some of them being defined by their provenance: "Milesian", "Chian", "Lemnian", etc. They are probably the victims of razzias and slave trade along the Anatolian coast.

The slave status, however, is not indicated in that case by the use of the word *do-e-ro*, equivalent to classical Greek *doulos*, "slave". This term is only used in connection with a genitive, indicating therefore a relation of private property, usually external to the palatial sphere. The word is attested in two major contexts. The first is a series of copies or extracts from private sale contracts of a slave, found at Cnossos. Two of them have been identified by Olivier (1987) and fragments of some others can be recognised in the A-series at Cnossos. The palace scribes register private transactions, perhaps because the palace has some interest in this. The important fact is that the slave is always the private property of an individual.

The second context in which the word *do-e-ro* is used is the land registers, where many "slaves of the deity", *te-o-jo do-e-ro*, are found. There is a tendency to interpret this as the title of a religious official or priest. But the other texts where *do-e-ro* appears in the clear sense of "slave" speak against this, as well as another text from Pylos. This tablet, PY Ae 303, mentions slaves *e-ne-ka ku-ru-so-jo i-je-ro-jo*, "because of the sacred gold". It can be argued that gold is a money (*Hackgold*, see infra), and in this case the text reveals the role of the temple as money-lender and the use of debt as a source of workforce, which is not a surprise given the widely attested Near Eastern practice. Debt slavery, known from Archaic Greece and from earlier times in Near Eastern sources (Old Babylonian, Hittite, Neo-Assyrian cuneiform but also the Old Testament laws), can be assumed to have existed in Mycenaean times, not only in the palatial system but also outside it, which could explain that it is not well represented in palatial texts.

The diversity of statuses of the workforce is a character of the Early Archaic period as well. The Athenian social crisis prior to the Solonian reforms was probably linked to the transition from some traditional forms to newer ones. Among the traditional ones we may list the kind of sharecropping and patronage defining the condition of the hectemoroi, as well as a form of debt servitude in which the debtor would work to pay his debt back (solutory form); both of these forms being probably subject to assimilation to the more severe form of debt slavery, where the debtor becomes definitively a slave (Zurbach 2009, 2013). This situation is clearly linked to the expansion of slavery as such, the Archaic period being the moment where the "society with slaves" is replaced by the "slave society" (Andreau & Descat 2006). In some places the outcome of the Archaic crises was the definition of collective forms of slavery, in the sense that the use of slaves was limited and controlled by the community. Not only in Sparta, where the status of Helots is quite well-known, but also in many other city-states did such categories appear during the Archaic period (van Wees 2003). The main factors of the definition of statuses are therefore the Early Archaic aristocratic initiative, intensifying exploitation of some categories; and the reaction of communities for the preservation of the free status of their members against debt slavery and a more balanced access to agricultural resources by its members (Zurbach 2013).

The difference between Mycenaean palaces and Early Archaic aristocrats therefore lies not in a diversity of forms – slavery as private property and debt slavery being fundamental – than in the use, the role attributed to these forms of control of the workforce. The system of obligations established by the palaces had disappeared, and no parallel can be found in the city-states. But the perspective may have to be corrected. The Homeric aristocrats rely on more different types of workforce (sharecropping, slaves, and wage earners) than the Hesiodic farmer, who relies only on slaves and exceptionally on wage-earners. The same could be true of the Mycenaean palaces: they rely on diversified modes of control of the workforce, linked or not to the personal status, whereas the only modes of control we find outside the palatial sphere are slavery, in some cases debt slavery, on the side of private individuals or the temples – the temples are in Mycenaean Greece institutions of quite modest size. This is a phenomenon which is well-known in the Near East as well: the institutions rely on diversified forms of control of the workforce, whereas the individuals have to rely mostly on slavery. In the Neo-Babylonian period, and perhaps earlier, this is paralleled by another contrast, non-palatial actors showing a much more intense relation to market places than the institution itself.

Some elements, therefore, begin to merge in a larger picture: slavery as a private property was known through the period; private property of the land was probably favoured by historical processes in Mycenaean times; the Mycenaean *damos* is registered as having slaves. But the sources concentrate on the institution of the palace or the crisis caused by aristocratic exploitation in the 7th century BC, leaving aside these elements of continuity.

Money

It is necessary to turn now to the last element of the triad. Here again the contrast is at its maximum. Finley (1957–1958) contends that the palatial economies attested in Linear B are based on equivalencies between products, not on money, since they are redistributive, not market economies. There are, accordingly, no prices. Archaic Greece, on the other hand, saw the introduction of coinage in the first half of the sixth century and its spread in the second half of that century. At the same time the city-states organized market institutions on the agora, with taxes, quality control and for part of them registration of contracts.

The appearance of coinage has been subject to a major historiographical shift in the last years. Works by Kroll and Descat notably have underlined the importance of the spread of weighed silver as non-coined money in the Early Archaic period. Kroll's hypothesis is that the Greek world did adopt the Near Eastern practice of using silver for all kinds of transactions. This can be seen from the texts, but for the moment not from treasures (see Kroll 2008; Balmuth 2001). The wide use of very small units in the first civic coinages in the second half of the 6th century demonstrated by Kim (2001a; 2001b) would then have to be seen in the perspective of a wide use of silver in the pre-coinage period. Descat underlines the importance of this highly probable use of silver bullion from the 7th century BC onwards, particularly in the transformation of the workforce, the new importance of debt slavery, and the definition of market places (Descat 2001; 2006a; 2006b). Silver was weighed (*Hacksilber*) and used as money in the Near East and Egypt from the 3rd millennium onwards.

Discussions on money in Mycenaean texts have focused on the system of multiple equivalencies, analogous in principle, if not in the goods involved, to the Homeric system based on oxen. It is widely accepted that no metal standard is attested in the Linear B texts, in contrast to the Near Eastern practice of *Hacksilber*. But this is probably due to the fact that mycenologists are looking for silver as a metal to be used as money (see the discussion by Sacconi 2005). It is certain that on one side payments are made by the palace in a quantity of different goods, for instance when paying for alum, the equivalent is in one case in wool, in another case in wool, goats, wine, figs and an unidentified product. The fiscal system seems to imply the existence of complex equivalencies between goods. But some texts in fact point to gold rather than silver money. Among them is the already quoted text PY Ae 303 on the slaves and the sacred gold; some other evidence can be added (Zurbach in press). It may be that this use of gold in Mycenaean Greece was a feature of temple, merchant or domestic economies, and therefore not well attested in palatial texts. This pattern of an institutional palatial economy relying on equivalencies in nature as opposed to private economies using metal standards is well-known in the Near East, as already mentioned (Jursa 2010).

The existence in Mycenaean Greece of such a system is coherent with other sets of data. The Near Eastern system is not immutable, even if in most periods silver was the preferred metal. In the Late Bronze and Early Iron Ages the use of gold as a standard is attested in Kassite Babylonia and the Levant. Mycenaean Greece would then have had an analogous system, which would be coherent with the intense trade networks known from this time. The situation in Early Iron Age Greece is not very well known on this point. Nevertheless, the role of gold in the Homeric poems, as well as the Eretria treasure of Late geometric date, which Kroll characterised as *Hackgold*, show that until *c.* 700 BC or later we can assume a system of gold money to have existed at least in some parts of Greece. The move towards silver, datable to the 7th century, is done in fact at the same time in Assyria and Greece (see Fales 2001, 163–165 on Assyrian sale documents, showing the passage to silver in the 7th century). It is obviously a sign of the Mediterraneanization of economies at that time, with very wide consequences.

Conclusion: dynamics of production and economic interaction

In all three fields – agrarian system, workforce, money – we found elements of analogy between the Late Bronze Age economies and the economic systems of the city-states. This is not to say that there is a complete continuity, notably in the field of private economies as opposed to institutional economies. It would be erroneous to argue that the private economy had gone unchanged through all the period. On the contrary, it is probable that the palace had a long-lasting effect on the community and the private sphere. But a certain degree of continuity lies in the fact that some fundamental practices – private appropriation of land, slavery, use of metallic money – were transmitted, and these were not only heirlooms since they were transformed and in continuous use. The link between Mycenaean and Archaic Greece lies therefore in historical processes where the interdependency of internal and external factors has a crucial role. The prime mover of the formation of city-states is probably the establishment of a new organization of the access to agricultural resources (Zurbach 2013). The Archaic crisis, on the other hand, would not be understandable without taking into account the Mediterranean scale, that is, the use of silver bullion. There is a similar long debate on the formation of Mycenaean palaces: are they to be explained through local factors or through Mediterranean connection? In both cases it appears that the interpretation of the interplay between dynamics of production and economic interaction is a pioneer front of historical research on early Greece.

Bibliography

Allegro, N. (1999), Imera. In E. Greco (ed.), *La città greca antica*, 269–302. Rome.

Amouretti, M.-Cl. (1976) Les instruments aratoires dans la Grèce archaïque. *Dialogues d'histoire ancienne* 2: 25–52

Amouretti, M.-Cl. (1985) La transformation des céréales dans les villes, un indicateur méconnu de la personnalité urbaine. L'exemple d'Athènes à l'époque classique, In P. Leveau (ed.), *L'origine des richesses dépensées dans la ville antique*, 133–146, Aix-en-Provence.

Andreau, J. & R. Descat (2006) *Esclave en Grèce et à Rome*, Paris.

Asheri, D. (1966) *Distribuzioni di terre nell'antica Grecia* (Memorie dell'Accademia delle Scienze di Torino, Classe di scienze morali, storiche e filologiche ser. 4/10), Turin.

Balmuth, M. S. (ed) (2001) *Hacksilber to Coinage: New Insights Into the Monetary History of the Near East and Greece* (Numismatic Studies 24), New York.

Bingen, J. (1983) Les cavaliers catoeques de l'Héracléopolite au Ier siècle. *In Egypt and the Hellenistic World* (Studia hellenistica 27), 1–11 Leuven.

Bourriot, F. (1976) *Génos*, Paris.

Broise, H., M. Gras & H. Tréziny (2005) *Mégara Hyblaea I 5. La ville archaïque*, Rome.

Buikstra, J. & A. Lagia (2009) Bioarchaeological approaches to Aegean archaeology. In L. A. Schepartz, S. C. Fox & Chr. Bourbou (eds), *New Directions in the Skeletal Biology of Greece* (*Hesperia* Supplement 43), 7–29, Princeton.

Carlier, P. (1984) *La royauté en Grèce avant Alexandre*, Strasbourg.

Carter, J. C. (2006) *Discovering the Greek Countryside at Metaponto*, Ann Arbor

De Fidio, P. (1989) L'artigianato del bronzo nei testi micenei di Pilo, *Klio* 71: 7–27.

De Polignac, Fr. (1984/1995) *La naissance de la cité grecque*, Paris.

Descat, R. (2001) Monnaie multiple et monnaie frappée en Grèce archaïque, *Revue numismatique*: 69–81.

Descat, R. (2006a) Le marché dans l'économie de la Grèce antique, *Revue de Synthèse* 127: 253–272

Descat, R. (2006b) Argyrônétos: les transformations de l'échange dans la Grèce archaïque. In P. van Alfen (ed.), *Agoranomia: Studies in Money and Exchange Presented to John H. Kroll*, 21–36, New York.

Dickinson, O. T. P. K. (2006) *The Aegean from Bronze Age to Iron Age: Continuity and Change Between the Twelfth and Eighth Centuries B.C.*, London.

Fales, M. (2001) *L'impero assiro. Storia e amministrazione (IX–VII secolo a.C.)*, Rome-Bari.

Finley, M. I. (1957–1958) The Mycenaean tablets and economic history, *Economic History Review* new series 10: 128–141.

Finley, M. I. (1960) Entre l'esclavage et la liberté. Reproduced in M. I. Finley (1984), *Économie et société en Grèce ancienne*, 172–194, Paris.

Finley, M. I. (1964) Les statuts serviles en Grèce ancienne. Reproduced in M. I. Finley (1984), *Économie et société en Grèce ancienne*, 195–219, Paris.

Forbes, H. A. (1995) The identification of pastoralist sites within the context of estate-based agriculture in ancient Greece: beyond the transhumance v. agro-pastoralism debate, Annual of the British School in Athens 90: 325–338.

Foxhall, L. (1995) Bronze to iron: agricultural systems and political structures in Late Bronze Age and Early Iron Age Greece, Annual of the British School in Athens 90: 239–250.

Garlan, Y. (1995) *Les esclaves en Grèce ancienne*, Paris.

Jursa, M. (2010) *Aspects of the Economic History of Babylonia in the First Millennium BC. Economic Geography, Economic Mentalities, Agriculture, the Use of Money and the Problem of Economic Growth*, Munster.

Kim, H. S. (2001a) Small change and the moneyed economy. In P. Cartledge, E. E. Cohen & L. Foxhall (eds), *Money, Labour and Land*, 44–51, London-New York.

Kim, H. S. (2001b) Archaic coinage as evidence for the use of money. In A. Meadows & K. Shipton (eds), *Money and its Uses in the Ancient Greek World*, 7–21, Oxford.

Kroll, J. H. (2008) The monetary use of weighed bullion in Archaic Greece. In W. V. Harris (ed.), *The Monetary Systems of the Greeks and Romans*, 12–37, Oxford.

Liverani, M. (1984) Land tenure and inheritance in the Ancient Near East: the interaction between "palace" and "family" sectors. In T. Khalidi (ed.), *Land Tenure and Social Transformation in the Middle East*, 33–44, Beyrouth.

Liverani, M. (2005) The Near East: the Bronze Age. In J. G. Manning & I. Morris (eds), *The Ancient Economy. Evidence and Models*, 47–57, Stanford.

Lombardo, M. (1993) Lo *Psephisma* di Lumbarda: note critiche e questioni esegetiche, *Hesperìa* 3: 161–188.
Manning, J. & I. Morris (2005) Introduction. In J. Manning & I. Morris (eds), *The Ancient Economy. Evidence and Models*, 1–44, Stanford.
Margaritis, E. (2014) The Kapeleio at Hellenistic Krania. Food consumption, disposal, and the use of space, *Hesperia* 83: 103–121.
Migeotte, L. (2014) *Les finances des cités grecques*, Paris.
Morris, I. (2000) *Archaeology as Cultural History: Words and Things in Iron Age Greece*, Oxford.
Olivier, J.-P. (1987) Des extraits de contrats de vente d'esclaves dans les tablettes de Knossos. In J. T. Killen, J. L. Melena & J.-P. Olivier (eds), *Studies in Mycenaean and Classical Greek Presented to John Chadwick* (*Minos* 20–22), 479–498, Salamanca.
Papazarkadas, N. (2011) *Sacred and Public Land in Ancient Athens*, Oxford.
Sacconi, A. (2005) La "monnaie" dans l'économie mycénienne. Le témoignage des textes. In R. Laffineur & E. Greco (eds), *Emporia: Aegeans in the Central and Eastern Mediterranean* (Aegaeum 25), 69–74, Liège-Austin.
Saller, R., W. Scheidel & I. Morris (2007), *The Cambridge Economic History of the Greco-Roman World*, Cambridge.
Schepartz, L. A., S. C. Fox & Chr. Bourbou (ed.) (2009), *New Directions in the Skeletal Biology of Greece* (Hesperia Supplements 430), Princeton.
Schmitt-Pantel, P. (1992 [2011]) *La cité au banquet. Histoire des repas publics dans les cités grecques*, Paris.
van Wees, H. (2003) Conquerors and serfs: wars of conquest and forced labour in archaic Greece. In S. Alcock & N. Luraghi (eds), *Helots and their Masters in Laconia and Messenia. Histories, Ideologies, Structures*, 33–80, Cambridge MA–London.
Zurbach, J. (2008) Pylos, Tirynthe, Cnossos: problèmes fonciers et diversité administrative. In A. Sacconi, M. Del Freo, L. Godart, M. Negri (ed.), *Colloquium Romanum*, 825–838, Pisa–Rome.
Zurbach, J. (2009) Paysanneries de la Grèce archaïque, *Histoire et sociétés rurales* 31: 9–44.
Zurbach, J. (2013) La formation des cités grecques. Statuts, classes et systèmes fonciers, *Annales.* Histoire, Sciences sociales 68: 957–998.
Zurbach, J. (in press), Esclaves, dette, monnaie en Grèce mycénienne. In H. Enegren, M.L. Nosch (ed.), *Acts of the 14th Mycenological Colloquium*, Copehagen 2015, in press.